PHILIP'S

STREET ATLAS Devon

Barnstaple, Exeter, Exmouth, Paignton, Plymouth, Torquay

www.philips-maps.co.uk
First published in 2003 by
Philip's, a division of
Octopus Publishing Group Ltd
www.octopusbooks.co.uk
Endeavour House
189 Shaftesbury Avenue
London WC2H 8JY
An Hachette UK Company
www.hachette.co.uk

Third edition 2011
Third impression 2014
DEVCA

ISBN 978-1-84907-295-3 (spiral)

Speed camera data provided by
PocketGPSWorld.com Ltd

Printed in China

Contents

Mobile safety cameras

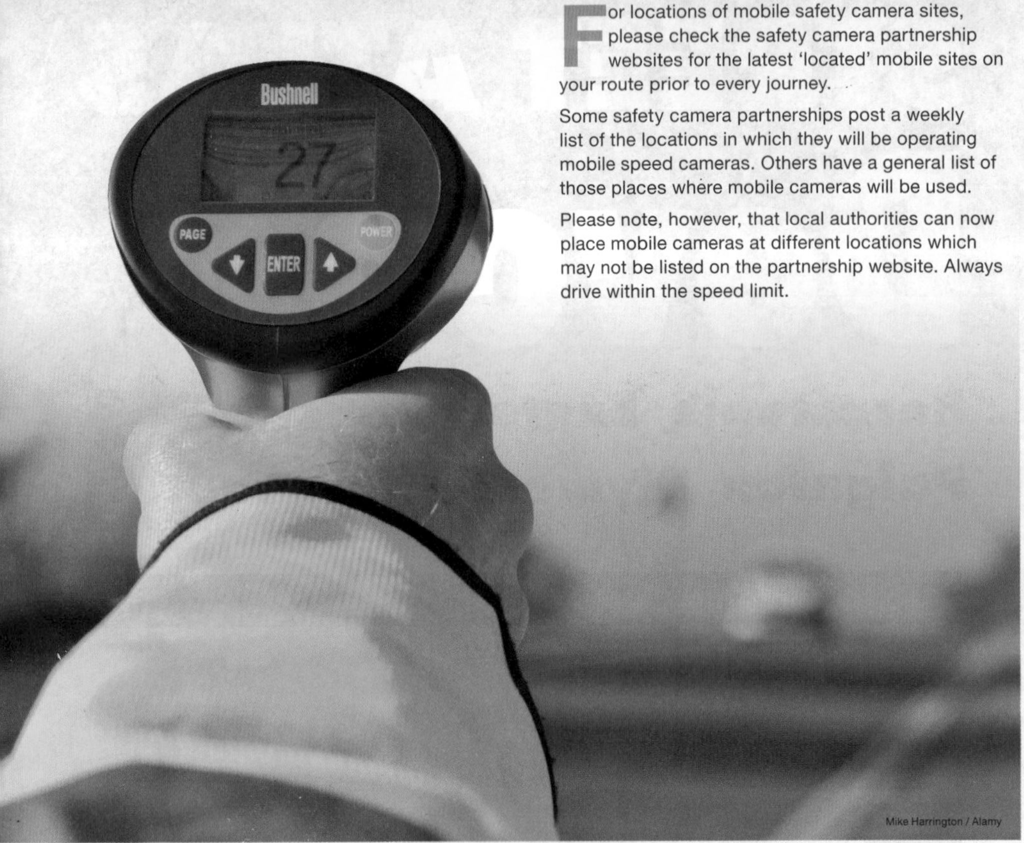

Mike Harrington / Alamy

For locations of mobile safety camera sites, please check the safety camera partnership websites for the latest 'located' mobile sites on your route prior to every journey.

Some safety camera partnerships post a weekly list of the locations in which they will be operating mobile speed cameras. Others have a general list of those places where mobile cameras will be used.

Please note, however, that local authorities can now place mobile cameras at different locations which may not be listed on the partnership website. Always drive within the speed limit.

Useful websites

Devon and Cornwall Safety Camera Partnership
www.dcsafetycameras.org

Dorset Safety Camera Partnership
www.dorsetsafetycameras.org.uk

Safecam
www.safecam.org.uk

Somerset Road Safety Partnership
www.roadsafetysomerset.org.uk

Further information
www.dvla.gov.uk
http://think.direct.gov.uk
www.dft.gov.uk
http://roadsafe.com

Key to map symbols

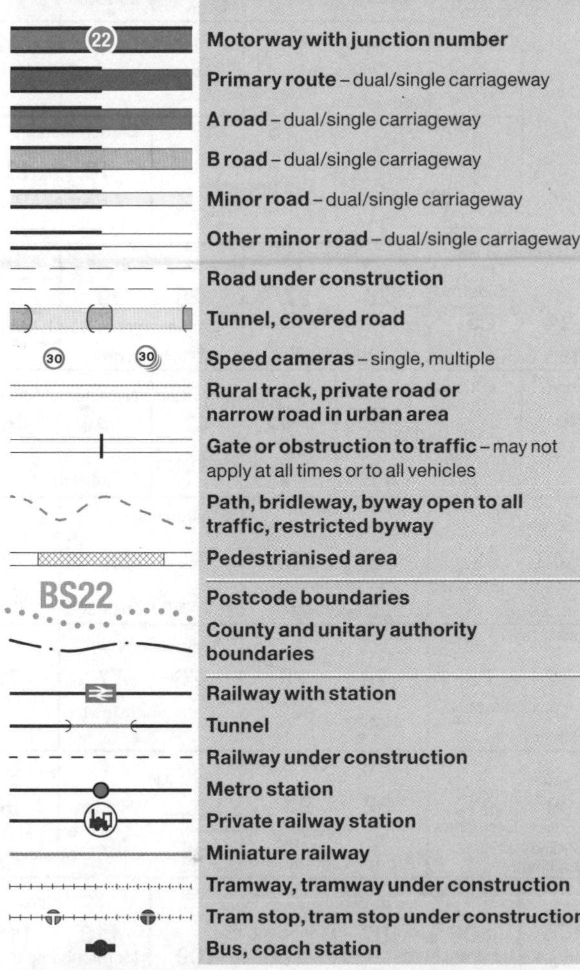

Motorway with junction number
Primary route – dual/single carriageway
A road – dual/single carriageway
B road – dual/single carriageway
Minor road – dual/single carriageway
Other minor road – dual/single carriageway
Road under construction
Tunnel, covered road
Speed cameras – single, multiple
Rural track, private road or narrow road in urban area
Gate or obstruction to traffic – may not apply at all times or to all vehicles
Path, bridleway, byway open to all traffic, restricted byway
Pedestrianised area
Postcode boundaries
County and unitary authority boundaries
Railway with station
Tunnel
Railway under construction
Metro station
Private railway station
Miniature railway
Tramway, tramway under construction
Tram stop, tram stop under construction
Bus, coach station

Abbreviations

Acad	Academy	Meml	Memorial
Allot Gdns	Allotments	Mon	Monument
Cemy	Cemetery	Mus	Museum
C Ctr	Civic centre	Obsy	Observatory
CH	Club house	Pal	Royal palace
Coll	College	PH	Public house
Crem	Crematorium	Recn Gd	Recreation ground
Ent	Enterprise	Resr	Reservoir
Ex H	Exhibition hall	Ret Pk	Retail park
Ind Est	Industrial Estate	Sch	School
IRB Sta	Inshore rescue boat station	Sh Ctr	Shopping centre
Inst	Institute	TH	Town hall / house
Ct	Law court	Trad Est	Trading estate
L Ctr	Leisure centre	Univ	University
LC	Level crossing	W Twr	Water tower
Liby	Library	Wks	Works
Mkt	Market	YH	Youth hostel

Ambulance station
Coastguard station
Fire station
Police station
Accident and Emergency entrance to hospital
Hospital
Place of worship
Information centre – open all year
Shopping centre
Parking
Park and Ride
Post Office
Camping site
Caravan site
Golf course
Picnic site
Church Non-Roman antiquity
ROMAN FORT Roman antiquity
Univ Important buildings, schools, colleges, universities and hospitals
Built-up area
Woods
River Medway Water name
River, weir
Stream
Canal, lock, tunnel
Water
Tidal water
263 58 87 Adjoining page indicators

The small numbers around the edges of the maps identify the 1-kilometre National Grid lines

The dark grey border on the inside edge of some pages indicates that the mapping does not continue onto the adjacent page

Enlarged maps only

Railway or bus station building
Place of interest
Parkland

The map scale on the pages numbered in green is 1¾ inches to 1 mile
2.76 cm to 1 km • 1:36206

0 ½ mile 1 mile 1½ miles 2 miles
0 500m 1 km 1½ km 2km

The map scale on the pages numbered in blue is 3½ inches to 1 mile
5.52 cm to 1 km • 1:18103

0 ¼ mile ½ mile ¾ mile 1 mile
0 250m 500m 750m 1km

The map scale on the pages numbered in red is 7 inches to 1 mile
11.04 cm to 1 km • 1:9051

0 220yds 440yds 660yds ½ mile
0 125m 250m 375m 500m

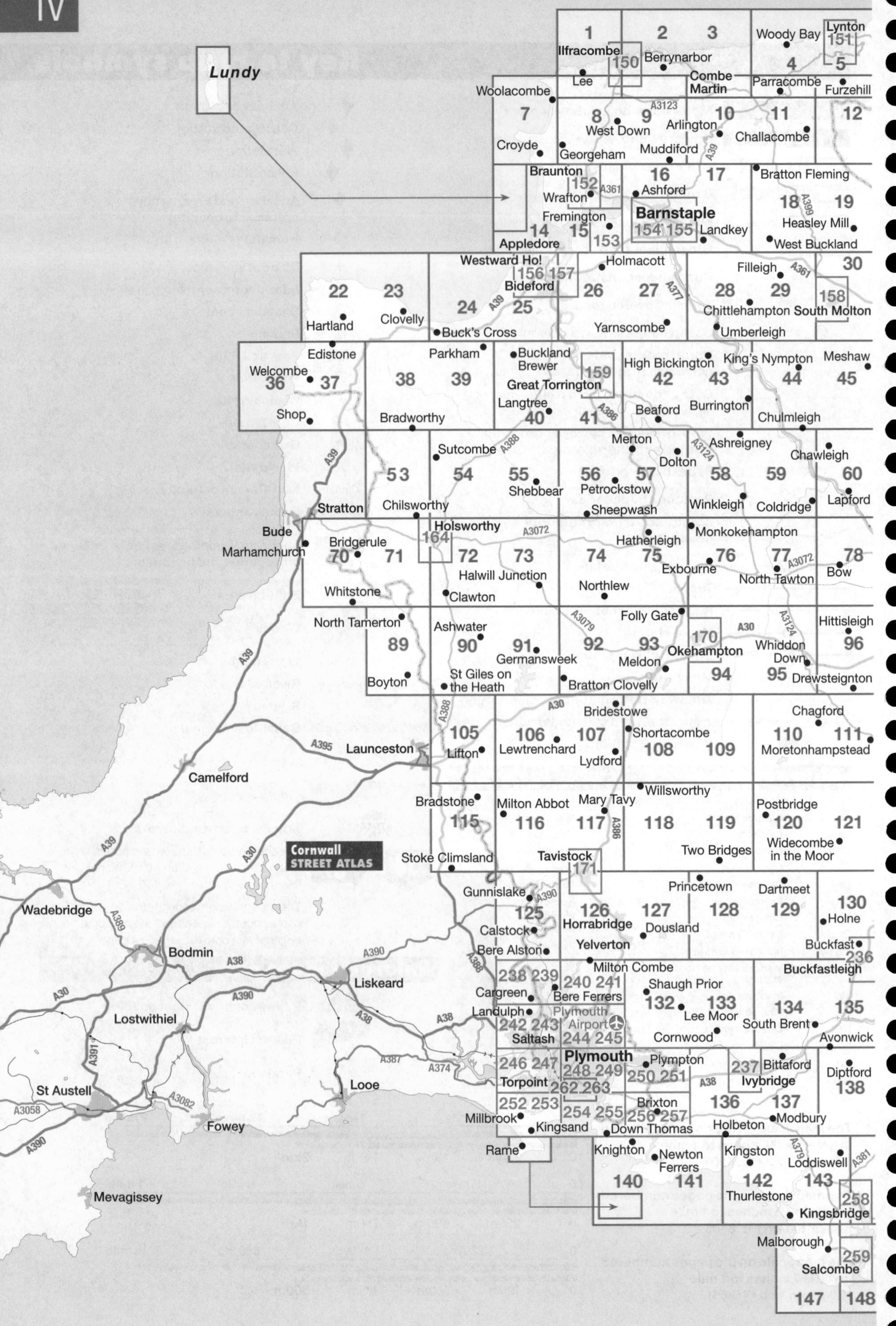

Lundy
Cornwall STREET ATLAS
Ilfracombe
Lee
Woolacombe
Berrynarbor
Combe Martin
Woody Bay
Lynton
Parracombe
Furzehill
West Down
Arlington
Challacombe
Croyde
Georgeham
Muddiford
Braunton
Wrafton
Ashford
Bratton Fleming
Barnstaple
Fremington
Landkey
Heasley Mill
West Buckland
Appledore
Westward Ho!
Bideford
Holmacott
Filleigh
South Molton
Hartland
Clovelly
Buck's Cross
Yarnscombe
Chittlehampton
Umberleigh
Edistone
Welcombe
Shop
Parkham
Bradworthy
Buckland Brewer
Great Torrington
Langtree
High Bickington
King's Nympton
Meshaw
Beaford
Burrington
Chulmleigh
Sutcombe
Merton
Dolton
Ashreigney
Chawleigh
Shebbear
Petrockstow
Sheepwash
Winkleigh
Coldridge
Lapford
Stratton
Chilsworthy
Bude
Marhamchurch
Bridgerule
Holsworthy
Hatherleigh
Monkokehampton
Exbourne
North Tawton
Bow
Halwill Junction
Whitstone
Clawton
Northlew
North Tamerton
Ashwater
Folly Gate
Hittisleigh
Okehampton
Whiddon Down
Germansweek
Meldon
Drewsteignton
Boyton
St Giles on the Heath
Bratton Clovelly
Bridestowe
Chagford
Shortacombe
Launceston
Lifton
Lewtrenchard
Lydford
Moretonhampstead
Camelford
Willsworthy
Bradstone
Milton Abbot
Mary Tavy
Postbridge
Widecombe in the Moor
Two Bridges
Stoke Climsland
Tavistock
Princetown
Dartmeet
Gunnislake
Wadebridge
Horrabridge
Dousland
Holne
Calstock
Bere Alston
Yelverton
Buckfast
Buckfastleigh
Bodmin
Milton Combe
Liskeard
Cargreen
Shaugh Prior
Bere Ferrers
Landulph
Plymouth Airport
Lee Moor
Lostwithiel
Saltash
Cornwood
South Brent
Avonwick
Plymouth
Plympton
Bittaford
Diptford
Torpoint
Ivybridge
Looe
St Austell
Brixton
Modbury
Millbrook
Fowey
Kingsand
Down Thomas
Holbeton
Rame
Knighton
Newton Ferrers
Kingston
Loddiswell
Thurlestone
Kingsbridge
Mevagissey
Malborough
Salcombe
A3123
A39
A361
A399
A377
A386
A388
A3124
A3072
A30
A3079
A395
A390
A38
A389
A391
A3082
A3058
A387
A374
A379
A381
1
2
3
4
5
7
8
9
10
11
12
14
15
16
17
18
19
22
23
24
25
26
27
28
29
30
36
37
38
39
40
41
42
43
44
45
53
54
55
56
57
58
59
60
70
71
72
73
74
75
76
77
78
89
90
91
92
93
94
95
96
105
106
107
108
109
110
111
115
116
117
118
119
120
121
125
126
127
128
129
130
132
133
134
135
136
137
138
140
141
142
143
147
148
150
151
152
153
154
155
156
157
158
159
164
170
171
236
237
238
239
240
241
242
243
244
245
246
247
248
249
250
251
252
253
254
255
256
257
258
259
262
263

Key to map pages

104	Map pages at 1¾ inches to 1 mile
166	Map pages at 3½ inches to 1 mile
261	Map pages at 7 inches to 1 mile

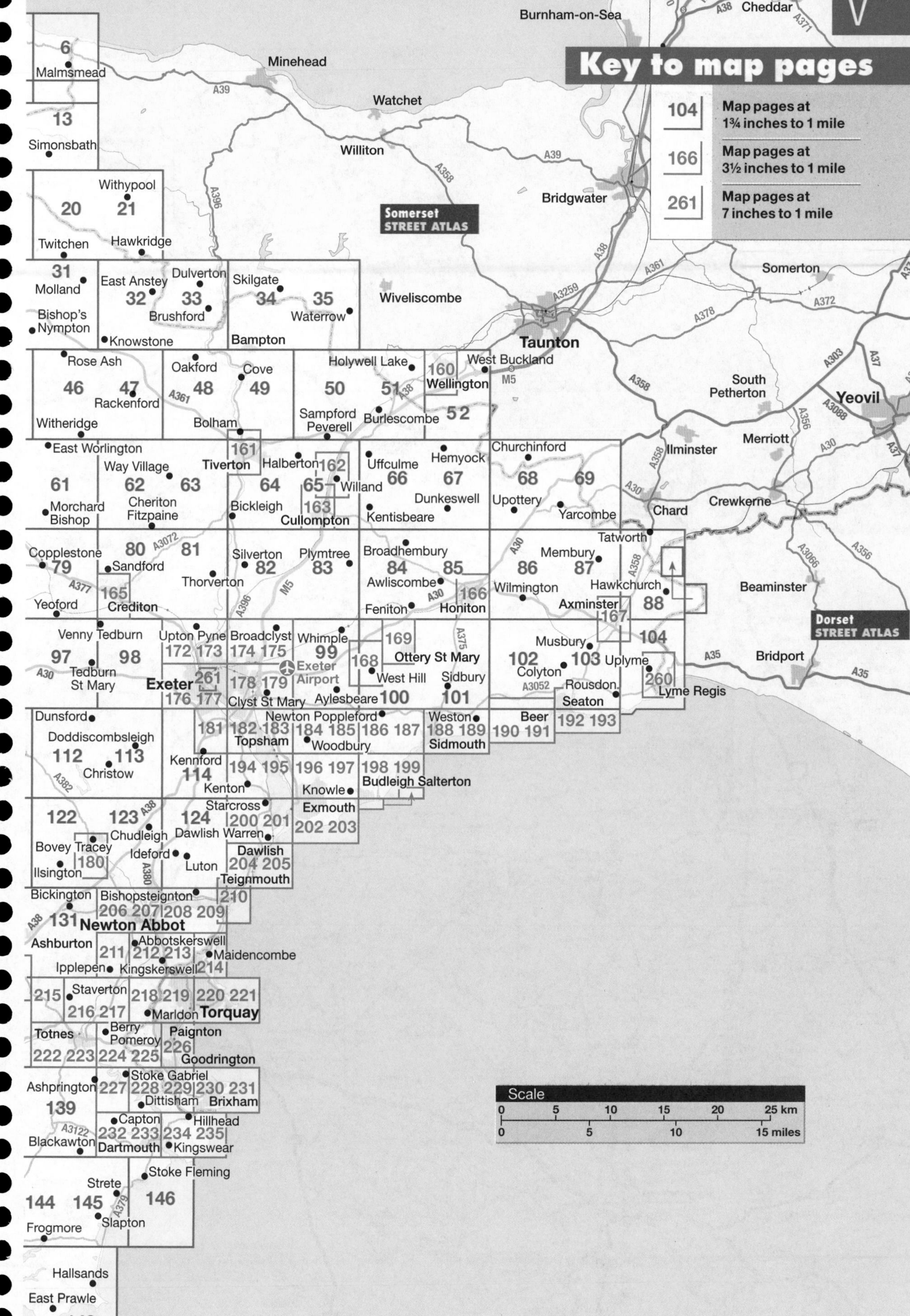

Route planning

Scale

0 5 10 km

0 5 miles

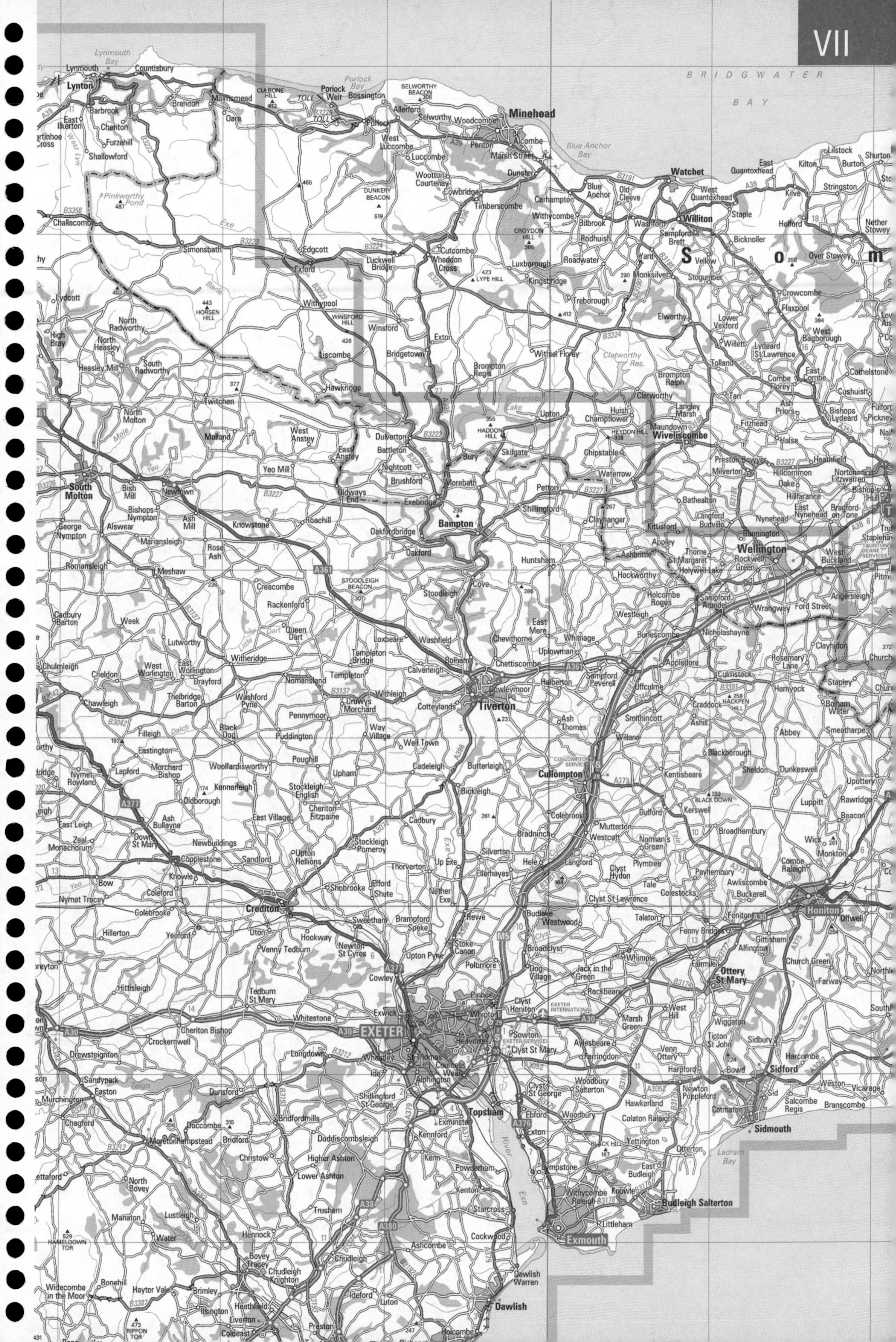
BRIDGWATER BAY
Lynmouth Bay
Lynmouth
Lynton
Countisbury
Porlock Bay
Porlock
Porlock Weir
Bossington
SELWORTHY BEACON
Minehead
Barbrook
Brendon
Malmsmead
Oare
Cheriton
Furzehill
Shallowford
Allerford
Selworthy
Woodcombe
Alcombe
Blue Anchor Bay
West Luccombe
Luccombe
Wootton Courtenay
Cowbridge
Timberscombe
Marsh Street
Dunster
Carhampton
Blue Anchor
Old Cleeve
Watchet
East Quantoxhead
West Quantoxhead
Williton
Kilve
Kilton
Lilstock
Shurton
Stringston
Holford
Nether Stowey
Over Stowey
Pinkworthy Pond
Challacombe
DUNKERY BEACON
Simonsbath
Exford
Edgcott
Luckwell Bridge
Cutcombe
Wheddon Cross
CROYDON HILL
LYPE HILL
Luxborough
Kingsbridge
Roadwater
Withycombe
Bilbrook
Rodhuish
Washford
Sampford Brett
Yard
Monksilver
Stogumber
Bicknoller
Vellow
Crowcombe
Flaxpool
Lydcott
HORSEN HILL
Withypool
WINSFORD HILL
Winsford
Exton
Treborough
Elworthy
Lower Vexford
West Bagborough
North Radworthy
North Heasley
High Bray
Heasley Mill
South Radworthy
Liscombe
Bridgetown
Brompton Regis
Withiel Florey
Clatworthy Res.
Willett
Lydeard St Lawrence
Tolland
Combe Florey
East Combe
Cothelstone
Hawkridge
Twitchen
North Molton
Molland
West Anstey
East Anstey
Dulverton
Battleton
Nightcott
Brushford
Yeo Mill
Wimbleball Lake
HADDON HILL
Upton
Skilgate
Bury
Morebath
Huish Champflower
HEYDON HILL
Chipstable
Waterrow
Clatworthy
Brompton Ralph
Langley Marsh
Maundown
Wiveliscombe
Fitzhead
Ash Priors
Bishops Lydeard
Halse
Preston Bowyer
Milverton
Hillcommon
Oake
Hillfarrance
Heathfield
Norton Fitzwarren
South Molton
Bish Mill
Newtown
Bishops Nympton
Alswear
George Nympton
Ash Mill
Knowstone
Roachill
Oldways End
Exebridge
Oakfordbridge
Bampton
Petton
Shillingford
Clayhanger
Bathealton
Langford Budville
Kittisford
Nynehead
East Nynehead
Bradford-on-Tone
Mariansleigh
Rose Ash
Oakford
Huntsham
Ashbrittle
Appley
Thorne St Margaret
Holywell Lake
Runnington
Wellington
Rockwell Green
West Buckland
Romansleigh
Meshaw
Creacombe
Rackenford
STOODLEIGH BEACON
Stoodleigh
Cove
Hockworthy
Holcombe Rogus
Sampford Arundel
Wrangway
Ford Street
Angersleigh
Cadbury Barton
Week
Queen Dart
Loxbeare
Washfield
East Mere
Chevithorne
Westleigh
Burlescombe
Whitnage
Nicholashayne
Lutworthy
Witheridge
Templeton Bridge
Templeton
Calverleigh
Bolham
Chettiscombe
Uplowman
Appledore
Rosemary Lane
Clayhidon
Chulmleigh
Cheldon
West Worlington
East Worlington
Brayford
Nomansland
Cowleymoor
Halberton
Sampford Peverell
Culmstock
Hemyock
Chawleigh
Thelbridge Barton
Washford Pyne
Cruwys Morchard
Withleigh
Cotteylands
Tiverton
Uffculme
Craddock
HACKPEN HILL
Stapley
Bolham Water
Pennymoor
Smithincott
Ashill
Fillleigh
Black Dog
Puddington
Way Village
Well Town
Ash Thomas
Willand
Abbey
Smeatharpe
Eastington
Blackborough
Lapford
Morchard Bishop
Woolfardisworthy
Poughill
Cadeleigh
Butterleigh
Cullompton
Kentisbeare
Sheldon
Dunkeswell
Nymet Rowland
Kennerleigh
Oldborough
Stockleigh English
Upham
Bickleigh
BLACK DOWN
Upottery
Luppitt
Rawridge
Ash Bullayne
East Village
Cheriton Fitzpaine
Cadbury
Colebrook
Dulford
Kerswell
Beacon
East Leigh
Zeal Monachorum
Down St Mary
Newbuildings
Stockleigh Pomeroy
Upton Hellions
Mutterton
Westcott
Norman's Green
Broadhembury
Wick
Monkton
Copplestone
Sandford
Thorverton
Up Exe
Silverton
Hele
Langford
Clyst Hydon
Plymtree
Payhembury
Combe Raleigh
Knowle
Bow
Coleford
Nymet Tracey
Shobrooke
Efford
Shute
Nether Exe
Ellerhayes
Tale
Colestocks
Awliscombe
Buckerell
Honiton
Offwell
Colebrooke
Crediton
Clyst St Lawrence
Bradlake
Westwood
Talaton
Feniton
Fenny Bridges
Gittisham
Hillerton
Yeoford
Uton
Sweetham
Brampford Speke
Hewe
Rewe
Hookway
Venny Tedburn
Newton St Cyres
Upton Pyne
Stoke Canon
Poltimore
Broadclyst
Whimple
Fairmile
Alfington
Church Green
Farway
Dog Village
Jack in the Green
Ottery St Mary
Cowley
Hittisleigh
Tedburn St Mary
Rockbeare
Pinhoe
Clyst Honiton
EXETER INTERNATIONAL
Marsh Green
West Hill
Wiggaton
Cheriton Bishop
Whitestone
Exwick
EXETER
Whipton
Sowton
EXETER SERVICES
Heavitree
Clyst St Mary
Aylesbeare
Tipton St John
Sidbury
Crockernwell
Drewsteignton
Longdown
Whitestone
Whitley
St Thomas
Ide
Countess Wear
Alphington
Farringdon
Venn Ottery
Harpford
Bowd
Sidford
Harcombe
Sandypark
Easton
Dunsford
Shillingford St George
Topsham
Clyst St George
Woodbury Salterton
Newton Poppleford
Weston
Vicarage
Murchington
Chagford
Doccombe
Bridfordmills
Exminster
Ebford
Hawkerland
Colaton Raleigh
Cotmaton
Salcombe Regis
Branscombe
Sidmouth
Moretonhampstead
Bridford
Doddiscombsleigh
Kennford
Exton
Woodbury
Yettington
Otterton
Ladram Bay
Christow
Higher Ashton
Kenn
Powderham
Lympstone
BLACK HILL
East Budleigh
North Bovey
Lower Ashton
Kenton
River Exe
Withycombe Raleigh
Knowle
Budleigh Salterton
Manaton
Lustleigh
Trusham
Starcross
Littleham
HAMELDOWN TOR
Water
Hennock
Cockwood
Exmouth
Ashcombe
Bovey Tracey
Chudleigh
Chudleigh Knighton
Dawlish Warren
Widecombe in the Moor
Bonehill
Haytor Vale
Brimley
Ideford
Luton
Dawlish
Heathfield
Ilsington
Liverton
RIPPON TOR
Coldeast
Preston
Holcombe
Exe
Barle
Mole
Yeo
Little Dart
Dalch
Teign
Culm
Clyst
Tale
Otter
Kenn
M5
A30
A38
A39
A361
A373
A375
A377
A379
A380
A396
A3052
B3212
B3223
B3224
B3227
B3137
B3042
B3181
B3191
B3178
B3179
B3180
B3174
B3177
B3391
B3440
TOLL

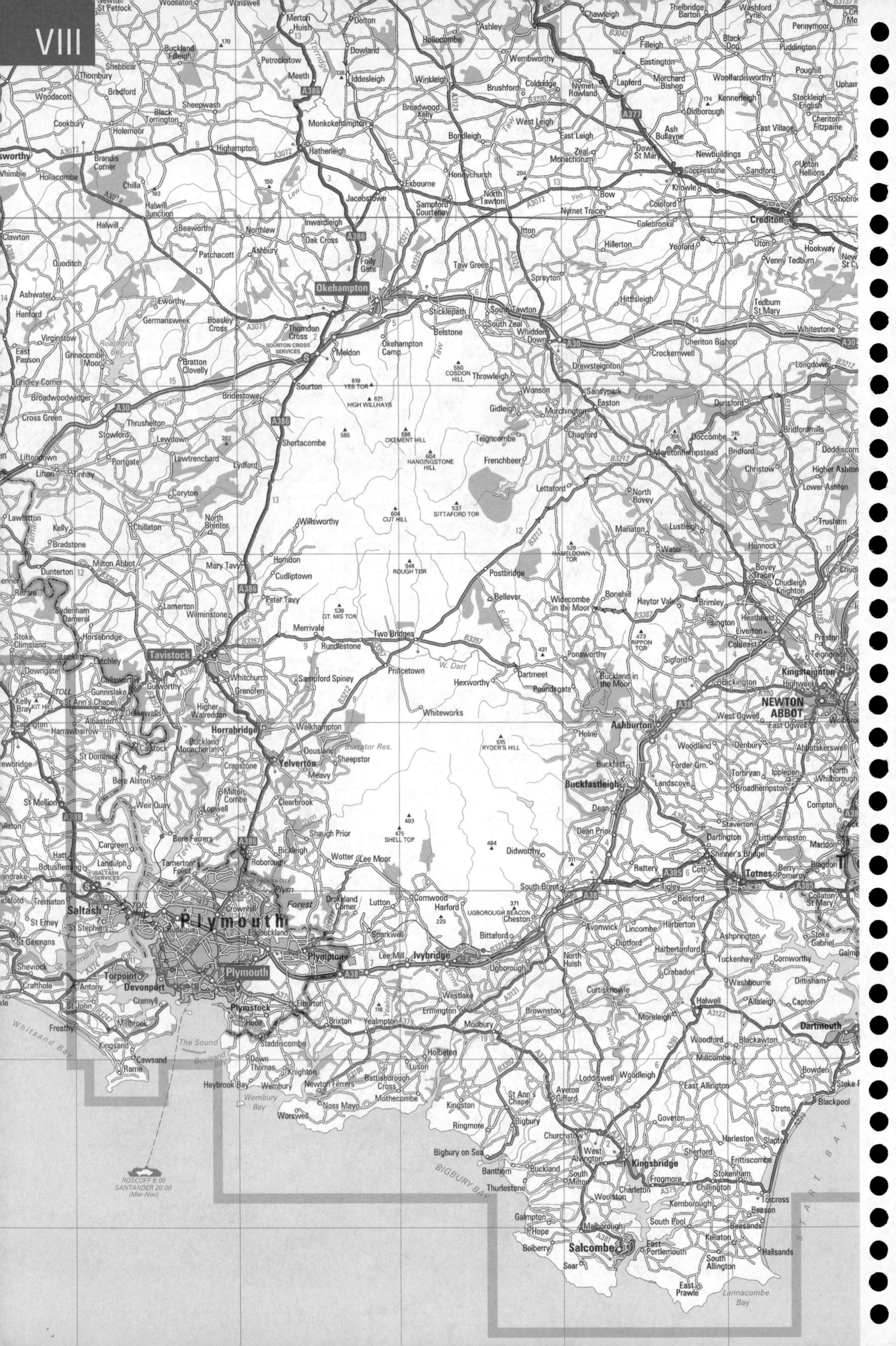
St Petrock
Woolfardisworthy
Winswell
Merton
Huish
Dolton
Chawleigh
Thelbridge Barton
Washford Pyne
Pennymoor
Buckland Filleigh
Petrockstow
Hollocombe
Ashley
Filleigh
Black Dog
Puddington
Torridge
Shebbear
Meeth
Iddesleigh
Dowland
Wembworthy
Eastington
Poughill
Thornbury
Winkleigh
Lapford
Morchard Bishop
Woolfardisworthy
Bradford
Brushford
Coldridge
Nymet Rowland
Kennerleigh
Stockleigh English
Woodacott
Sheepwash
Black Torrington
Broadwood Kelly
Oldborough
Cheriton Fitzpaine
Cookbury
Holemoor
Monkokehampton
West Leigh
East Leigh
Ash Bullayne
East Village
Bondleigh
Zeal Monachorum
Down St Mary
Newbuildings
Upton Hellions
Highampton
Hatherleigh
Honeychurch
Copplestone
Sandford
Brandis Corner
Hollacombe
Chilla
Exbourne
Knowle
Halwill Junction
Jacobstowe
North Tawton
Bow
Coleford
Sampford Courtenay
Nymet Tracey
Crediton
Halwill
Beaworthy
Inwardleigh
Colebrooke
Clawton
Northlew
Oak Cross
Itton
Hillerton
Yeoford
Uton
Hookway
Patchacott
Ashbury
Venny Tedburn
Quoditch
Folly Gate
Taw Green
Spreyton
Ashwater
Okehampton
Hittisleigh
Eworthy
Tedburn St Mary
Henford
Germansweek
Boasley Cross
Sticklepath
South Tawton
South Zeal
Whiddon Down
Belstone
Virginstow
Thorndon Cross
SOURTON CROSS SERVICES
Cheriton Bishop
Whitestone
East Panson
Roadford Res.
Meldon
Okehampton Camp
Crockernwell
Grinacombe Moor
Bratton Clovelly
COSDON HILL
Throwleigh
Drewsteignton
Longdown
Gridley Corner
Sourton
YES TOR
HIGH WILLHAYS
Wonson
Sandypark
Easton
Teign
Dunsford
Broadwoodwidger
Bridestowe
Gidleigh
Murchington
Cross Green
Thrushelton
Chagford
Doccombe
Bridford
Bridfordmills
Stowford
Lewdown
Shortacombe
OKEMENT HILL
Teigncombe
Moretonhampstead
Doddiscombe
Liftondown
Portgate
Lewtrencharrd
Lydford
HANGINGSTONE HILL
Frenchbeer
Christow
Higher Ashton
Lifton
Tinhay
Lettaford
Lower Ashton
Coryton
North Bovey
Lawhitton
SITTAFORD TOR
Kelly
Chillaton
North Brentor
Willsworthy
CUT HILL
Manaton
Lustleigh
Trusham
Bradstone
HAMELDOWN TOR
Water
Hennock
Milton Abbot
Horndon
ROUGH TOR
Dunterton
Mary Tavy
Cudliptown
Postbridge
Bovey Tracey
Chudleigh Knighton
Rezare
Peter Tavy
Bellever
Bonehill
Haytor Vale
Brimley
Sydenham Damerel
Lamerton
Wilminstone
GT. MIS TOR
Widecombe in the Moor
Ilsington
Heathfield
Horsebridge
Merrivale
Two Bridges
RIPPON TOR
Liverton
Stoke Climsland
Rundlestone
Coldeast
Preston
Tavistock
Ponsworthy
Teigngrace
Latchley
Princetown
W. Dart
Sigford
Downgate
Chilsworthy
Whitchurch
Sampford Spiney
Dartmeet
Buckland in the Moor
Kingsteignton
Gunnislake
Gulworthy
Grenofen
Hexworthy
Poundsgate
Bickington
Highweek
Kelly Bray
St Ann's Chapel
TOLL
NEWTON ABBOT
Drakewalls
Higher Walreddon
Whiteworks
West Ogwell
Callington
Albaston
East Ogwell
Harrowbarrow
Horrabridge
Walkhampton
Ashburton
Holne
Calstock
Buckland Monachorum
Burrator Res.
RYDER'S HILL
Woodland
Denbury
Abbotskerswell
St Dominick
Dousland
Sheepstor
Buckfast
Yelverton
Forder Grn.
Torbryan
Ipplepen
North Whilborough
Crapstone
Meavy
Buckfastleigh
Landscove
Broadhempston
Bere Alston
St Mellion
Milton Combe
Clearbrook
Dean
Compton
Weir Quay
Lopwell
Staverton
Pillaton
Dean Prior
Plym
Shaugh Prior
SHELL TOP
Dartington
Littlehempston
Bere Ferrers
Marldon
Hatt
Cargreen
Bickleigh
Didworthy
Shinner's Bridge
Botusfleming
Landulph
Wotter
Lee Moor
Rattery
Cott
Totnes
Berry Pomeroy
Blagdon
Tamerton Foliot
Roborough
Landrake
SALTASH SERVICES
South Brent
Tigley
Belsford
Collaton St Mary
Trematon
Saltash
Plymouth
Forest
Drakeland Corner
Lutton
Cornwood
Harford
UGBOROUGH BEACON
Cheston
St Erney
St Stephens
St Budeaux
Crownhill
Eggbuckland
Sparkwell
Bittaford
Avonwick
Lincombe
Harberton
Ashprington
Stoke Gabriel
St Germans
Plympton
Lee Mill
Ivybridge
Ugborough
Diptford
Harbertonford
Tuckenhay
Cornworthy
Galmpton
Sheviock
Torpoint
Devonport
North Huish
Crabadon
Crafthole
Antony
Washbourne
Dittisham
Cremyll
Westlake
Curtisknowle
St John
Plymstock
Elburton
Ermington
Brownston
Moreleigh
Halwell
Allaleigh
Capton
Hooe
Millbrook
Freathy
Whitsand Bay
Brixton
Yealmpton
Modbury
Dartmouth
Kingsand
The Sound
Staddiscombe
Woodford
Blackawton
Cawsand
Bovisand Bay
Down Thomas
Holbeton
Rame
Millcombe
Heybrook Bay
Wembury
Knighton
Battisborough Cross
Luson
Aveton Gifford
Loddiswell
Woodleigh
Bowden
East Allington
Stoke Fleming
Wembury Bay
Newton Ferrers
Noss Mayo
Mothecombe
Kingston
St Ann's Chapel
Blackpool
Worswell
Ringmore
Bigbury
Goveton
Strete
Churchstow
Bigbury on Sea
West Alvington
Kingsbridge
Harleston
Slapton
Sherford
Frittiscombe
Bantham
Buckland
South Milton
Charleton
Stokenham
ROSCOFF 6:00
SANTANDER 20:00
(Mar-Nov)
BIGBURY BAY
Thurlestone
Chillington
Torcross
Woolston
Kernborough
Beeson
Galmpton
Malborough
South Pool
Beesands
Hope
Bolberry
Salcombe
East Portlemouth
Kellaton
Hallsands
Soar
South Allington
East Prawle
Lannacombe Bay
START BAY

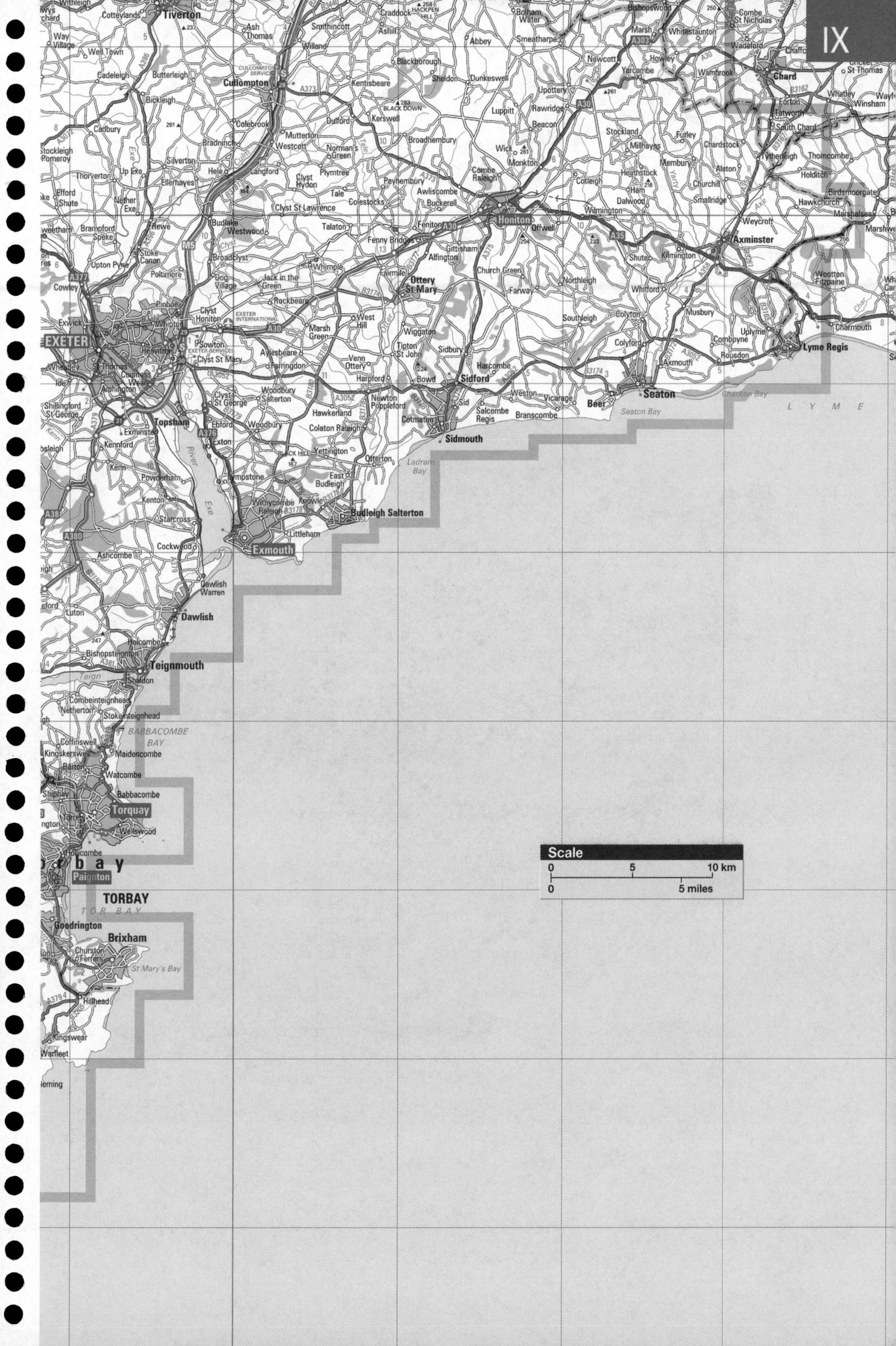
IX
Tiverton
Cullompton
Chard
Honiton
Axminster
EXETER
Exmouth
Budleigh Salterton
Sidmouth
Sidford
Ottery St Mary
Seaton
Beer
Lyme Regis
Charmouth
Topsham
Dawlish
Teignmouth
Torquay
Paignton
Brixham
TORBAY
BABBACOMBE BAY
TOR BAY
Seaton Bay
Ladram Bay
Charlton Bay
L Y M E
River Exe
Scale
0
5
10 km
0
5 miles

Major administrative and Postcode boundaries

Scale: 1¾ inches to 1 mile
0 ¼ ½ mile
0 250m 500m 750m 1 km

2

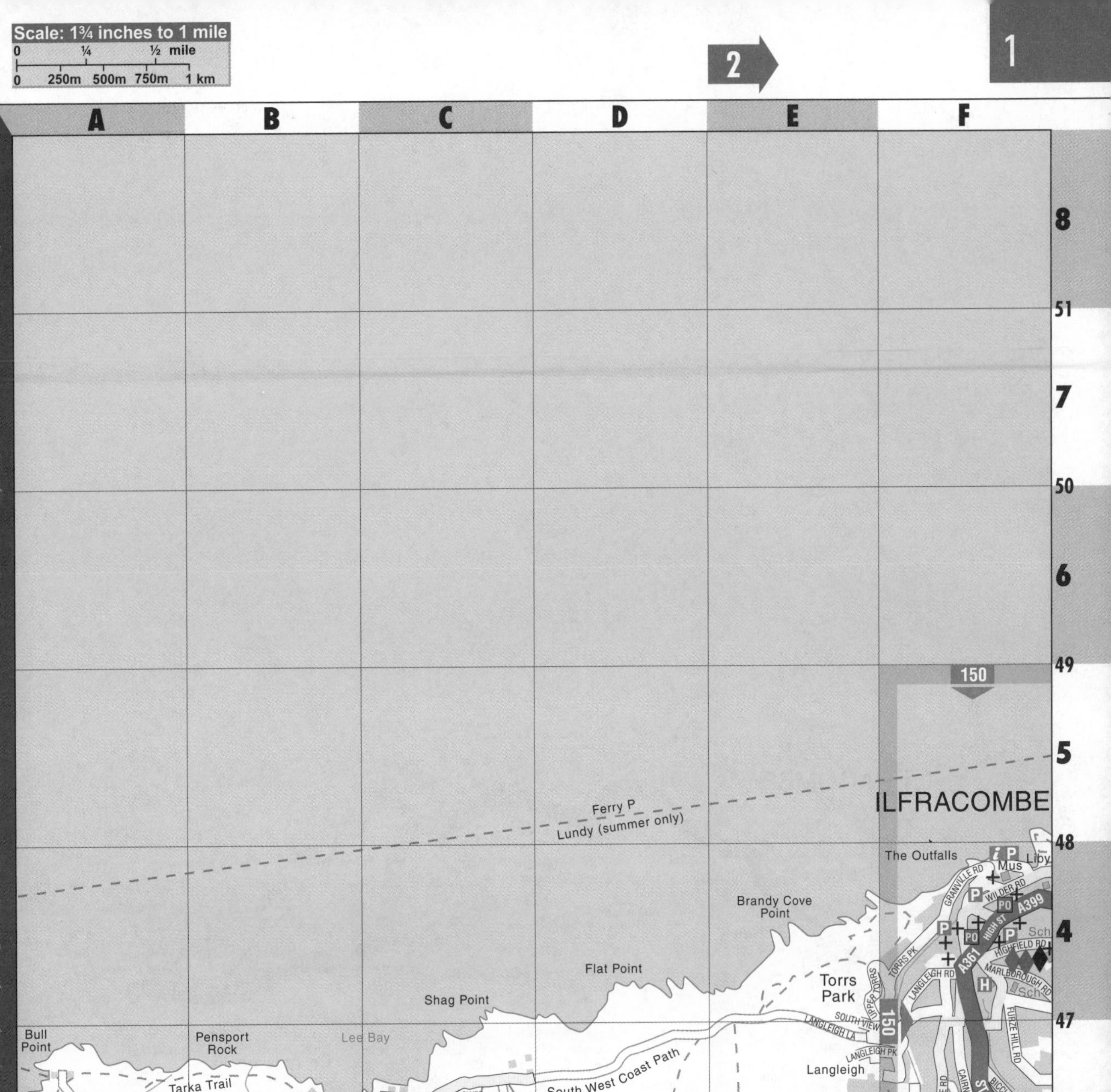

7
8
2
For full street detail of the highlighted area see page 150.

1

Scale: 1¾ inches to 1 mile

0 ¼ ½ mile

0 250m 500m 750m 1 km

ILFRACOMBE
Berrynarbor
Chambercombe
Hele
Goosewell
Widmouth
Two Pots
EX34

BERRY LA 1
NEWBERRY LA 2
NEWBERRY RD 3
THE GABLES 4
WHITEGATES 5
SEASIDE HILL 6
HANGMAN PATH 7
CROSS ST 8
MOORY MDW 9
REW'S CL 10
LIBRA GDNS 11
KING ST 12
UMBER CL 13
TRENODE AVE 14
BELMONT AVE 15

150

9

For full street detail of the highlighted area see page 150.

1

9

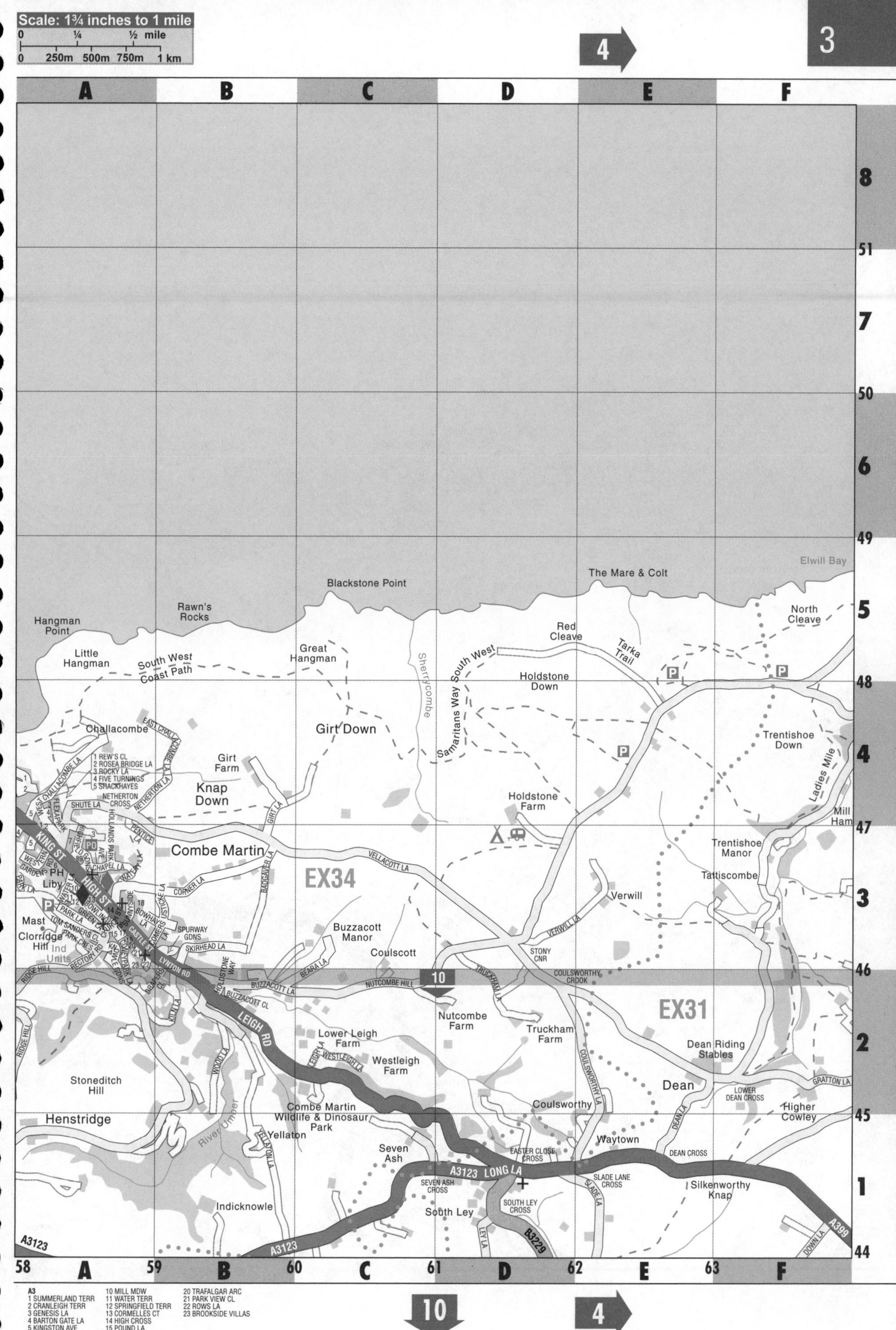

A3
1 SUMMERLAND TERR
2 CRANLEIGH TERR
3 GENESIS LA
4 BARTON GATE LA
5 KINGSTON AVE
6 MANSION TERR
7 VALLEY LA
8 KINGSLEY TERR
9 ORCHARD CL
10 MILL MDW
11 WATER TERR
12 SPRINGFIELD TERR
13 CORMELLES CT
14 HIGH CROSS
15 POUND LA
16 ROCK LA
17 WET LA
18 SUNNYSIDE COTTS
19 UMBERSIDE
20 TRAFALGAR ARC
21 PARK VIEW CL
22 ROWS LA
23 BROOKSIDE VILLAS

3

Scale: 1¾ inches to 1 mile
0 ¼ ½ mile
0 250m 500m 750m 1 km

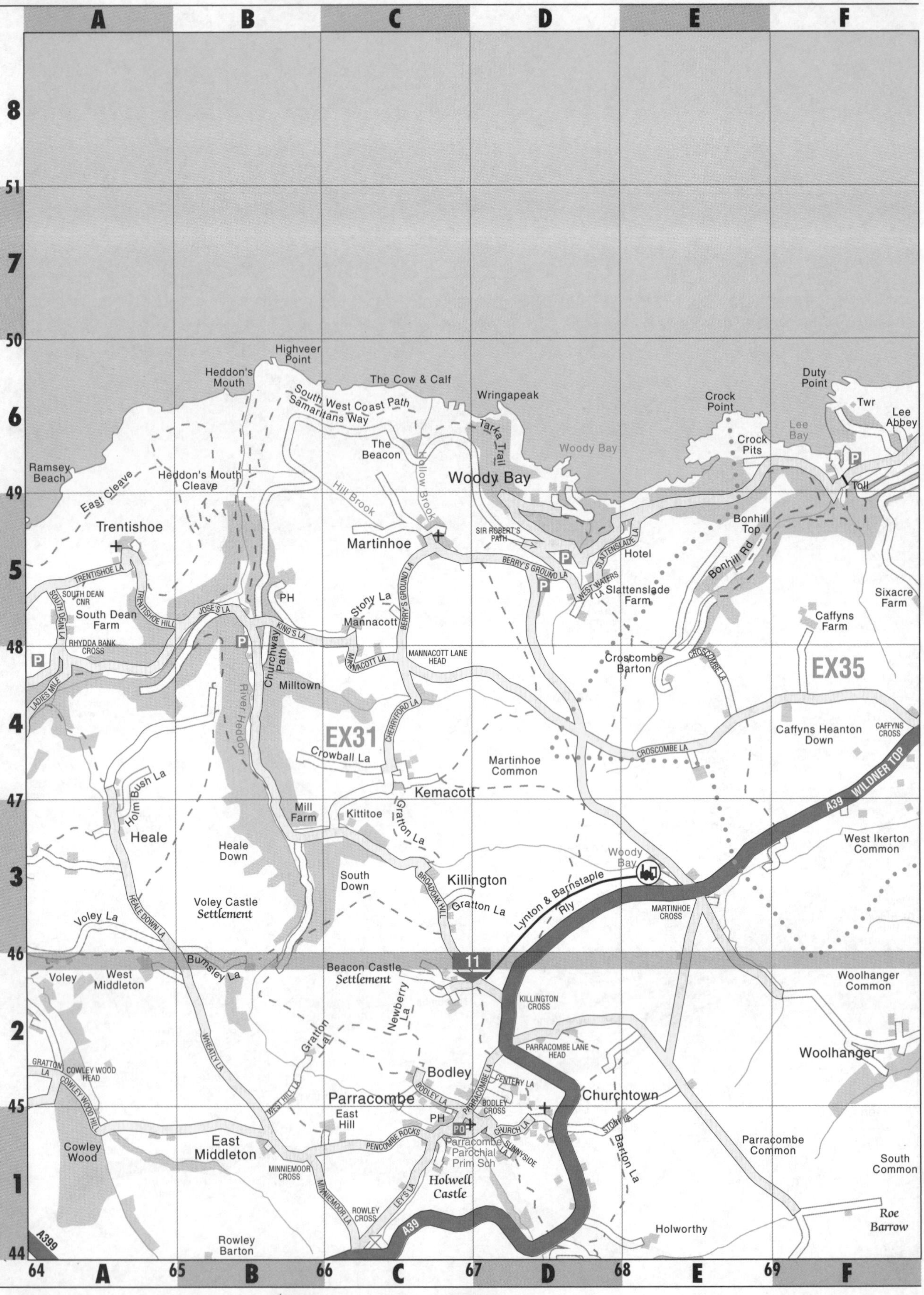

Highveer Point
Heddon's Mouth
The Cow & Calf
South West Coast Path
Samaritans Way
Wringapeak
Tarka Trail
Crock Point
Duty Point
Twr
Lee Abbey
Lee Bay
Woody Bay
Crock Pits
The Beacon
Hollow Brook
Hill Brook
Ramsey Beach
East Cleave
Heddon's Mouth Cleave
Woody Bay
Toll
Trentishoe
Martinhoe
Sir Robert's Path
Bonhill Top
Hotel
Berry's Ground La
Slattenslade La
West Waters La
Slattenslade Farm
Bonhill Rd
Sixacre Farm
Trentishoe La
South Dean CNR
South Dean La
Trentishoe Hill
South Dean Farm
Jose's La
PH
Stony La
Mannacott
King's La
Caffyns Farm
Rhydda Bank Cross
Mannacott La
Mannacott Lane Head
Croscombe Barton
Croscombe La
EX35
Churchway Path
Milltown
River Heddon
Ladies Mile
Cherryford La
EX31
Caffyns Heanton Down
Caffyns Cross
Croscombe La
Crowball La
Martinhoe Common
Holm Bush La
Kemacott
A39 Wildner Top
Mill Farm
Kittitoe
Gratton La
Heale
Heale Down
West Ikerton Common
Woody Bay
South Down
Killington
Lynton & Barnstaple Rly
Broadoak Hill
Gratton La
Martinhoe Cross
Voley Castle Settlement
Voley La
Heale Down La
Bumsley La
Beacon Castle Settlement
Voley
West Middleton
Woolhanger Common
Killington Cross
Newberry La
Gratton La
Wheatley La
Woolhanger
Paracombe Lane Head
Gratton La
Cowley Wood Head
Cowley Wood Hill
Bodley
Paracombe La
Centery La
Churchtown
West Hill La
Bodley La
Parracombe
Bodley Cross
East Hill
PH
PO
Church La
Stony La
Barton La
Cowley Wood
East Middleton
Pencombe Rocks
Parracombe Parochial Prim Sch
Sunnyside
Parracombe Common
South Common
Minniemoor Cross
Minniemoor La
Ley's La
Holwell Castle
Rowley Cross
Roe Barrow
A399
A39
Rowley Barton
Holworthy

Grid: A B C D E F; 8, 7, 6, 5, 4, 3, 2, 1; 51, 50, 49, 48, 47, 46, 45, 44; 64, 65, 66, 67, 68, 69

3

11

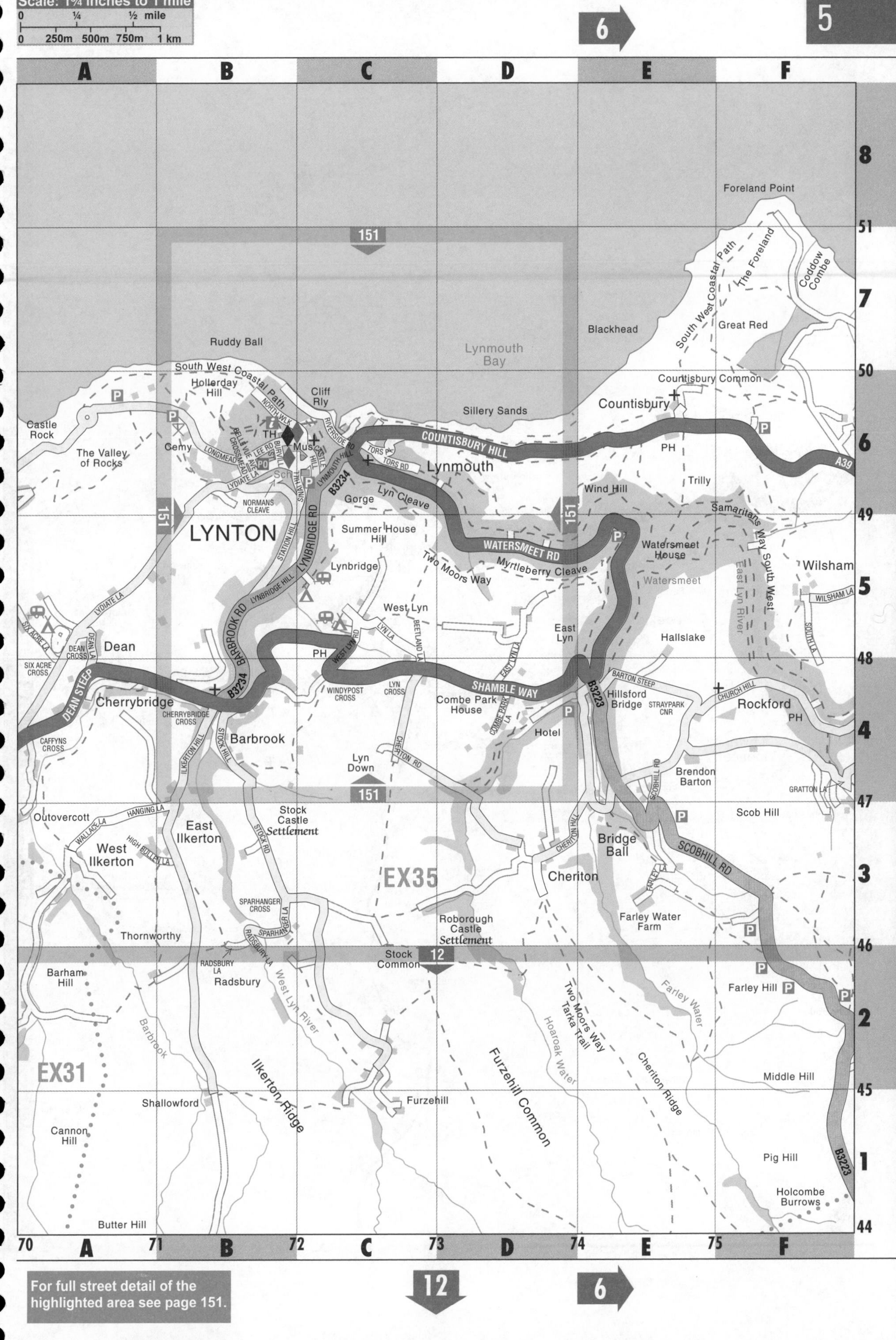

For full street detail of the highlighted area see page 151.

5

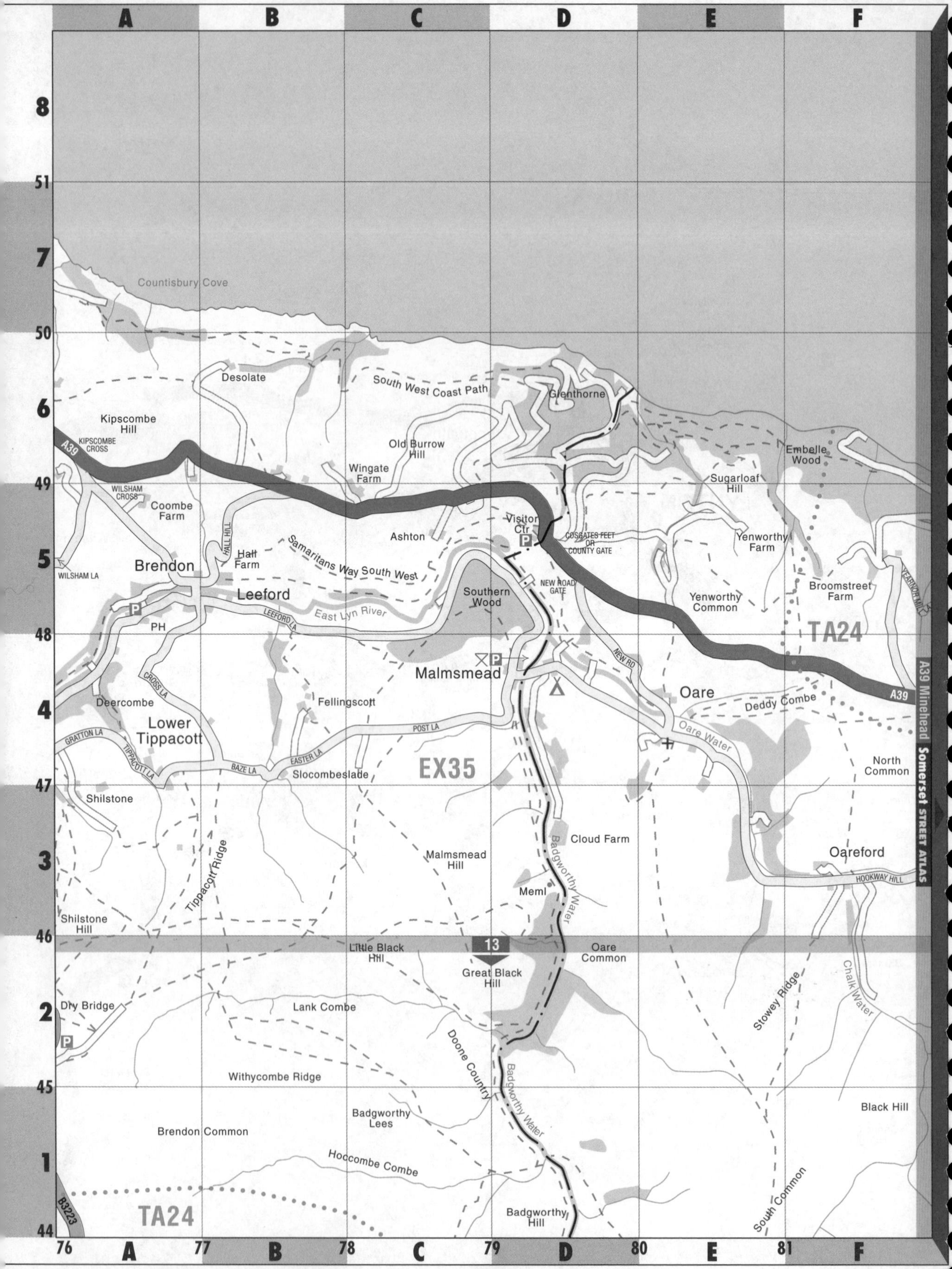
Scale: 1¾ inches to 1 mile
0 ¼ ½ mile
0 250m 500m 750m 1 km
A B C D E F
8
51
7
50
6
49
5
48
4
47
3
46
2
45
1
44
76 77 78 79 80 81
Countisbury Cove
Desolate
South West Coast Path
Glenthorne
Kipscombe Hill
KIPSCOMBE CROSS
A39
Old Burrow Hill
Embelle Wood
Wingate Farm
Sugarloaf Hill
WILSHAM CROSS
Coombe Farm
Visitor Ctr
Ashton
COSGATES FEET OR COUNTY GATE
Yenworthy Farm
HALL HILL
Hall Farm
Samaritans Way South West
Brendon
WILSHAM LA
NEW ROAD GATE
Southern Wood
Broomstreet Farm
Leeford
Yenworthy Common
LEEFORD LA
East Lyn River
PH
TA24
Malmsmead
NEW RD
CROSS LA
Deercombe
Fellingscott
Oare
Deddy Combe
A39
A39 Minehead
Lower Tippacott
POST LA
Oare Water
GRATTON LA
TIPPACOTT LA
BAZE LA
EASTER LA
Slocombeslade
EX35
North Common
Shilstone
Somerset STREET ATLAS
Cloud Farm
Tippacott Ridge
Malmsmead Hill
Oareford
HOOKWAY HILL
Badgworthy Water
Meml
Shilstone Hill
Little Black Hill
13
Oare Common
Great Black Hill
Chalk Water
Stowey Ridge
Dry Bridge
Lank Combe
Doone Country
Badgworthy Water
Withycombe Ridge
Black Hill
Badgworthy Lees
Brendon Common
Hoccombe Combe
B3223
South Common
TA24
Badgworthy Hill

5

13

Scale: 1¾ inches to 1 mile

7
Scale: 1¾ inches to 1 mile
0 ¼ ½ mile
0 250m 500m 750m 1 km

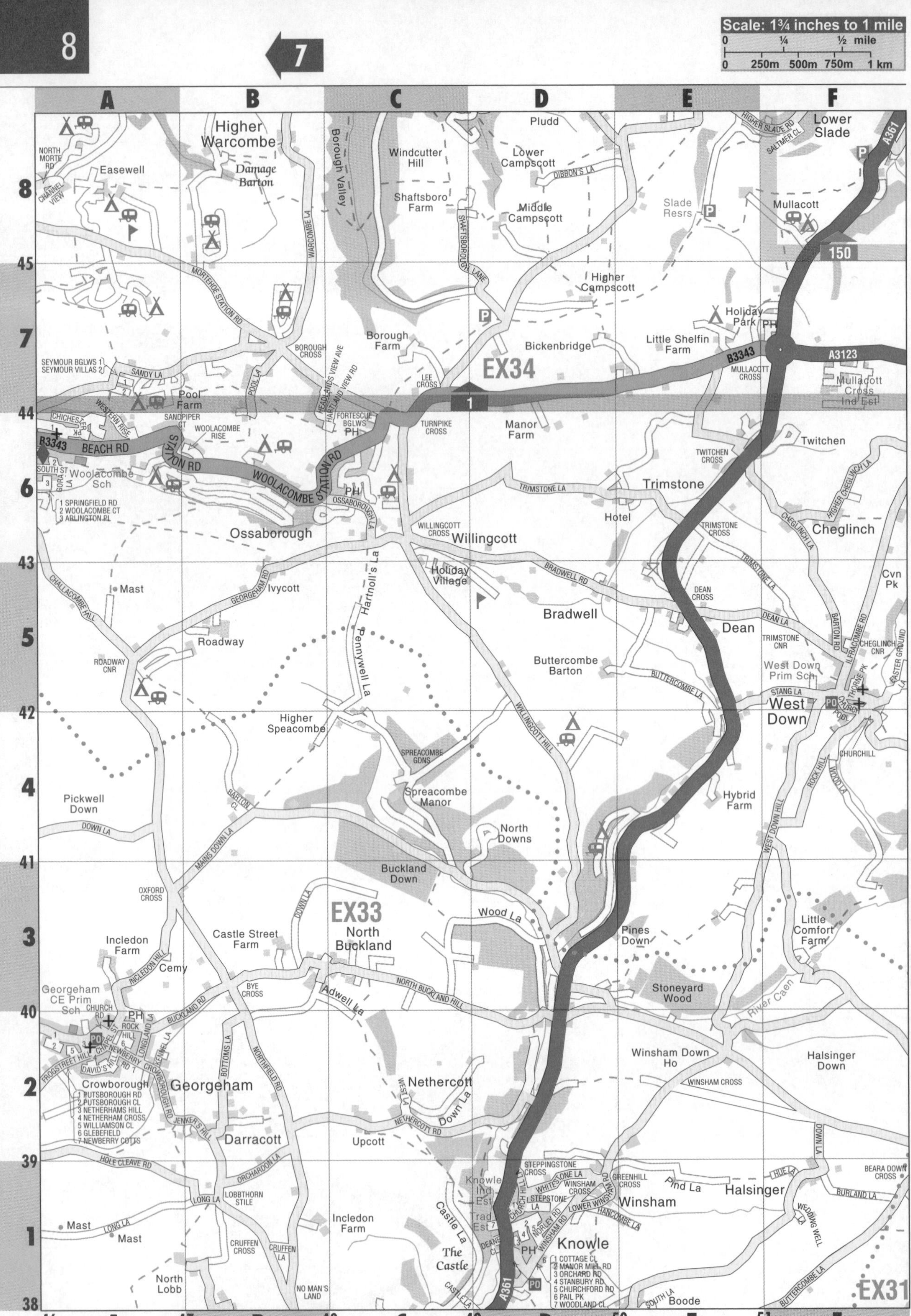

7
15

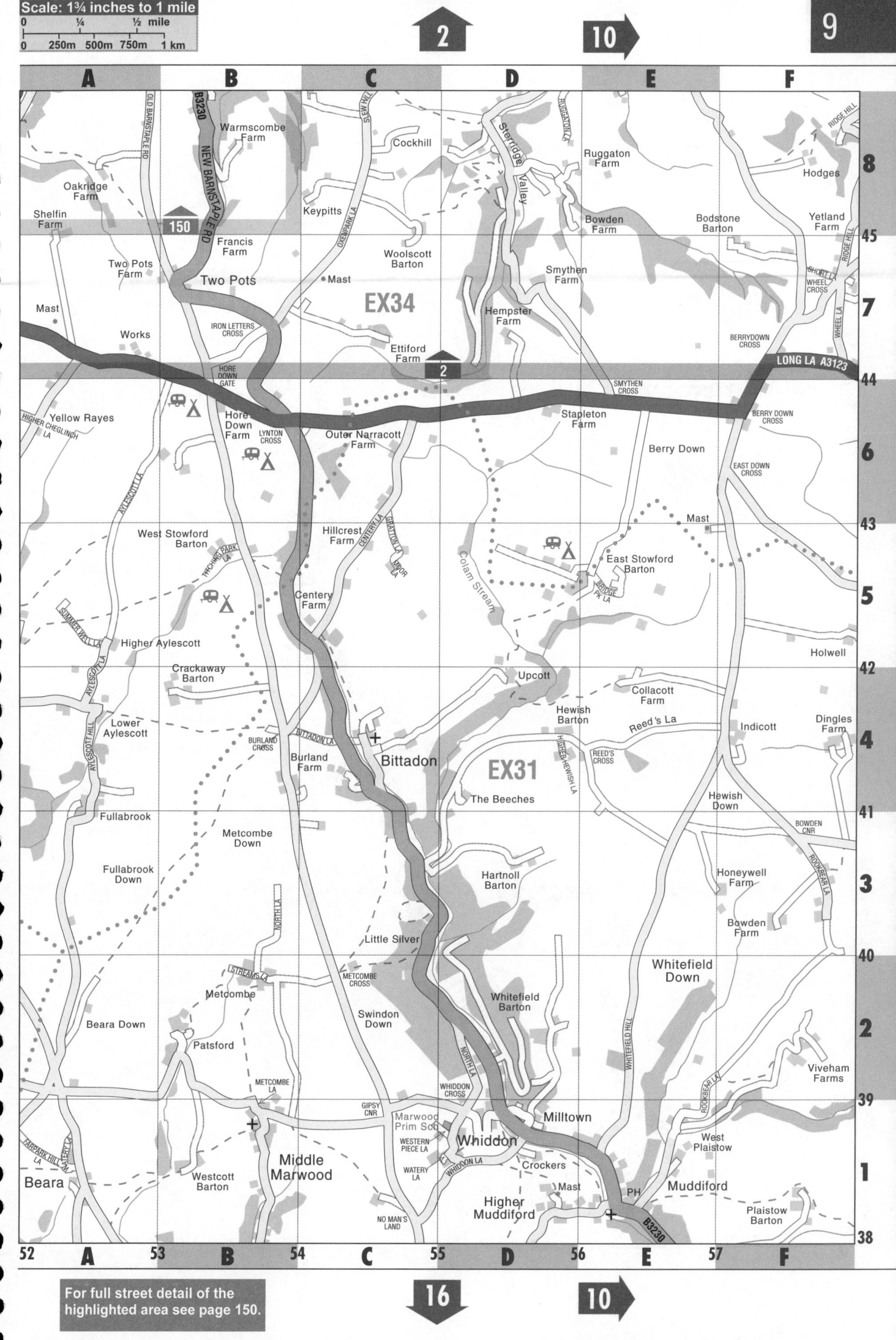

For full street detail of the highlighted area see page 150.

9
3

Scale: 1¾ inches to 1 mile
0 ¼ ½ mile
0 250m 500m 750m 1 km

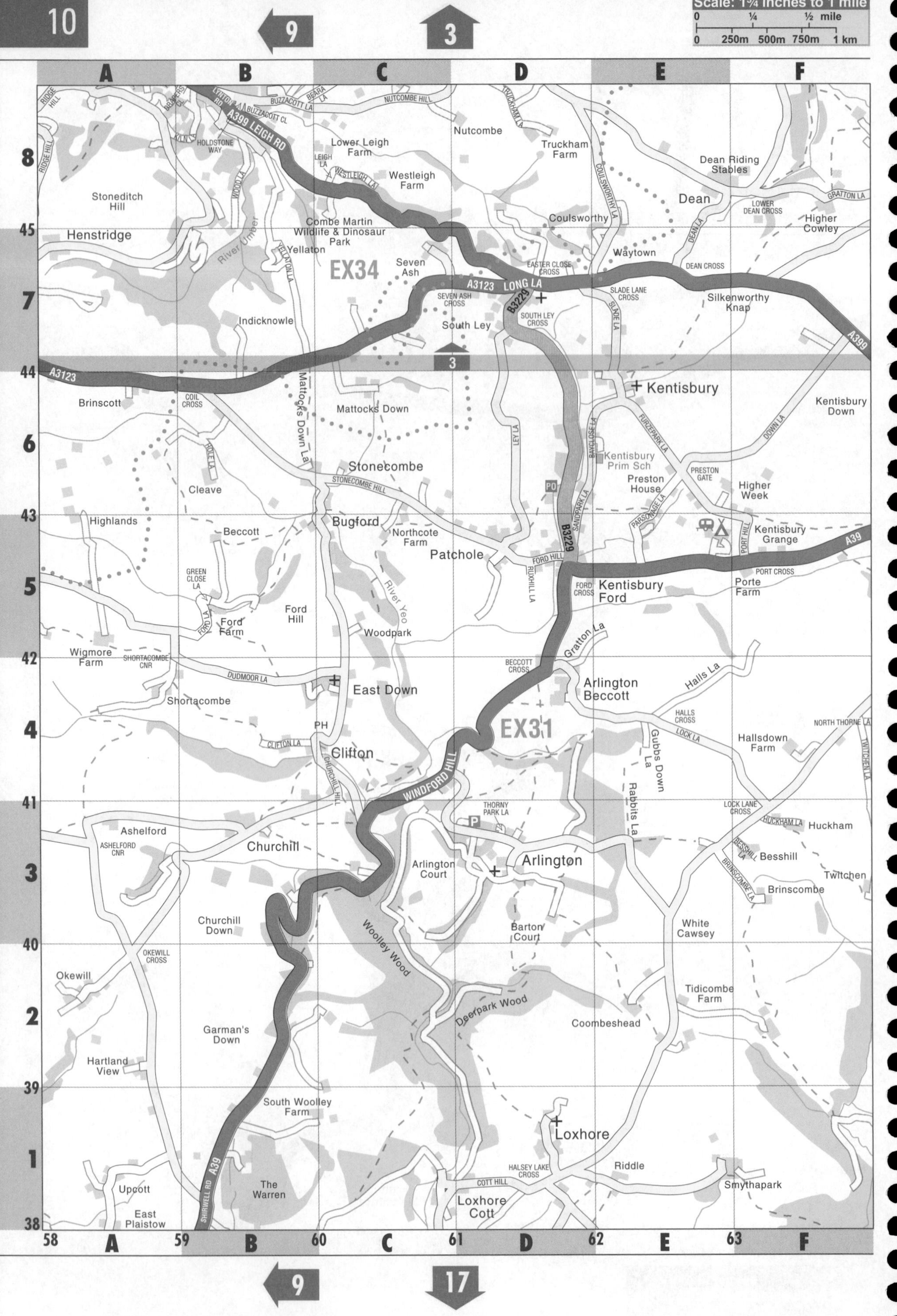

9
17

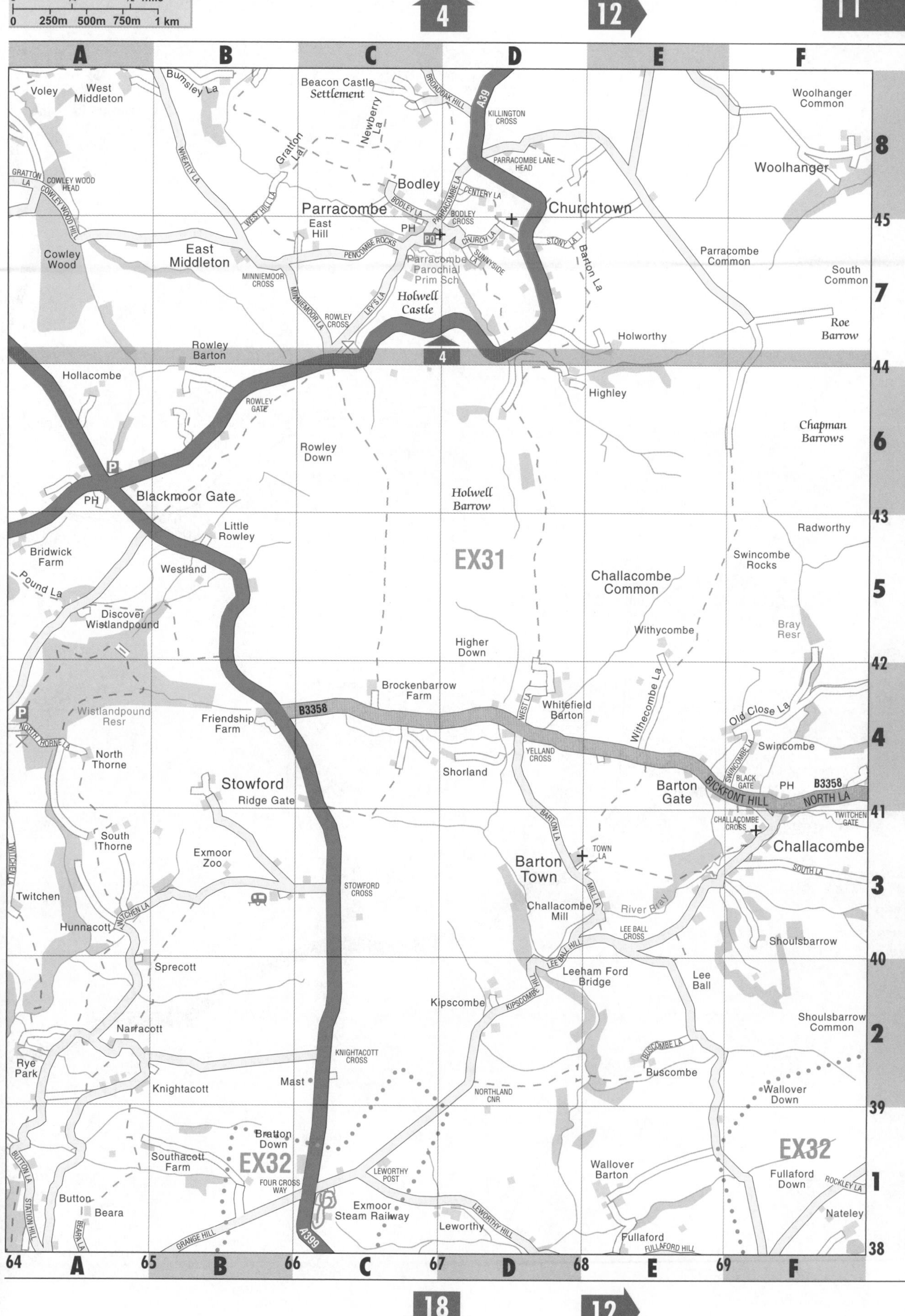
Scale: 1¾ inches to 1 mile
0 ¼ ½ mile
0 250m 500m 750m 1 km
4
12
Beacon Castle
Settlement
Voley
West Middleton
Bumsley La
Newberry La
Gratton La
Bodley
Parracombe
Churchtown
Woolhanger Common
Woolhanger
East Hill
East Middleton
Cowley Wood
Parracombe Common
South Common
Parracombe Parochial Prim Sch
Holwell Castle
Holworthy
Roe Barrow
Rowley Barton
Hollacombe
Highley
Rowley Down
Chapman Barrows
Blackmoor Gate
Holwell Barrow
Little Rowley
Radworthy
Bridwick Farm
Westland
EX31
Swincombe Rocks
Pound La
Challacombe Common
Discover Wistlandpound
Withycombe
Bray Resr
Higher Down
Brockenbarrow Farm
Whitefield Barton
Old Close La
Wistlandpound Resr
Friendship Farm
B3358
Withecombe La
North Thorne
Swincombe
Shorland
Stowford
Ridge Gate
Barton Gate
PH
South Thorne
Challacombe
Exmoor Zoo
Barton Town
Twitchen
Challacombe Mill
River Bray
Hunnacott
Shoulsbarrow
Sprecott
Leeham Ford Bridge
Lee Ball
Kipscombe
Narracott
Shoulsbarrow Common
Rye Park
Buscombe
Mast
Knightacott
Wallover Down
Bratton Down
Southacott Farm
EX32
Wallover Barton
Fullaford Down
Button
Beara
Exmoor Steam Railway
Leworthy
Nateley
Fullaford
8
45
7
44
6
43
5
42
4
41
3
40
2
39
1
38
A B C D E F
64 65 66 67 68 69
18
12

11
5

Scale: 1¾ inches to 1 mile

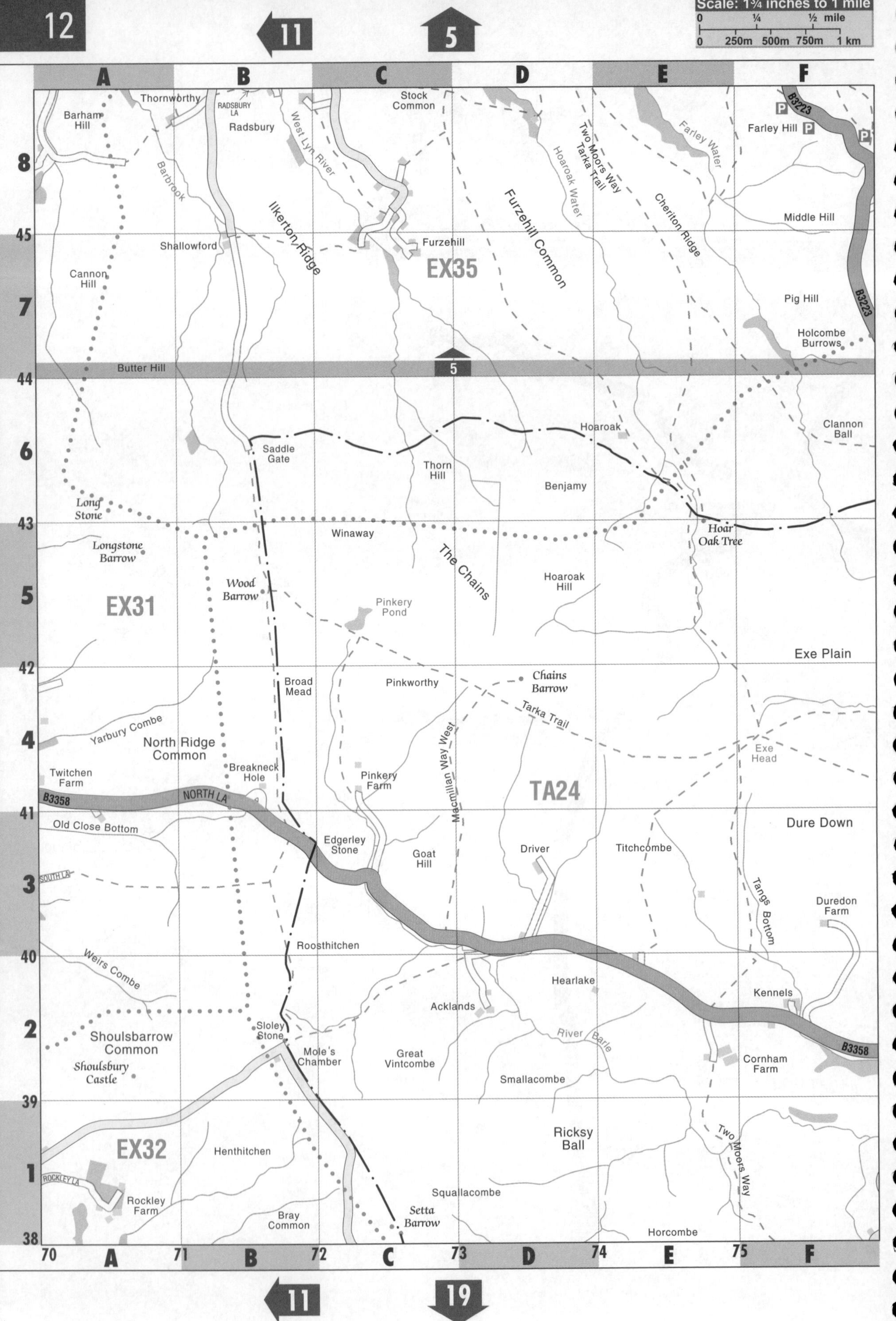

11
19

Scale: 1¾ inches to 1 mile
0 ¼ ½ mile
0 250m 500m 750m 1 km

6

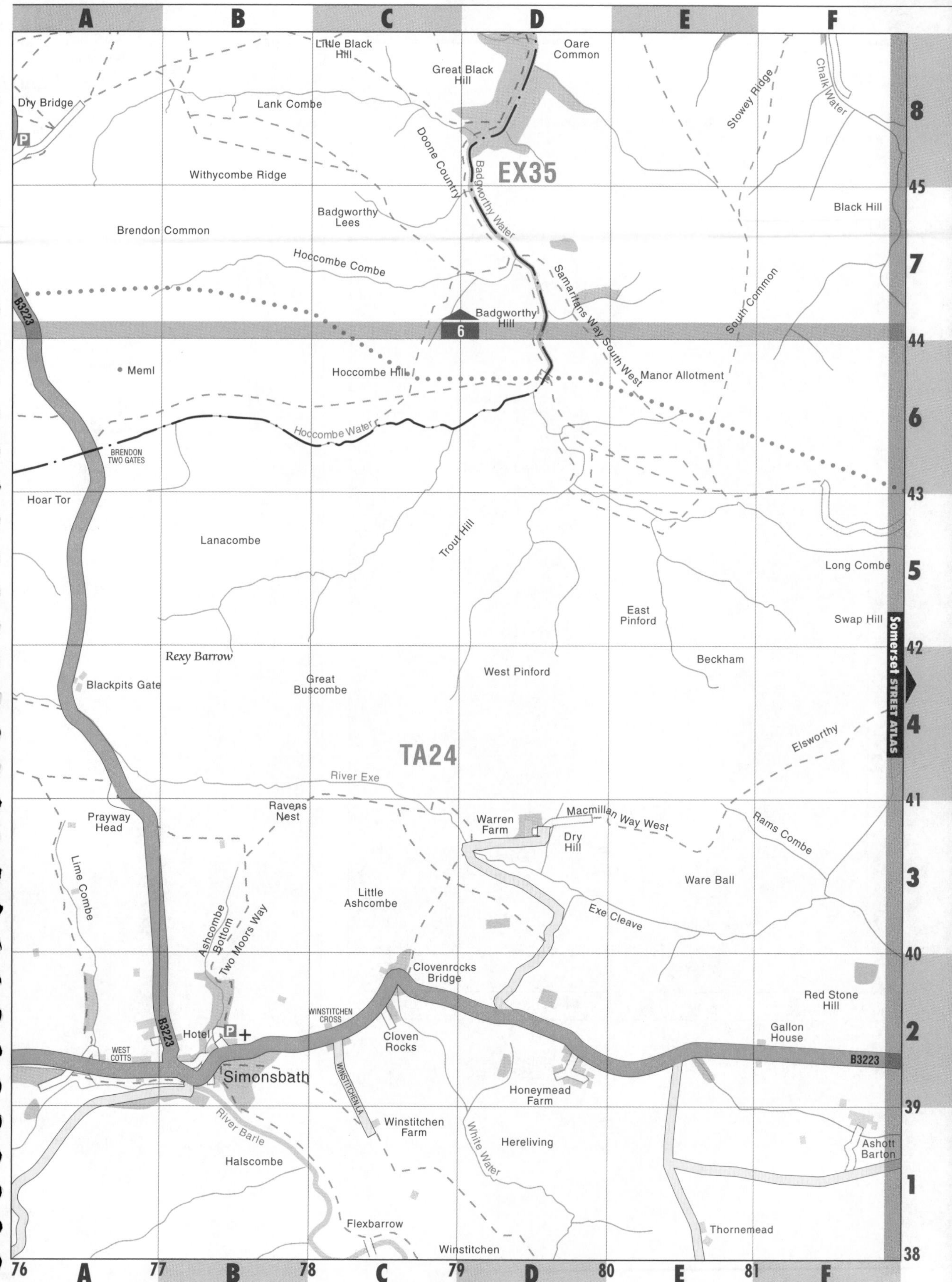

20

7

Scale: 1¾ inches to 1 mile

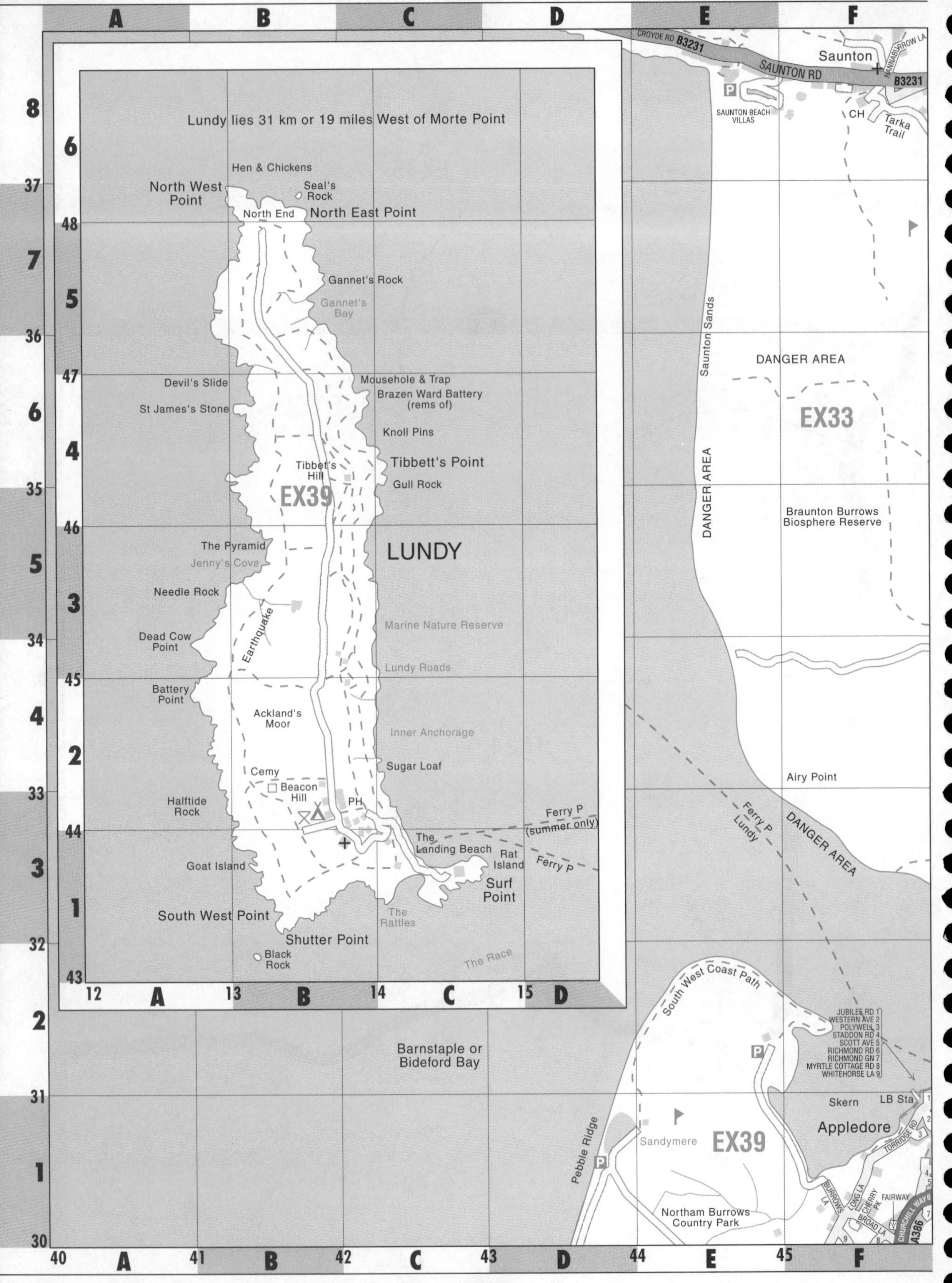

A1
1 FACTORY OPE
2 MARKET ST
3 SILVER ST
4 ONE END ST
5 APPLETREE MEWS
6 NEW ST
7 BACKFIELD
8 PITT CT
9 RICHMOND TERR
10 KINGSLEY AVE
11 LONGFIELD
12 PITT AVE
13 TOMOUTH TERR
14 TOMOUTH CRES
15 TOMOUTH SQ
16 SOUTH RD
17 MYRTLE ST
18 SCOTT AVE
19 THE HOLT
20 YEO DR
21 THE MALTINGS
22 ODUN RD
23 GREEN LA
24 ALPHA PL
25 VERNONS LA
26 CHURCHFIELD RD
27 MYRA CT
28 IVY CT
29 THE PATH
30 HILLCLIFFE TERR
31 GREYSAND CRES
32 THE MOUNT
33 MARINER'S WAY
34 ODUN PL
35 Appledore Com Prim Sch
36 ODUN TERR

B1
1 LANE END CL
2 WHITEHOUSE CL
3 STONEYWELL
4 INSTOW HO
5 KILN CLOSE LA
6 BATH TERR
7 BRIDGE LA
8 OLD QUAY LA
9 CHANDLERS CT
10 MILLARDS HILL
11 CHICHESTER CL
12 THE DUNES
13 SYCAMORE CL
14 MARSH COTTS

26

16

For full street detail of the highlighted area see pages 152 and 153.

15
9

Scale: 1¾ inches to 1 mile

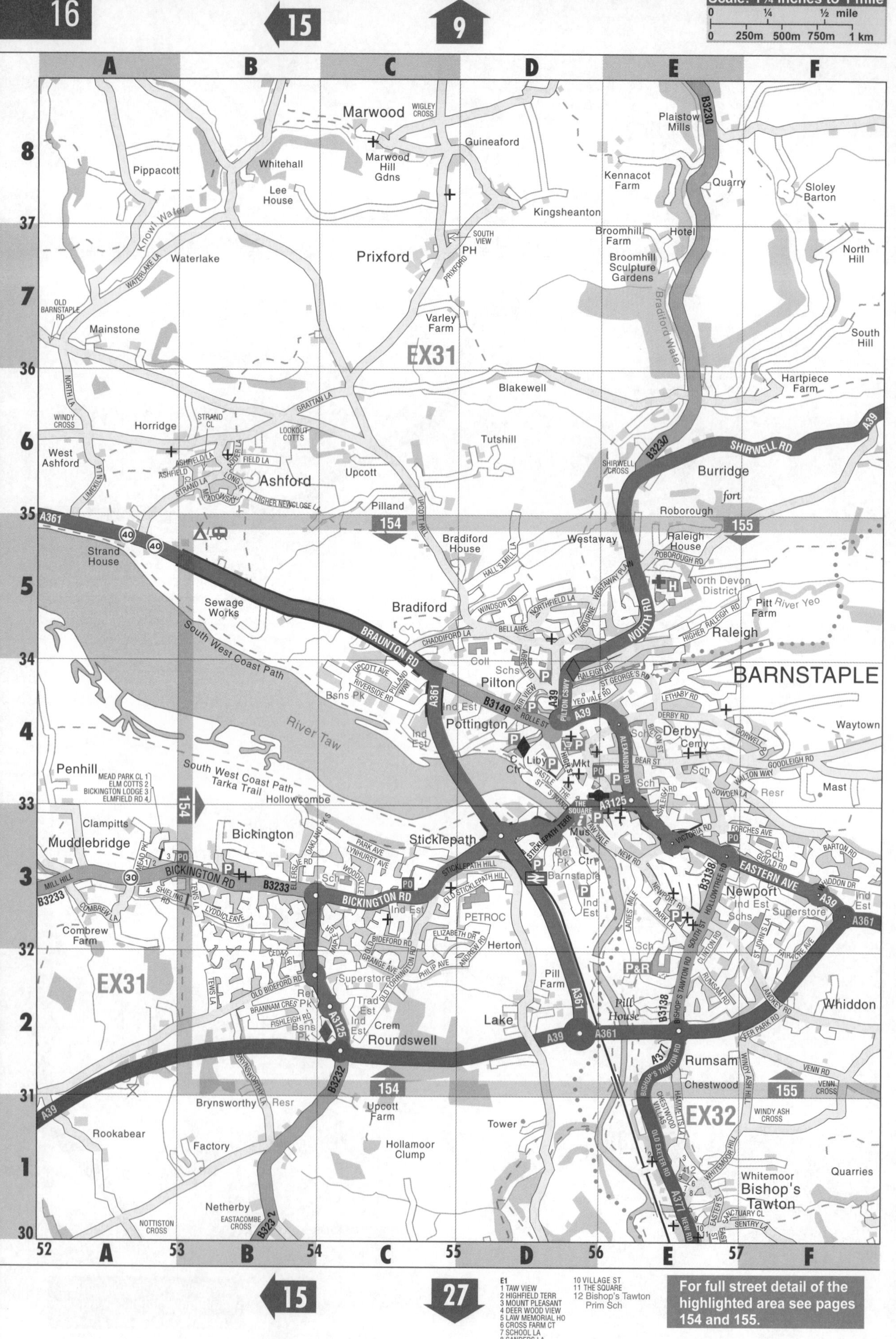

E1
1 TAW VIEW
2 HIGHFIELD TERR
3 MOUNT PLEASANT
4 DEER WOOD VIEW
5 LAW MEMORIAL HO
6 CROSS FARM CT
7 SCHOOL LA
8 SANDERS LA
9 ROSE COTTS
10 VILLAGE ST
11 THE SQUARE
12 Bishop's Tawton Prim Sch

For full street detail of the highlighted area see pages 154 and 155.

15
27

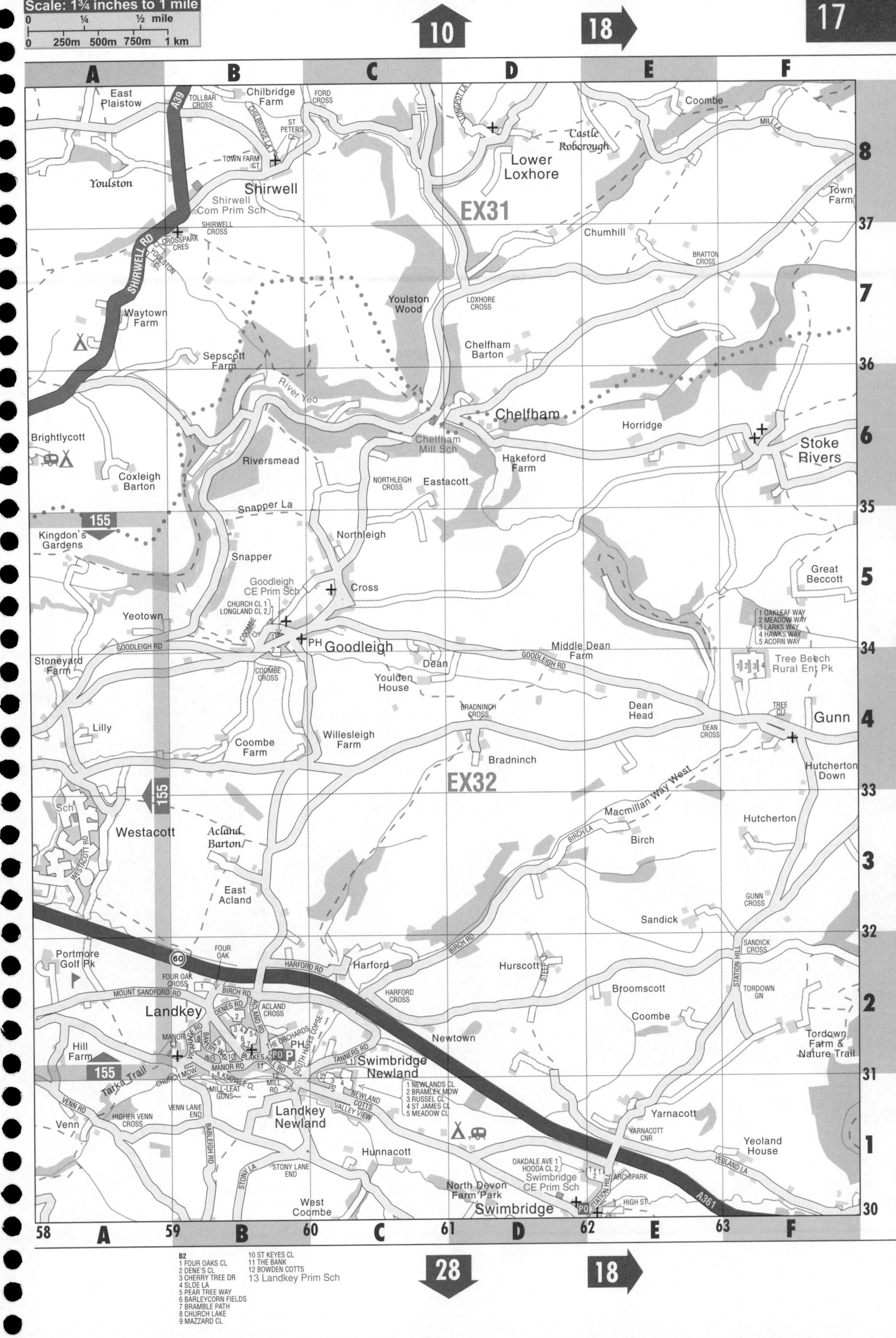
Scale: 1¾ inches to 1 mile
0 ¼ ½ mile
0 250m 500m 750m 1 km
10
18
A B C D E F
8
37
7
36
6
35
5
34
4
33
3
32
2
31
1
30
58 A 59 B 60 C 61 D 62 E 63 F
East Plaistow
A39
TOLLBAR CROSS
Chilbridge Farm
CHILBRIDGE LA
FORD CROSS
ST PETERS CL
TOWN FARM CT
Youlston
Shirwell
Shirwell Com Prim Sch
SHIRWELL CROSS
CROSSPARK CRES
YOULSTON CL
SHIRWELL RD
LONGPOT LA
Lower Loxhore
Castle Roborough
Coombe
MILL LA
Town Farm
EX31
Chumhill
BRATTON CROSS
Youlston Wood
LOXHORE CROSS
Waytown Farm
Sepscott Farm
Chelfham Barton
River Yeo
Chelfham
Horridge
Stoke Rivers
Brightlycott
Coxleigh Barton
Riversmead
Chelfham Mill Sch
Hakeford Farm
NORTHLEIGH CROSS
Eastacott
Snapper La
155
Kingdon's Gardens
Northleigh
Snapper
Goodleigh CE Prim Sch
Cross
Great Beccott
CHURCH CL 1
LONGLAND CL 2
Yeotown
COOMBE CL
PH
Goodleigh
Middle Dean Farm
1 OAKLEAF WAY
2 MEADOW WAY
3 LARKS WAY
4 HAWKS WAY
5 ACORN WAY
Tree Beech Rural Ent Pk
GOODLEIGH RD
Stoneyard Farm
COOMBE CROSS
Youlden House
Dean
Dean Head
BRADNINCH CROSS
TREE CL
Gunn
DEAN CROSS
Lilly
Coombe Farm
Willesleigh Farm
Bradninch
Hutcherton Down
EX32
Macmillan Way West
Sch
Westacott
Acland Barton
BIRCH LA
Birch
Hutcherton
WESTACOTT RD
East Acland
GUNN CROSS
Sandick
Portmore Golf Pk
FOUR OAK
60
HARFORD RD
Harford
BIRCH RD
Hurscott
STEEP LA
SANDICK CROSS
STATION HILL
TORDOWN GN
FOUR OAK CROSS
MOUNT SANDFORD RD
BIRCH RD
Landkey
DENES RD
ACLAND RD
ACLAND CROSS
HARFORD CROSS
Broomscott
Coombe
Tordown Farm & Nature Trail
Hill Farm
MANOR CL
VICARAGE RD
BAKERY WAY
MANOR RD
BLAKES HILL RD
THE ORCHARDS
SOUTH HAYES COPSE
TANNERS RD
PH
PO
P
Swimbridge Newland
Newtown
Tarka Trail
CHURCH MDW
KNOWLE CL
MILL-LEAT GDNS
MILL RD
NEWLAND COTTS
VALLEY VIEW
1 NEWLANDS CL
2 BRAMLEY MDW
3 RUSSEL CL
4 ST JAMES CL
5 MEADOW CL
VENN RD
HIGHER VENN CROSS
VENN LANE END
Landkey Newland
Yarnacott
YARNACOTT CNR
Venn
Yeoland House
YEOLAND LA
BABLEIGH RD
Hunnacott
STONY LA
STONY LANE END
OAKDALE AVE 1
HOODA CL 2
Swimbridge CE Prim Sch
ARCHIPARK
North Devon Farm Park
West Coombe
Swimbridge
HIGH ST
A361
B2
1 FOUR OAKS CL
2 DENE'S CL
3 CHERRY TREE DR
4 SLOE LA
5 PEAR TREE WAY
6 BARLEYCORN FIELDS
7 BRAMBLE PATH
8 CHURCH LAKE
9 MAZZARD CL
10 ST KEYES CL
11 THE BANK
12 BOWDEN COTTS
13 Landkey Prim Sch
28
18

17 11

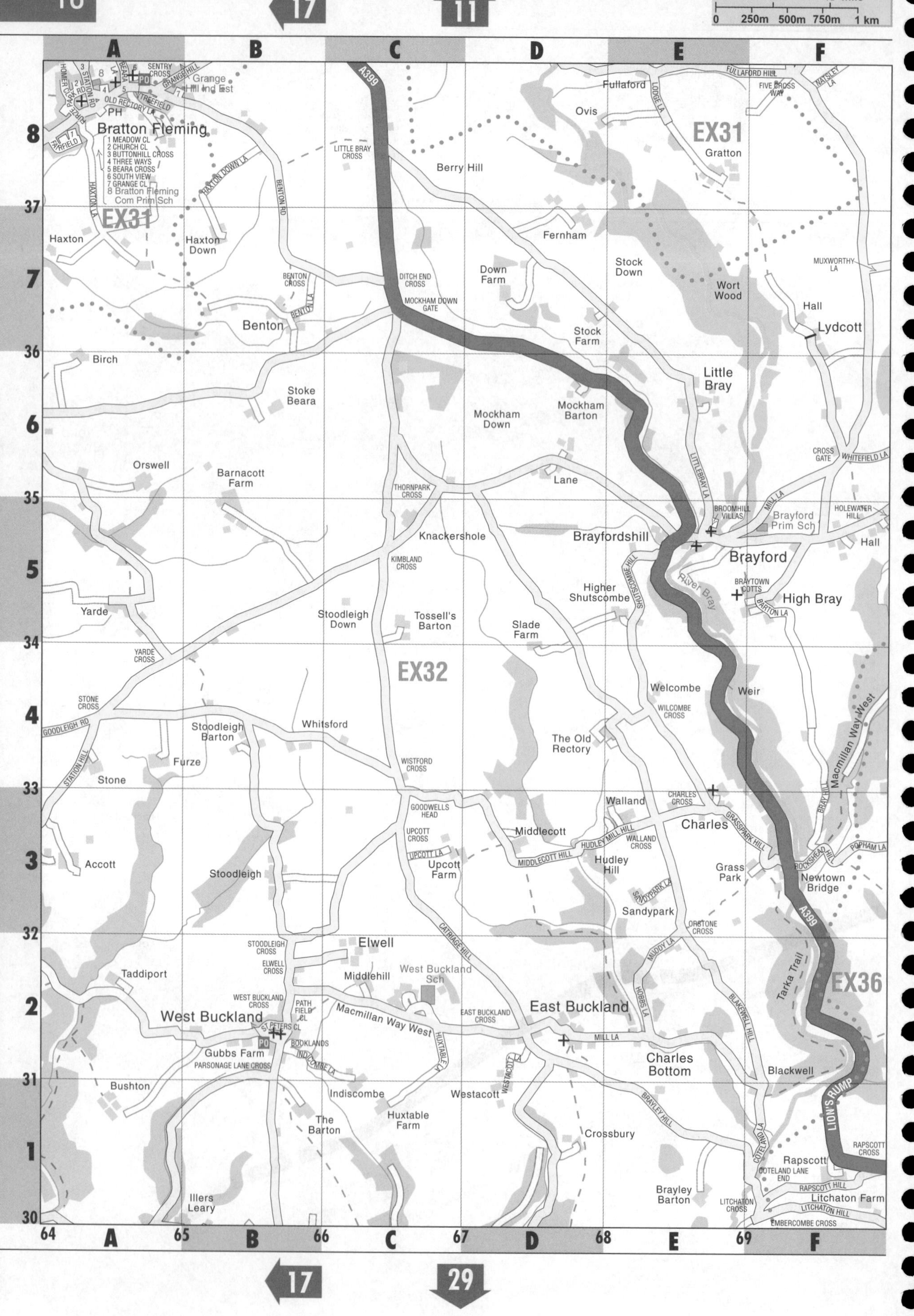
Scale: 1¾ inches to 1 mile
0 ¼ ½ mile
0 250m 500m 750m 1 km
A B C D E F
Bratton Fleming
1 MEADOW CL
2 CHURCH CL
3 BUTTONHILL CROSS
4 THREE WAYS
5 BEARA CROSS
6 SOUTH VIEW
7 GRANGE CL
8 Bratton Fleming Com Prim Sch
Grange Hill Ind Est
SENTRY CROSS
GRANGE HILL
OLD RECTORY LA
TREEFIELD
STATION RD
FAIRFIELD
PH
PO
EX31
Haxton
HAXTON LA
HAXTON DOWN LA
Haxton Down
BENTON RD
BENTON CROSS
Benton
Birch
LITTLE BRAY CROSS
A399
Berry Hill
DITCH END CROSS
MOCKHAM DOWN GATE
Down Farm
Fernham
Fullaford
Ovis
LODGE LA
FULLAFORD HILL
FIVE CROSS WAY
NATSLEY LA
Gratton
Stock Down
Wort Wood
MUXWORTHY LA
Hall
Lydcott
Stock Farm
Little Bray
Stoke Beara
Mockham Down
Mockham Barton
LITTLEBRAY LA
CROSS GATE
WHITEFIELD LA
Orswell
Barnacott Farm
THORNPARK CROSS
Lane
BROOMHILL VILLAS
Brayford Prim Sch
MILL LA
HOLEWATER HILL
Knackershole
Brayfordshill
Brayford
Hall
KIMBLAND CROSS
SHUTSCOMBE HILL
Higher Shutscombe
River Bray
BRAYTOWN COTTS
High Bray
BARTON LA
Yarde
Stoodleigh Down
Tossell's Barton
Slade Farm
YARDE CROSS
EX32
Welcombe
Weir
STONE CROSS
GOODLEIGH RD
WILCOMBE CROSS
Macmillan Way West
Stoodleigh Barton
Whitsford
The Old Rectory
STATION HILL
Furze
Stone
WISTFORD CROSS
Walland
CHARLES CROSS
GOODWELLS HEAD
Charles
GRASSPARK HILL
Middlecott
UPCOTT CROSS
HUDLEY MILL HILL
WALLAND CROSS
BRAY HILL
POPHAM LA
Accott
UPCOTT LA
Upcott Farm
MIDDLECOTT HILL
Hudley Hill
Grass Park
ROCKSHEAD HILL
Newtown Bridge
Stoodleigh
SANDYPARK LA
Sandypark
ORSTONE CROSS
STOODLEIGH CROSS
Elwell
CATRIAGE HILL
MUDDY LA
ELWELL CROSS
West Buckland Sch
Tarka Trail
EX36
Taddiport
Middlehill
WEST BUCKLAND CROSS
PATH FIELD CL
East Buckland
HOBBS LA
BLAKEWELL HILL
West Buckland
EAST BUCKLAND CROSS
ST PETERS CL
Gubbs Farm
BOOKLANDS
MILL LA
PARSONAGE LANE CROSS
INDICOMBE LA
HUXTABLE LA
WESTACOTT LA
Charles Bottom
Blackwell
Bushton
Indiscombe
Westacott
BRAYLEY HILL
LION'S RUMP
The Barton
Huxtable Farm
Crossbury
COTELAND LA
RAPSCOTT CROSS
Rapscott
COTELAND LANE END
RAPSCOTT HILL
Illers Leary
Brayley Barton
LITCHATON CROSS
Litchaton Farm
LITCHATON HILL
EMBERCOMBE CROSS
8 37 7 36 6 35 5 34 4 33 3 32 2 31 1 30
64 65 66 67 68 69

17 29

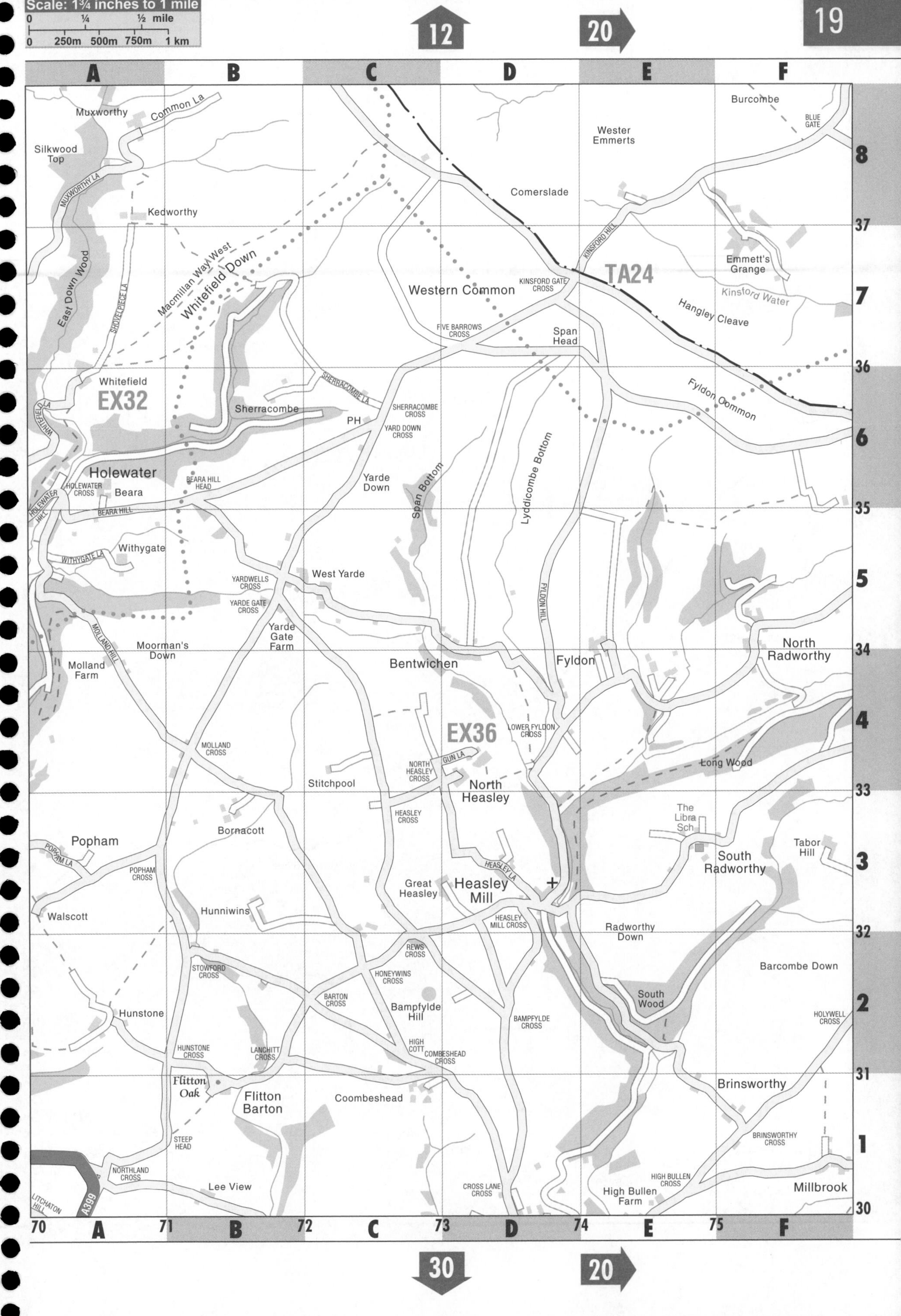
Scale: 1¾ inches to 1 mile
0
¼
½ mile
0
250m
500m
750m
1 km
12
20
30
20
A
B
C
D
E
F
8
37
7
36
6
35
5
34
4
33
3
32
2
31
1
30
70
71
72
73
74
75
Muxworthy
Common La
Silkwood Top
Muxworthy La
Kedworthy
East Down Wood
Shovelpiece La
Macmillan Way West
Whitefield Down
Burcombe
Blue Gate
Wester Emmerts
Comerslade
Kinsford Hill
TA24
Emmett's Grange
Kinsford Water
Hangley Cleave
Western Common
Kinsford Gate Cross
Five Barrows Cross
Span Head
Fyldon Common
Whitefield
Whitefield La
EX32
Sherracombe
Sherracombe La
Sherracombe Cross
Yard Down Cross
PH
Holewater
Holewater Cross
Holewater Hill
Beara
Beara Hill
Beara Hill Head
Yarde Down
Span Bottom
Lyddicombe Bottom
Withygate
Withygate La
Yardwells Cross
West Yarde
Yarde Gate Cross
Yarde Gate Farm
Fyldon Hill
Molland Hill
Moorman's Down
Molland Farm
Bentwichen
Fyldon
North Radworthy
EX36
Lower Fyldon Cross
Long Wood
Molland Cross
Gun La
North Heasley Cross
North Heasley
Stitchpool
Heasley Cross
Bornacott
The Libra Sch
Popham
Popham La
Popham Cross
South Radworthy
Tabor Hill
Heasley La
Great Heasley
Heasley Mill
Heasley Mill Cross
Walscott
Hunniwins
Radworthy Down
Rews Cross
Stowford Cross
Honeywins Cross
Barcombe Down
Barton Cross
Bampfylde Hill
South Wood
Hunstone
Bampfylde Cross
Holywell Cross
Hunstone Cross
Lanchitt Cross
High Cott
Combeshead Cross
Flitton Oak
Flitton Barton
Coombeshead
Brinsworthy
Steep Head
Brinsworthy Cross
Northland Cross
Lee View
Cross Lane Cross
High Bullen Cross
High Bullen Farm
Millbrook
Litchaton Hill
A399

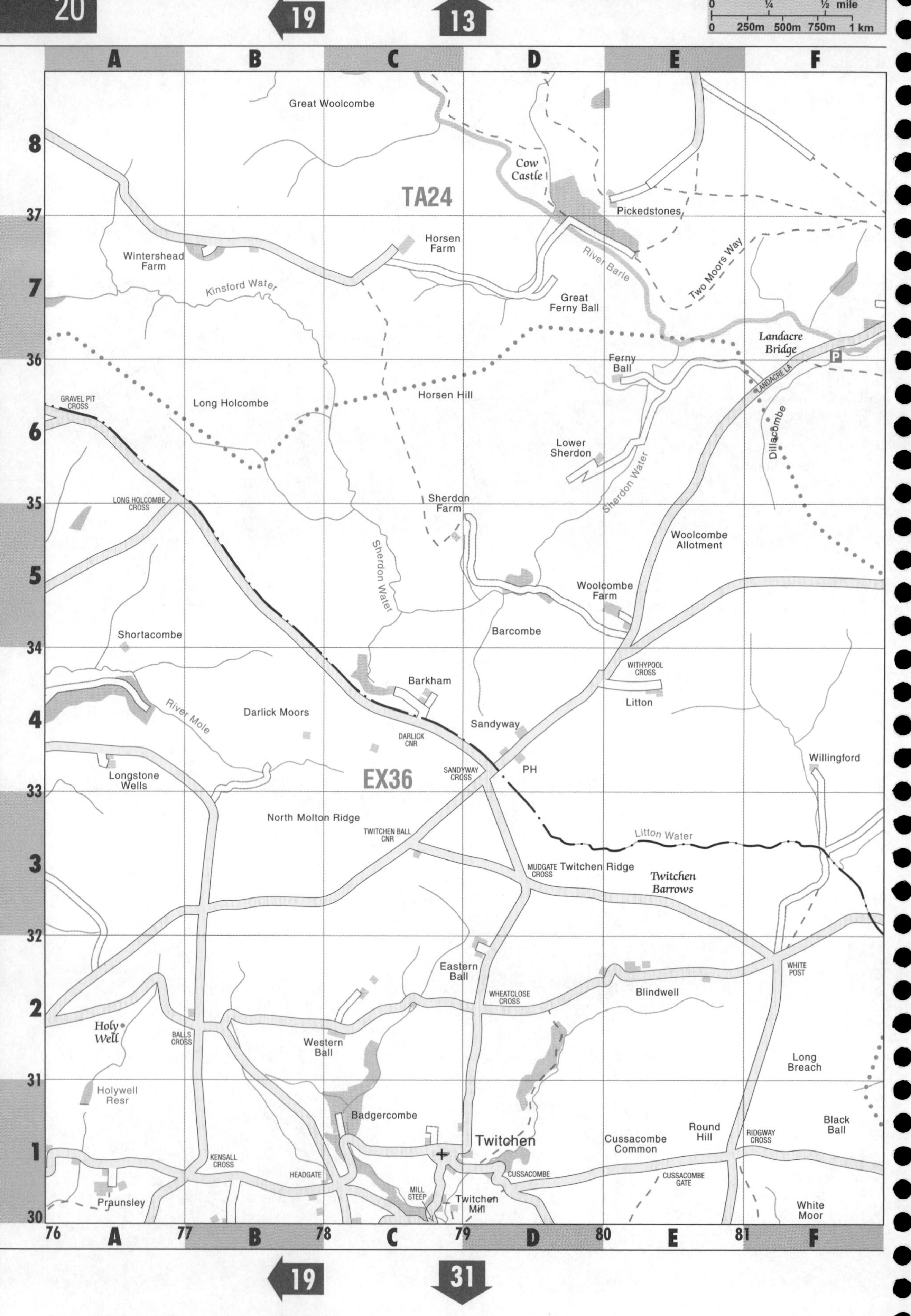
19
13
Scale: 1¾ inches to 1 mile
0 ¼ ½ mile
0 250m 500m 750m 1 km
A B C D E F
Great Woolcombe
Cow Castle
TA24
Pickedstones
Horsen Farm
Wintershead Farm
River Barle
Two Moors Way
Kinsford Water
Great Ferny Ball
Landacre Bridge
P
Ferny Ball
LANDACRE LA
GRAVEL PIT CROSS
Long Holcombe
Horsen Hill
Dillacombe
Lower Sherdon
Sherdon Water
LONG HOLCOMBE CROSS
Sherdon Farm
Woolcombe Allotment
Sherdon Water
Woolcombe Farm
Shortacombe
Barcombe
WITHYPOOL CROSS
Barkham
Litton
River Mole
Darlick Moors
Sandyway
DARLICK CNR
Willingford
Longstone Wells
EX36
SANDYWAY CROSS
PH
North Molton Ridge
TWITCHEN BALL CNR
Litton Water
MUDGATE CROSS
Twitchen Ridge
Twitchen Barrows
Eastern Ball
WHITE POST
WHEATCLOSE CROSS
Blindwell
Holy Well
BALLS CROSS
Western Ball
Long Breach
Holywell Resr
Badgercombe
Black Ball
Round Hill
Twitchen
Cussacombe Common
RIDGWAY CROSS
KENSALL CROSS
HEADGATE
CUSSACOMBE
CUSSACOMBE GATE
MILL STEEP
Twitchen Mill
Praunsley
White Moor
8
37
7
36
6
35
5
34
4
33
3
32
2
31
1
30
76 77 78 79 80 81

19
31

Scale: 1¾ inches to 1 mile

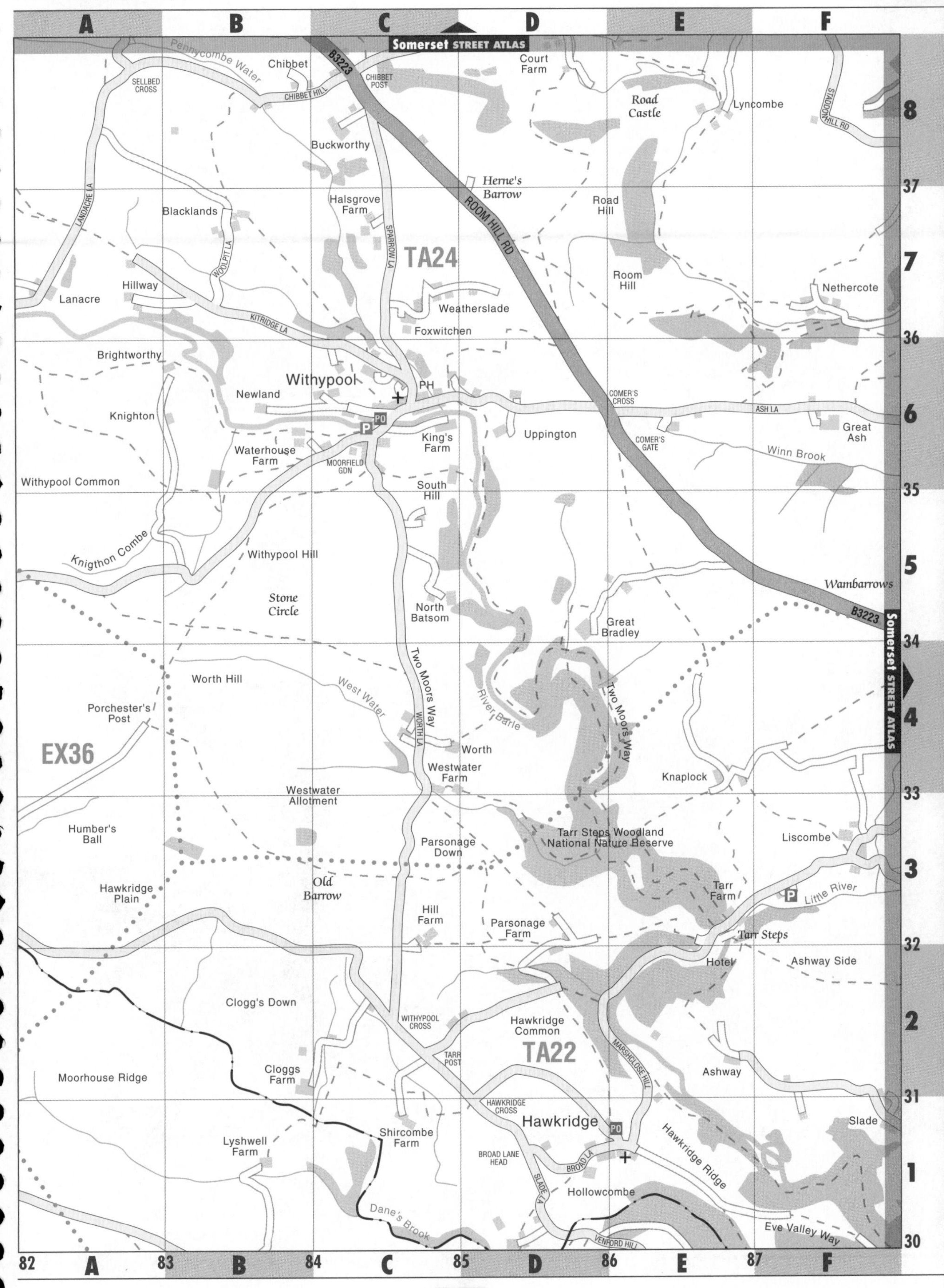

32

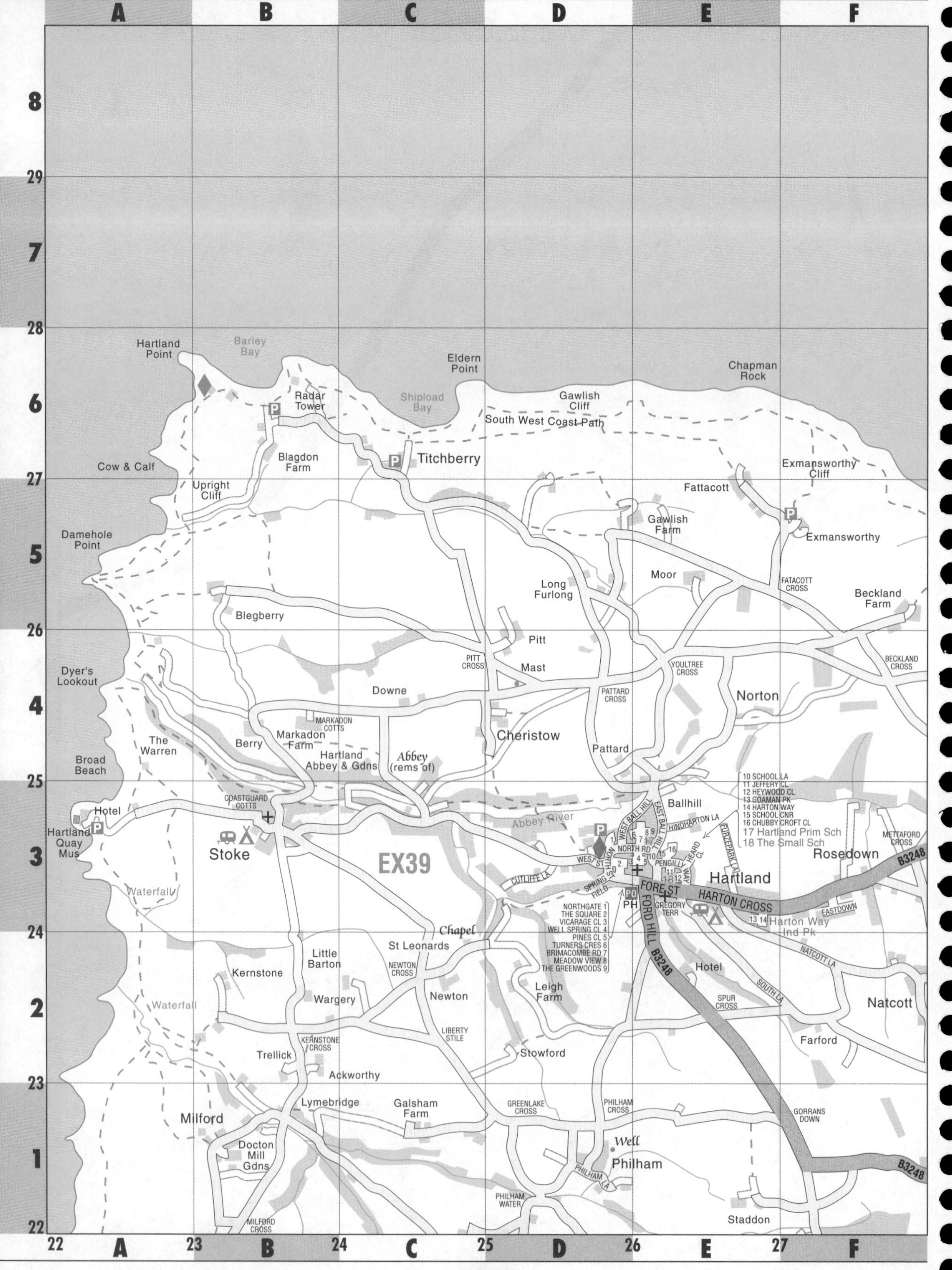
Scale: 1¾ inches to 1 mile
Hartland Point
Barley Bay
Radar Tower
Shipload Bay
Eldern Point
Gawlish Cliff
Chapman Rock
South West Coast Path
Cow & Calf
Blagdon Farm
Titchberry
Upright Cliff
Exmansworthy Cliff
Fattacott
Gawlish Farm
Exmansworthy
Damehole Point
Long Furlong
Moor
Fatacott Cross
Beckland Farm
Blegberry
Pitt
Pitt Cross
Mast
Youltree Cross
Beckland Cross
Dyer's Lookout
Downe
Pattard Cross
Norton
Markadon Cotts
The Warren
Berry
Markadon Farm
Cheristow
Pattard
Broad Beach
Hartland Abbey & Gdns
Abbey (rems of)
Hotel
Coastguard Cotts
Ballhill
Hartland Quay Mus
Stoke
EX39
Abbey River
Hartland
Rosedown
Mettaford Cross
Waterfall
Cutliffe La
Fore St
Harton Cross
Ford Hill
Gregory Terr
Harton Way Ind Pk
Eastdown
10 School La
11 Jeffery Cl
12 Heywood Cl
13 Goaman Pk
14 Harton Way
15 School Cnr
16 Chubby Croft Cl
17 Hartland Prim Sch
18 The Small Sch
Northgate 1
The Square 2
Vicarage Cl 3
Well Spring Cl 4
Pines Cl 5
Turners Cres 6
Brimacombe Rd 7
Meadow View 8
The Greenwoods 9
Chapel
Little Barton
St Leonards
Kernstone
Newton Cross
Newton
Leigh Farm
Hotel
Natcott La
South La
Natcott
Wargery
Spur Cross
Waterfall
Liberty Stile
Farford
Trellick
Kernstone Cross
Stowford
Ackworthy
Milford
Lymebridge
Galsham Farm
Greenlake Cross
Philham Cross
Gorrans Down
Docton Mill Gdns
Well
Philham
Philham La
Philham Water
Staddon
Milford Cross
B3248

37

Scale: 1¾ inches to 1 mile

24

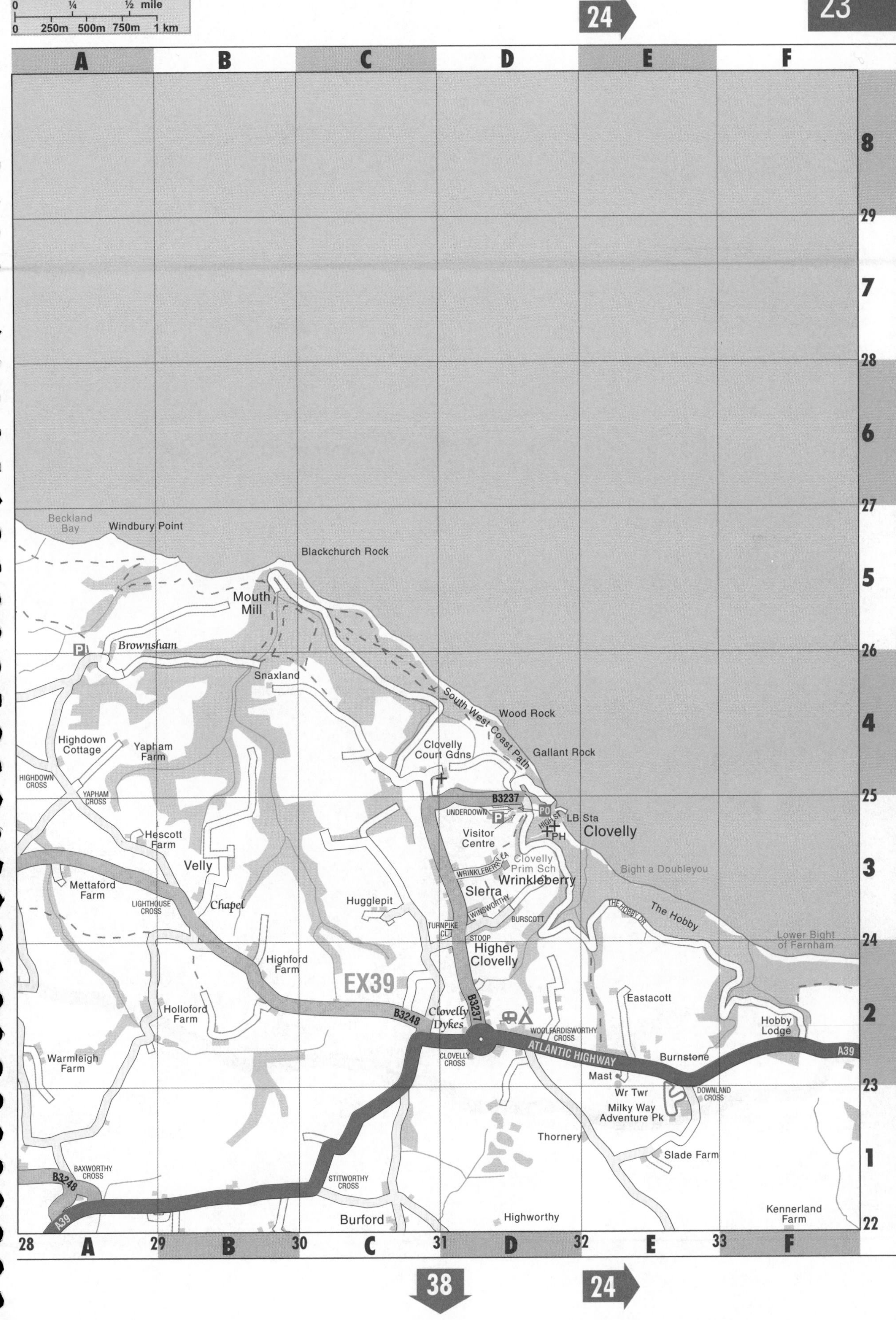

38

24

23

Scale: 1¾ inches to 1 mile
0 ¼ ½ mile
0 250m 500m 750m 1 km

A B C D E F

8
29
7
28
6
27
5
26
4
25
3
24
2
23
1
22

Babbacombe Mouth
Babbacombe Cliff
Higher Rowden
Portledge
Chiddlecombe
Castle
Gauter Point
Peppercombe
Gilscott
A39
South West Coast Path
Sloo
Holiday Village
Buck's Mills
Northway
Hoops PH
PH
Horns Cross
A39
ATLANTIC HIGHWAY
Holwell
ACRE RD
ACRE CL
ACRE
PO
EX39
Buck's Cross
Watershute
DOTHERIDGE LA
Cemy
Waytown
Goldworthy
Bitworthy
Walland
Foxdown Manor
BREWERS HILL
Broad Parkham
Limebury
Newhaven
PARKHAM CROSS

34 A 35 B 36 C 37 D 38 E 39 F

23
39

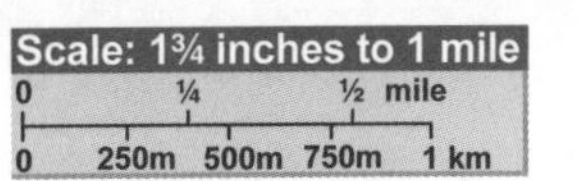

26

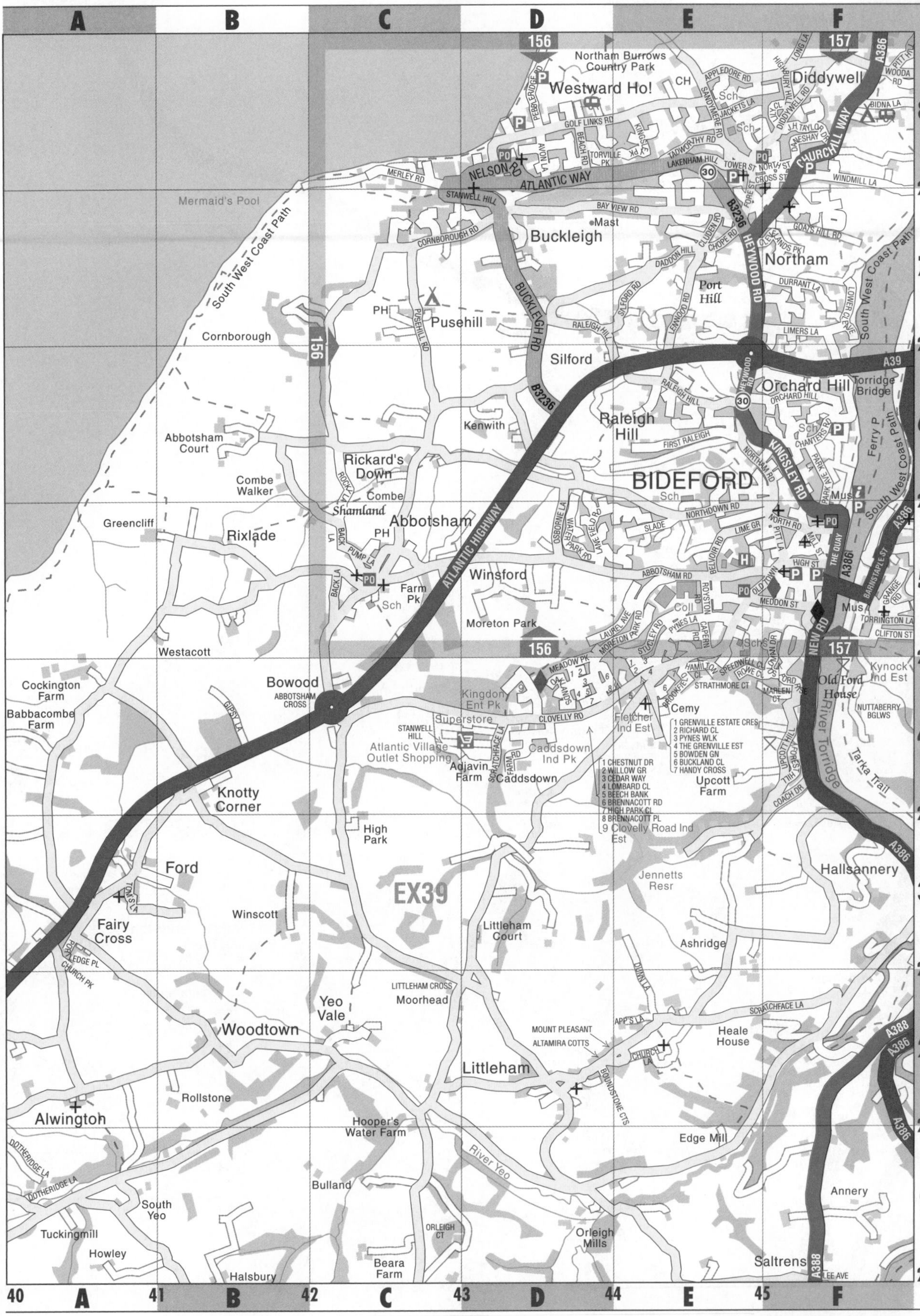

40

26

For full street detail of the highlighted area see pages 156 and 157.

25
15

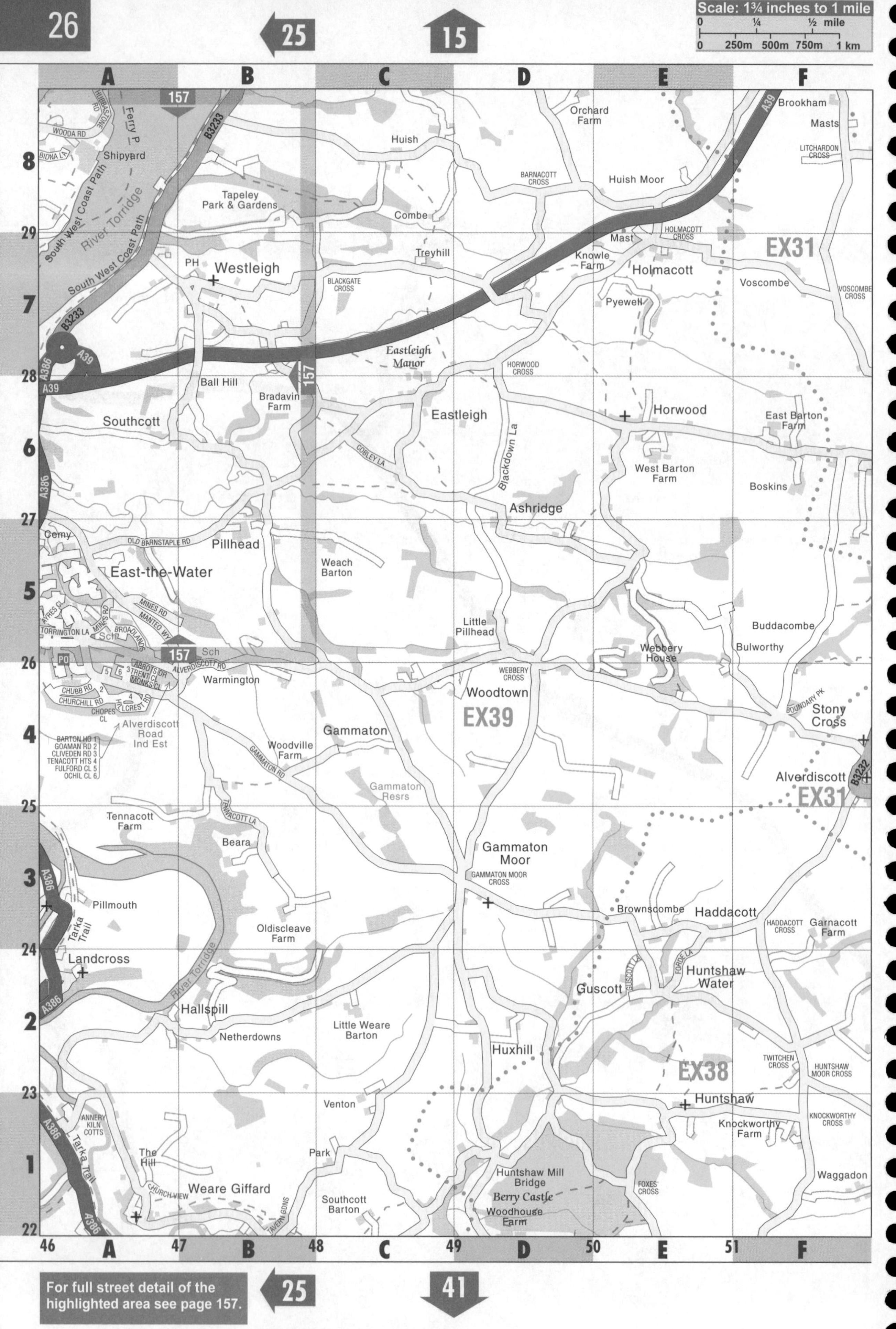

For full street detail of the highlighted area see page 157.
25
41

Scale: 1¾ inches to 1 mile
0 ¼ ½ mile
0 250m 500m 750m 1 km

16
28

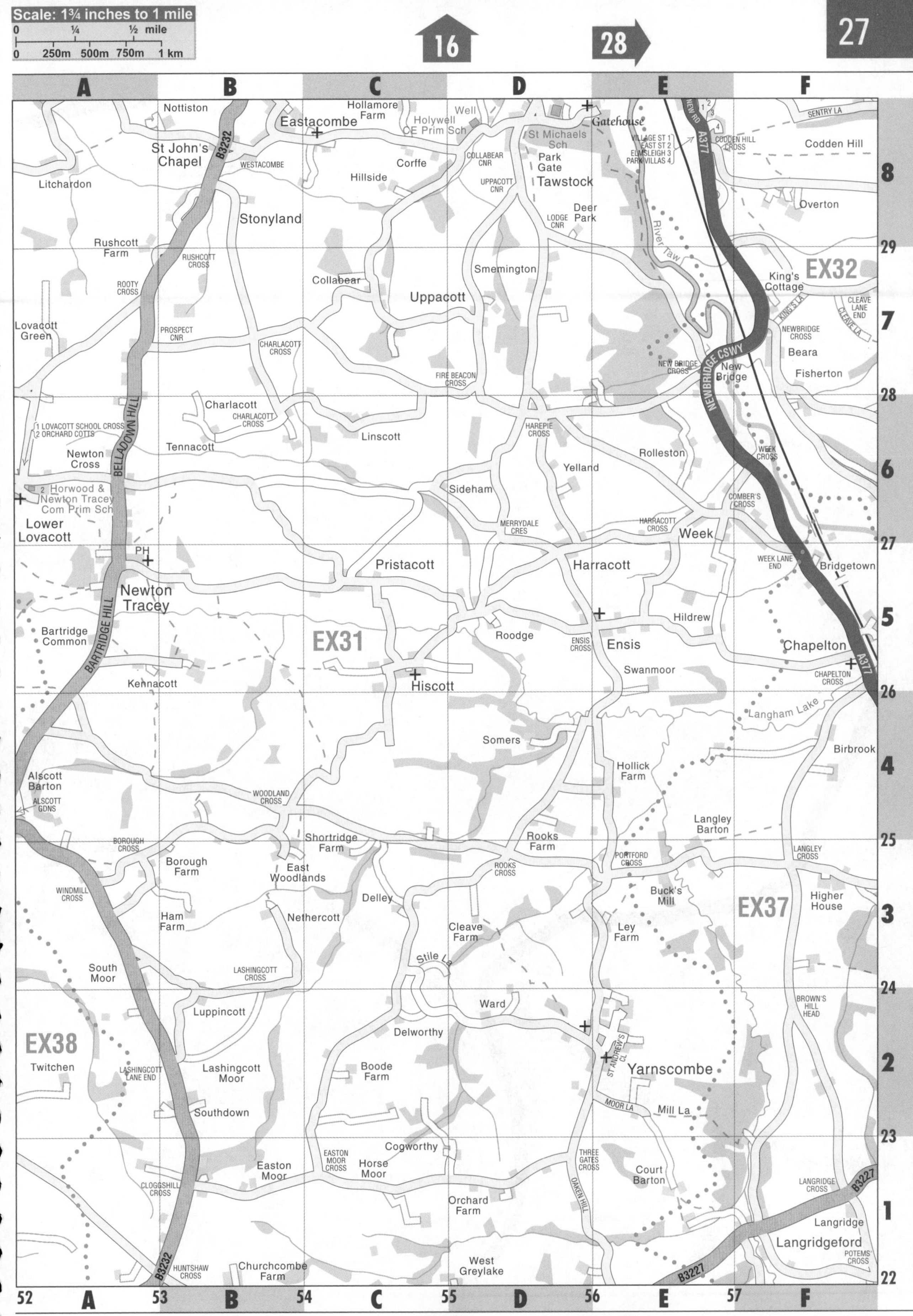

42
28

27
17

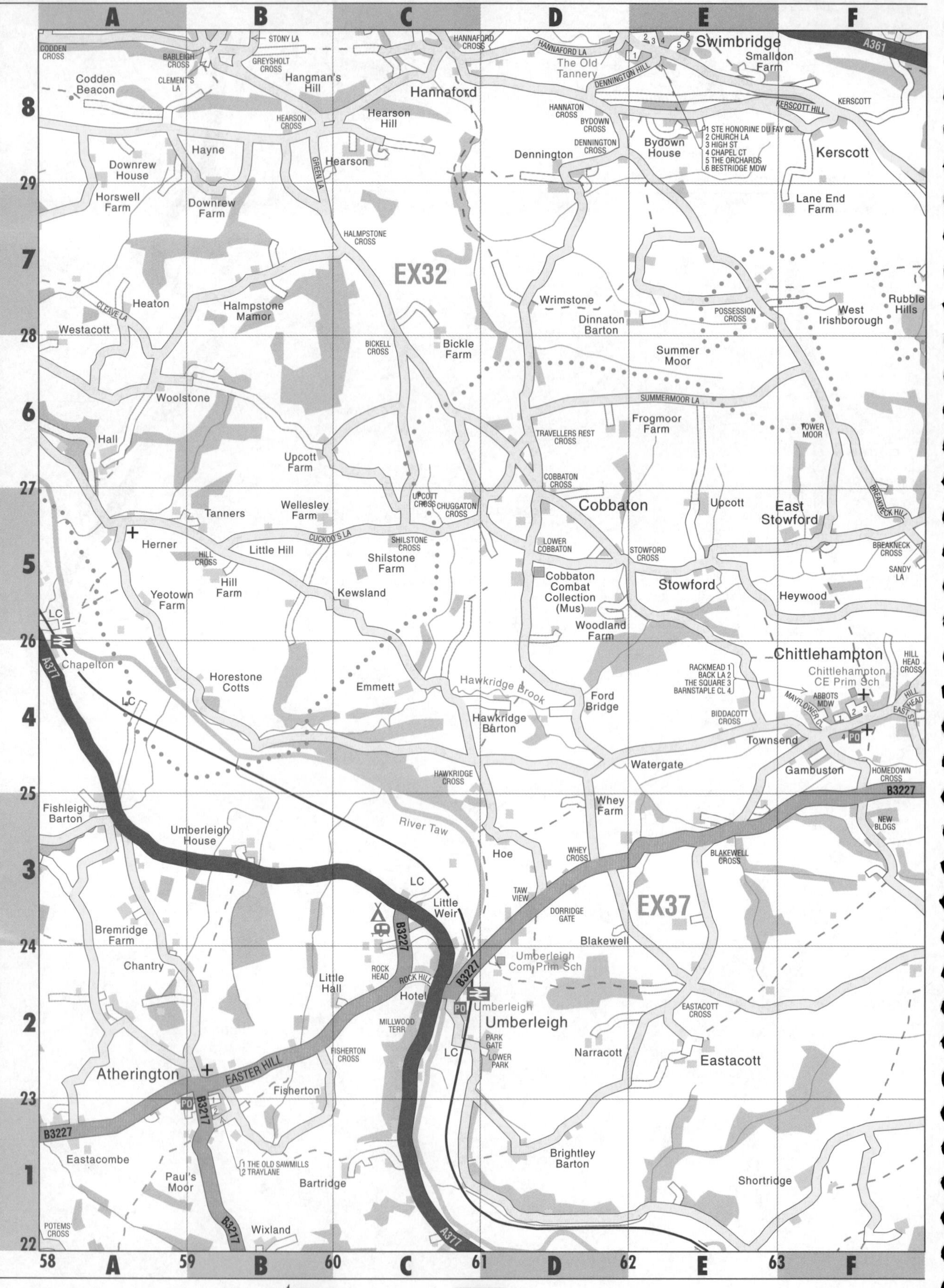
Scale: 1¾ inches to 1 mile
0 ¼ ½ mile
0 250m 500m 750m 1 km
A B C D E F
Swimbridge
Smalldon Farm
The Old Tannery
Hannaford
Hangman's Hill
Codden Beacon
Hearson Hill
Hearson
Dennington
Bydown House
Kerscott
Downrew House
Hayne
Horswell Farm
Downrew Farm
Lane End Farm
EX32
Wrimstone
Dinnaton Barton
Heaton
Halmpstone Manor
Westacott
Bickle Farm
Summer Moor
West Irishborough
Rubble Hills
Woolstone
Hall
Upcott Farm
Frogmoor Farm
Cobbaton
Upcott
East Stowford
Tanners
Wellesley Farm
Herner
Little Hill
Shilstone Farm
Stowford
Yeotown Farm
Hill Farm
Kewsland
Cobbaton Combat Collection (Mus)
Heywood
Woodland Farm
Chapelton
Chittlehampton
Chittlehampton CE Prim Sch
Horestone Cotts
Emmett
Hawkridge Brook
Hawkridge Barton
Ford Bridge
Townsend
Watergate
Gambuston
Fishleigh Barton
Umberleigh House
River Taw
Whey Farm
Hoe
Little Weir
EX37
Bremridge Farm
Blakewell
Chantry
Little Hall
Hotel
Umberleigh Com Prim Sch
Umberleigh
Atherington
Narracott
Eastacott
Fisherton
Eastacombe
Paul's Moor
Bartridge
Brightley Barton
Shortridge
Wixland
A361
A377
B3227
B3217
1 STE HONORINE DU FAY CL
2 CHURCH LA
3 HIGH ST
4 CHAPEL CT
5 THE ORCHARDS
6 BESTRIDGE MDW
RACKMEAD 1
BACK LA 2
THE SQUARE 3
BARNSTAPLE CL 4
1 THE OLD SAWMILLS
2 TRAYLANE
8 29 7 28 6 27 5 26 4 25 3 24 2 23 1 22
58 59 60 61 62 63

27
43

Scale: 1¾ inches to 1 mile

18
30

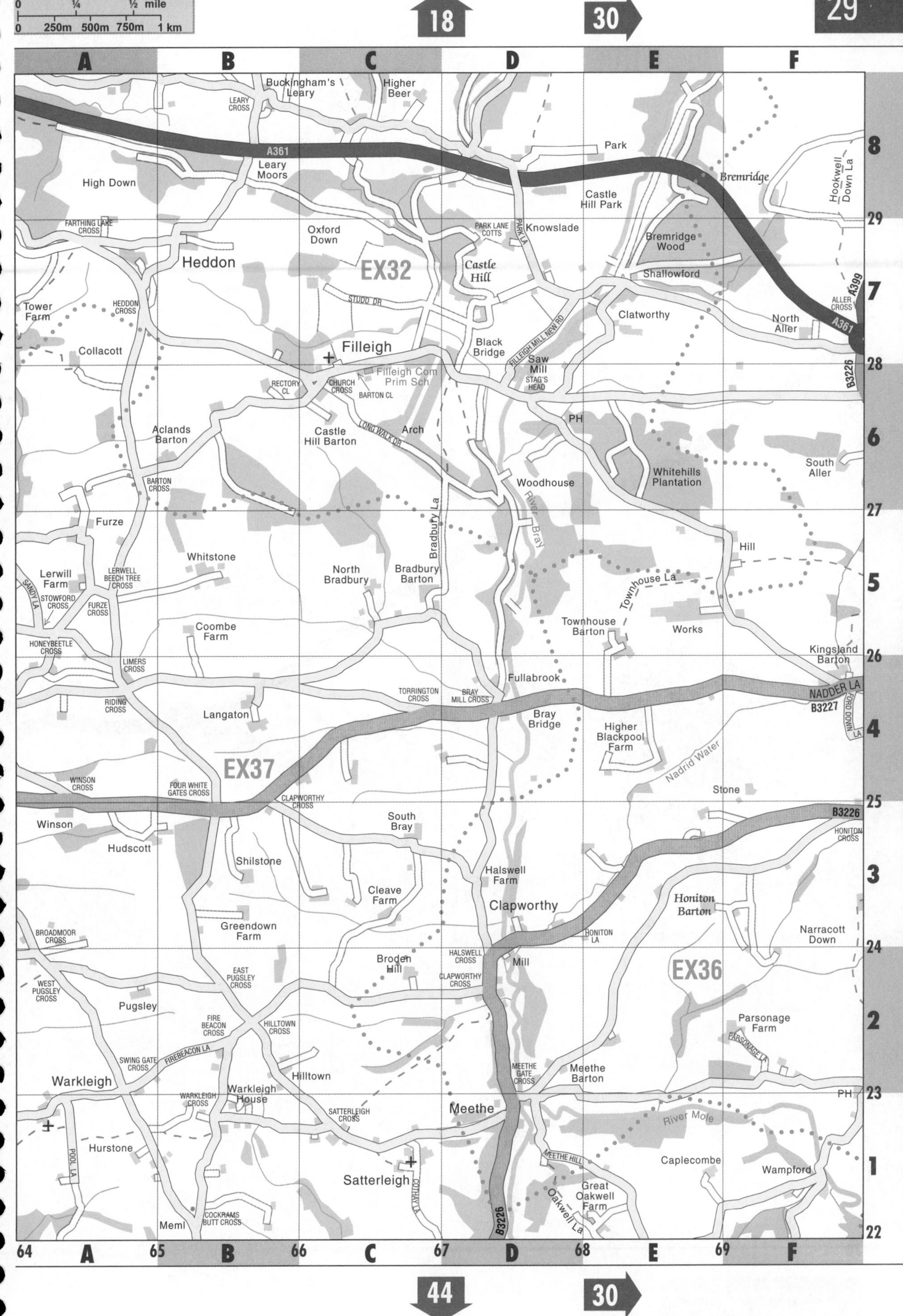

44
30

29

19

Scale: 1¾ inches to 1 mile
0 ¼ ½ mile
0 250m 500m 750m 1 km

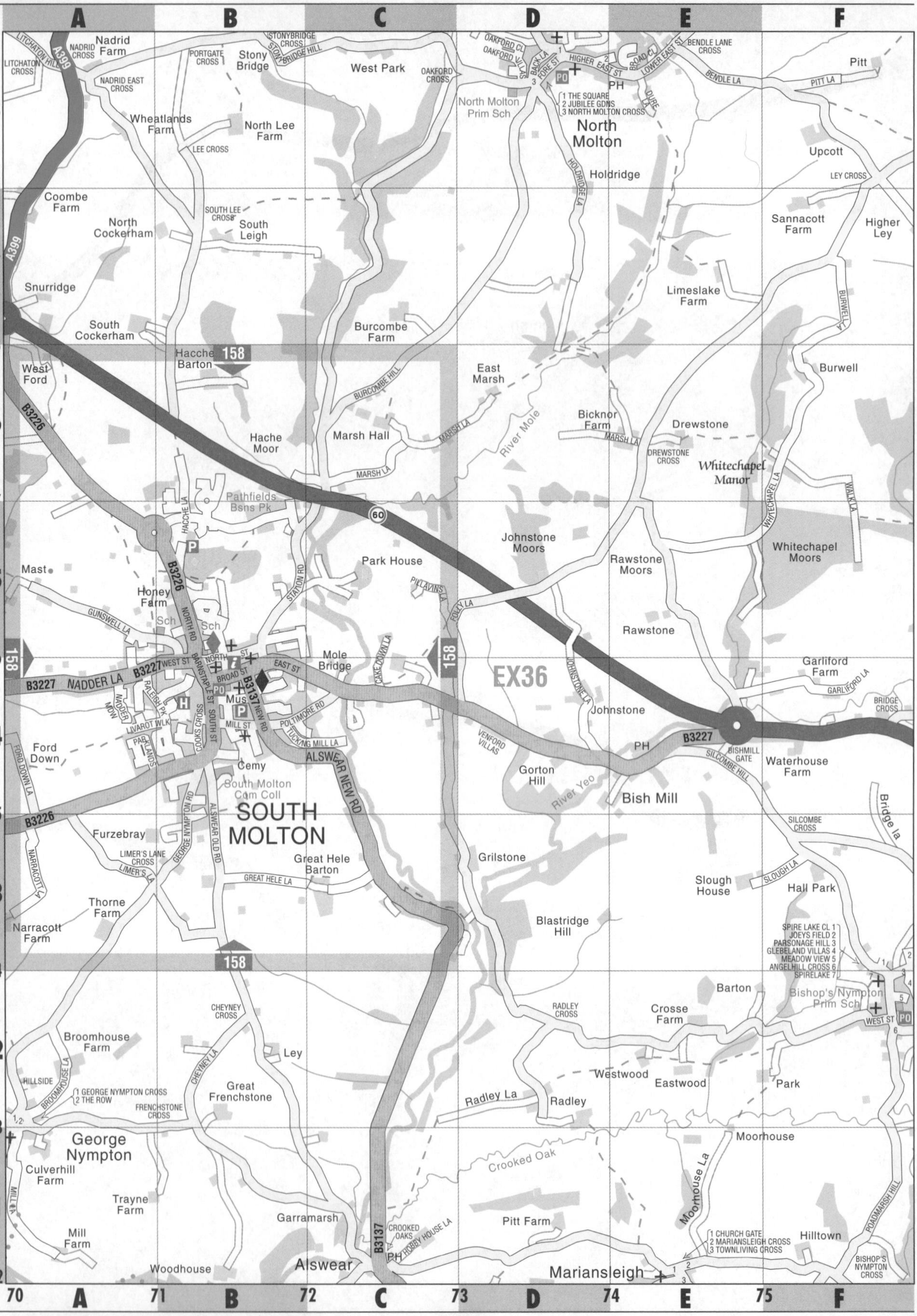

A B C D E F

8
29
7
28
6
27
5
26
4
25
3
24
2
23
1
22

Nadrid Farm
LITCHATON HILL
LITCHATON CROSS
NADRID CROSS
A399
NADRID EAST CROSS
PORTGATE CROSS
Stony Bridge
STONYBRIDGE CROSS
STONY BRIDGE HILL
West Park
OAKFORD CROSS
OAKFORD CL
OAKFORD VILLAS
BACK LA
FORE ST
HIGHER EAST ST
BROAD CL
LOWER EAST ST
BENDLE LANE CROSS
BENDLE LA
Pitt
PITT LA
PO
PH
DUKE LA
1 THE SQUARE
2 JUBILEE GDNS
3 NORTH MOLTON CROSS
North Molton Prim Sch
North Molton
Wheatlands Farm
North Lee Farm
LEE CROSS
Holdridge
HOLDRIDGE LA
Upcott
LEY CROSS
Coombe Farm
North Cockerham
SOUTH LEE CROSS
South Leigh
Sannacott Farm
Higher Ley
Snurridge
Limeslake Farm
BURWELL LA
South Cockerham
Burcombe Farm
Hacche Barton
158
West Ford
East Marsh
Burwell
B3226
BURCOMBE HILL
Bicknor Farm
Drewstone
Hache Moor
Marsh Hall
MARSH LA
River Mole
DREWSTONE CROSS
Whitechapel Manor
WHITECHAPEL LA
WALK LA
Pathfields Bsns Pk
60
HACCHE LA
P
Johnstone Moors
Rawstone Moors
Whitechapel Moors
Mast
Park House
STATION RD
PILLAVINS LA
FOLLY LA
Honey Farm
B3226
NORTH RD
GUNSWELL LA
Sch
Rawstone
158
B3227
WEST ST
NORTH ST
EAST ST
Mole Bridge
CAKE DOWN LA
158
EX36
Garliford Farm
GARLIFORD LA
BRIDGE CROSS
B3227 NADDER LA
RALEIGH PK
BARNSTAPLE ST
BROAD ST
PO
B3137
Mus
H
P
NEW RD
NADDER MDW
LIVAROT WLK
PARK LANDS
COOKS CROSS
SOUTH ST
MILL ST
POLTIMORE RD
TUCKING MILL LA
JOHNSTONE LA
Johnstone
Ford Down
FORD DOWN LA
Cemy
ALSWEAR NEW RD
VENFORD VILLAS
Gorton Hill
PH
B3227
BISHMILL GATE
SILCOMBE HILL
Waterhouse Farm
South Molton Com Coll
River Yeo
Bish Mill
Bridge la
B3226
SOUTH MOLTON
SILCOMBE CROSS
Furzebray
GEORGE NYMPTON RD
ALSWEAR OLD RD
LIMER'S LANE CROSS
LIMER'S LA
Great Hele Barton
Grilstone
NARRACOTT LA
GREAT HELE LA
SLOUGH LA
Slough House
Hall Park
Thorne Farm
Narracott Farm
Blastridge Hill
SPIRE LAKE CL 1
JOEYS FIELD 2
PARSONAGE HILL 3
GLEBELAND VILLAS 4
MEADOW VIEW 5
ANGELHILL CROSS 6
SPIRELAKE 7
158
Barton
Bishop's Nympton Prim Sch
CHEYNEY CROSS
RADLEY CROSS
Crosse Farm
WEST ST
PO
Broomhouse Farm
Ley
CHEYNEY LA
HILLSIDE
BROOMHOUSE LA
1 GEORGE NYMPTON CROSS
2 THE ROW
Great Frenchstone
FRENCHSTONE CROSS
Westwood
Eastwood
Park
Radley La
Radley
George Nympton
Moorhouse
Culverhill Farm
Crooked Oak
Moorhouse La
MILL LA
Trayne Farm
POADMARSH HILL
Garramarsh
Pitt Farm
Mill Farm
B3137
CROOKED OAKS
HOBBY HOUSE LA
1 CHURCH GATE
2 MARIANSLEIGH CROSS
3 TOWNLIVING CROSS
Hilltown
Woodhouse
Alswear
PH
Mariansleigh
BISHOP'S NYMPTON CROSS

70 A 71 B 72 C 73 D 74 E 75 F

For full street detail of the highlighted area see page 158.

29

45

Scale: 1¾ inches to 1 mile

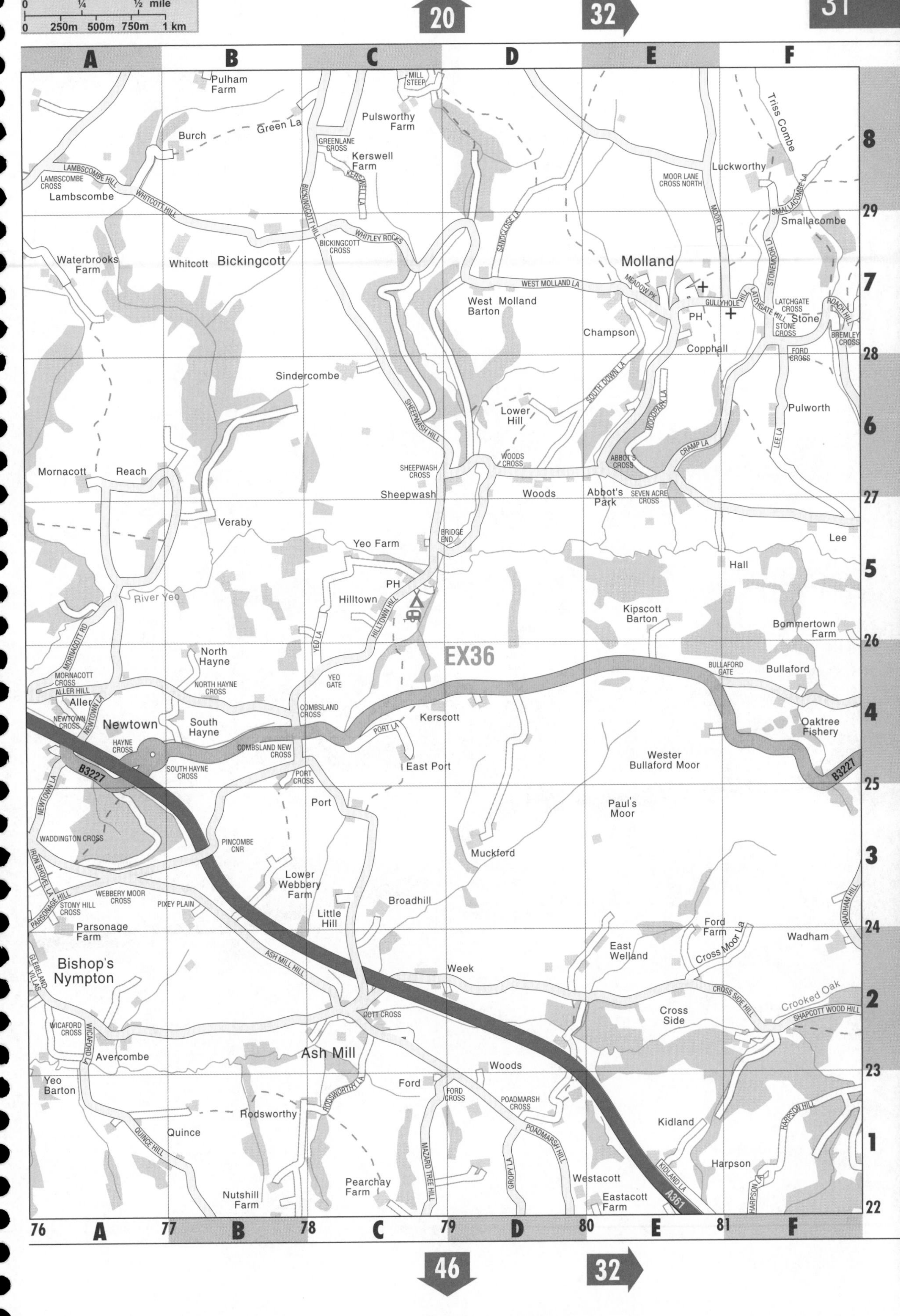

31
21

Scale: 1¾ inches to 1 mile

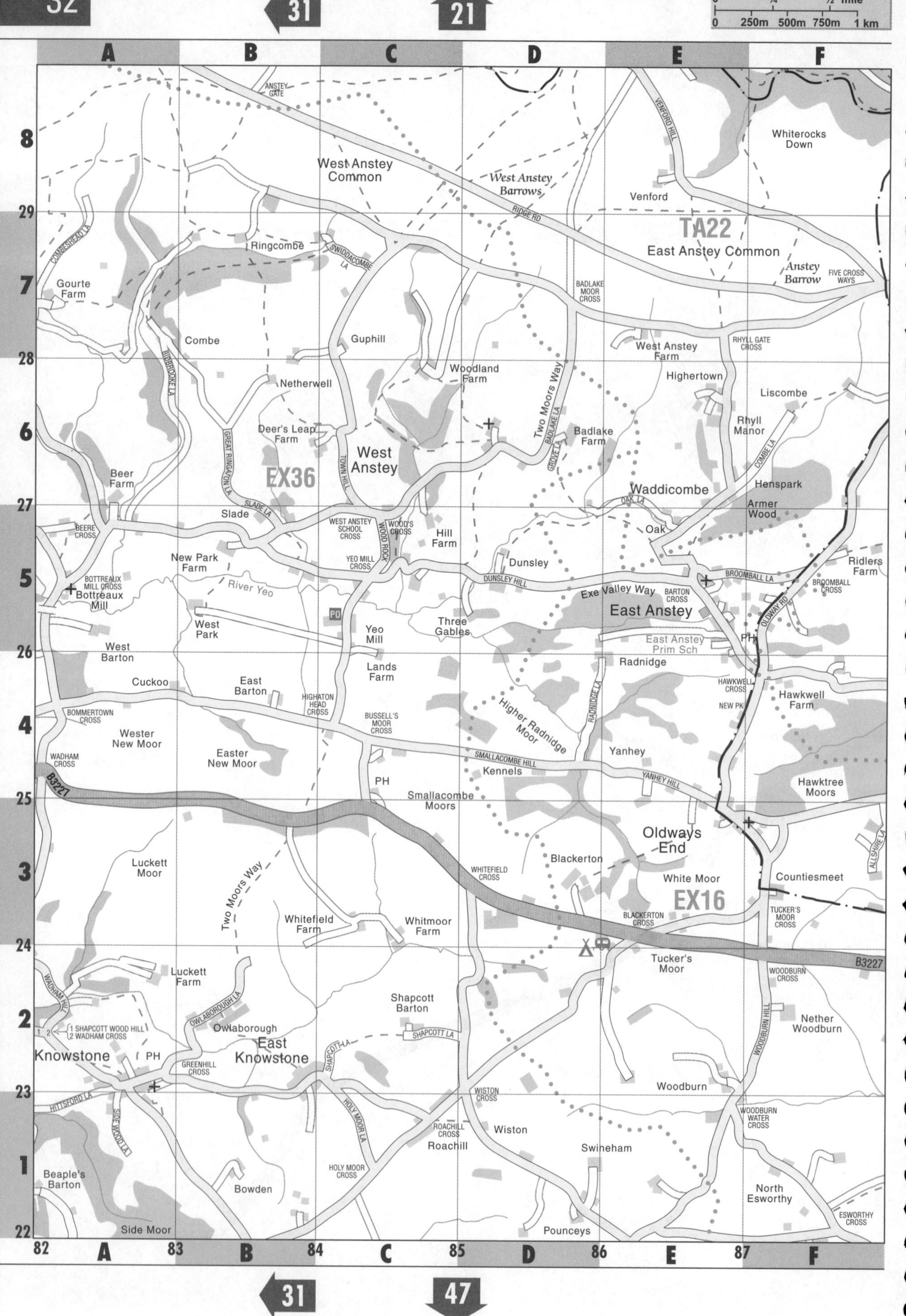

31
47

34

A B C D E F

Somerset STREET ATLAS

A396 Dunster

Brewer's Castle
Mounsey Castle
Draydon Farm
B3223
Court Down
Stockham
STOCKHAM HILL
A396
Oxgrove Farm
MARSH HILL
Marsh Hill House
New Invention
Hinam Farm
LOOSEALL LA
Northcombe
MARSHBRIDGE CROSS
Northmoor
NORTHCOMBE LA
Barlynch Farm
LOUISA GATE
HOLLAM CROSS
Barlynch Woods
CHILCOTT CROSS
WINDBALL HILL
NORTHMOOR RD
NEWGATE CROSS
HINAM CROSS
Exe Valley Way
Old Shute
Oldberry Castle
B3223
Holland House
HOLLAM LA
1 EXMOOR GDNS
2 THE PADDOCK
3 BANK SQ
4 FORE ST
5 UNION ST
6 CHURCH LA
7 VICARAGE HILL
8 BRIDGE ST
9 BARNSCLOSE N
10 HERBERT RD
11 BARNSCLOSE
12 BARNSCLOSE W
13 PICTON PL
MINEHEAD LA
Bury Hill
SHELDON'S LA
THE GARDENS
WEIR HEAD COTTS
HANOVER CT
CHILCOTT LA
OLDSHUTE LA
Old Berry Farm
TOWN MARSH
BEECH TREE CROSS
PO
Hele Bridge
OLDBERRY LA
KEMPS WAY
LADY ST
PH
HOLLAM DR
Chilcott
P
HIGH ST
JURY RD
JURY HILL
B3222
MACHINE CROSS
OLDWAY RD
GREAT MEAD
ROSEMARY LA
FISHERS MEAD
AMORY RD
BATH PL
MEADOW DR
Cawkett Farm
Liby & Visitor Ctr
KING'S CNR
CHAPEL ST
VALENTINES
PIXTON WAY
LADY VICTORIA'S DR
Wilway
ANDREW'S HILL CROSS
COTTAGE LA
B3222
MILLHAM LA
MUSGRAVES
Dulverton
WILWAY LA
ANDREW
BARNES CLOSE MEAD
Barns Close Ind Est
Streamcombe
COMBE LA
BATTLETON
THREE GATES CROSS
Pixton Park
STREAMCOMBE LA
CLAYFORD RD
All Saints CE Sch
Dulverton Mid & Com Sch
Beasley Farm
Bury Castle
Bere
Combe
TA22
Allers Wood
Weir House
DYEHOUSE CROSS
DYEHOUSE LA
Knowle Farm
Gulland
CLAYFORD LA
Clayford
Pixton Hill
Pixy Copse
BEER LA
POOLE HILL
Beer Moors
IRON POST
Mast
Ashill
Brockey River
Venn
Brushford
THE GREEN
ELLERSDOWN LA
Perry Farm
Nightcott
MARKET CL
PERRY NEW RD
West Knowle
1
2
BRUSHFORD NEW RD
VERDALE CL
DENNINGTON LA
Exe Valley Way
River Exe
LANGALLER HILL
MOOR LA
TWELVE ACRE POST
1 NICHOLAS CL
2 POUNDSCLOSE
Langaller Farm
Kents Hill
Hulverton Hill
CROFT LA
Poole Farm
Upcott
Croft Farm
Exebridge Ind Est
ALLSHIRE LA
TRACKFORDMOOR CROSS
Wind Pump
Rocks
Riphay Barton
RIPHAY CROSS
RIVER VIEW
Sowerhill
Exe Valley Fishery
Langridge
Exebridge
Wilsons Farm
B3222
Den Brook
PH
Hele Manor Farm
Higher Grants Farm
BLIGH'S HILL
West Tapps
GRANT'S HILL
Red Deer Farm
Great Highleigh
East Tapps
Western Farm
EAST TAPPS LA
NEW LA
Combe Water
Mast
Combe Head
Newhouse Farm
BLACKALLER LA
East Mildon
Hutswell Farm
EX16
East Loosemoor
West Mildon
OLDWAY LA
Benshayes Farm
HIGH BOLHAM
Ford Farm
B3227
A396
Westbrook Farmhouse
B3227

8
29
7
28
6
27
5
26
4
25
3
24
2
23
1
22

88 A 89 B 90 C 91 D 92 E 93 F

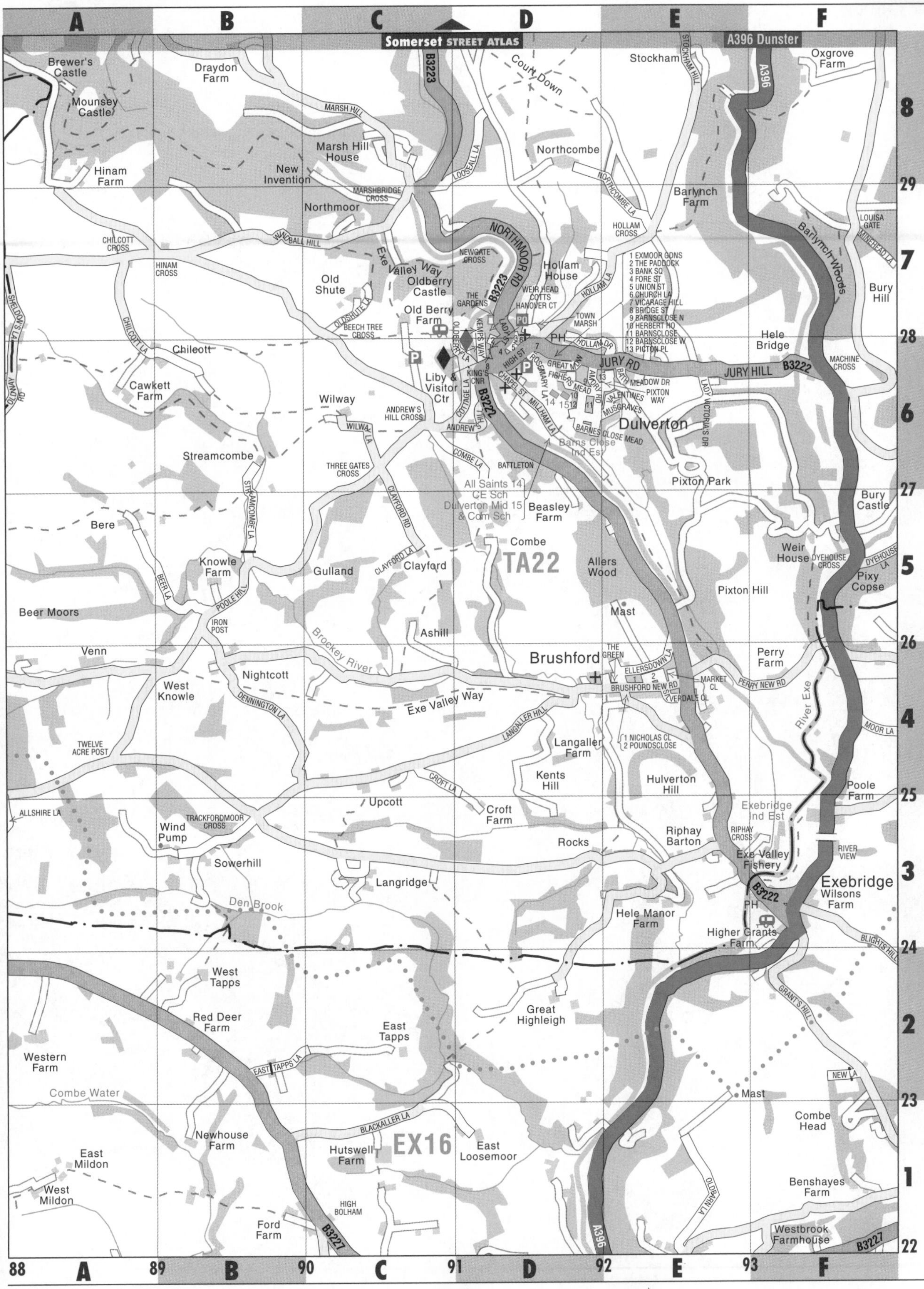

48

34

33

Scale: 1¾ inches to 1 mile
0 ¼ ½ mile
0 250m 500m 750m 1 km

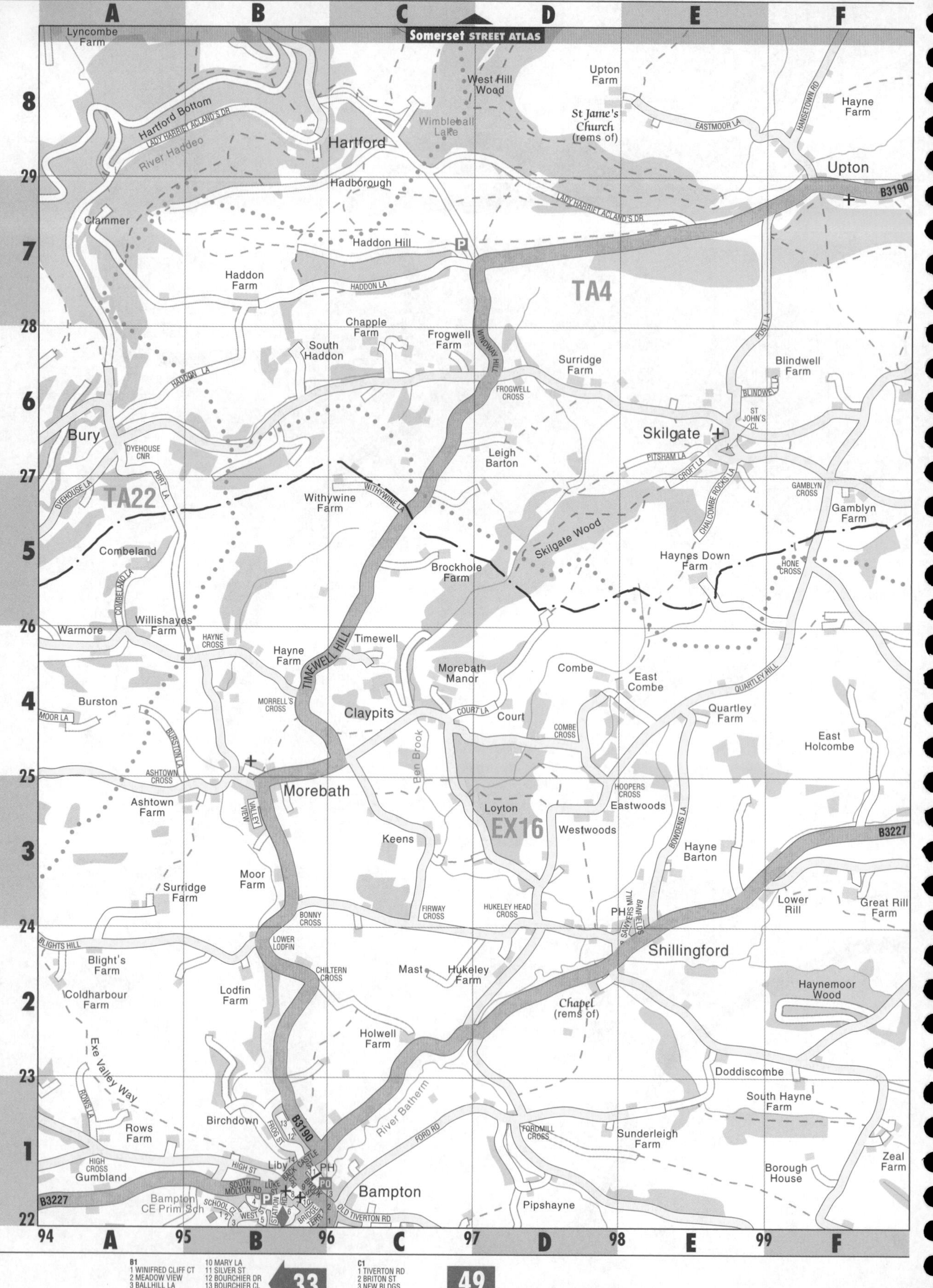

B1
1 WINIFRED CLIFF CT
2 MEADOW VIEW
3 BALLHILL LA
4 MARKET CL
5 LORDS MEADOW LA
6 BARNHAY
7 CHURCH TERR
8 NEWTON SQ
9 FORE ST
10 MARY LA
11 SILVER ST
12 BOURCHIER DR
13 BOURCHIER CL
14 NEWTON CT

C1
1 TIVERTON RD
2 BRITON ST
3 NEW BLDGS

33

49

Scale: 1¾ inches to 1 mile

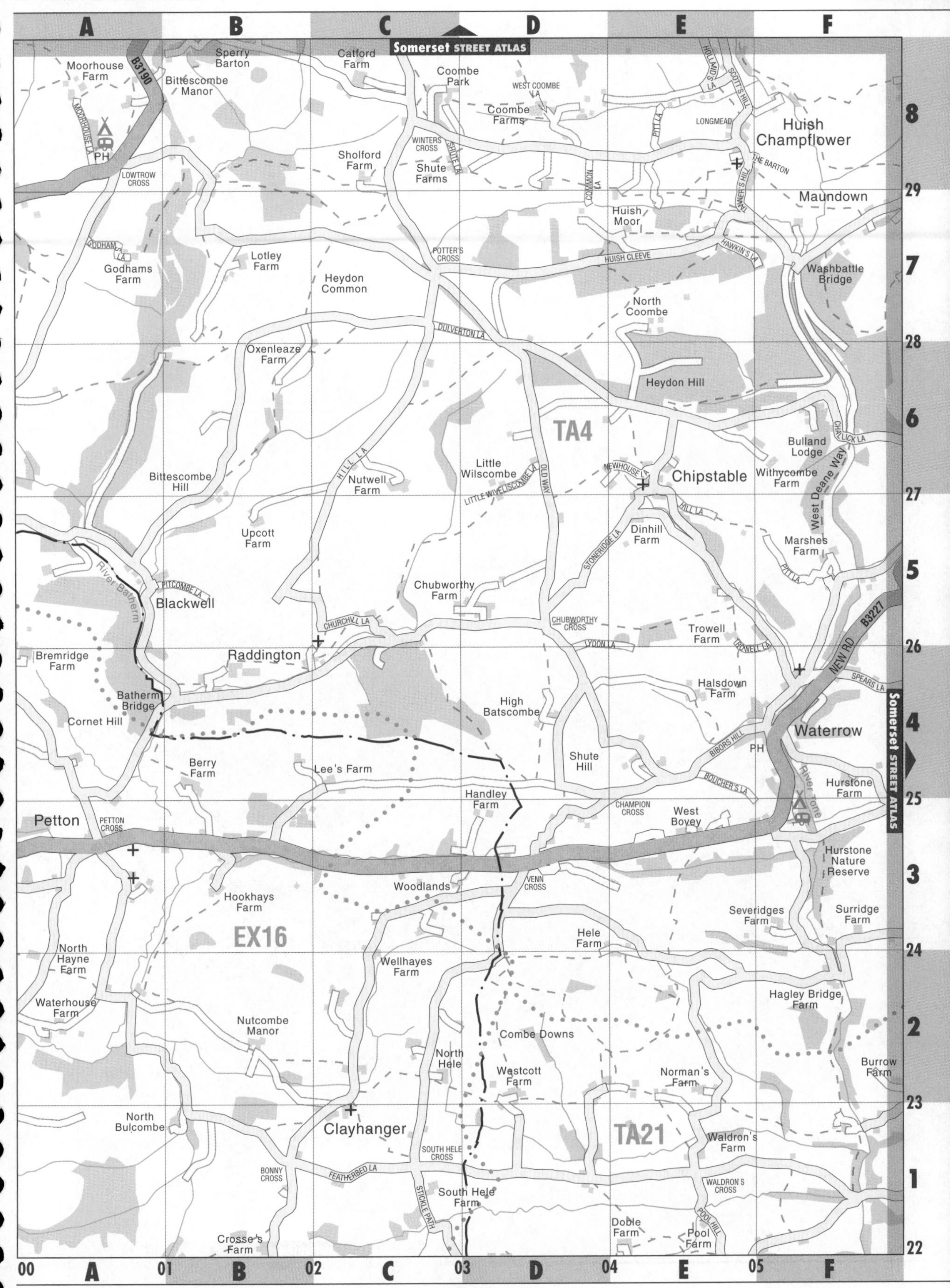

50

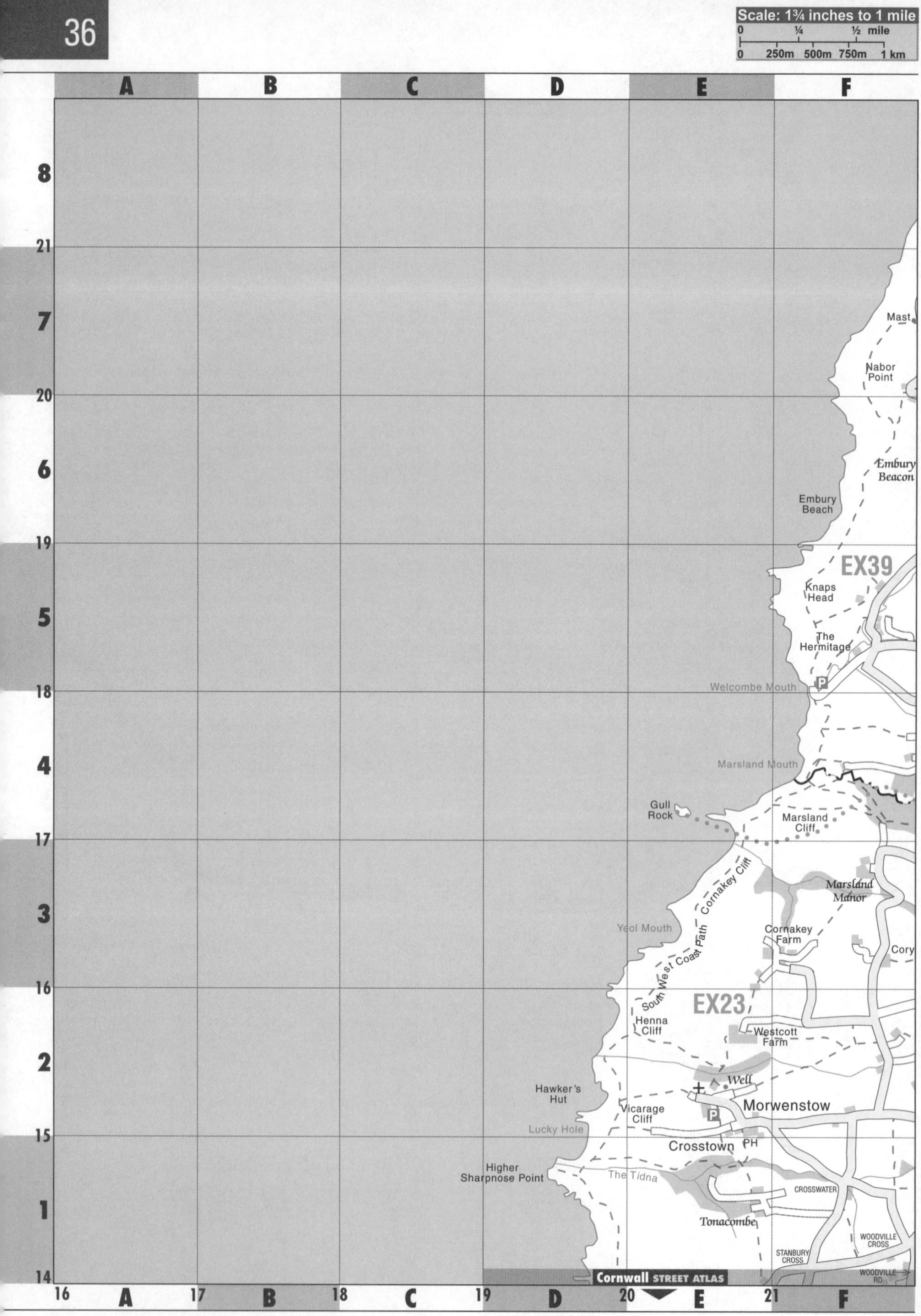

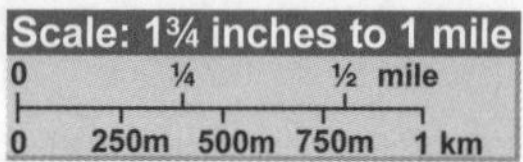

Mast
Nabor Point
Embury Beacon
Embury Beach
EX39
Knaps Head
The Hermitage
Welcombe Mouth
Marsland Mouth
Gull Rock
Marsland Cliff
Cornakey Cliff
Marsland Manor
Yeol Mouth
South West Coast Path
Cornakey Farm
Cory
EX23
Henna Cliff
Westcott Farm
Well
Hawker's Hut
Morwenstow
Vicarage Cliff
Lucky Hole
Crosstown
PH
Higher Sharpnose Point
The Tidna
CROSSWATER
Tonacombe
STANBURY CROSS
WOODVILLE CROSS
WOODVILLE RD

Cornwall STREET ATLAS

A B C D E F
8 7 6 5 4 3 2 1
21 20 19 18 17 16 15 14
16 17 18 19 20 21

Scale: 1¾ inches to 1 mile

22
38

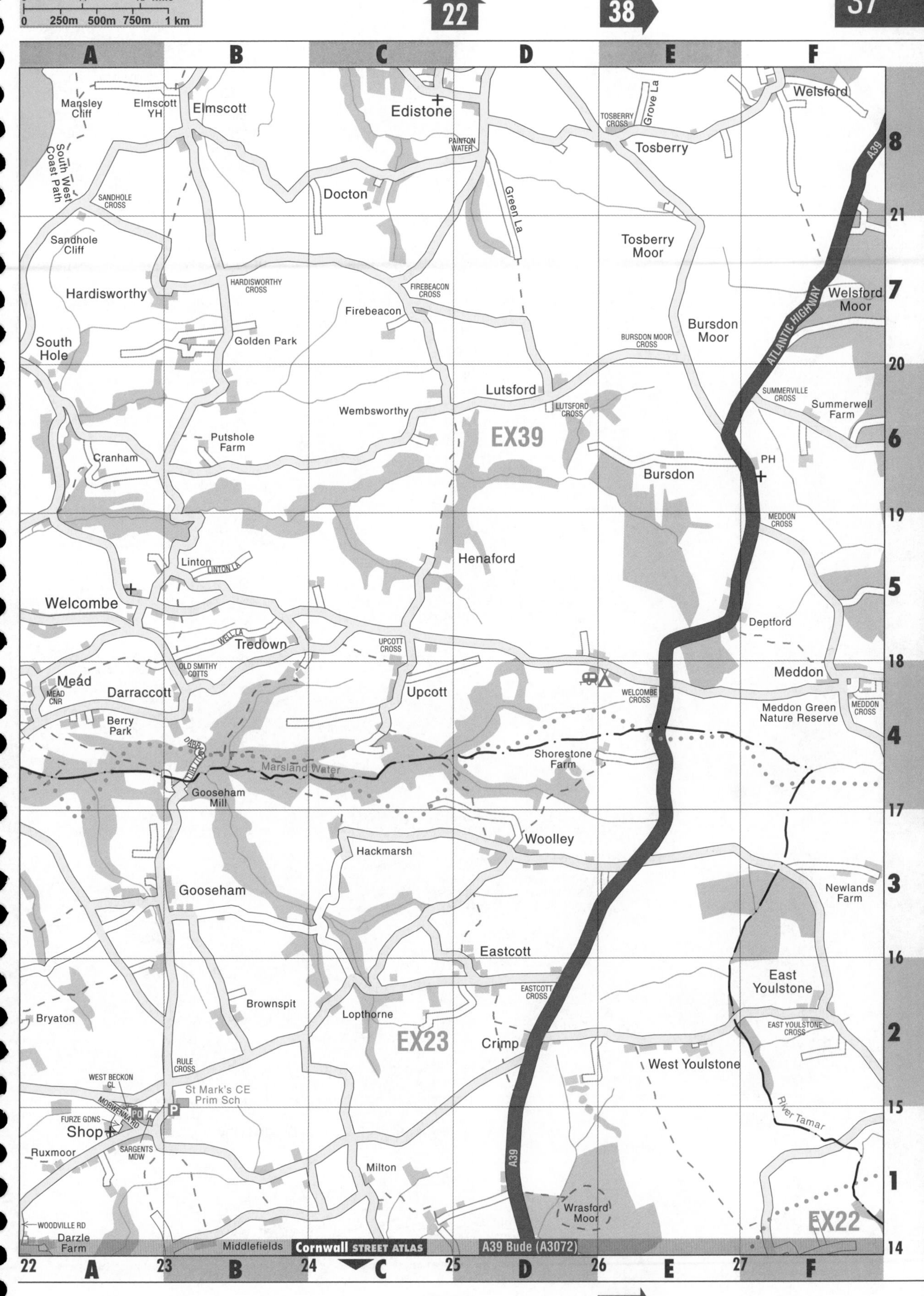

38

37 23

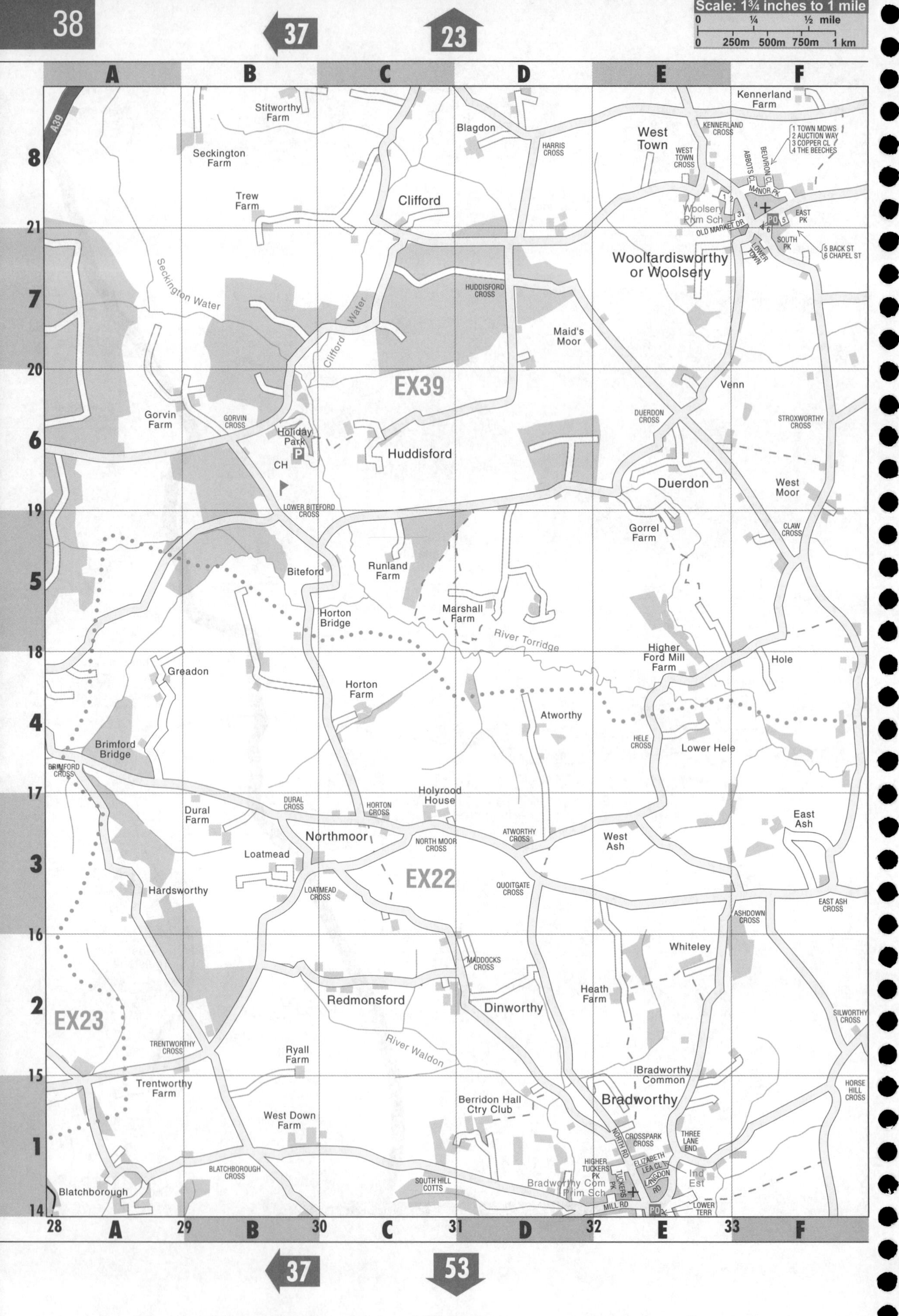
Scale: 1¾ inches to 1 mile
0 ¼ ½ mile
0 250m 500m 750m 1 km
A B C D E F
A39
Stitworthy Farm
Seckington Farm
Trew Farm
Clifford
Blagdon
HARRIS CROSS
West Town
WEST TOWN CROSS
Kennerland Farm
KENNERLAND CROSS
1 TOWN MDWS
2 AUCTION WAY
3 COPPER CL
4 THE BEECHES
ABBOTS CL
BEUVRON CL
MANOR PK
Woolsery Prim Sch
OLD MARKET DR
EAST PK
SOUTH PK
LOWER TOWN
5 BACK ST
6 CHAPEL ST
Woolfardisworthy or Woolsery
Seckington Water
Clifford Water
HUDDISFORD CROSS
Maid's Moor
EX39
Venn
Gorvin Farm
GORVIN CROSS
Holiday Park
CH
Huddisford
DUERDON CROSS
STROXWORTHY CROSS
Duerdon
West Moor
LOWER BITEFORD CROSS
Gorrel Farm
CLAW CROSS
Biteford
Runland Farm
Marshall Farm
Horton Bridge
River Torridge
Higher Ford Mill Farm
Hole
Greadon
Horton Farm
Atworthy
HELE CROSS
Lower Hele
Brimford Bridge
BRIMFORD CROSS
Holyrood House
Dural Farm
DURAL CROSS
HORTON CROSS
Northmoor
NORTH MOOR CROSS
ATWORTHY CROSS
West Ash
East Ash
Loatmead
EX22
QUOITGATE CROSS
Hardsworthy
LOATMEAD CROSS
EAST ASH CROSS
ASHDOWN CROSS
Whiteley
MADDOCKS CROSS
Heath Farm
Redmonsford
Dinworthy
EX23
SILWORTHY CROSS
TRENTWORTHY CROSS
Ryall Farm
River Waldon
Bradworthy Common
Trentworthy Farm
Berridon Hall Ctry Club
Bradworthy
HORSE HILL CROSS
West Down Farm
NORTH RD
CROSSPARK CROSS
THREE LANE END
BLATCHBOROUGH CROSS
HIGHER TUCKERS PK
ELIZABETH
LEA CL
LANGDON RD
Ind Est
Blatchborough
SOUTH HILL COTTS
Bradworthy Com Prim Sch
TUCKERS PK
MILL RD
PO
LOWER TERR
8 21 7 20 6 19 5 18 4 17 3 16 2 15 1 14
28 29 30 31 32 33

37 53

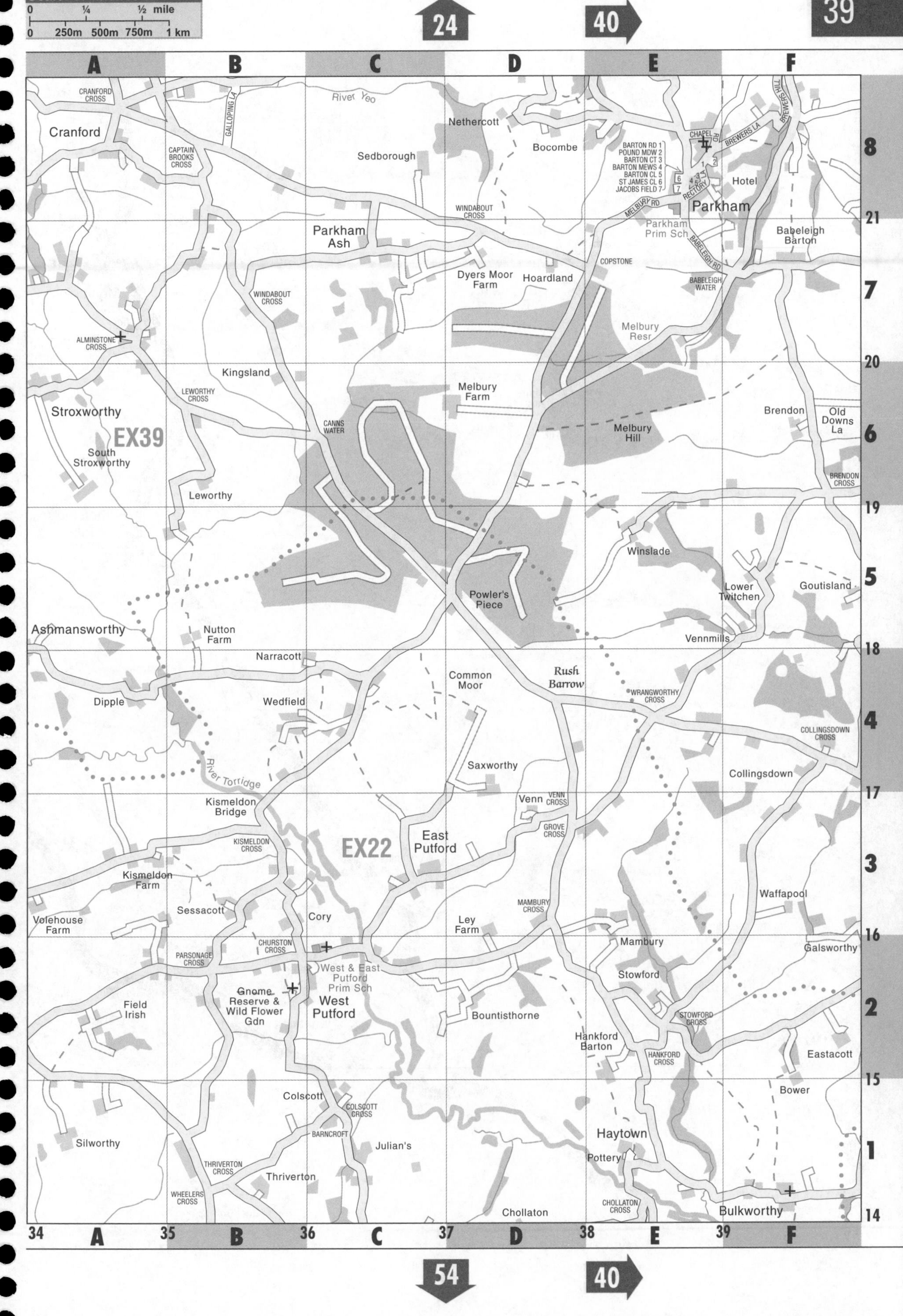

Scale: 1¾ inches to 1 mile
0 ¼ ½ mile
0 250m 500m 750m 1 km
24
40
A B C D E F
Cranford Cross
Cranford
Galloping La
Captain Brooks Cross
River Yeo
Sedborough
Nethercott
Bocombe
Chapel Rd
Brewers La
Brewers Hill
Barton Rd 1
Pound Mdw 2
Barton Ct 3
Barton Mews 4
Barton Cl 5
St James Cl 6
Jacobs Field 7
Rectory La
Hotel
Melbury Rd
Parkham
Parkham Prim Sch
Babeleigh Rd
Babeleigh Barton
Windabout Cross
Parkham Ash
Copstone
Dyers Moor Farm
Hoardland
Babeleigh Water
Windabout Cross
Alminstone Cross
Melbury Resr
Kingsland
Lenworthy Cross
Melbury Farm
Stroxworthy
EX39
South Stroxworthy
Canns Water
Brendon
Old Downs La
Melbury Hill
Brendon Cross
Leworthy
Winslade
Powler's Piece
Lower Twitchen
Goutisland
Ashmansworthy
Nutton Farm
Vennmills
Narracott
Common Moor
Rush Barrow
Wrangworthy Cross
Dipple
Wedfield
Collingsdown Cross
Saxworthy
Collingsdown
River Torridge
Kismeldon Bridge
Venn
Venn Cross
Grove Cross
Kismeldon Cross
EX22
East Putford
Kismeldon Farm
Waffapool
Sessacott
Mambury Cross
Volehouse Farm
Cory
Ley Farm
Churston Cross
Mambury
Galsworthy
Parsonage Cross
West & East Putford Prim Sch
Stowford
Gnome Reserve & Wild Flower Gdn
West Putford
Field Irish
Bountisthorne
Stowford Cross
Hankford Barton
Hankford Cross
Eastacott
Bower
Colscott
Colscott Cross
Barncroft
Julian's
Haytown
Silworthy
Pottery
Thriverton Cross
Thriverton
Wheelers Cross
Chollaton
Chollaton Cross
Bulkworthy
8 21 7 20 6 19 5 18 4 17 3 16 2 15 1 14
34 35 36 37 38 39
54
40

39
25

Scale: 1¾ inches to 1 mile

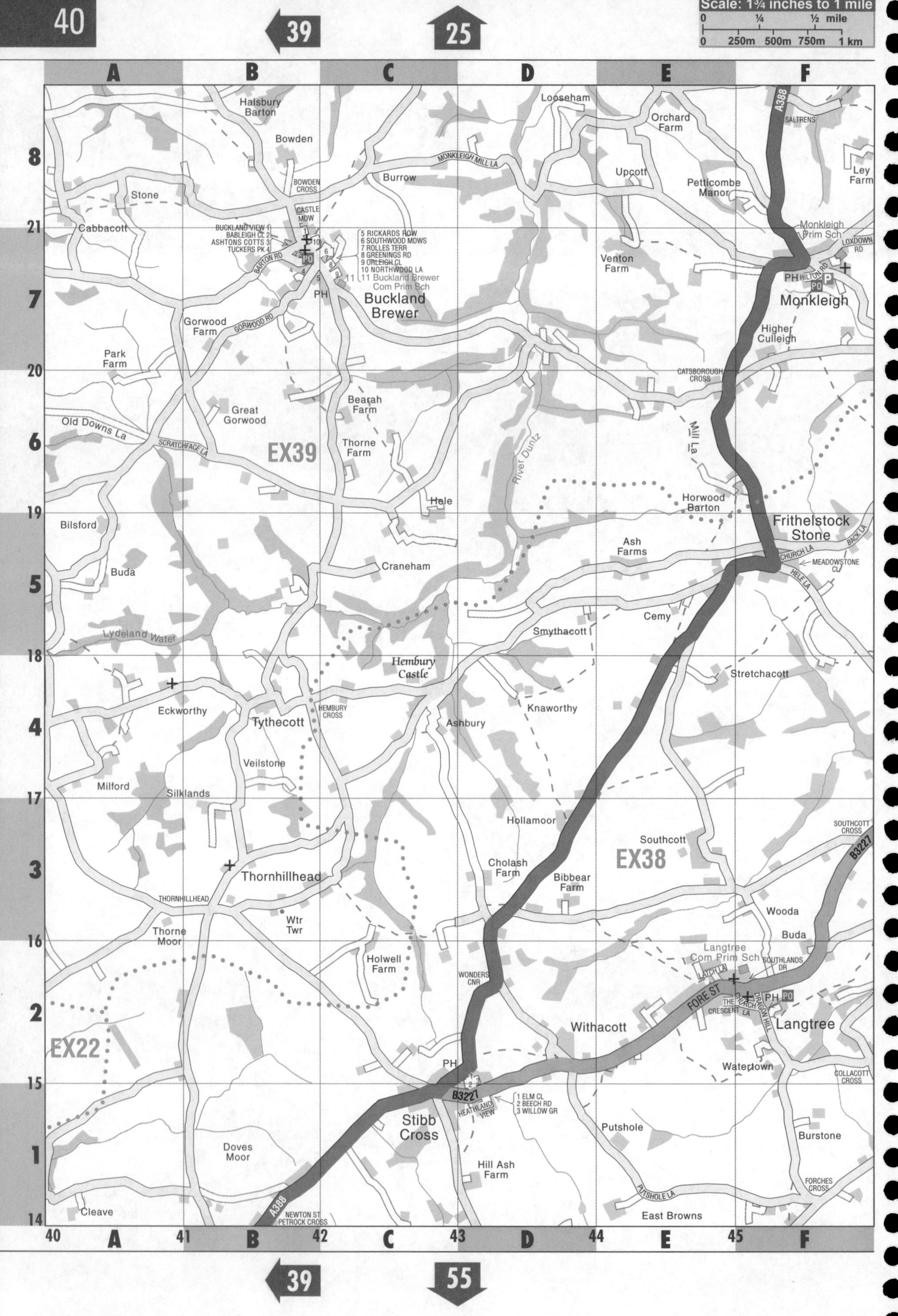

39
55

Scale: 1¾ inches to 1 mile

26
42

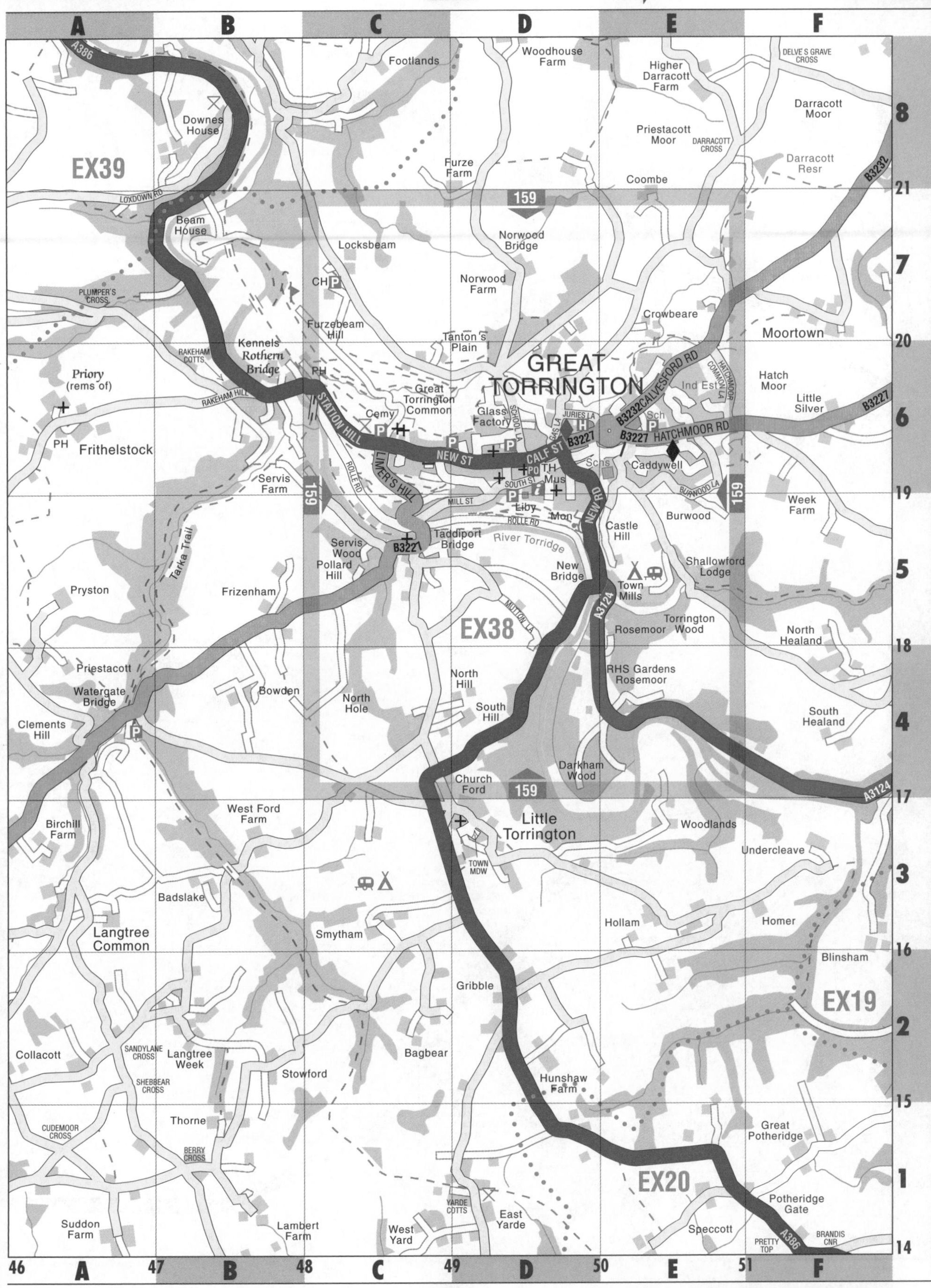

56
42
For full street detail of the highlighted area see page 159.

41
27

Scale: 1¾ inches to 1 mile
0 ¼ ½ mile
0 250m 500m 750m 1 km

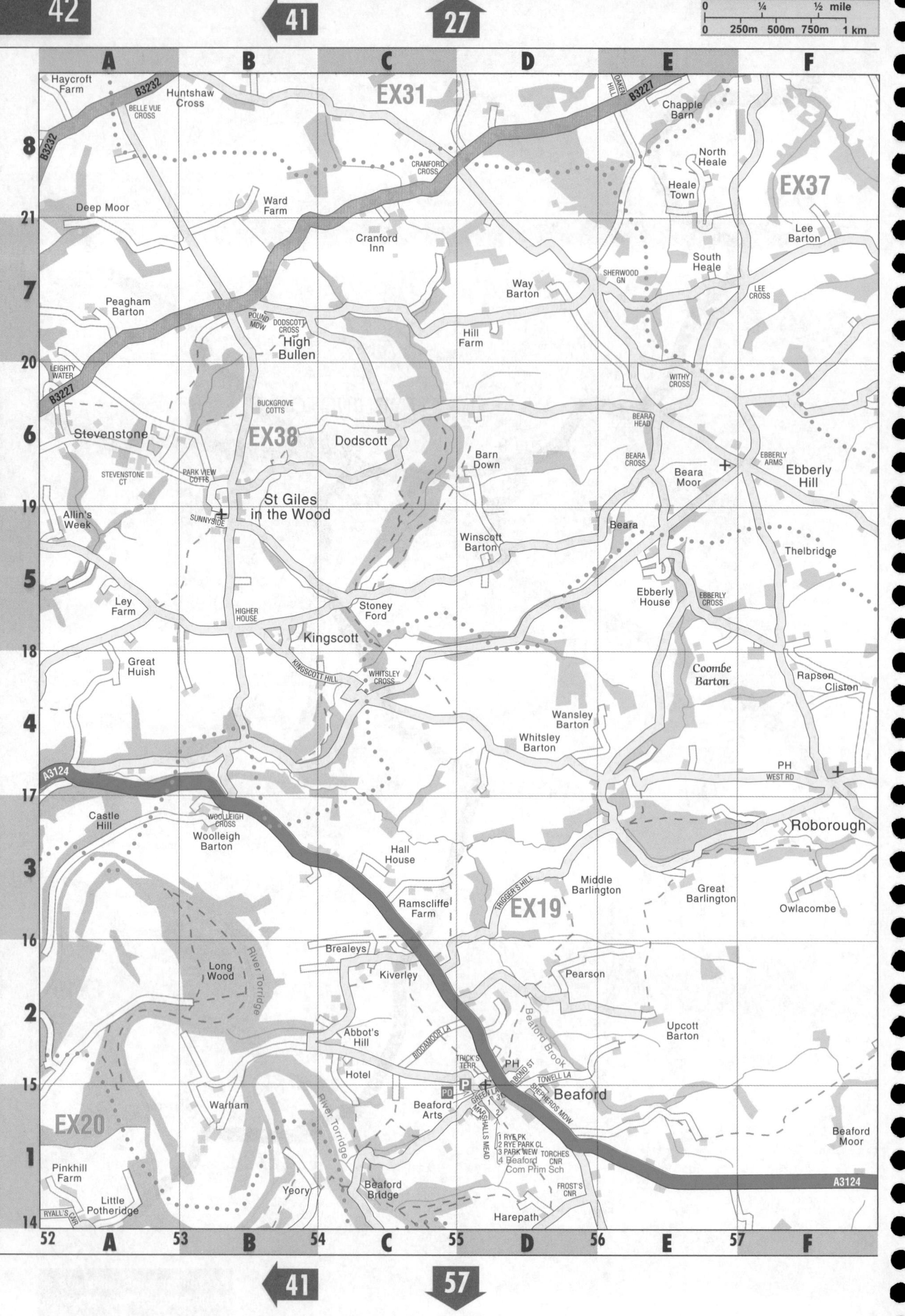

41
57

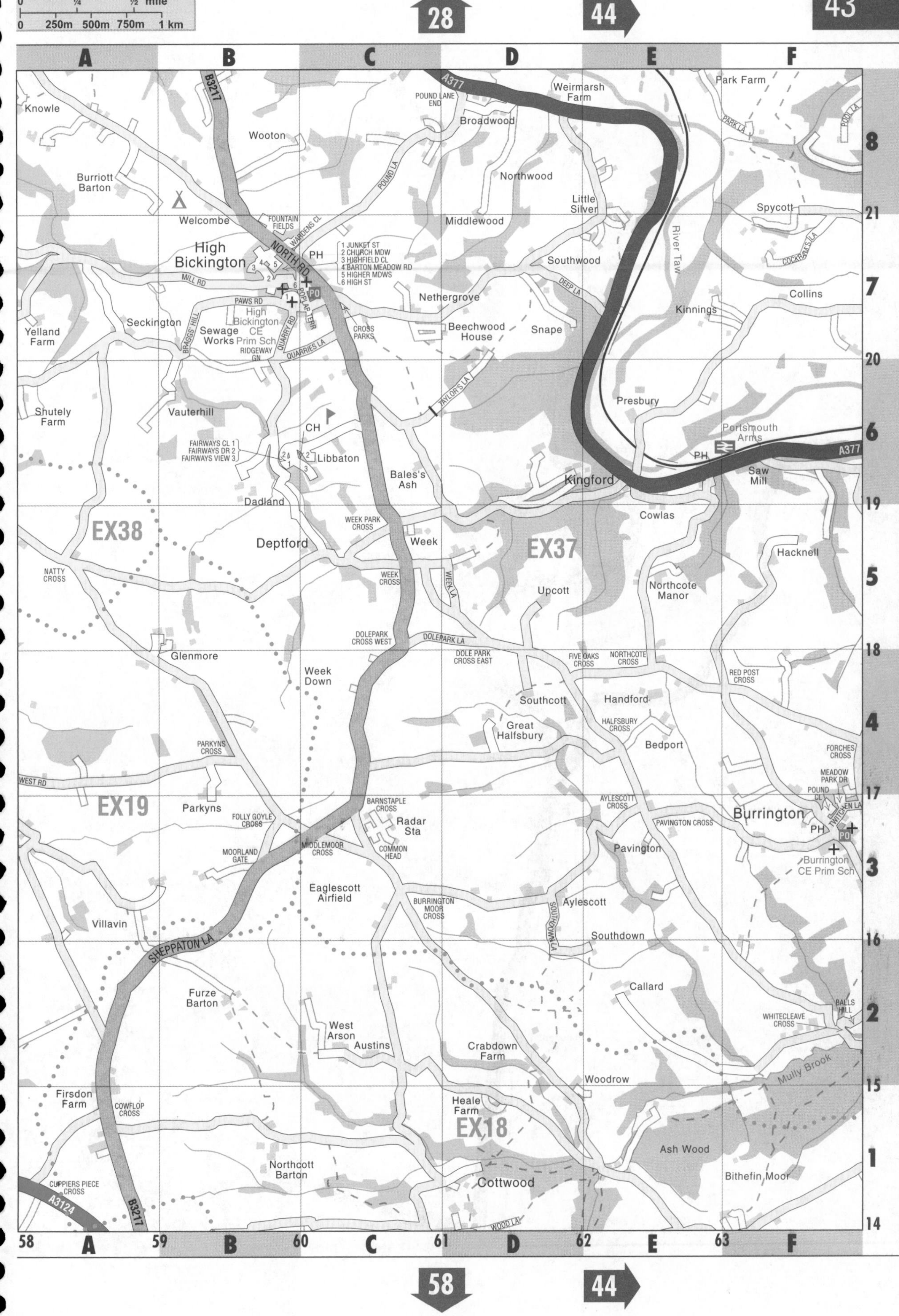
Scale: 1¾ inches to 1 mile
0 ¼ ½ mile
0 250m 500m 750m 1 km
28
44
A B C D E F
Knowle
Wooton
Burriott Barton
Welcombe
High Bickington
Seckington
Yelland Farm
Sewage Works
High Bickington CE Prim Sch
Shutely Farm
Vauterhill
Libbaton
Dadland
Deptford
NATTY CROSS
Glenmore
Week Down
PARKYNS CROSS
WEST RD
Parkyns
FOLLY GOYLE CROSS
MOORLAND GATE
MIDDLEMOOR CROSS
Villavin
SHEPPATON LA
Furze Barton
Firsdon Farm
COWFLOP CROSS
CUPPIERS PIECE CROSS
A3124
B3217
Northcott Barton
West Arson
Austins
Eaglescott Airfield
Radar Sta
BARNSTAPLE CROSS
COMMON HEAD
BURRINGTON MOOR CROSS
Crabdown Farm
Heale Farm
Cottwood
WOOD LA
Woodrow
Ash Wood
Bithefin Moor
Mully Brook
Callard
WHITECLEAVE CROSS
BALLS HILL
Southdown
Aylescott
SOUTHDOWN LA
Pavington
PAVINGTON CROSS
AYLESCOTT CROSS
Burrington
Burrington CE Prim Sch
POUND CL
TWITCHEN LA
MEADOW PARK DR
FORCHES CROSS
Bedport
HALFSBURY CROSS
Great Halfsbury
Southcott
Handford
FIVE OAKS CROSS
NORTHCOTE CROSS
RED POST CROSS
DOLE PARK CROSS EAST
DOLEPARK LA
DOLEPARK CROSS WEST
WEEK CROSS
WEEK LA
Week
WEEK PARK CROSS
Bales's Ash
Upcott
Northcote Manor
Hacknell
Cowlas
Kingford
Saw Mill
Portsmouth Arms
A377
Presbury
Kinnings
Collins
River Taw
Spycott
COCKRAM'S LA
Park Farm
PARK LA
POOL LA
Weirmarsh Farm
Broadwood
POUND LANE END
POUND LA
Northwood
Little Silver
Middlewood
Southwood
DEEP LA
Nethergrove
Beechwood House
Snape
TAYLOR'S LA
CROSS PARKS
FOUNTAIN FIELDS
WARDENS CL
NORTH RD
POPLAR TERR
QUARRY RD
QUARRIES LA
RIDGEWAY GN
PAWS RD
BRAGGS HILL
MILL RD
1 JUNKET ST
2 CHURCH MDW
3 HIGHFIELD CL
4 BARTON MEADOW RD
5 HIGHER MDWS
6 HIGH ST
FAIRWAYS CL 1
FAIRWAYS DR 2
FAIRWAYS VIEW 3
CH
PH
PO
EX38
EX37
EX19
EX18
8
21
7
20
6
19
5
18
4
17
3
16
2
15
1
14
58 59 60 61 62 63
58
44

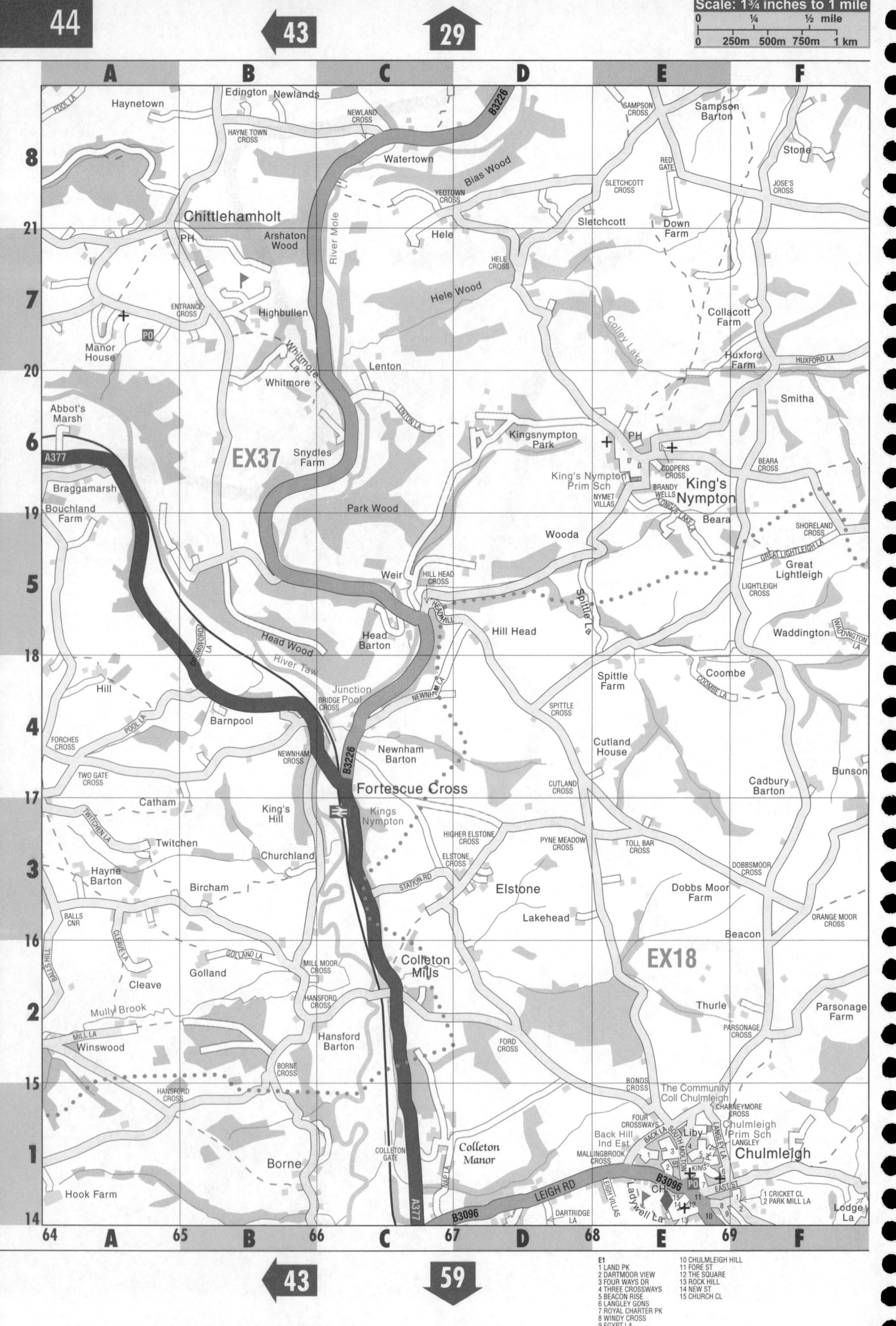
44
43
29
59
Scale: 1¾ inches to 1 mile
0 ¼ ½ mile
0 250m 500m 750m 1 km
A
B
C
D
E
F
Haynetown
Edington
Newlands
Newland Cross
Hayne Town Cross
Sampson Cross
Sampson Barton
Stone
Watertown
Bias Wood
Red Gate
Sletchcott Cross
Jose's Cross
Yeotown Cross
Chittlehamholt
PH
Arshaton Wood
River Mole
Hele
Sletchcott
Down Farm
Hele Cross
Hele Wood
Entrance Cross
Highbullen
PO
Manor House
Whitmore La
Whitmore
Colley Lake
Collacott Farm
Huxford Farm
Huxford La
Lenton
Lenton La
Smitha
Abbot's Marsh
A377
EX37
Snydles Farm
Kingsnympton Park
PH
Coopers Cross
Beara Cross
King's Nympton Prim Sch
Brandy Wells
Nymet Villas
King's Nympton
Longlake La
Beara
Braggamarsh
Bouchland Farm
Park Wood
Wooda
Shoreland Cross
Great Lightleigh La
Great Lightleigh
Weir
Hill Head Cross
Spittle La
Lightleigh Cross
Head Hill
Hill Head
Waddington
Waddington La
Head Barton
Head Wood
River Taw
Drumsford La
Spittle Farm
Coombe
Coombe La
Hill
Junction Pool
Bridge Cross
Newnham La
Spittle Cross
Pool La
Barnpool
Forches Cross
Newnham Cross
B3226
Newnham Barton
Cutland House
Two Gate Cross
Bunson
Fortescue Cross
Cadbury Barton
Catham
Cutland Cross
King's Hill
Kings Nympton
Twitchen La
Twitchen
Higher Elstone Cross
Pyne Meadow Cross
Toll Bar Cross
Churchland
Elstone Cross
Hayne Barton
Dobbsmoor Cross
Station Rd
Bircham
Elstone
Dobbs Moor Farm
Balls Cnr
Cleave La
Lakehead
Orange Moor Cross
Beacon
Balls Hill
Golland La
Colleton Mills
Mill Moor Cross
EX18
Golland
Cleave
Mully Brook
Hansford Cross
Thurle
Parsonage Farm
Mill La
Hansford Barton
Parsonage Cross
Winswood
Ford Cross
Borne Cross
Hansford Cross
Bonds Cross
The Community Coll Chulmleigh
Charneymore Cross
Four Crossways
Back La
South Molton St
Liby
Langley La
Chulmleigh Prim Sch
Langley
Back Hill Ind Est
Colleton Gate
Colleton Manor
Mallingbrook Cross
Chulmleigh
Borne
Hook Farm
Leigh Rd
B3096
Leigh Villas
Ladywell La
CH
East St
1 Cricket Cl
2 Park Mill La
Lodge La
Dartridge La
Vorn La
64
65
66
67
68
69
8
21
7
20
6
19
5
18
4
17
3
16
2
15
1
14
E1
1 Land Pk
2 Dartmoor View
3 Four Ways Dr
4 Three Crossways
5 Beacon Rise
6 Langley Gdns
7 Royal Charter Pk
8 Windy Cross
9 Egypt La
10 Chulmleigh Hill
11 Fore St
12 The Square
13 Rock Hill
14 New St
15 Church Cl

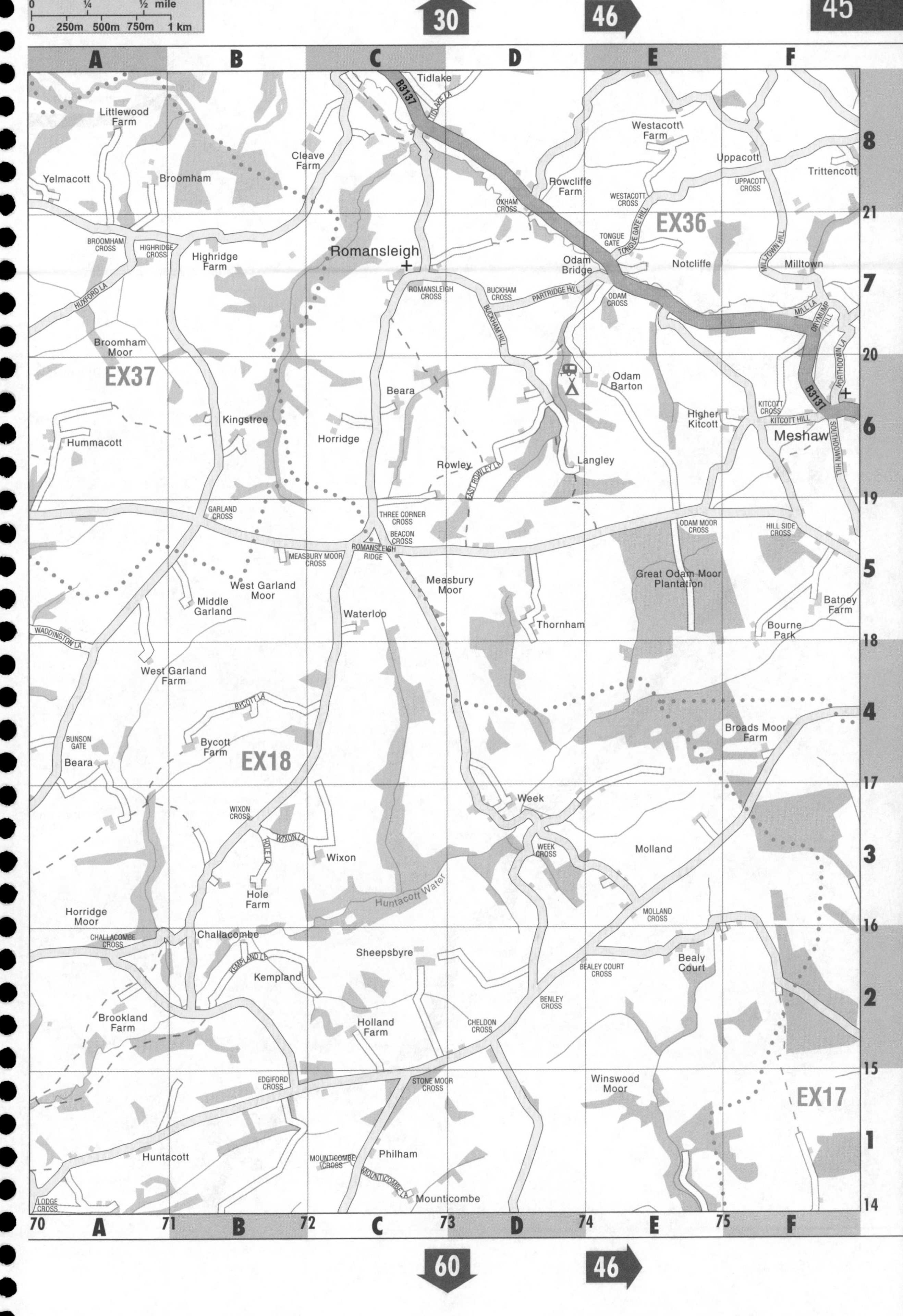
Scale: 1¾ inches to 1 mile
0 ¼ ½ mile
0 250m 500m 750m 1 km
30
46
A B C D E F
Tidlake
B3137
TIDLAKE LA
Littlewood Farm
Westacott Farm
Cleave Farm
Uppacott
Trittencott
Yelmacott
Broomham
Rowcliffe Farm
UPPACOTT CROSS
OXHAM CROSS
WESTACOTT CROSS
EX36
BROOMHAM CROSS
HIGHRIDGE CROSS
Highridge Farm
Romansleigh
TONGUE GATE
TONGUE GATE HILL
Odam Bridge
Notcliffe
MILLTOWN HILL
Milltown
HUXFORD LA
ROMANSLEIGH CROSS
BUCKHAM CROSS
PARTRIDGE HILL
ODAM CROSS
MILL LA
DRYHUMP HILL
BUCKHAM HILL
Broomham Moor
EX37
Odam Barton
NORTHDOWN LA
Beara
Higher Kitcott
KITCOTT CROSS
KITCOTT HILL
Kingstree
Meshaw
Hummacott
Horridge
SOUTHDOWN HILL
Rowley
EAST ROWLEY LA
Langley
GARLAND CROSS
THREE CORNER CROSS
BEACON CROSS
ODAM MOOR CROSS
HILL SIDE CROSS
ROMANSLEIGH RIDGE
MEASBURY MOOR CROSS
West Garland Moor
Measbury Moor
Great Odam Moor Plantation
Middle Garland
Waterloo
Batney Farm
WADDINGTON LA
Thornham
Bourne Park
West Garland Farm
BYCOTT LA
BUNSON GATE
Bycott Farm
Broads Moor Farm
Beara
EX18
WIXON CROSS
Week
HOLE LA
WIXON LA
WEEK CROSS
Molland
Wixon
Hole Farm
Huntacott Water
Horridge Moor
MOLLAND CROSS
CHALLACOMBE CROSS
Challacombe
Sheepsbyre
Bealy Court
KEMPLAND LA
Kempland
BEALEY COURT CROSS
BENLEY CROSS
Brookland Farm
Holland Farm
CHELDON CROSS
EDGIFORD CROSS
STONE MOOR CROSS
Winswood Moor
EX17
Huntacott
Philham
MOUNTICOMBE CROSS
MOUNTICOMBE LA
Mounticombe
LODGE CROSS
8 21 7 20 6 19 5 18 4 17 3 16 2 15 1 14
70 71 72 73 74 75
60
46

45
31

Scale: 1¾ inches to 1 mile
0 ¼ ½ mile
0 250m 500m 750m 1 km

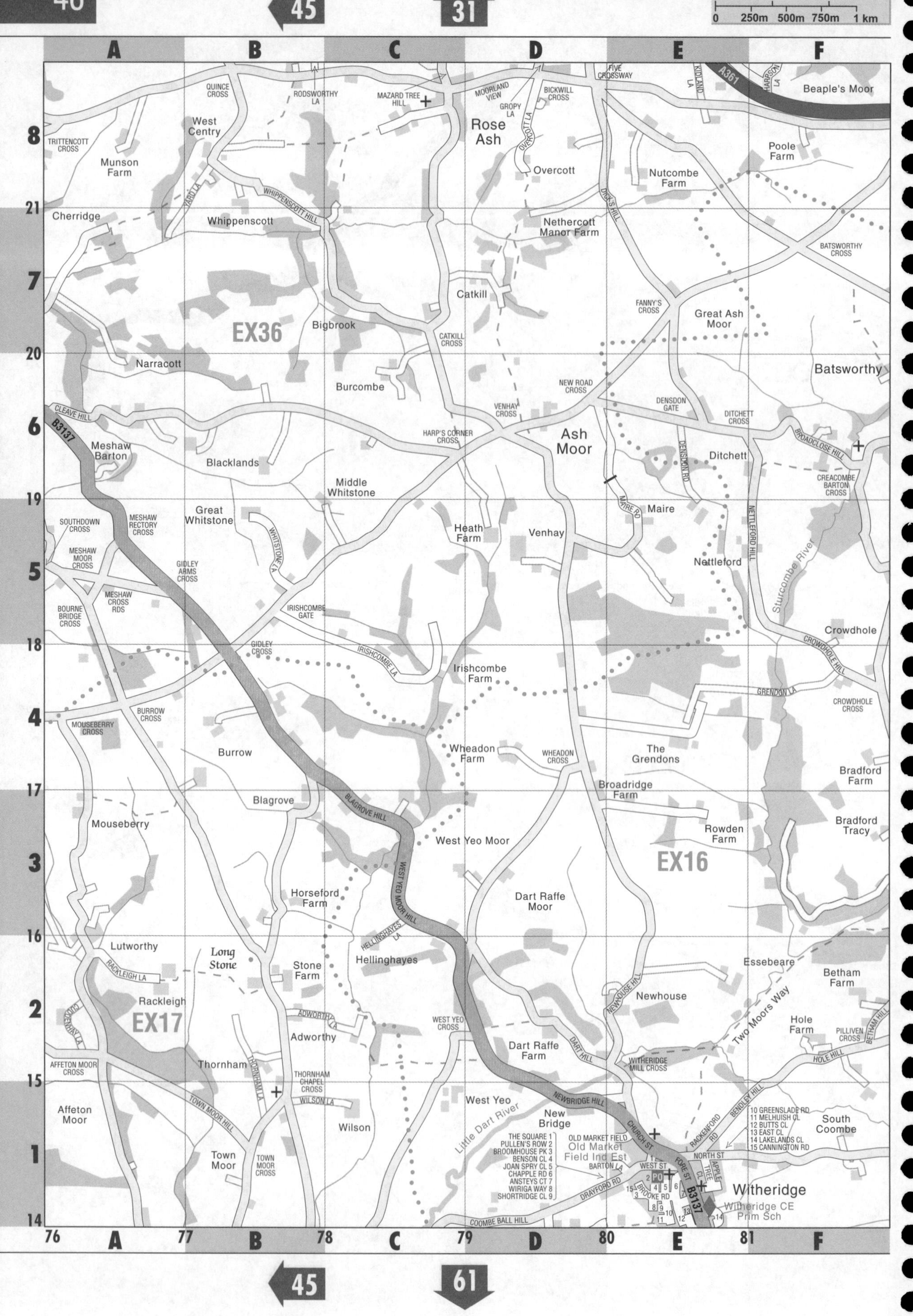

45
61

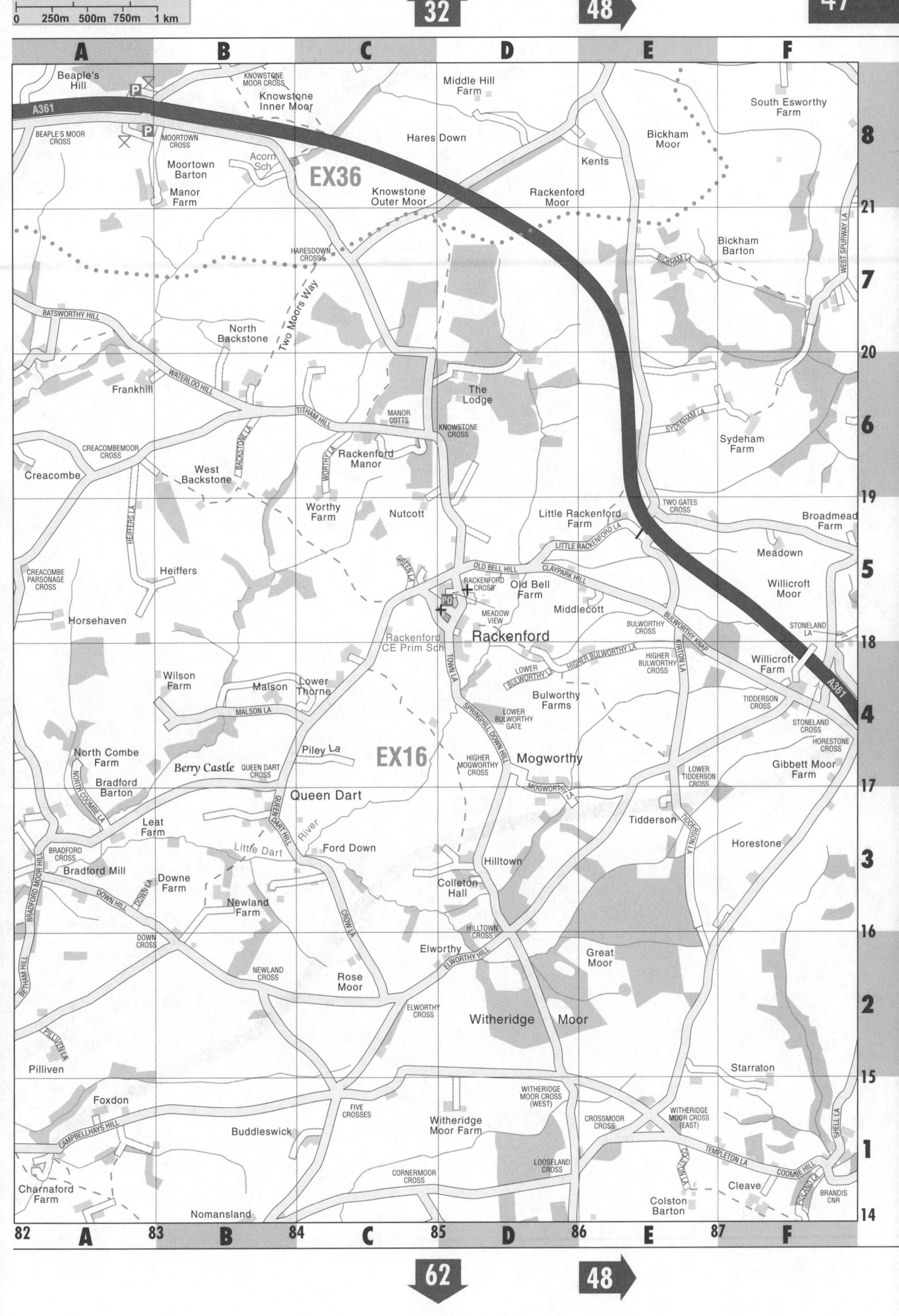
Scale: 1¾ inches to 1 mile
0 ¼ ½ mile
0 250m 500m 750m 1 km
32
48
A B C D E F
Beaple's Hill
Knowstone Moor Cross
Knowstone Inner Moor
Middle Hill Farm
South Esworthy Farm
A361
Beaple's Moor Cross
Moortown Cross
Hares Down
Bickham Moor
Kents
Moortown Barton
Acorn Sch
EX36
Manor Farm
Knowstone Outer Moor
Rackenford Moor
Bickham Barton
Haresdown Cross
Bickham La
West Spurway La
Two Moors Way
Batsworthy Hill
North Backstone
Frankhill
Waterloo Hill
The Lodge
Titham Hill
Manor Cotts
Knowstone Cross
Sydenham La
Sydeham Farm
Creacombemoor Cross
Backstone La
Worthy La
Rackenford Manor
Creacombe
West Backstone
Worthy Farm
Nutcott
Two Gates Cross
Little Rackenford Farm
Broadmead Farm
Heiffers La
Little Rackenford La
Meadown
Green La
Old Bell Hill
Claypark Hill
Creacombe Parsonage Cross
Heiffers
Rackenford Cross
Old Bell Farm
Willicroft Moor
PO
Middlecott
Horsehaven
Meadow View
Bulworthy Cross
Stoneland La
Bulworthy Knap
Rackenford
Rackenford CE Prim Sch
Kirton La
Higher Bulworthy La
Willicroft Farm
Higher Bulworthy Cross
Town La
Lower Bulworthy La
Wilson Farm
Malson
Lower Thorne
Bulworthy Farms
Tidderson Cross
Malson La
Springhill Down Hill
Lower Bulworthy Gate
Stoneland Cross
North Combe Farm
Piley La
EX16
Horestone Cross
Berry Castle
Queen Dart Cross
Higher Mogworthy Cross
Mogworthy
Gibbett Moor Farm
Lower Tidderson Cross
North Coombe La
Bradford Barton
Queen Dart
Mogworthy La
Leat Farm
Queen Dart Hill
Tidderson
Tidderson La
River Little Dart
Bradford Cross
Ford Down
Horestone
Bradford Mill
Hilltown
Bradford Moor Hill
Downe Farm
Colleton Hall
Down La
Down Hill
Newland Farm
Crow La
Down Cross
Hilltown Cross
Elworthy
Great Moor
Elworthy Hill
Betham Hill
Newland Cross
Rose Moor
Elworthy Cross
Witheridge Moor
Pilliven La
Pilliven
Starraton
Foxdon
Witheridge Moor Cross (West)
Five Crosses
Crossmoor Cross
Witheridge Moor Cross (East)
Campbellhays Hill
Buddleswick
Witheridge Moor Farm
Shell La
Templeton La
Looseland Cross
Colston La
Charnaford Farm
Cornermoor Cross
Coombe Hill
Cleave
Pidland La
Brandis Cnr
Colston Barton
Nomansland
8 21 7 20 6 19 5 18 4 17 3 16 2 15 1 14
82 83 84 85 86 87
62
48

47
33

Scale: 1¾ inches to 1 mile

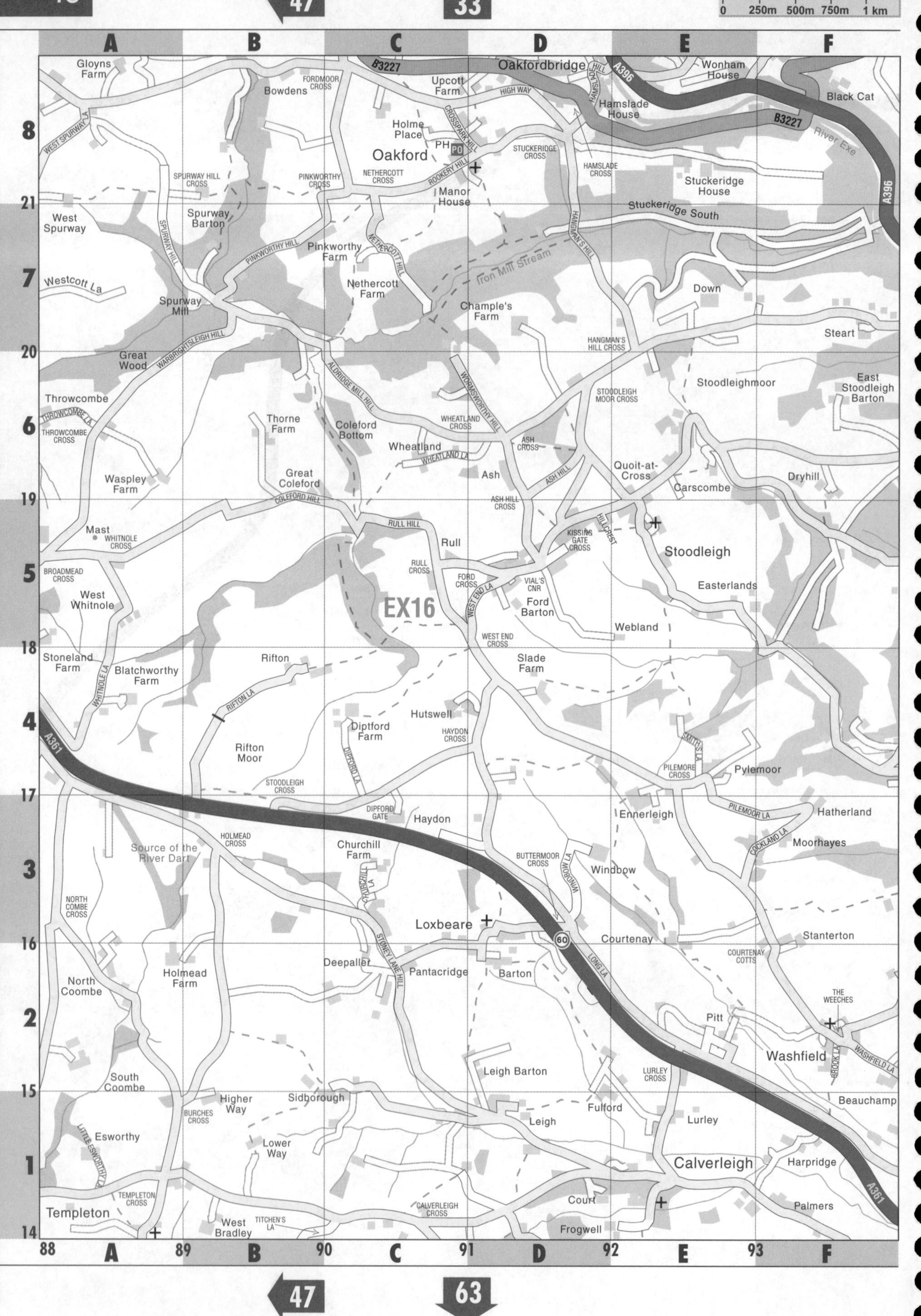

47
63

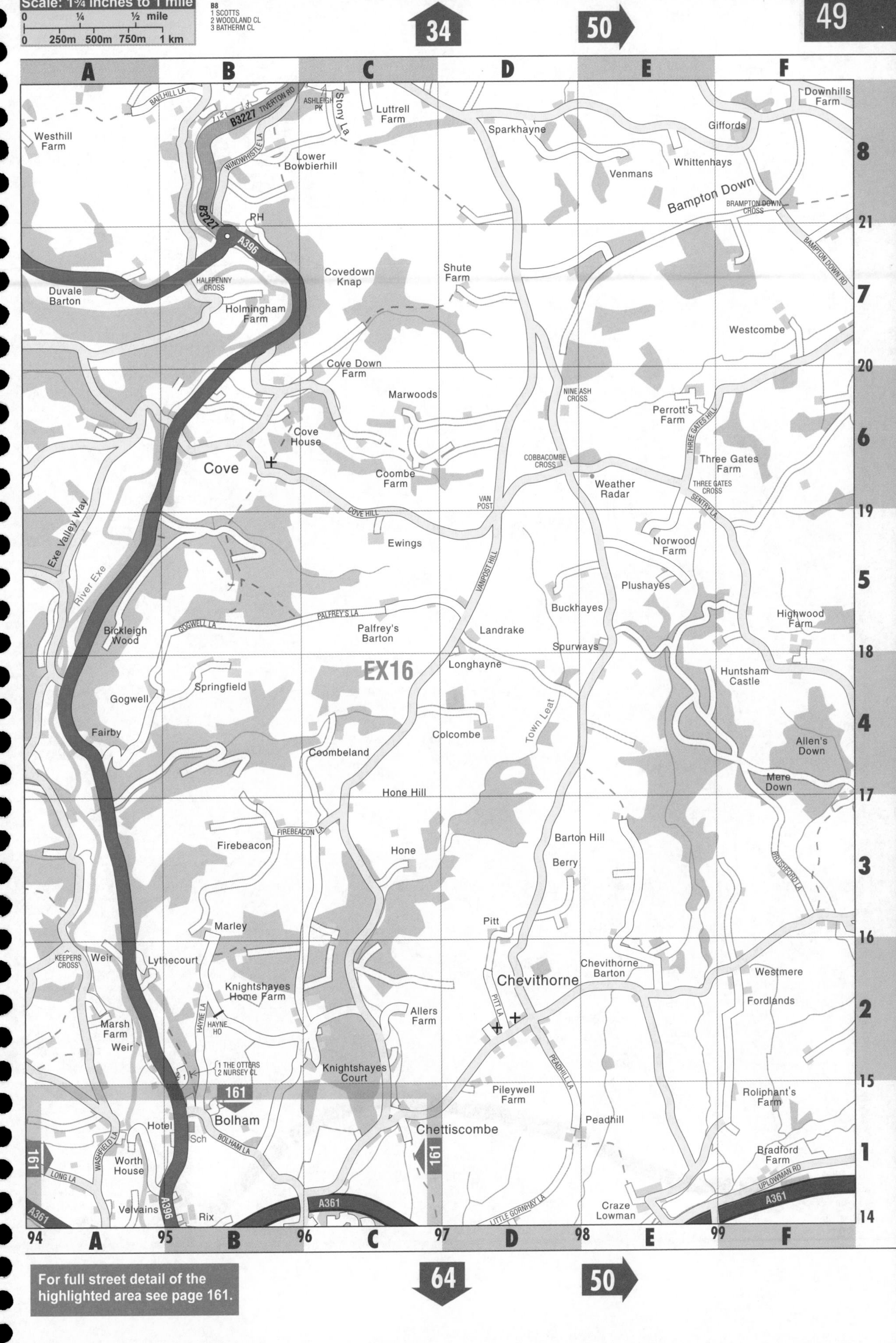

For full street detail of the highlighted area see page 161.

49
35

Scale: 1¾ inches to 1 mile
0 ¼ ½ mile
0 250m 500m 750m 1 km

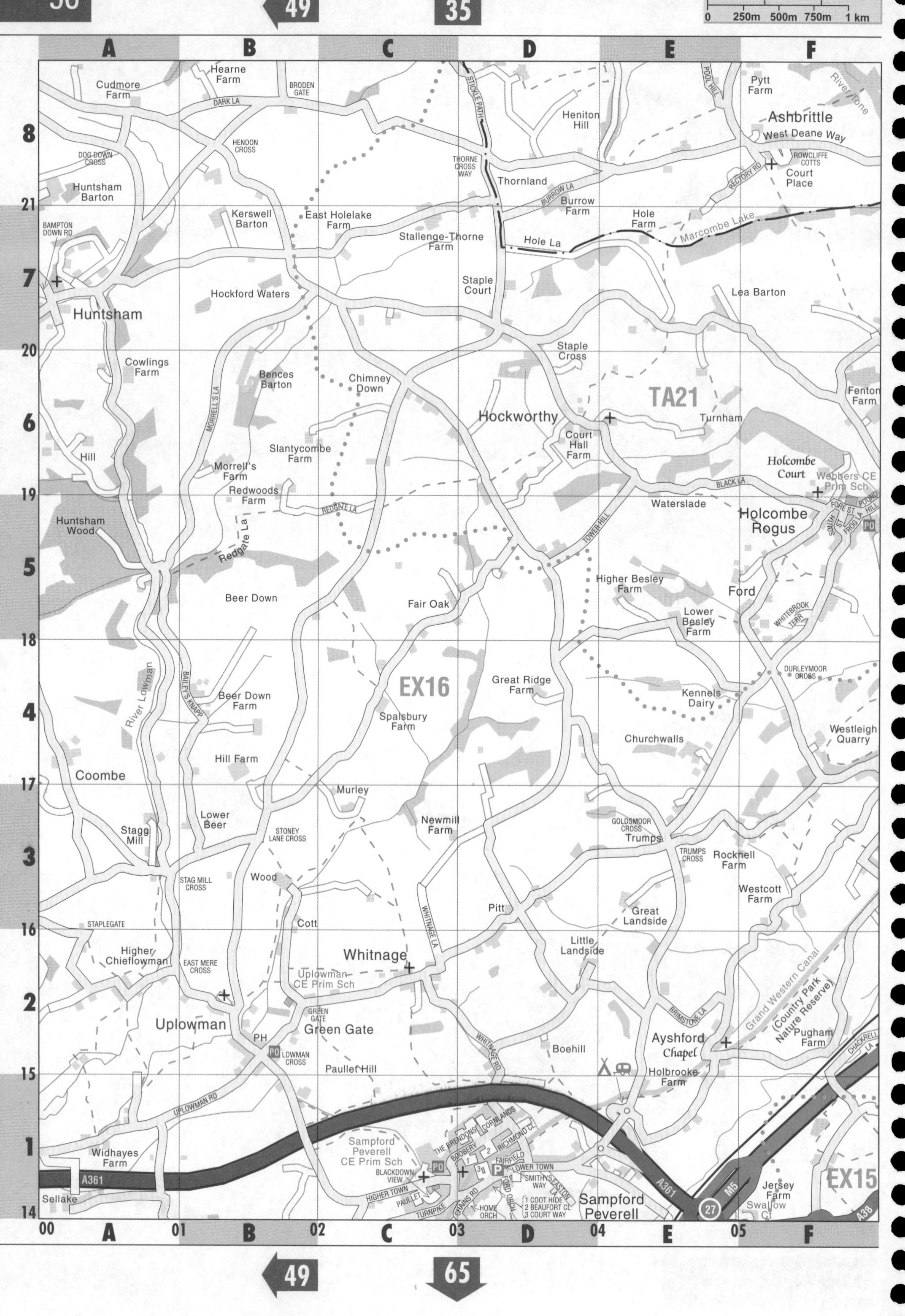

49
65

52

Somerset STREET ATLAS

A B C D E F

Wellisford
Runnington
Hill Farm
PH
West Deane Way
Appley
Tracebridge
Stawley Prim Sch
Meadland
Cothay Manor & Gardens
Thorne St Margaret
Rewe Farm
Harpford Farm
River Tone
Steels
Appley Cross
Elworthy Farm
Payton
Bishop's Barton
Greenham
Ramsey Farm
Kytton Barton
Greenham Hall
Holy Well
Holywell Lake
Westford
TA21
Freathingcott Farm
Greenham Barton
Chitterwell
Burrow Farm
Bazeley Farm
Woolcombe
Pinksmoor
Burnhill Farm
Ridge Farm
Perry Elm
Wiseburrow Farm
White Ball
Beam Bridge
Beacon Hill
Four Elms
Greenham Bsns Pk
Sampford Arundel Com Prim Sch
Broadleigh
Easterlands
Sampford Arundel
Whipcott
White Ball Hill
Broadways
Werescote
Marlands
Sampford Moor
Fenacre Farm
Hallhays
Redhill Farm
Westleigh Quarry
Henegar
Dykes Farm
Mill
Canonsleigh House
Eastbrook House
Red Ball
Westleigh
Upcott Farm
Burlescombe CE Prim Sch
Burlescombe
Danisco Pack Westward
North End
Sampford Point
Windwhistle
Woodlands Bsns Pk
EX16
Tucker's Farm
Nicholashayne
Black Down Common
Pound Farm
Maiden Down
Maidenhead Cross
Gipsy Town
Gallops
Waterslade
Sunnyside
Southdown Cross
Old Beat
Axon Farm
Combeshead Farm
Tithe Barn Cross
Woodgate
Culmstock Beacon
Southdown Farms
Henborough Farm
Almshayne Farm
Higher Cross
Dalwood Farm
Pithayne Farm
Culliford Farm
EX15
Appledore
Prescott
Culmstock Prim Sch
Clement's Farm
Lower Cross
Old Hall
Pitt Farm
Spiceland
Millmoor

1 South View
2 Hensons Dr
3 Pear Tree Cl
4 Harris Cl
5 Furlong Cotts

1 Great Cl
2 Hunter's Way
3 Valley View
4 Linhay Cl

A38 M5 B3391

8 21 7 20 6 19 5 18 4 17 3 16 2 15 1 14

06 A 07 B 08 C 09 D 10 E 11 F

66
52

51

Scale: 1¾ inches to 1 mile

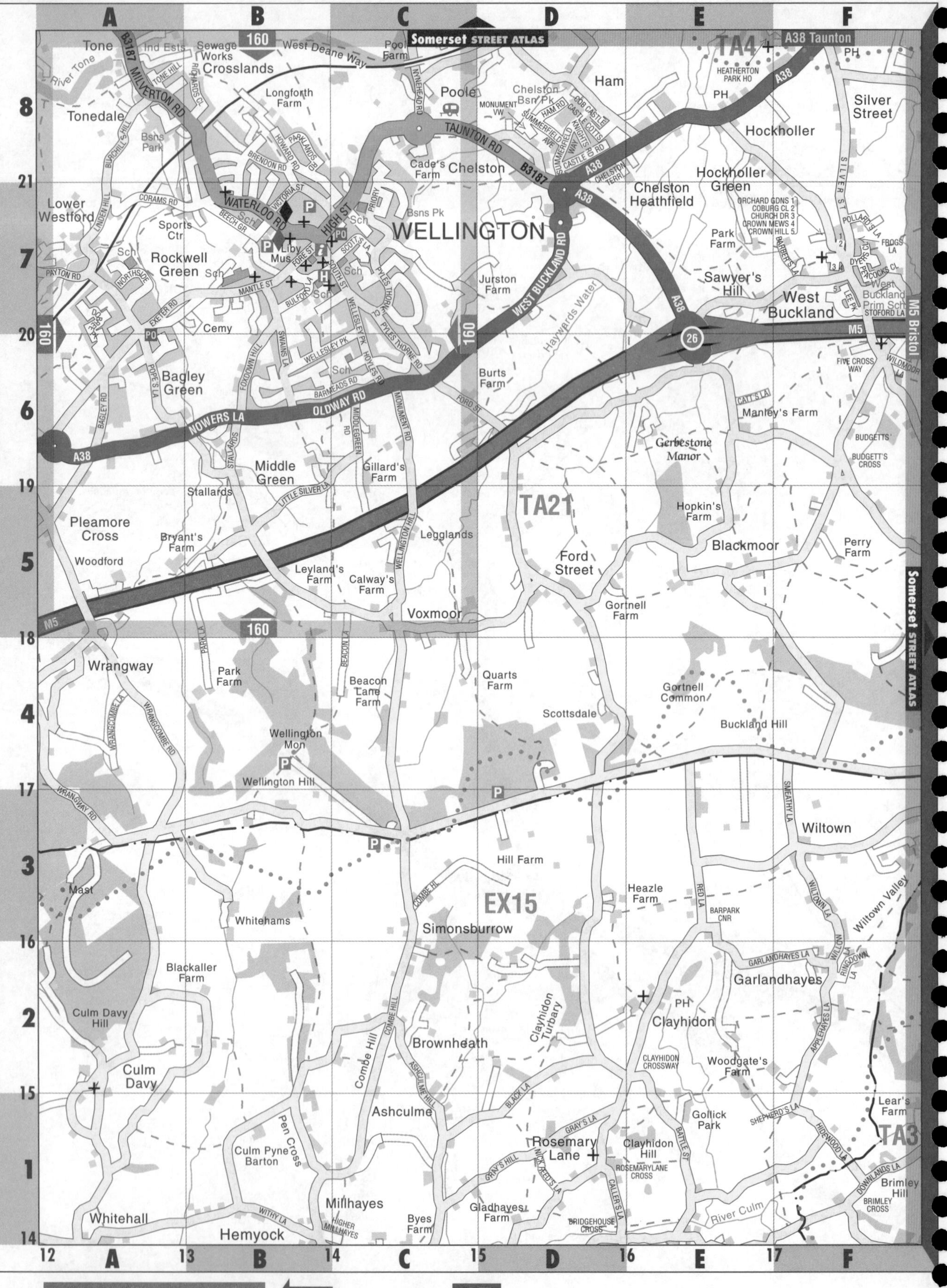

For full street detail of the highlighted area see page 160.

51

67

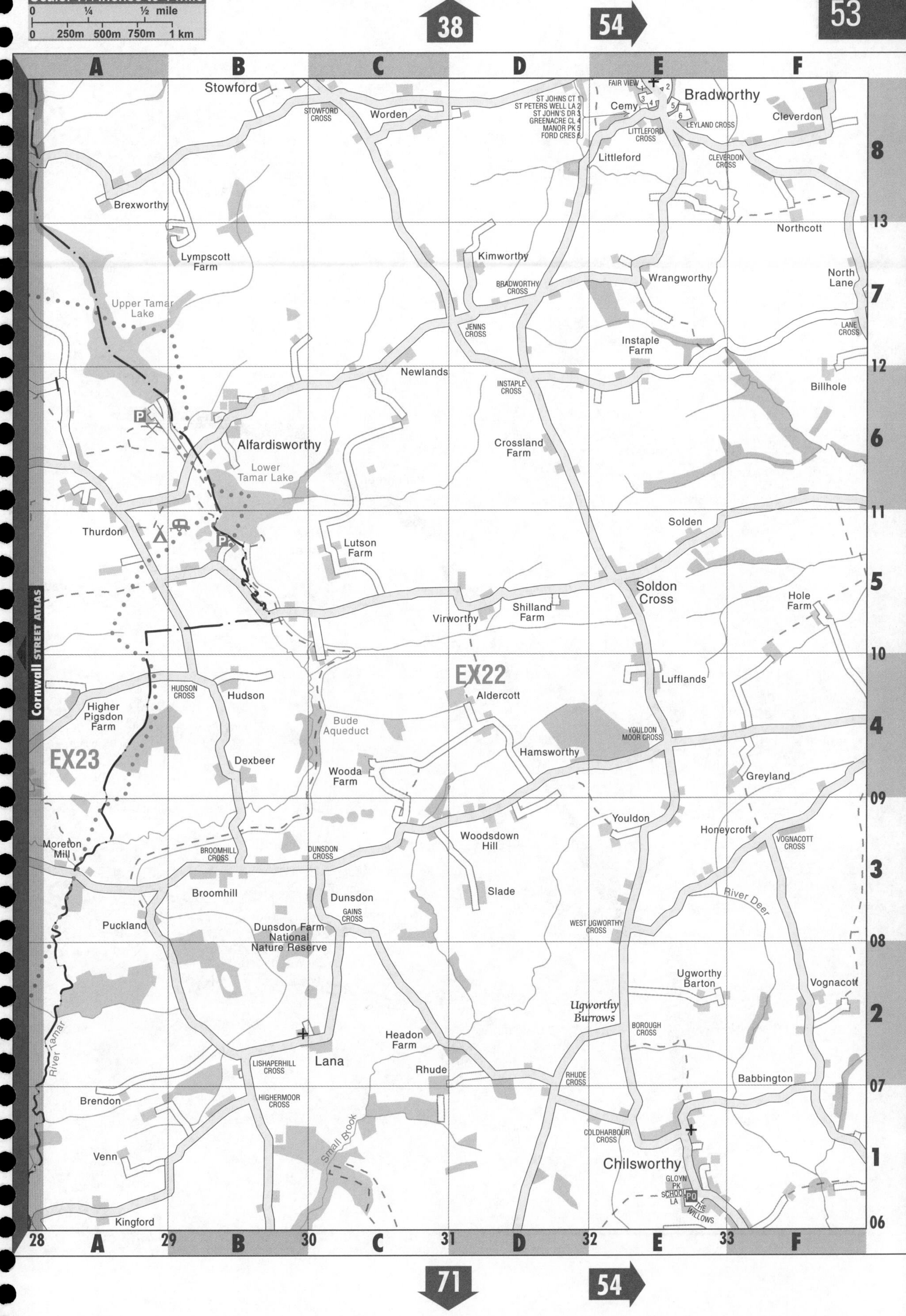
Scale: 1¾ inches to 1 mile
0 ¼ ½ mile
0 250m 500m 750m 1 km
38
54
A B C D E F
Stowford
Stowford Cross
Worden
Fair View
Cemy
Bradworthy
Cleverdon
St Johns Ct 1
St Peters Well La 2
St John's Dr 3
Greenacre Cl 4
Manor Pk 5
Ford Cres 6
Littleford Cross
Leyland Cross
Littleford
Cleverdon Cross
Brexworthy
Northcott
Lympscott Farm
Kimworthy
Wrangworthy
North Lane
Bradworthy Cross
Upper Tamar Lake
Jenns Cross
Instaple Farm
Lane Cross
Newlands
Instaple Cross
Billhole
Alfardisworthy
Crossland Farm
Lower Tamar Lake
Thurdon
Solden
Lutson Farm
Soldon Cross
Hole Farm
Virworthy
Shilland Farm
EX22
Hudson Cross
Hudson
Lufflands
Higher Pigsdon Farm
Aldercott
Bude Aqueduct
Youldon Moor Cross
EX23
Dexbeer
Hamsworthy
Wooda Farm
Greyland
Youldon
Honeycroft
Moreton Mill
Woodsdown Hill
Vognacott Cross
Broomhill Cross
Dunsdon Cross
Broomhill
Slade
Dunsdon
River Deer
Gains Cross
Puckland
Dunsdon Farm National Nature Reserve
West Ugworthy Cross
Ugworthy Barton
Vognacott
Ugworthy Burrows
Borough Cross
Headon Farm
Lishaperhill Cross
Lana
Rhude
Rhude Cross
Babbington
River Tamar
Brendon
Highermoor Cross
Small Brook
Coldharbour Cross
Chilsworthy
Venn
Gloyn Pk
School La
The Willows
Kingford
Cornwall STREET ATLAS
13 12 11 10 09 08 07 06
8 7 6 5 4 3 2 1
28 29 30 31 32 33
71
54

53
39

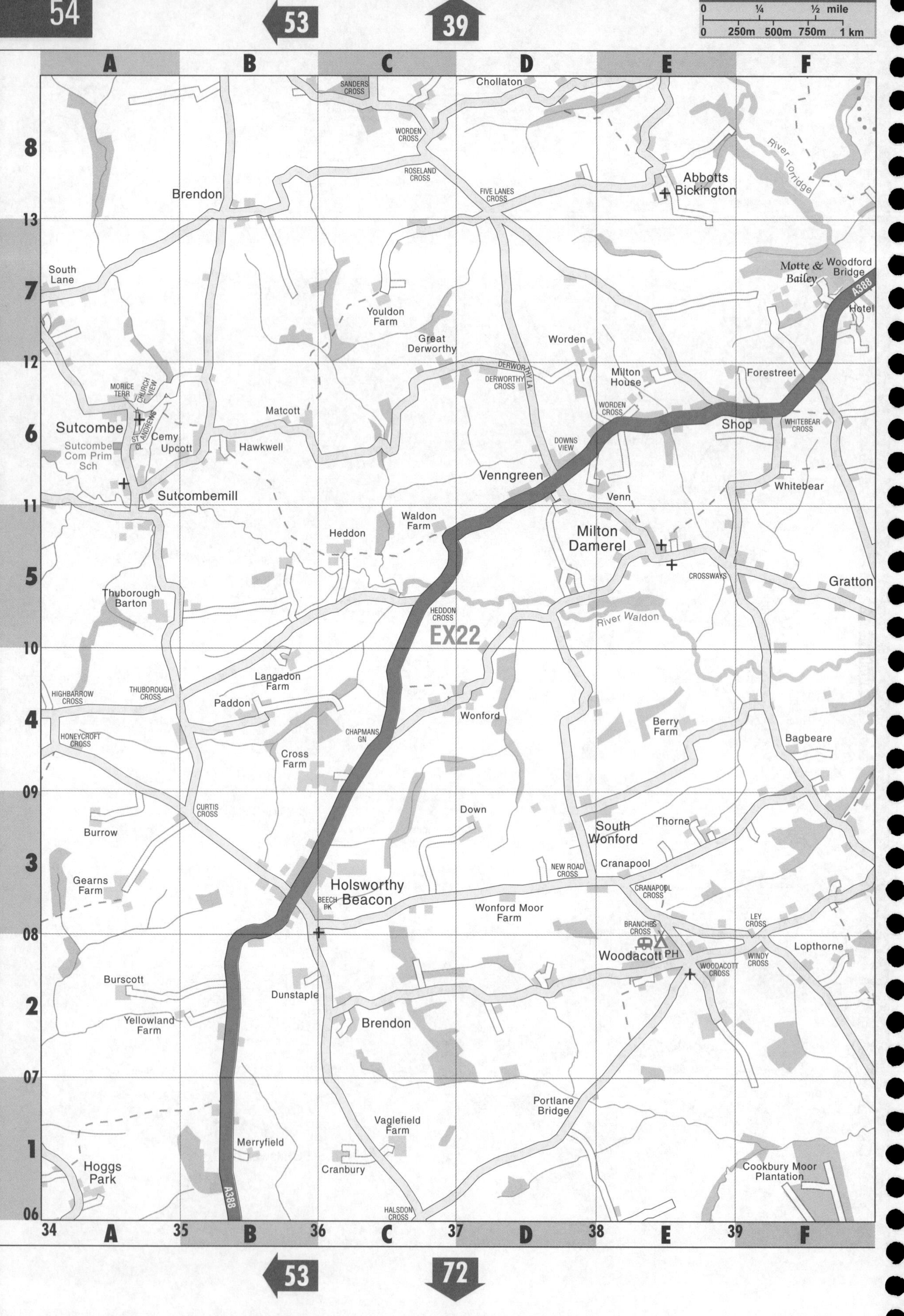
Scale: 1¾ inches to 1 mile
0
¼
½ mile
0
250m
500m
750m
1 km
A
B
C
D
E
F
Chollaton
SANDERS CROSS
WORDEN CROSS
ROSELAND CROSS
FIVE LANES CROSS
Abbotts Bickington
River Torridge
Brendon
South Lane
Motte & Bailey
Woodford Bridge
A388
Hotel
Youldon Farm
Great Derworthy
Worden
DERWORTHY LA
DERWORTHY CROSS
Milton House
Forestreet
MORICE TERR
CHURCH VIEW
Sutcombe
Matcott
WORDEN CROSS
Shop
WHITEBEAR CROSS
ST ANDREWS CL
Cemy
Upcott
Hawkwell
DOWNS VIEW
Sutcombe Com Prim Sch
Venngreen
Whitebear
Sutcombemill
Venn
Waldon Farm
Heddon
Milton Damerel
CROSSWAYS
Gratton
Thuborough Barton
HEDDON CROSS
River Waldon
EX22
Langadon Farm
HIGHBARROW CROSS
THUBOROUGH CROSS
Paddon
Wonford
Berry Farm
HONEYCROFT CROSS
CHAPMANS GN
Bagbeare
Cross Farm
CURTIS CROSS
Down
South Wonford
Thorne
Burrow
Gearns Farm
NEW ROAD CROSS
Cranapool
Holsworthy Beacon
CRANAPOOL CROSS
BEECH PK
Wonford Moor Farm
BRANCHES CROSS
LEY CROSS
Lopthorne
Woodacott
PH
WOODACOTT CROSS
WINDY CROSS
Burscott
Dunstaple
Yellowland Farm
Brendon
Portlane Bridge
Vaglefield Farm
Merryfield
Hoggs Park
Cranbury
Cookbury Moor Plantation
HALSDON CROSS
8
13
7
12
6
11
5
10
4
09
3
08
2
07
1
06
34
35
36
37
38
39

53
72

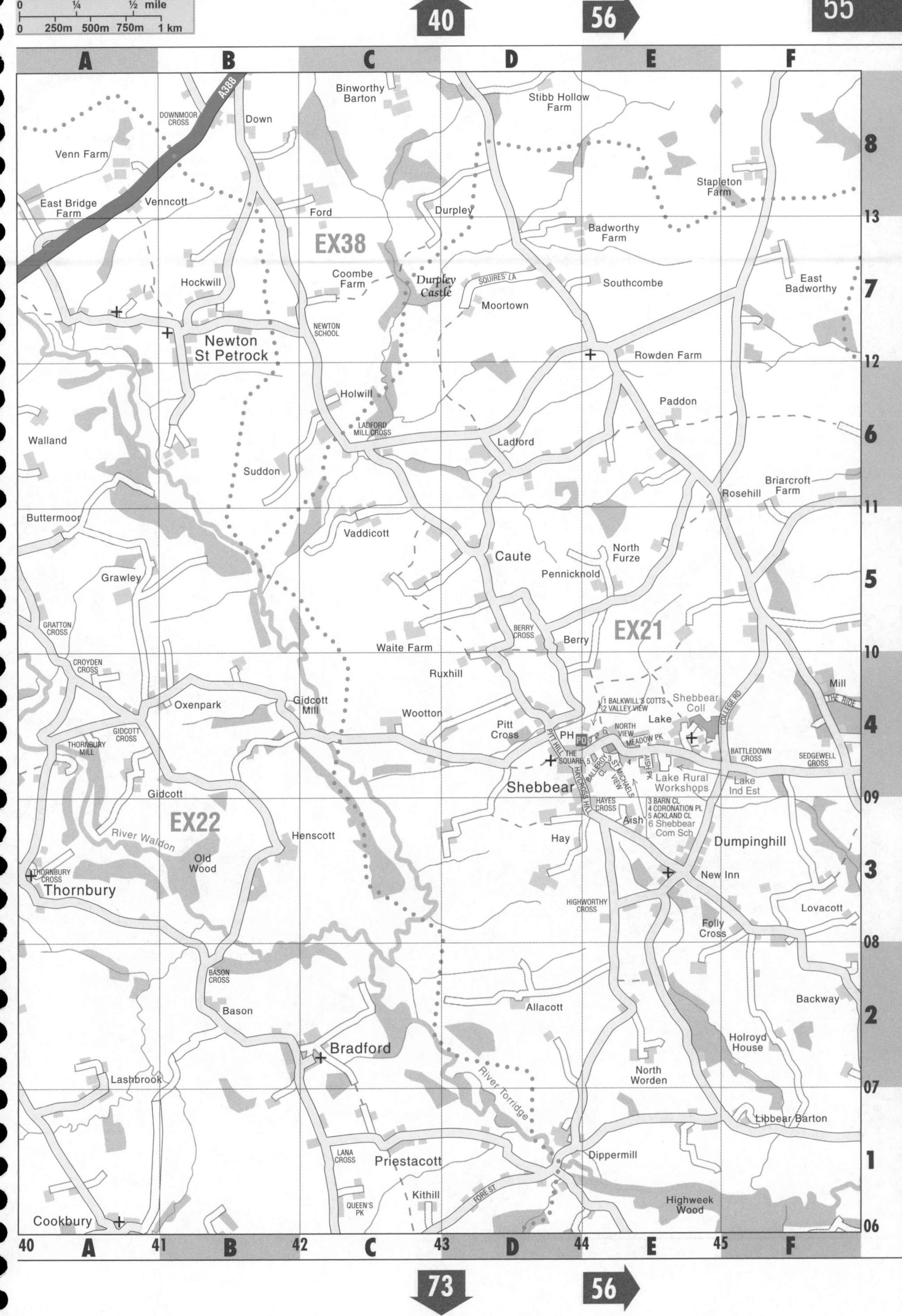
Scale: 1¾ inches to 1 mile
0 ¼ ½ mile
0 250m 500m 750m 1 km
40
56
A B C D E F
Venn Farm
DOWNMOOR CROSS
A388
Down
Binworthy Barton
Stibb Hollow Farm
East Bridge Farm
Venncott
Ford
Durpley
Stapleton Farm
Badworthy Farm
EX38
Hockwill
Coombe Farm
Durpley Castle
SQUIRES' LA
Moortown
Southcombe
East Badworthy
NEWTON SCHOOL
Newton St Petrock
Rowden Farm
Holwill
Paddon
Walland
LADFORD MILL CROSS
Ladford
Suddon
Rosehill
Briarcroft Farm
Buttermoor
Vaddicott
Caute
North Furze
Pennicknold
Grawley
EX21
GRATTON CROSS
BERRY CROSS
Berry
Waite Farm
Ruxhill
CROYDEN CROSS
Oxenpark
Gidcott Mill
Wootton
1 BALKWILL'S COTTS
2 VALLEY VIEW
Shebbear Coll
Lake
Mill
THE RIDE
COLLEGE RD
Pitt Cross
PH
PO
NORTH VIEW
MEADOW PK
GIDCOTT CROSS
THORNBURY MILL
PITT HILL
THE SQUARE
BALLROY CL
ST MICHAELS VIEW
AISH PK
BATTLEDOWN CROSS
SEDGEWELL CROSS
Shebbear
Lake Rural Workshops
Lake Ind Est
Gidcott
HAYES CROSS
HAYCROSS HILL
3 BARN CL
4 CORONATION PL
5 ACKLAND CL
6 Shebbear Com Sch
EX22
Aish
River Waldon
Henscott
Hay
Dumpinghill
Old Wood
THORNBURY CROSS
Thornbury
New Inn
HIGHWORTHY CROSS
Lovacott
Folly Cross
BASON CROSS
Bason
Allacott
Backway
Bradford
Holroyd House
River Torridge
North Worden
Lashbrook
Libbear Barton
LANA CROSS
Priestacott
Dippermill
Kithill
FORE ST
QUEEN'S PK
Highweek Wood
Cookbury
8 13 7 12 6 11 5 10 4 09 3 08 2 07 1 06
40 41 42 43 44 45
73
56

55
41

Scale: 1¾ inches to 1 mile

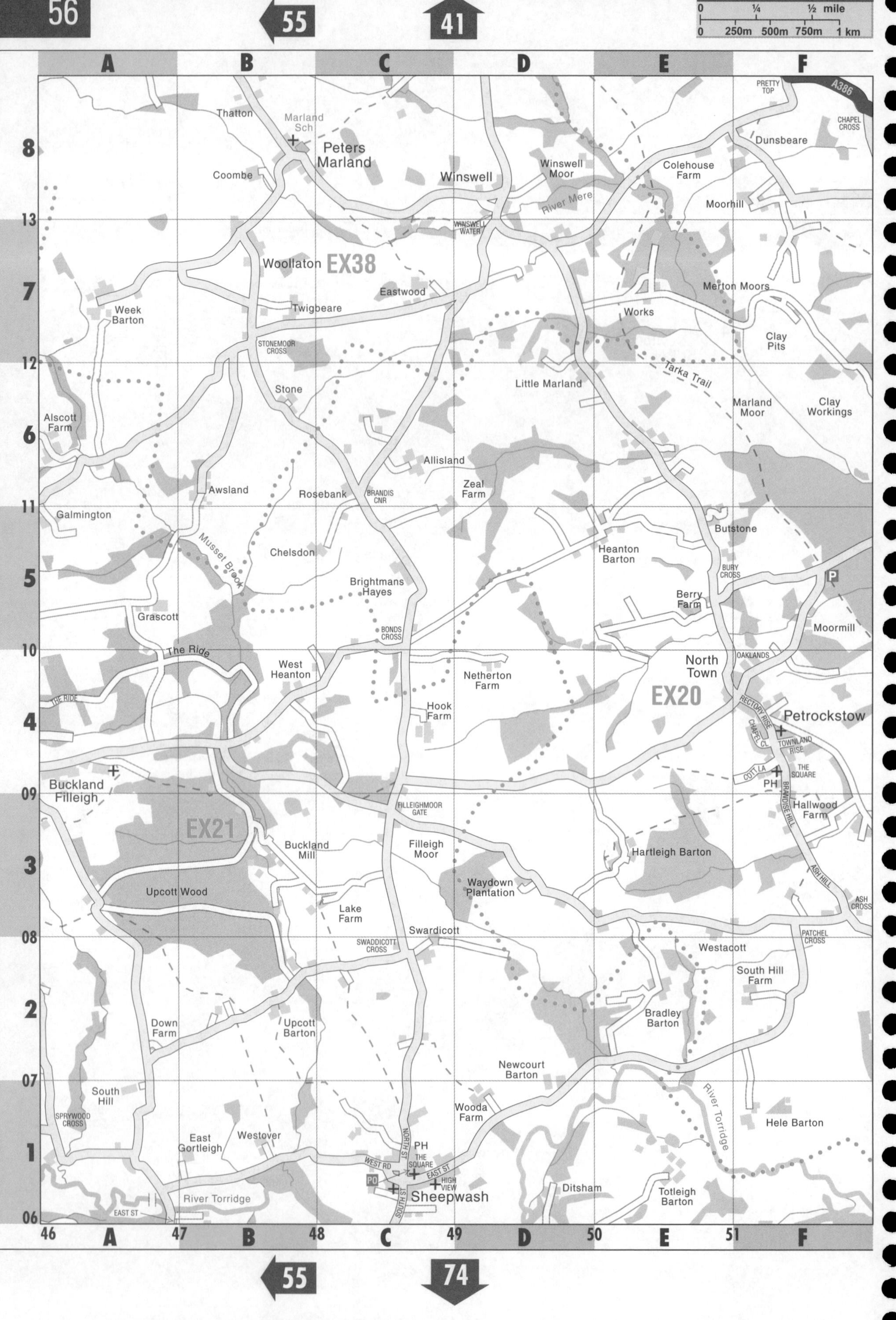

55
74

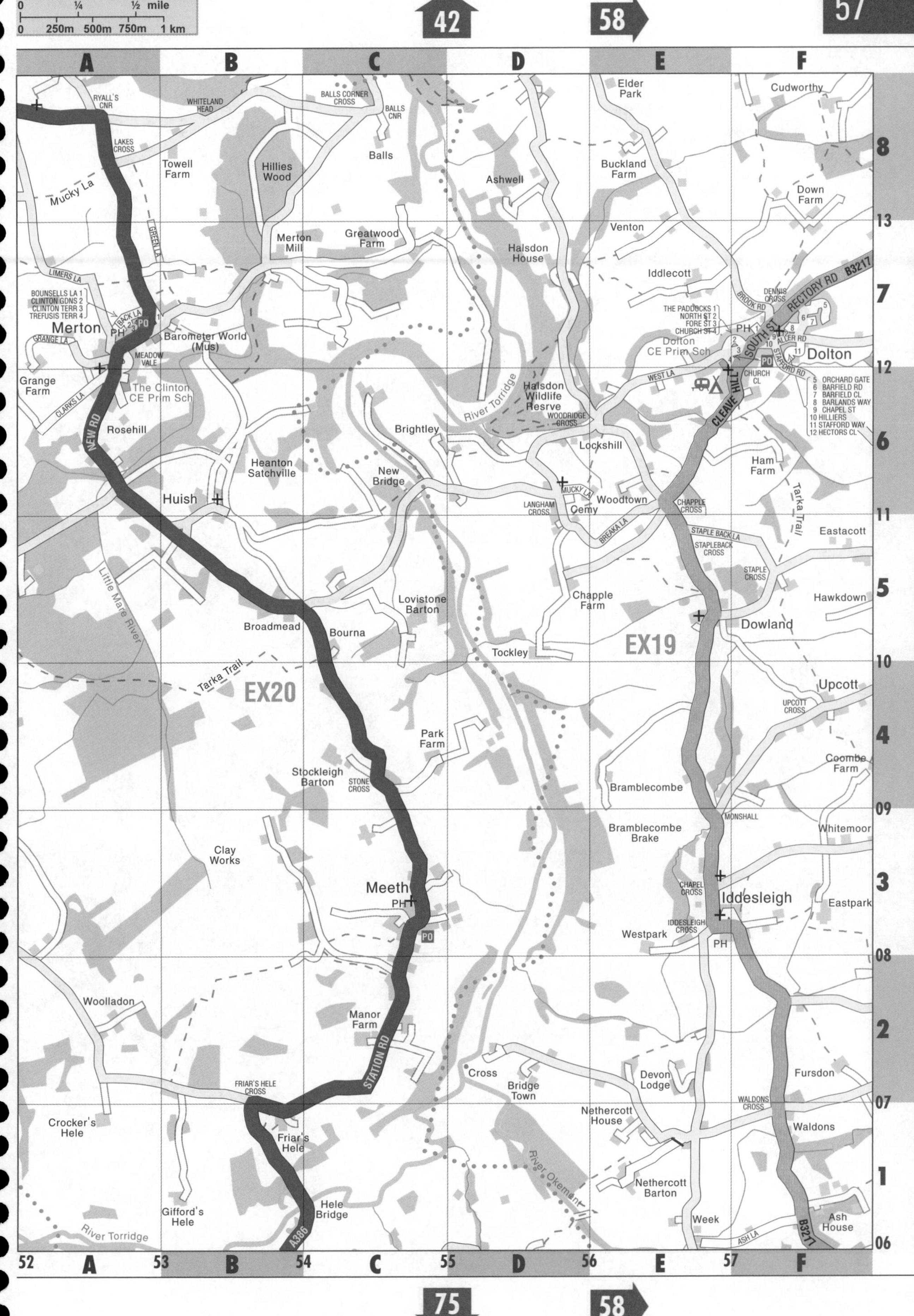
Scale: 1¾ inches to 1 mile
0 ¼ ½ mile
0 250m 500m 750m 1 km
42
58
A B C D E F
Ryall's Cnr
Whiteland Head
Balls Corner Cross
Balls Cnr
Elder Park
Cudworthy
Lakes Cross
Towell Farm
Hillies Wood
Balls
Ashwell
Buckland Farm
Down Farm
Mucky La
Green La
Merton Mill
Greatwood Farm
Halsdon House
Venton
Limers La
Iddlecott
Rectory Rd
B3217
Bounsells La 1
Clinton Gdns 2
Clinton Terr 3
Trefusis Terr 4
Back La
Merton
PH
PO
Barometer World (Mus)
Grange La
Meadow Vale
Grange Farm
Clarks La
The Clinton CE Prim Sch
Brook Rd
Dennis Cross
The Paddocks 1
North St 2
Fore St 3
Church St 4
South St
Alfer Rd
Dolton CE Prim Sch
Dolton
Stafford Rd
Church Cl
West La
5 Orchard Gate
6 Barfield Rd
7 Barfield Cl
8 Barlands Way
9 Chapel St
10 Hilliers
11 Stafford Way
12 Hectors Cl
Cleave Hill
Halsdon Wildlife Resrve
Woodridge Cross
River Torridge
New Rd
Rosehill
Brightley
Lockshill
Heanton Satchville
New Bridge
Ham Farm
Huish
Mucky La
Langham Cross
Cemy
Woodtown
Chapple Cross
Breaka La
Tarka Trail
Eastacott
Staple Back La
Stapleback Cross
Staple Cross
Little Mare River
Lovistone Barton
Chapple Farm
Hawkdown
Broadmead
Bourna
Dowland
EX19
Tockley
Tarka Trail
EX20
Upcott
Upcott Cross
Park Farm
Stockleigh Barton
Stone Cross
Coombe Farm
Bramblecombe
Monshall
Bramblecombe Brake
Whitemoor
Clay Works
Meeth
Chapel Cross
Iddesleigh
Eastpark
Iddesleigh Cross
Westpark
Woolladon
Manor Farm
Station Rd
Cross
Devon Lodge
Fursdon
Bridge Town
Friar's Hele Cross
Waldons Cross
Nethercott House
Waldons
Crocker's Hele
Friar's Hele
River Okement
Nethercott Barton
Gifford's Hele
Hele Bridge
Week
Ash House
River Torridge
A386
Ash La
B3217
8
13
7
12
6
11
5
10
4
09
3
08
2
07
1
06
52 53 54 55 56 57
75
58

57
43

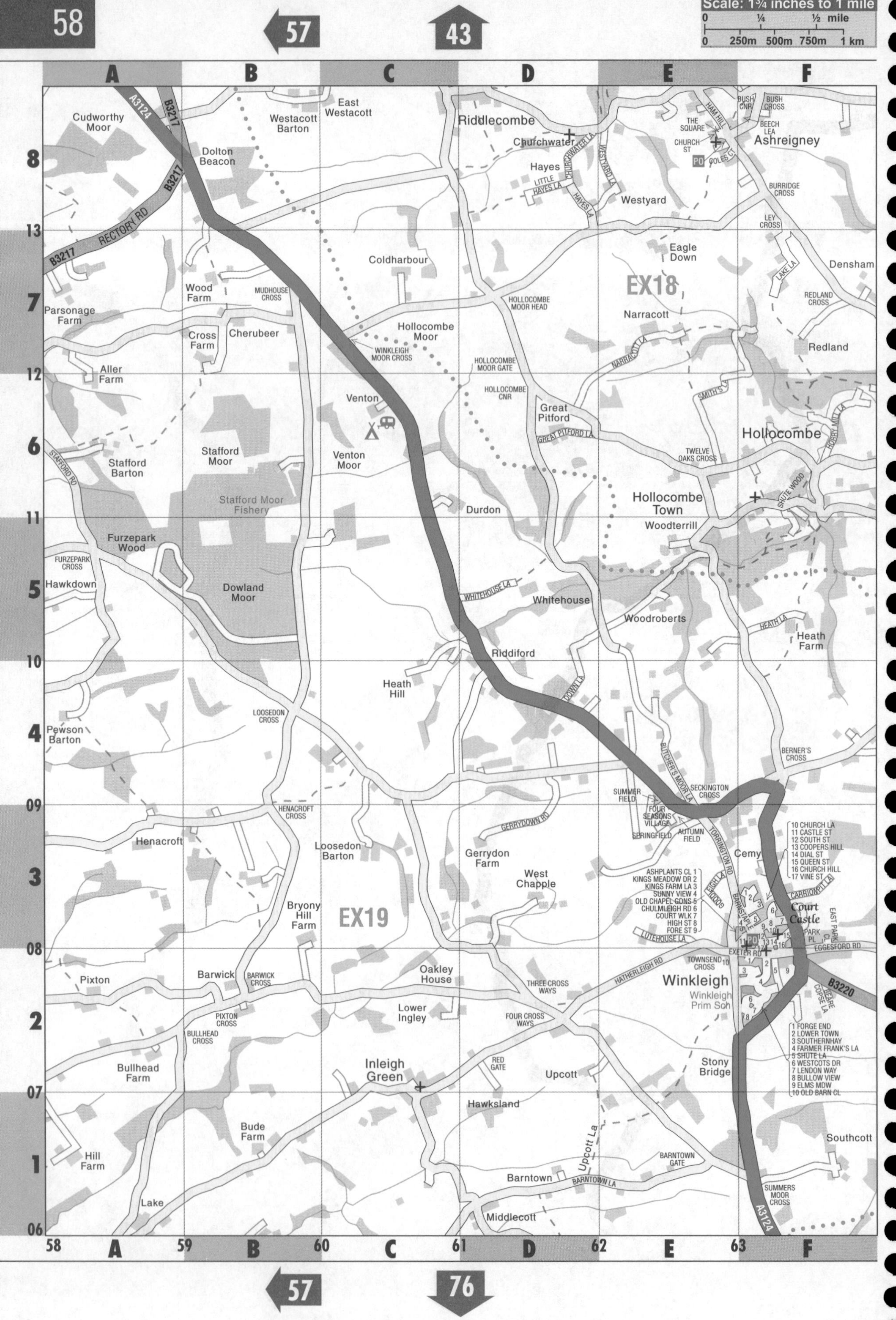
Scale: 1¾ inches to 1 mile
0 ¼ ½ mile
0 250m 500m 750m 1 km
A B C D E F
Cudworthy Moor
Westacott Barton
East Westacott
Riddlecombe
Churchwater
Hayes
Little Hayes La
Churchwater La
Westyard La
Hayes La
Westyard
The Square
Church St
Ham Hill
Bush Cnr
Bush Cross
Beech Lea
Ashreigney
Goles Ct
Burridge Cross
Ley Cross
Dolton Beacon
A3124
B3217
Rectory Rd
Coldharbour
Eagle Down
EX18
Densham
Lake La
Wood Farm
Mudhouse Cross
Hollocombe Moor Head
Redland Cross
Parsonage Farm
Narracott
Narracott La
Cross Farm
Cherubeer
Hollocombe Moor
Winkleigh Moor Cross
Redland
Aller Farm
Hollocombe Moor Gate
Hollocombe Cnr
Venton
Great Pitford
Great Pitford La
Smith's La
Hollocombe
Hobby Mill La
Stafford Rd
Stafford Barton
Stafford Moor
Venton Moor
Twelve Oaks Cross
Stafford Moor Fishery
Durdon
Hollocombe Town
Shute Wood
Woodterrill
Furzepark Wood
Furzepark Cross
Hawkdown
Dowland Moor
Whitehouse La
Whitehouse
Woodroberts
Heath La
Heath Farm
Riddiford
Heath Hill
Down La
Loosedon Cross
Pewson Barton
Butcher's Moor La
Berner's Cross
Summer Field
Seckington Cross
Four Seasons Village
Springfield
Autumn Field
Torrington Rd
Henacroft Cross
Henacroft
Loosedon Barton
Gerrydown Rd
Gerrydon Farm
Cemy
West Chapple
10 Church La
11 Castle St
12 South St
13 Coopers Hill
14 Dial St
15 Queen St
16 Church Hill
17 Vine St
Carrions La
Ashplants Cl 1
Kings Meadow Dr 2
Kings Farm La 3
Sunny View 4
Old Chapel Gdns 5
Chulmleigh Rd 6
Court Wlk 7
High St 8
Fore St 9
Court Castle
East Park Cl
Park Pl
Eggesford Rd
Bryony Hill Farm
EX19
Lutehouse La
Exeter Rd
Townsend Cross
Hatherleigh Rd
Pixton
Barwick
Barwick Cross
Oakley House
Three Cross Ways
Winkleigh
Winkleigh Prim Sch
B3220
Beere Copse La
Pixton Cross
Lower Ingley
Four Cross Ways
Bullhead Cross
1 Forge End
2 Lower Town
3 Southernhay
4 Farmer Frank's La
5 Shute La
6 Westcots Dr
7 Lendon Way
8 Bullow View
9 Elms Mdw
10 Old Barn Cl
Bullhead Farm
Inleigh Green
Red Gate
Upcott
Stony Bridge
Hawksland
Upcott La
Southcott
Bude Farm
Hill Farm
Barntown Gate
Barntown
Barntown La
Summers Moor Cross
Lake
Middlecott
A3124
8
13
7
12
6
11
5
10
4
09
3
08
2
07
1
06
58 59 60 61 62 63

57
76

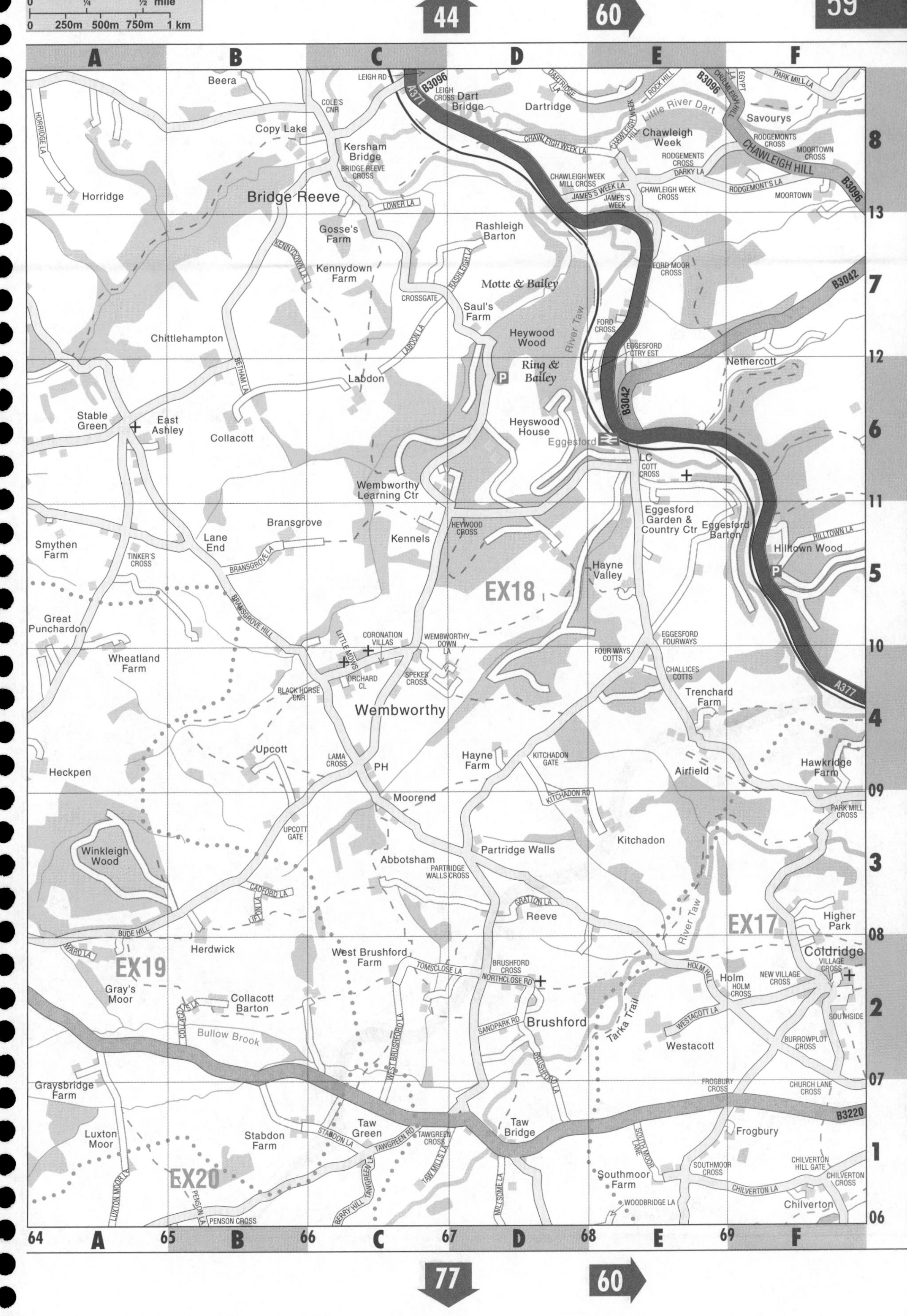
Scale: 1¾ inches to 1 mile
44
60
Beera
Copy Lake
Kersham Bridge
Bridge Reeve
Dart Bridge
Dartridge
Chawleigh Week
Savourys
Little River Dart
Horridge
Gosse's Farm
Rashleigh Barton
Kennydown Farm
Motte & Bailey
Saul's Farm
Heywood Wood
Ring & Bailey
River Taw
Chittlehampton
Labdon
Nethercott
Stable Green
East Ashley
Collacott
Heyswood House
Eggesford
Wembworthy Learning Ctr
Bransgrove
Kennels
Eggesford Garden & Country Ctr
Eggesford Barton
Hilltown Wood
Smythen Farm
Lane End
Hayne Valley
EX18
Great Punchardon
Wheatland Farm
Wembworthy
Trenchard Farm
Upcott
Heckpen
Hayne Farm
Airfield
Hawkridge Farm
PH
Moorend
Kitchadon
Winkleigh Wood
Partridge Walls
Abbotsham
Reeve
Higher Park
EX17
Herdwick
EX19
West Brushford Farm
Coldridge
Holm
Gray's Moor
Collacott Barton
Brushford
Bullow Brook
Tarka Trail
Westacott
Graysbridge Farm
Taw Green
Taw Bridge
Frogbury
Luxton Moor
Stabdon Farm
EX20
Southmoor Farm
Chilverton
A377
B3096
B3042
B3220
77
60

59
45

Scale: 1¾ inches to 1 mile
0 ¼ ½ mile
0 250m 500m 750m 1 km

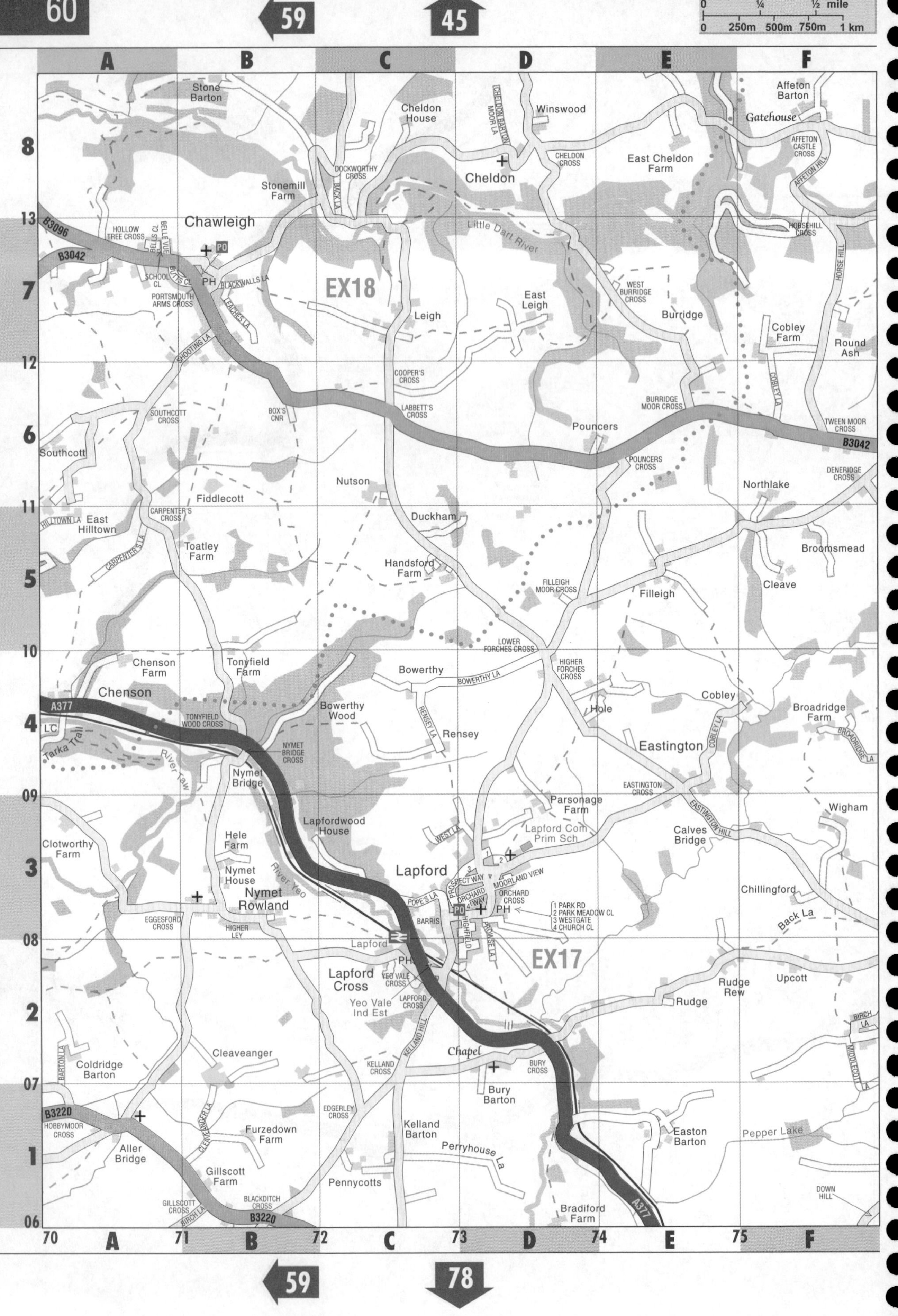

59
78

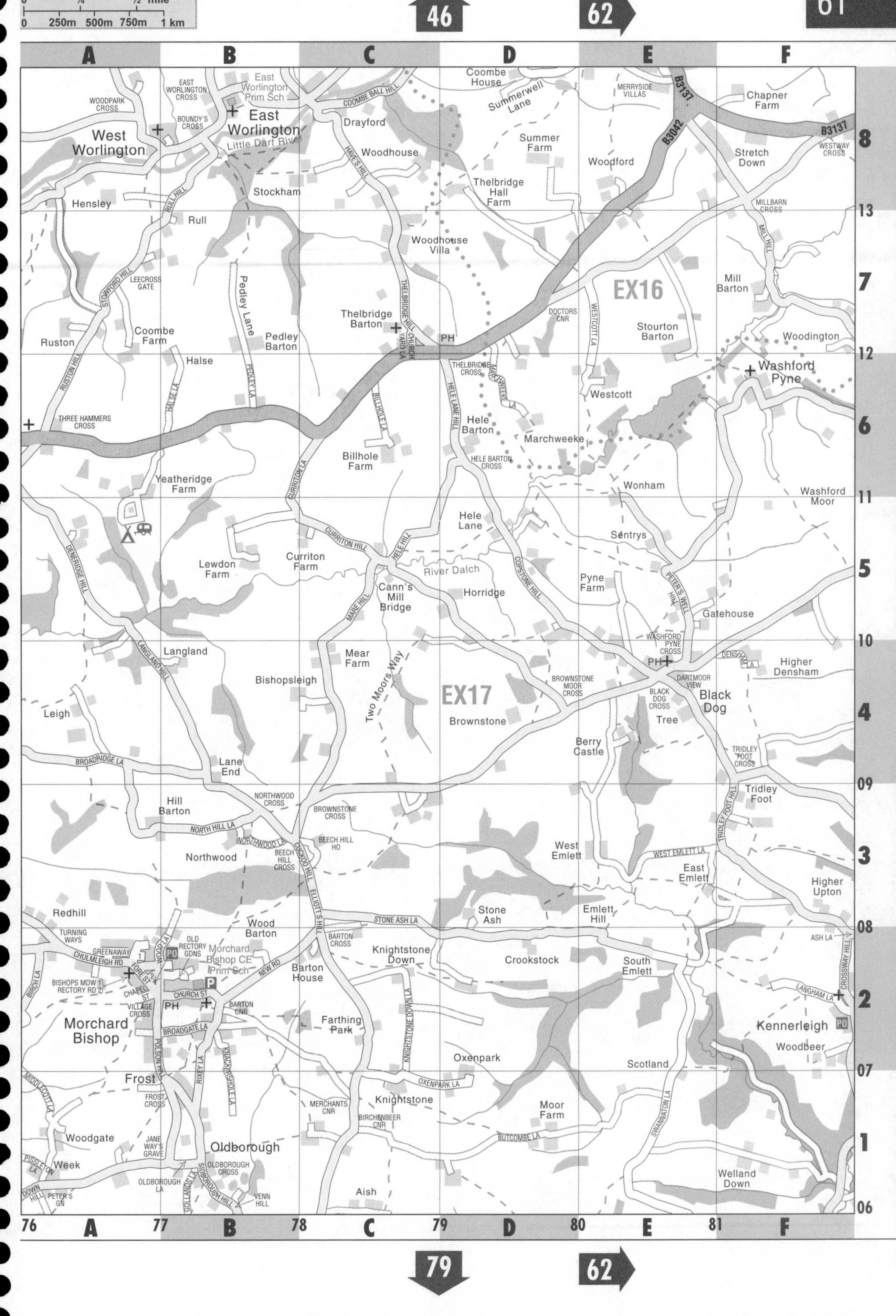

Scale: 1¾ inches to 1 mile
0 ¼ ½ mile
0 250m 500m 750m 1 km
46
62
A B C D E F
West Worlington
East Worlington
East Worlington Prim Sch
Little Dart River
WOODPARK CROSS
EAST WORLINGTON CROSS
BOUNDY'S CROSS
COOMBE BALL HILL
Drayford
Coombe House
Summerwell Lane
MERRYSIDE VILLAS
B3137
B3042
Chapner Farm
Summer Farm
Woodhouse
HAVE'S HILL
Stretch Down
WESTWAY CROSS
Woodford
Thelbridge Hall Farm
Stockham
Hensley
Rull
RULL HILL
MILLBARN CROSS
MILL HILL
Woodhouse Villa
LEECROSS GATE
STOWFORD HILL
Pedley Lane
THELBRIDGE HILL
CHURCH YARD LA
EX16
Mill Barton
Thelbridge Barton
DOCTORS CNR
WESTCOTT LA
Stourton Barton
Ruston
Coombe Farm
Pedley Barton
PH
Woodington
Halse
THELBRIDGE CROSS
Washford Pyne
RUSTON HILL
HALSE LA
PEDLEY LA
BILLHOLE LA
HELE LANE HILL
MARCHWEEKE LA
Westcott
THREE HAMMERS CROSS
Hele Barton
Marchweeke
Billhole Farm
HELE BARTON CROSS
Yeatheridge Farm
CURRITON LA
Wonham
Washford Moor
Hele Lane
Sentrys
DENERIDGE HILL
CURRITON HILL
HELE HILL
Lewdon Farm
Curriton Farm
River Dalch
Cann's Mill Bridge
Horridge
COPSTONE HILL
Pyne Farm
PETER'S WELL HILL
MARE HILL
Gatehouse
Langland
LANGLAND HILL
Mear Farm
WASHFORD PYNE CROSS
PH
DENSHAM LA
Higher Densham
Bishopsleigh
Two Moors Way
EX17
BROWNSTONE MOOR CROSS
DARTMOOR VIEW
Black Dog
BLACK DOG CROSS
Leigh
Brownstone
Tree
Berry Castle
BROADRIDGE LA
Lane End
TRIDLEY FOOT CROSS
Tridley Foot
Hill Barton
NORTHWOOD CROSS
BROWNSTONE CROSS
TRIDLEY FOOT HILL
NORTH HILL LA
NORTHWOOD LA
BEECH HILL HO
West Emlett
Northwood
BEECH HILL CROSS
CUCKOO HILL
ELLIOTT'S HILL
WEST EMLETT LA
East Emlett
Higher Upton
Redhill
Stone Ash
Emlett Hill
Wood Barton
STONE ASH LA
TURNING WAYS
GREENAWAY
OLD RECTORY GDNS
Morchard Bishop CE Prim Sch
BARTON CROSS
ASH LA
CROSSWAY HILL
CHULMLEIGH RD
FORE ST
NEW RD
Knightstone Down
Crookstock
South Emlett
Barton House
BIRCH LA
BISHOPS MDW 1
RECTORY RD 2
CHAPEL ST
CHURCH ST
LANGHAM LA
VILLAGE CROSS
PH
BARTON CNR
Morchard Bishop
BROADGATE LA
Farthing Park
KNIGHTSTONE DOWN LA
Kennerleigh
Woodbeer
POLSON HILL
RIXEY LA
KNACKERSHOLE LA
Oxenpark
Scotland
Frost
OXENPARK LA
MIDDLECOTT LA
FROST CROSS
MERCHANTS CNR
Knightstone
Moor Farm
BIRCHENBEER CNR
SWANNATON LA
Woodgate
JANE WAY'S GRAVE
Oldborough
BUTCOMBE LA
PISSLETON LA
Week
OLDBOROUGH CROSS
OLDBOROUGH LA
Welland Down
DOWN HILL
PETER'S GN
GOLLANDS LA
SIDBOROUGH HILL
VENN HILL
Aish
8 13 7 12 6 11 5 10 4 09 3 08 2 07 1 06
76 77 78 79 80 81
79
62

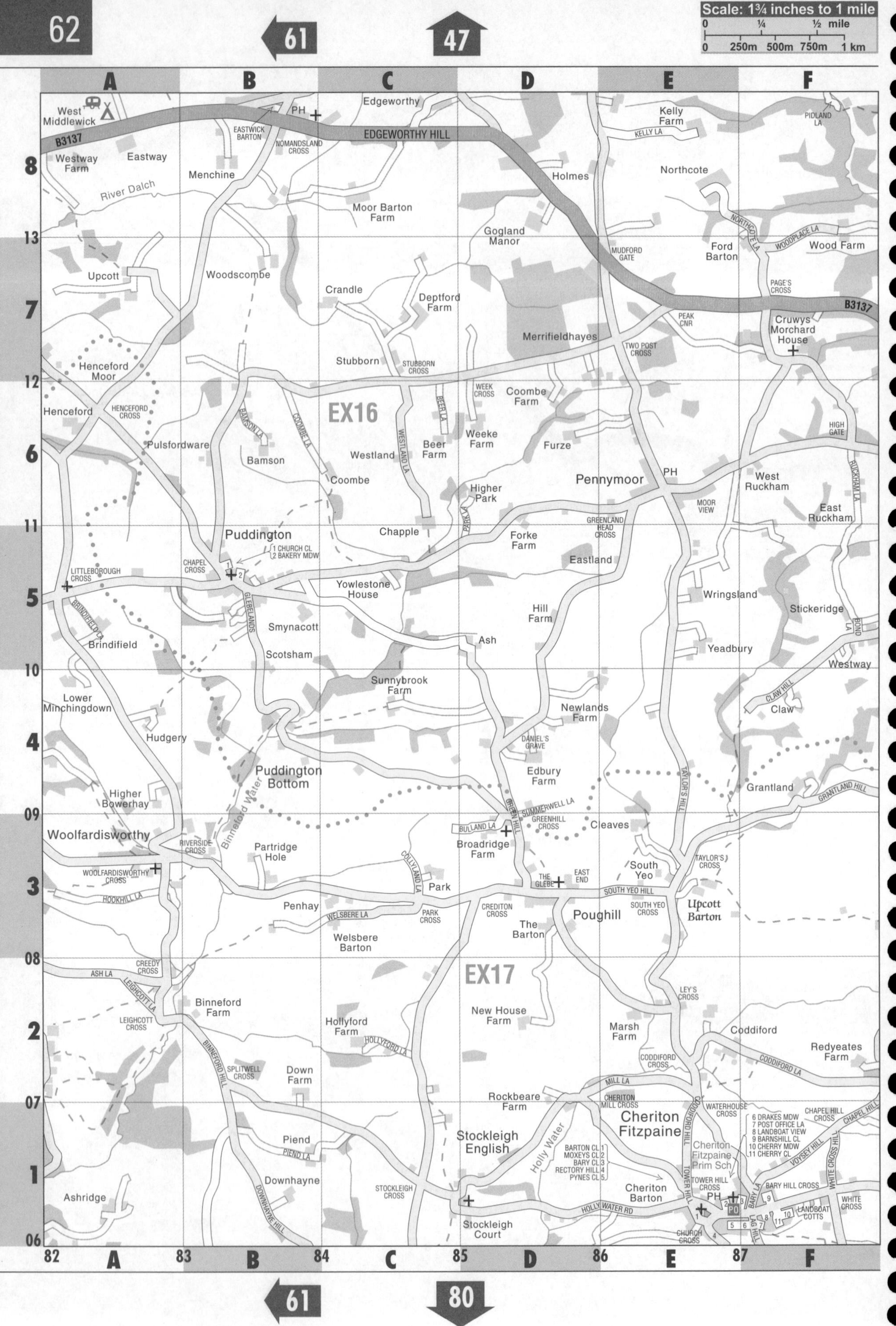
61
47
Scale: 1¾ inches to 1 mile
0 ¼ ½ mile
0 250m 500m 750m 1 km
A
B
C
D
E
F
8
13
7
12
6
11
5
10
4
09
3
08
2
07
1
06
82
83
84
85
86
87
West Middlewick
B3137
Westway Farm
Eastway
EASTWICK BARTON
PH
NOMANSLAND CROSS
Edgeworthy
EDGEWORTHY HILL
Menchine
River Dalch
Moor Barton Farm
Kelly Farm
KELLY LA
PIDLAND LA
Northcote
Holmes
Gogland Manor
MUDFORD GATE
NORTHCOTE LA
WOODPLACE LA
Ford Barton
Wood Farm
Upcott
Woodscombe
Crandle
Deptford Farm
PAGE'S CROSS
B3137
PEAK CNR
Cruwys Morchard House
Merrifieldhayes
TWO POST CROSS
Henceford Moor
Stubborn
STUBBORN CROSS
WEEK CROSS
Coombe Farm
Henceford
HENCEFORD CROSS
EX16
BAMSON LA
COOMBE LA
BEER LA
WESTLAND LA
Weeke Farm
HIGH GATE
Pulsfordware
Bamson
Westland
Beer Farm
Furze
PH
West Ruckham
Coombe
Pennymoor
Higher Park
MOOR VIEW
RUCKHAM LA
East Ruckham
Puddington
Chapple
Forke Farm
GREENLAND HEAD CROSS
1 CHURCH CL
2 BAKERY MDW
LITTLEBOROUGH CROSS
CHAPEL CROSS
Yowlestone House
Eastland
GLEBELANDS
Wringsland
BRINDIFIELD LA
Smynacott
Hill Farm
Stickeridge
Brindifield
Ash
Yeadbury
Scotsham
BOND LA
Westway
Sunnybrook Farm
CLAW HILL
Lower Minchingdown
Newlands Farm
Claw
Hudgery
DANIEL'S GRAVE
Puddington Bottom
Edbury Farm
Higher Bowerhay
Grantland
GRANTLAND HILL
SUMMERWELL LA
GREEN HILL
Woolfardisworthy
Binneford Water
BULLAND LA
GREENHILL CROSS
Cleaves
RIVERSIDE CROSS
Partridge Hole
Broadridge Farm
COLLYLAND LA
South Yeo
TAYLOR'S HILL
TAYLOR'S CROSS
WOOLFARDISWORTHY CROSS
THE GLEBE
EAST END
Park
SOUTH YEO HILL
HOOKHILL LA
Penhay
CREDITON CROSS
SOUTH YEO CROSS
Upcott Barton
WELSBERE LA
PARK CROSS
Poughill
The Barton
Welsbere Barton
CREEDY CROSS
EX17
ASH LA
LEIGHCOTT LA
LEY'S CROSS
Binneford Farm
New House Farm
LEIGHCOTT CROSS
Hollyford Farm
Marsh Farm
Coddiford
HOLLYFORD LA
Redyeates Farm
BINNEFORD HILL
SPLITWELL CROSS
Down Farm
CODDIFORD CROSS
CODDIFORD LA
MILL LA
Rockbeare Farm
CHERITON MILL CROSS
WATERHOUSE CROSS
CHAPEL HILL CROSS
CHAPEL HILL
Cheriton Fitzpaine
CODDIFORD HILL
6 DRAKES MDW
7 POST OFFICE LA
8 LANDBOAT VIEW
9 BARNSHILL CL
10 CHERRY MDW
11 CHERRY CL
Stockleigh English
Holly Water
Piend
PIEND LA
BARTON CL 1
MOXEYS CL 2
BARY CL 3
RECTORY HILL 4
PYNES CL 5
Cheriton Fitzpaine Prim Sch
VOYSEY HILL
WHITE CROSS HILL
Downhayne
TOWER HILL
TOWER HILL CROSS
BARY LA
BARY HILL CROSS
Ashridge
STOCKLEIGH CROSS
Cheriton Barton
PH
PO
WHITE CROSS
DOWNHAYNE HILL
HOLLY WATER RD
LANDBOAT COTTS
LAG HILL
Stockleigh Court
CHURCH CROSS
82
A
83
B
84
C
85
D
86
E
87
F
61
80

Scale: 1¾ inches to 1 mile
0 ¼ ½ mile
0 250m 500m 750m 1 km

48
64

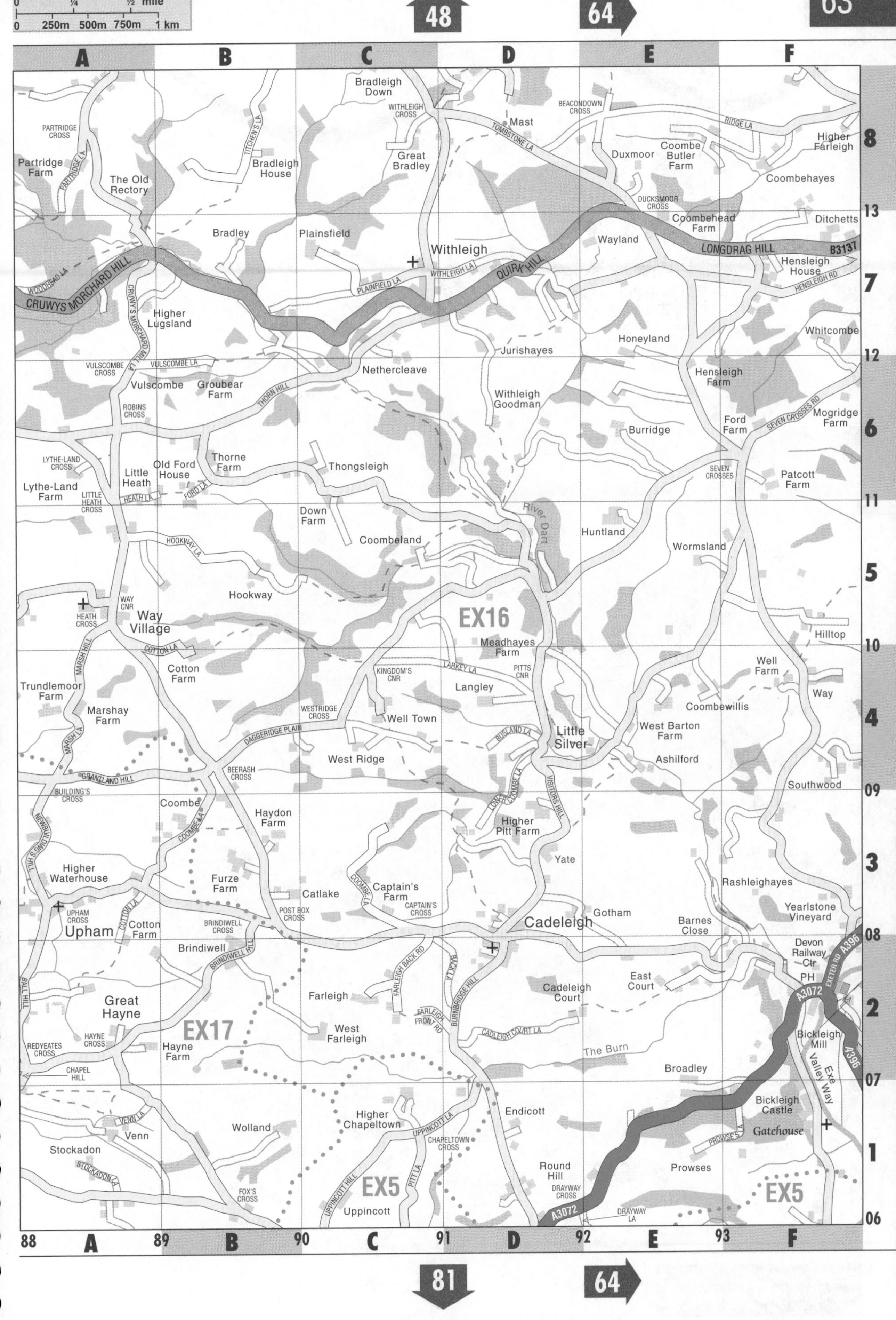

81
64

63
49

D7
1 LIME TREE MEAD
2 RENNIE RD
3 WESLEY CL
4 FRANCIS CRES
5 CHILCOTT CL
6 MARINA WAY
7 CHICHESTER PL
8 COLERIDGE RD
9 PUGSLEY RD
10 STARKEY CL
11 TIDCOMBE CL
12 ST LAWRENCE CL
13 RAYER RD
14 POLWHELE RD
15 WESTCOTT RD
16 RYDER CL
17 RIPPON CL
18 TIDCOMBE WLK

Scale: 1¾ inches to 1 mile
0 ¼ ½ mile
0 250m 500m 750m 1 km

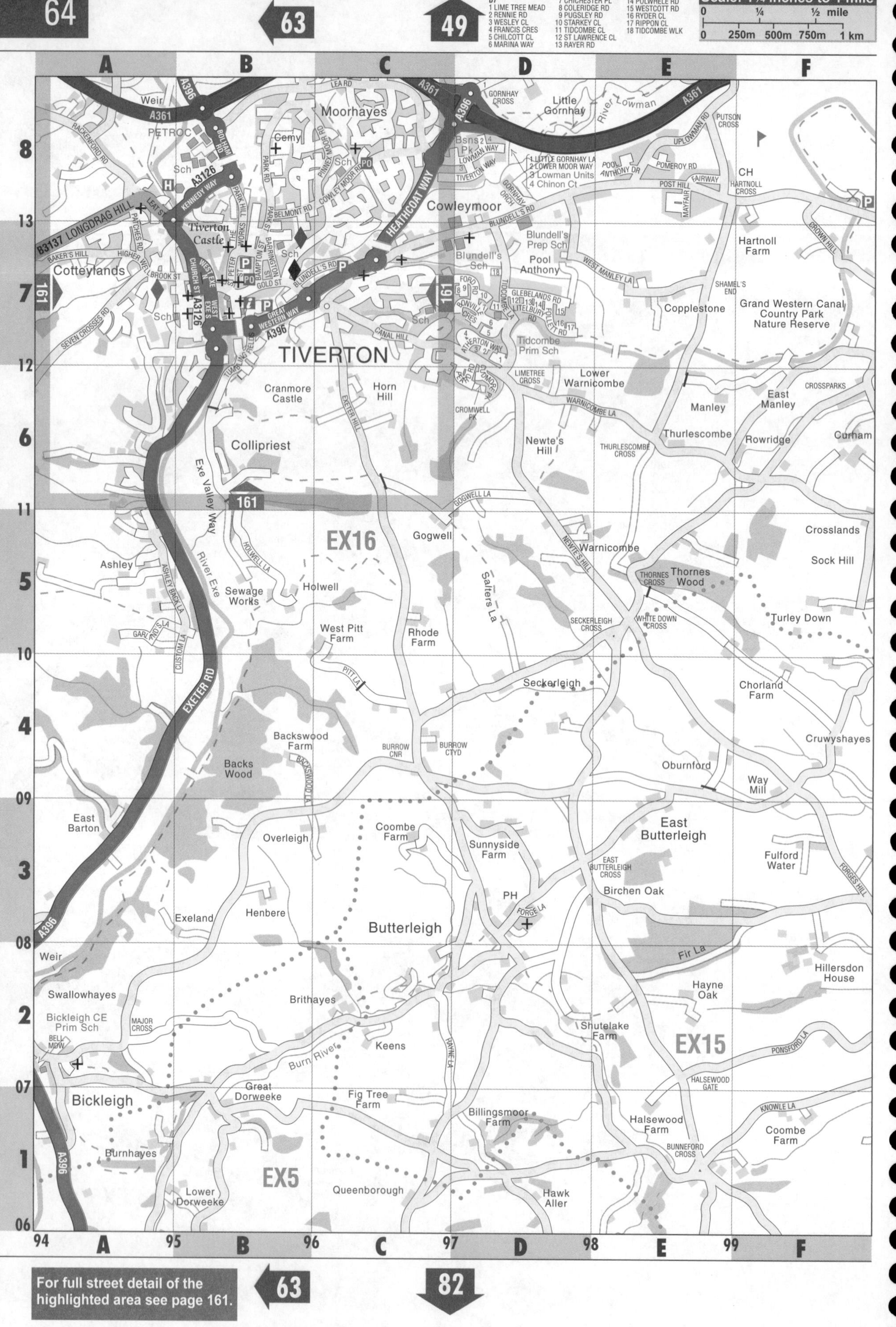

For full street detail of the highlighted area see page 161.
63
82

Scale: 1¾ inches to 1 mile

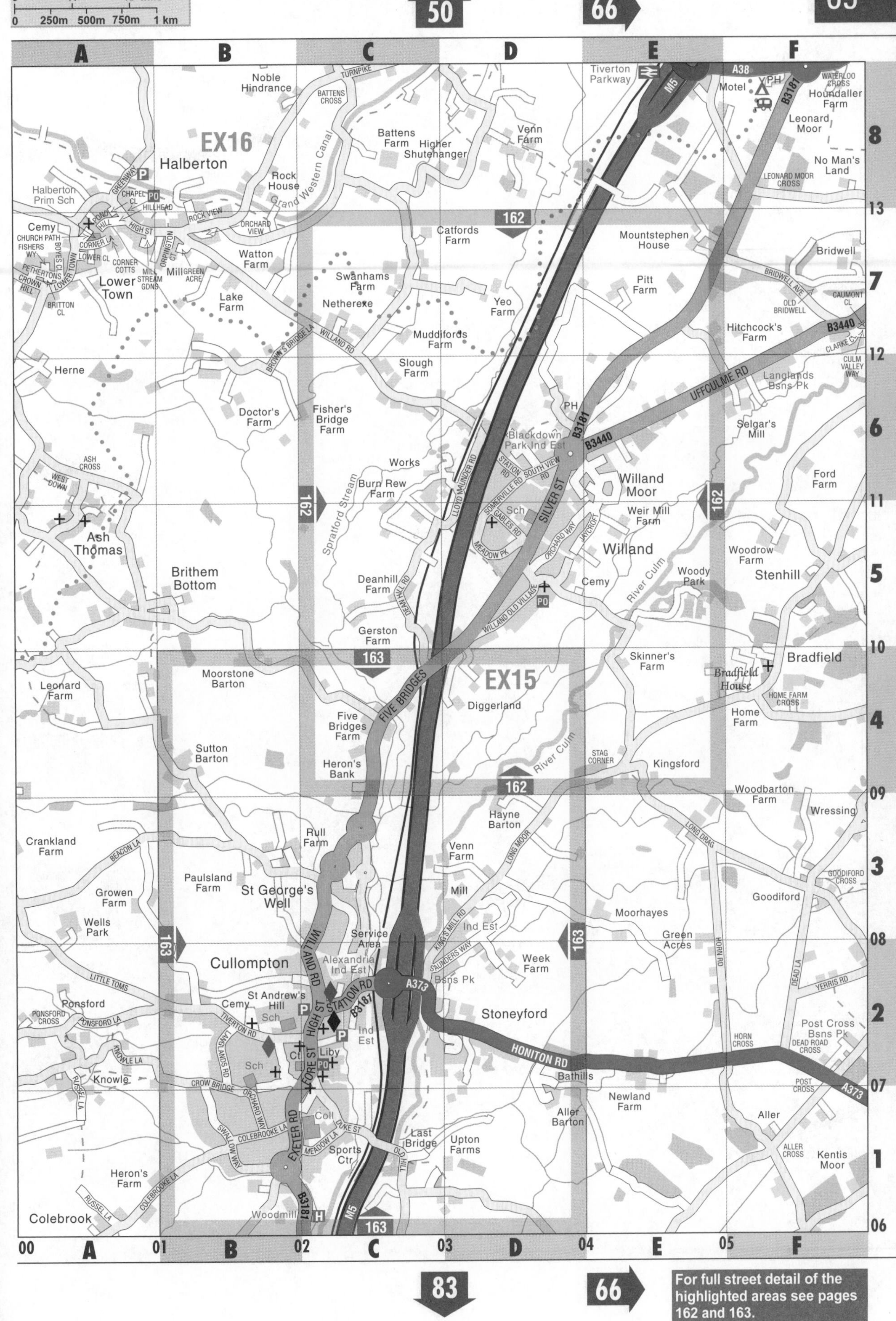

For full street detail of the highlighted areas see pages 162 and 163.

65
51

Scale: 1¾ inches to 1 mile

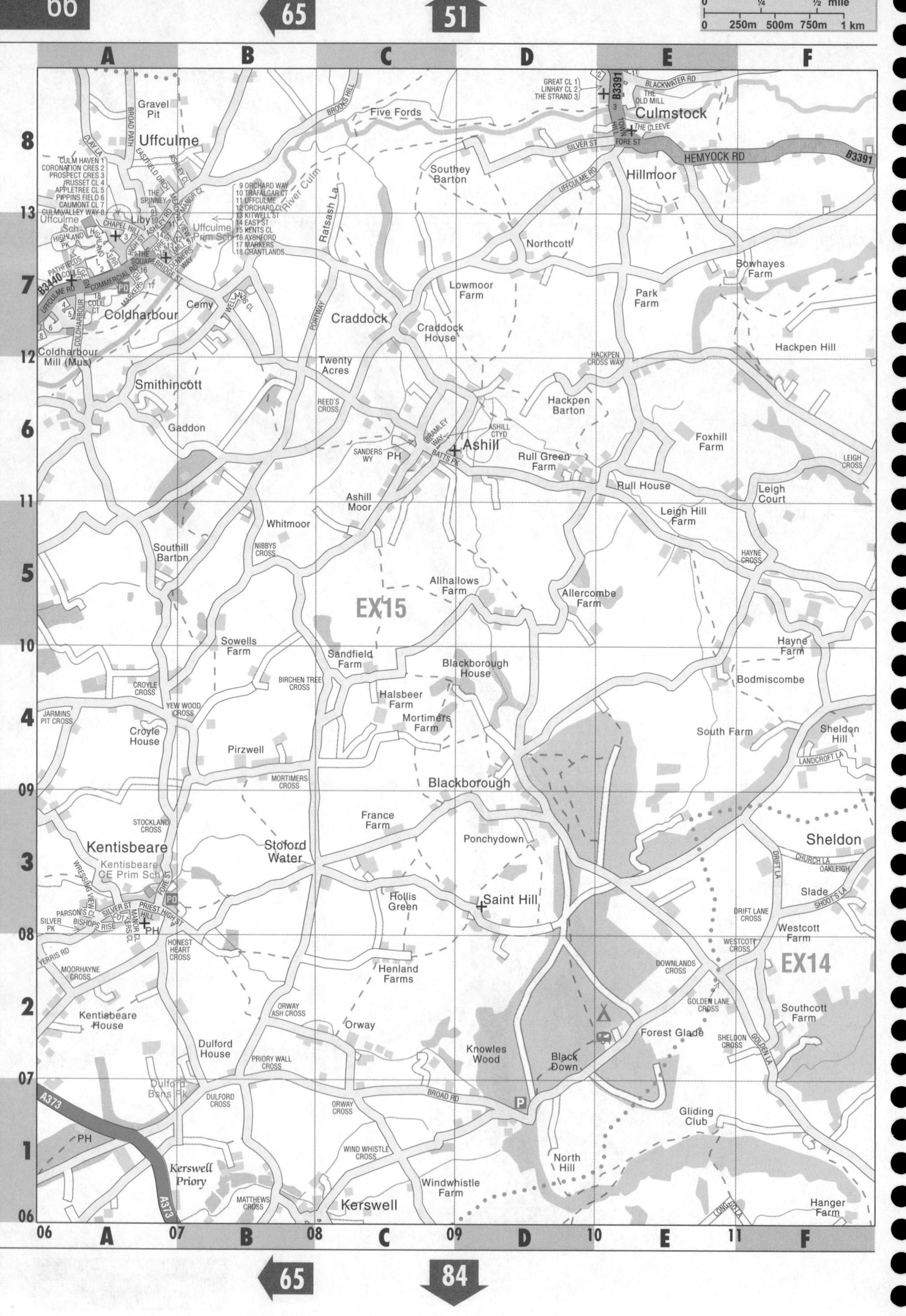

65
84

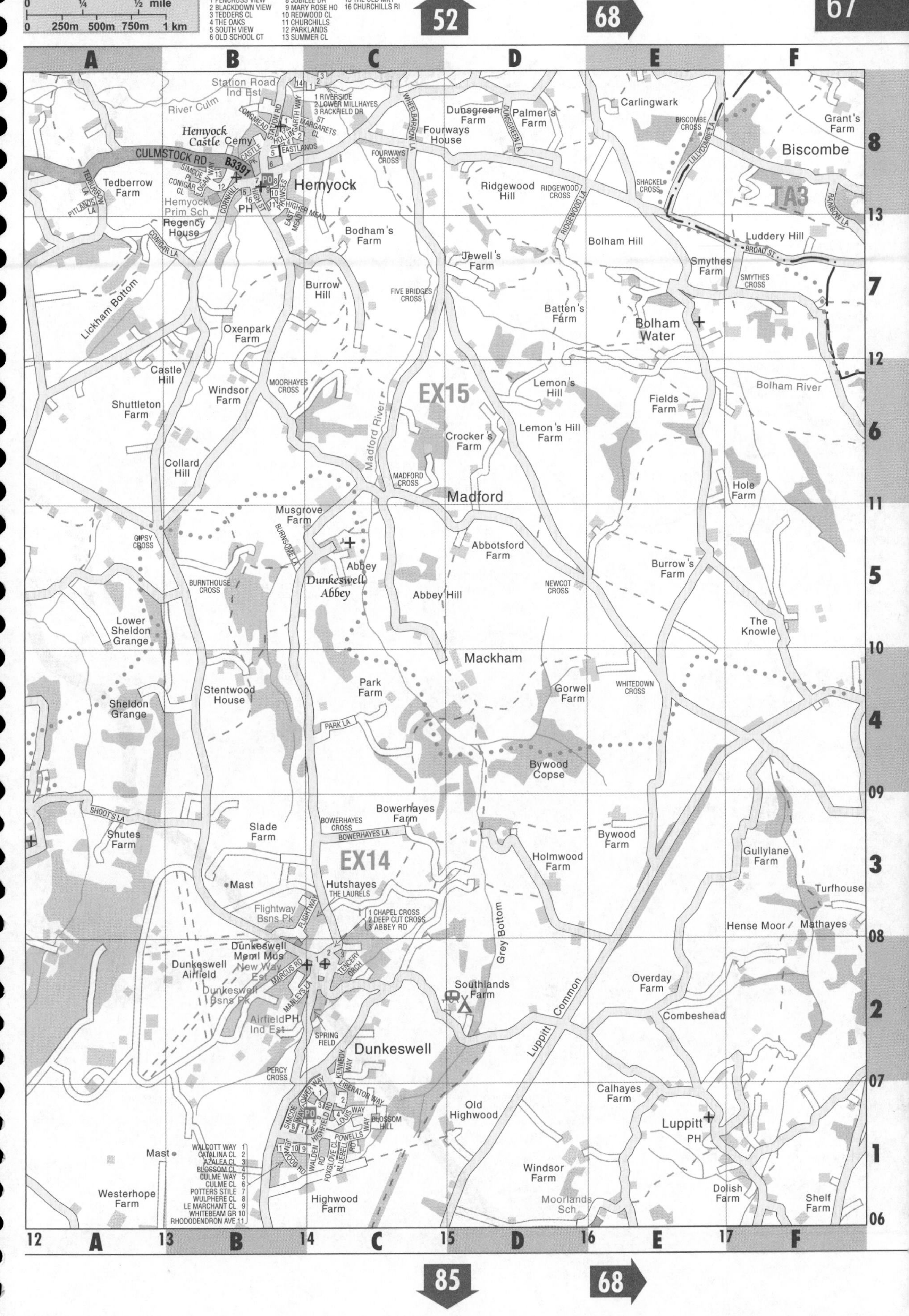
Scale: 1¾ inches to 1 mile
0 ¼ ½ mile
0 250m 500m 750m 1 km
B8
1 PENCROSS VIEW
2 BLACKDOWN VIEW
3 TEDDERS CL
4 THE OAKS
5 SOUTH VIEW
6 OLD SCHOOL CT
7 FORE ST
8 JUBILEE DR
9 MARY ROSE HO
10 REDWOOD CL
11 CHURCHILLS
12 PARKLANDS
13 SUMMER CL
14 MILL LEAT
15 THE OLD MKT
16 CHURCHILLS RI
52
68
A
B
C
D
E
F
Station Road Ind Est
River Culm
Hemyock Castle
Cemy
1 RIVERSIDE
2 LOWER MILLHAYES
3 RACKFIELD DR
ST MARGARETS CL
EASTLANDS
LONGMEAD
STATION RD
HOLLINGARTH WAY
WHEELBARROW LA
Dunsgreen Farm
DUNSGREEN LA
Palmer's Farm
Fourways House
FOURWAYS CROSS
Carlingwark
BISCOMBE CROSS
LILLYCOMBE LA
Grant's Farm
Biscombe
CULMSTOCK RD
B3391
SIMCOE PL
LOGAN WAY
CASTLE PK
CONIGAR CL
CORNHILL
HIGH ST
PROWSES
PO
PH
Hemyock
Tedberrow Farm
TEDBURROW LA
PITLANDS LA
Hemyock Prim Sch
Regency House
CONIGAR LA
EAST MEAD
HIGHER MEAD
Ridgewood Hill
RIDGEWOOD CROSS
RIDGEWOOD LA
SHACKEL CROSS
TA3
RAINBOW LA
Luddery Hill
BROAD ST
Bodham's Farm
Jewell's Farm
Bolham Hill
Smythes Farm
SMYTHES CROSS
Lickham Bottom
Burrow Hill
FIVE BRIDGES CROSS
Batten's Farm
Bolham Water
Oxenpark Farm
Castle Hill
Windsor Farm
MOORHAYES CROSS
EX15
Lemon's Hill
Bolham River
Fields Farm
Shuttleton Farm
Madford River
Crocker's Farm
Lemon's Hill Farm
Collard Hill
MADFORD CROSS
Madford
Hole Farm
Musgrove Farm
GIPSY CROSS
BURNSOME LA
Abbotsford Farm
Abbey
Burrow's Farm
BURNTHOUSE CROSS
Dunkeswell Abbey
Abbey Hill
NEWCOT CROSS
Lower Sheldon Grange
The Knowle
Mackham
Stentwood House
Park Farm
Gorwell Farm
WHITEDOWN CROSS
Sheldon Grange
PARK LA
Bywood Copse
SHOOT'S LA
Slade Farm
Bowerhayes Farm
BOWERHAYES CROSS
BOWERHAYES LA
Shutes Farm
Bywood Farm
Holmwood Farm
Gullylane Farm
EX14
Mast
Hutshayes
THE LAURELS
Turfhouse
Flightway Bsns Pk
FLIGHT WAY
1 CHAPEL CROSS
2 DEEP CUT CROSS
3 ABBEY RD
Grey Bottom
Hense Moor
Mathayes
Dunkeswell Meml Mus
New Way Est
Dunkeswell Airfield
MARCUS RD
TENCERY ORCH
Dunkeswell Bsns Pk
MANLEYS LA
Southlands Farm
Overday Farm
Airfield Ind Est
PH
Luppitt Common
Combeshead
SPRING FIELD
Dunkeswell
PERCY CROSS
KENNEDY WAY
LIBERATOR WAY
Calhayes Farm
Old Highwood
SIMCOE WAY
LOWER WAY
HIGHFIELD RD
LOUIS WAY
BLOSSOM HILL
POWELLS WAY
Luppitt
PH
WALCOTT WAY 1
CATALINA CL 2
AZALEA CL 3
BLOSSOM CL 4
CULME WAY 5
CULME CL 6
POTTERS STILE 7
WULPHERE CL 8
LE MARCHANT CL 9
WHITEBEAM GR 10
RHODODENDRON AVE 11
Mast
WALDEN RD
FOXGLOVE CL
BLUEBELL RD
JENWOOD RD
Windsor Farm
Westerhope Farm
Highwood Farm
Moorlands Sch
Dolish Farm
Shelf Farm
8
13
7
12
6
11
5
10
4
09
3
08
2
07
1
06
12
13
14
15
16
17
85
68

67

Scale: 1¾ inches to 1 mile

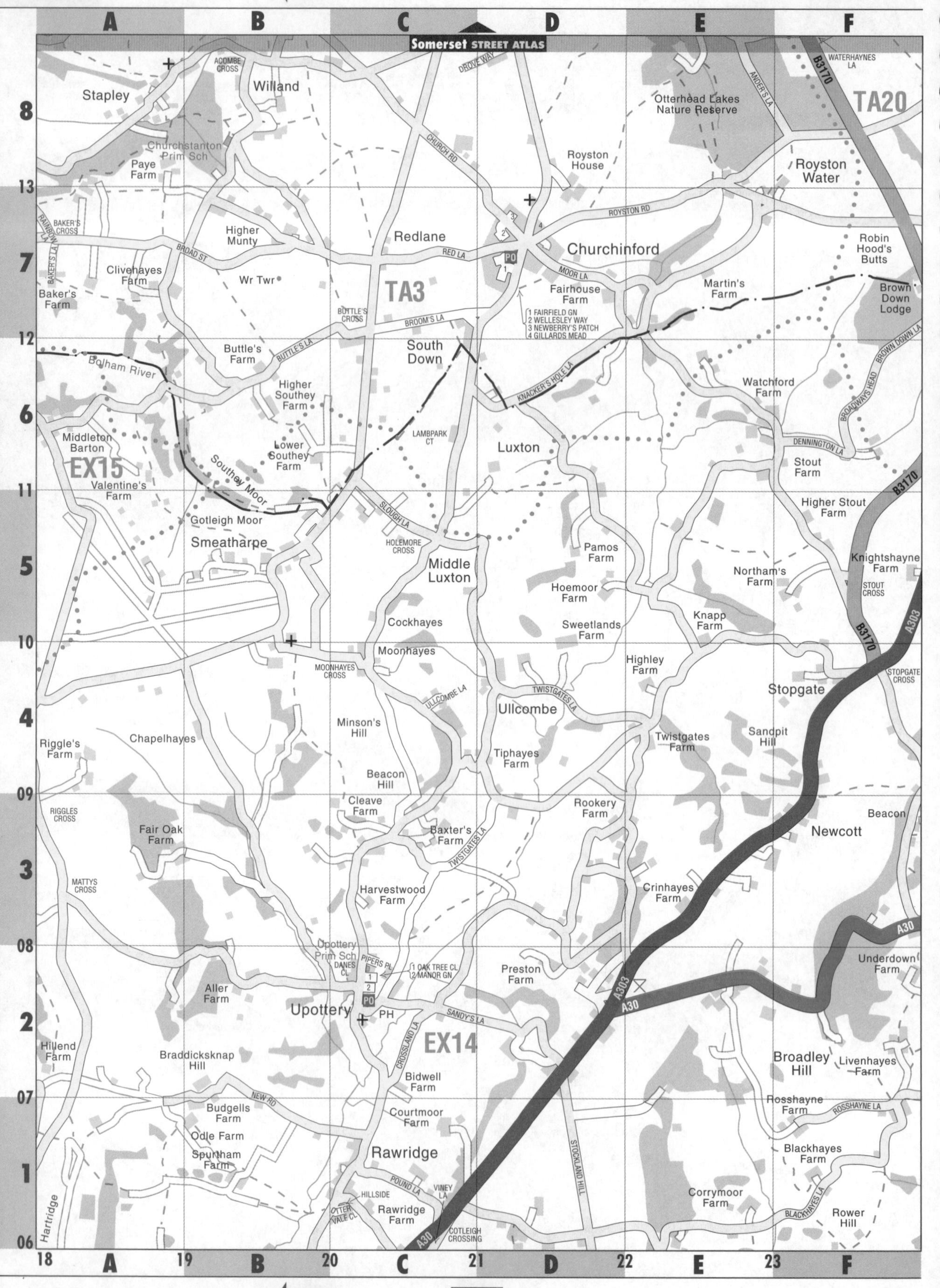

67

86

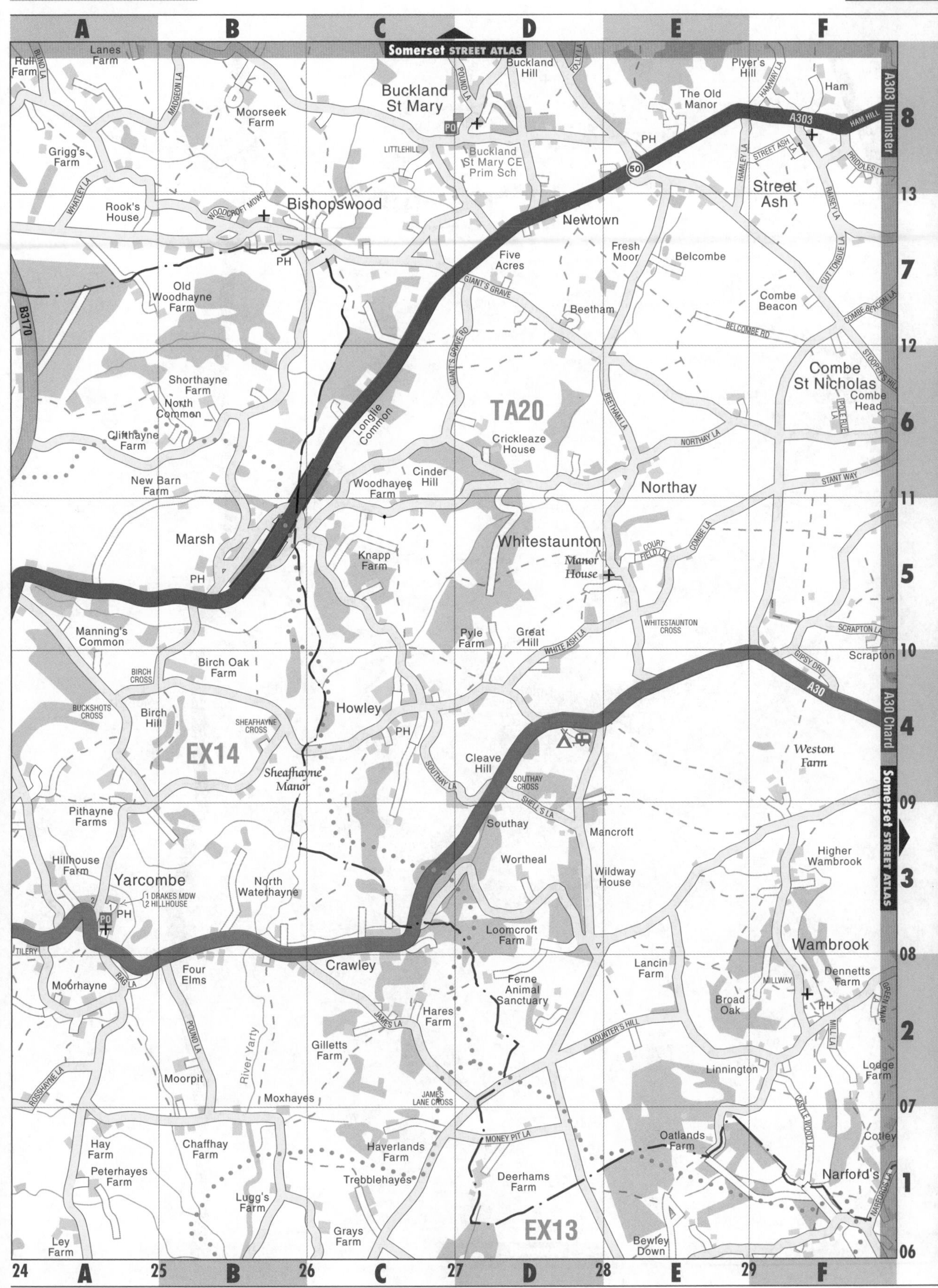
Scale: 1¾ inches to 1 mile
Somerset STREET ATLAS
Buckland St Mary
Bishopswood
Newtown
Street Ash
Combe St Nicholas
TA20
Northay
Whitestaunton
Marsh
Howley
EX14
Yarcombe
Crawley
Wambrook
EX13
A303 Ilminster
A30 Chard

Scale: 1¾ inches to 1 mile

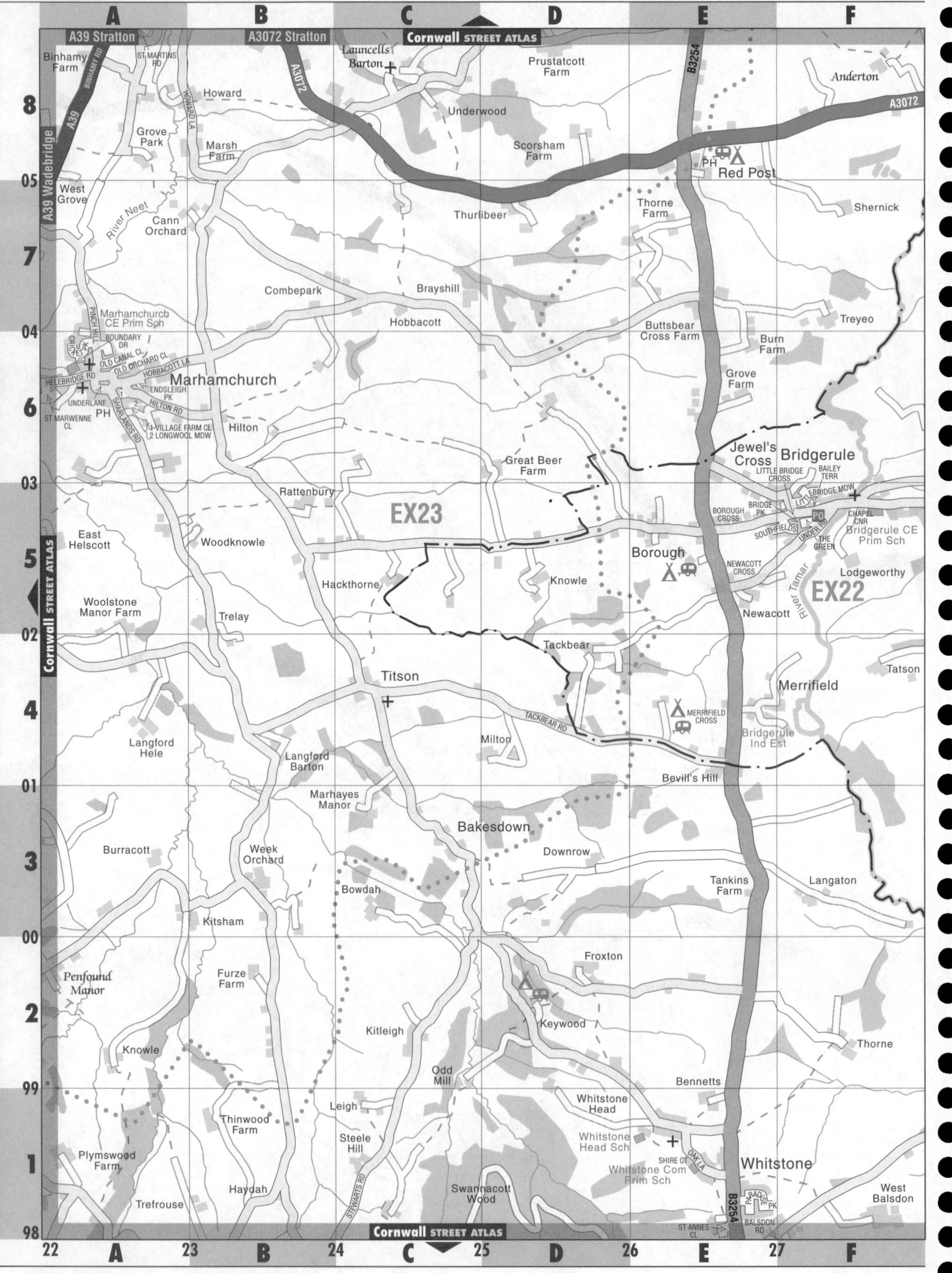

Cornwall STREET ATLAS

Scale: 1¾ inches to 1 mile

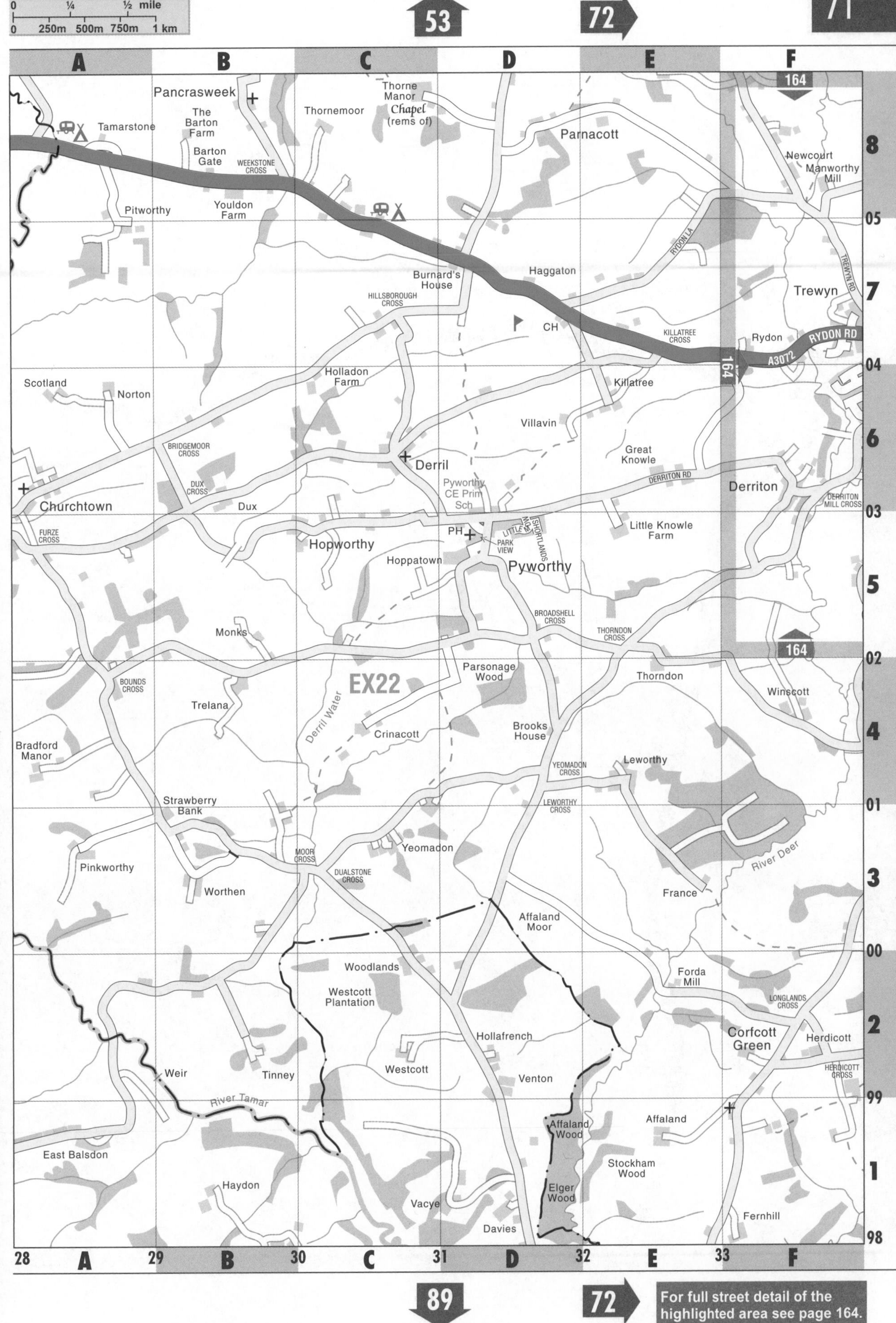

89
72
For full street detail of the highlighted area see page 164.

Scale: 1¾ inches to 1 mile
0 ¼ ½ mile
0 250m 500m 750m 1 km

For full street detail of the highlighted area see page 164.

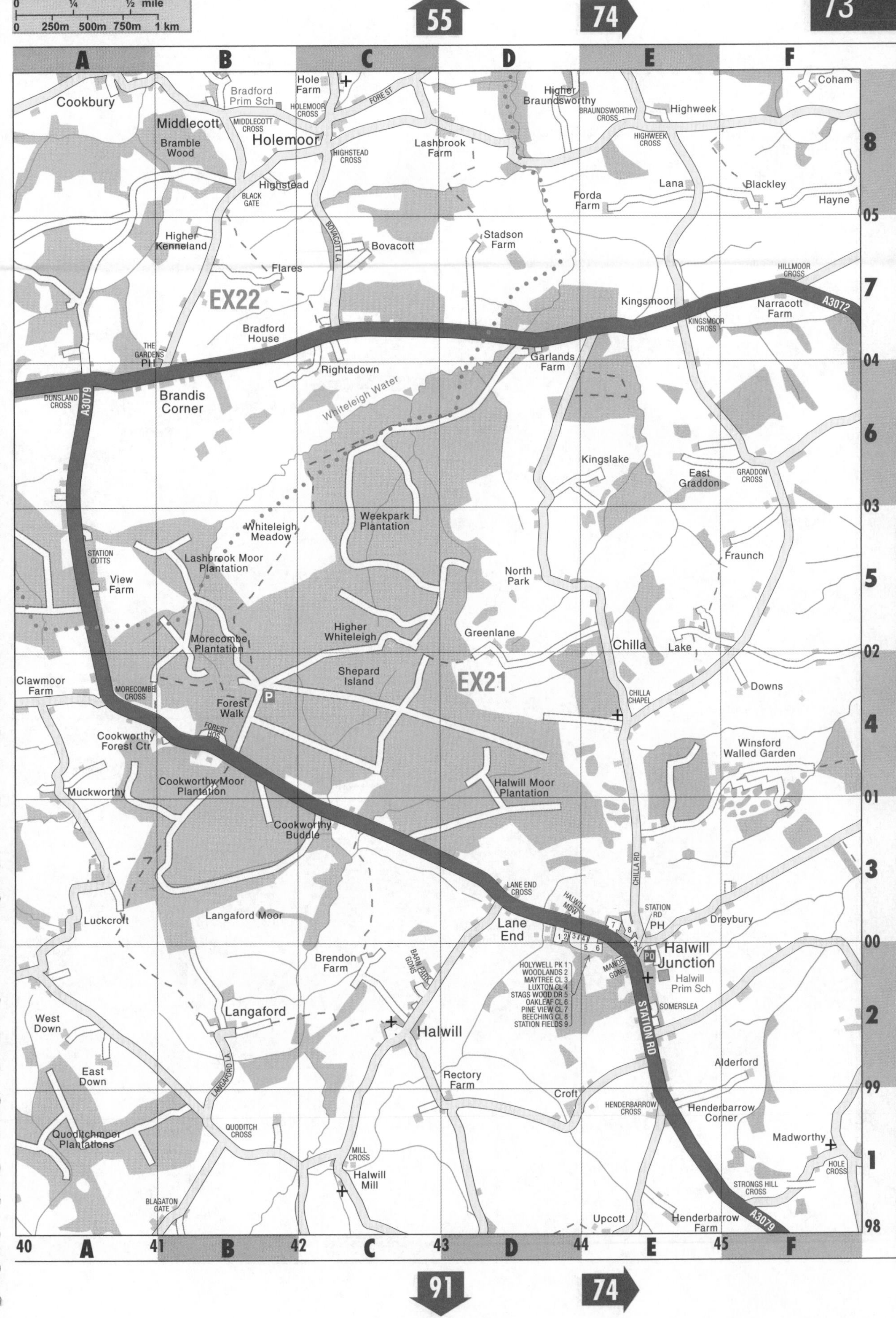
Scale: 1¾ inches to 1 mile
0 ¼ ½ mile
0 250m 500m 750m 1 km
55
74
Cookbury
Bradford Prim Sch
Hole Farm
Holemoor
Middlecott
Bramble Wood
Highstead
Lashbrook Farm
Higher Braundsworthy
Highweek
Coham
Lana
Blackley
Hayne
Forda Farm
Higher Kenneland
Bovacott
Flares
Stadson Farm
EX22
Kingsmoor
Narracott Farm
A3072
Bradford House
Rightadown
Garlands Farm
Brandis Corner
Whiteleigh Water
Kingslake
East Graddon
Weekpark Plantation
Whiteleigh Meadow
Lashbrook Moor Plantation
View Farm
North Park
Fraunch
Higher Whiteleigh
Greenlane
Chilla
Lake
Morecombe Plantation
Shepard Island
EX21
Downs
Clawmoor Farm
Forest Walk
Cookworthy Forest Ctr
Winsford Walled Garden
Muckworthy
Cookworthy Moor Plantation
Halwill Moor Plantation
Cookworthy Buddle
Luckcroft
Langaford Moor
Lane End
Dreybury
Halwill Junction
Halwill Prim Sch
Brendon Farm
HOLYWELL PK 1
WOODLANDS 2
MAYTREE CL 3
LUXTON CL 4
STAGS WOOD DR 5
OAKLEAF CL 6
PINE VIEW CL 7
BEECHING CL 8
STATION FIELDS 9
West Down
Langaford
Halwill
East Down
Rectory Farm
Alderford
Croft
Henderbarrow Corner
Quoditchmoor Plantations
Madworthy
Halwill Mill
Upcott
Henderbarrow Farm
A3079
STATION RD
91
74

73
56

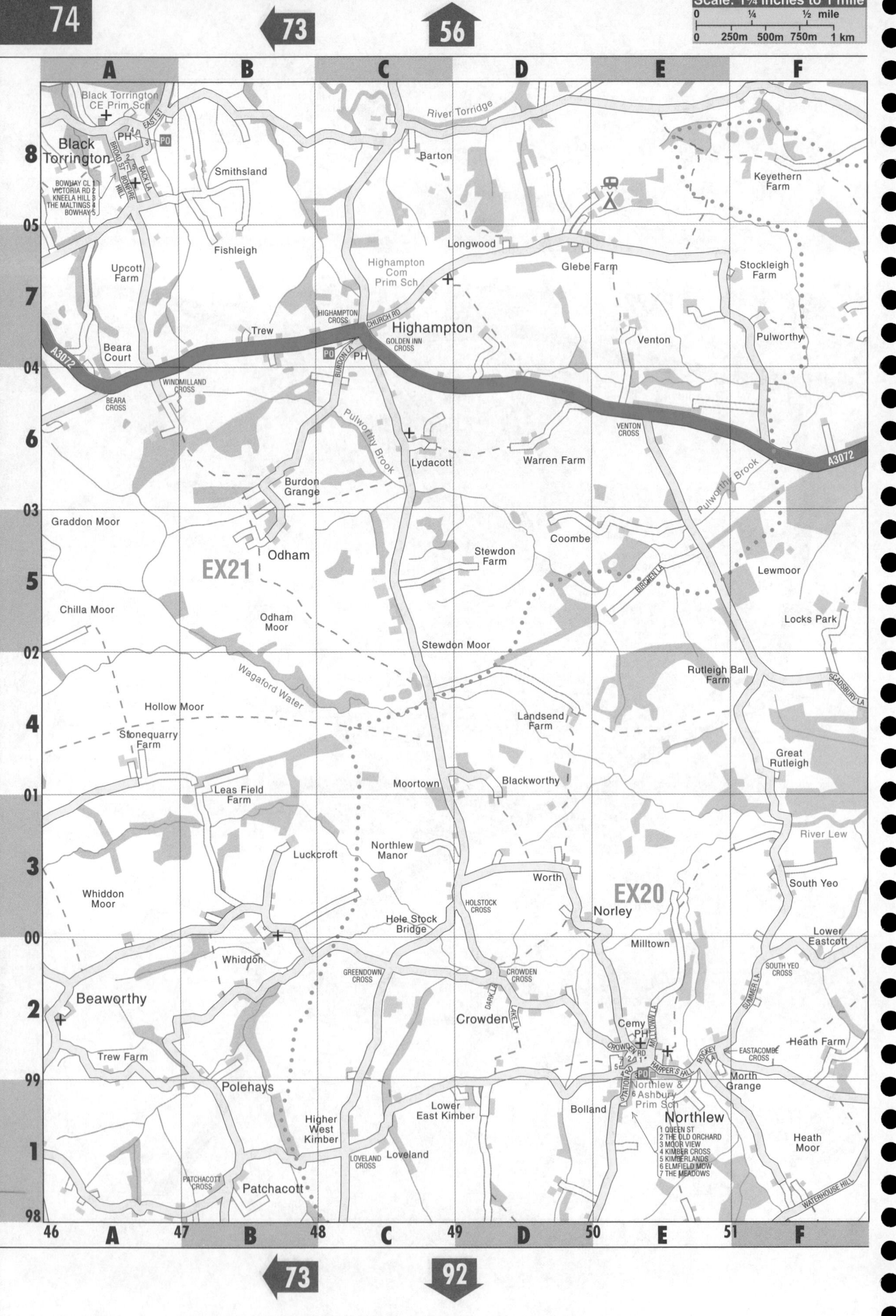
Scale: 1¾ inches to 1 mile
Black Torrington
Black Torrington CE Prim Sch
Smithsland
Fishleigh
Upcott Farm
Beara Court
Trew
Barton
River Torridge
Longwood
Highampton Com Prim Sch
Highampton
Glebe Farm
Keyethern Farm
Stockleigh Farm
Venton
Pulworthy
A3072
Lydacott
Warren Farm
Burdon Grange
Pulworthy Brook
Graddon Moor
Odham
EX21
Stewdon Farm
Coombe
Lewmoor
Chilla Moor
Odham Moor
Stewdon Moor
Locks Park
Wagaford Water
Hollow Moor
Stonequarry Farm
Landsend Farm
Rutleigh Ball Farm
Great Rutleigh
Leas Field Farm
Moortown
Blackworthy
Luckcroft
Northlew Manor
River Lew
Whiddon Moor
Worth
EX20
Norley
South Yeo
Hole Stock Bridge
Lower Eastcott
Whiddon
Milltown
Beaworthy
Crowden
Heath Farm
Trew Farm
Polehays
Lower East Kimber
Bolland
Northlew
Morth Grange
Higher West Kimber
Loveland
Heath Moor
Patchacott
Northlew & Ashbury Prim Sch
1 QUEEN ST
2 THE OLD ORCHARD
3 MOOR VIEW
4 KIMBER CROSS
5 KIMBERLANDS
6 ELMFIELD MDW
7 THE MEADOWS

73
92

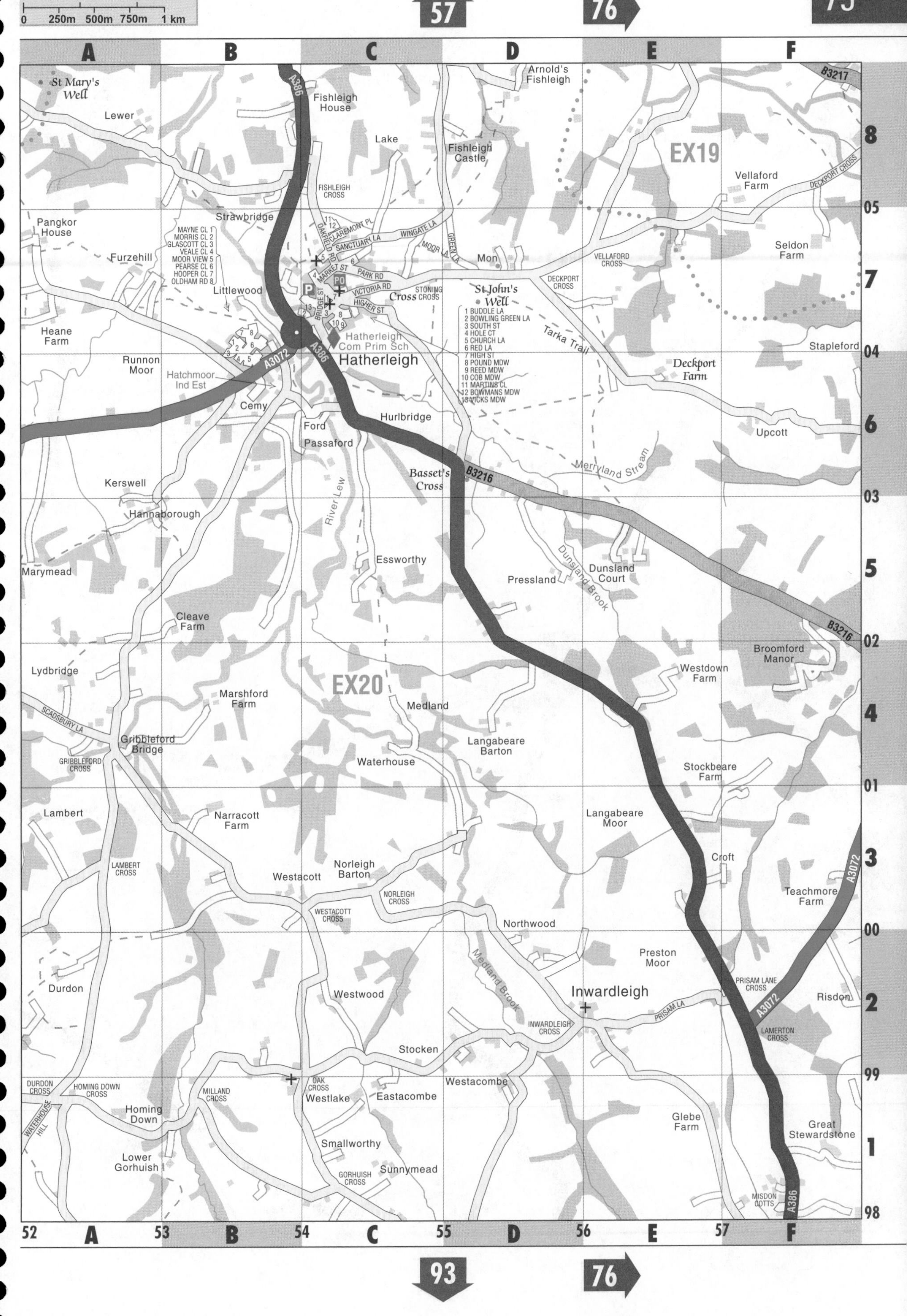

Scale: 1¾ inches to 1 mile
0 ¼ ½ mile
0 250m 500m 750m 1 km
57
76
A B C D E F
8
05
7
04
6
03
5
02
4
01
3
00
2
99
1
98
52 53 54 55 56 57
St Mary's Well
Lewer
Fishleigh House
Arnold's Fishleigh
B3217
Lake
Fishleigh Castle
EX19
Vellaford Farm
DECKPORT CROSS
FISHLEIGH CROSS
Pangkor House
Strawbridge
MAYNE CL 1
MORRIS CL 2
GLASCOTT CL 3
VEALE CL 4
MOOR VIEW 5
PEARSE CL 6
HOOPER CL 7
OLDHAM RD 8
CLAREMONT PL
WINGATE LA
OAKFIELD RD
SANCTUARY LA
MOOR LA
GREEN LA
Furzehill
MARKET ST
PARK RD
Mon
VELLAFORD CROSS
Seldon Farm
Littlewood
VICTORIA RD
BRIDGE ST
HIGHER ST
STONING CROSS
Cross
St John's Well
DECKPORT CROSS
Heane Farm
1 BUDDLE LA
2 BOWLING GREEN LA
3 SOUTH ST
4 HOLE CT
5 CHURCH LA
6 RED LA
7 HIGH ST
8 POUND MDW
9 REED MDW
10 COB MDW
11 MARTINS CL
12 BOWMANS MDW
13 VICKS MDW
Tarka Trail
Stapleford
Hatherleigh Com Prim Sch
Hatherleigh
Runnon Moor
Hatchmoor Ind Est
A3072
A386
Deckport Farm
Cemy
Ford
Hurlbridge
Passaford
Upcott
Basset's Cross
B3216
Merryland Stream
Kerswell
Hannaborough
River Lew
Dunsland Brook
Essworthy
Dunsland Court
Pressland
Marymead
Cleave Farm
B3216
Broomford Manor
Lydbridge
Westdown Farm
EX20
Marshford Farm
Medland
SCADSBURY LA
Gribbleford Bridge
Langabeare Barton
GRIBBLEFORD CROSS
Waterhouse
Stockbeare Farm
Lambert
Narracott Farm
Langabeare Moor
Croft
LAMBERT CROSS
Norleigh Barton
Westacott
A3072
Teachmore Farm
NORLEIGH CROSS
WESTACOTT CROSS
Northwood
Preston Moor
Medland Brook
Durdon
Westwood
Inwardleigh
PRISAM LANE CROSS
Risdon
PRISAM LA
INWARDLEIGH CROSS
LAMERTON CROSS
Stocken
DURDON CROSS
HOMING DOWN CROSS
MILLAND CROSS
OAK CROSS
Westlake
Eastacombe
Westacombe
WATERHOUSE HILL
Homing Down
Glebe Farm
Great Stewardstone
Smallworthy
Lower Gorhuish
GORHUISH CROSS
Sunnymead
MISDON COTTS
A386
93
76

75
58

Scale: 1¾ inches to 1 mile
0 ¼ ½ mile
0 250m 500m 750m 1 km

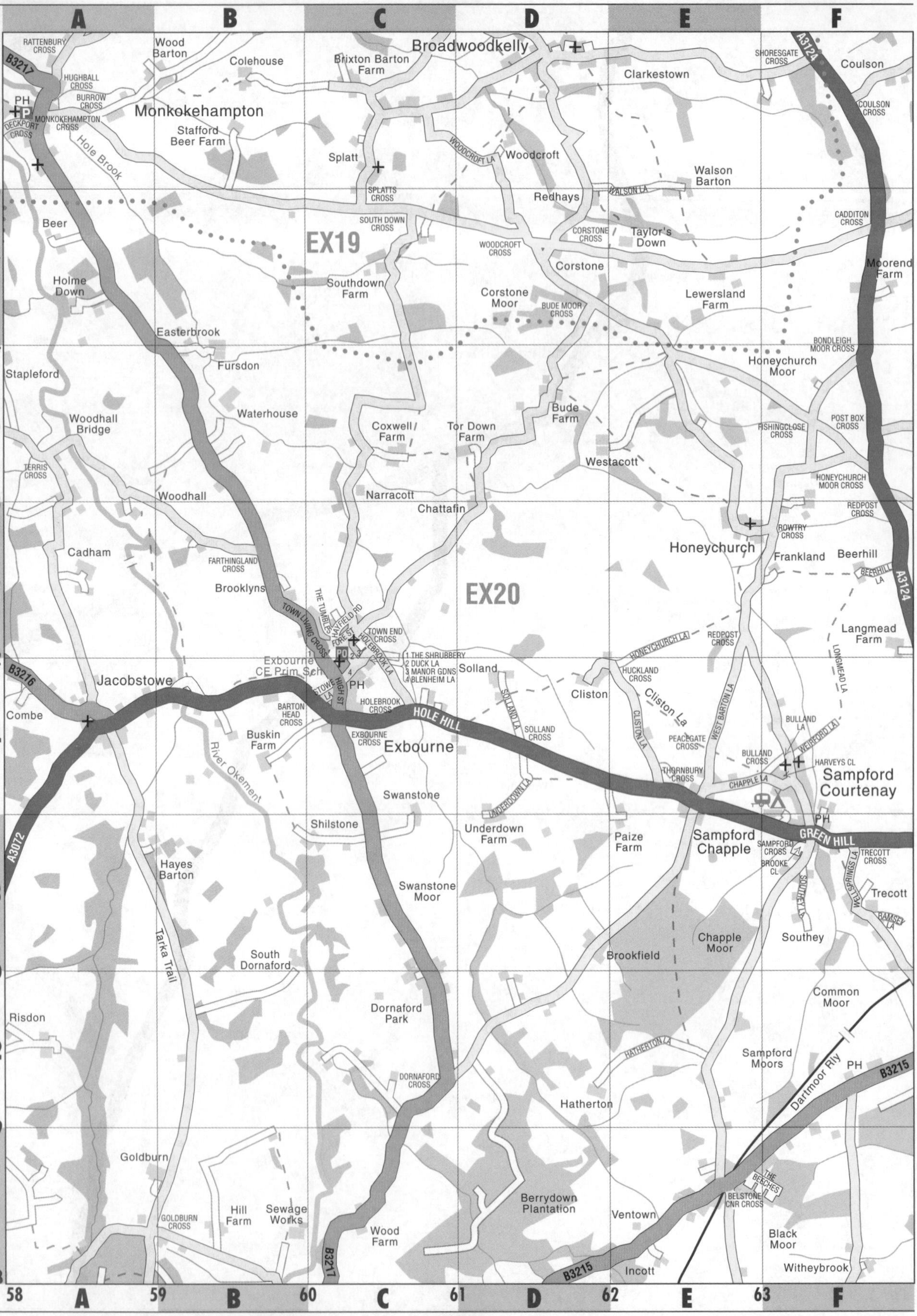

Broadwoodkelly
Monkokehampton
Jacobstowe
Exbourne
Honeychurch
Sampford Courtenay
Sampford Chapple
EX19
EX20
Wood Barton
Colehouse
Brixton Barton Farm
Clarkestown
Coulson
Stafford Beer Farm
Splatt
Woodcroft
Walson Barton
Redhays
Taylor's Down
Beer
Holme Down
Southdown Farm
Corstone
Corstone Moor
Lewersland Farm
Moorend Farm
Easterbrook
Fursdon
Honeychurch Moor
Stapleford
Waterhouse
Bude Farm
Woodhall Bridge
Coxwell Farm
Tor Down Farm
Westacott
Narracott
Chattafin
Woodhall
Cadham
Frankland
Beerhill
Brooklyns
Langmead Farm
Exbourne CE Prim Sch
Solland
Cliston
Combe
Buskin Farm
Swanstone
Shilstone
Underdown Farm
Paize Farm
Hayes Barton
Swanstone Moor
Trecott
Chapple Moor
Southey
South Dornaford
Brookfield
Common Moor
Risdon
Dornaford Park
Sampford Moors
Hatherton
Goldburn
Berrydown Plantation
Hill Farm
Sewage Works
Wood Farm
Ventown
Black Moor
Incott
Witheybrook
Hole Brook
River Okement
Tarka Trail
Dartmoor Rly
B3217
B3216
B3215
A3072
A3124
HOLE HILL
GREEN HILL
Clisto Lane
PH
PO
1 THE SHRUBBERY
2 DUCK LA
3 MANOR GDNS
4 BLENHEIM LA

75
94

Scale: 1¾ inches to 1 mile
0 ¼ ½ mile
0 250m 500m 750m 1 km

59
78

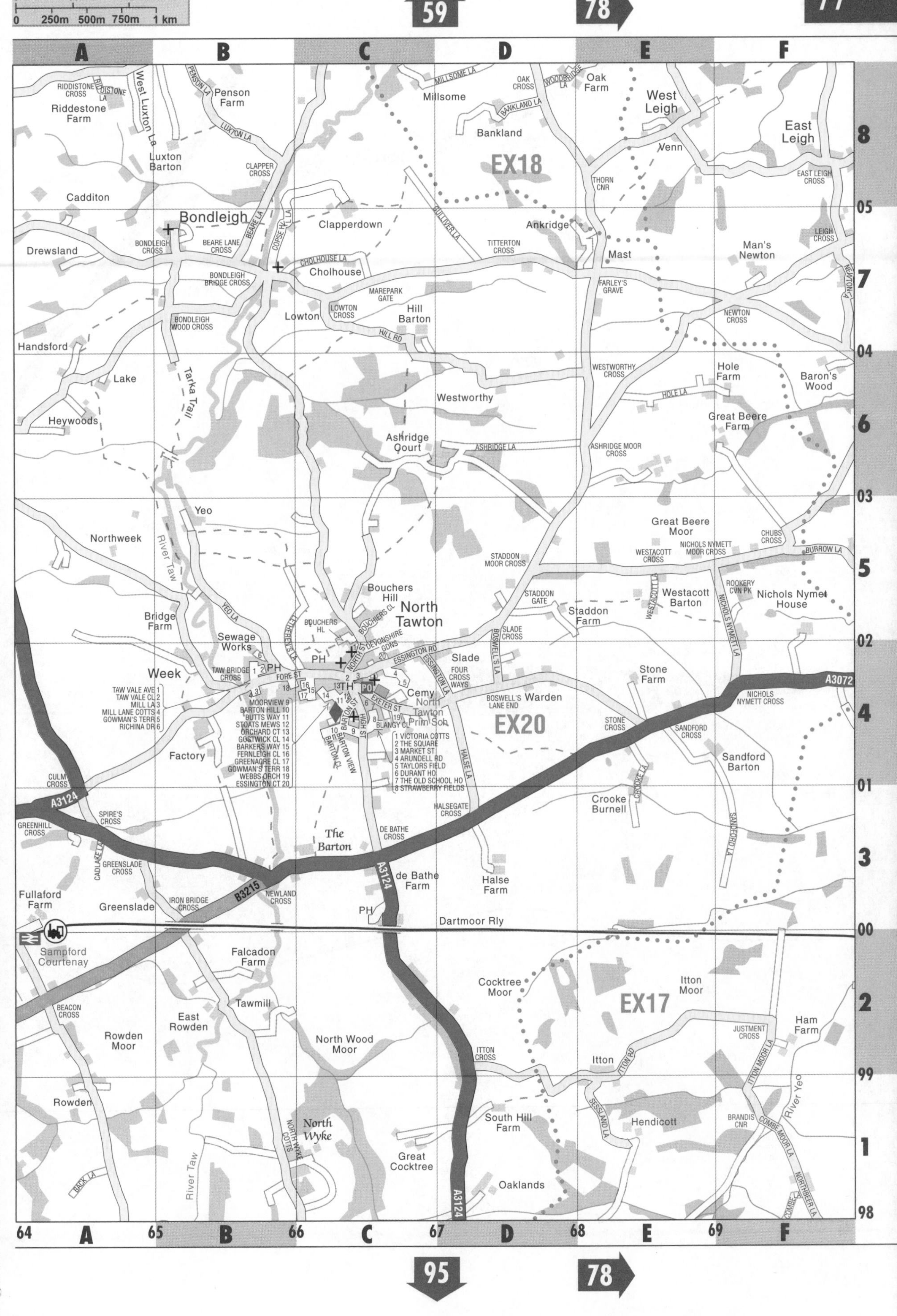

95
78

77 60

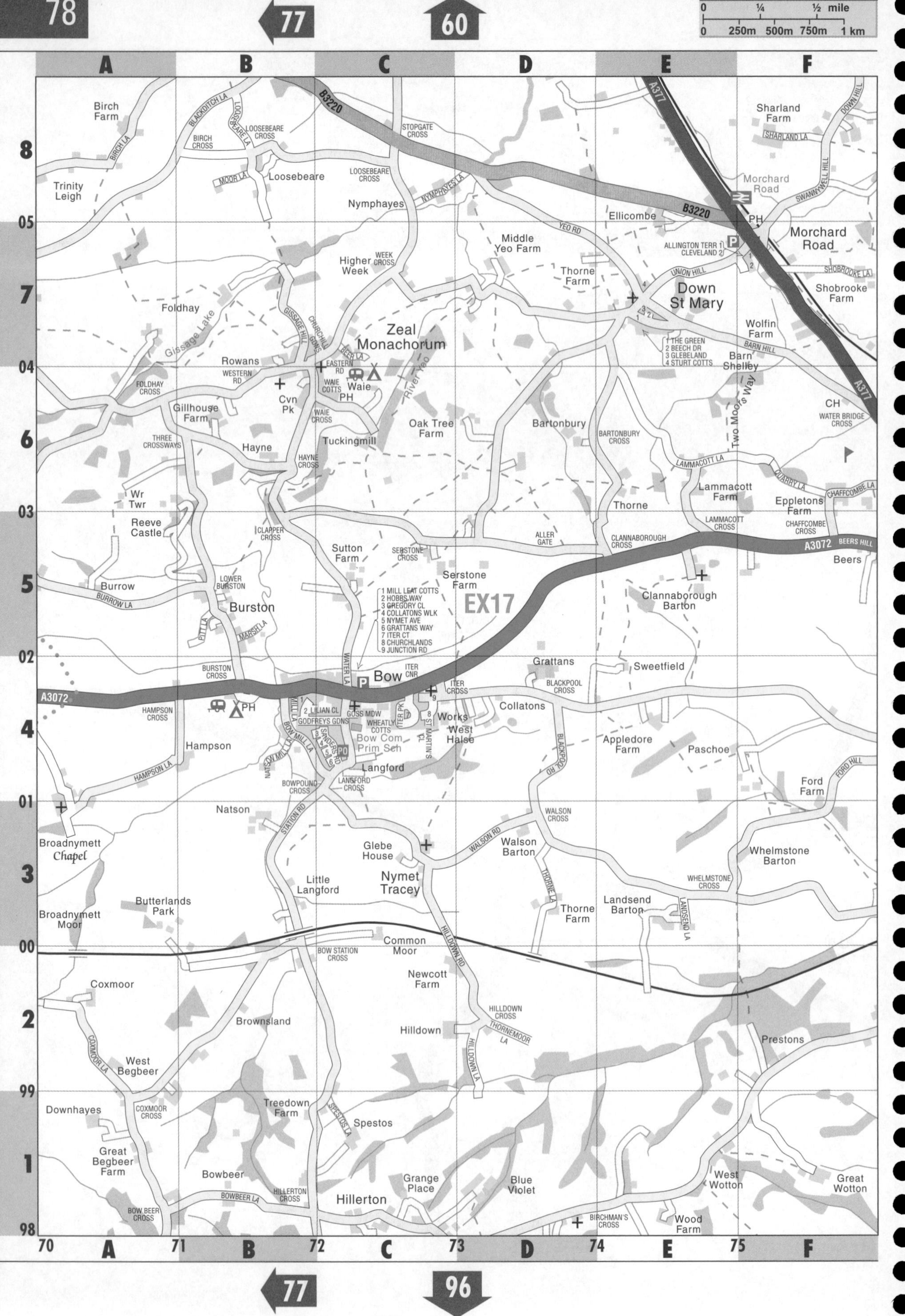
Scale: 1¾ inches to 1 mile
0 ¼ ½ mile
0 250m 500m 750m 1 km
A B C D E F
8 05 7 04 6 03 5 02 4 01 3 00 2 99 1 98
70 71 72 73 74 75
B3220
A377
A3072
Birch Farm
Trinity Leigh
Loosebeare
Nymphayes
Higher Week
Foldhay
Rowans
Gillhouse Farm
Hayne
Reeve Castle
Burrow
Burston
Bow
Hampson
Natson
Broadnymett Chapel
Broadnymett Moor
Butterlands Park
Coxmoor
West Begbeer
Downhayes
Great Begbeer Farm
Bowbeer
Brownsland
Treedown Farm
Spestos
Hillerton
Grange Place
Blue Violet
Hilldown
Newcott Farm
Common Moor
Little Langford
Glebe House
Nymet Tracey
Langford
Zeal Monachorum
Waie
Tuckingmill
Oak Tree Farm
Sutton Farm
Serstone Farm
EX17
Middle Yeo Farm
Thorne Farm
Bartonbury
Thorne
Grattans
Collatons
Works
West Halse
Walson Barton
Thorne Farm
Landsend Barton
Appledore Farm
Sweetfield
Clannaborough Barton
Paschoe
Ellicombe
Down St Mary
Morchard Road
Sharland Farm
Shobrooke Farm
Wolfin Farm
Barn Shelley
Lammacott Farm
Eppletons Farm
Beers
Ford Farm
Whelmstone Barton
Prestons
West Wotton
Great Wotton
Wood Farm
Two Moors Way
River Yeo
Gissage Lake
Bow Com Prim Sch
1 MILL LEAT COTTS
2 HOBBS WAY
3 GREGORY CL
4 COLLATONS WLK
5 NYMET AVE
6 GRATTANS WAY
7 ITER CT
8 CHURCHLANDS
9 JUNCTION RD
1 THE GREEN
2 BEECH DR
3 GLEBELAND
4 STURT COTTS

77 96

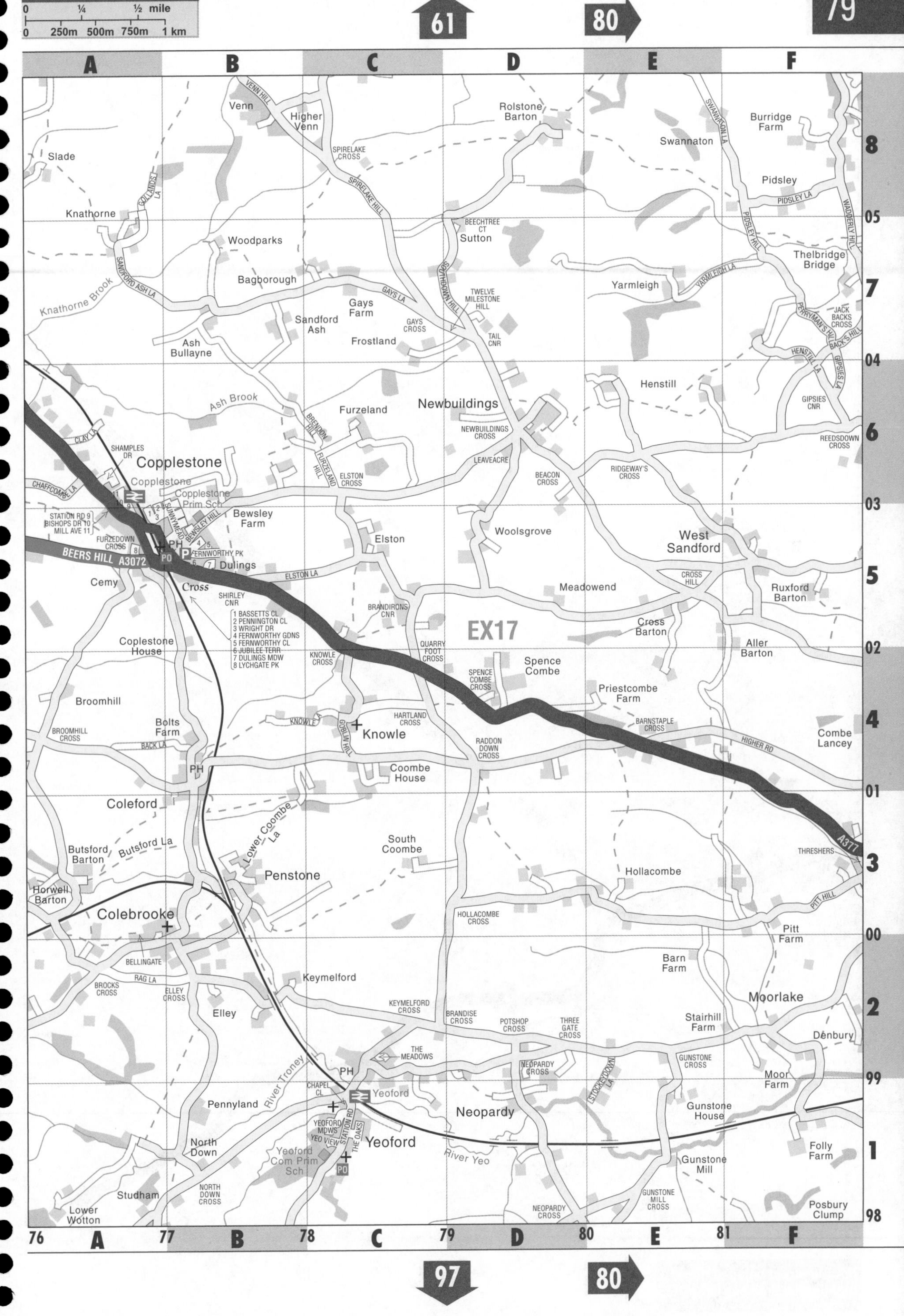
Scale: 1¾ inches to 1 mile
61
80
Copplestone
Venn
Higher Venn
Slade
Knathorne
Woodparks
Bagborough
Sandford Ash
Gays Farm
Frostland
Ash Bullayne
Rolstone Barton
Swannaton
Burridge Farm
Pidsley
Sutton
Yarmleigh
Thelbridge Bridge
Henstill
Newbuildings
Furzeland
Elston
Woolsgrove
West Sandford
Bewsley Farm
Dulings
Cemy
Cross
Meadowend
Ruxford Barton
EX17
Cross Barton
Aller Barton
Coplestone House
Spence Combe
Priestcombe Farm
Broomhill
Bolts Farm
Knowle
Coombe House
Combe Lancey
Coleford
South Coombe
Butsford Barton
Penstone
Hollacombe
Horwell Barton
Colebrooke
Pitt Farm
Barn Farm
Keymelford
Moorlake
Elley
Stairhill Farm
Denbury
Moor Farm
Pennyland
Yeoford
Neopardy
Gunstone House
North Down
Folly Farm
Gunstone Mill
Studham
Lower Wotton
Posbury Clump
River Yeo
River Troney
97
80

79
62

Scale: 1¾ inches to 1 mile
0 ¼ ½ mile
0 250m 500m 750m 1 km

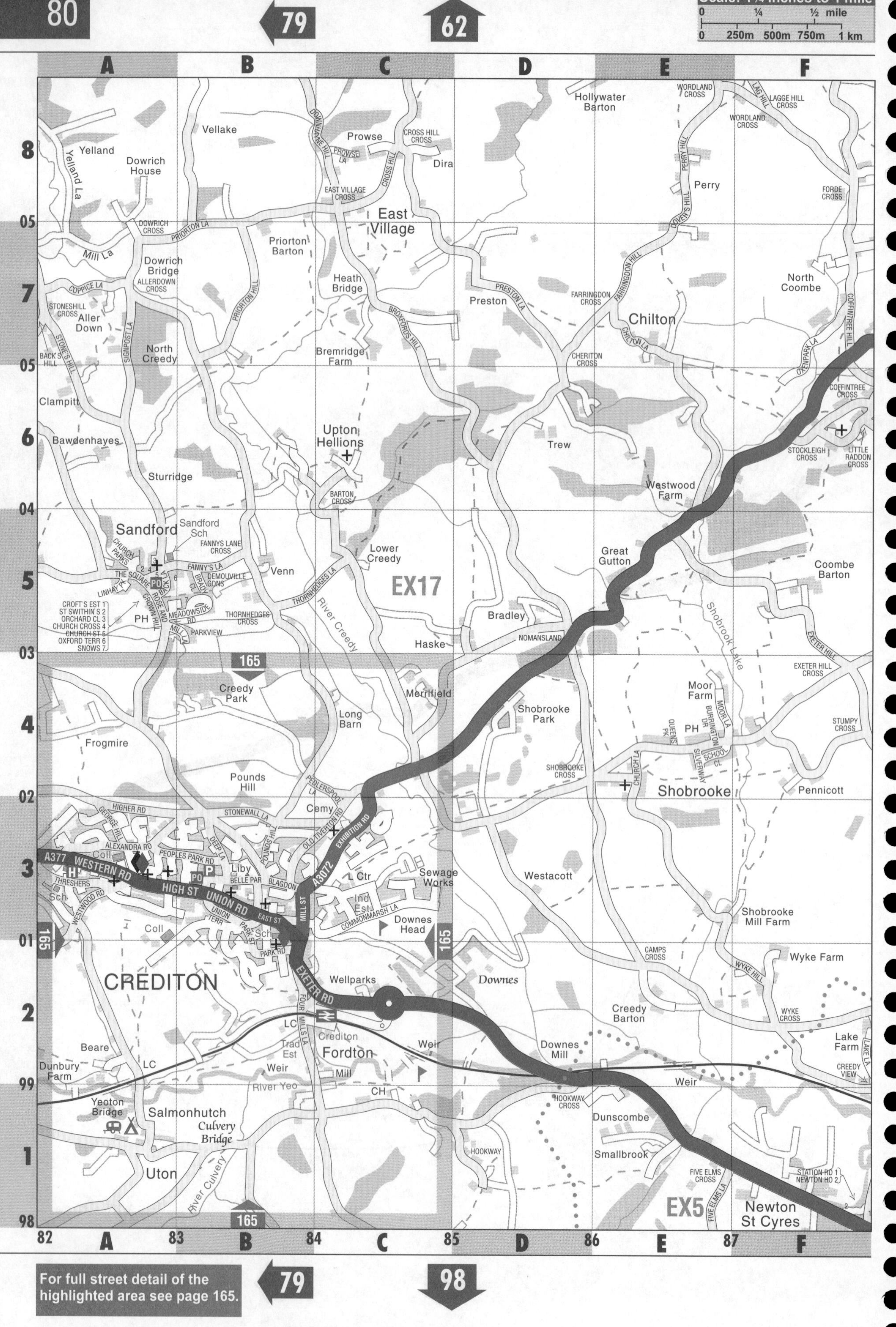

For full street detail of the highlighted area see page 165.
79
98

Scale: 1¾ inches to 1 mile

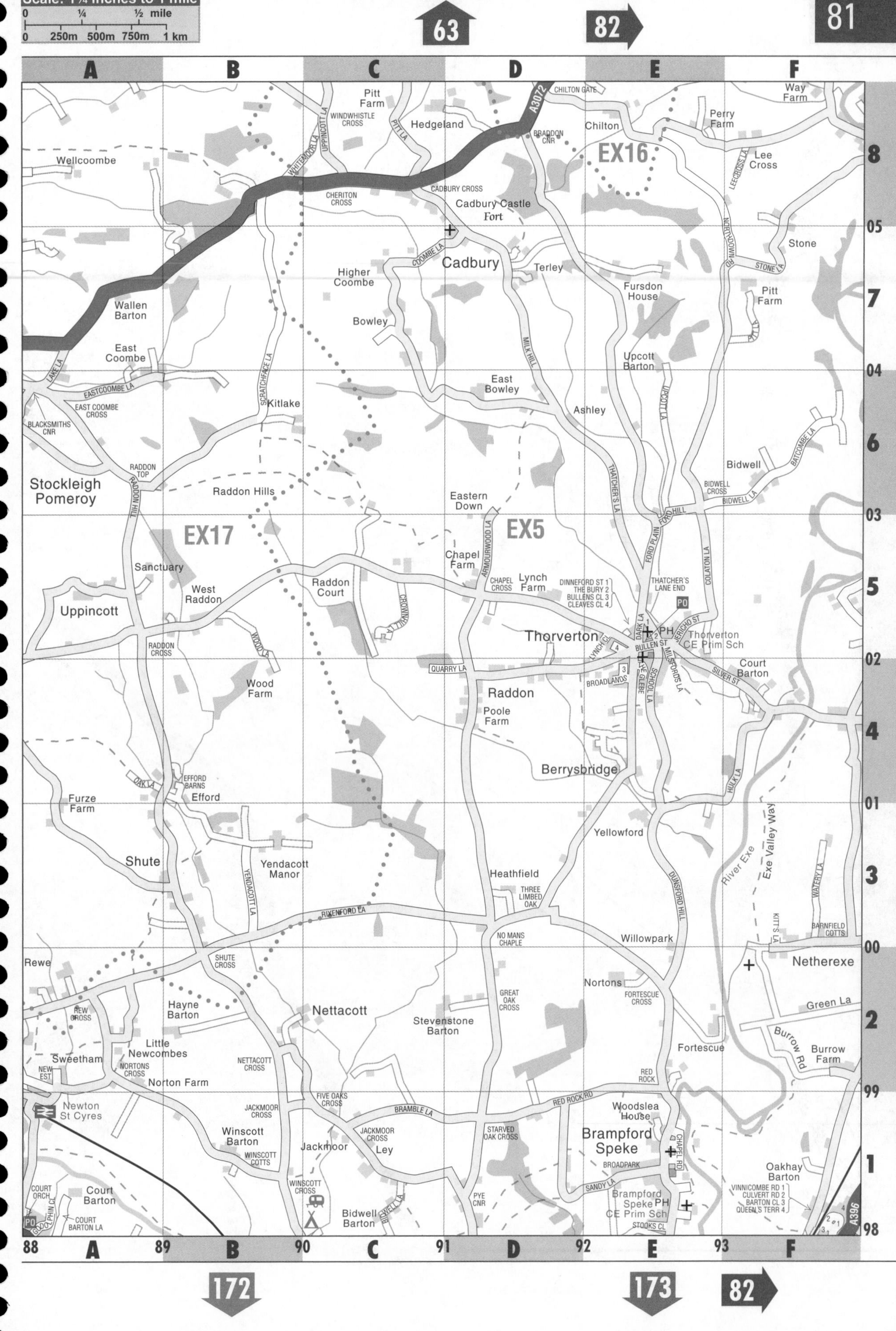

81
64

Scale: 1¾ inches to 1 mile
0 ¼ ½ mile
0 250m 500m 750m 1 km

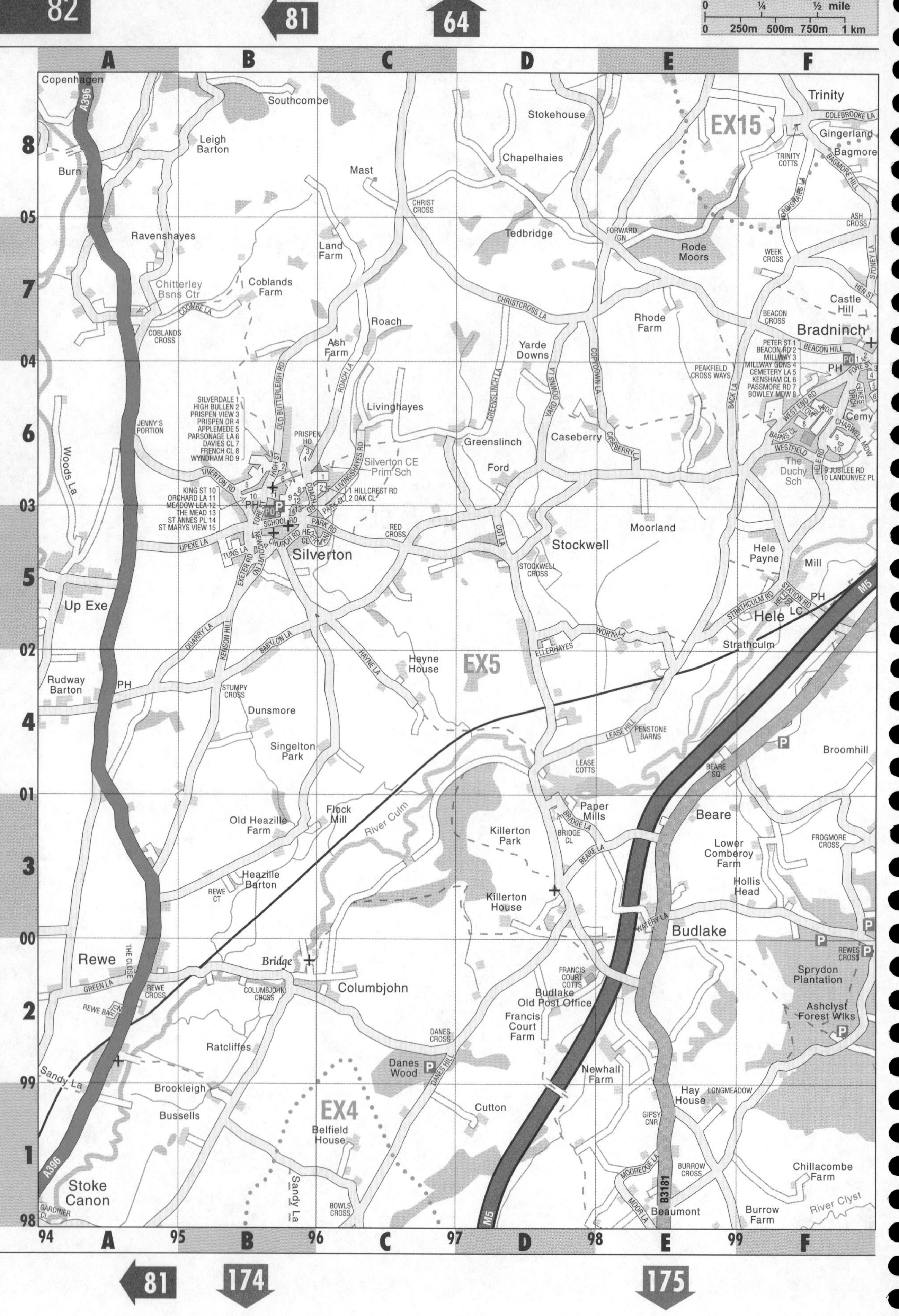

81
174
175

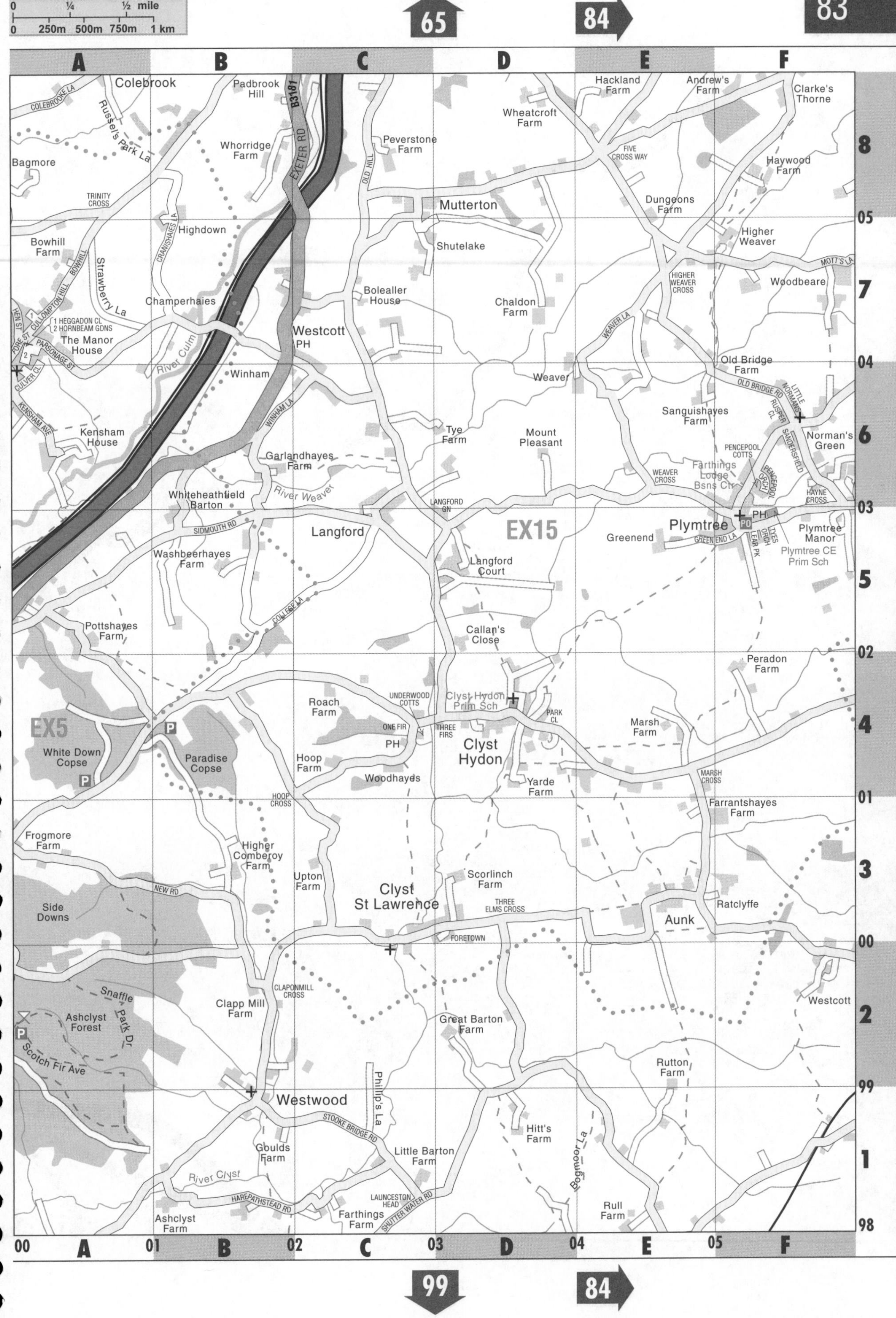
Scale: 1¾ inches to 1 mile
0 ¼ ½ mile
0 250m 500m 750m 1 km
65
84
A B C D E F
Colebrook
Padbrook Hill
B3181
Hackland Farm
Andrew's Farm
Clarke's Thorne
Wheatcroft Farm
Russel's Park La
Whorridge Farm
EXETER RD
Peverstone Farm
FIVE CROSS WAY
Haywood Farm
Bagmore
OLD HILL
TRINITY CROSS
Mutterton
Dungeons Farm
Highdown
CRANISHAIES LA
Higher Weaver
Bowhill Farm
Shutelake
BOWHILL
CULLOMPTON HILL
Strawberry La
HIGHER WEAVER CROSS
Woodbeare
MOTT'S LA
Champerhaies
Bolealler House
Chaldon Farm
HEN ST
FORE ST
1 HEGGADON CL
2 HORNBEAM GDNS
PARSONAGE ST
The Manor House
Westcott
PH
WEAVER LA
River Culm
Old Bridge Farm
CULVER CL
Winham
Weaver
OLD BRIDGE RD
LITTLE NORMANS
RUSPER CL
WINHAM LA
KENSHAM AVE
Kensham House
Tye Farm
Mount Pleasant
Sanguishayes Farm
SANDERSFIELD
Norman's Green
Garlandhayes Farm
PENCEPOOL COTTS
Farthings Lodge Bsns Ctr
WEAVER CROSS
PENCEPOOL ORCH
River Weaver
HAYNE CROSS
Whiteheathfield Barton
LANGFORD GN
SIDMOUTH RD
Langford
EX15
Plymtree
PH
PO
Greenend
GREEN END LA
LEAR PK
DYES ORCH
Plymtree Manor
Plymtree CE Prim Sch
Washbeerhayes Farm
Langford Court
COLLEGE LA
Pottshayes Farm
Callan's Close
Peradon Farm
Roach Farm
UNDERWOOD COTTS
Clyst Hydon Prim Sch
PARK CL
EX5
ONE FIR
THREE FIRS
Marsh Farm
White Down Copse
Paradise Copse
PH
Clyst Hydon
Hoop Farm
Woodhayes
Yarde Farm
MARSH CROSS
HOOP CROSS
Farrantshayes Farm
Frogmore Farm
Higher Comberoy Farm
NEW RD
Scorlinch Farm
Upton Farm
Clyst St Lawrence
THREE ELMS CROSS
Ratclyffe
Side Downs
Aunk
FORETOWN
CLAPONMILL CROSS
Snaffle Park Dr
Westcott
Clapp Mill Farm
Ashclyst Forest
Great Barton Farm
Scotch Fir Ave
Rutton Farm
Phillip's La
Westwood
STOOKE BRIDGE RD
Hitt's Farm
Goulds Farm
Little Barton Farm
Bogmoor La
River Clyst
HAREPATHSTEAD RD
LAUNCESTON HEAD
SHUTTER WATER RD
Farthings Farm
Rull Farm
Ashclyst Farm
8
05
7
04
6
03
5
02
4
01
3
00
2
99
1
98
00 01 02 03 04 05
99
84

83
66

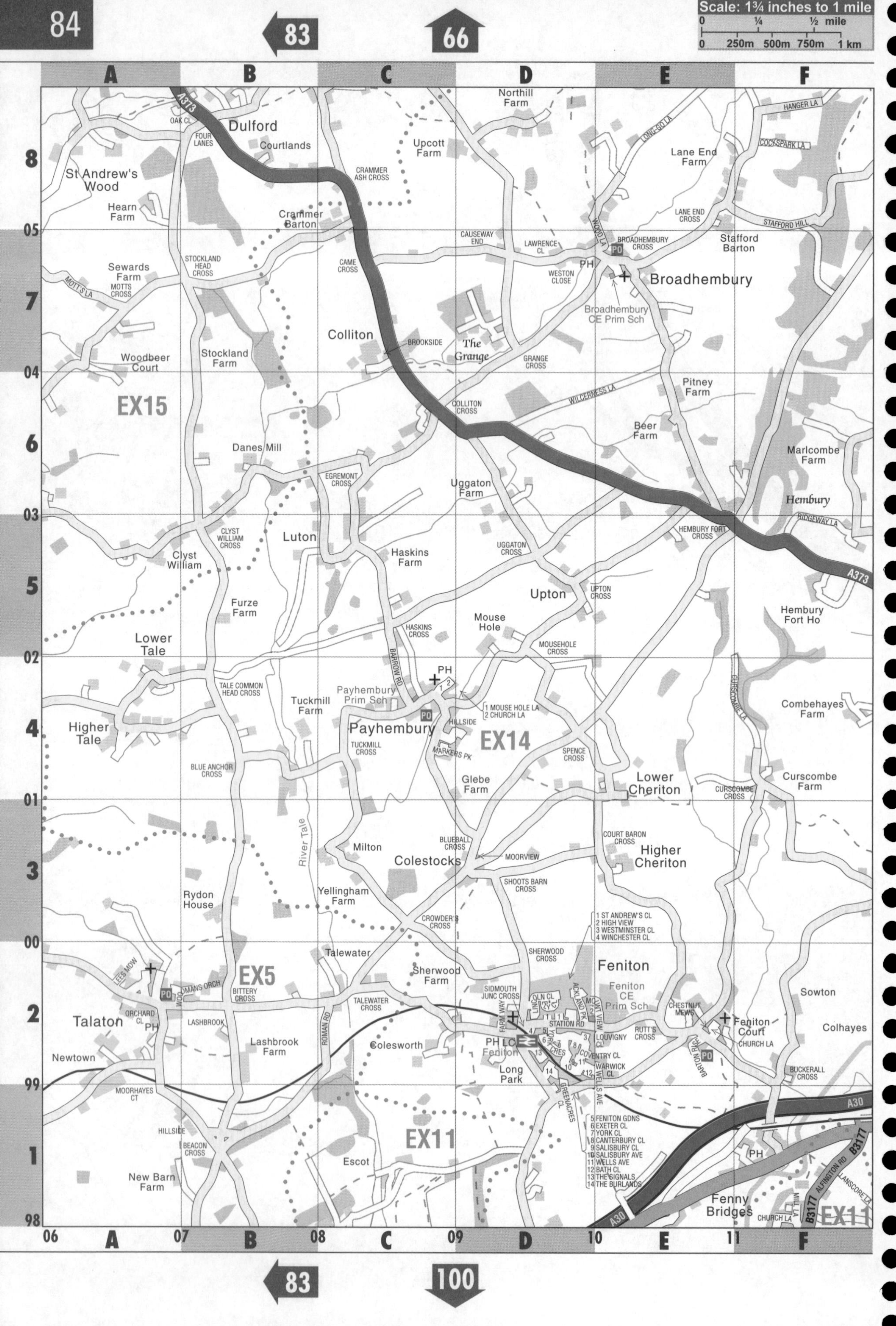
Scale: 1¾ inches to 1 mile
0 ¼ ½ mile
0 250m 500m 750m 1 km
A B C D E F
8
05
7
04
6
03
5
02
4
01
3
00
2
99
1
98
06 07 08 09 10 11
Dulford
Courtlands
St Andrew's Wood
Hearn Farm
Crammer Barton
Sewards Farm
Woodbeer Court
Stockland Farm
EX15
Danes Mill
Luton
Clyst William
Furze Farm
Lower Tale
Higher Tale
Tuckmill Farm
Payhembury
Payhembury Prim Sch
Milton
Colestocks
Rydon House
Yellingham Farm
Talewater
Sherwood Farm
EX5
Talaton
Newtown
Lashbrook Farm
Colesworth
New Barn Farm
Escot
EX11
Upcott Farm
Northill Farm
Colliton
The Grange
Uggaton Farm
Haskins Farm
Upton
Mouse Hole
EX14
Glebe Farm
Lower Cheriton
Higher Cheriton
Feniton
Feniton CE Prim Sch
Long Park
Lane End Farm
Broadhembury
Broadhembury CE Prim Sch
Stafford Barton
Pitney Farm
Beer Farm
Marlcombe Farm
Hembury
Hembury Fort Ho
Combehayes Farm
Curscombe Farm
Sowton
Colhayes
Feniton Court
Fenny Bridges
A373
A30
B3177
River Tale
1 MOUSE HOLE LA
2 CHURCH LA
1 ST ANDREW'S CL
2 HIGH VIEW
3 WESTMINSTER CL
4 WINCHESTER CL
5 FENITON GDNS
6 EXETER CL
7 YORK CL
8 CANTERBURY CL
9 SALISBURY CL
10 SALISBURY AVE
11 WELLS AVE
12 BATH CL
13 THE SIGNALS
14 THE BURLANDS

83
100

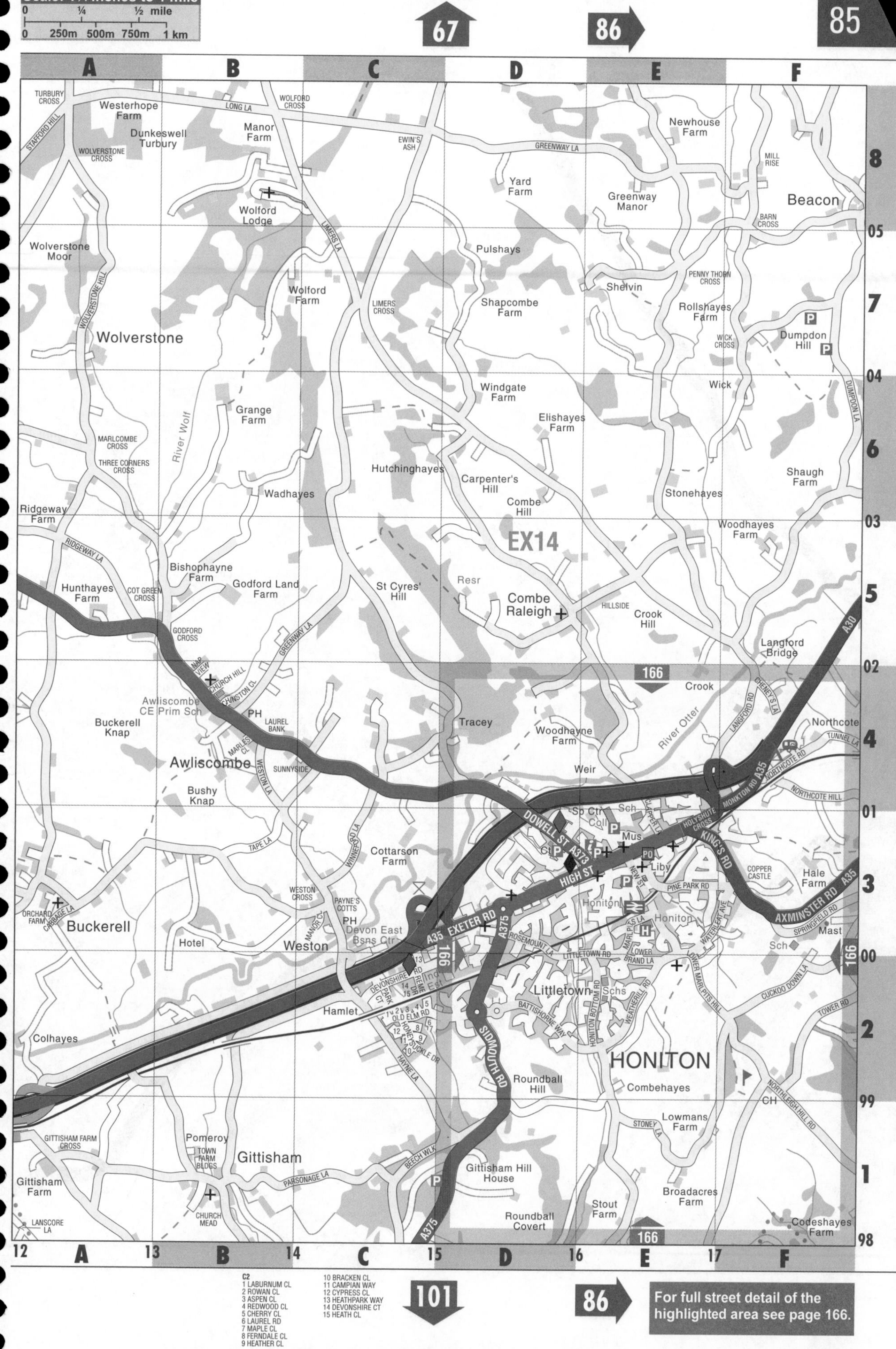
Scale: 1¾ inches to 1 mile
0 ¼ ½ mile
0 250m 500m 750m 1 km
67
86
A B C D E F
8 05 7 04 6 03 5 02 4 01 3 00 2 99 1 98
12 13 14 15 16 17
TURBURY CROSS
STAFFORD HILL
Westerhope Farm
Dunkeswell Turbury
WOLVERSTONE CROSS
LONG LA
WOLFORD CROSS
Manor Farm
EWIN'S ASH
GREENWAY LA
Newhouse Farm
MILL RISE
Beacon
BARN CROSS
Yard Farm
Greenway Manor
Wolford Lodge
LIMERS LA
Wolverstone Moor
Pulshays
Wolford Farm
LIMERS CROSS
Shelvin
PENNY THORN CROSS
Rollshayes Farm
Shapcombe Farm
WOLVERSTONE HILL
Wolverstone
WICK CROSS
Dumpdon Hill
Wick
DUMPDON LA
Windgate Farm
Grange Farm
Elishayes Farm
River Wolf
MARLCOMBE CROSS
THREE CORNERS CROSS
Hutchinghayes
Carpenter's Hill
Combe Hill
Shaugh Farm
Wadhayes
Stonehayes
Ridgeway Farm
Woodhayes Farm
RIDGEWAY LA
EX14
Bishophayne Farm
Godford Land Farm
St Cyres' Hill
Resr
Hunthayes Farm
COT GREEN CROSS
Combe Raleigh
HILLSIDE
Crook Hill
GODFORD CROSS
GREENWAY LA
Langford Bridge
A30
NAP VIEW
CHURCH HILL
166
Crook
Awliscombe CE Prim Sch
PH
LAUREL BANK
LANGFORD RD
CHENEY'S LA
Buckerell Knap
Tracey
Woodhayne Farm
River Otter
Northcote
TUNNEL LA
MARLES CL
SUNNYSIDE
WESTON LA
Awliscombe
Weir
NORTHCOTE RD
A35
Bushy Knap
NORTHCOTE HILL
MONKTON RD
DOWELL ST
Sp Ctr
Coll
Sch
HOLYSHUTE CROSS
TAPE LA
WINNERS RD LA
A373
Mus
KING'S RD
Cottarson Farm
PO
HIGH ST
Liby
COPPER CASTLE
Hale Farm
Buckerell
WESTON CROSS
NEW ST
PINE PARK RD
ORCHARD FARM
CABBAGE LA
PAYNE'S COTTS
Honiton
AXMINSTER RD
Hotel
Weston
Devon East Bsns Ctr
EXETER RD
A375
ROSEMOUNT LA
MARLPITS LA
SPRINGFIELD RD
Mast
Sch
LITTLETOWN RD
LOWER BRAND LA
WATERLEAT AVE
DEVONSHIRE RD
Ind Est
Littletown
Schs
CUCKOO DOWN LA
Hamlet
OLD ELM RD
BATTISHORNE WAY
HONITON BOTTOM RD
WEATHERILL RD
LOWER MARLPITS HILL
TOWER RD
Colhayes
HONEYSUCKLE DR
SIDMOUTH RD
HAYNE LA
HONITON
Roundball Hill
Combehayes
NORTHLEIGH HILL RD
CH
GITTISHAM FARM CROSS
Pomeroy
STONEY LA
Lowmans Farm
TOWN FARM BLDGS
Gittisham
BEECH WLK
Gittisham Hill House
Gittisham Farm
PARSONAGE LA
Broadacres Farm
Stout Farm
LANSCORE LA
CHURCH MEAD
Roundball Covert
Codeshayes Farm
C2
1 LABURNUM CL
2 ROWAN CL
3 ASPEN CL
4 REDWOOD CL
5 CHERRY CL
6 LAUREL RD
7 MAPLE CL
8 FERNDALE CL
9 HEATHER CL
10 BRACKEN CL
11 CAMPIAN WAY
12 CYPRESS CL
13 HEATHPARK WAY
14 DEVONSHIRE CT
15 HEATH CL
101
86
For full street detail of the highlighted area see page 166.

Scale: 1¾ inches to 1 mile

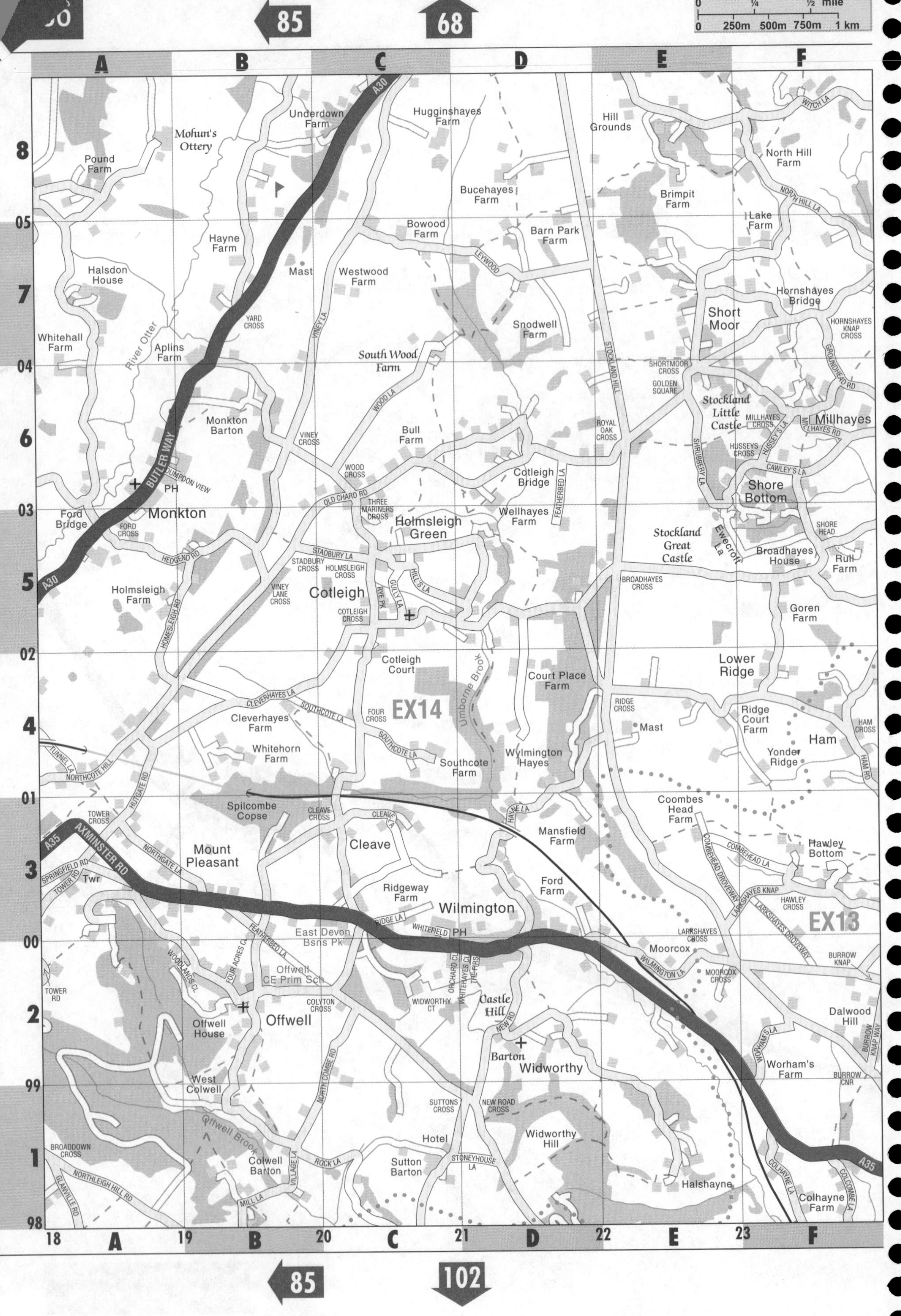

Scale: 1¾ inches to 1 mile
0 ¼ ½ mile
0 250m 500m 750m 1 km

69
88

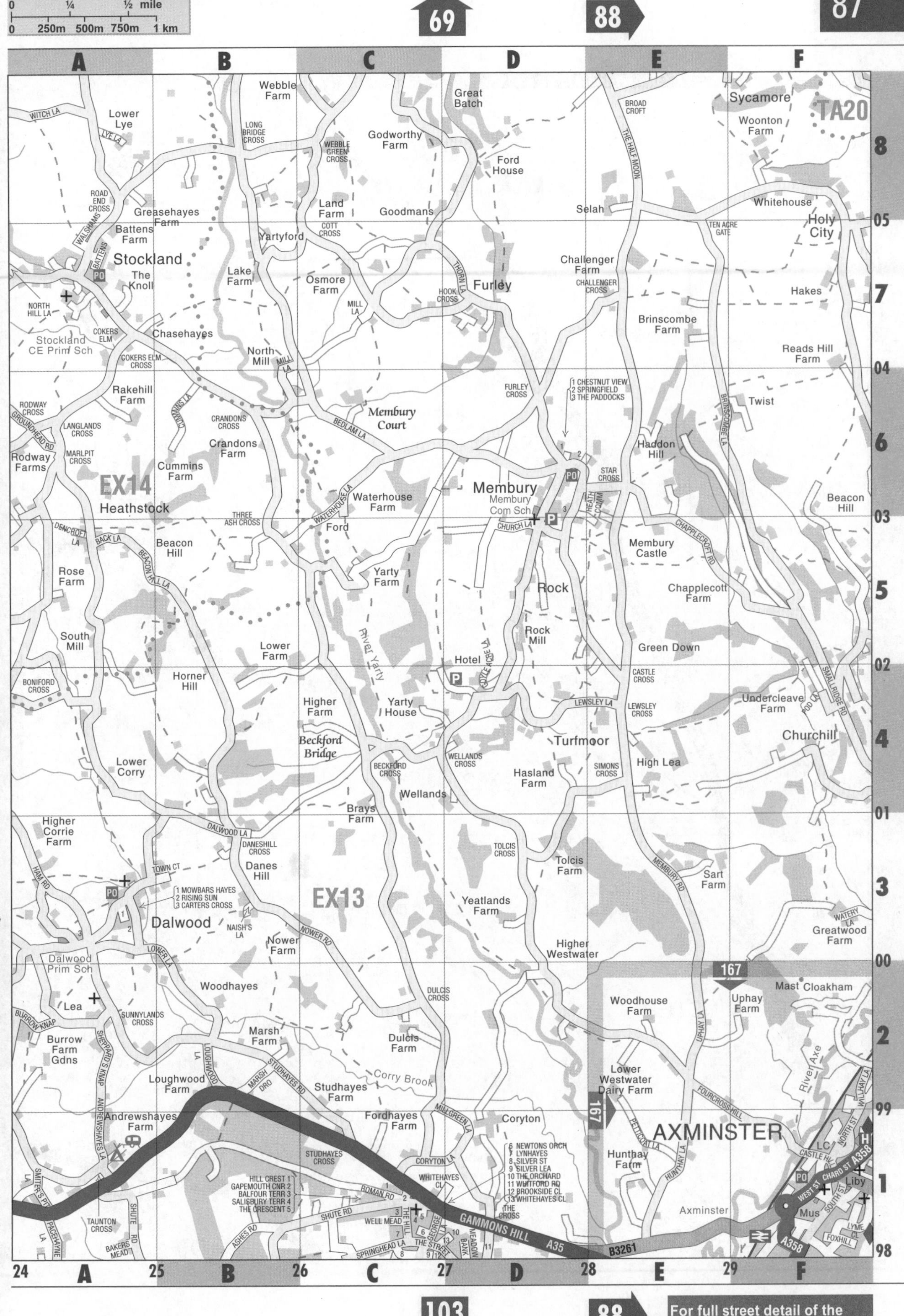

103
88
For full street detail of the highlighted area see page 167.

87

Scale: 1¾ inches to 1 mile

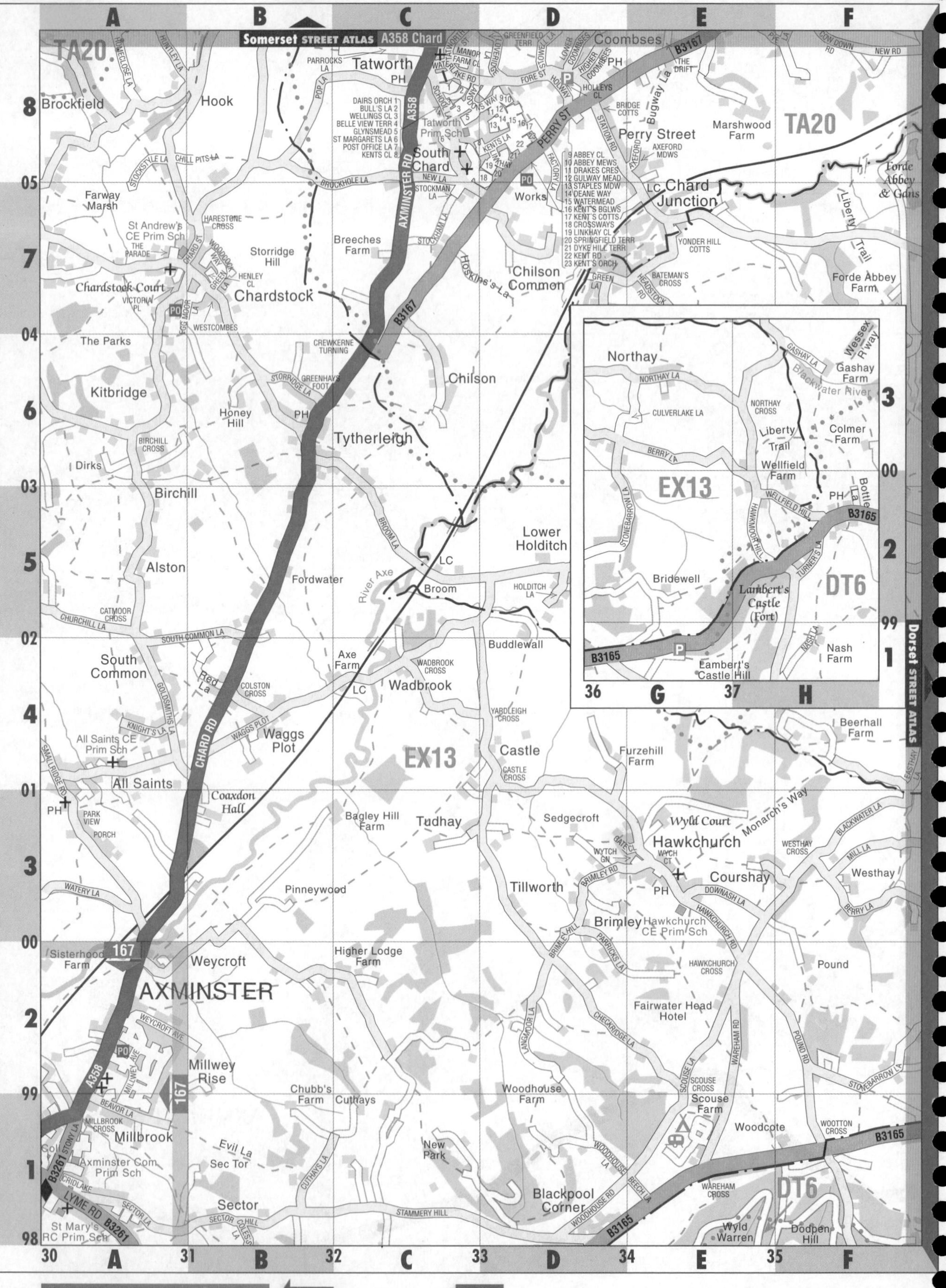

For full street detail of the highlighted area see page 167.

87

104

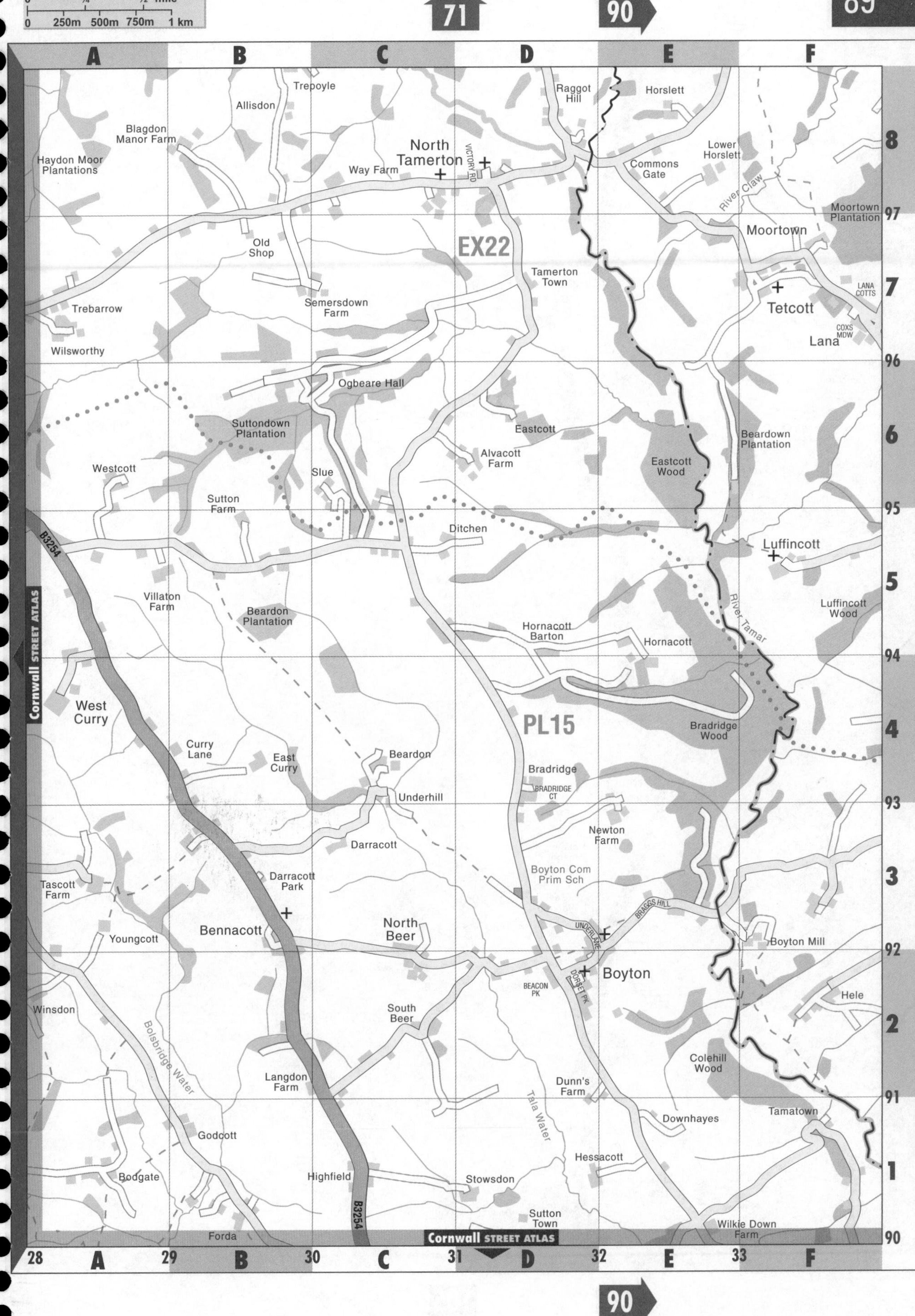
Scale: 1¾ inches to 1 mile
0 ¼ ½ mile
0 250m 500m 750m 1 km
71
90
A B C D E F
Trepoyle
Allisdon
Raggot Hill
Horslett
Blagdon Manor Farm
North Tamerton
VICTORY RD
Haydon Moor Plantations
Way Farm
Commons Gate
Lower Horslett
River Claw
Moortown Plantation
Moortown
Old Shop
EX22
Tamerton Town
Trebarrow
Semersdown Farm
Tetcott
LANA COTTS
COXS MDW
Lana
Wilsworthy
Ogbeare Hall
Suttondown Plantation
Eastcott
Beardown Plantation
Alvacott Farm
Eastcott Wood
Westcott
Slue
Sutton Farm
Ditchen
Luffincott
B3254
Villaton Farm
Beardon Plantation
Luffincott Wood
Hornacott Barton
Hornacott
River Tamar
Cornwall STREET ATLAS
West Curry
PL15
Bradridge Wood
Curry Lane
East Curry
Beardon
Bradridge
BRADRIDGE CT
Underhill
Newton Farm
Darracott
Boyton Com Prim Sch
Tascott Farm
Darracott Park
BRIGGS HILL
UNDERLANE
Bennacott
North Beer
Youngcott
Boyton Mill
Boyton
DORSET PK
BEACON PK
Hele
Winsdon
South Beer
Bolsbridge Water
Colehill Wood
Langdon Farm
Dunn's Farm
Tala Water
Downhayes
Tamatown
Godcott
Hessacott
Bodgate
Highfield
Stowsdon
Sutton Town
Wilkie Down Farm
Forda
98 8 97 7 96 6 95 5 94 4 93 3 92 2 91 1 90
28 29 30 31 32 33

90

89 72

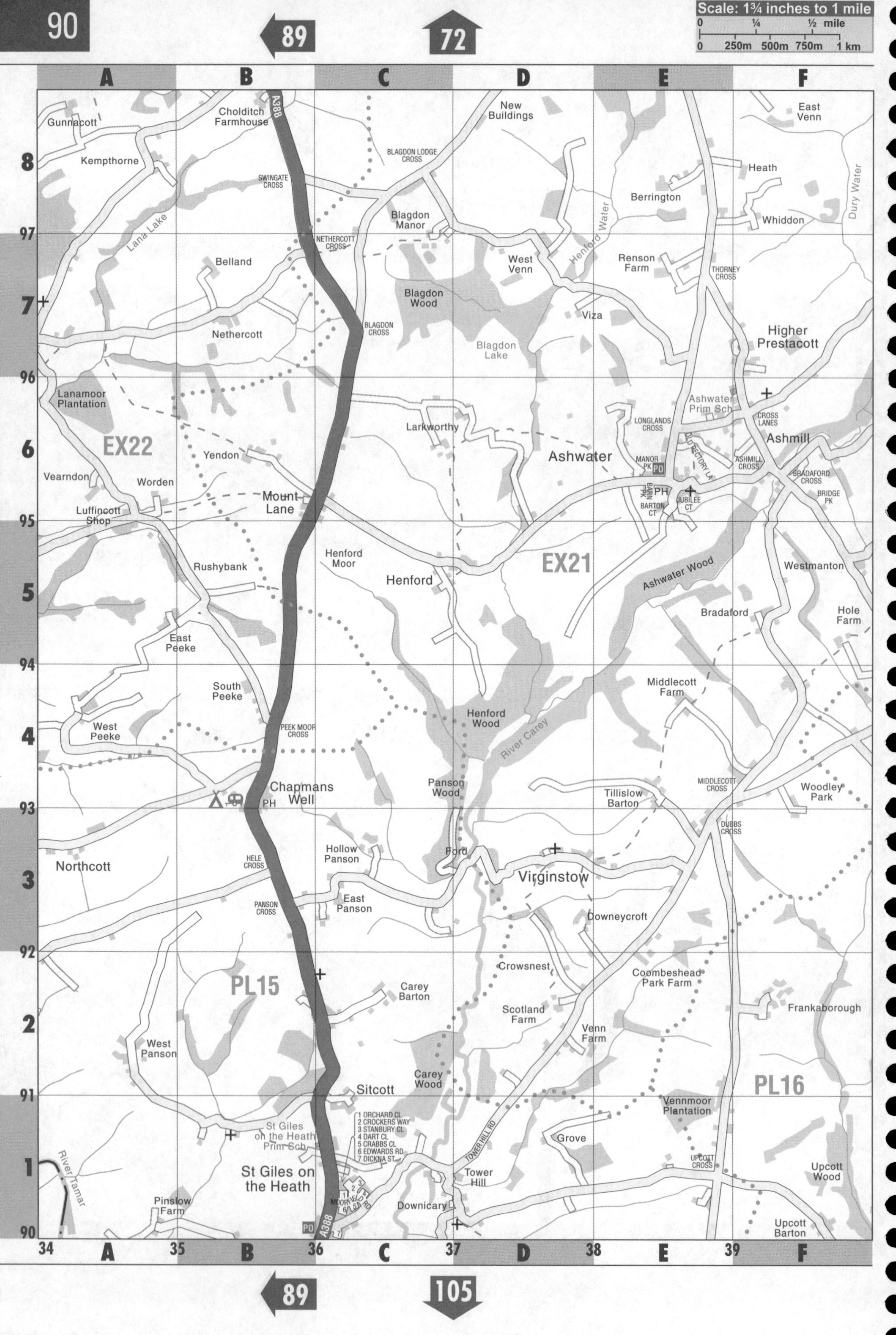
Scale: 1¾ inches to 1 mile
0 ¼ ½ mile
0 250m 500m 750m 1 km
A B C D E F
Gunnacott
Choldlitch Farmhouse
A388
New Buildings
East Venn
Kempthorne
BLAGDON LODGE CROSS
SWINGATE CROSS
Heath
Berrington
Blagdon Manor
Dury Water
Whiddon
Lana Lake
NETHERCOTT CROSS
Henford Water
West Venn
Renson Farm
Belland
THORNEY CROSS
Blagdon Wood
BLAGDON CROSS
Viza
Nethercott
Higher Prestacott
Blagdon Lake
Lanamoor Plantation
Ashwater Prim Sch
LONGLANDS CROSS
CROSS LANES
Larkworthy
Ashmill
EX22
Ashwater
Yendon
MANOR PK
PO
OLD RECTORY LA
ASHMILL CROSS
BRADAFORD CROSS
Vearndon
Worden
BARN PK
PH
Mount Lane
JUBILEE CT
BRIDGE PK
Luffincott Shop
BARTON CT
Henford Moor
EX21
Westmanton
Rushybank
Henford
Ashwater Wood
Bradaford
Hole Farm
East Peeke
Middlecott Farm
South Peeke
Henford Wood
West Peeke
PEEK MOOR CROSS
River Carey
Panson Wood
Chapmans Well
PH
MIDDLECOTT CROSS
Tillislow Barton
Woodley Park
DUBBS CROSS
Northcott
HELE CROSS
Hollow Panson
Ford
Virginstow
PANSON CROSS
East Panson
Downeycroft
Crowsnest
PL15
Carey Barton
Coombeshead Park Farm
Scotland Farm
Frankaborough
Venn Farm
West Panson
Carey Wood
PL16
Sitcott
Vennmoor Plantation
1 ORCHARD CL
2 CROCKERS WAY
3 STANBURY CL
4 DART CL
5 CRABBS CL
6 EDWARDS RD
7 DICKNA ST
St Giles on the Heath Prim Sch
TOWER HILL RD
Grove
River Tamar
St Giles on the Heath
Tower Hill
UPCOTT CROSS
Upcott Wood
Pinslow Farm
MOORFIELD RD
Downicary
PO
A388
Upcott Barton
8 97 7 96 6 95 5 94 4 93 3 92 2 91 1 90
34 35 36 37 38 39

89 105

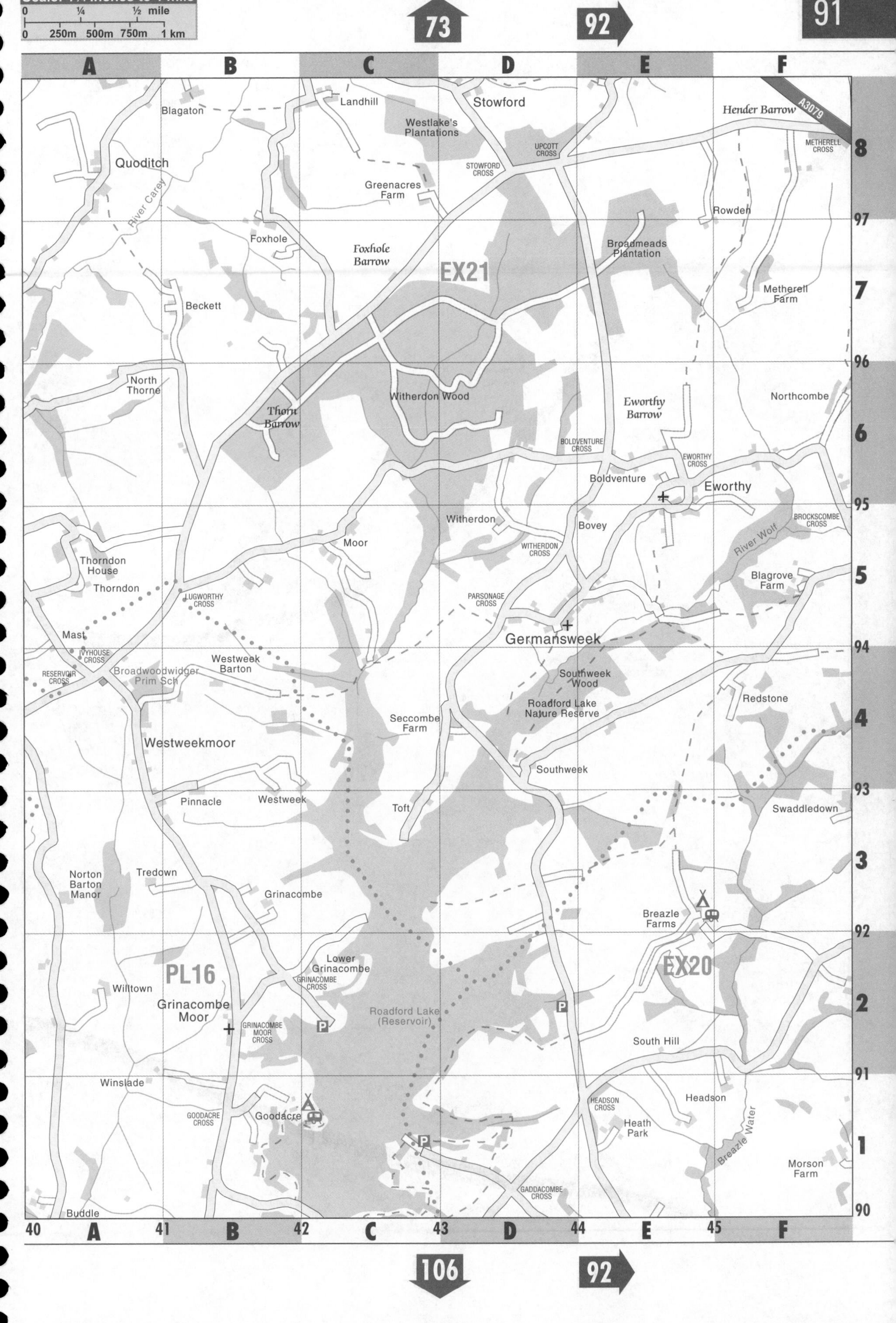
Scale: 1¾ inches to 1 mile
0 ¼ ½ mile
0 250m 500m 750m 1 km
73
92
A
B
C
D
E
F
Blagaton
Landhill
Stowford
Hender Barrow
A3079
Westlake's Plantations
UPCOTT CROSS
METHERELL CROSS
Quoditch
STOWFORD CROSS
Greenacres Farm
River Carey
Rowden
Foxhole
Foxhole Barrow
Broadmeads Plantation
EX21
Beckett
Metherell Farm
North Thorne
Witherdon Wood
Northcombe
Thorn Barrow
Eworthy Barrow
BOLDVENTURE CROSS
EWORTHY CROSS
Boldventure
Eworthy
Witherdon
Bovey
BROCKSCOMBE CROSS
Moor
WITHERDON CROSS
River Wolf
Thorndon House
Thorndon
Blagrove Farm
LUGWORTHY CROSS
PARSONAGE CROSS
Mast
Germansweek
IVYHOUSE CROSS
Westweek Barton
RESERVOIR CROSS
Broadwoodwidger Prim Sch
Southweek Wood
Redstone
Roadford Lake Nature Reserve
Seccombe Farm
Westweekmoor
Southweek
Pinnacle
Westweek
Toft
Swaddledown
Norton Barton Manor
Tredown
Grinacombe
Breazle Farms
Lower Grinacombe
PL16
GRINACOMBE CROSS
EX20
Willtown
Grinacombe Moor
Roadford Lake (Reservoir)
GRINACOMBE MOOR CROSS
South Hill
Winslade
Headson
HEADSON CROSS
GOODACRE CROSS
Goodacre
Heath Park
Breazle Water
Morson Farm
GADDACOMBE CROSS
Buddle
8
97
7
96
6
95
5
94
4
93
3
92
2
91
1
90
40
41
42
43
44
45
106
92

91
74

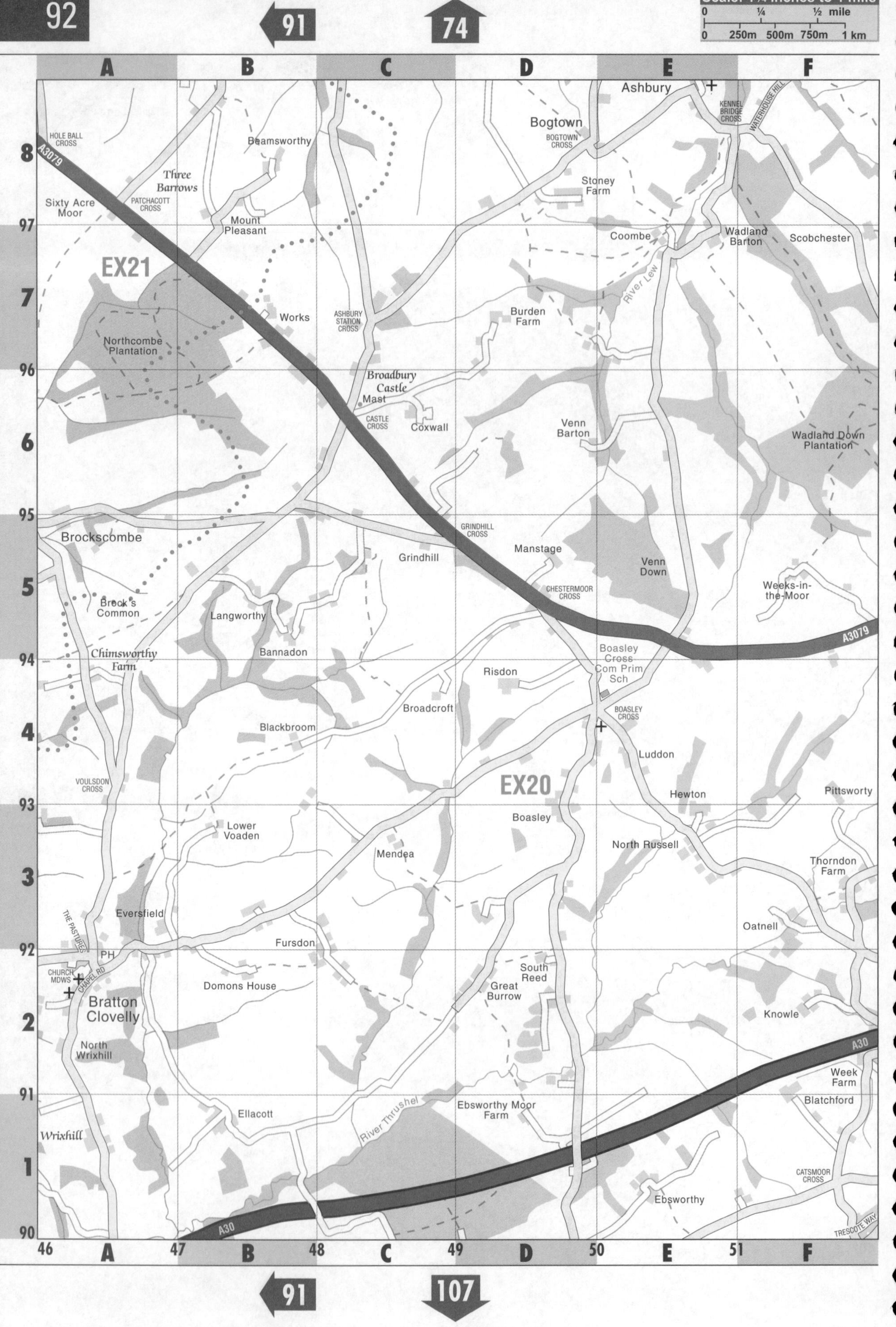
Scale: 1¾ inches to 1 mile
0 ¼ ½ mile
0 250m 500m 750m 1 km
Ashbury
Bogtown
Beamsworthy
Three Barrows
Sixty Acre Moor
Mount Pleasant
Stoney Farm
Coombe
Wadland Barton
Scobchester
EX21
Works
Burden Farm
Northcombe Plantation
Broadbury Castle
Mast
Coxwall
Venn Barton
Wadland Down Plantation
Brockscombe
Grindhill
Manstage
Venn Down
Weeks-in-the-Moor
Brock's Common
Langworthy
Chimsworthy Farm
Bannadon
Risdon
Boasley Cross Com Prim Sch
Broadcroft
Blackbroom
Luddon
EX20
Hewton
Pittsworty
Lower Voaden
Boasley
North Russell
Mendea
Thorndon Farm
Eversfield
Oatnell
Fursdon
PH
South Reed
Great Burrow
Domons House
Bratton Clovelly
Knowle
North Wrixhill
Week Farm
Ellacott
Ebsworthy Moor Farm
Blatchford
Wrixhill
River Thrushel
River Lew
Ebsworthy
A3079
A30
46 47 48 49 50 51
A B C D E F
8 97 7 96 6 95 5 94 4 93 3 92 2 91 1 90

91
107

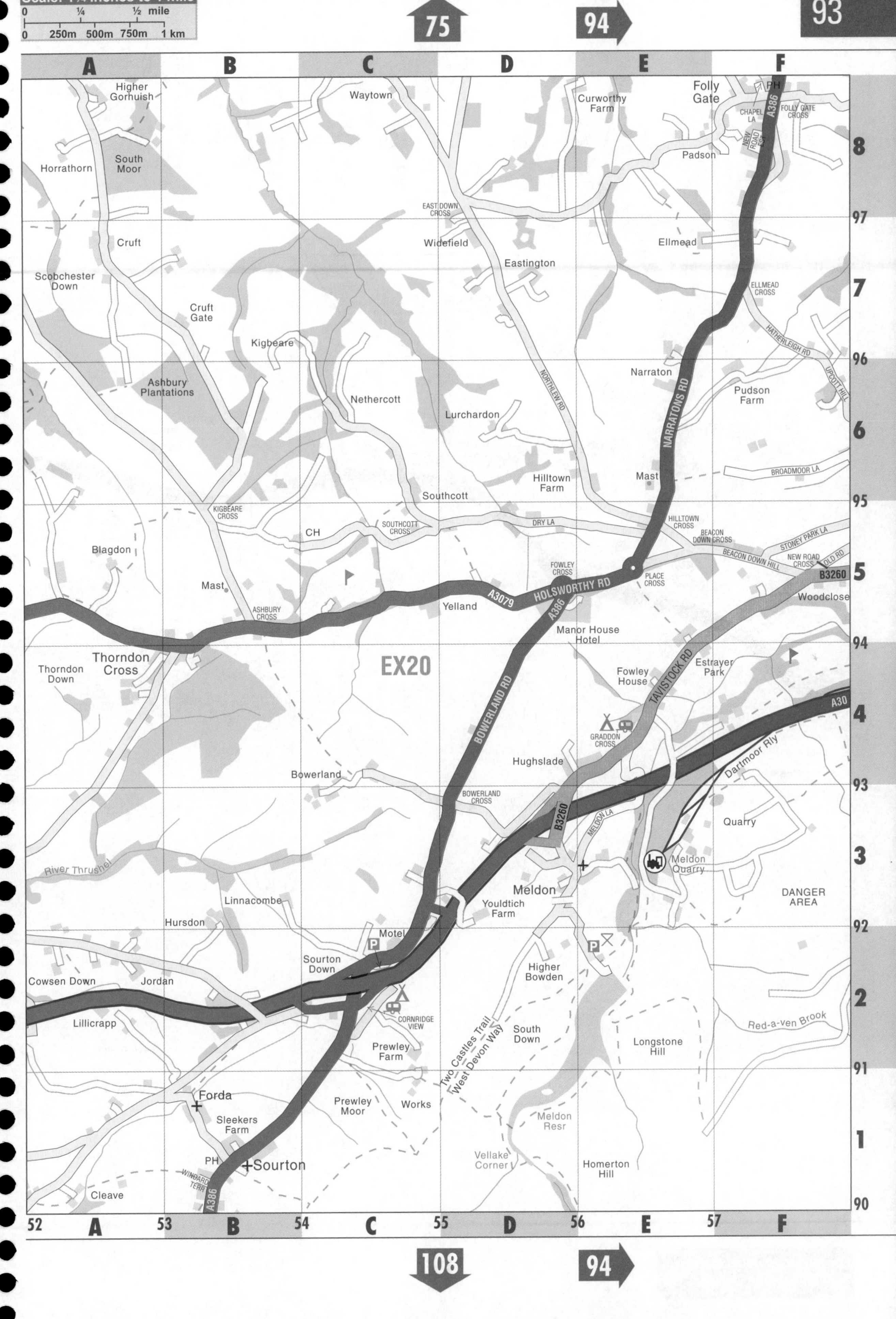
Scale: 1¾ inches to 1 mile
0 ¼ ½ mile
0 250m 500m 750m 1 km
75
94
A B C D E F
8 97 7 96 6 95 5 94 4 93 3 92 2 91 1 90
52 53 54 55 56 57
Higher Gorhuish
Waytown
Curworthy Farm
Folly Gate
PH
A386
CHAPEL LA
FOLLY GATE CROSS
NEW ROAD EST
Padson
Horrathorn
South Moor
EAST DOWN CROSS
Widefield
Ellmead
Cruft
Eastington
Scobchester Down
ELLMEAD CROSS
Cruft Gate
HATHERLEIGH RD
Kigbeare
Narraton
Ashbury Plantations
Nethercott
NORTHLEW RD
Pudson Farm
UPCOTT HILL
Lurchardon
NARRATONS RD
Mast
Hilltown Farm
BROADMOOR LA
Southcott
KIGBEARE CROSS
SOUTHCOTT CROSS
CH
DRY LA
HILLTOWN CROSS
BEACON DOWN CROSS
STONEY PARK LA
Blagdon
BEACON DOWN HILL
NEW ROAD CROSS
OLD RD
FOWLEY CROSS
PLACE CROSS
B3260
Mast
HOLSWORTHY RD
A3079
Yelland
Woodclose
ASHBURY CROSS
Manor House Hotel
Thorndon Cross
Thorndon Down
EX20
Fowley House
TAVISTOCK RD
Estrayer Park
BOWERLAND RD
A30
GRADDON CROSS
Hughslade
Dartmoor Rly
Bowerland
BOWERLAND CROSS
Quarry
MELDON LA
River Thrushel
Meldon Quarry
DANGER AREA
Meldon
Youldtich Farm
Linnacombe
Hursdon
Motel
Sourton Down
Higher Bowden
Cowsen Down
Jordan
CORNRIDGE VIEW
Lillicrapp
South Down
Red-a-ven Brook
Longstone Hill
Prewley Farm
Two Castles Trail
West Devon Way
Forda
Prewley Moor
Works
Sleekers Farm
Meldon Resr
Vellake Corner
Homerton Hill
PH
Sourton
WINDARD TERR
Cleave
108
94

93
76

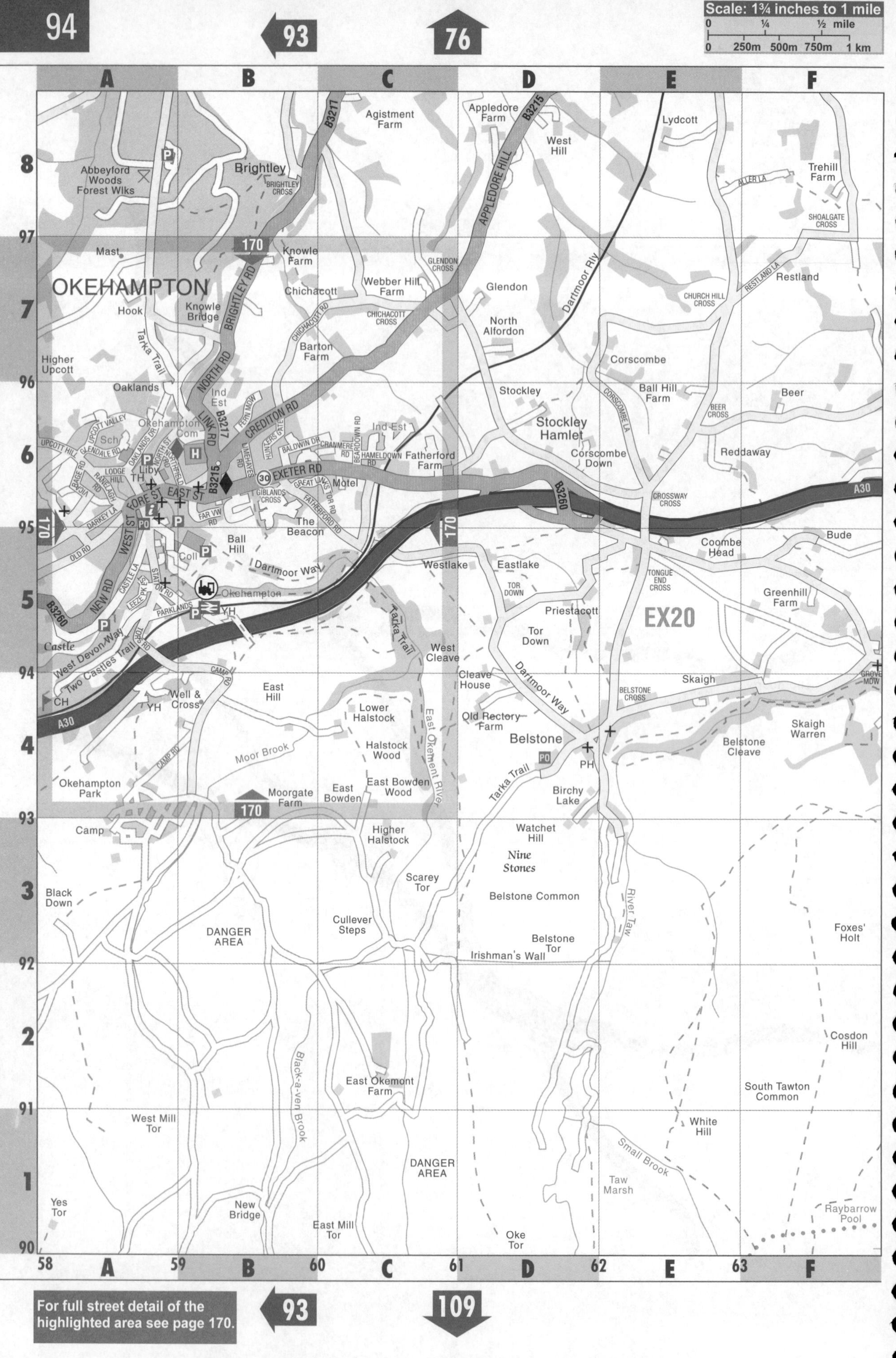

For full street detail of the highlighted area see page 170.
93
109

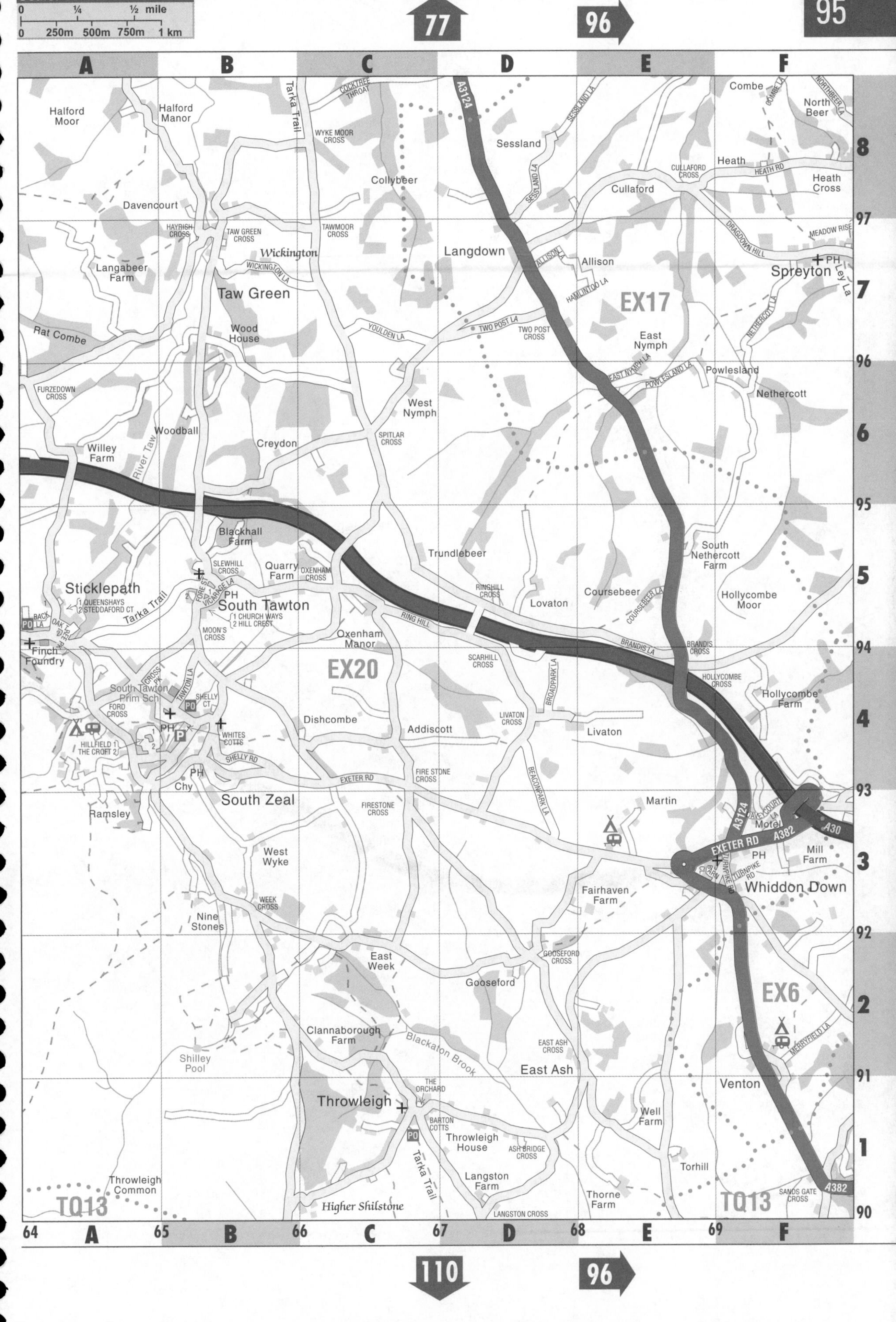
Scale: 1¾ inches to 1 mile
77
96
110
96
EX17
EX20
EX6
TQ13
TQ13
South Tawton
South Zeal
Sticklepath
Taw Green
Spreyton
Whiddon Down
Throwleigh
Halford Moor
Halford Manor
Davencourt
Langabeer Farm
Rat Combe
Willey Farm
Woodball
Creydon
Wood House
Collybeer
Langdown
Sessland
Cullaford
Heath
Heath Cross
Combe
North Beer
Allison
East Nymph
Powlesland
Nethercott
West Nymph
Trundlebeer
Coursebeer
Lovaton
South Nethercott Farm
Hollycombe Moor
Hollycombe Farm
Blackhall Farm
Quarry Farm
Oxenham Manor
Dishcombe
Addiscott
Livaton
Martin
Motel
Mill Farm
Fairhaven Farm
Finch Foundry
Ramsley
Chy
West Wyke
Nine Stones
East Week
Gooseford
Clannaborough Farm
Shilley Pool
East Ash
Well Farm
Torhill
Venton
Throwleigh House
Langston Farm
Thorne Farm
Throwleigh Common
Higher Shilstone
Tarka Trail
River Taw
Blackaton Brook
A3124
A382
A30
Wickington
South Tawton Prim Sch

95
78

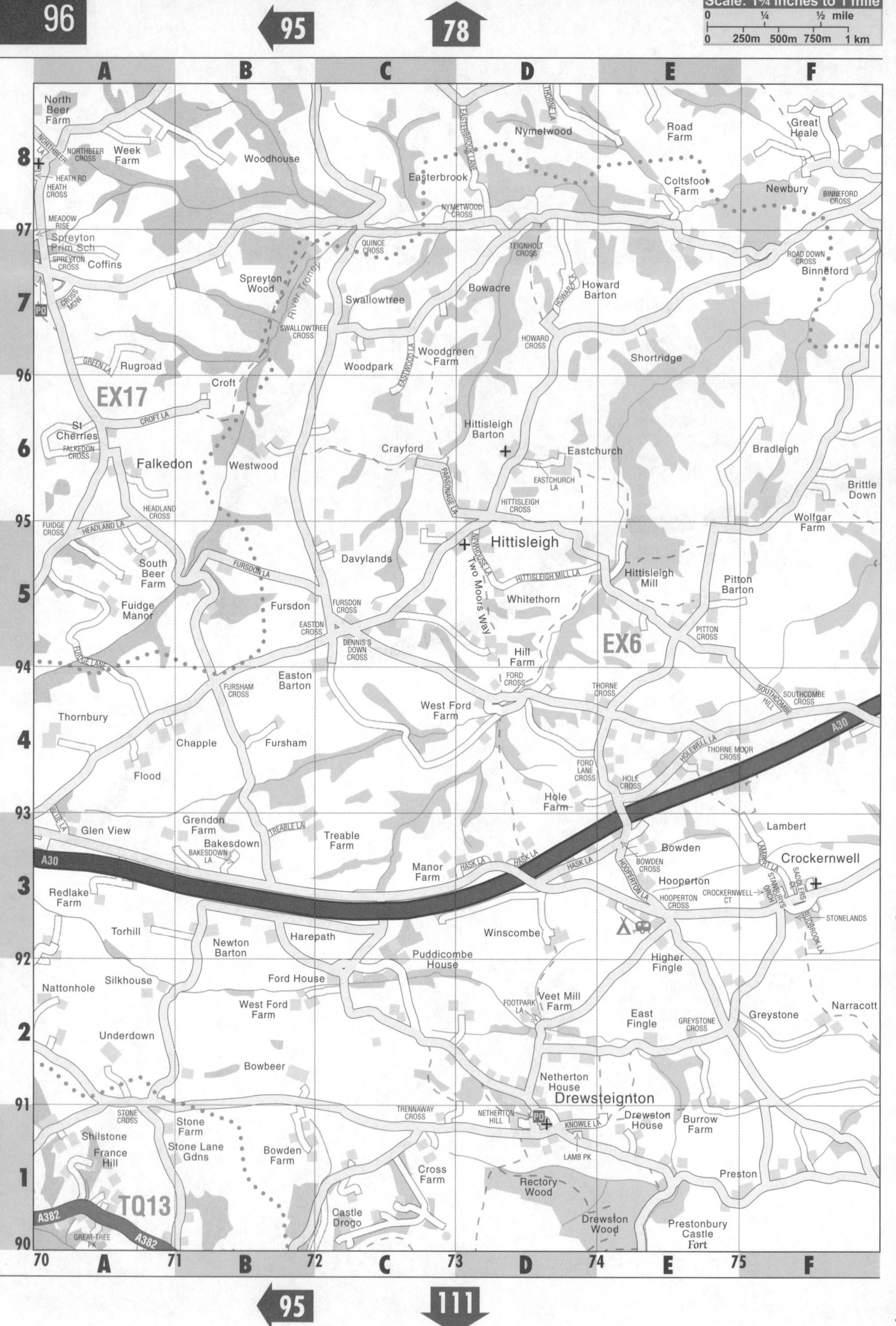
Scale: 1¾ inches to 1 mile
0 ¼ ½ mile
0 250m 500m 750m 1 km
A B C D E F
North Beer Farm
Week Farm
Woodhouse
Easterbrook
Nymetwood
Road Farm
Great Heale
Coltsfoot Farm
Newbury
BINNEFORD CROSS
Spreyton Prim Sch
Coffins
Spreyton Wood
River Troney
Swallowtree
Bowacre
Howard Barton
Binneford
Woodgreen Farm
Woodpark
Shortridge
Rugroad
Croft
EX17
St Cherries
Falkedon
Westwood
Crayford
Hittisleigh Barton
Eastchurch
Bradleigh
Brittle Down
Wolfgar Farm
Hittisleigh
Two Moors Way
South Beer Farm
Davylands
Hittisleigh Mill
Pitton Barton
Fuidge Manor
Fursdon
Whitethorn
EX6
Hill Farm
Easton Barton
Thornbury
West Ford Farm
Chapple
Fursham
Flood
Hole Farm
A30
Glen View
Grendon Farm
Bakesdown
Treable Farm
Lambert
Bowden
Crockernwell
Manor Farm
Hooperton
Redlake Farm
Torhill
Newton Barton
Harepath
Winscombe
Higher Fingle
Puddicombe House
Nattonhole
Silkhouse
Ford House
Veet Mill Farm
Narracott
West Ford Farm
East Fingle
Greystone
Underdown
Bowbeer
Netherton House
Drewsteignton
Drewston House
Burrow Farm
Shilstone
Stone Farm
Stone Lane Gdns
France Hill
Bowden Farm
Cross Farm
Preston
Rectory Wood
TQ13
Castle Drogo
Drewston Wood
Prestonbury Castle Fort
A382
GREAT TREE PK
70 71 72 73 74 75
90 1 91 2 92 3 93 4 94 5 95 6 96 7 97 8

95
111

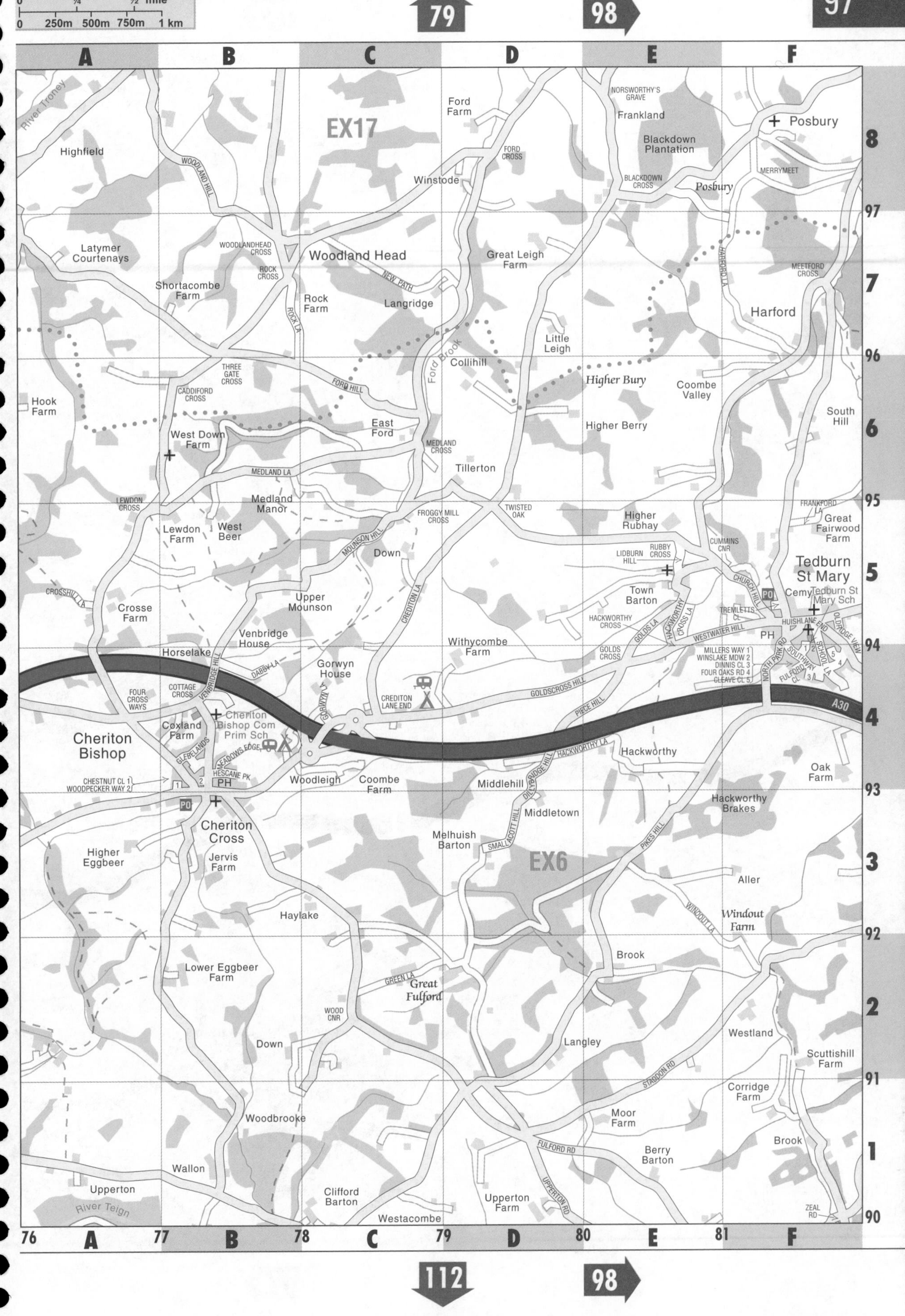
Scale: 1¾ inches to 1 mile
0 ¼ ½ mile
0 250m 500m 750m 1 km
79
98
A B C D E F
EX17
EX6
Highfield
Woodland Head
Latymer Courtenays
Shortacombe Farm
Rock Farm
Langridge
Winstode
Ford Farm
Frankland
Blackdown Plantation
Posbury
Great Leigh Farm
Harford
Little Leigh
Collihill
Higher Bury
Coombe Valley
Hook Farm
West Down Farm
East Ford
Higher Berry
South Hill
Tillerton
Medland Manor
Lewdon Farm
West Beer
Down
Higher Rubhay
Great Fairwood Farm
Town Barton
Tedburn St Mary
Cemy
Tedburn St Mary Sch
Crosse Farm
Upper Mounson
Venbridge House
Horselake
Withycombe Farm
Gorwyn House
Cheriton Bishop
Coxland Farm
Cheriton Bishop Com Prim Sch
Woodleigh
Coombe Farm
Middlehill
Hackworthy
Oak Farm
Cheriton Cross
Middletown
Hackworthy Brakes
Higher Eggbeer
Jervis Farm
Melhuish Barton
Aller
Windout Farm
Haylake
Brook
Lower Eggbeer Farm
Great Fulford
Down
Langley
Westland
Scuttishill Farm
Corridge Farm
Woodbrooke
Moor Farm
Brook
Berry Barton
Wallon
Upperton
Clifford Barton
Westacombe
Upperton Farm
River Troney
River Teign
Ford Brook
A30
PH
PO
8 97 7 96 6 95 5 94 4 93 3 92 2 91 1 90
76 77 78 79 80 81
112
98

97
80
172

Scale: 1¾ inches to 1 mile
0 ¼ ½ mile
0 250m 500m 750m 1 km

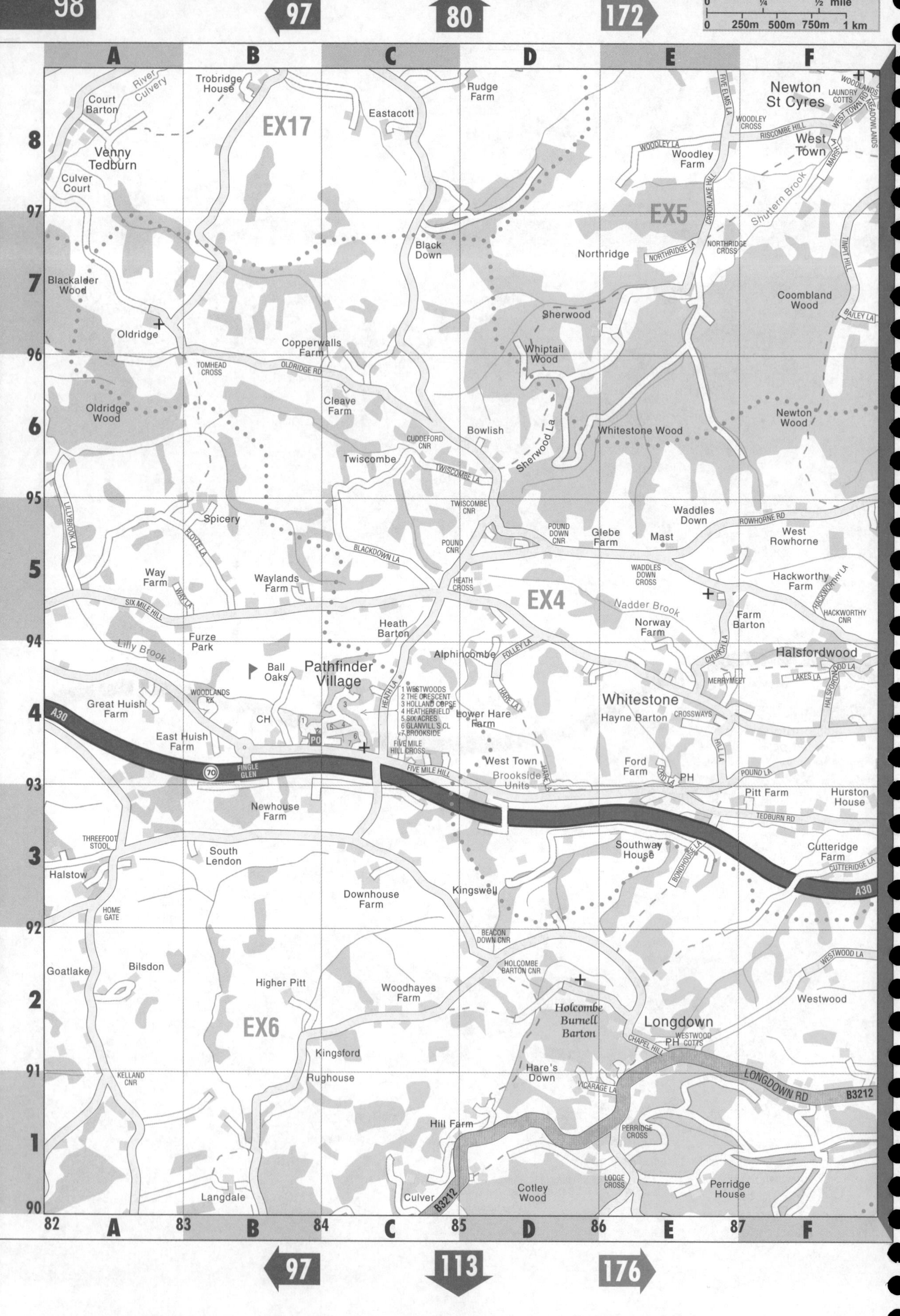

97
113
176

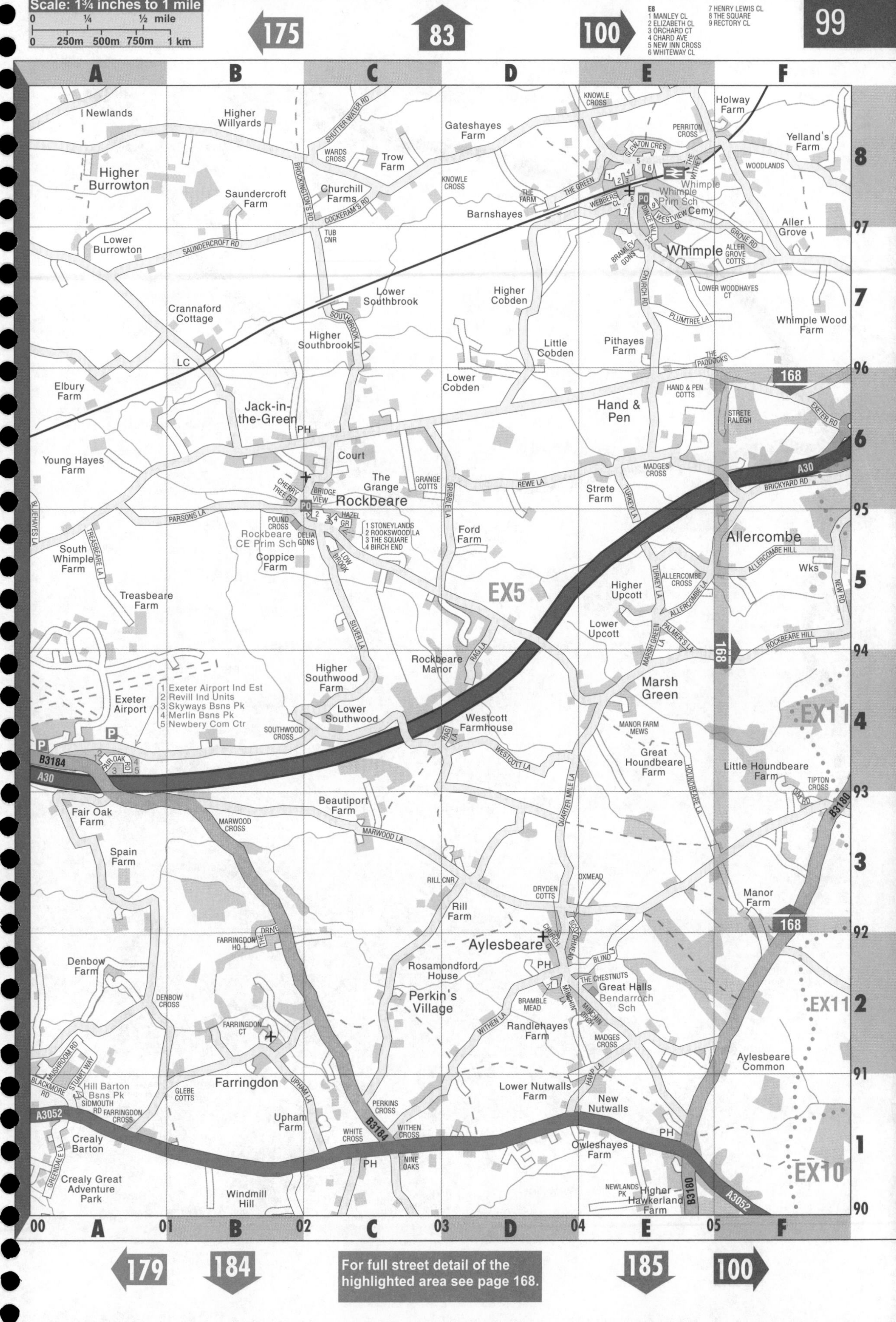

175
83
100
168
179
184
For full street detail of the highlighted area see page 168.
185
100

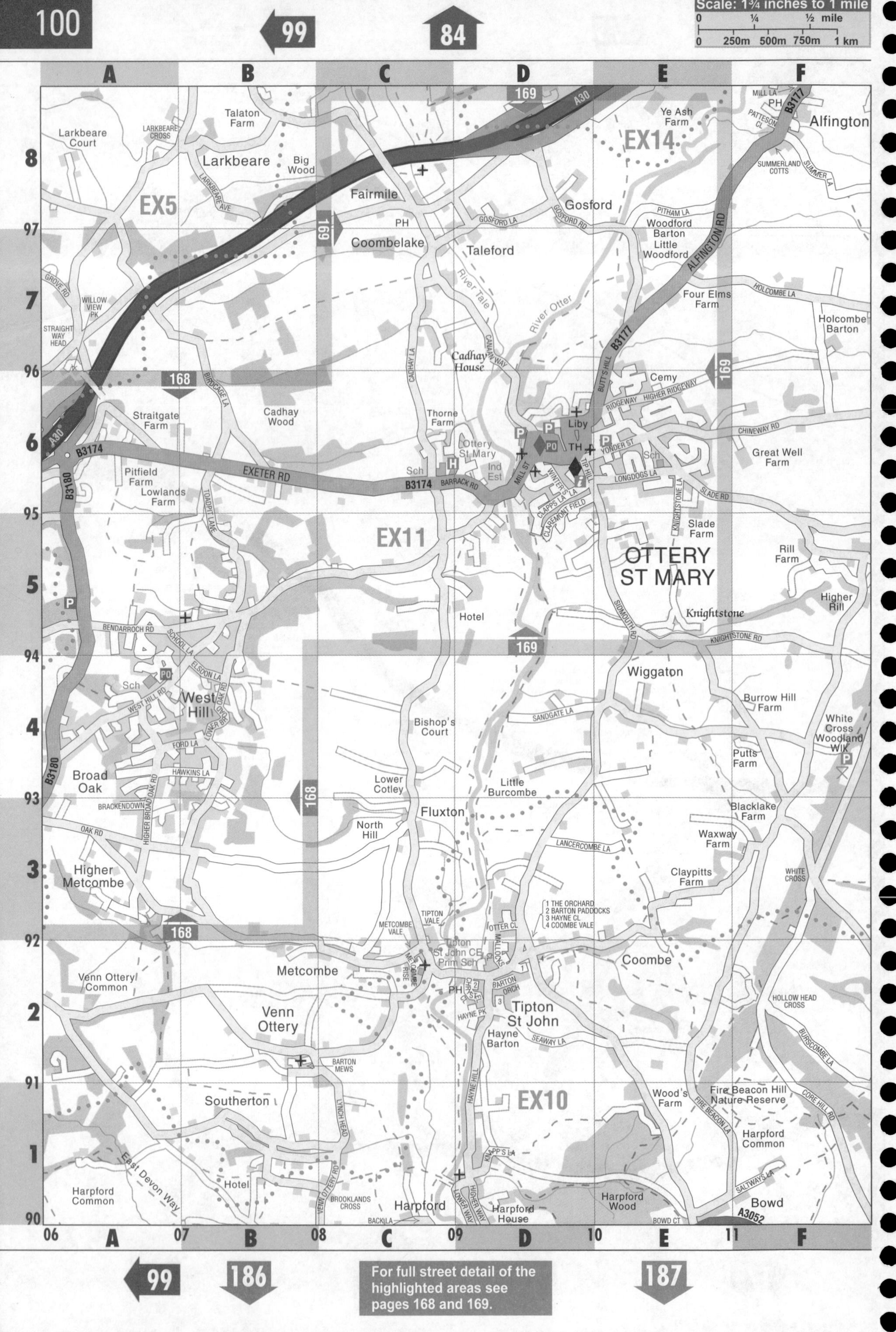

99
84
Scale: 1¾ inches to 1 mile
0
¼
½ mile
0
250m
500m
750m
1 km
A
B
C
D
E
F
169
A30
Talaton Farm
Larkbeare Court
LARKBEARE CROSS
Larkbeare
Big Wood
EX5
LARKBEARE AVE
Fairmile
PH
169
Coombelake
GOSFORD LA
Taleford
Gosford
GOSFORD RD
Ye Ash Farm
EX14
MILL LA
PH
PATTESON CL
B3177
Alfington
SUMMERLAND COTTS
SUMMER LA
PITHAM LA
Woodford Barton
Little Woodford
ALFINGTON RD
GROVE RD
WILLOW VIEW PK
STRAIGHT WAY HEAD
River Tale
River Otter
Four Elms Farm
HOLCOMBE LA
Holcombe Barton
CADHAY LA
Cadhay House
CANAAN WAY
B3177
BUTT'S HILL
168
BIRDCAGE LA
Cadhay Wood
Straitgate Farm
Thorne Farm
Cemy
RIDGEWAY
HIGHER RIDGEWAY
169
Liby
A30
B3174
Ottery St Mary
TH
YONDER ST
CHINEWAY RD
Great Well Farm
Pitfield Farm
Lowlands Farm
B3180
EXETER RD
Sch
H
Ind Est
B3174
BARRACK RD
MILL ST
WINTER'S LA
TIP HILL
Sch
LONGDOGS LA
KNIGHTSTONE LA
SLADE RD
CLAPPS LA
CLAREMONT FIELD
TOADPIT LANE
EX11
Slade Farm
OTTERY ST MARY
Rill Farm
P
Hotel
Knightstone
Higher Rill
SIDMOUTH RD
BENDARROCH RD
SCHOOL LA
169
KNIGHTSTONE RD
ELSDON LA
Sch
West Hill
WEST HILL RD
OAK RD
LOWER BROAD
Wiggaton
Bishop's Court
SANDGATE LA
Burrow Hill Farm
White Cross Woodland Wlk
FORD LA
HAWKINS LA
Putts Farm
B3180
Broad Oak
HIGHER BROAD OAK RD
168
Lower Cotley
Little Burcombe
BRACKENDOWN
Fluxton
Blacklake Farm
OAK RD
North Hill
Waxway Farm
LANCERCOMBE LA
Higher Metcombe
Claypitts Farm
WHITE CROSS
1 THE ORCHARD
2 BARTON PADDOCKS
3 HAYNE CL
4 COOMBE VALE
TIPTON VALE
METCOMBE VALE
OTTER CL
168
MALLOCKS CL
Tipton St John CE Prim Sch
Coombe
Venn Ottery Common
Metcombe
METCOMBE RISE
PH
CHRISTIE CL
BARTON ORCH
HOLLOW HEAD CROSS
Venn Ottery
HAYNE PK
Tipton St John
Hayne Barton
SEAWAY LA
BURSCOMBE LA
BARTON MEWS
Southerton
LYNCH HEAD
HAYNE HILL
EX10
Wood's Farm
Fire Beacon Hill Nature Reserve
FIRE BEACON LA
CORE HILL RD
Harpford Common
KNAPP'S LA
East Devon Way
VENN OTTERY RD
Harpford Common
Hotel
BROOKLANDS CROSS
Harpford
LOWER WAY
HIGHER WAY
Harpford House
Harpford Wood
SALTWAYS LA
Bowd
A3052
BACKLLA
BOWD CT
8
97
7
96
6
95
5
94
4
93
3
92
2
91
1
90
06
07
08
09
10
11

99
186
187

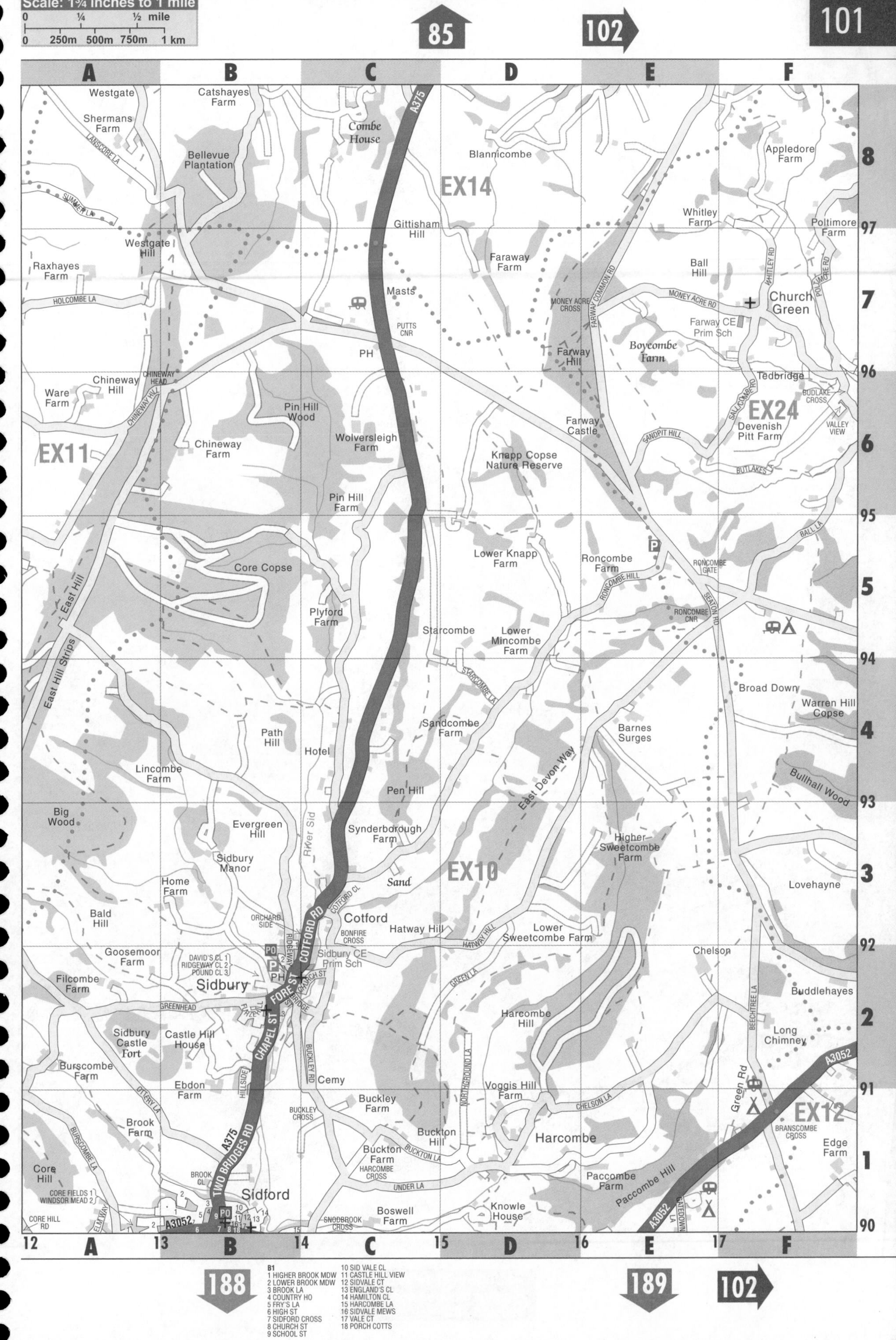
Scale: 1¾ inches to 1 mile
0 ¼ ½ mile
0 250m 500m 750m 1 km
85
102
A B C D E F
Westgate
Catshayes Farm
Shermans Farm
LANSCORE LA
Combe House
A375
Bellevue Plantation
Blannicombe
EX14
Appledore Farm
SUMMER LA
Gittisham Hill
Whitley Farm
Poltimore Farm
Westgate Hill
Faraway Farm
Ball Hill
Raxhayes Farm
Masts
WHITLEY RD
HOLCOMBE LA
MONEY ACRE CROSS
FARWAY COMMON RD
MONEY ACRE RD
Church Green
PUTTS CNR
Farway CE Prim Sch
PH
Boycombe Farm
Farway Hill
Chineway Hill
CHINEWAY HEAD
Tedbridge
Ware Farm
Pin Hill Wood
BUDLAKE CROSS
Farway Castle
EX24
CHINEWAY HILL
Devenish Pitt Farm
SANDPIT HILL
VALLEY VIEW
Wolversleigh Farm
EX11
Chineway Farm
Knapp Copse Nature Reserve
BUTLAKES
Pin Hill Farm
BALL LA
Lower Knapp Farm
Roncombe Farm
RONCOMBE GATE
Core Copse
RONCOMBE HILL
SEATON RD
East Hill
Plyford Farm
RONCOMBE CNR
Starcombe
Lower Mincombe Farm
East Hill Strips
STARCOMBE LA
Broad Down
Warren Hill Copse
Sandcombe Farm
Barnes Surges
Path Hill
Hotel
East Devon Way
Lincombe Farm
Bullhall Wood
Pen Hill
Big Wood
Evergreen Hill
Synderborough Farm
River Sid
Higher Sweetcombe Farm
Sidbury Manor
EX10
Sand
Home Farm
Lovehayne
COTFORD CL
Cotford
Bald Hill
ORCHARD SIDE
COTFORD RD
BONFIRE CROSS
Hatway Hill
HATWAY HILL
Lower Sweetcombe Farm
Goosemoor Farm
DAVID'S CL 1
RIDGEWAY CL 2
POUND CL 3
RIDGEWAY
Sidbury CE Prim Sch
Chelson
PH
CHURCH ST
GREEN LA
Filcombe Farm
Sidbury
FORE ST
Buddlehayes
GREENHEAD
BRIDGE
Harcombe Hill
CHAPEL ST
Sidbury Castle Fort
Castle Hill House
Long Chimney
BEECHTREE LA
Burscombe Farm
BUCKLEY RD
Cemy
NORTHGROUND LA
A3052
HILLSIDE
Ebdon Farm
OTTERY LA
Voggis Hill Farm
Green Rd
Buckley Farm
CHELSON LA
BUCKLEY CROSS
EX12
Brook Farm
BURSCOMBE LA
TWO BRIDGES RD
A375
Buckton Hill
Harcombe
BRANSCOMBE CROSS
Buckton Farm
BUCKTON LA
Edge Farm
Core Hill
HARCOMBE CROSS
Paccombe Hill
BROOK CL
UNDER LA
Paccombe Farm
CORE FIELDS 1
WINDSOR MEAD 2
Sidford
Knowle House
GATEDOWN LA
ELM WAY
CORE HILL RD
A3052
SNODBROOK CROSS
Boswell Farm
8 97 7 96 6 95 5 94 4 93 3 92 2 91 1 90
12 13 14 15 16 17
188
B1
1 HIGHER BROOK MDW
2 LOWER BROOK MDW
3 BROOK LA
4 COUNTRY HO
5 FRY'S LA
6 HIGH ST
7 SIDFORD CROSS
8 CHURCH ST
9 SCHOOL ST
10 SID VALE CL
11 CASTLE HILL VIEW
12 SIDVALE CT
13 ENGLAND'S CL
14 HAMILTON CL
15 HARCOMBE LA
16 SIDVALE MEWS
17 VALE CT
18 PORCH COTTS
189
102

101
86

Scale: 1¾ inches to 1 mile
0 ¼ ½ mile
0 250m 500m 750m 1 km

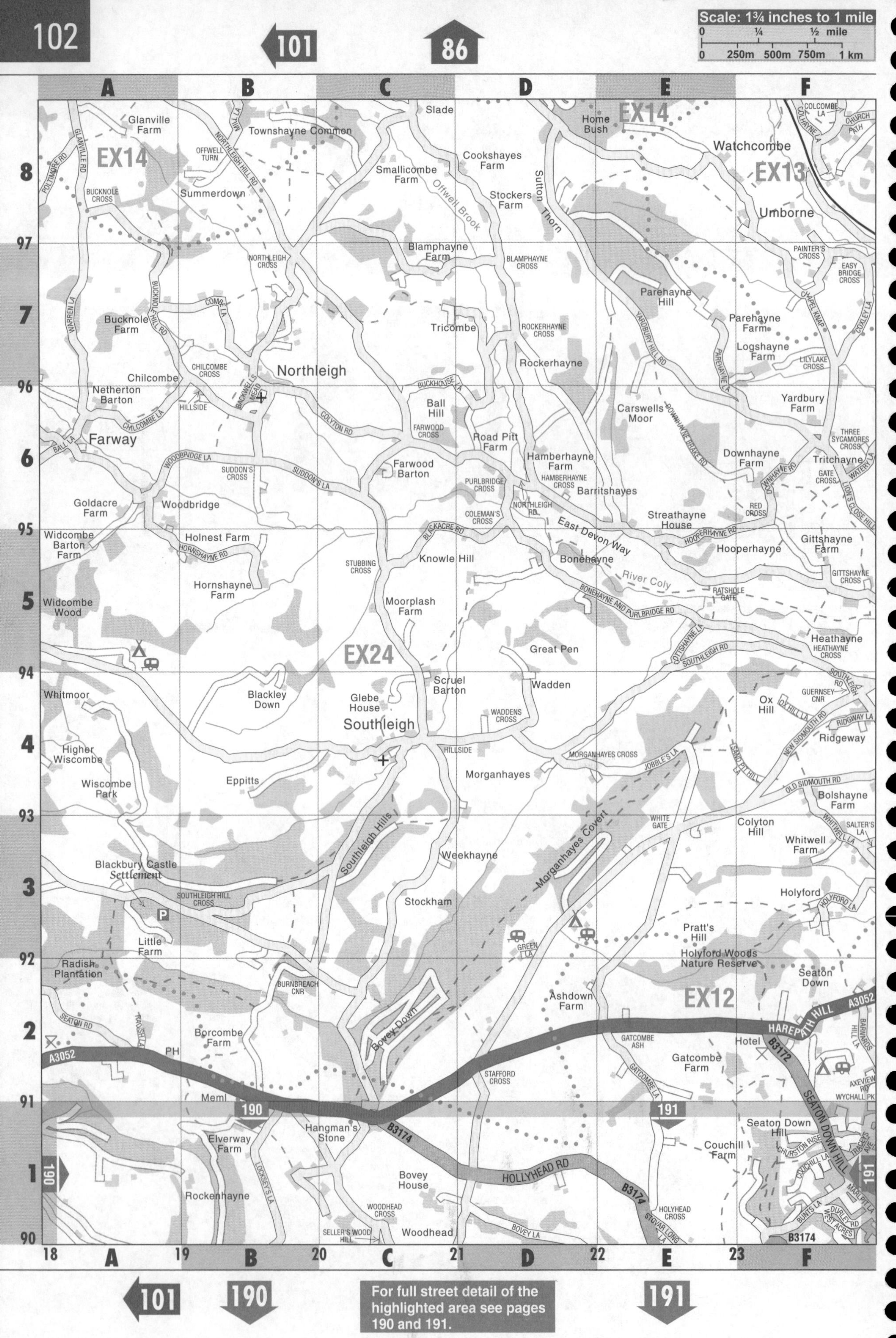

101
190
For full street detail of the highlighted area see pages 190 and 191.
191

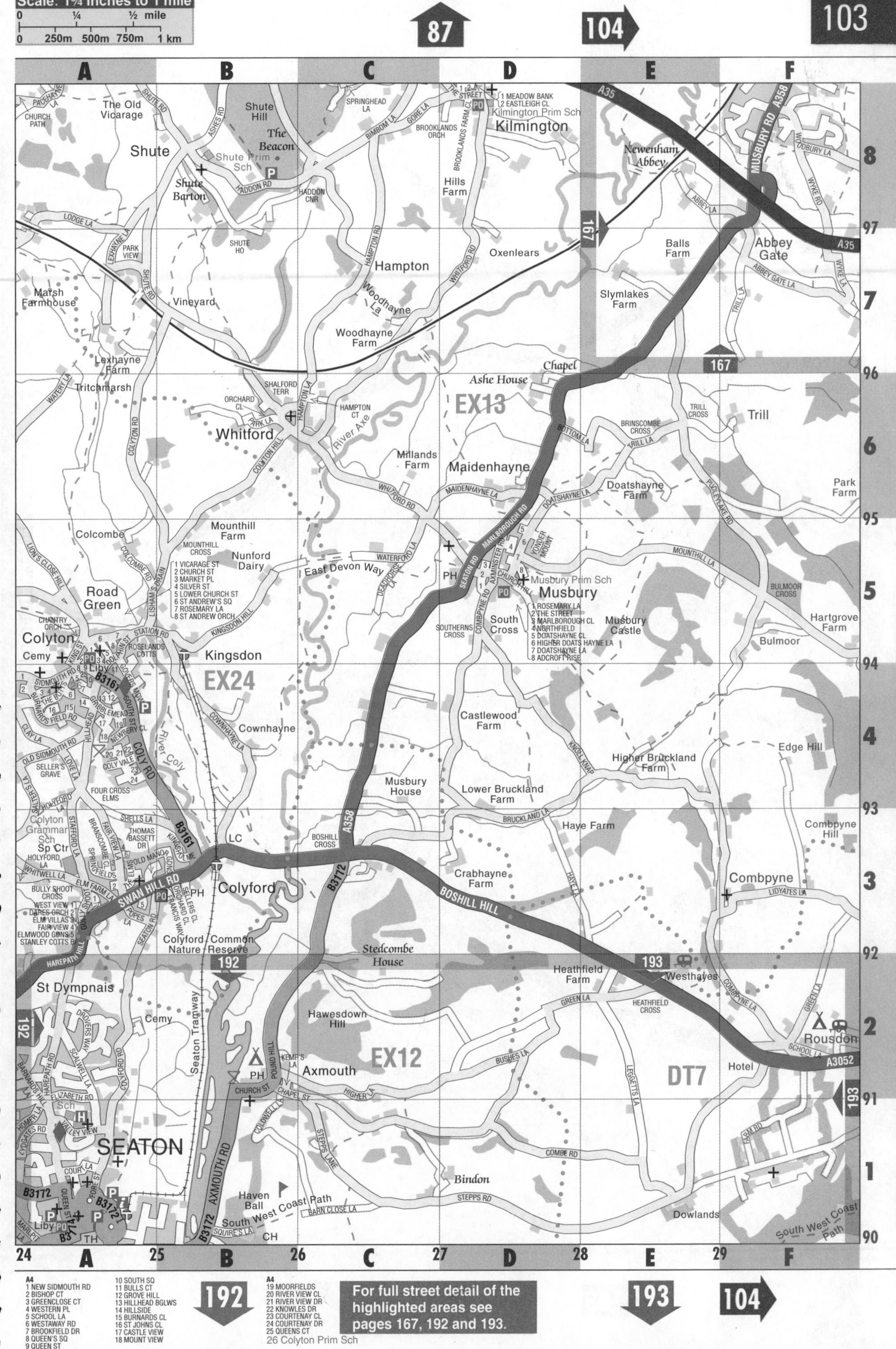
Scale: 1¾ inches to 1 mile
0 ¼ ½ mile
0 250m 500m 750m 1 km
87
104
A B C D E F
Shute
The Old Vicarage
Shute Hill
The Beacon
Shute Prim Sch
Shute Barton
Kilmington
1 MEADOW BANK
2 EASTLEIGH CL
Kilmington Prim Sch
Newenham Abbey
Hills Farm
Hampton
Oxenlears
Balls Farm
Abbey Gate
Slymlakes Farm
Marsh Farmhouse
Vineyard
Woodhayne La
Woodhayne Farm
Lexhayne Farm
Tritchmarsh
Ashe House
Chapel
EX13
Trill
Whitford
River Axe
Millands Farm
Maidenhayne
Doatshayne Farm
Park Farm
Colcombe
Mounthill Farm
Nunford Dairy
East Devon Way
1 VICARAGE ST
2 CHURCH ST
3 MARKET PL
4 SILVER ST
5 LOWER CHURCH ST
6 ST ANDREW'S SQ
7 ROSEMARY LA
8 ST ANDREW ORCH
Musbury Prim Sch
Musbury
Road Green
Colyton
Cemy
Kingsdon
South Cross
Musbury Castle
Hartgrove Farm
Bulmoor
1 ROSEMARY LA
2 THE STREET
3 MARLBOROUGH CL
4 NORTHFIELD
5 DOATSHAYNE CL
6 HIGHER DOATS HAYNE LA
7 DOATSHAYNE LA
8 ADCROFT RISE
EX24
Castlewood Farm
Cownhayne
River Coly
Higher Bruckland Farm
Edge Hill
Musbury House
Lower Bruckland Farm
Haye Farm
Combpyne Hill
Colyton Grammar Sch
Sp Ctr
Colyford
Crabhayne Farm
Combpyne
BOSHILL HILL
Colyford Common Nature Reserve
Stedcombe House
St Dympnais
Heathfield Farm
Westhayes
Cemy
Hawesdown Hill
EX12
Rousdon
Axmouth
Hotel
DT7
SEATON
Seaton Tramway
Bindon
Haven Ball
South West Coast Path
Dowlands
South West Coast Path
24 25 26 27 28 29
A B C D E F
97 96 95 94 93 92 91 90
192
A4
1 NEW SIDMOUTH RD
2 BISHOP CT
3 GREENCLOSE CT
4 WESTERN PL
5 SCHOOL LA
6 WESTAWAY RD
7 BROOKFIELD DR
8 QUEEN'S SQ
9 QUEEN ST
10 SOUTH SQ
11 BULLS CT
12 GROVE HILL
13 HILLHEAD BGLWS
14 HILLSIDE
15 BURNARDS CL
16 ST JOHNS CL
17 CASTLE VIEW
18 MOUNT VIEW
A4
19 MOORFIELDS
20 RIVER VIEW CL
21 RIVER VIEW DR
22 KNOWLES DR
23 COURTENAY CL
24 COURTENAY DR
25 QUEENS CT
26 Colyton Prim Sch
For full street detail of the highlighted areas see pages 167, 192 and 193.
193
104

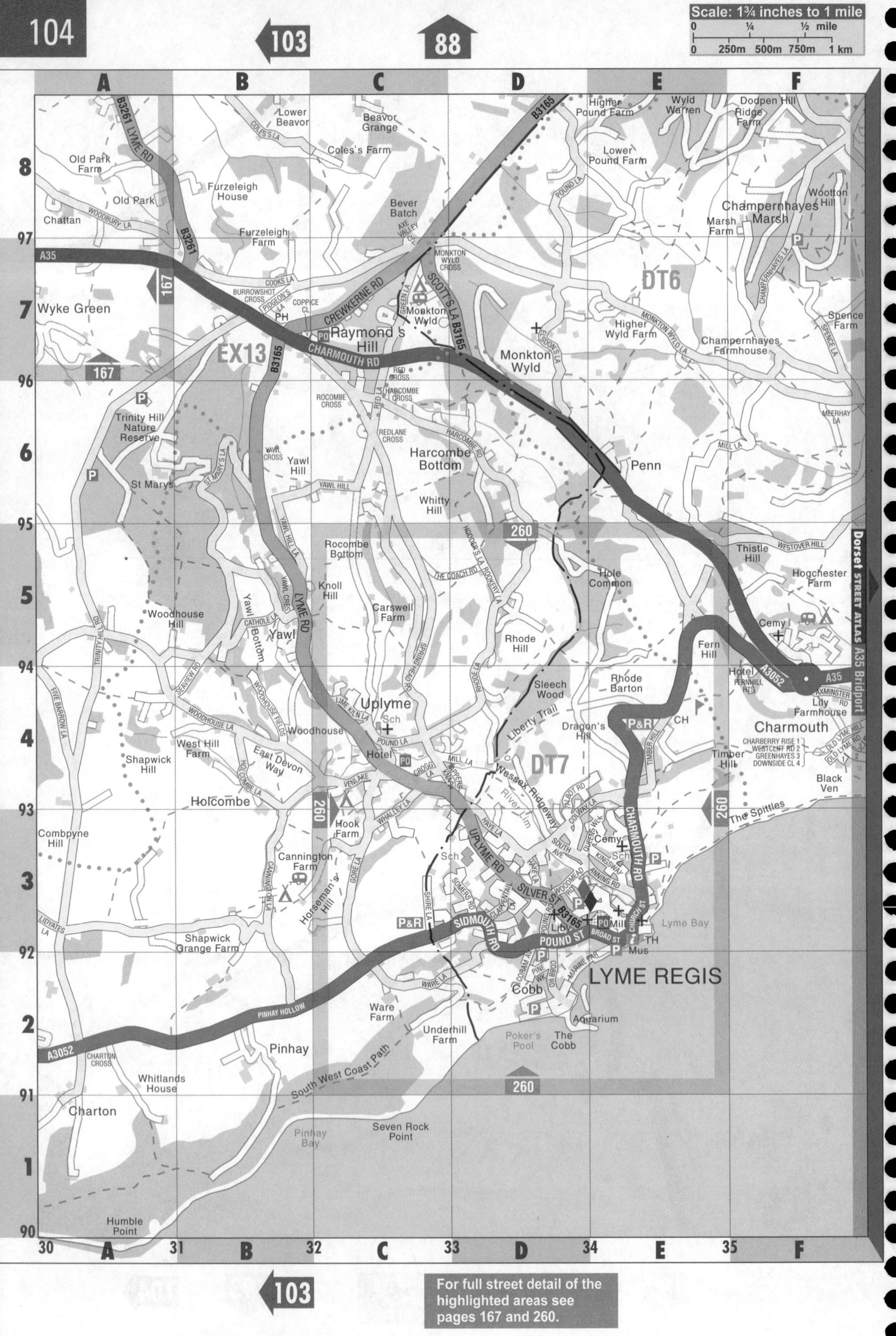

103

For full street detail of the highlighted areas see pages 167 and 260.

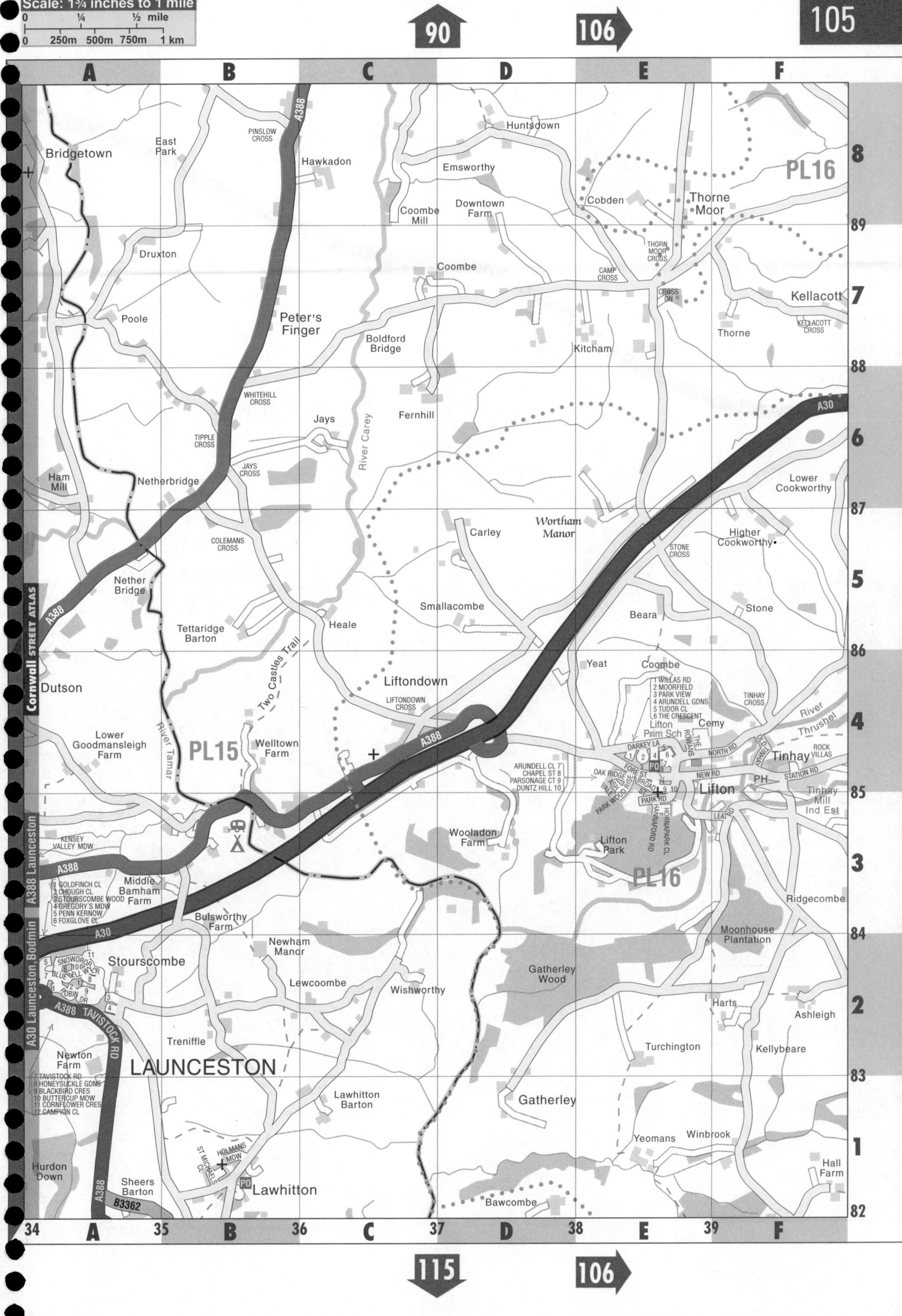
Scale: 1¾ inches to 1 mile
0 ¼ ½ mile
0 250m 500m 750m 1 km
90
106
A B C D E F
8
89
7
88
6
87
5
86
4
85
3
84
2
83
1
82
34 35 36 37 38 39
Bridgetown
East Park
PINSLOW CROSS
A388
Hawkadon
Huntsdown
Emsworthy
Coombe Mill
Downtown Farm
Cobden
Thorne Moor
PL16
Druxton
THORN MOOR CROSS
Coombe
CAMP CROSS
CROSS GN
Kellacott
Poole
Peter's Finger
Boldford Bridge
Kitcham
Thorne
KELLACOTT CROSS
WHITEHILL CROSS
Jays
Fernhill
River Carey
A30
TIPPLE CROSS
JAYS CROSS
Ham Mill
Netherbridge
Lower Cookworthy
Carley
Wortham Manor
Higher Cookworthy
COLEMANS CROSS
STONE CROSS
Nether Bridge
A388
Smallacombe
Beara
Stone
Tettaridge Barton
Heale
Two Castles Trail
Yeat
Coombe
Dutson
Liftondown
1 WILLAS RD
2 MOORFIELD
3 PARK VIEW
4 ARUNDELL GDNS
5 TUDOR CL
6 THE CRESCENT
TINHAY CROSS
LIFTONDOWN CROSS
Lifton Prim Sch
Cemy
River Thrushel
Lower Goodmansleigh Farm
River Tamar
PL15
Welltown Farm
A388
DARKEY LA
THE ROWANS
NORTH RD
OLD TINHAY
Tinhay
ROCK VILLAS
ARUNDELL CL 7
CHAPEL ST 8
PARSONAGE CT 9
DUNTZ HILL 10
OAK RIDGE
FORE ST
BROAD ST
ASH VALE
PARK WOOD RISE
NEW RD
PH
STATION RD
Lifton
Tinhay Mill Ind Est
PARK RD
HORNAPARK CL
HANNAFORD RD
LEAT RD
KENSEY VALLEY MDW
Wooladon Farm
Lifton Park
A388
PL16
1 GOLDFINCH CL
2 CHOUGH CL
3 STOURSCOMBE WOOD
4 GREGORY'S MDW
5 PENN KERNOW
6 FOXGLOVE CL
Middle Bamham Farm
Bulsworthy Farm
Ridgecombe
A30
Newham Manor
Moonhouse Plantation
Stourscombe
SNOWDROP
BLUEBELL WLK
ROBIN DR
Gatherley Wood
Lewcoombe
Wishworthy
Harts
Ashleigh
A388 TAVISTOCK RD
Treniffle
Turchington
Kellybeare
Newton Farm
LAUNCESTON
7 TAVISTOCK RD
8 HONEYSUCKLE GDNS
9 BLACKBIRD CRES
10 BUTTERCUP MDW
11 CORNFLOWER CRES
12 CAMPION CL
Lawhitton Barton
Gatherley
Yeomans
Winbrook
Hurdon Down
ST MICHAELS CL
HOLMANS MDW
Hall Farm
Sheers Barton
PO
Lawhitton
A388
B3362
Bawcombe
Cornwall STREET ATLAS
A388 Launceston
A30 Launceston, Bodmin
A30 Launceston, Bodmin
115
106

105
91

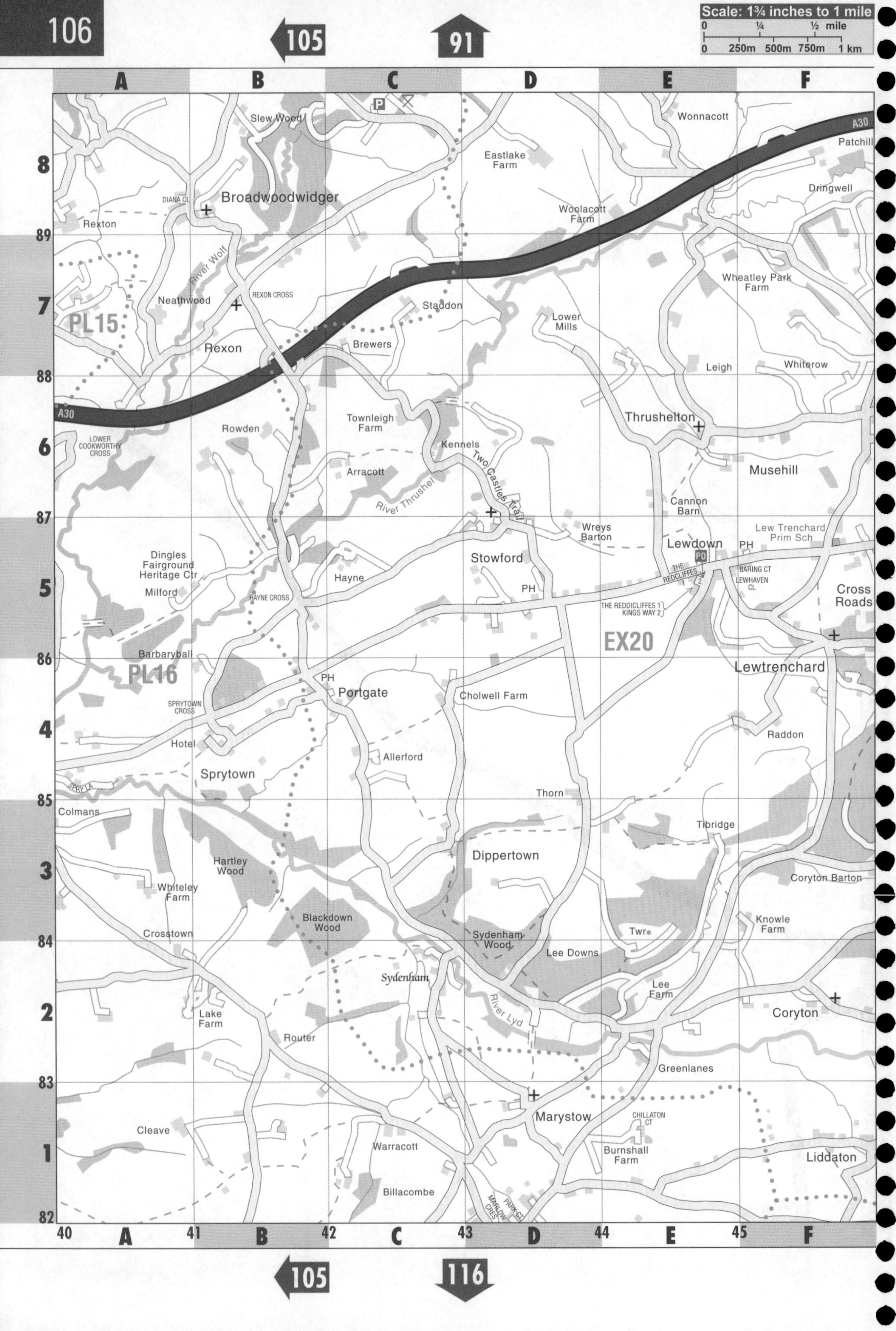

105
116

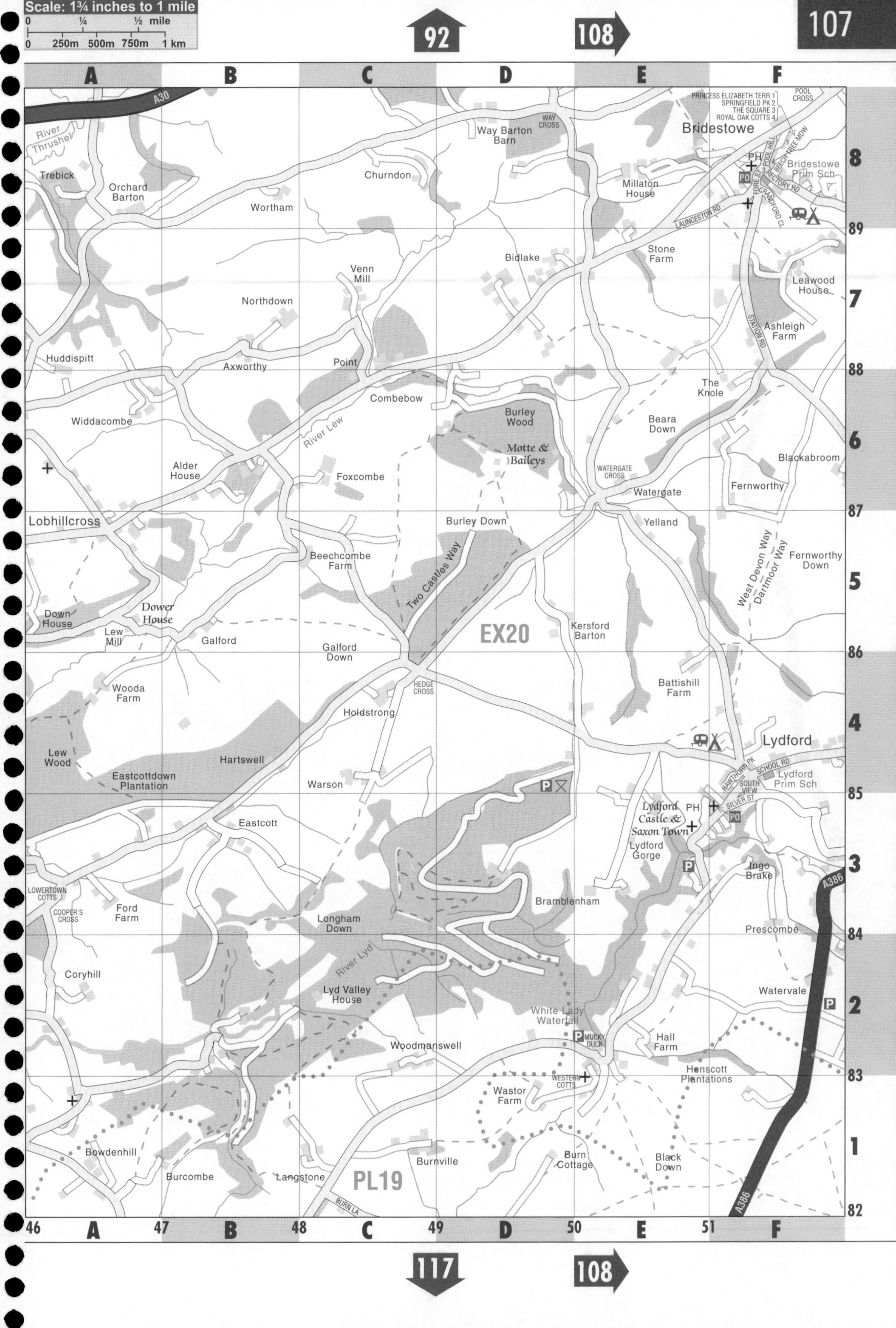
Scale: 1¾ inches to 1 mile
0 ¼ ½ mile
0 250m 500m 750m 1 km
92
108
A B C D E F
A30
River Thrushel
Trebick
Orchard Barton
Wortham
Churndon
Way Barton Barn
WAY CROSS
PRINCESS ELIZABETH TERR 1
SPRINGFIELD PK 2
THE SQUARE 3
ROYAL OAK COTTS 4
POOL CROSS
Bridestowe
Bridestowe Prim Sch
Millaton House
LAUNCESTON RD
RECTORY RD
CRANDFORD CL
FORE ST
POOL HILL
BEECH TREE MDW
Stone Farm
Bidlake
Venn Mill
Northdown
Leawood House
Ashleigh Farm
STATION RD
Huddispitt
Axworthy
Point
The Knole
Combebow
Widdacombe
Burley Wood
Beara Down
River Lew
Motte & Baileys
Blackabroom
Alder House
Foxcombe
WATERGATE CROSS
Watergate
Fernworthy
Lobhillcross
Burley Down
Yelland
Beechcombe Farm
Two Castles Way
West Devon Way
Dartmoor Way
Fernworthy Down
Down House
Dower House
Lew Mill
Galford
EX20
Kersford Barton
Galford Down
HEDGE CROSS
Wooda Farm
Holdstrong
Battishill Farm
Lew Wood
Hartswell
Lydford
Eastcottdown Plantation
Warson
HAWTHORN PK
SCHOOL RD
Lydford Prim Sch
SOUTH VIEW
SILVER ST
Eastcott
Lydford Castle & Saxon Town
PH
Lydford Gorge
LOWERTOWN COTTS
COOPER'S CROSS
Ford Farm
Longham Down
Bramblenham
Ingo Brake
A386
Prescombe
River Lyd
Coryhill
Lyd Valley House
Watervale
White Lady Waterfall
MUCKY DUCK
Woodmanswell
Hall Farm
Henscott Plantations
WESTERN COTTS
Wastor Farm
Bowdenhill
Burcombe
Langstone
PL19
Burnville
Burn Cottage
Black Down
BURN LA
8 89 7 88 6 87 5 86 4 85 3 84 2 83 1 82
46 47 48 49 50 51
117
108

107 93

Scale: 1¾ inches to 1 mile
0 ¼ ½ mile
0 250m 500m 750m 1 km

A B C D E F

8 89 7 88 6 87 5 86 4 85 3 84 2 83 1 82

East Tor
Sourton Tors
Shelstone Tor
Black Tor
West Devon Way
Dartmoor Way
A386
Collaven Manor
Black-a-Tor Copse National Nature Reserve
Tor Wood
Branscombe Loaf
PIGS LEG CROSS
Two Castles Trail
PH
Lake Down
Corn Ridge
Slipper Stones
West Okement River
DANGER AREA
Fordsland Ledge
Lake
West Coombe
Lyn Head
Southerly
Bridestowe and Sourton Common
Steng-a-Tor
Logan Rock
Logan Stone
Gren Tor
Sandy Ford
Southerly Down
Woodcock Hill
EX20
Great Nodden
Kitty Tor
STATION RD
Shortacombe
White Links Tor
Great Links Tor
FOX & HOUNDS CROSS
Bleak House
PH
Arms Tor
Dunna Goat
Nodden Gate
Green Tor
Vale Down
Rattle Brook
DANGER AREA
Amicombe Hill
Widgery Cross
Bray Tor
Rattlebrook Hill
SCHOOL RD
P
Doetor Brook
Chat Tor
PH
High Down
Doe Tor
Sharp Tor
Doetor Common
DANGER AREA
A386
River Lyd
Bearwalls
Beardon
Hare Tor
DANGER AREA
Willsworthy Range
Watern Oke
Amicombe Brook
PL19
White Hill
Rifle Ranges
Ger Tor
Tavy Cleave
Nattor Down
River Tavy
The Meads
DANGER AREA
P
Nat Tor
Lane End
DANGER AREA

52 A 53 B 54 C 55 D 56 E 57 F

107 118

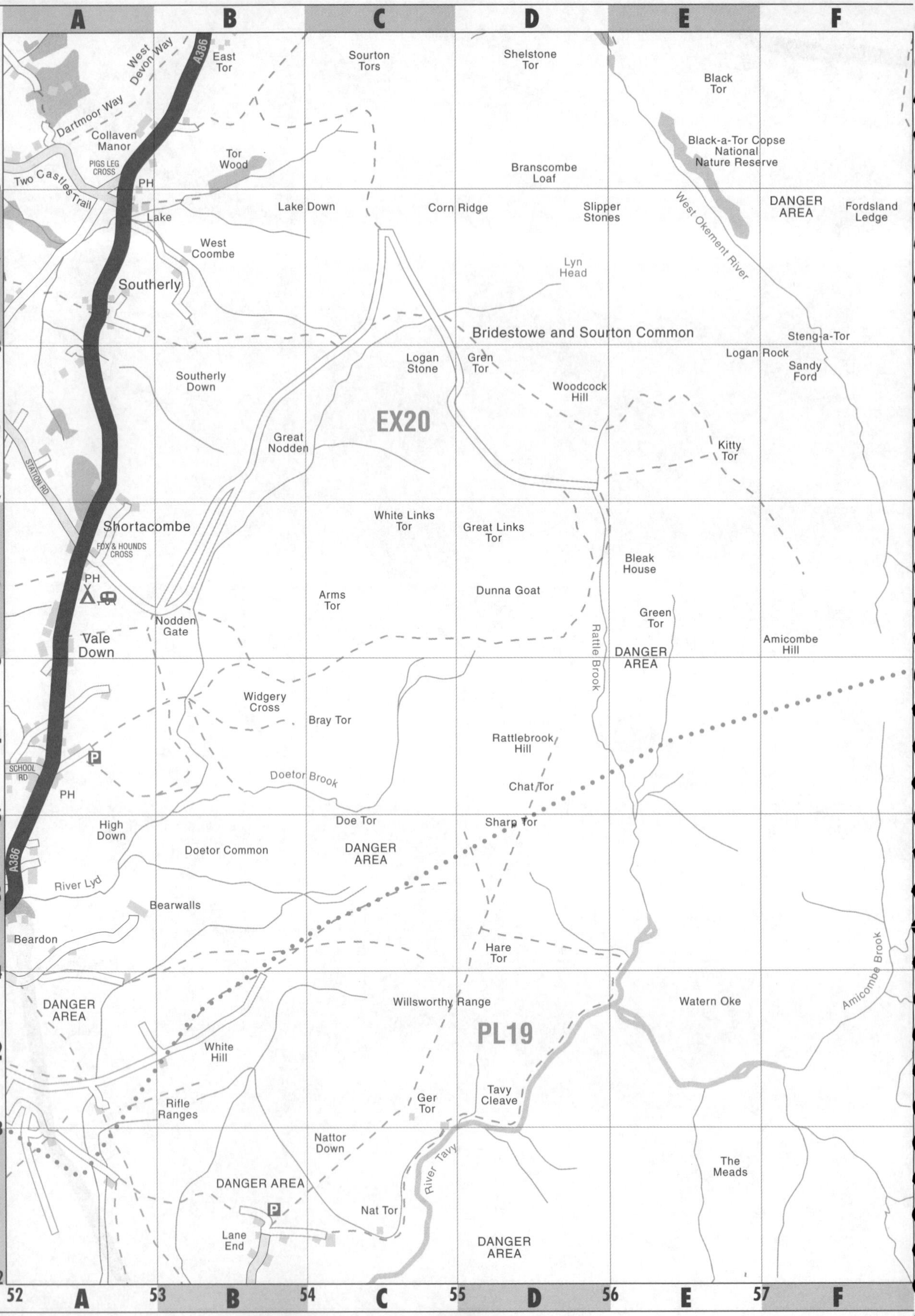

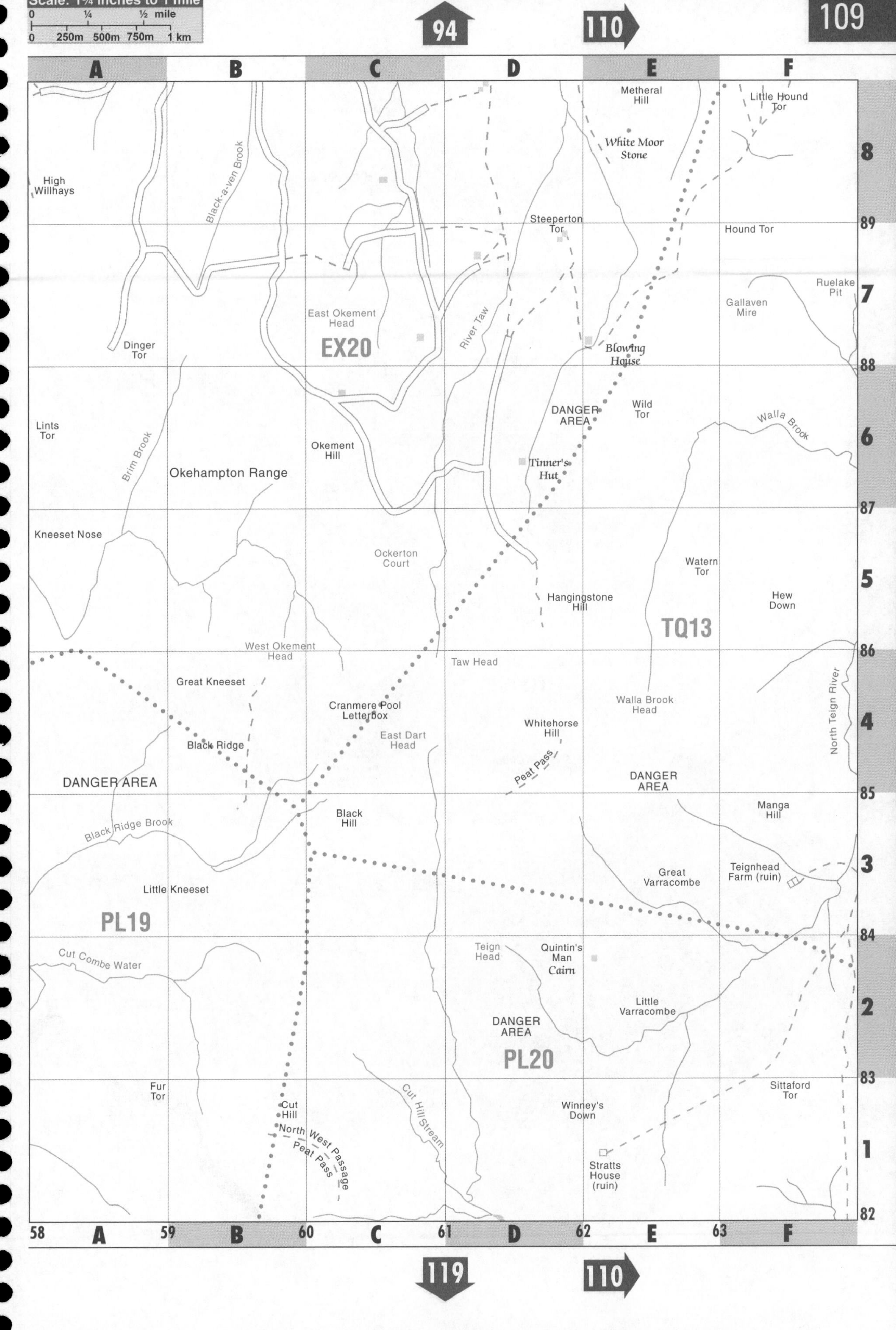
Scale: 1¾ inches to 1 mile
0 ¼ ½ mile
0 250m 500m 750m 1 km
94
110
A B C D E F
8 89 7 88 6 87 5 86 4 85 3 84 2 83 1 82
58 59 60 61 62 63
Metheral Hill
Little Hound Tor
White Moor Stone
High Willhays
Black-a-ven Brook
Steeperton Tor
Hound Tor
Ruelake Pit
Gallaven Mire
East Okement Head
EX20
River Taw
Dinger Tor
Blowing House
DANGER AREA
Wild Tor
Lints Tor
Walla Brook
Okement Hill
Tinner's Hut
Brim Brook
Okehampton Range
Kneeset Nose
Ockerton Court
Watern Tor
Hangingstone Hill
Hew Down
TQ13
West Okement Head
Taw Head
North Teign River
Great Kneeset
Cranmere Pool Letterbox
Walla Brook Head
Whitehorse Hill
East Dart Head
Black Ridge
Peat Pass
DANGER AREA
DANGER AREA
Manga Hill
Black Hill
Black Ridge Brook
Teignhead Farm (ruin)
Great Varracombe
Little Kneeset
PL19
Teign Head
Quintin's Man Cairn
Cut Combe Water
Little Varracombe
DANGER AREA
PL20
Fur Tor
Sittaford Tor
Cut Hill
Cut Hill Stream
Winney's Down
North West Passage
Peat Pass
Stratts House (ruin)
119
110

109
95

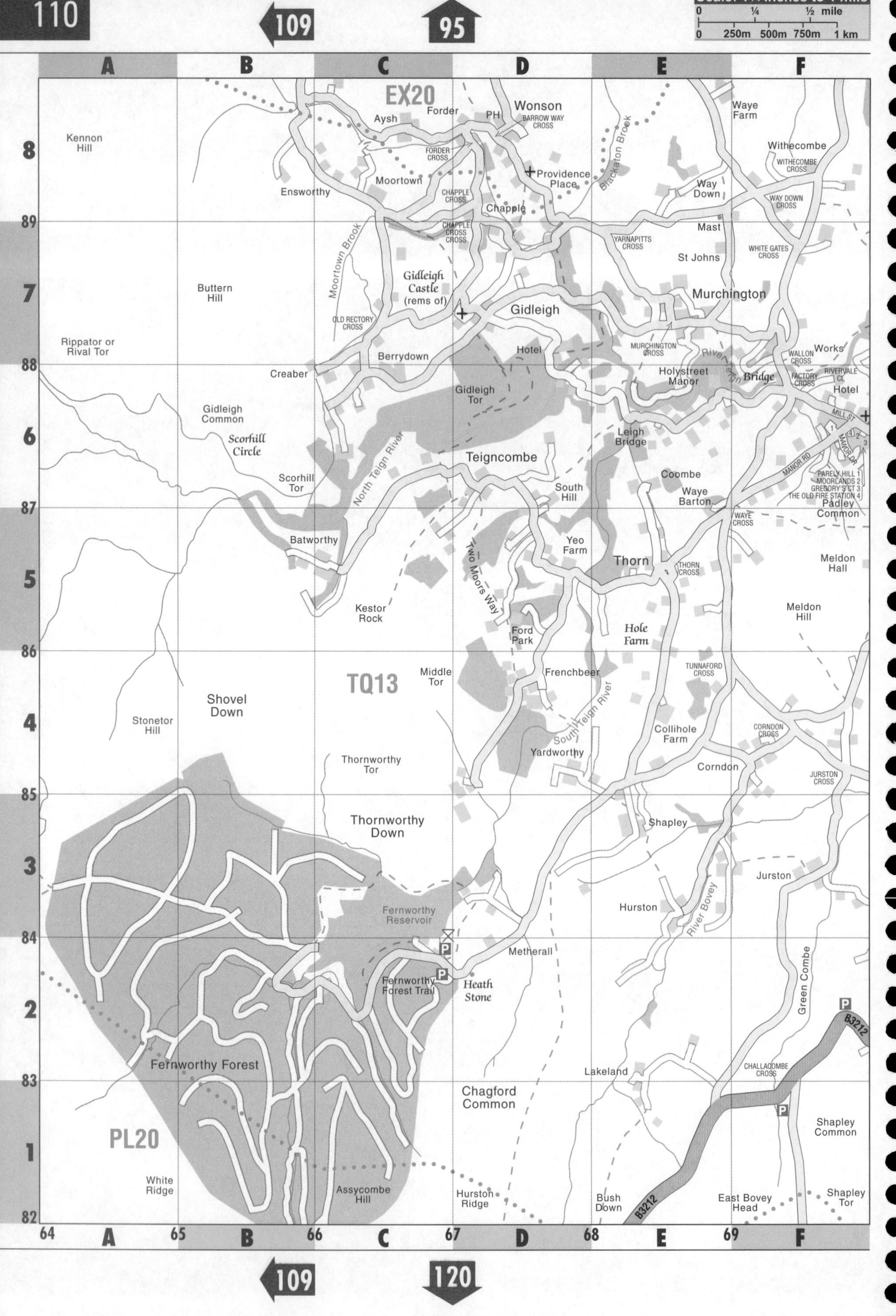

109
120

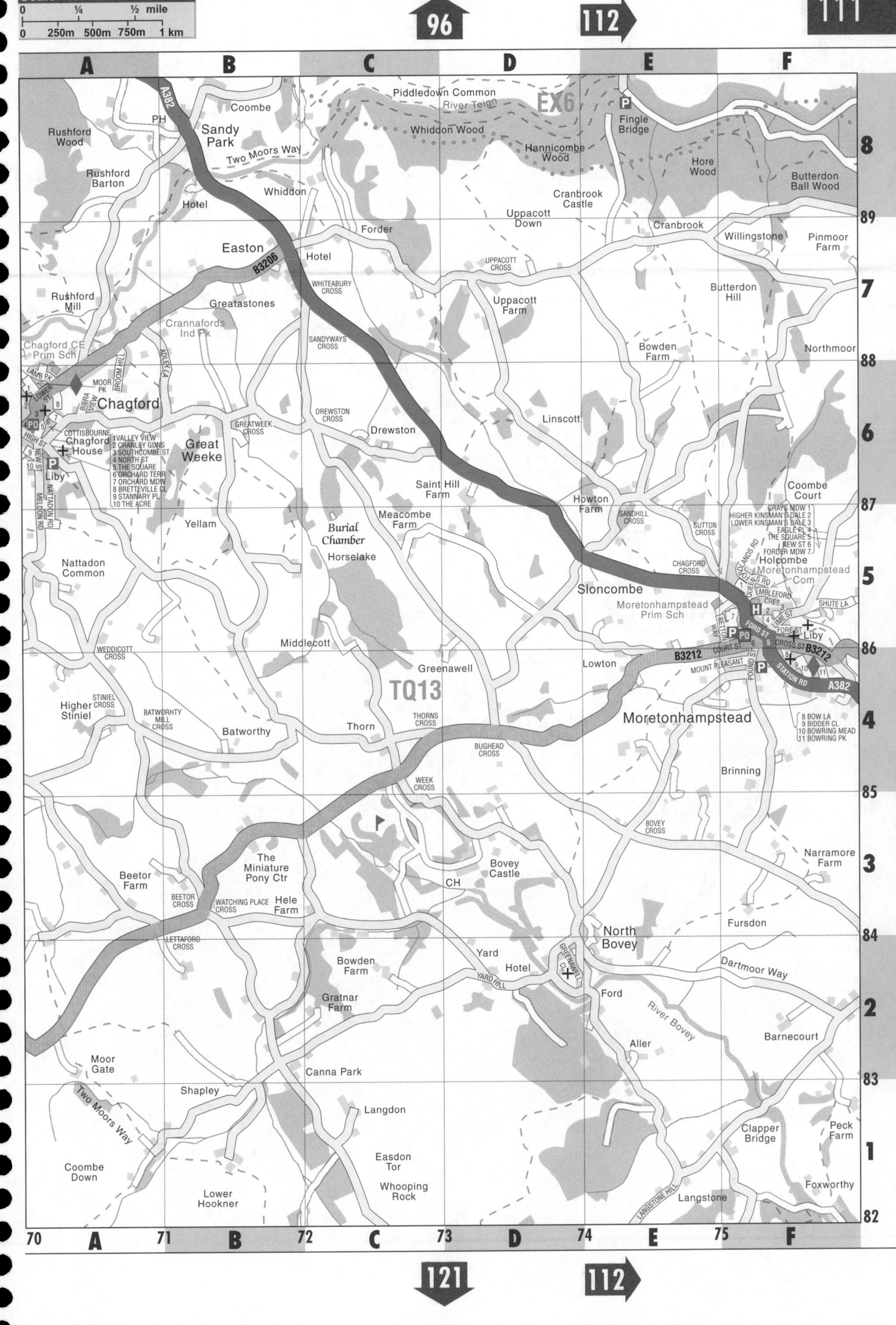

Scale: 1¾ inches to 1 mile
0 ¼ ½ mile
0 250m 500m 750m 1 km
96
112
A B C D E F
Piddledown Common
River Teign
EX6
Fingle Bridge
Coombe
PH
Sandy Park
Rushford Wood
Whiddon Wood
Hannicombe Wood
Hore Wood
Butterdon Ball Wood
Two Moors Way
Rushford Barton
Hotel
Whiddon
Cranbrook Castle
Uppacott Down
Cranbrook
Forder
Willingstone
Pinmoor Farm
Easton
B3206
Hotel
Uppacott Cross
Whiteabury Cross
Rushford Mill
Greatastones
Uppacott Farm
Butterdon Hill
Crannafords Ind Pk
Sandyways Cross
Bowden Farm
Chagford CE Prim Sch
Northmoor
Chagford
Drewston Cross
Linscott
Greatweek Cross
Drewston
Chagford House
Great Weeke
1 Valley View
2 Cranley Gdns
3 Southcombe St
4 North St
5 The Square
6 Orchard Terr
7 Orchard Mdw
8 Bretteville Cl
9 Stannary Pl
10 The Acre
Liby
Saint Hill Farm
Howton Farm
Coombe Court
Yellam
Meacombe Farm
Sandhill Cross
Burial Chamber
Horselake
Sutton Cross
Nattadon Common
Chagford Cross
Holcombe
Moretonhampstead Com
Sloncombe
Moretonhampstead Prim Sch
Middlecott
Weddicott Cross
Greenawell
Lowton
B3212
TQ13
Higher Stiniel
Stiniel Cross
Batworhty Mill Cross
Batworthy
Thorn
Thorns Cross
Moretonhampstead
8 Bow La
9 Bidder Cl
10 Bowring Mead
11 Bowring Pk
Bughead Cross
A382
Brinning
Week Cross
Bovey Cross
The Miniature Pony Ctr
Narramore Farm
Beetor Farm
Bovey Castle
CH
Beetor Cross
Watching Place Cross
Hele Farm
Fursdon
Lettaford Cross
North Bovey
Yard
Bowden Farm
Hotel
Dartmoor Way
Ford
Gratnar Farm
River Bovey
Barnecourt
Aller
Moor Gate
Canna Park
Shapley
Langdon
Two Moors Way
Clapper Bridge
Peck Farm
Coombe Down
Easdon Tor
Whooping Rock
Foxworthy
Lower Hookner
Langstone
70 71 72 73 74 75
89 88 87 86 85 84 83 82
8 7 6 5 4 3 2 1
121
112

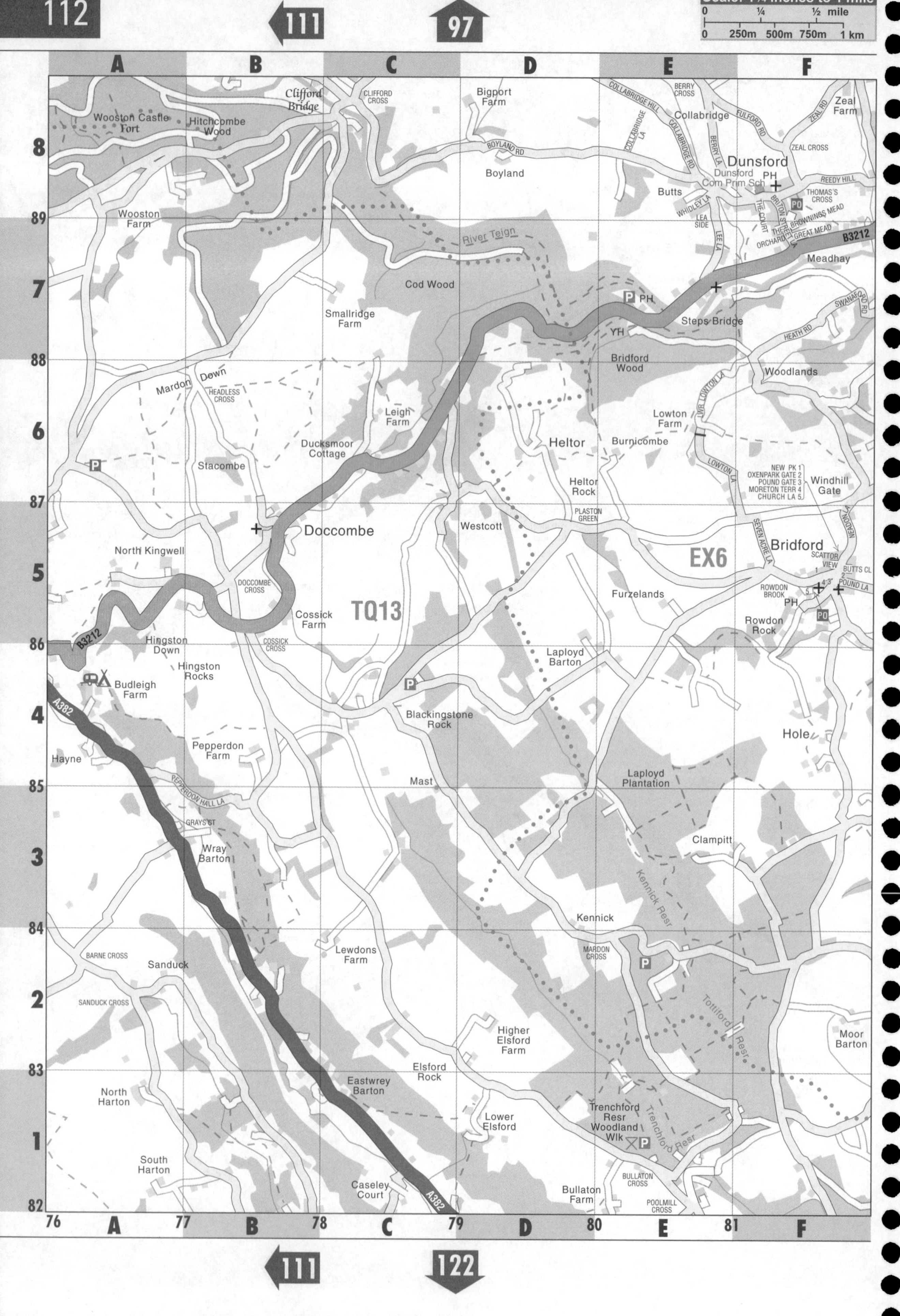
111
97
Scale: 1¾ inches to 1 mile
0 ¼ ½ mile
0 250m 500m 750m 1 km
A B C D E F
8 89 7 88 6 87 5 86 4 85 3 84 2 83 1 82
76 77 78 79 80 81
Wooston Castle Fort
Hitchcombe Wood
Clifford Bridge
CLIFFORD CROSS
Bigport Farm
BOYLAND RD
Boyland
COLLABRIDGE HILL
BERRY CROSS
Collabridge
FULFORD RD
ZEAL RD
Zeal Farm
ZEAL CROSS
Dunsford
Dunsford Com Prim Sch
PH
REEDY HILL
Butts
THOMAS'S CROSS
WHIDLEY LA
LEA SIDE
LEE LA
THE COURT
BRITON STREET
BROWNINGS MEAD
THE ORCHARD
GREAT MEAD
B3212
Meadhay
Wooston Farm
River Teign
Cod Wood
PH
YH
Steps Bridge
SWANAFORD RD
HEATH RD
Smallridge Farm
Bridford Wood
Woodlands
Mardon Down
HEADLESS CROSS
Leigh Farm
UPR LOWTON LA
Lowton Farm
Ducksmoor Cottage
Heltor
Burnicombe
Stacombe
LOWTON LA
NEW PK 1
OXENPARK GATE 2
POUND GATE 3
MORETON TERR 4
CHURCH LA 5
Windhill Gate
Heltor Rock
PLASTON GREEN
Westcott
Doccombe
SEVEN ACRE LA
Bridford
North Kingwell
EX6
SCATTOR VIEW
BUTTS CL
POUND LA
DOCCOMBE CROSS
TQ13
Furzelands
ROWDON BROOK
PH
Cossick Farm
Rowdon Rock
B3212
Hingston Down
COSSICK CROSS
Laployd Barton
Hingston Rocks
Budleigh Farm
A382
Blackingstone Rock
Hole
Hayne
Pepperdon Farm
Laployd Plantation
Mast
PEPPERDON HALL LA
GRAYS CT
Wray Barton
Clampitt
Kennick Resr
Kennick
Lewdons Farm
MARDON CROSS
BARNE CROSS
Sanduck
SANDUCK CROSS
Tottiford Resr
Higher Elsford Farm
Moor Barton
Elsford Rock
North Harton
Eastwrey Barton
Trenchford Resr Woodland Wlk
Lower Elsford
Trenchford Resr
South Harton
Caseley Court
A382
Bullaton Farm
BULLATON CROSS
POOLMILL CROSS
111
122

Scale: 1¾ inches to 1 mile

98
114

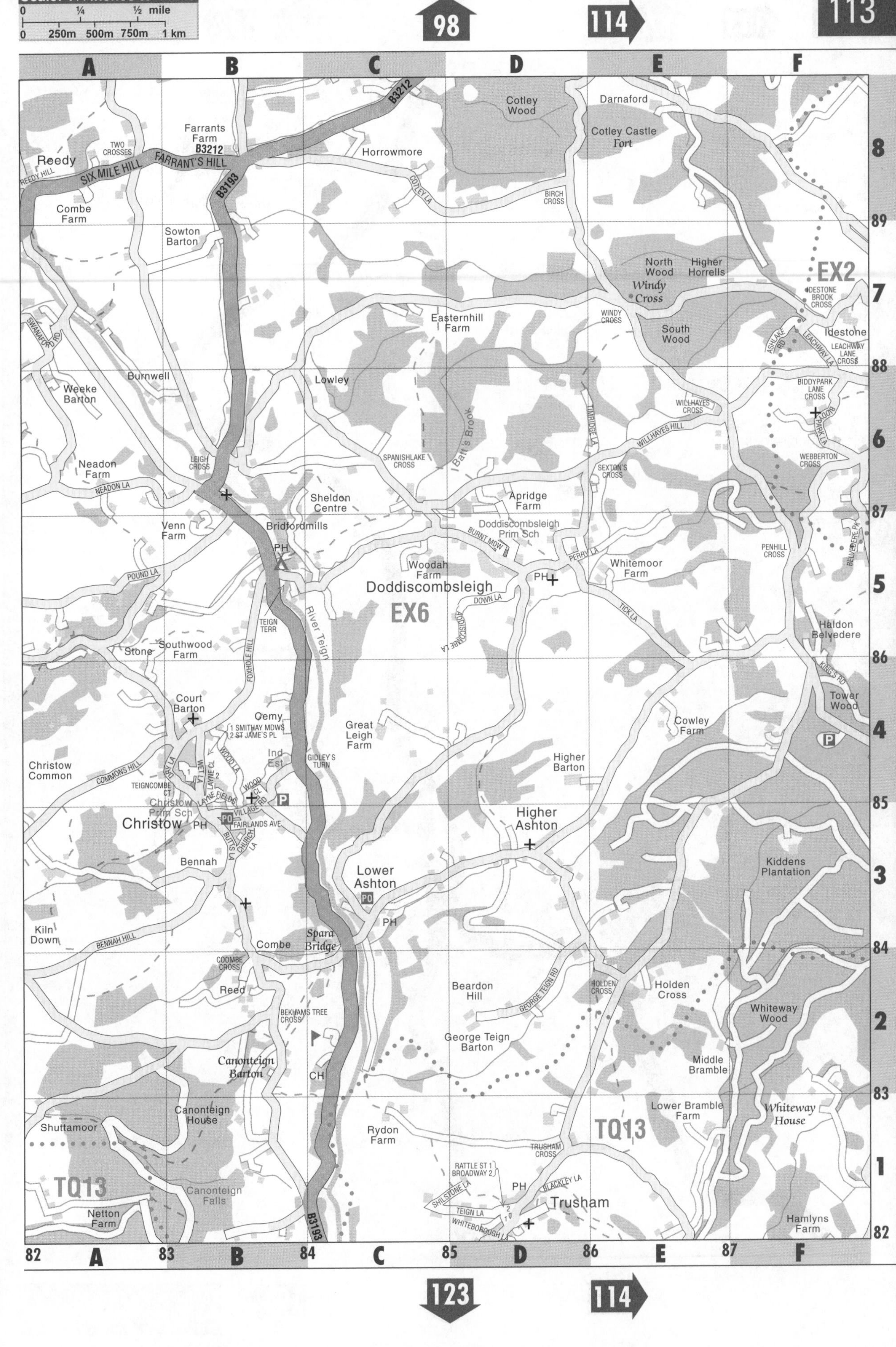

123
114

113 176 177 182

Scale: 1¾ inches to 1 mile

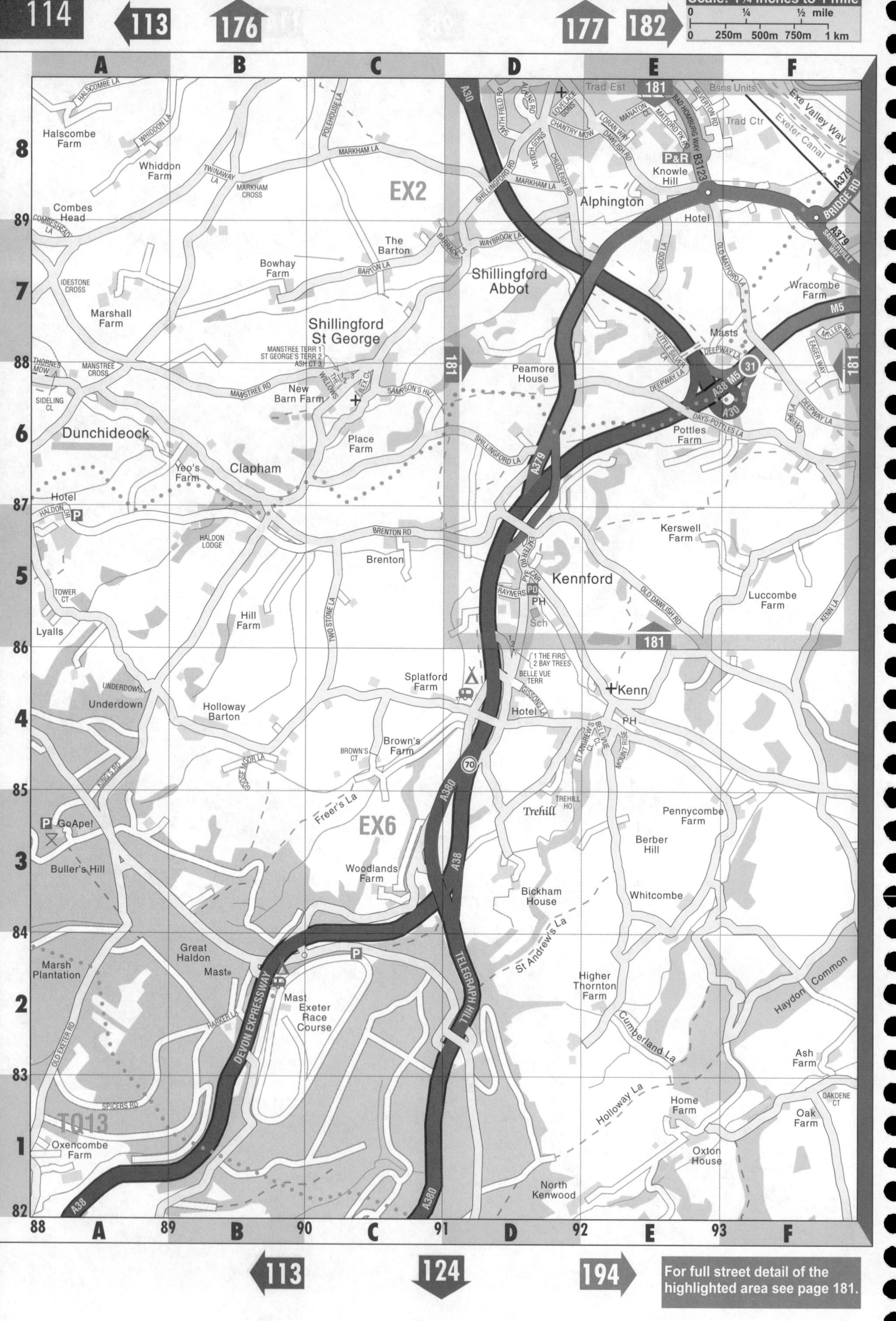

For full street detail of the highlighted area see page 181.

113 124 194

Scale: 1¾ inches to 1 mile

105
116

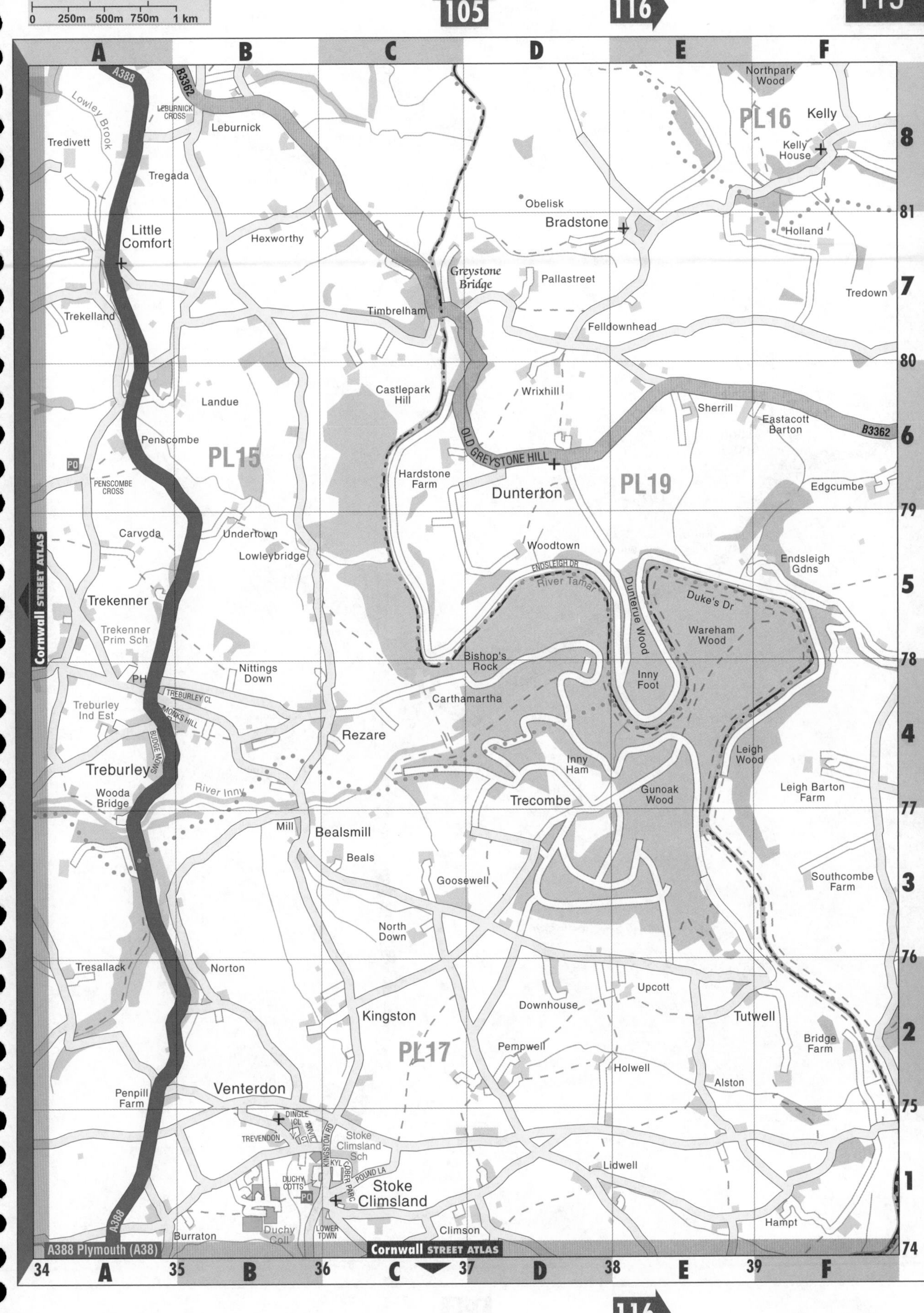

116

115
106

Scale: 1¾ inches to 1 mile

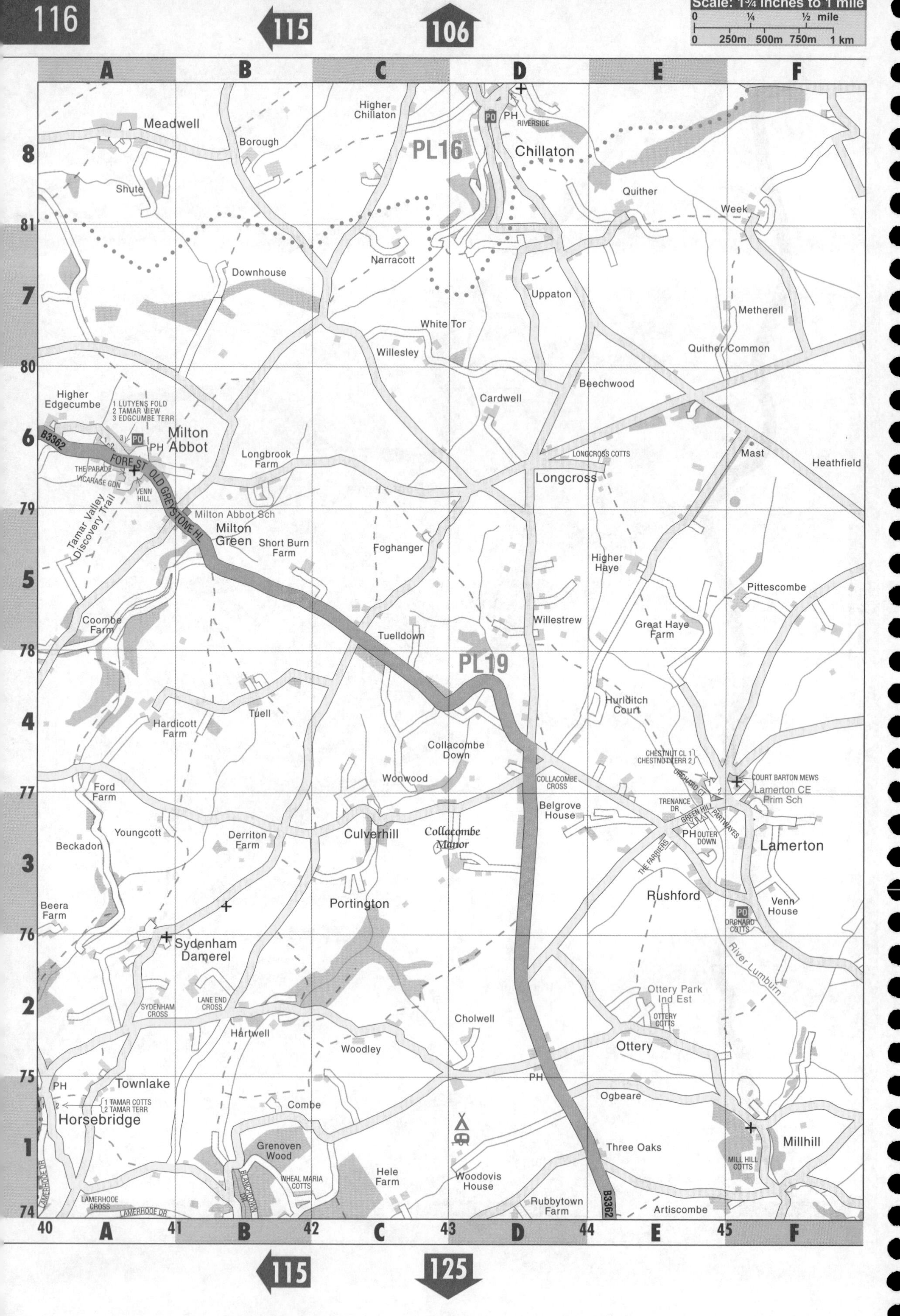

115
125

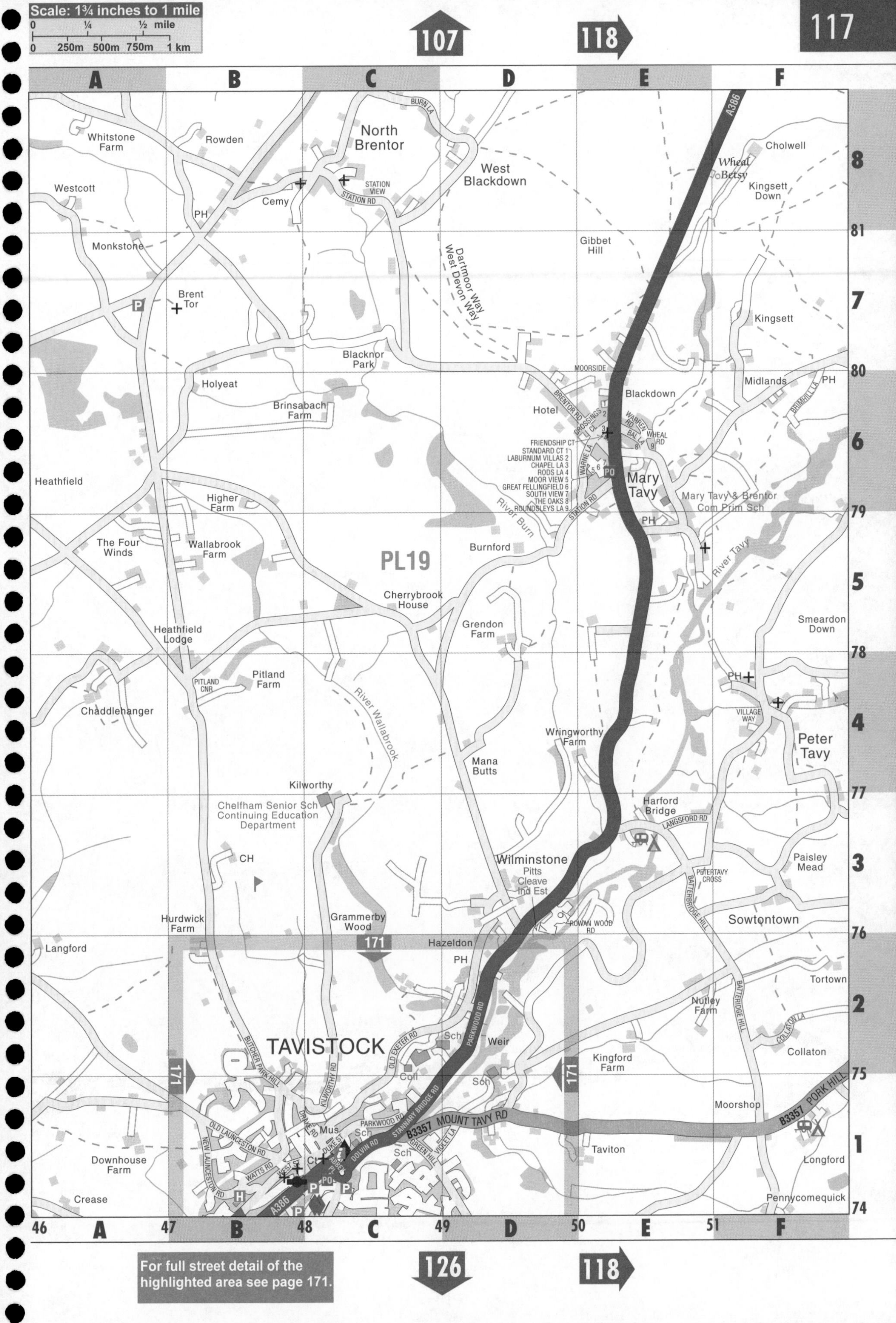

For full street detail of the highlighted area see page 171.

117
108

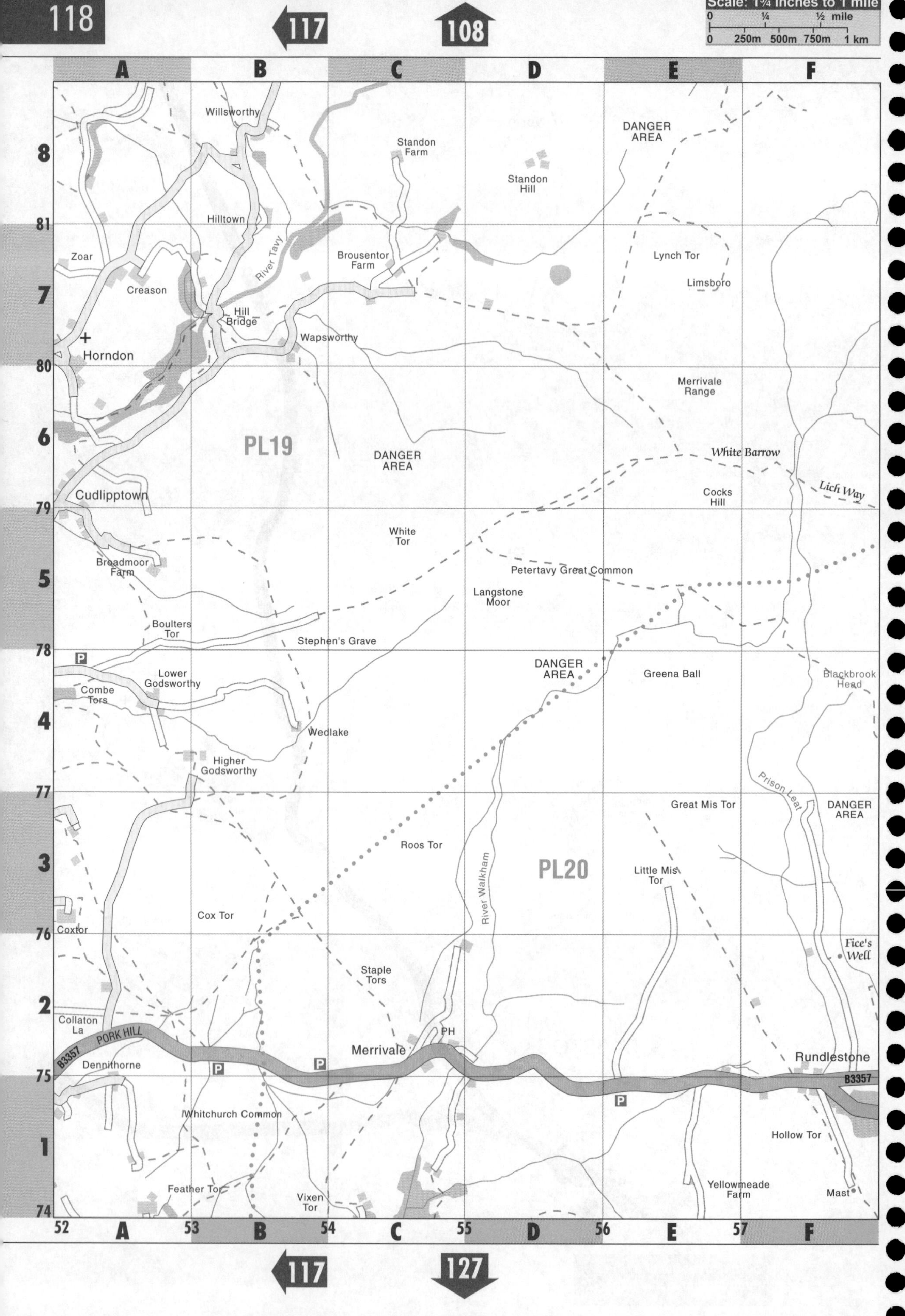

117
127

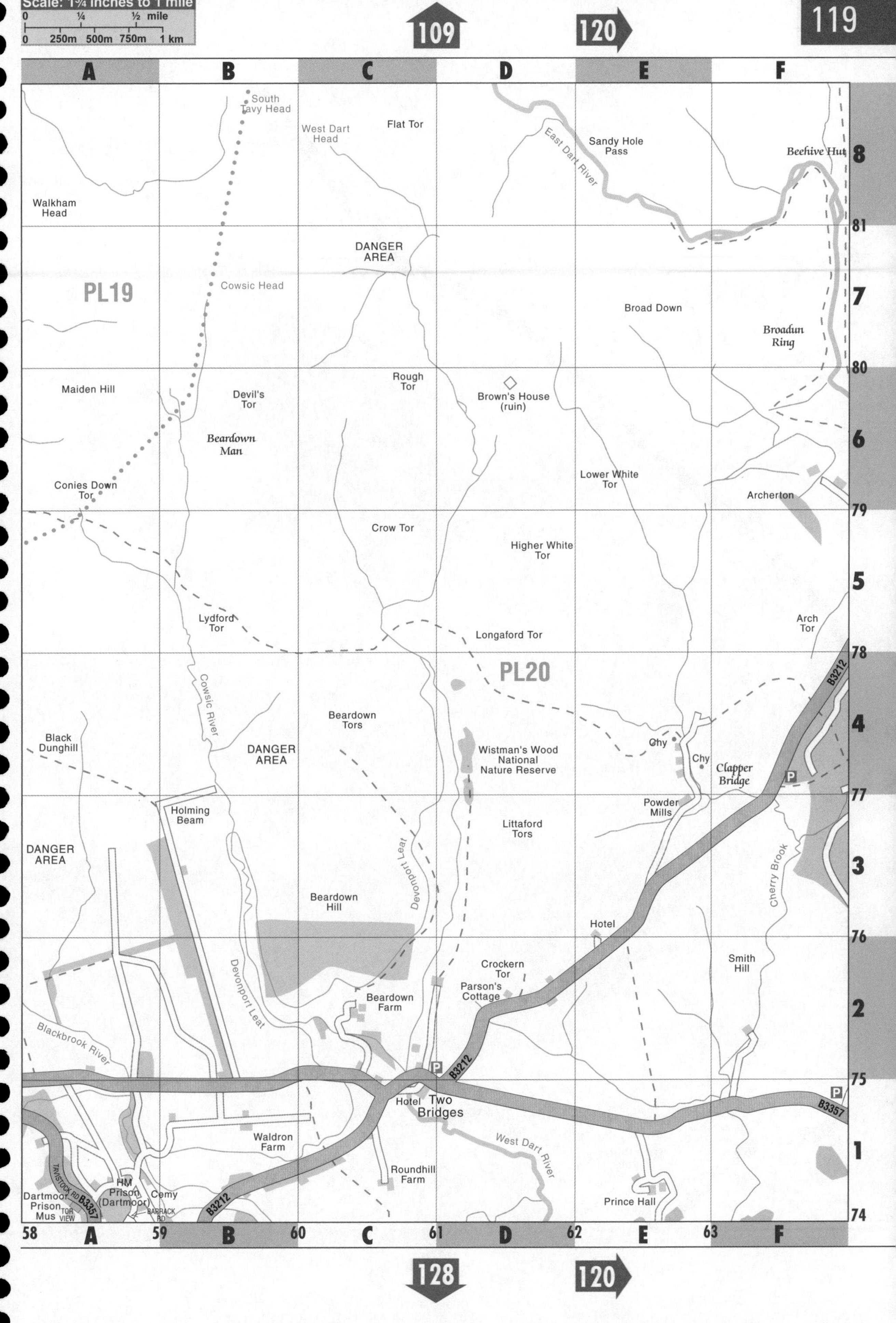
Scale: 1¾ inches to 1 mile
0 ¼ ½ mile
0 250m 500m 750m 1 km
109
120
A B C D E F
South Tavy Head
West Dart Head
Flat Tor
East Dart River
Sandy Hole Pass
Beehive Hut
Walkham Head
DANGER AREA
PL19
Cowsic Head
Broad Down
Broadun Ring
Maiden Hill
Devil's Tor
Rough Tor
Brown's House (ruin)
Beardown Man
Conies Down Tor
Lower White Tor
Archerton
Crow Tor
Higher White Tor
Lydford Tor
Longaford Tor
Arch Tor
PL20
Cowsic River
Beardown Tors
Black Dunghill
DANGER AREA
Wistman's Wood National Nature Reserve
Chy
Chy
Clapper Bridge
B3212
Holming Beam
Powder Mills
Littaford Tors
DANGER AREA
Devonport Leat
Cherry Brook
Beardown Hill
Hotel
Devonport Leat
Crockern Tor
Smith Hill
Parson's Cottage
Beardown Farm
Blackbrook River
B3212
P
Hotel
Two Bridges
B3357
Waldron Farm
West Dart River
Roundhill Farm
HM Prison (Dartmoor)
Cemy
Dartmoor Prison Mus
TAVISTOCK RD
B3357
TOR VIEW
BARRACK RD
B3212
Prince Hall
8
81
7
80
6
79
5
78
4
77
3
76
2
75
1
74
58 59 60 61 62 63
128
120

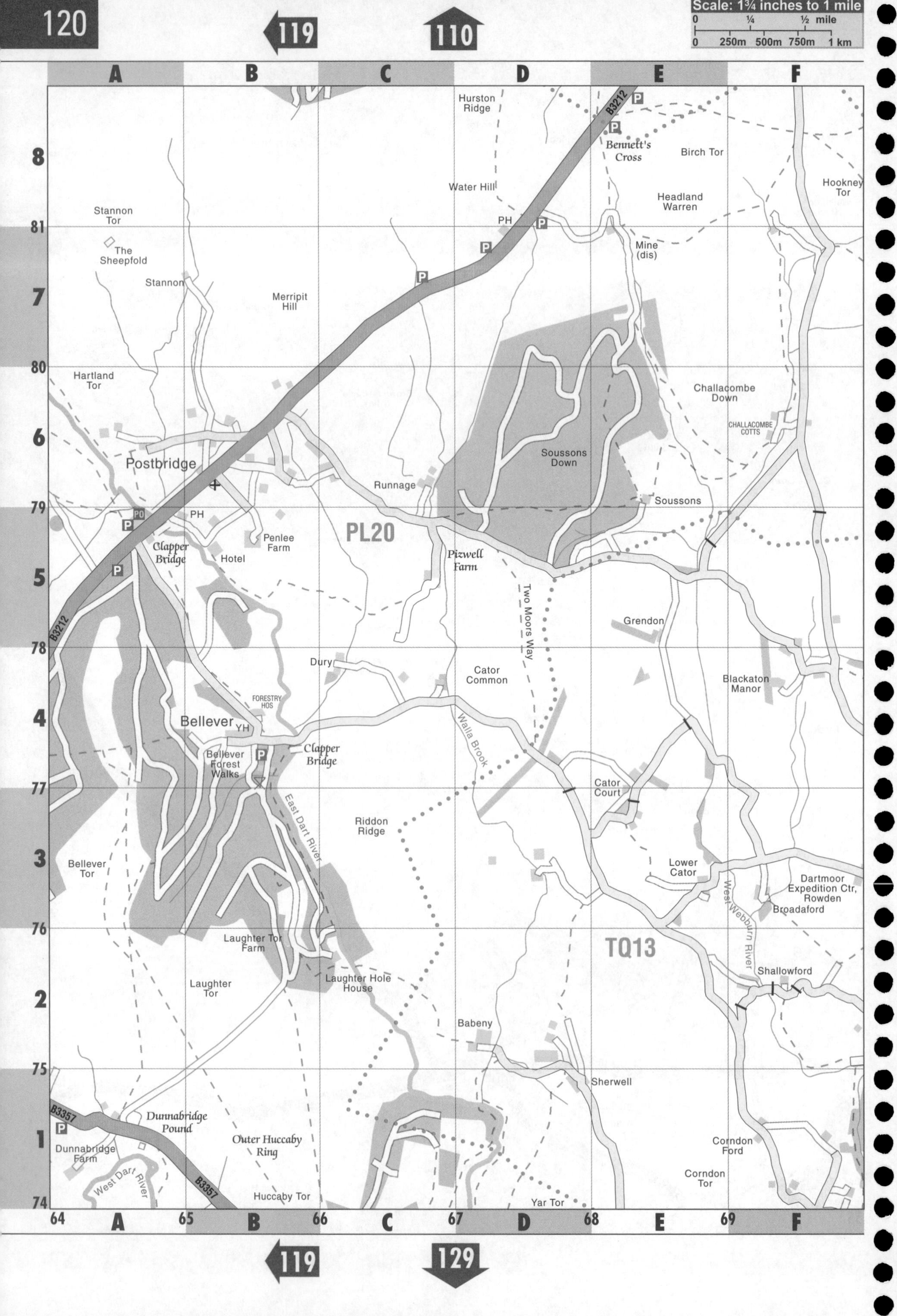
119
110
Scale: 1¾ inches to 1 mile
0
¼
½ mile
0
250m
500m
750m
1 km
A
B
C
D
E
F
Hurston Ridge
B3212
Bennett's Cross
Birch Tor
Water Hill
Hookney Tor
Stannon Tor
Headland Warren
PH
The Sheepfold
Mine (dis)
Stannon
Merripit Hill
Hartland Tor
Challacombe Down
CHALLACOMBE COTTS
Postbridge
Soussons Down
Runnage
Soussons
PO
PH
PL20
Clapper Bridge
Penlee Farm
Hotel
Pizwell Farm
Two Moors Way
Grendon
Dury
Cator Common
Blackaton Manor
FORESTRY HOS
Bellever
YH
Walla Brook
Clapper Bridge
Bellever Forest Walks
Cator Court
East Dart River
Riddon Ridge
Bellever Tor
Lower Cator
Dartmoor Expedition Ctr, Rowden
West Webburn River
Broadaford
Laughter Tor Farm
TQ13
Laughter Tor
Laughter Hole House
Shallowford
Babeny
Sherwell
B3357
Dunnabridge Pound
Outer Huccaby Ring
Corndon Ford
Dunnabridge Farm
West Dart River
Corndon Tor
Huccaby Tor
Yar Tor
8
81
7
80
6
79
5
78
4
77
3
76
2
75
1
74
64
65
66
67
68
69
119
129

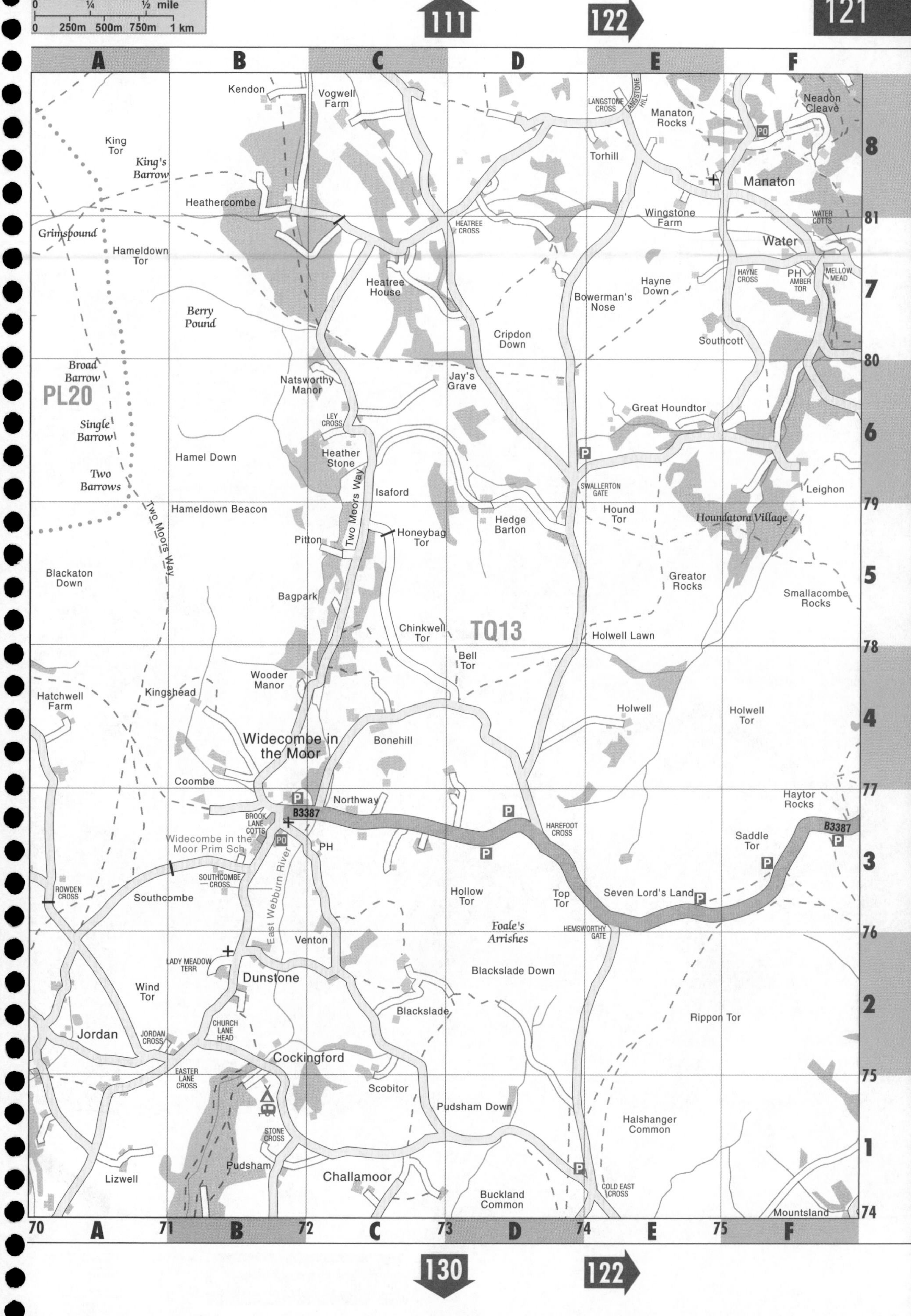
Scale: 1¾ inches to 1 mile
0 ¼ ½ mile
0 250m 500m 750m 1 km
111
122
A B C D E F
Kendon
Vogwell Farm
Langstone Cross
Langstone Hill
Manaton Rocks
Neadon Cleave
PO
King Tor
King's Barrow
Torhill
Manaton
Heathercombe
Heatree Cross
Wingstone Farm
Water Cotts
Water
Grimspound
Hameldown Tor
Heatree House
Hayne Down
Hayne Cross
PH
Amber Tor
Mellow Mead
Bowerman's Nose
Berry Pound
Cripdon Down
Southcott
Broad Barrow
Natsworthy Manor
Jay's Grave
PL20
Ley Cross
Great Houndtor
Single Barrow
Hamel Down
Heather Stone
Two Barrows
Two Moors Way
Isaford
Swallerton Gate
Leighon
Hameldown Beacon
Hedge Barton
Hound Tor
Houndatora Village
Pitton
Honeybag Tor
Blackaton Down
Greator Rocks
Smallacombe Rocks
Bagpark
Chinkwell Tor
TQ13
Holwell Lawn
Bell Tor
Wooder Manor
Hatchwell Farm
Kingshead
Holwell
Holwell Tor
Widecombe in the Moor
Bonehill
Coombe
Northway
Haytor Rocks
B3387
Brook Lane Cotts
Harefoot Cross
Saddle Tor
Widecombe in the Moor Prim Sch
PO
PH
Rowden Cross
Southcombe Cross
Southcombe
East Webburn River
Hollow Tor
Top Tor
Seven Lord's Land
Foale's Arrishes
Hemsworthy Gate
Venton
Lady Meadow Terr
Dunstone
Blackslade Down
Wind Tor
Blackslade
Rippon Tor
Jordan
Jordan Cross
Church Lane Head
Cockingford
Easter Lane Cross
Scobitor
Pudsham Down
Halshanger Common
Stone Cross
Pudsham
Challamoor
Lizwell
Buckland Common
Cold East Cross
Mountsland
8
81
7
80
6
79
5
78
4
77
3
76
2
75
1
74
70 71 72 73 74 75
130
122

121 112

Scale: 1¾ inches to 1 mile
0 ¼ ½ mile
0 250m 500m 750m 1 km

A B C D E F

Raven's Tor
Lustleigh Cleave
Sharpitor
Nut Crackers
Lustleigh
PO
PETHYBRIDGE
Wrayland
LOWER BROOKFIELD COTTS
KNOWLE RD
KELLY CROSS
A382
Kelly
SLADE CROSS
Beadon Farm
BEADON LA
SHAPTOR CROSS
HAWKMOOR
Shaptor Rock
HAWKMOOR COTTS
BOWDEN LA
Cerny
Knowle
Houndtor Wood
Hisley
Becky Falls
Becka Brook
LOWER KNOWLE RD
HATHERLEIGH LA
Gradner Rocks
Stonelands Waste
FORDER LA
KING'S CROSS
HIGHER ALLER LA
FURZELEIGH CROSS
LITTLE JOHN'S WLK
River Bovey
ASHWELL LA
Wolleigh House
LOWER ALLER LA
Beckaford Farm
Trendlebere Down
Pullabrook Farm
TQ13
Dartmoor Way
Stone Row
Whitstone
MORETONHAMPSTEAD RD
FURZELEIGH LA
Southbrook
Reddaford Water
Shewte
180
Black Hill
Yarner Wood
Yarner Wood Nature Trail
GIPSY CNR
SHEWTE CROSS
East Dartmoor Woods & Heaths National Nature Reserve
Parke
Bovey Tracey
MARY ST
EAST ST
Sch
Liby
FORE ST
PO
LOWERDOWN
Lower Down
LOWERDOWN CROSS
Mine (dis)
Yarner
B3387
MONKS WAY
STATION RD
B3344
Craft Ctr
Bovey Tracey
Haytor Down
Challabrook Farm
CHAPPLE RD
Ullacombe Farm
Colehayes Park
Whisselwell Farm
CHALLABROOK LA
ASHBURTON RD
NEWTON RD
Indio
HAYTOR CT.
PH
Hotel
HAYTOR VALE
STENTIFORD LA
LINDER LA
BRIMLEY RD
BRIMLEY LA
WALLFIELD RD
POTTERY RD
Brimley
Bsns Pk
GREEN LA
Green Lane
180
B3387
Slade Mead
LAKESIDE CL
Ind Est
A382
Pinchaford
Narracombe
Langaller
SMOKEY CROSS
Hotel
PO
Ilsington CE Prim Sch
Ilsington
WOODHOUSE CROSS
Wilsworthy
TIPLEYHILL LA
LEWTHORN CROSS
HONEYWELL LA
OLD TOWN HILL
Belle Vue
Bag Tor
HILLCREST 1
DREWSMEAD 2
TOWN MDW 3
SIMMS HILL
TIPLEYHILL CROSS
Great Plantation
BIRCHANGER CROSS
LENDA LA
Lenda
Liverton
Bagtor House
SIGFORD CROSS
FOUR CROSS
Lounston
WILLIS'S CROSS
KEL CL
Coldeast
PH
180
SHAPLEY WAY
BENEDICTS RD
TQ12
FIVE CROSS
Rora Wood
HALFORD CROSS
MOUNTHILL COTTS
BARN PK
Rora House
Halford
BETHELCOMBE CROSS
Higher Sigford
Blackpool CE Prim Sch
Blackpool
A38
STAPLEHILL RD
Horridge
BETHEL CROSS
Ramshorn Down

8 81 7 80 6 79 5 78 4 77 3 76 2 75 1 74

76 A 77 B 78 C 79 D 80 E 81 F

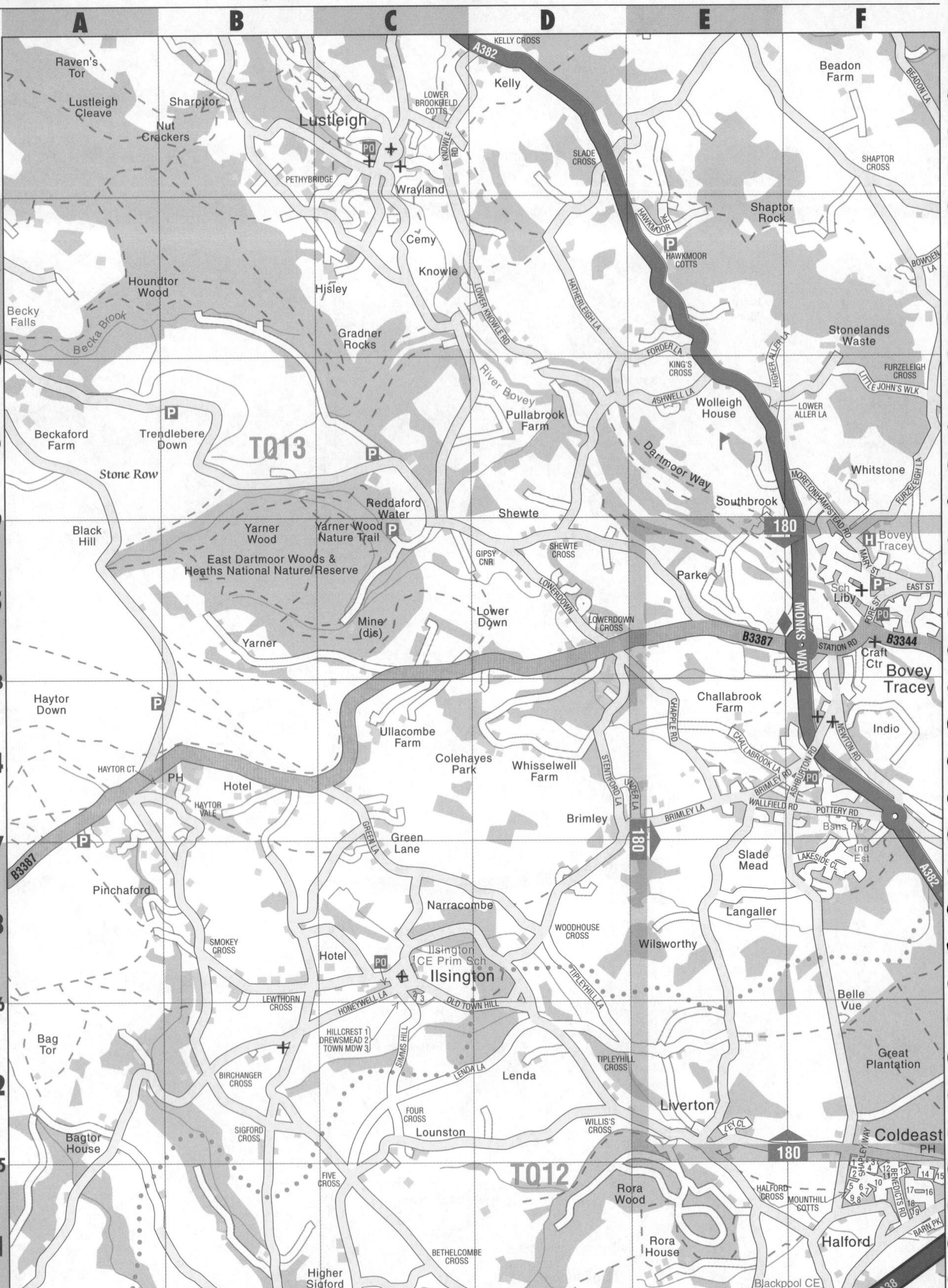

121 131

For full street detail of the highlighted area see page 180.

F1
1 LASKEYS HEATH
2 TAYLORS NEWTAKE
3 LEAT MDW
4 ROWELLS MEAD
5 BEAUMONT CL
6 DIVETT DR
7 MUNRO MEAD
8 POMEROY PL
9 FLOWERS MDW
10 KITTERSLEY DR
11 CHAPEL LA
12 BEANHAY CL
13 BENLEARS ACRE
14 BICKFORDS GN
15 SUMMERLANDS CT
16 SUMMERHILL RD
17 SUMMERHILL CRES
18 SUMMERHILL CL
19 BENEDICTS CL

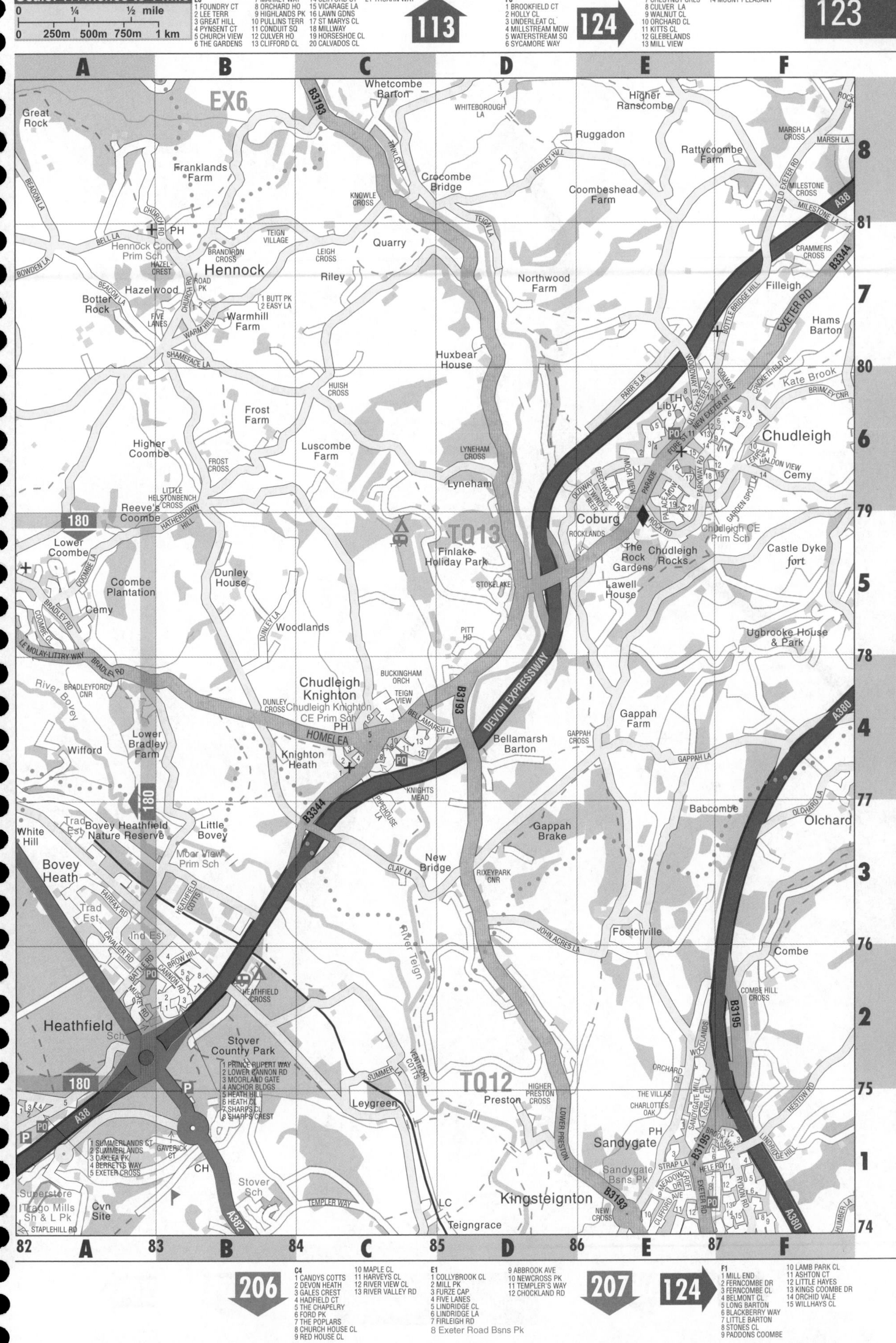

Scale: 1¾ inches to 1 mile
0 ¼ ½ mile
0 250m 500m 750m 1 km
E6
1 FOUNDRY CT
2 LEE TERR
3 GREAT HILL
4 PYNSENT CT
5 CHURCH VIEW
6 THE GARDENS
7 MARKET WAY
8 ORCHARD HO
9 HIGHLANDS PK
10 PULLINS TERR
11 CONDUIT SQ
12 CULVER HO
13 CLIFFORD CL
14 CLIFFORD ST
15 VICARAGE LA
16 LAWN GDNS
17 ST MARYS CL
18 MILLWAY
19 HORSESHOE CL
20 CALVADOS CL
21 TROARN WAY
113
F6
1 BROOKFIELD CT
2 HOLLY CL
3 UNDERLEAT CL
4 MILLSTREAM MDW
5 WATERSTREAM SQ
6 SYCAMORE WAY
124
7 CHESTNUT CRES
8 CULVER LA
9 WALNUT CL
10 ORCHARD CL
11 KITTS CL
12 GLEBELANDS
13 MILL VIEW
14 MOUNT PLEASANT
123
A B C D E F
EX6
Great Rock
Whetcombe Barton
Higher Ranscombe
Ruggadon
Rattycoombe Farm
Franklands Farm
Crocombe Bridge
Coombeshead Farm
Hennock Com Prim Sch
Hennock
Quarry
Riley
Northwood Farm
Filleigh
Hazelwood
Botter Rock
Warmhill Farm
Hams Barton
Huxbear House
Kate Brook
Frost Farm
Luscombe Farm
Chudleigh
Higher Coombe
Lyneham
Cemy
Reeve's Coombe
Coburg
Chudleigh CE Prim Sch
180
Lower Coombe
TQ13
Finlake Holiday Park
The Rock Gardens
Chudleigh Rocks
Castle Dyke fort
Coombe Plantation
Dunley House
Lawell House
Cemy
Woodlands
Ugbrooke House & Park
River Bovey
Chudleigh Knighton
Chudleigh Knighton CE Prim Sch
Gappah Farm
Lower Bradley Farm
Wifford
Bellamarsh Barton
Knighton Heath
DEVON EXPRESSWAY
Babcombe
Olchard
White Hill
Trad Est
Bovey Heathfield Nature Reserve
Little Bovey
Gappah Brake
Bovey Heath
Moor View Prim Sch
New Bridge
Trad Est
Ind Est
River Teign
Fosterville
Combe
Heathfield
Stover Country Park
TQ12
Preston
Leygreen
Sandygate
Sandygate Bsns Pk
Superstore
Trago Mills Sh & L Pk
Cvn Site
Stover Sch
Kingsteignton
Teigngrace
B3193 B3344 B3195 A38 A380 A382
82 83 84 85 86 87
81 80 79 78 77 76 75 74
8 7 6 5 4 3 2 1
206
C4
1 CANDYS COTTS
2 DEVON HEATH
3 GALES CREST
4 HADFIELD CT
5 THE CHAPELRY
6 FORD PK
7 THE POPLARS
8 CHURCH HOUSE CL
9 RED HOUSE CL
10 MAPLE CL
11 HARVEYS CL
12 RIVER VIEW CL
13 RIVER VALLEY RD
E1
1 COLLYBROOK CL
2 MILL PK
3 FURZE CAP
4 FIVE LANES
5 LINDRIDGE CL
6 LINDRIDGE LA
7 FIRLEIGH RD
8 Exeter Road Bsns Pk
9 ABBROOK AVE
10 NEWCROSS PK
11 TEMPLER'S WAY
12 CHOCKLAND RD
207
124
F1
1 MILL END
2 FERNCOMBE DR
3 FERNCOMBE CL
4 BELMONT CL
5 LONG BARTON
6 BLACKBERRY WAY
7 LITTLE BARTON
8 STONES CL
9 PADDONS COOMBE
10 LAMB PARK CL
11 ASHTON CT
12 LITTLE HAYES
13 KINGS COOMBE DR
14 ORCHID VALE
15 WILLHAYS CL

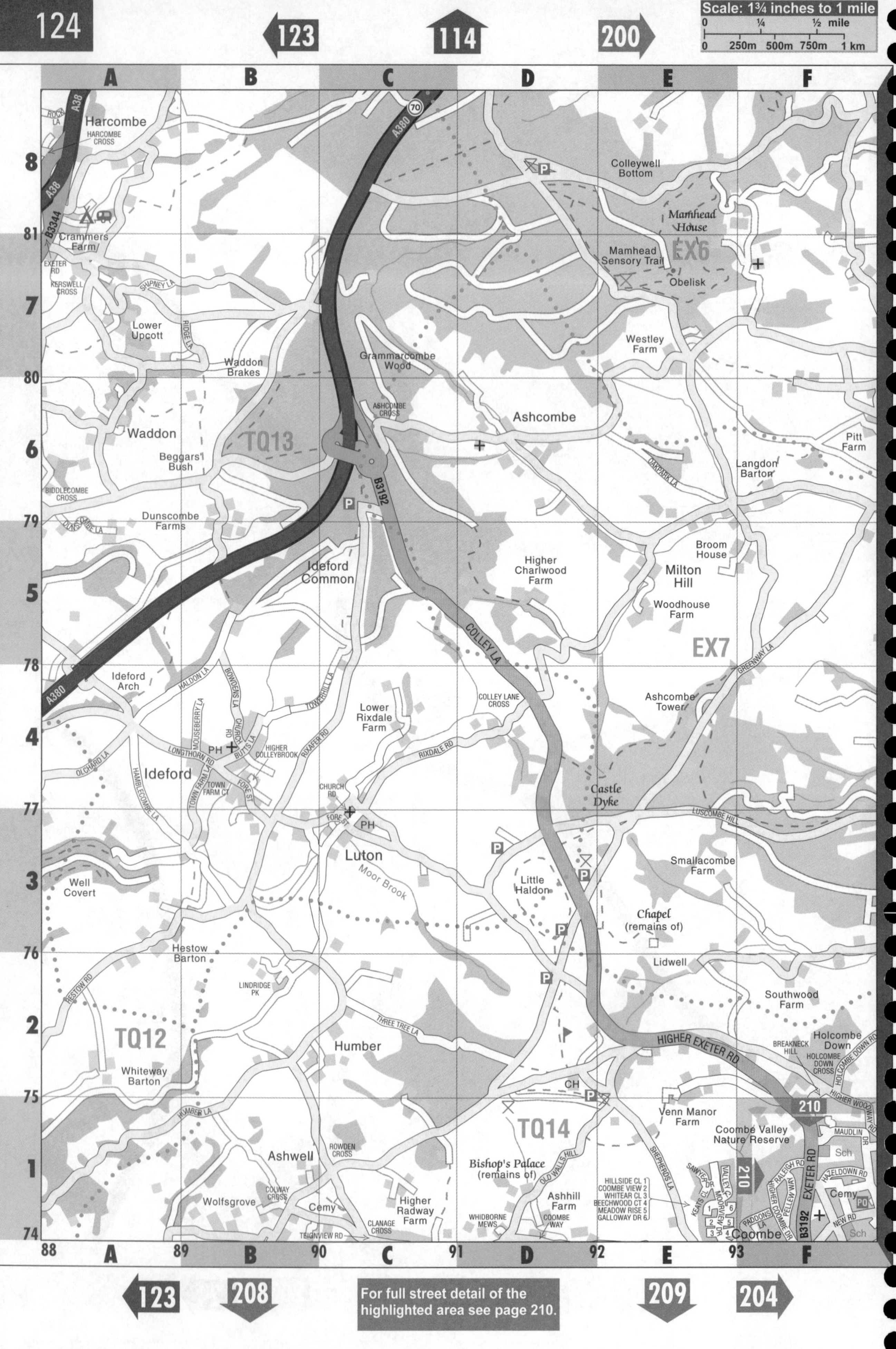
124
123
114
200
Scale: 1¾ inches to 1 mile
0
¼
½ mile
0
250m
500m
750m
1 km
A
B
C
D
E
F
8
81
7
80
6
79
5
78
4
77
3
76
2
75
1
74
88
89
90
91
92
93
A38
A380
B3344
B3192
70
Rock La
Harcombe
Harcombe Cross
Crammers Farm
Exeter Rd
Kerswell Cross
Shipney La
Lower Upcott
Ridge La
Waddon Brakes
Waddon
Beggars' Bush
Biddlecombe Cross
Dunscombe La
Dunscombe Farms
TQ13
Grammarcombe Wood
Ashcombe Cross
Ashcombe
Colleywell Bottom
Mamhead House
Mamhead Sensory Trail
EX6
Obelisk
Westley Farm
Oakpark La
Pitt Farm
Langdon Barton
Broom House
Milton Hill
Woodhouse Farm
Higher Charlwood Farm
Ideford Common
EX7
Greenway La
Colley La
Colley Lane Cross
Ashcombe Tower
Ideford Arch
Haldon La
Bowdens La
Mouseberry La
Church Rd
Butts La
Higher Colleybrook
Towerhill La
Lower Rixdale Farm
Rixdale Rd
Rixafer Rd
PH
Longthorn Rd
Olchard La
Ideford
Hamblecombe La
Town Farm La
Town Farm Ct
Fore St
Church Rd
Fore St
PH
Castle Dyke
Luscombe Hill
Luton
Moor Brook
Little Haldon
Smallacombe Farm
Well Covert
Chapel (remains of)
Hestow Barton
Lidwell
Hestow Rd
Lindridge Pk
Southwood Farm
Three Tree La
TQ12
Humber
Higher Exeter Rd
Holcombe Down
Breakneck Hill
Holcombe Down Cross
Holcombe Down Rd
Whiteway Barton
CH
Higher Woodway Rd
210
Humber La
TQ14
Venn Manor Farm
Maudlin Dr
Coombe Valley Nature Reserve
Sch
Rowden Cross
Ashwell
Bishop's Palace (remains of)
Old Walls Hill
Shepherds La
Sawyers Dr
Valley Cl
Moorview Dr
Keats Cl
Raleigh Rd
Pellew Way
Higher Coombe Dr
Exeter Rd
Hazeldown Rd
Cemy
PO
Hillside Cl 1
Coombe View 2
Whitear Cl 3
Beechwood Ct 4
Meadow Rise 5
Galloway Dr 6
Ashhill Farm
Colway Cross
Wolfsgrove
Cemy
Higher Radway Farm
Whidborne Mews
Coombe Way
Paddons La
New Rd
Clanage Cross
Teignview Rd
Coombe
Sch
123
208
For full street detail of the highlighted area see page 210.
209
204

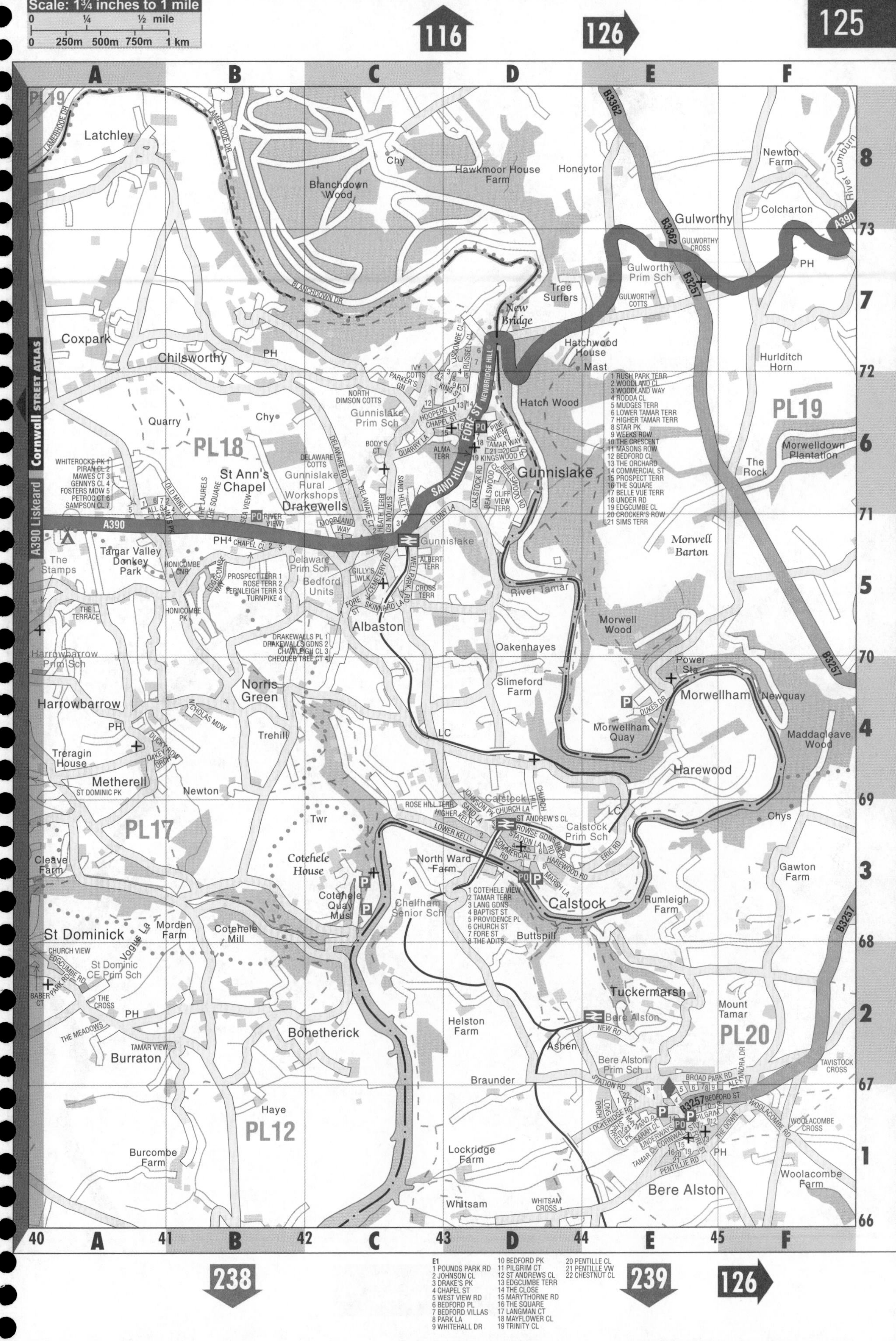
Scale: 1¾ inches to 1 mile
0 ¼ ½ mile
0 250m 500m 750m 1 km
116
126
Latchley
Coxpark
Chilsworthy
Blanchdown Wood
Chy
Hawkmoor House Farm
Honeytor
Newton Farm
Colcharton
Gulworthy
Gulworthy Prim Sch
Gulworthy Cotts
Tree Surfers
New Bridge
Hatchwood House
Mast
Hurlditch Horn
Hatch Wood
PL19
PL18
Quarry
St Ann's Chapel
Gunnislake Prim Sch
Gunnislake
Gunnislake Rural Workshops
Drakewells
Morwelldown Plantation
The Rock
Morwell Barton
1 RUSH PARK TERR
2 WOODLAND CL
3 WOODLAND WAY
4 RODDA CL
5 MUDGES TERR
6 LOWER TAMAR TERR
7 HIGHER TAMAR TERR
8 STAR PK
9 WEEKS ROW
10 THE CRESCENT
11 MASONS ROW
12 BEDFORD CL
13 THE ORCHARD
14 COMMERCIAL ST
15 PROSPECT TERR
16 THE SQUARE
17 BELLE VUE TERR
18 UNDER RD
19 EDGCUMBE CL
20 CROCKER'S ROW
21 SIMS TERR
WHITEROCKS PK 1
PIRAN CL 2
MAWES CT 3
GENNYS CL 4
FOSTERS MDW 5
PETROC CT 6
SAMPSON CL 7
A390 Liskeard
Tamar Valley Donkey Park
The Stamps
Delaware Prim Sch
Bedford Units
Albaston
River Tamar
Morwell Wood
Oakenhayes
Slimeford Farm
Power Sta
Morwellham
Newquay
Morwellham Quay
Maddacleave Wood
Harewood
Harrowbarrow Prim Sch
Harrowbarrow
Norris Green
Treragin House
Metherell
Trehill
Newton
PL17
Twr
Cotehele House
Calstock
Calstock Prim Sch
Chys
Cleave Farm
North Ward Farm
Gawton Farm
Cotehele Quay Mus
Chelfham Senior Sch
Rumleigh Farm
1 COTEHELE VIEW
2 TAMAR TERR
3 LANG GDNS
4 BAPTIST ST
5 PROVIDENCE PL
6 CHURCH ST
7 FORE ST
8 THE ADITS
St Dominick
Morden Farm
Cotehele Mill
Buttspill
St Dominic CE Prim Sch
Tuckermarsh
Mount Tamar
Helston Farm
Bere Alston
PL20
Bohetherick
Burraton
Ashen
Bere Alston Prim Sch
Braunder
Tavistock Cross
Haye
PL12
Burcombe Farm
Lockridge Farm
Woolacombe Cross
Woolacombe Farm
Whitsam
Whitsam Cross
A390
B3362
B3257
238
239
126
E1
1 POUNDS PARK RD
2 JOHNSON CL
3 DRAKE'S PK
4 CHAPEL ST
5 WEST VIEW RD
6 BEDFORD PL
7 BEDFORD VILLAS
8 PARK LA
9 WHITEHALL DR
10 BEDFORD PK
11 PILGRIM CT
12 ST ANDREWS CL
13 EDGCUMBE TERR
14 THE CLOSE
15 MARYTHORNE RD
16 THE SQUARE
17 LANGMAN CT
18 MAYFLOWER CL
19 TRINITY CL
20 PENTILLIE CL
21 PENTILLIE VW
22 CHESTNUT CL

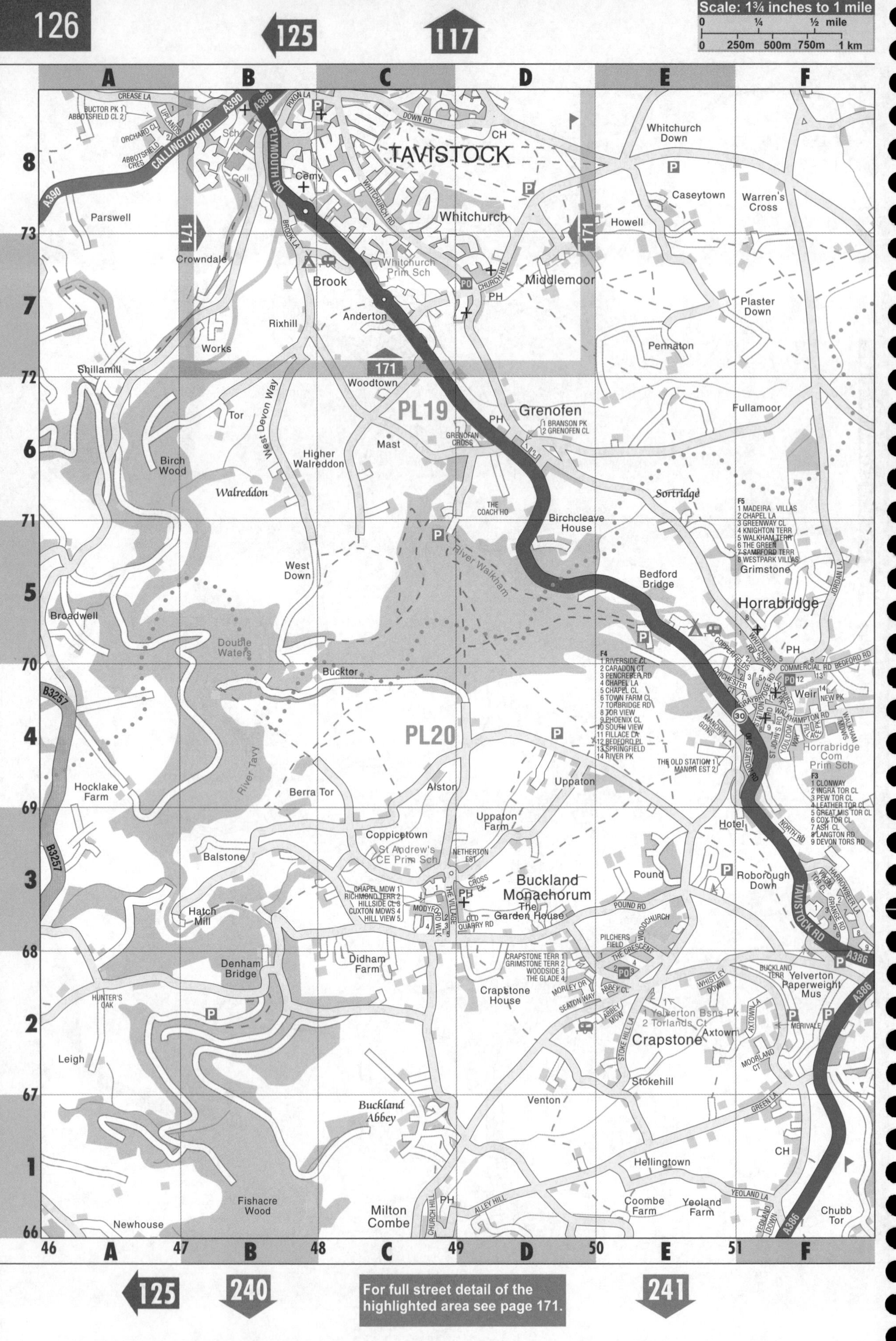

125
240
For full street detail of the highlighted area see page 171.
241

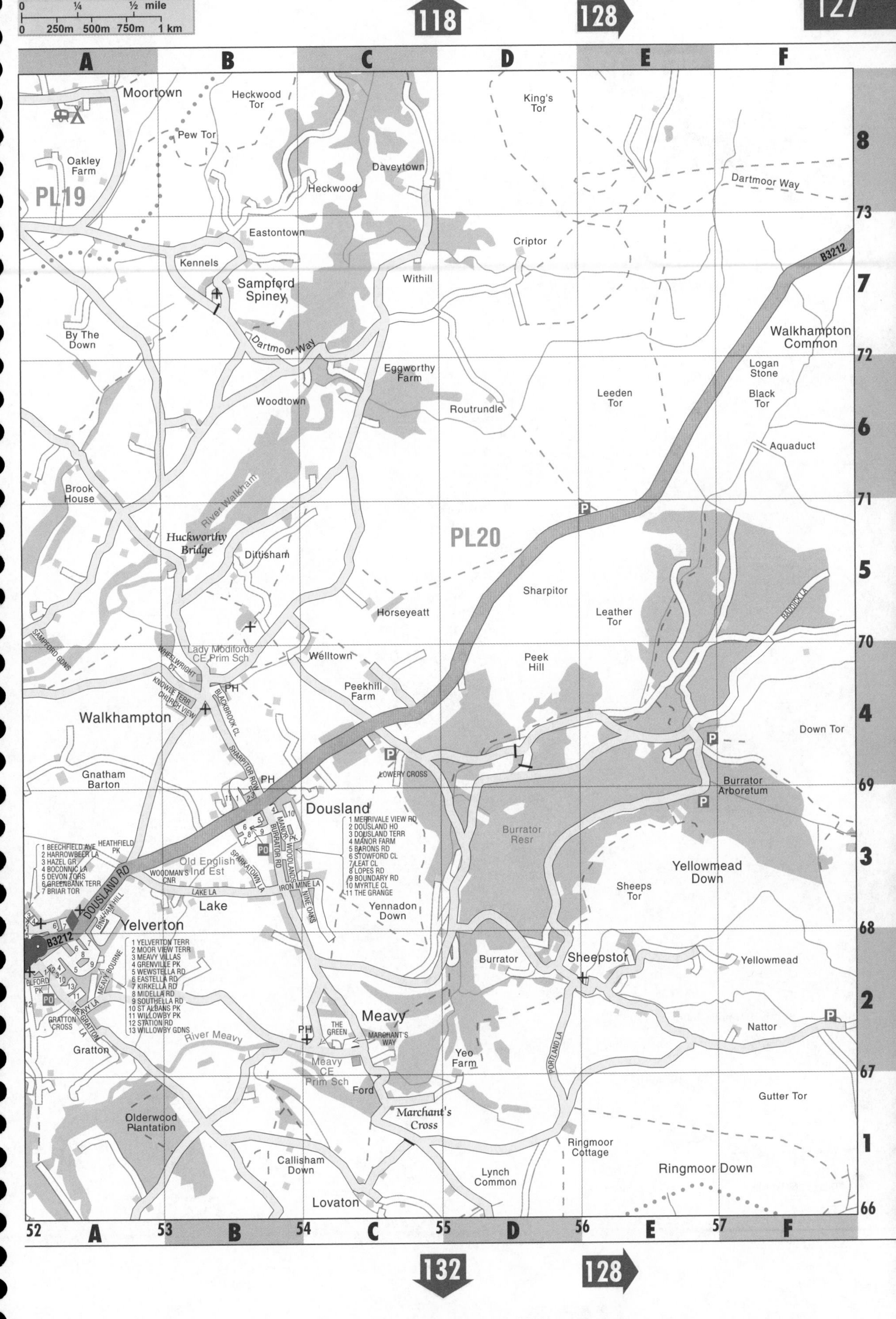

Scale: 1¾ inches to 1 mile
0 ¼ ½ mile
0 250m 500m 750m 1 km
118
128
A B C D E F
8 73 7 72 6 71 5 70 4 69 3 68 2 67 1 66
52 53 54 55 56 57
Moortown
Heckwood Tor
Pew Tor
King's Tor
Oakley Farm
PL19
Daveytown
Heckwood
Dartmoor Way
Eastontown
Criptor
Kennels
Sampford Spiney
Withill
B3212
By The Down
Walkhampton Common
Logan Stone
Eggworthy Farm
Leeden Tor
Black Tor
Woodtown
Routrundle
Aquaduct
Brook House
River Walkham
Huckworthy Bridge
PL20
Dittisham
Sharpitor
Leather Tor
Horseyeatt
SAMPFORD GDNS
WHEELWRIGHT CT
Lady Modifords CE Prim Sch
Welltown
Peek Hill
RADDICK LA
KNOWLE TERR
CHURCH VIEW
PH
Peekhill Farm
Walkhampton
BLACKBROOK CL
Down Tor
SHARPITOR ROW
LOWERY CROSS
Gnatham Barton
PH
Burrator Arboretum
Dousland
1 MERRIVALE VIEW RD
2 DOUSLAND HO
3 DOUSLAND TERR
4 MANOR FARM
5 BARONS RD
6 STOWFORD CL
7 LEAT CL
8 LOPES RD
9 BOUNDARY RD
10 MYRTLE CL
11 THE GRANGE
MANOR RD
BURRATOR RD
WOODLANDS
Burrator Resr
1 BEECHFIELD AVE
2 HARROWBEER LA
3 HAZEL GR
4 BOCONNIC LA
5 DEVON TORS
6 GREENBANK TERR
7 BRIAR TOR
HEATHFIELD PK
Old English Ind Est
SPARKATOWN LA
WOODMAN'S CNR
DOUSLAND RD
Yellowmead Down
Sheeps Tor
LAKE LA
IRON MINE LA
NINE OAKS
Lake
Yennadon Down
BINKHAM HILL
Yelverton
B3212
1 YELVERTON TERR
2 MOOR VIEW TERR
3 MEAVY VILLAS
4 GRENVILLE PK
5 WEWSTELLA RD
6 EASTELLA RD
7 KIRKELLA RD
8 MIDELLA RD
9 SOUTHELLA RD
10 ST ALBANS PK
11 WILLOWBY PK
12 STATION RD
13 WILLOWBY GDNS
MEAVY BOURNE
Burrator
Sheepstor
Yellowmead
ELFORD PK
PO
MEAVY LA
GRATTON CROSS
GRATTON LA
Meavy
THE GREEN
MARCHANT'S WAY
Nattor
River Meavy
PH
Gratton
Meavy CE Prim Sch
Yeo Farm
PORTLAND LA
Ford
Gutter Tor
Olderwood Plantation
Marchant's Cross
Ringmoor Cottage
Callisham Down
Lynch Common
Ringmoor Down
Lovaton
132
128

127
119

Scale: 1¾ inches to 1 mile

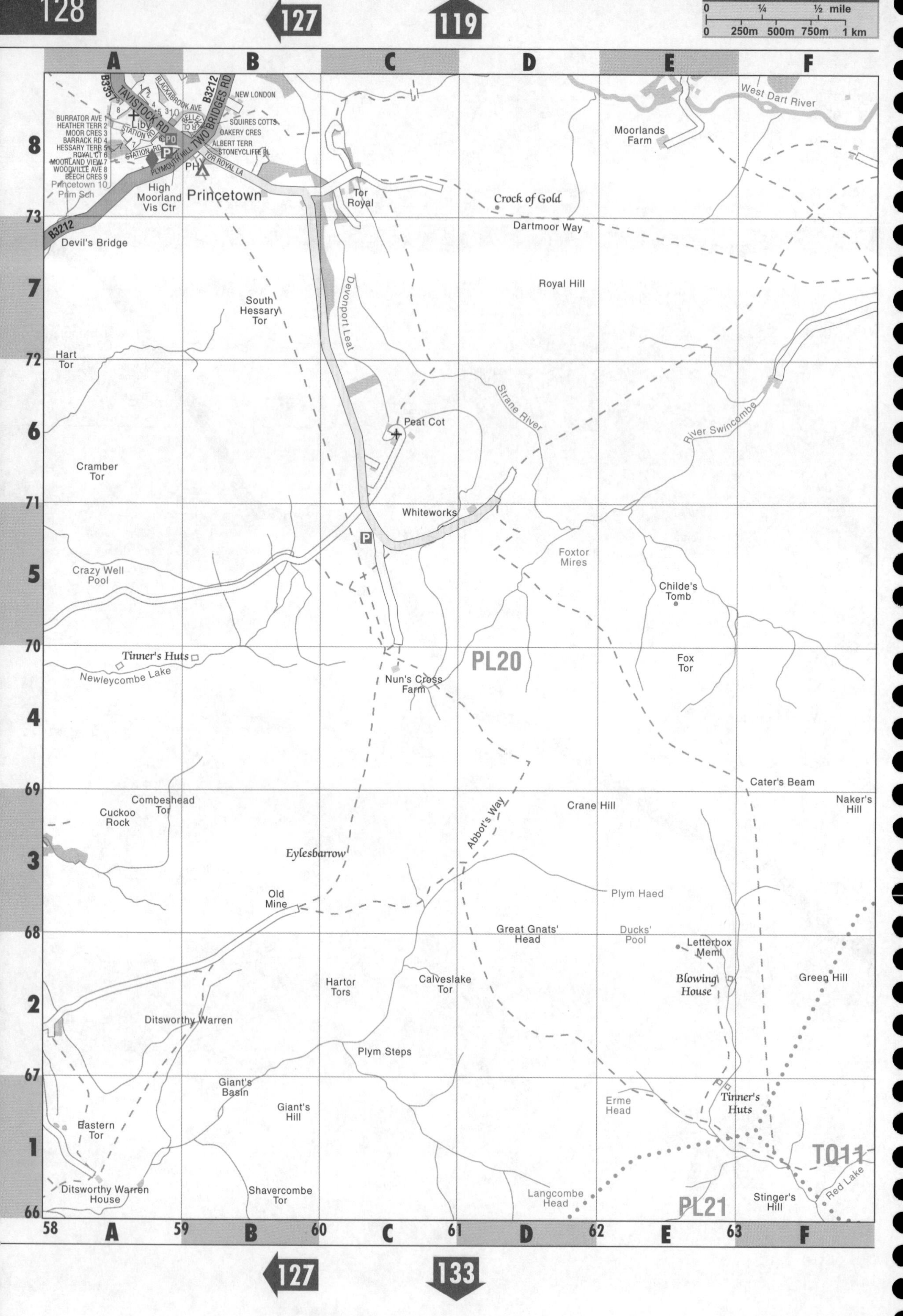

127
133

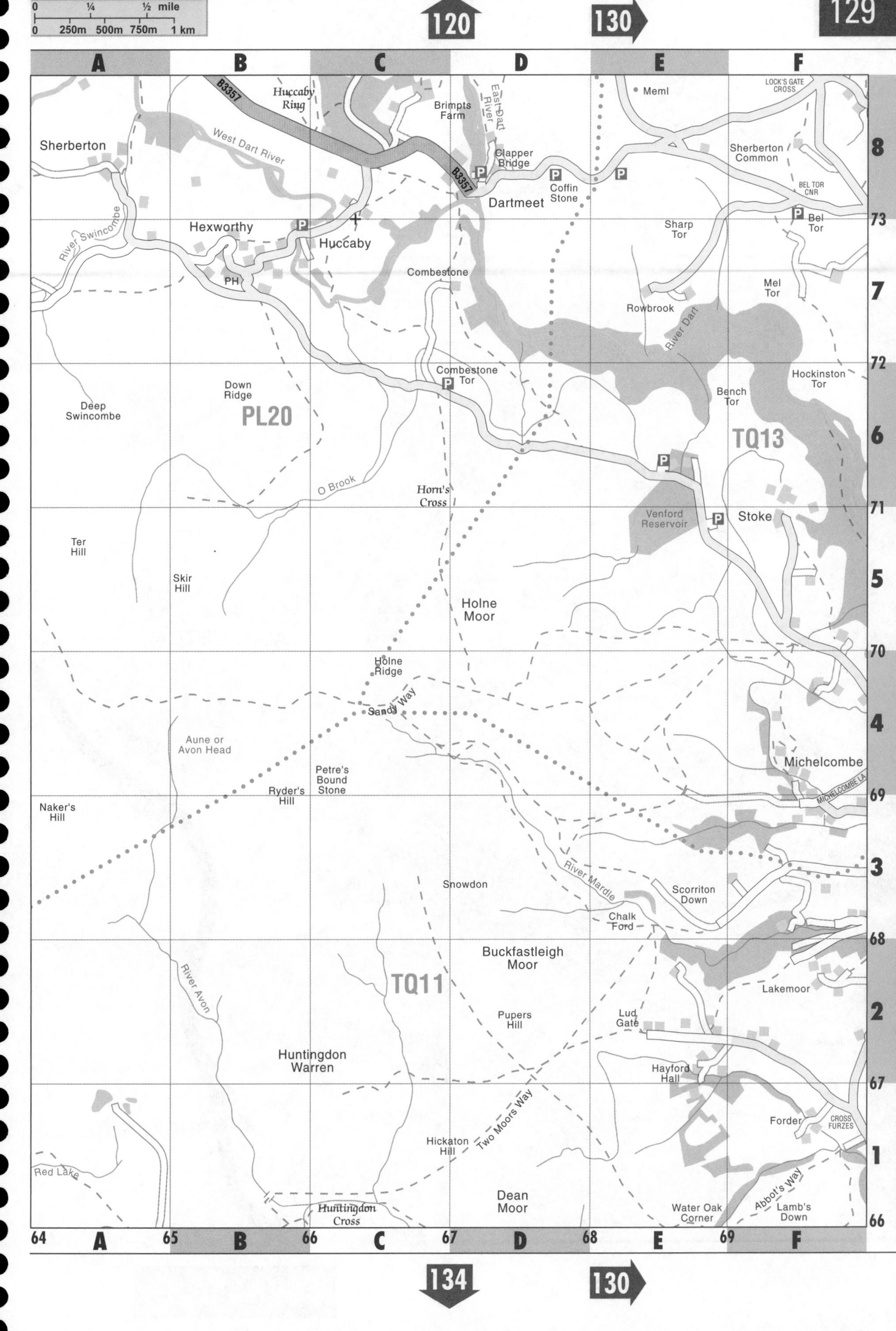
Scale: 1¾ inches to 1 mile
0 ¼ ½ mile
0 250m 500m 750m 1 km
120
130
A B C D E F
Sherberton
Huccaby Ring
Brimpts Farm
East Dart River
Meml
LOCK'S GATE CROSS
West Dart River
B3357
Clapper Bridge
Sherberton Common
Coffin Stone
Dartmeet
BEL TOR CNR
Bel Tor
Hexworthy
Huccaby
Sharp Tor
River Swincombe
PH
Combestone
Mel Tor
Rowbrook
River Dart
Combestone Tor
Hockinston Tor
Down Ridge
PL20
Bench Tor
Deep Swincombe
TQ13
O Brook
Horn's Cross
Venford Reservoir
Stoke
Ter Hill
Skir Hill
Holne Moor
Holne Ridge
Sandy Way
Aune or Avon Head
Michelcombe
Petre's Bound Stone
MICHELCOMBE LA
Ryder's Hill
Naker's Hill
River Mardle
Snowdon
Scorriton Down
Chalk Ford
Buckfastleigh Moor
River Avon
TQ11
Lakemoor
Pupers Hill
Lud Gate
Huntingdon Warren
Hayford Hall
Two Moors Way
Forder
CROSS FURZES
Hickaton Hill
Red Lake
Abbot's Way
Dean Moor
Huntingdon Cross
Water Oak Corner
Lamb's Down
8 73 7 72 6 71 5 70 4 69 3 68 2 67 1 66
64 65 66 67 68 69
134
130

129
121

Scale: 1¾ inches to 1 mile

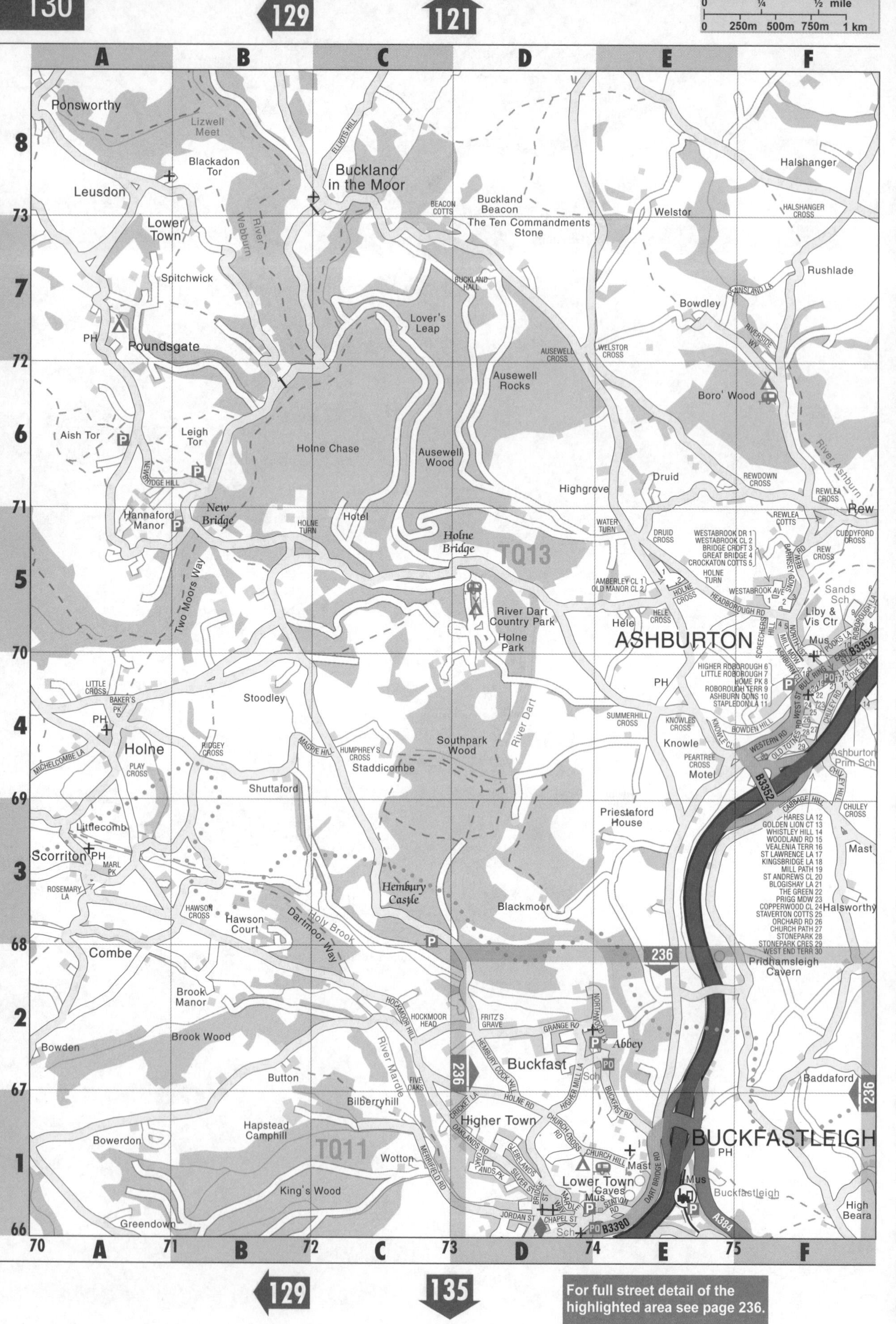

129
135
For full street detail of the highlighted area see page 236.

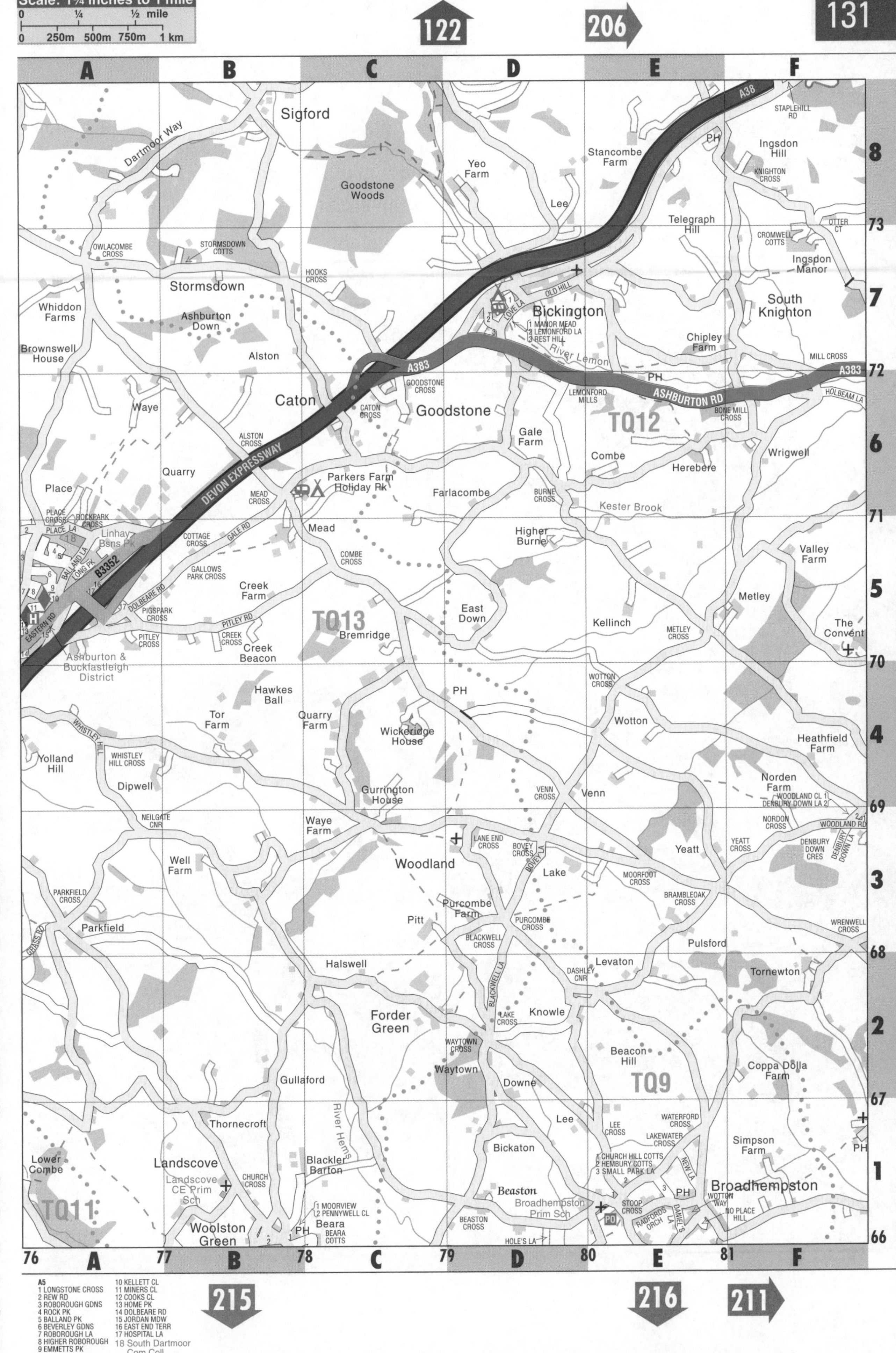
Scale: 1¾ inches to 1 mile
0 ¼ ½ mile
0 250m 500m 750m 1 km
122
206
131
A B C D E F
Sigford
Dartmoor Way
Goodstone Woods
Yeo Farm
Stancombe Farm
Lee
A38
STAPLEHILL RD
PH
Ingsdon Hill
KNIGHTON CROSS
Telegraph Hill
OTTER CT
CROMWELL COTTS
Ingsdon Manor
South Knighton
OWLACOMBE CROSS
STORMSDOWN COTTS
Stormsdown
HOOKS CROSS
OLD HILL
LOVE LA
Bickington
1 MANOR MEAD
2 LEMONFORD LA
3 REST HILL
Whiddon Farms
Ashburton Down
Brownswell House
Alston
River Lemon
Chipley Farm
MILL CROSS
A383
Waye
Caton
GOODSTONE CROSS
CATON CROSS
Goodstone
LEMONFORD MILLS
PH
ASHBURTON RD
TQ12
BONE MILL CROSS
HOLBEAM LA
ALSTON CROSS
DEVON EXPRESSWAY
Gale Farm
Combe
Herebere
Wrigwell
Quarry
Parkers Farm Holiday Pk
Farlacombe
BURNE CROSS
Kester Brook
Place
MEAD CROSS
PLACE CROSS
ROCKPARK CROSS
PLACE LA
Linhay Bsns Pk
GALE RD
Mead
Higher Burne
COTTAGE CROSS
BALLAND LA
LONG PK
B3352
GALLOWS PARK CROSS
COMBE CROSS
Valley Farm
Creek Farm
DOLBEARE RD
East Down
Metley
PIGSPARK CROSS
TQ13
PITLEY RD
Bremridge
Kellinch
METLEY CROSS
The Convent
EASTERN RD
PITLEY CROSS
CREEK CROSS
Creek Beacon
Ashburton & Buckfastleigh District
Hawkes Ball
PH
WOTTON CROSS
WHISTLEY HILL
Tor Farm
Quarry Farm
Wickeridge House
Wotton
Heathfield Farm
Yolland Hill
WHISTLEY HILL CROSS
Dipwell
Gurrington House
VENN CROSS
Venn
Norden Farm
WOODLAND CL 1
DENBURY DOWN LA 2
NEILGATE CNR
Waye Farm
LANE END CROSS
BOVEY CROSS
BOVEY LA
NORDON CROSS
WOODLAND RD
YEATT CROSS
Yeatt
DENBURY DOWN CRES
DENBURY DOWN LA
Well Farm
Woodland
Lake
MOORFOOT CROSS
PARKFIELD CROSS
BRAMBLEOAK CROSS
Purcombe Farm
Pitt
PURCOMBE CROSS
GRASS RD
Parkfield
BLACKWELL CROSS
Pulsford
WRENWELL CROSS
Halswell
Levaton
Tornewton
DASHLEY CNR
BLACKWELL LA
Forder Green
LAKE CROSS
Knowle
WAYTOWN CROSS
Beacon Hill
Waytown
Coppa Dolla Farm
Gullaford
Downe
TQ9
River Hems
Thornecroft
Lee
LEE CROSS
WATERFORD CROSS
LAKEWATER CROSS
Simpson Farm
Lower Combe
Bickaton
PH
Landscove
Blackler Barton
1 CHURCH HILL COTTS
2 HEMBURY COTTS
3 SMALL PARK LA
NEW LA
Landscove CE Prim Sch
CHURCH CROSS
Broadhempston
Beaston
PH
WOTTON WAY
1 MOORVIEW
2 PENNYWELL CL
Broadhempston Prim Sch
TQ11
STOOP CROSS
NO PLACE HILL
Woolston Green
Beara
BEARA COTTS
BEASTON CROSS
RADFORDS ORCH
DANIEL'S LA
PH
PO
HOLE'S LA
73 72 71 70 69 68 67 66
8 7 6 5 4 3 2 1
76 77 78 79 80 81
A5
1 LONGSTONE CROSS
2 REW RD
3 ROBOROUGH GDNS
4 ROCK PK
5 BALLAND PK
6 BEVERLEY GDNS
7 ROBOROUGH LA
8 HIGHER ROBOROUGH
9 EMMETTS PK
10 KELLETT CL
11 MINERS CL
12 COOKS CL
13 HOME PK
14 DOLBEARE RD
15 JORDAN MDW
16 EAST END TERR
17 HOSPITAL LA
18 South Dartmoor Com Coll
215
216
211

241
127

Scale: 1¾ inches to 1 mile

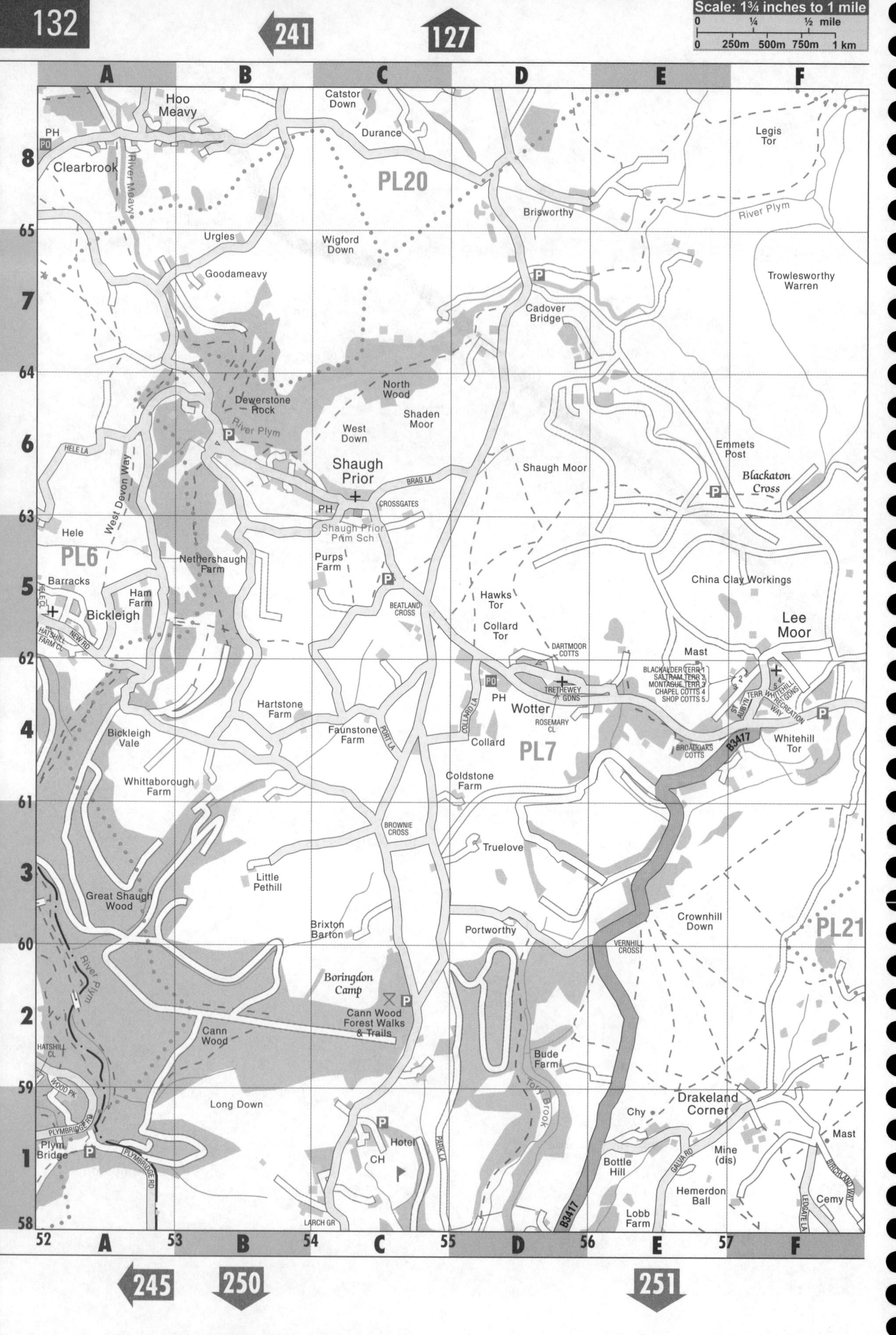

245
250
251

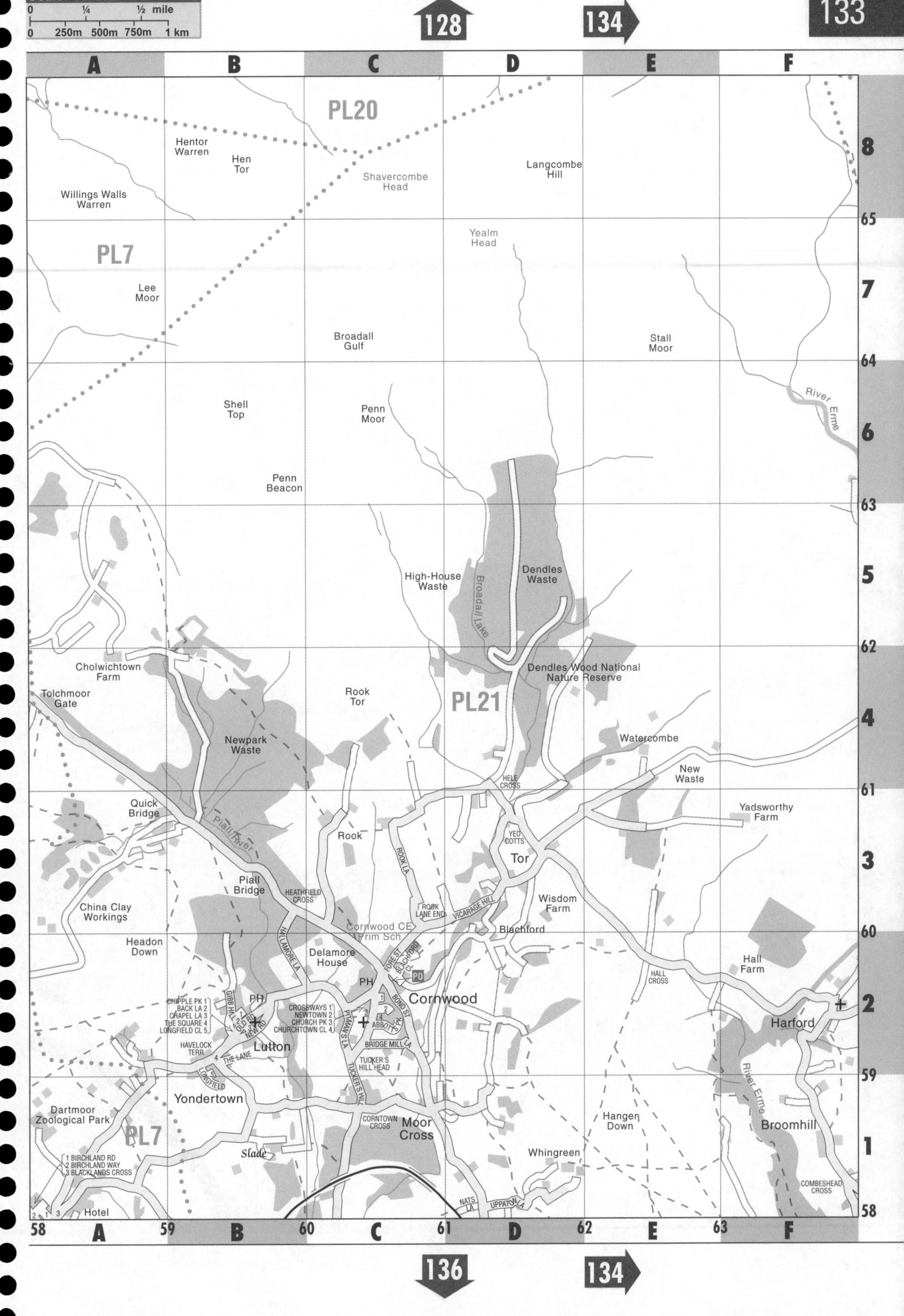
Scale: 1¾ inches to 1 mile
0 ¼ ½ mile
0 250m 500m 750m 1 km
128
134
A B C D E F
PL20
Hentor Warren
Hen Tor
Shavercombe Head
Langcombe Hill
Willings Walls Warren
Yealm Head
PL7
Lee Moor
Broadall Gulf
Stall Moor
River Erme
Shell Top
Penn Moor
Penn Beacon
High-House Waste
Broadall Lake
Dendles Waste
Cholwichtown Farm
Dendles Wood National Nature Reserve
Tolchmoor Gate
Rook Tor
PL21
Newpark Waste
Watercombe
New Waste
HELE CROSS
Quick Bridge
Yadsworthy Farm
Piall River
Rook
YEO COTTS
Tor
ROOK LA
Piall Bridge
HEATHFIELD CROSS
ROOK LANE END
VICARAGE HILL
Wisdom Farm
China Clay Workings
Cornwood CE Prim Sch
Blachford
Headon Down
HALLAMORE LA
Delamore House
FORE ST
BLACHFORD CL
PO
Hall Farm
HALL CROSS
PH
PH
Cornwood
BOND ST
CHIPPLE PK 1
BACK LA 2
CHAPEL LA 3
THE SQUARE 4
LONGFIELD CL 5
GIBB HILL
OLD RD
NEW RD
CROSSWAYS 1
NEWTOWN 2
CHURCH PK 3
CHURCHTOWN CL 4
PITMAN'S LA
ABBOTTS PK
Harford
BRIDGE MILL LA
HAVELOCK TERR
THE LANE
Lutton
TUCKER'S HILL HEAD
TUCKER'S HILL
LONGFIELD
River Erme
Yondertown
Dartmoor Zoological Park
CORNTOWN CROSS
Moor Cross
Hangen Down
Broomhill
PL7
1 BIRCHLAND RD
2 BIRCHLAND WAY
3 BLACKLANDS CROSS
Slade
Whingreen
COMBESHEAD CROSS
NATS LA
UPPATON LA
Hotel
58 59 60 61 62 63
65 64 63 62 61 60 59 58
8 7 6 5 4 3 2 1
136
134

133
129

Scale: 1¾ inches to 1 mile
0 ¼ ½ mile
0 250m 500m 750m 1 km

A B C D E F

Brown Heath
Crossways
Bishop's Mead
Dean Moor
Water Oak Corner
Lambs Down
Avon Dam Reservoir
TQ11
Petre's Cross
White Barrows
Gripper's Hill
Avon Dam
Harbourne Head
Standing Stone
Quickbeam Hill
Broad Rushes
Smallbrook Plains
Ryder's Rocks
Ryder's Rings
Knatta Barrow
Dockwell Hole
Brent Moor
Woolholes
Dockwell Farm
Black Tor
Hunters Stone
Shipley Tor
Old Hill
Shipley Bridge
Yalland
Two Moors Way
Harford Moor
Three Barrows
Red Brook
Bala Brook
Zeal
YALLAND CROSS
DOWNSTOW CROSS
Downstow
DIDWORTHY BGLWS
Ugborough Moor
Hickley Plain
Didworthy
Overbrent
DIAMOND LA
TQ10
Badworthy
River Erme
Higher Piles
Sharp Tor
Brent Fore Hill
River Avon
Ball Gate
Binnamore
BINNAMORE CROSS
Staddon
Lutton
Lower Piles
PL21
Piles Hill
Corringdon Ball
Aish Ridge
Lydia Bridge
Aish
VICARAGE RD
Hobajons Cross
Blowing House
STATION APP
Great Aish
South Brent
PO
AISH LA
PH
Kingswood Ct
Brent Mill
Brent Mill Ind Est
PLYMOUTH RD
Glaze Brook
Owley
LONG MDW
AISH LANE END
EXETER ROAD
B3372
Hangershell Rock
Beacon Plain
BEGGAR'S BUSH
GLAZEBROOK CT
Hotel
A38
Ugborough Beacon
Weatherdon Hill
Eastern Beacon
PH
Butterdon Hill
CHESTON CROSS
Cheston
FOLLY CROSS
Mast
Higher Turtley
Zeaston
Black Pool
Cuckoo Ball
CH
GOLF LINKS RD
MARWOOD'S CROSS
SHUTE CROSS
CUTWELL CROSS

8 65 7 64 6 63 5 62 4 61 3 60 2 59 1 58

64 A 65 B 66 C 67 D 68 E 69 F

133
137

F2
1 WOODHAYE TERR
2 WOODHAYE CL
3 CLOBELLS
4 BEACON TERR
5 ST MICHAELS TERR
6 CORN PK
7 GREENFIELD DR
8 BEACON VIEW
9 NEW ORCHARD
10 AVONDALE HO
11 AVONDALE WLK

F3
1 BELMONT TERR
2 HILLSIDE
3 BISHOPS MEAD
4 BROOKWOOD CL
5 ASHWOOD
6 CHAPEL FIELDS
7 BALMORAL LA
8 STATION RD
9 MANOR CT
10 TOTNES RD
11 MONS TERR
12 CLIFTON TERR
13 FORE ST
14 CHURCH ST
15 WELLINGTON SQ

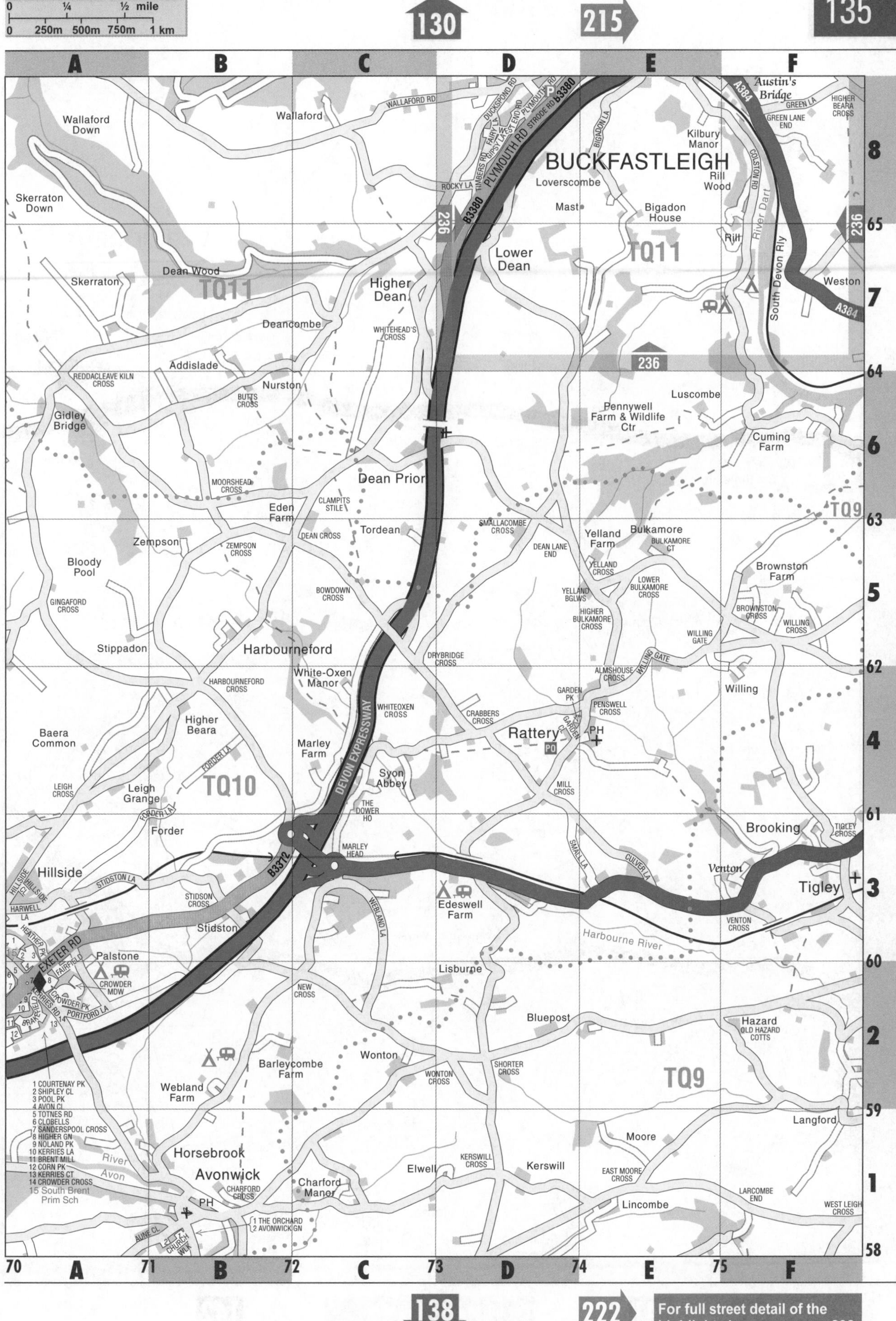

130
215
138
222
For full street detail of the highlighted area see page 236.

251
133

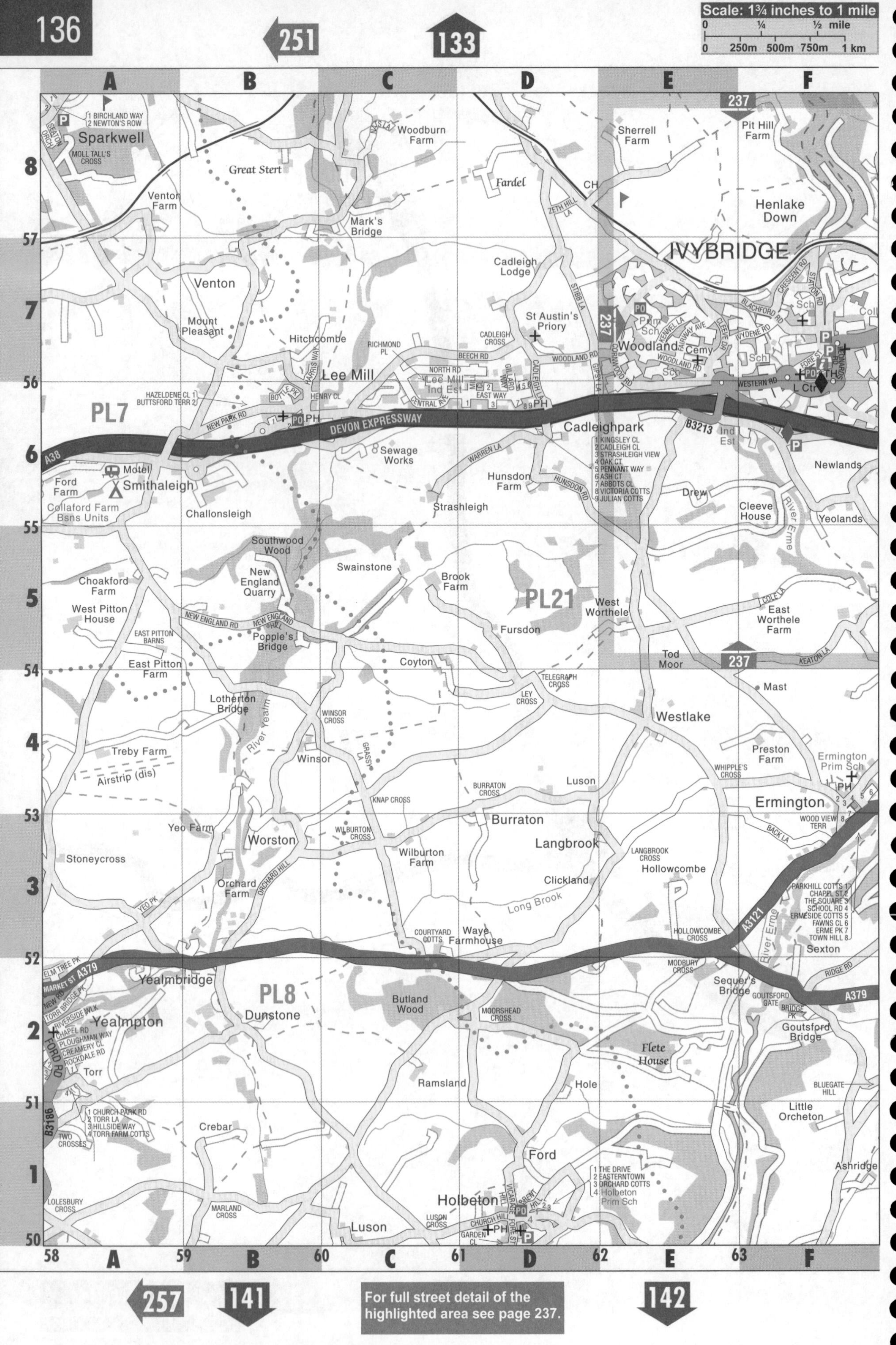

257
141
For full street detail of the highlighted area see page 237.
142

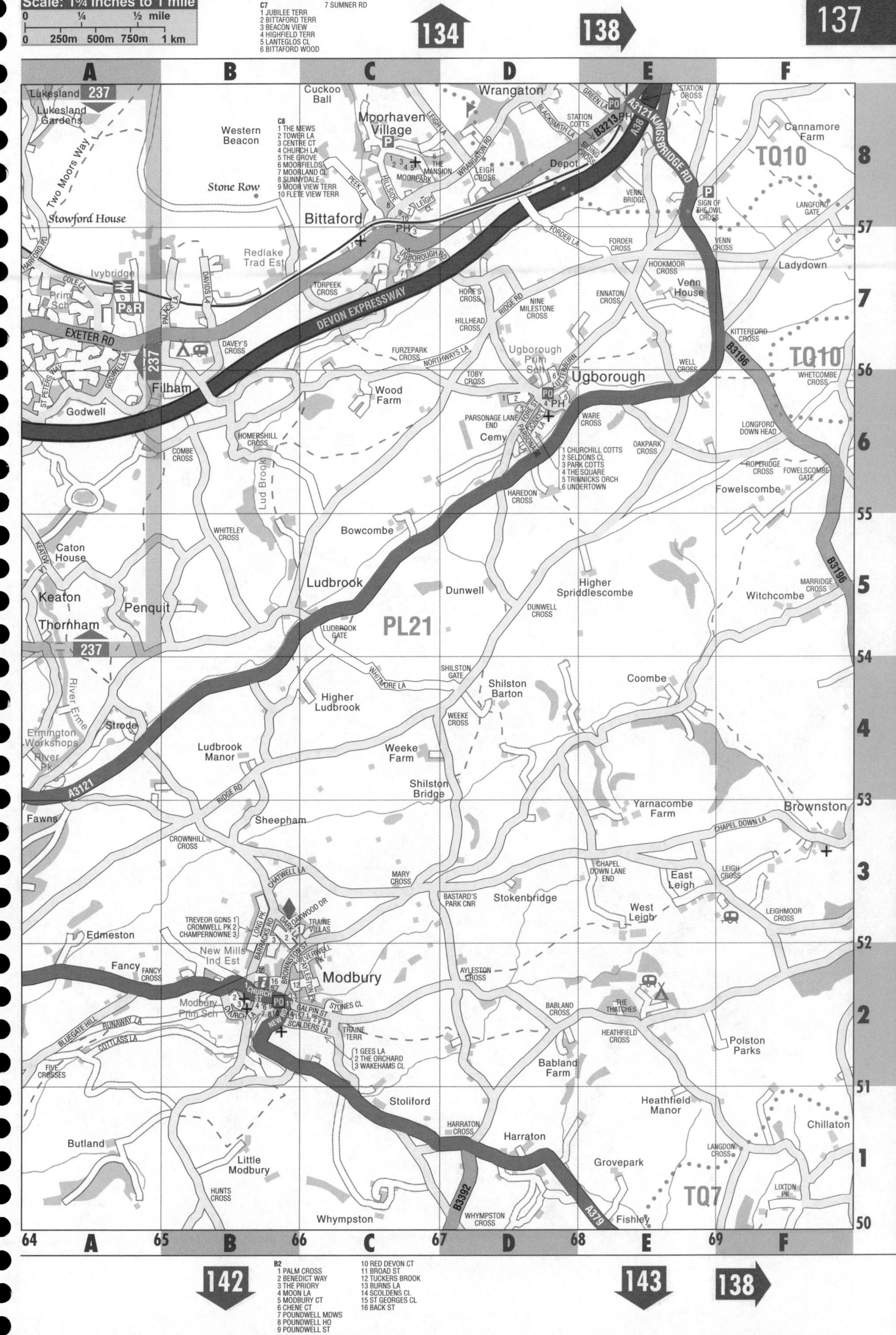
Scale: 1¾ inches to 1 mile
0 ¼ ½ mile
0 250m 500m 750m 1 km
C7
1 JUBILEE TERR
2 BITTAFORD TERR
3 BEACON VIEW
4 HIGHFIELD TERR
5 LANTEGLOS CL
6 BITTAFORD WOOD
7 SUMNER RD
134
138
A B C D E F
Lukesland 237
Lukesland Gardens
Two Moors Way
Western Beacon
Stone Row
Stowford House
Cuckoo Ball
C8
1 THE MEWS
2 TOWER LA
3 CENTRE CT
4 CHURCH LA
5 THE GROVE
6 MOORFIELDS
7 MOORLAND CL
8 SUNNYDALE
9 MOOR VIEW TERR
10 FLETE VIEW TERR
Moorhaven Village
THE MANSION
MOORPARK
HILLSIDE
PEEK LA
LEIGH CL
LEIGH LA
Wrangaton
WRANGATON RD
LEIGH CROSS
BLACKSMITH LA
STATION COTTS
GREEN LA
B3213
A3121
A38
KINGSBRIDGE RD
STATION CROSS
SIDING CROSS
Depot
VENN BRIDGE
SIGN OF THE OWL CROSS
Cannamore Farm
TQ10
LANGFORD GATE
Bittaford
PH
Redlake Trad Est
HARFORD RD
Ivybridge
COLE LA
Prim Sch
P&R
DAVIDS LA
PALACE LA
UGBOROUGH RD
TORPEEK CROSS
DEVON EXPRESSWAY
FORDER LA
FORDER CROSS
HOOKMOOR CROSS
VENN CROSS
Ladydown
Venn House
HORE'S CROSS
RIDGE RD
NINE MILESTONE CROSS
ENNATON CROSS
HILLHEAD CROSS
EXETER RD
DAVEY'S CROSS
237
GODWELL LA
ST PETERS WAY
Filham
Godwell
FURZEPARK CROSS
NORTHWAYS LA
KITTERFORD CROSS
TQ10
B3196
WELL CROSS
WHETCOMBE CROSS
Ugborough Prim Sch
LUTTERBURN
Ugborough
TOBY CROSS
Wood Farm
PO
PH
PARSONAGE LANE END
FORE ST
PARSONAGE
Cemy
WARE CROSS
OAKPARK CROSS
LONGFORD DOWN HEAD
HOMERSHILL CROSS
COMBE CROSS
1 CHURCHILL COTTS
2 SELDONS CL
3 PARK COTTS
4 THE SQUARE
5 TRINNICKS ORCH
6 UNDERTOWN
ROPERIDGE CROSS
FOWELSCOMBE GATE
Fowelscombe
Lud Brook
HAREDON CROSS
WHITELEY CROSS
Bowcombe
KEATON
Caton House
Keaton
Thornham
237
Penquit
Ludbrook
Dunwell
Higher Spriddlescombe
Witchcombe
MARRIDGE CROSS
B3196
DUNWELL CROSS
PL21
LUDBROOK GATE
WHITMORE LA
SHILSTON GATE
Shilston Barton
Coombe
River Erme
Higher Ludbrook
WEEKE CROSS
Ermington Workshops
River Pk
Strode
Ludbrook Manor
Weeke Farm
Shilston Bridge
A3121
RIDGE RD
Fawns
Sheepham
Yarnacombe Farm
Brownston
CHAPEL DOWN LA
CROWNHILL CROSS
CHATWELL LA
MARY CROSS
CHAPEL DOWN LANE END
East Leigh
LEIGH CROSS
BASTARD'S PARK CNR
Stokenbridge
West Leigh
LEIGHMOOR CROSS
TREVEOR GDNS 1
CROMWELL PK 2
CHAMPERNOWNE 3
LONG PK
BARRACKS RD
DARK LA
OAKWOOD DR
TRAINE VILLAS
Edmeston
New Mills Ind Est
BROWNSTON ST
SILVERWELL PK
AYLESTON PK
Fancy
FANCY CROSS
Modbury
AYLESTON CROSS
CHURCH ST
PO
STONES CL
GALPIN ST
SCALDERS LA
NEW RD
Modbury Prim Sch
CHURCH LA
BLUEGATE HILL
RUNAWAY LA
COTTLASS LA
TRAINE TERR
1 GEES LA
2 THE ORCHARD
3 WAKEHAMS CL
BABLAND CROSS
THE THATCHES
HEATHFIELD CROSS
Polston Parks
Babland Farm
FIVE CROSSES
Stoliford
Heathfield Manor
Chillaton
HARRATON CROSS
Harraton
LANGDON CROSS
Butland
Little Modbury
Grovepark
B3392
A379
TQ7
LIXTON PK
HUNTS CROSS
Whympston
WHYMPSTON CROSS
Fishley
8 57 7 56 6 55 5 54 4 53 3 52 2 51 1 50
64 65 66 67 68 69
B2
1 PALM CROSS
2 BENEDICT WAY
3 THE PRIORY
4 MOON LA
5 MODBURY CT
6 CHENE CT
7 POUNDWELL MDWS
8 POUNDWELL HO
9 POUNDWELL ST
10 RED DEVON CT
11 BROAD ST
12 TUCKERS BROOK
13 BURNS LA
14 SCOLDENS CL
15 ST GEORGES CL
16 BACK ST
142
143
138

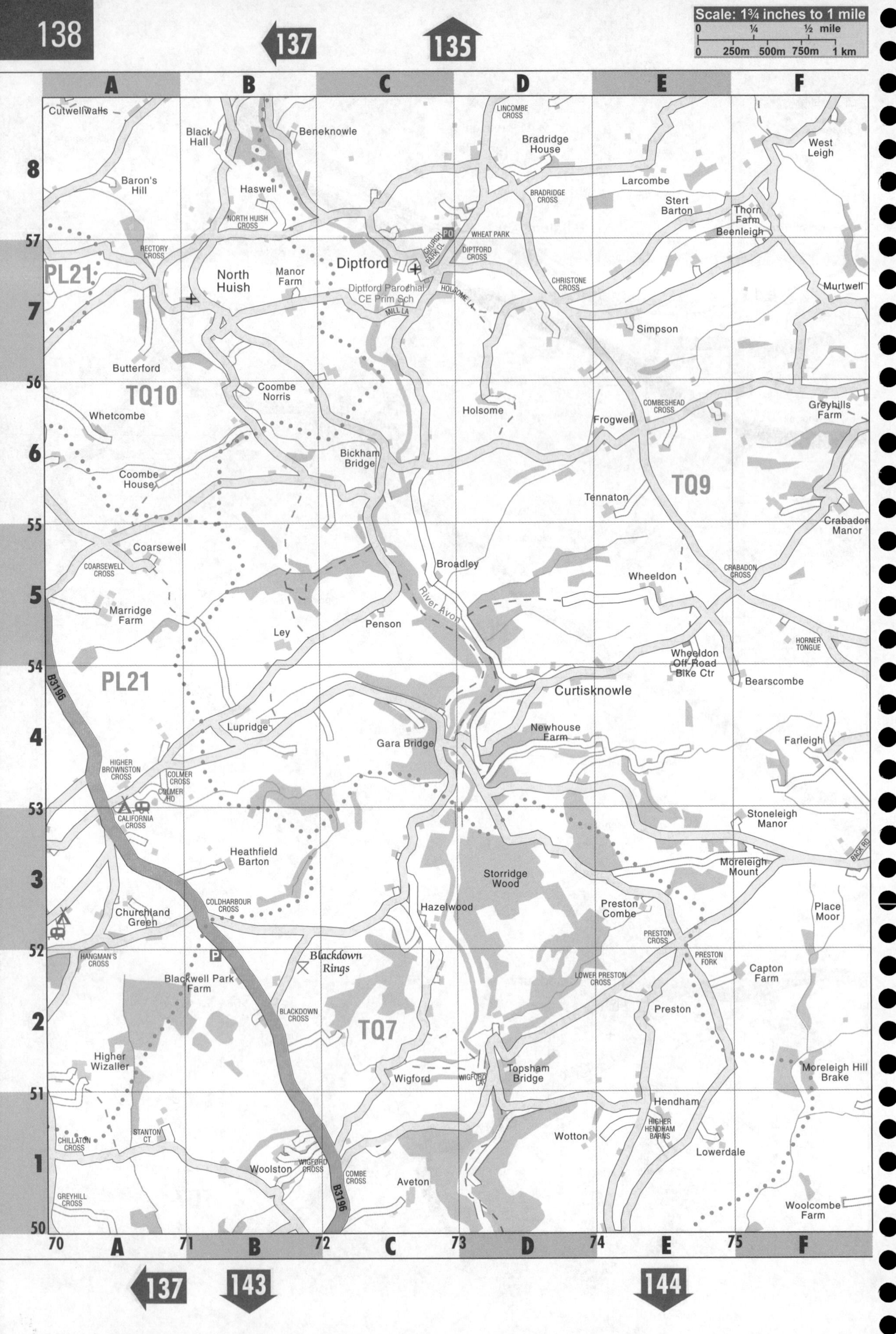
137
135
Scale: 1¾ inches to 1 mile
0 ¼ ½ mile
0 250m 500m 750m 1 km
A B C D E F
8 7 6 5 4 3 2 1
57 56 55 54 53 52 51 50
70 71 72 73 74 75
Cutwellwalls
Black Hall
Beneknowle
LINCOMBE CROSS
Bradridge House
West Leigh
Baron's Hill
Haswell
Larcombe
BRADRIDGE CROSS
Stert Barton
Thorn Farm
Beenleigh
NORTH HUISH CROSS
CHURCH PARK CL
PO
WHEAT PARK
RECTORY CROSS
DIPTFORD CROSS
PL21
North Huish
Manor Farm
Diptford
Diptford Parochial CE Prim Sch
HOLSOME LA
CHRISTONE CROSS
Murtwell
MILL LA
Simpson
Butterford
Coombe Norris
TQ10
COMBESHEAD CROSS
Greyhills Farm
Whetcombe
Holsome
Frogwell
Bickham Bridge
Coombe House
Tennaton
TQ9
Crabadon Manor
Coarsewell
COARSEWELL CROSS
Broadley
Wheeldon
CRABADON CROSS
River Avon
Marridge Farm
Penson
Ley
HORNER TONGUE
Wheeldon Off-Road Bike Ctr
Bearscombe
B3196
PL21
Curtisknowle
Lupridge
Newhouse Farm
Gara Bridge
Farleigh
HIGHER BROWNSTON CROSS
COLMER CROSS
COLMER HO
CALIFORNIA CROSS
Stoneleigh Manor
Heathfield Barton
Moreleigh Mount
BACK RD
Storridge Wood
Place Moor
COLDHARBOUR CROSS
Churchland Green
Hazelwood
Preston Combe
PRESTON CROSS
HANGMAN'S CROSS
P
Blackdown Rings
PRESTON FORK
Capton Farm
Blackwell Park Farm
LOWER PRESTON CROSS
BLACKDOWN CROSS
Preston
TQ7
Higher Wizaller
Moreleigh Hill Brake
Wigford
WIGFORD LA
Topsham Bridge
Hendham
HIGHER HENDHAM BARNS
STANTON CT
CHILLATON CROSS
Wotton
Lowerdale
Woolston
WIGFORD CROSS
COMBE CROSS
Aveton
GREYHILL CROSS
B3196
Woolcombe Farm
137
143
144

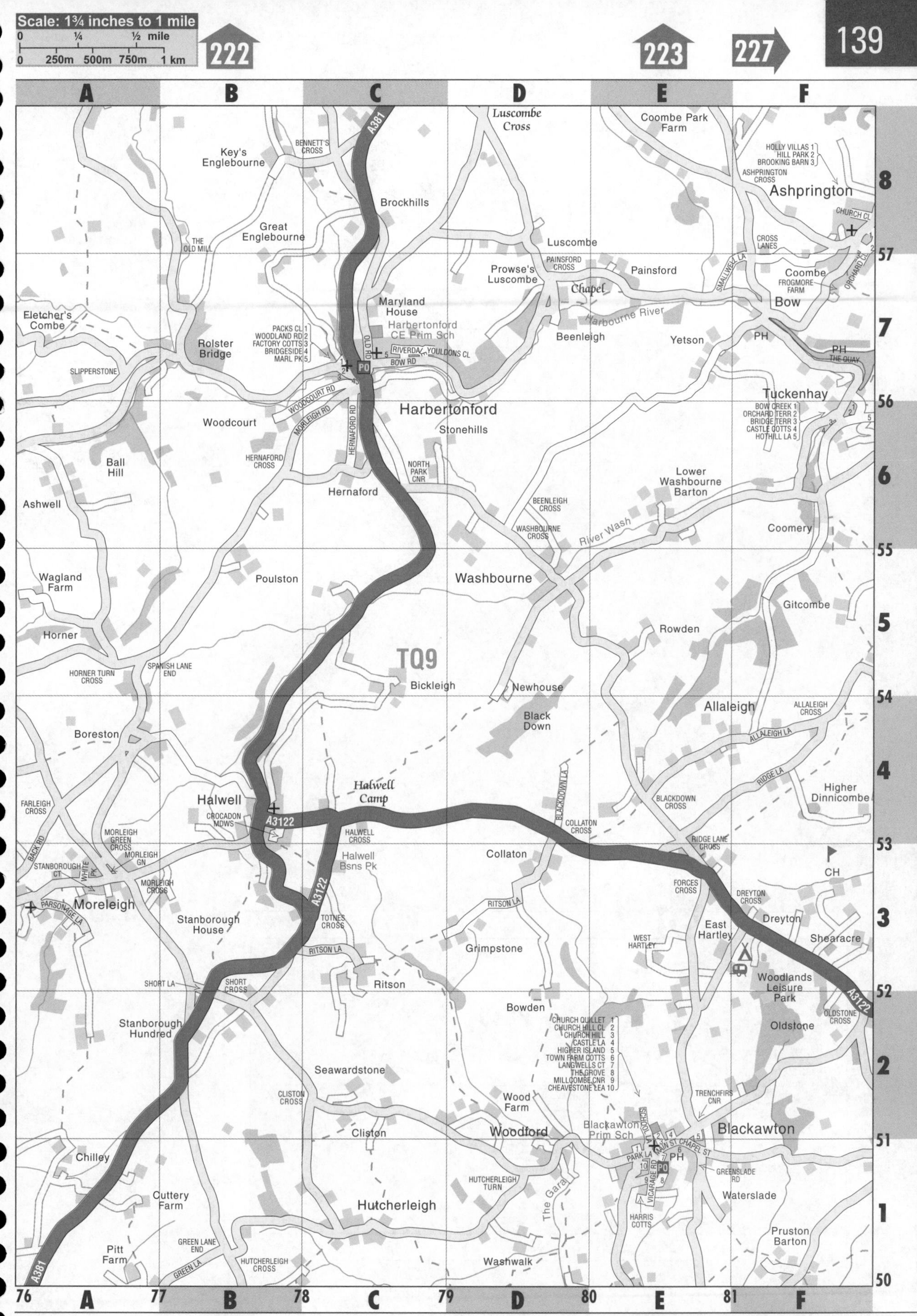

Scale: 1¾ inches to 1 mile
222
223
227
A B C D E F
Harbertonford
Ashprington
Tuckenhay
Washbourne
Halwell
Moreleigh
Blackawton
Allaleigh
TQ9
A381
A3122
144
145
232

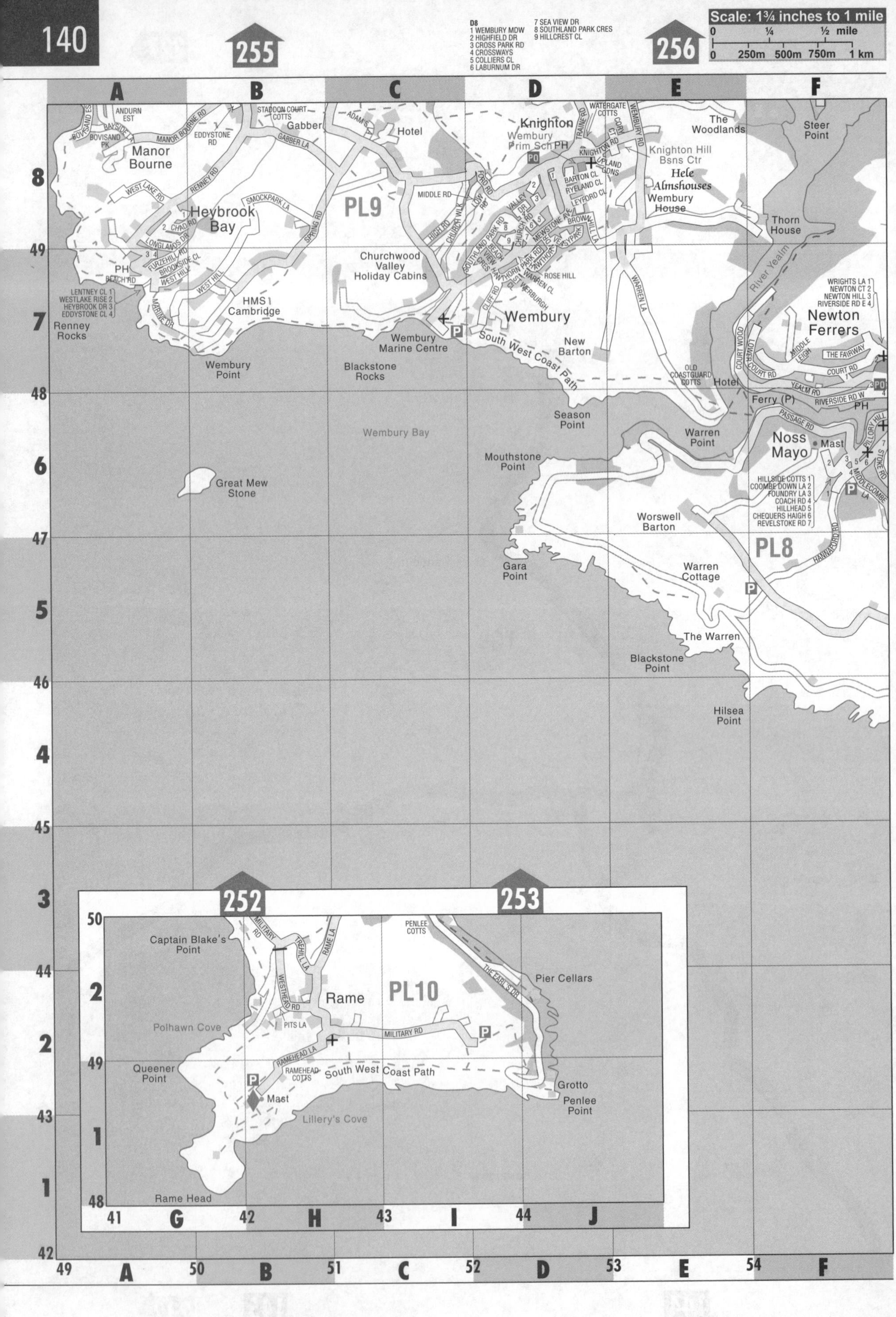
255
256
D8
1 WEMBURY MDW
2 HIGHFIELD DR
3 CROSS PARK RD
4 CROSSWAYS
5 COLLIERS CL
6 LABURNUM DR
7 SEA VIEW DR
8 SOUTHLAND PARK CRES
9 HILLCREST CL
Scale: 1¾ inches to 1 mile
0 ¼ ½ mile
0 250m 500m 750m 1 km
A B C D E F
8 49 7 48 6 47 5 46 4 45 3 44 2 43 1 42
49 50 51 52 53 54
ANDURN EST
BOVISAND EST
BAYSIDE LA
BOVISAND PK
MANOR BOURNE RD
Manor Bourne
EDDYSTONE RD
STADDON COURT COTTS
Gabber
GABBER LA
ADAM'S LA
Hotel
Knighton
Wembury Prim Sch
PH
WATERGATE COTTS
TRAINE RD
CORY CT
WEMBURY RD
KNIGHTON RD
UPLAND GDNS
The Woodlands
Steer Point
Knighton Hill Bsns Ctr
Hele Almshouses
Wembury House
BARTON CL
RYELAND CL
LEYFORD CL
BROWNHILL LA
MEWSTONE AV
WEST LAKE RD
RENNEY RD
SMOCKPARK LA
Heybrook Bay
PL9
MIDDLE RD
FORD RD
LOW RD
CHURCH WLK
HIGH RD
VALLEY DR
CHURCH RD
SPRING RD
CHAD RD
LONGLANDS DR
FURZEHILL RD
BROOKSIDE CL
WEST HILL
PH
BEACH RD
LENTNEY CL 1
WESTLAKE RISE 2
HEYBROOK DR 3
EDDYSTONE CL 4
Renney Rocks
MARINE DR
HMS Cambridge
Churchwood Valley Holiday Cabins
SOUTHLAND PARK RD
BEACH VIEW CRES
HAWTHORN PARK RD
ROSE HILL
WARREN CL
ST WERBURGH
CLIFF RD
Wembury
Wembury Marine Centre
South West Coast Path
WARREN LA
New Barton
Thorn House
River Yealm
WRIGHTS LA 1
NEWTON CT 2
NEWTON HILL 3
RIVERSIDE RD E 4
Newton Ferrers
COURT WOOD
LOWER COURT RD
MIDDLE LEIGH
THE FAIRWAY
COURT RD
OLD COASTGUARD COTTS
Hotel
YEALM RD
Ferry (P)
RIVERSIDE RD W
PH
Wembury Point
Blackstone Rocks
Wembury Bay
Season Point
Warren Point
PASSAGE RD
Noss Mayo
Mast
PILLORY HILL
STOKE RD
MIDDLECOMBE LA
HILLSIDE COTTS 1
COOMBE DOWN LA 2
FOUNDRY LA 3
COACH RD 4
HILLHEAD 5
CHEQUERS HAIGH 6
REVELSTOKE RD 7
Mouthstone Point
Great Mew Stone
Worswell Barton
PL8
HANNAFORD RD
Gara Point
Warren Cottage
The Warren
Blackstone Point
Hilsea Point
252
253
50 49 48
41 42 43 44
G H I J
2 1
Captain Blake's Point
MILITARY RD
TREHILL LA
RAME LA
PENLEE COTTS
THE EARL'S DR
Pier Cellars
WESTHEAD RD
Rame
PL10
Polhawn Cove
PITS LA
MILITARY RD
Queener Point
RAMEHEAD LA
RAMEHEAD COTTS
South West Coast Path
Grotto
Penlee Point
Mast
Lillery's Cove
Rame Head

257
136
142

Scale: 1¾ inches to 1 mile
0 ¼ ½ mile
0 250m 500m 750m 1 km

A8
1 CHURCH PARK RD
2 CHURCH PK
3 NEWTON CL
4 YEALM RD
5 COURT RD
6 ST CATHERINES PK
7 MEADOW CL
8 ARCHERS CT
9 Newton Ferrers CE Prim Sch

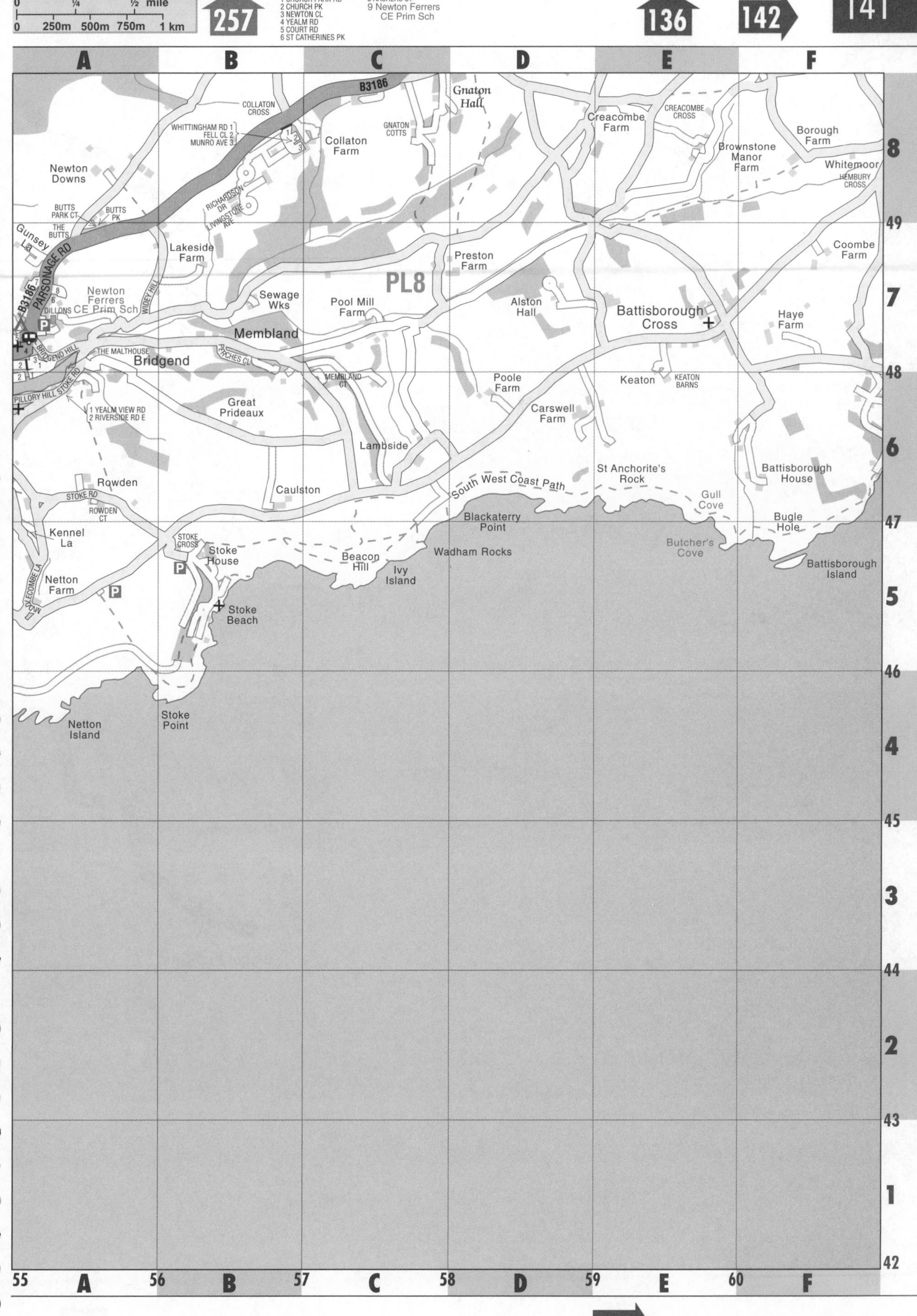

142

141 136 137

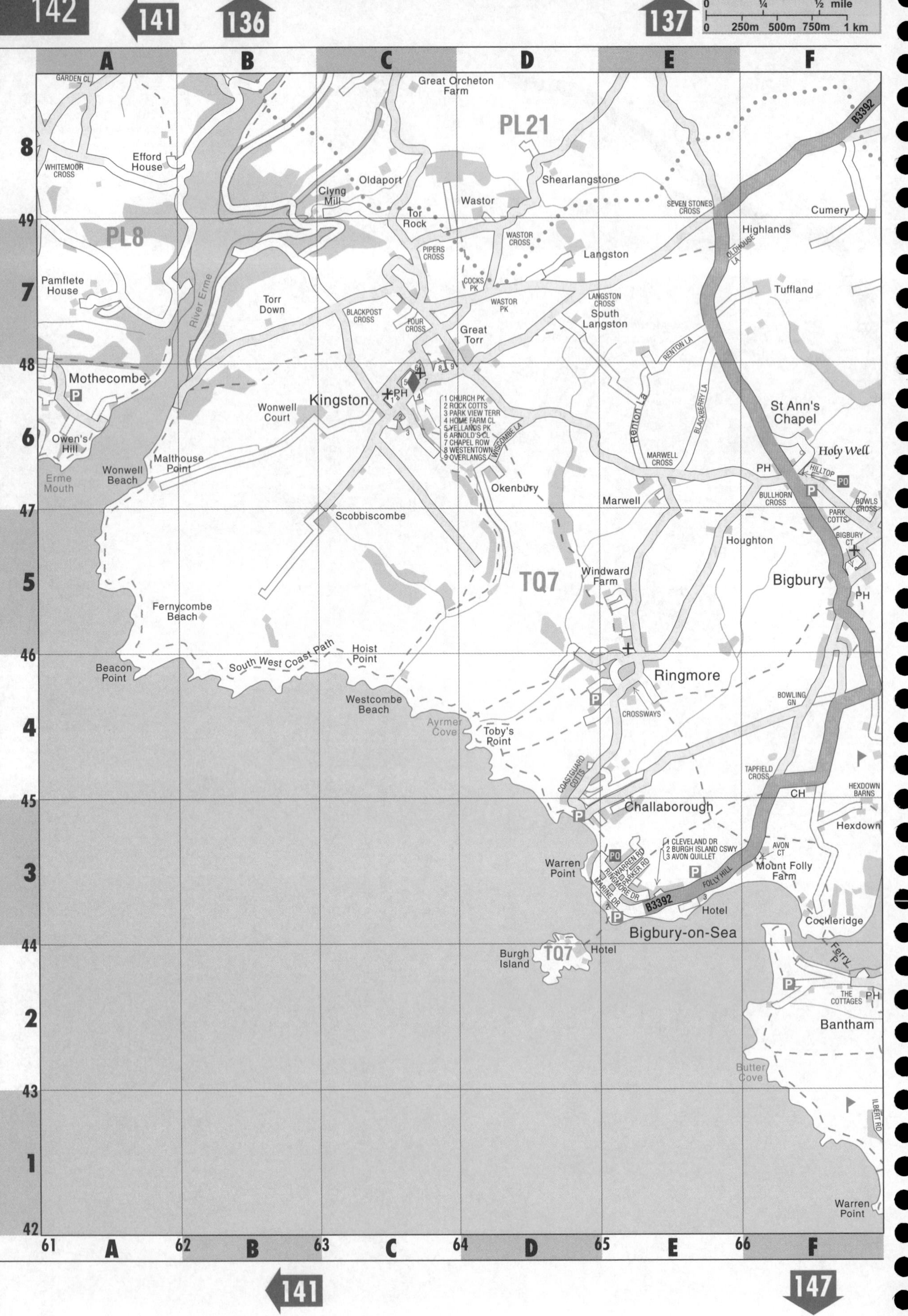

141 147

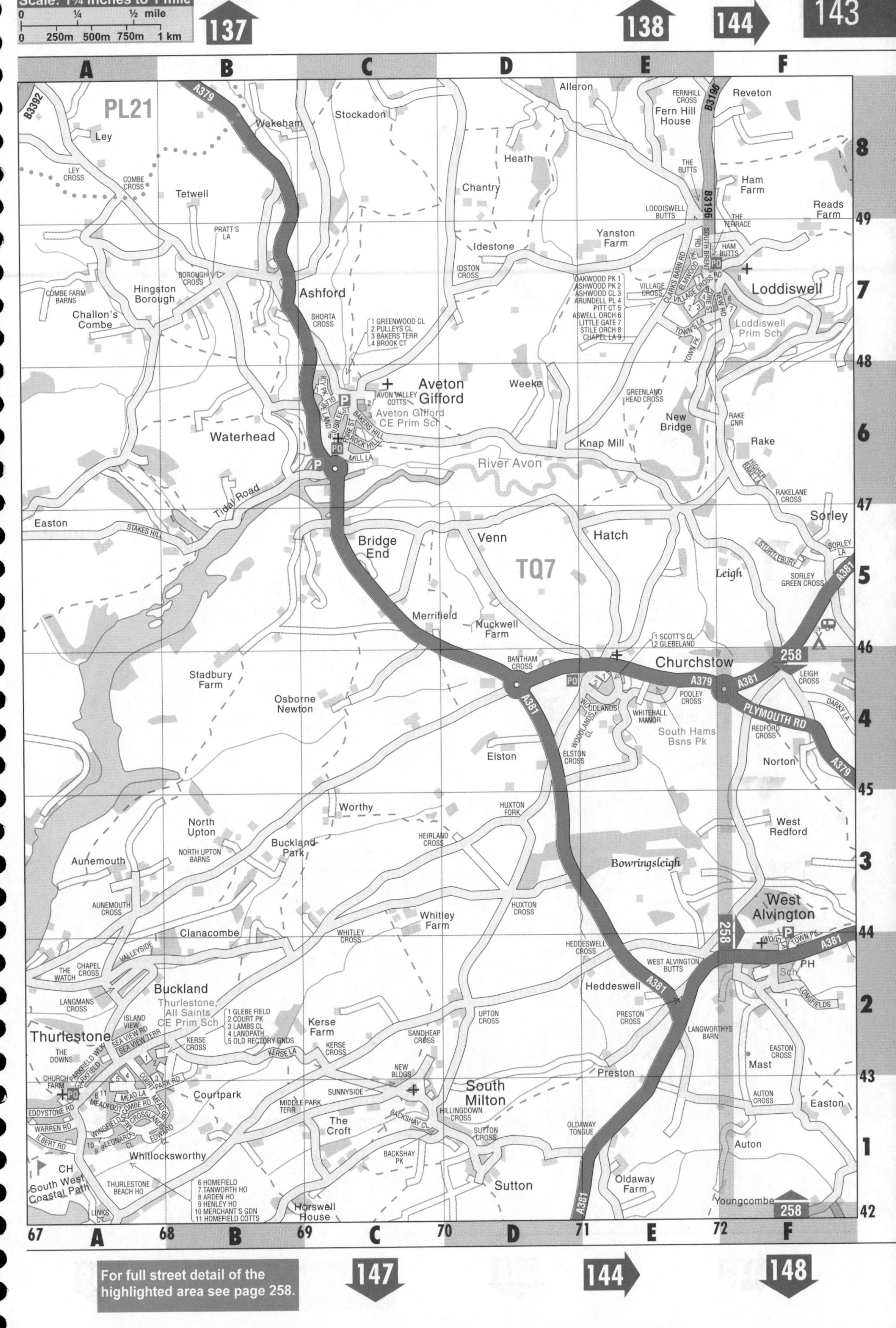

For full street detail of the highlighted area see page 258.

143 138 139

Scale: 1¾ inches to 1 mile

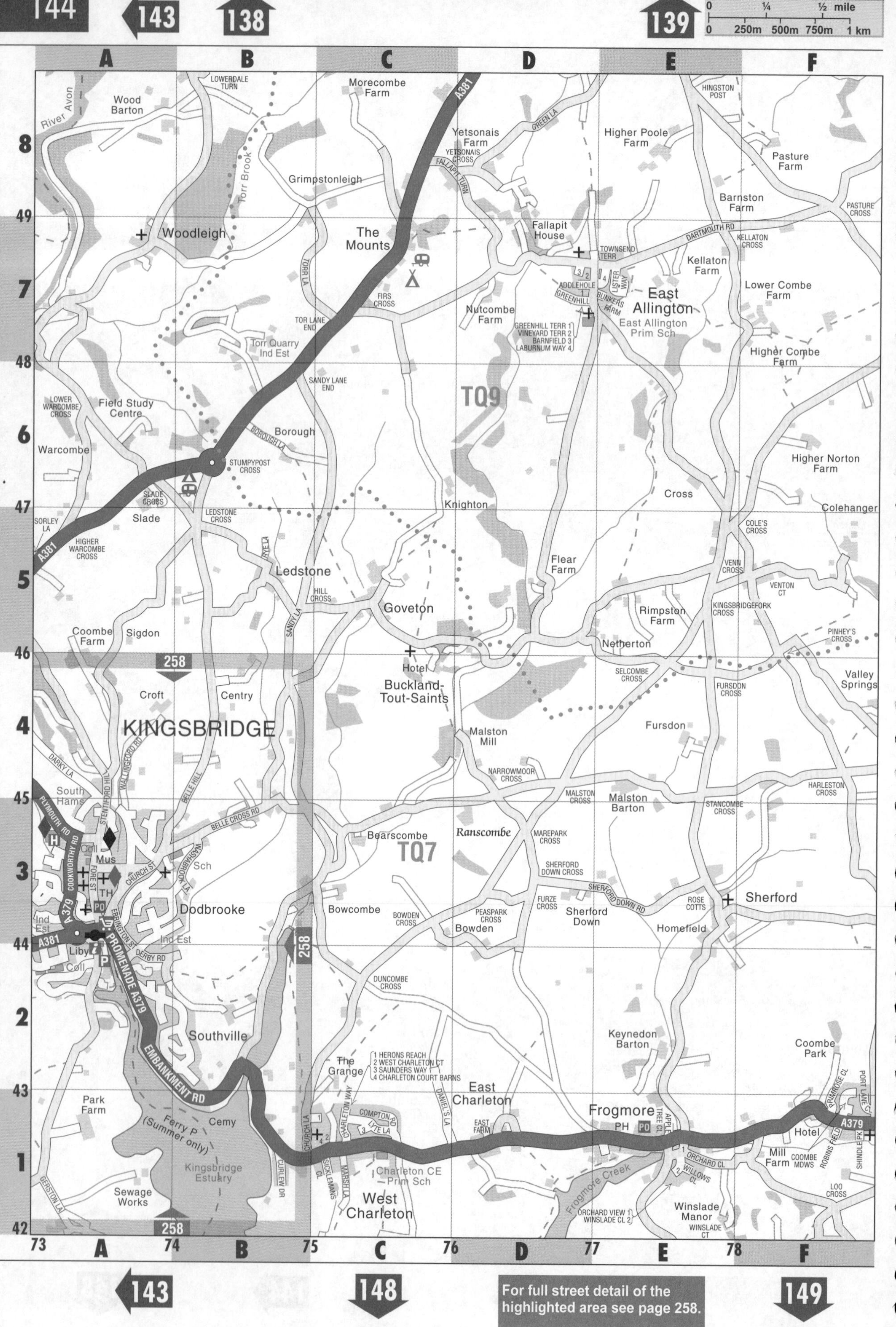

143 148 149

For full street detail of the highlighted area see page 258.

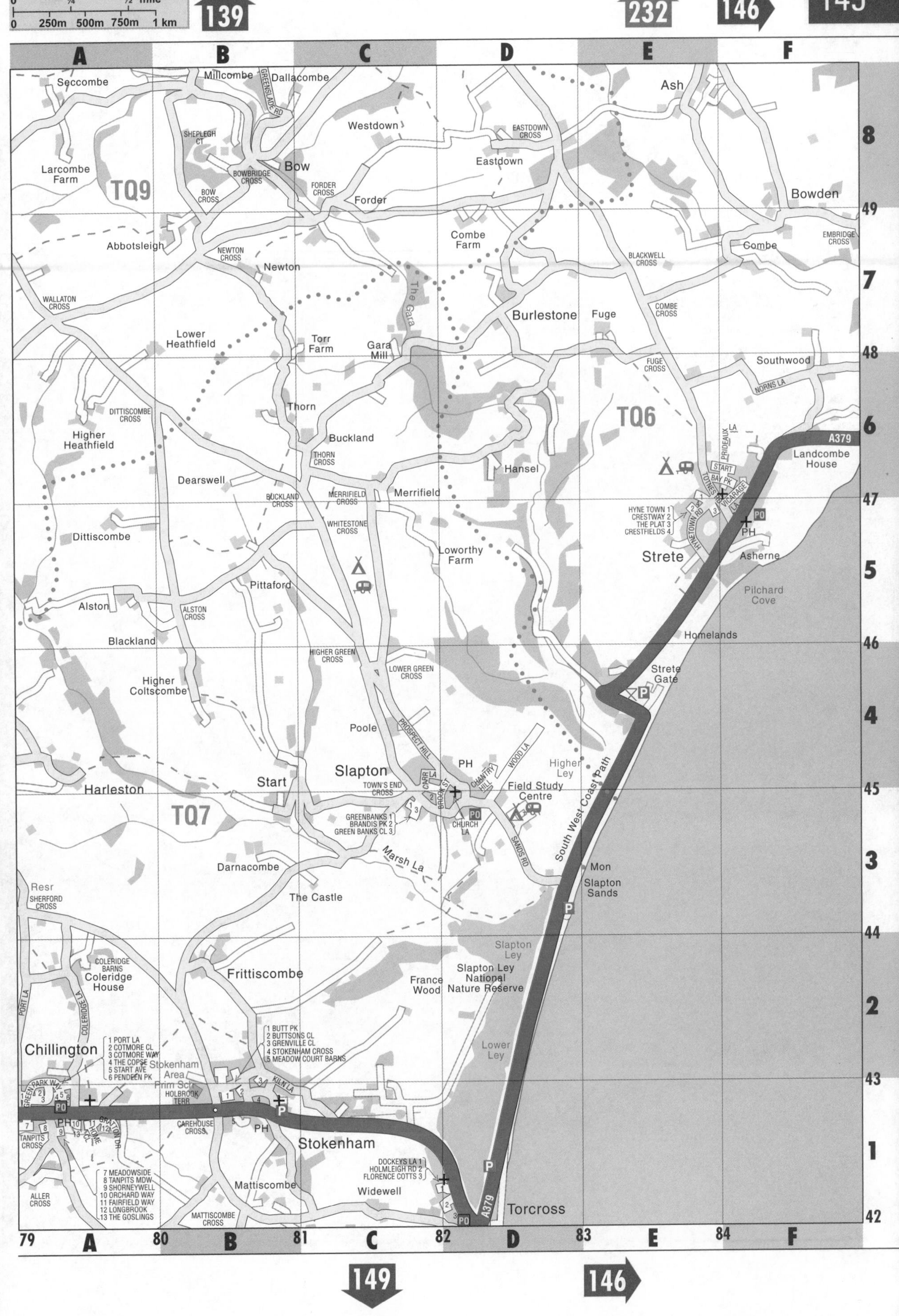
Scale: 1¾ inches to 1 mile
0 ¼ ½ mile
0 250m 500m 750m 1 km
139
232
146
Seccombe
Millcombe
Dallacombe
Ash
Westdown
Larcombe Farm
TQ9
Bow
Eastdown
Forder
Bowden
Abbotsleigh
Combe Farm
Combe
Newton
Burlestone
Fuge
Lower Heathfield
Torr Farm
Gara Mill
Southwood
Thorn
TQ6
Higher Heathfield
Buckland
Landcombe House
Dearswell
Hansel
Merrifield
Dittiscombe
Loworthy Farm
Strete
Asherne
Pittaford
Alston
Pilchard Cove
Blackland
Homelands
Higher Coltscombe
Strete Gate
Poole
Slapton
Start
Harleston
TQ7
Field Study Centre
Higher Ley
Darnacombe
The Castle
Slapton Sands
Resr
Frittiscombe
Slapton Ley National Nature Reserve
France Wood
Coleridge House
Chillington
Lower Ley
Stokenham
Mattiscombe
Widewell
Torcross
South West Coast Path
A379
149
146

145 233 234

Scale: 1¾ inches to 1 mile

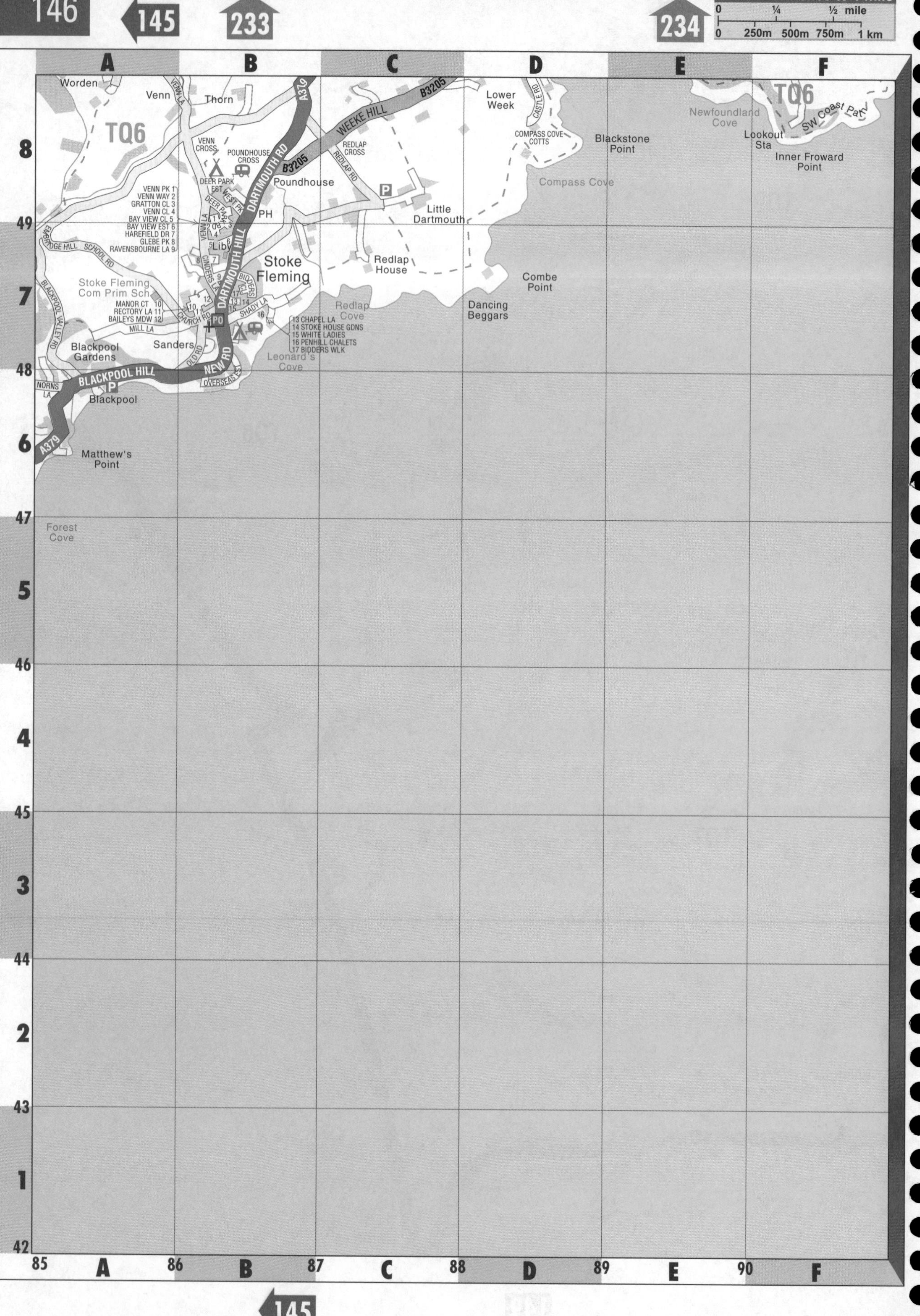

145

143
148

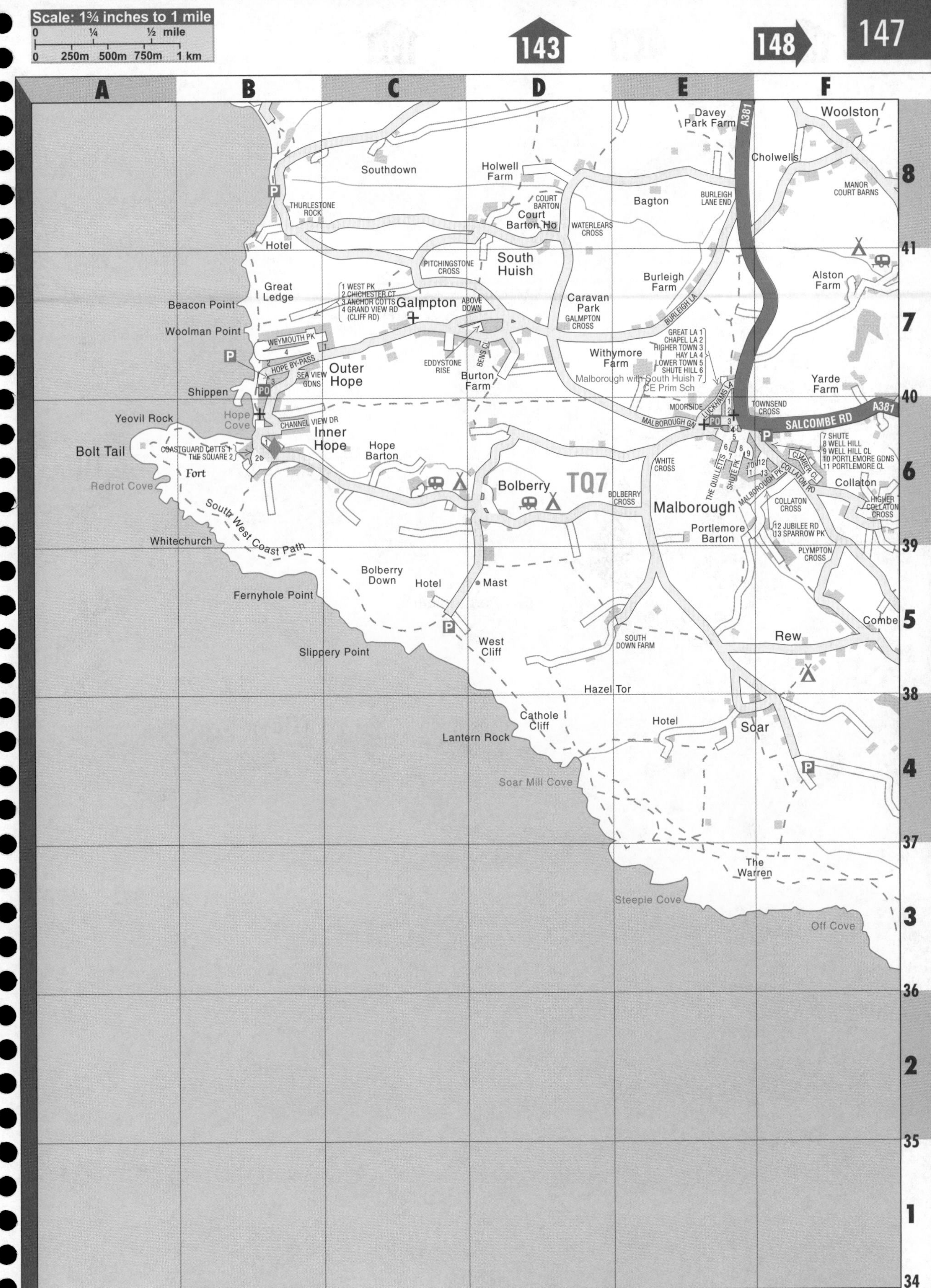
Scale: 1¾ inches to 1 mile
0 ¼ ½ mile
0 250m 500m 750m 1 km
A B C D E F
8 41 7 40 6 39 5 38 4 37 3 36 2 35 1 34
66 67 68 69 70 71
Davey Park Farm
A381
Woolston
Cholwells
Southdown
Holwell Farm
Bagton
BURLEIGH LANE END
MANOR COURT BARNS
THURLESTONE ROCK
COURT BARTON
Court Barton Ho
WATERLEARS CROSS
Hotel
South Huish
PITCHINGSTONE CROSS
Burleigh Farm
Alston Farm
Great Ledge
1 WEST PK
2 CHICHESTER CT
3 ANCHOR COTTS
4 GRAND VIEW RD (CLIFF RD)
Galmpton
ABOVE DOWN
Caravan Park
GALMPTON CROSS
BURLEIGH LA
Beacon Point
Woolman Point
WEYMOUTH PK
HOPE BY-PASS
SEA VIEW GDNS
Outer Hope
EDDYSTONE RISE
BENS CL
Burton Farm
Withymore Farm
GREAT LA 1
CHAPEL LA 2
HIGHER TOWN 3
HAY LA 4
LOWER TOWN 5
SHUTE HILL 6
Malborough with South Huish 7 CE Prim Sch
Yarde Farm
Shippen
Hope Cove
Yeovil Rock
CHANNEL VIEW DR
Inner Hope
LUCKHAMS LA
MOORSIDE
MALBOROUGH GN
TOWNSEND CROSS
SALCOMBE RD
Bolt Tail
COASTGUARD COTTS 1
THE SQUARE 2
Hope Barton
7 SHUTE
8 WELL HILL
9 WELL HILL CL
10 PORTLEMORE GDNS
11 PORTLEMORE CL
Fort
Redrot Cove
Bolberry
TQ7
WHITE CROSS
BOLBERRY CROSS
THE QUILLETTS
SHUTE PK
MALBOROUGH PK
COLLATON RD
CUMBER CL
Collaton
HIGHER COLLATON CROSS
South West Coast Path
Malborough
COLLATON CROSS
Portlemore Barton
12 JUBILEE RD
13 SPARROW PK
Whitechurch
PLYMPTON CROSS
Bolberry Down
Hotel
Mast
Fernyhole Point
Combe
SOUTH DOWN FARM
Rew
West Cliff
Slippery Point
Hazel Tor
Cathole Cliff
Hotel
Soar
Lantern Rock
Soar Mill Cove
The Warren
Steeple Cove
Off Cove

148

Scale: 1¾ inches to 1 mile

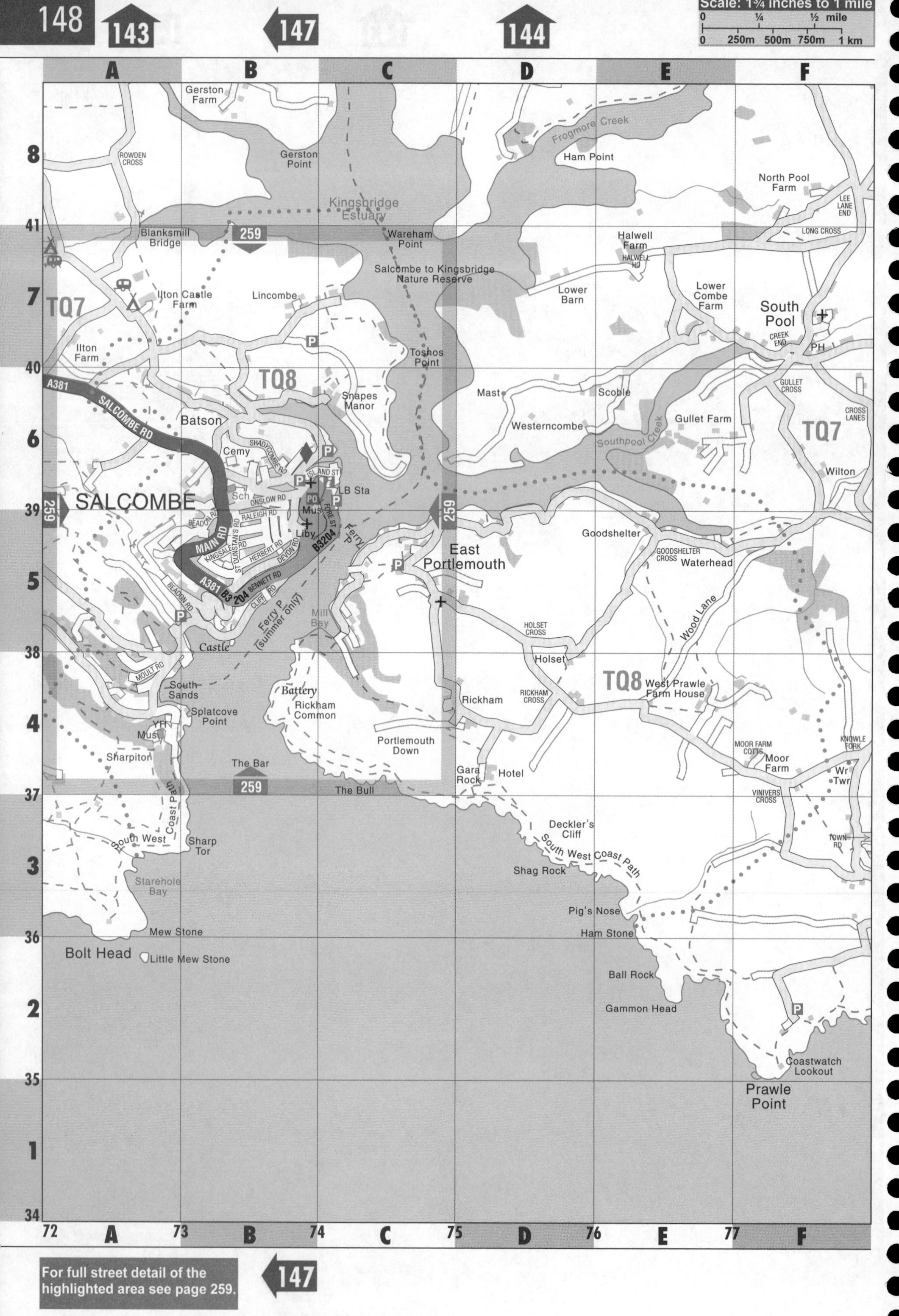

For full street detail of the highlighted area see page 259.

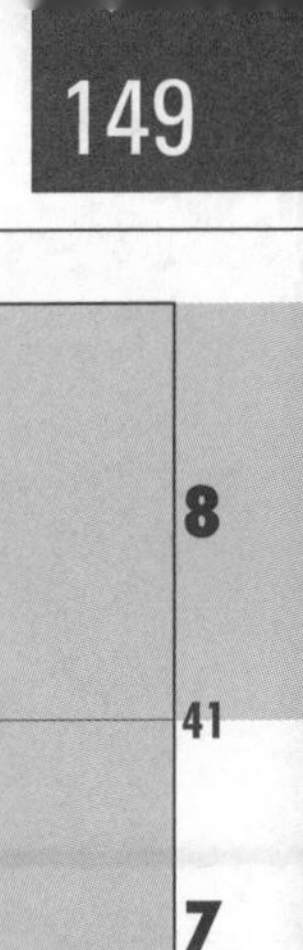

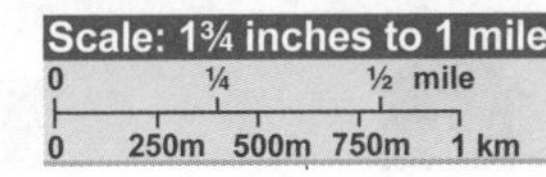

144

A B C D E F

RIDGE CROSS
MARBER CROSS
Molescombe
DURLESTONE CROSS
Mast
Hotel
Widdicombe House
Cotmore
EASTPARK
Kernborough
BEESON POOL
SUNNYDALE
8
CHESTNUT PK
BEESON CROSS
41
Burial Gd
Moyson
ORCHARD CL
FORD CROSS
Beeson
HUCKHAM BARN CROSS
Beesands
7
THE COUNCIL HOUSES
Dunstone
DUNSTONE CROSS
Huccombe
Ford
PH
40
Higher Middlecombe Farm
COUSIN'S CROSS
Kellaton
Batton Farm
Tinsey Head
South West Coast Path
TQ7
KELLATON CROSS
6
HILL PK
Muckwell
Chivelstone
39
Greenstraight
FORDWORTH COTTS
BICKERTON TOP
NEW HOUSES
Bickerton
Hotel
Hallsands
CHIVELSTONE CROSS
THE MALTINGS
South Allington
5
LANNACOMBE GN
IVYCOMBE LA
HOLLOWCOMBE HEAD
38
Down Farm
HIGHER BOROUGH
Masts
Lower Borough
Start Farm
Nestley Point
4
Woodcombe Farm
Lannacombe Beach
Start Point
The Narrows
37
TOWN RD
Raven's Cove
HIGHER PK
Maelcombe House
East Prawle
PH
Lannacombe Bay
3
SEAVIEW
36
2
Langerstone Point
35
1
34

78 A 79 B 80 C 81 D 82 E 83 F

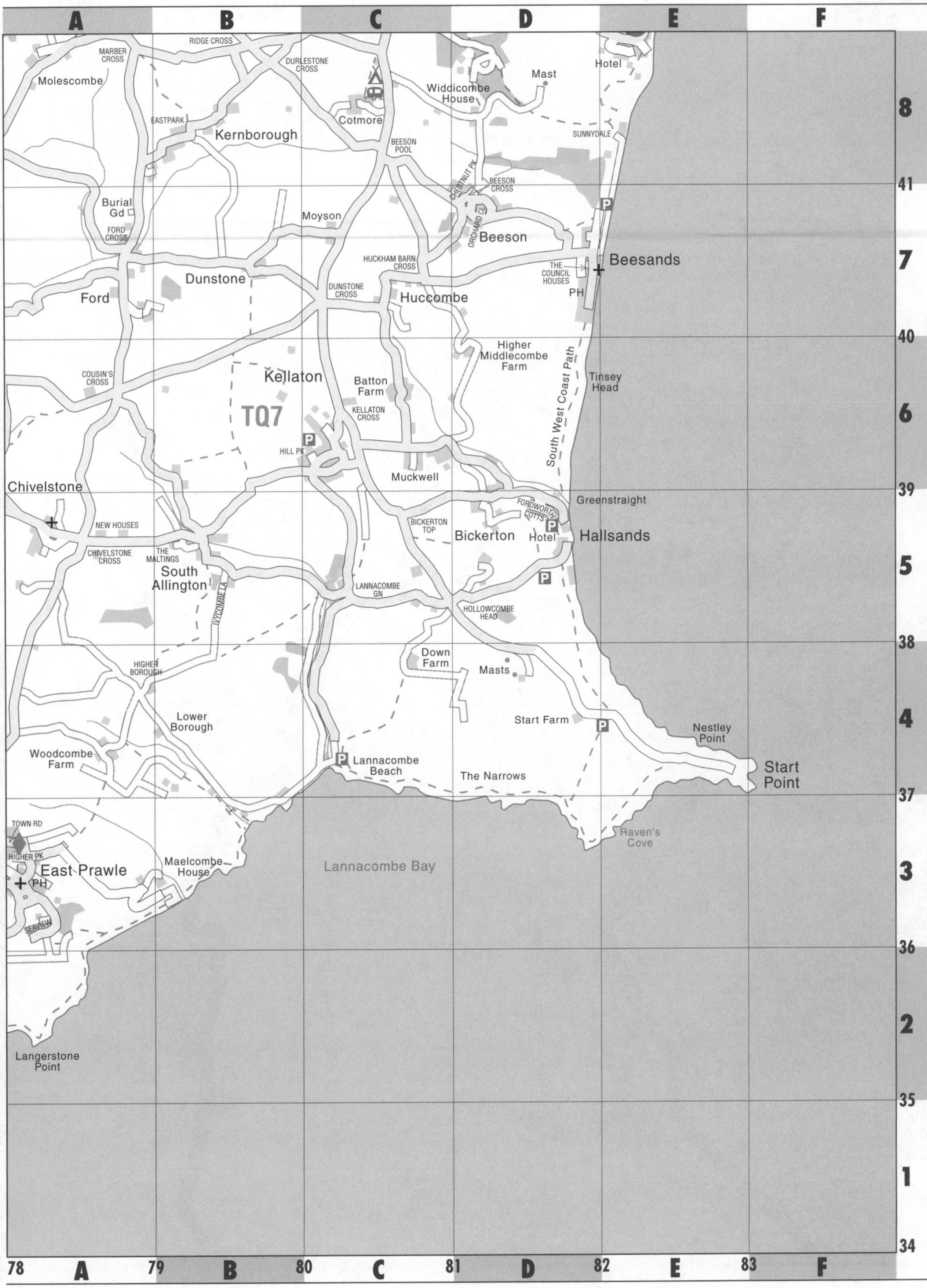

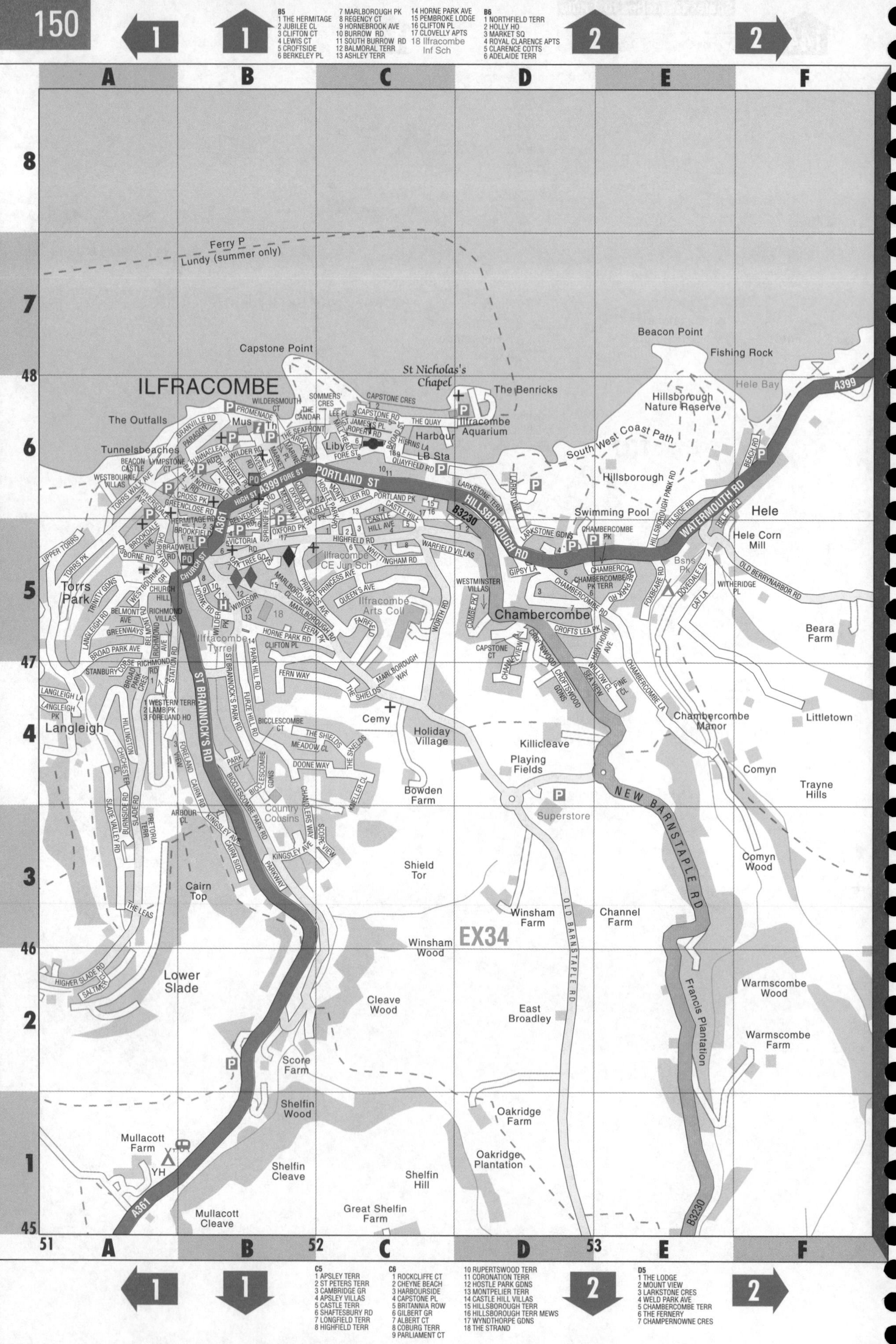
B5
1 THE HERMITAGE
2 JUBILEE CL
3 CLIFTON CT
4 LEWIS CT
5 CROFTSIDE
6 BERKELEY PL
7 MARLBOROUGH PK
8 REGENCY CT
9 HORNEBROOK AVE
10 BURROW RD
11 SOUTH BURROW RD
12 BALMORAL TERR
13 ASHLEY TERR
14 HORNE PARK AVE
15 PEMBROKE LODGE
16 CLIFTON PL
17 CLOVELLY APTS
18 Ilfracombe Inf Sch
B6
1 NORTHFIELD TERR
2 HOLLY HO
3 MARKET SQ
4 ROYAL CLARENCE APTS
5 CLARENCE COTTS
6 ADELAIDE TERR
A B C D E F
8
7
48
6
5
47
4
3
46
2
1
45
51 52 53
Ferry P
Lundy (summer only)
Capstone Point
ILFRACOMBE
St Nicholas's Chapel
The Benricks
Beacon Point
Fishing Rock
Hele Bay
A399
Hillsborough Nature Reserve
South West Coast Path
The Outfalls
Tunnelsbeaches
Mus
Th
Harbour
Ilfracombe Aquarium
Liby
LB Sta
Hillsborough
PORTLAND ST
HILLSBOROUGH RD
WATERMOUTH RD
B3230
A361
Swimming Pool
Hele
Hele Corn Mill
Bsns Pk
Torrs Park
Ilfracombe CE Jun Sch
Ilfracombe Arts Coll
Chambercombe
Beara Farm
Ilfracombe Tyrrell
Langleigh
Cemy
Holiday Village
Killicleave
Playing Fields
Chambercombe Manor
Littletown
Comyn
Trayne Hills
Bowden Farm
Superstore
Country Cousins
ST BRANNOCK'S RD
NEW BARNSTAPLE RD
Shield Tor
Comyn Wood
Cairn Top
Winsham Farm
Channel Farm
EX34
Winsham Wood
OLD BARNSTAPLE RD
Lower Slade
Warmscombe Wood
Cleave Wood
East Broadley
Francis Plantation
Warmscombe Farm
Score Farm
Shelfin Wood
Oakridge Farm
Mullacott Farm
YH
Oakridge Plantation
Shelfin Cleave
Shelfin Hill
Mullacott Cleave
Great Shelfin Farm
C5
1 APSLEY TERR
2 ST PETERS TERR
3 CAMBRIDGE GR
4 APSLEY VILLAS
5 CASTLE TERR
6 SHAFTESBURY RD
7 LONGFIELD TERR
8 HIGHFIELD TERR
C6
1 ROCKCLIFFE CT
2 CHEYNE BEACH
3 HARBOURSIDE
4 CAPSTONE PL
5 BRITANNIA ROW
6 GILBERT GR
7 ALBERT CT
8 COBURG TERR
9 PARLIAMENT CT
10 RUPERTSWOOD TERR
11 CORONATION TERR
12 HOSTLE PARK GDNS
13 MONTPELIER TERR
14 CASTLE HILL VILLAS
15 HILLSBOROUGH TERR
16 HILLSBOROUGH TERR MEWS
17 WYNDTHORPE GDNS
18 THE STRAND
D5
1 THE LODGE
2 MOUNT VIEW
3 LARKSTONE CRES
4 WELD PARK AVE
5 CHAMBERCOMBE TERR
6 THE FERNERY
7 CHAMPERNOWNE CRES

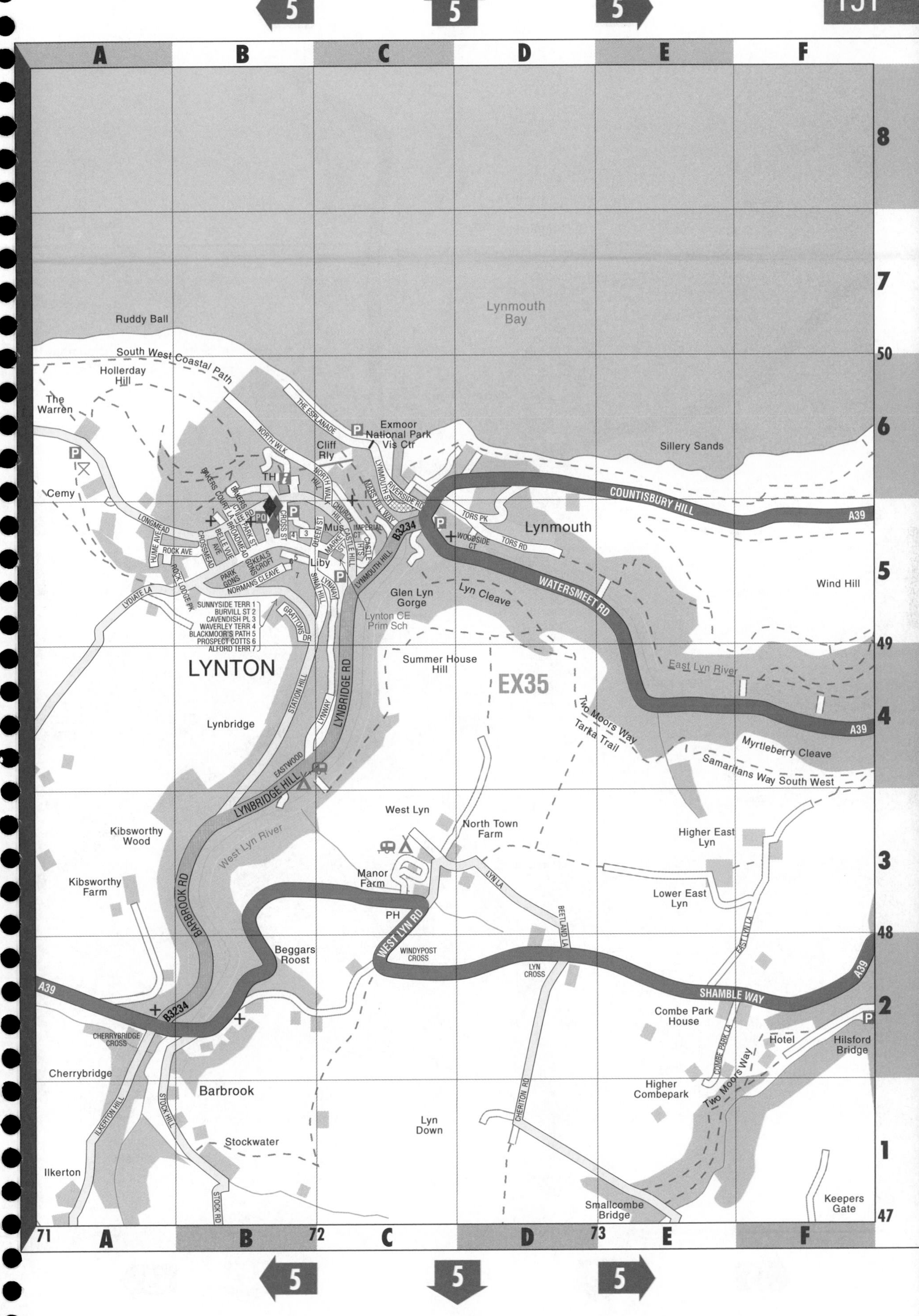
5
5
5
A
B
C
D
E
F
8
7
6
5
4
3
2
1
50
49
48
47
71
72
73
Lynmouth Bay
Ruddy Ball
South West Coastal Path
Hollerday Hill
The Warren
Cemy
THE ESPLANADE
NORTH WLK
Exmoor National Park Vis Ctr
Cliff Rly
Sillery Sands
COUNTISBURY HILL
A39
TH
LONGMEAD
CROSSMEAD
HUME AVE
ROCK AVE
ROCK LODGE PK
LYDIATE LA
PARK GDNS
NORMANS CLEAVE
KEALS CROFT
BELLE VUE AVE
BROADMEAD
CROSS ST
QUEEN ST
Mus
Liby
SINAI HILL
LYNWAY
CASTLE HILL
CASTLE HTS
IMPERIAL CT
LYNMOUTH ST
MARS HILL WAY
RIVERSIDE RD
LYNMOUTH HILL
B3234
TORS PK
TORS RD
WOODSIDE CT
Lynmouth
WATERSMEET RD
Wind Hill
Glen Lyn Gorge
Lyn Cleave
Lynton CE Prim Sch
SUNNYSIDE TERR 1
BURVILL ST 2
CAVENDISH PL 3
WAVERLEY TERR 4
BLACKMOOR'S PATH 5
PROSPECT COTTS 6
ALFORD TERR 7
GRATTONS DR
LYNTON
Summer House Hill
EX35
East Lyn River
Two Moors Way
Tarka Trail
Myrtleberry Cleave
Samaritans Way South West
STATION HILL
LYNBRIDGE RD
Lynbridge
EASTWOOD
LYNBRIDGE HILL
West Lyn
North Town Farm
Higher East Lyn
Kibsworthy Wood
West Lyn River
Kibsworthy Farm
Manor Farm
LYN LA
Lower East Lyn
BARBROOK RD
PH
WEST LYN RD
BEETLAND LA
EAST LYN LA
Beggars Roost
WINDYPOST CROSS
LYN CROSS
SHAMBLE WAY
Combe Park House
COMBE PARK LA
Hotel
Hilsford Bridge
CHERRYBRIDGE CROSS
Cherrybridge
Barbrook
ILKERTON HILL
STOCK HILL
Higher Combepark
Lyn Down
CHERITON RD
Stockwater
Ilkerton
STOCK RD
Smallcombe Bridge
Keepers Gate

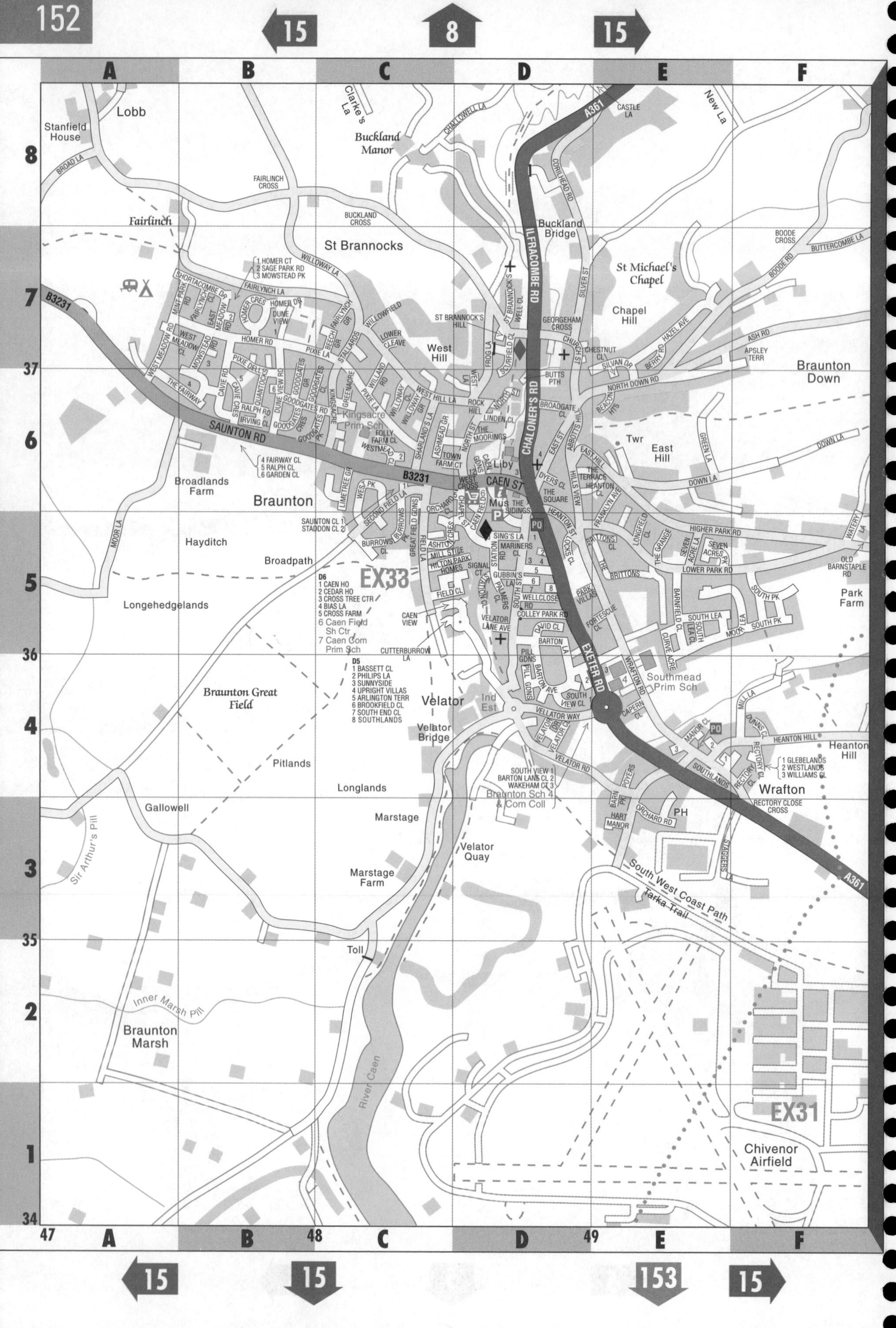
15
8
15
Lobb
Stanfield House
Buckland Manor
Fairlinch
St Brannocks
Buckland Bridge
St Michael's Chapel
Chapel Hill
West Hill
Braunton Down
East Hill
Broadlands Farm
Braunton
Haydicth
Broadpath
EX33
Longehedgelands
Park Farm
Braunton Great Field
Velator
Velator Bridge
Heanton Hill
Wrafton
Pitlands
Longlands
Gallowell
Marstage
Velator Quay
Marstage Farm
South West Coast Path
Tarka Trail
Toll
Inner Marsh Pill
Braunton Marsh
River Caen
EX31
Chivenor Airfield
Sir Arthur's Pill
B3231
SAUNTON RD
A361
ILFRACOMBE RD
CHALONER'S RD
EXETER RD
CAEN ST
Kingsacre Prim Sch
Southmead Prim Sch
Braunton Sch & Com Coll
1 HOMER CT
2 SAGE PARK RD
3 MOWSTEAD PK
4 FAIRWAY CL
5 RALPH CL
6 GARDEN CL
D6
1 CAEN HO
2 CEDAR HO
3 CROSS TREE CTR
4 BIAS LA
5 CROSS FARM
6 Caen Field Sh Ctr
7 Caen Com Prim Sch
D5
1 BASSETT CL
2 PHILIPS LA
3 SUNNYSIDE
4 UPRIGHT VILLAS
5 ARLINGTON TERR
6 BROOKFIELD CL
7 SOUTH END CL
8 SOUTHLANDS
SOUTH VIEW 1
BARTON LANE CL 2
WAKEHAM CT 3
1 GLEBELANDS
2 WESTLANDS
3 WILLIAMS CL
SAUNTON CL 1
STADDON CL 2
A B C D E F
8 7 6 5 4 3 2 1
37 36 35 34
47 48 49
15
15
153
15

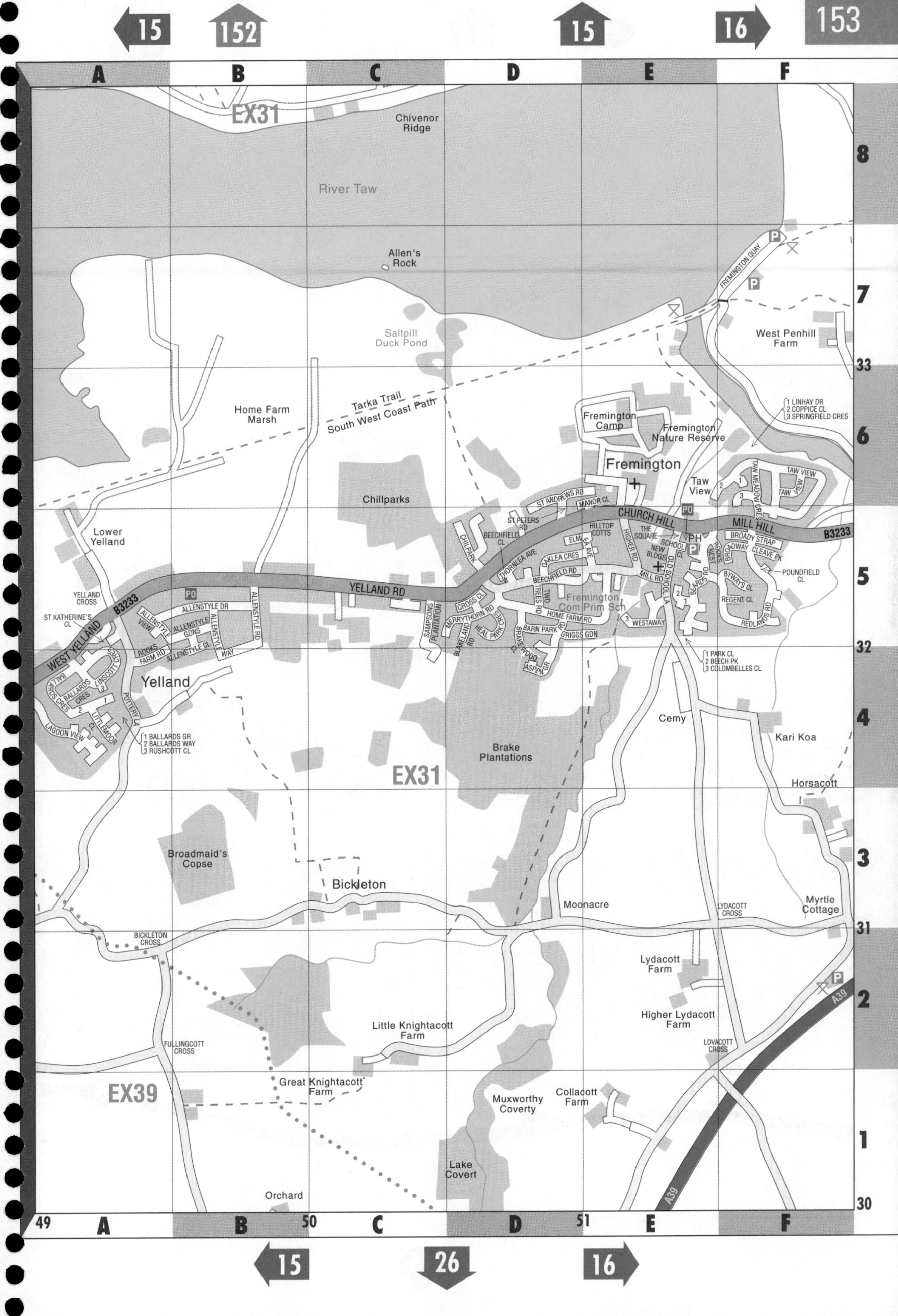
15
152
15
16
EX31
Chivenor Ridge
River Taw
Allen's Rock
Saltpill Duck Pond
West Penhill Farm
FREMINGTON QUAY
Home Farm Marsh
Tarka Trail
South West Coast Path
Fremington Camp
Fremington Nature Reserve
Fremington
1 LINHAY DR
2 COPPICE CL
3 SPRINGFIELD CRES
Taw View
TAW VIEW
Chillparks
Lower Yelland
CHURCH HILL
MILL HILL
B3233
YELLAND RD
Fremington Com Prim Sch
POUNDFIELD CL
REGENT CL
WESTAWAY
YELLAND CROSS
ST KATHERINE'S CL
WEST YELLAND
ALLENSTYLE DR
Yelland
1 BALLARDS GR
2 BALLARDS WAY
3 RUSHCOTT CL
1 PARK CL
2 BEECH PK
3 COLOMBELLES CL
Cemy
Kari Koa
Brake Plantations
EX31
Horsacott
Broadmaid's Copse
Bickleton
Moonacre
LYDACOTT CROSS
Myrtle Cottage
BICKLETON CROSS
Lydacott Farm
Higher Lydacott Farm
Little Knightacott Farm
FULLINGCOTT CROSS
LOVACOTT CROSS
A39
EX39
Great Knightacott Farm
Muxworthy Coverty
Collacott Farm
Lake Covert
Orchard
49
50
51
15
26
16

16 16

F5
1 GREEN LA
2 NORAH BELLOT CT
3 LOVERINGS CT
4 MARKET ST
5 CASTLE QUAY CT
6 HOLLAND ST
7 PAIGES LA
8 PATERNOSTER ROW
9 ST PETER'S TERR
10 CHURCH LA
11 HORWOOD SQ
12 RIVERSIDE CT
13 QUEEN ANNE'S MEWS
14 QUEEN ANNE'S CT
15 BRIDGE CHAMBERS
16 THEATRE LA
17 MAIDEN ST
18 BRIDGE BLDGS
19 BEDFORD ROW
20 SOMERSET PL
21 DIAMOND ST
22 BELLE MEADOW CT
23 GAMMON WLK

F6
1 ST MARGARETS GDN
2 LOWER ALMSHOUSES
3 REFORM ST
4 CRANLEIGH
5 YEO VALE HO
6 HALDENE TERR
7 MAPLES CT
8 WARWICK TERR
9 KINGSLEY AVE
10 MARGROVE TERR
11 BOUTPORT ST (MERMAID WLK)
12 GEORGE ST
13 KING EDWARD ST
14 CHARLES ST
15 SEVEN TH ST

A B C D E F

8 7 34 6 5 33 4 3 32 2 1 31

EX31

Beara Cottage
Ashford Inn Farm
Sewage Works
South West Coast Path
Bradiford House
Bradiford
Riverside Units
Pottington Bsns Pk
River Taw
Hotel
River View Commercial Ctr
Pottington Ind Est
Pottington
Two Rivers Ind Est
Taw Trade Pk
Pilton
Pilton Com Coll
Pathfield Sch
Pilton Inf Sch
EX32

CHURCH PATH 1
DARK LA 2
FEOFFE COTTS 3
BEECHGROVE TERR 4
MASEFIELD AVE 5
RALEIGH LAWN 6
Pilton Bluecoat CE Jun Sch 7

Swing Bridge
C Ctr
Castle Green & Mound
Liby
Green Lanes
Mkt
Heritage Ctr
Long Bridge
THE SQUARE
Mus
North Devon L Ctr
South West Coast Path Tarka Trail
Hollowcombe
North Down Farm
Bickington

1 OAKLANDS GDNS
2 OAKLANDS CT
3 BEECHWOOD CL

Sticklepath
Barnstaple Ret Pk
Barnstaple
Seven Brethren Ind Est
Tarka Tennis Ctr
Sticklepath Com Sch
Aviemore Ind Est
PETROC
Herton
Superstore
Gratton Ct
Roundswell
Ret Pk
Bsns Pk
Brannam Ct
Trad Est
Williams Ct
Crem
EX31
Baron Ct
Ind Est
Brynhyfryd
Pill Farm
Lake
Larkbear Plantation
Brynsworthy Manor
Brynsworthy Farm
Tallyns
Clanton
Tallins Moor

A361 A39 A3125 B3149 B3233 B3232
BRAUNTON RD
BRAUNTON ROAD
ROLLE ST
BICKINGTON RD
STICKLEPATH HL

53 A B 54 C D 55 E F

A2
1 THE COOMBES
2 WOODLARK LA
3 SKYLARK SPINNEY
4 HIGHER WESTLAKE RD
5 LARK RISE
6 WESTER-MOOR CL

B3
1 YELLAFORD WAY
2 HONEYSUCKLE CL
3 MEADOWSWEET LA
4 CORNFLOWER CL

C2
1 HORNBEAM HOLLOW
2 ROWAN PK
3 ALMOND CT
4 HAZEL GR
5 SILVER BIRCH CT

C3
1 DUNNING GN
2 DEPTFORD VILLAS
3 OAKHILL RISE

16 16

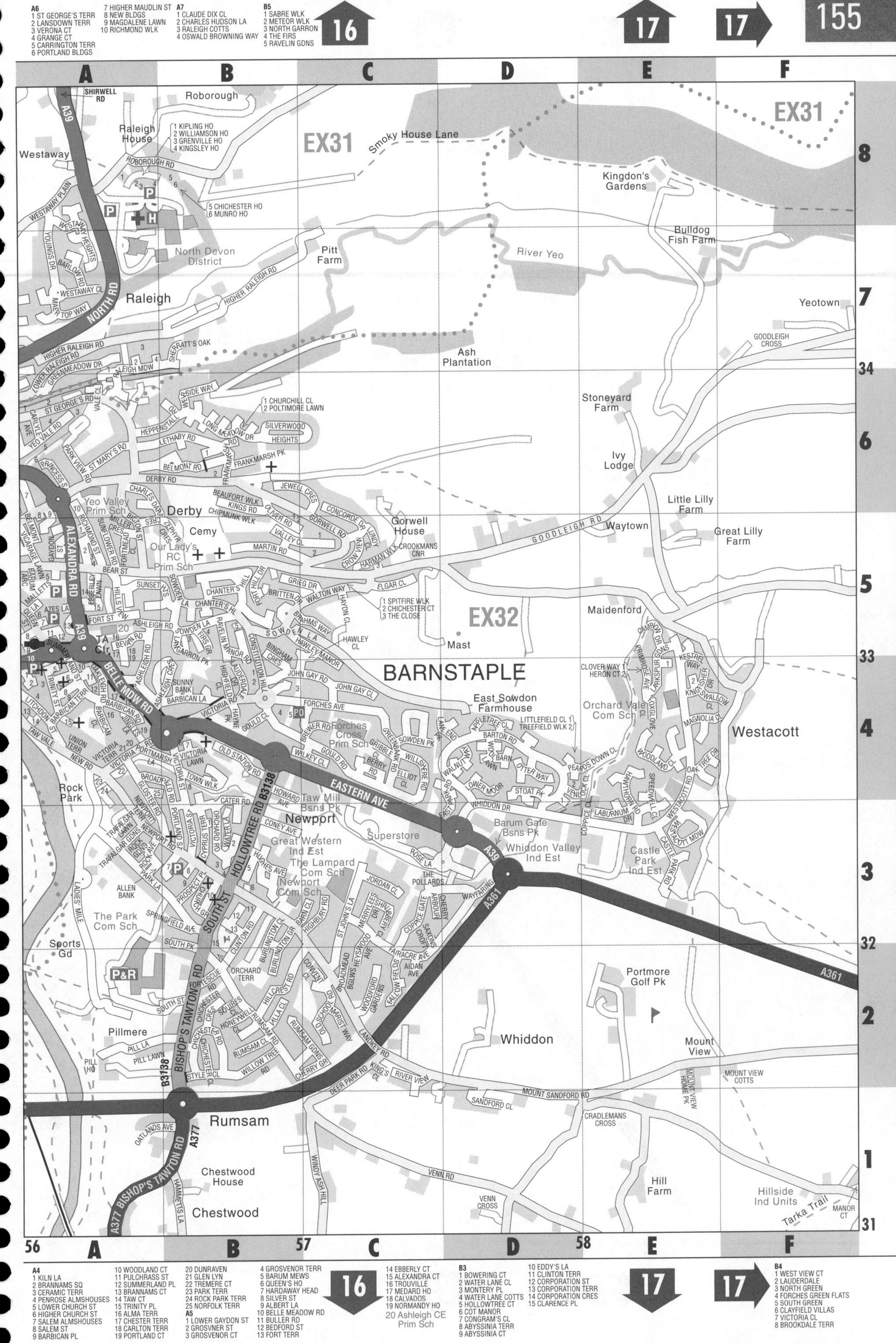
A6
1 ST GEORGE'S TERR
2 LANSDOWN TERR
3 VERONA CT
4 GRANGE CT
5 CARRINGTON TERR
6 PORTLAND BLDGS
7 HIGHER MAUDLIN ST
8 NEW BLDGS
9 MAGDALENE LAWN
10 RICHMOND WLK
A7
1 CLAUDE DIX CL
2 CHARLES HUDSON LA
3 RALEIGH COTTS
4 OSWALD BROWNING WAY
B5
1 SABRE WLK
2 METEOR WLK
3 NORTH GARRON
4 THE FIRS
5 RAVELIN GDNS
16
17
17
A
B
C
D
E
F
8
7
34
6
5
33
4
3
32
2
1
31
56
57
58
EX31
EX31
EX32
Roborough
Raleigh House
Westaway
Smoky House Lane
Kingdon's Gardens
Bulldog Fish Farm
North Devon District
Pitt Farm
River Yeo
Raleigh
NORTH RD
Yeotown
GOODLEIGH CROSS
Ash Plantation
Stoneyard Farm
Ivy Lodge
Little Lilly Farm
Great Lilly Farm
Waytown
GOODLEIGH RD
Derby
Cemy
Our Lady's RC Prim Sch
Yeo Valley Prim Sch
Gorwell House
CROOKMANS CNR
Maidenford
Mast
BARNSTAPLE
East Sowdon Farmhouse
Orchard Vale Com Sch
Westacott
Forches Cross Prim Sch
EASTERN AVE
Taw Mill Bsns Pk
Newport
Superstore
Great Western Ind Est
The Lampard Com Sch
Newport Com Sch
Barum Gate Bsns Pk
Whiddon Valley Ind Est
Castle Park Ind Est
Rock Park
ALLEN BANK
The Park Com Sch
Sports Gd
Portmore Golf Pk
Whiddon
Mount View
MOUNT VIEW COTTS
Pillmere
PILL HO
Rumsam
CRADLEMANS CROSS
Chestwood House
Chestwood
Hill Farm
Hillside Ind Units
Tarka Trail
MANOR CT
VENN CROSS
A39
A361
A377
B3138
BISHOP'S TAWTON RD
A4
1 KILN LA
2 BRANNAMS SQ
3 CERAMIC TERR
4 PENROSE ALMSHOUSES
5 LOWER CHURCH ST
6 HIGHER CHURCH ST
7 SALEM ALMSHOUSES
8 SALEM ST
9 BARBICAN PL
10 WOODLAND CT
11 PULCHRASS ST
12 SUMMERLAND PL
13 BRANNAMS CT
14 TAW CT
15 TRINITY PL
16 ALMA TERR
17 CHESTER TERR
18 CARLTON TERR
19 PORTLAND CT
20 DUNRAVEN
21 GLEN LYN
22 TREMERE CT
23 PARK TERR
24 ROCK PARK TERR
25 NORFOLK TERR
A5
1 LOWER GAYDON ST
2 GROSVNER ST
3 GROSVENOR CT
4 GROSVENOR TERR
5 BARUM MEWS
6 QUEEN'S HO
7 HARDAWAY HEAD
8 SILVER ST
9 ALBERT LA
10 BELLE MEADOW RD
11 BULLER RD
12 BEDFORD ST
13 FORT TERR
14 EBBERLY CT
15 ALEXANDRA CT
16 TROUVILLE
17 MEDARD HO
18 CALVADOS
19 NORMANDY HO
20 Ashleigh CE Prim Sch
B3
1 BOWERING CT
2 WATER LANE CL
3 MONTERY PL
4 WATER LANE COTTS
5 HOLLOWTREE CT
6 COT MANOR
7 CONGRAM'S CL
8 ABYSSINIA TERR
9 ABYSSINIA CT
10 EDDY'S LA
11 CLINTON TERR
12 CORPORATION ST
13 CORPORATION TERR
14 CORPORATION CRES
15 CLARENCE PL
B4
1 WEST VIEW CT
2 LAUDERDALE
3 NORTH GREEN
4 FORCHES GREEN FLATS
5 SOUTH GREEN
6 CLAYFIELD VILLAS
7 VICTORIA CL
8 BROOKDALE TERR

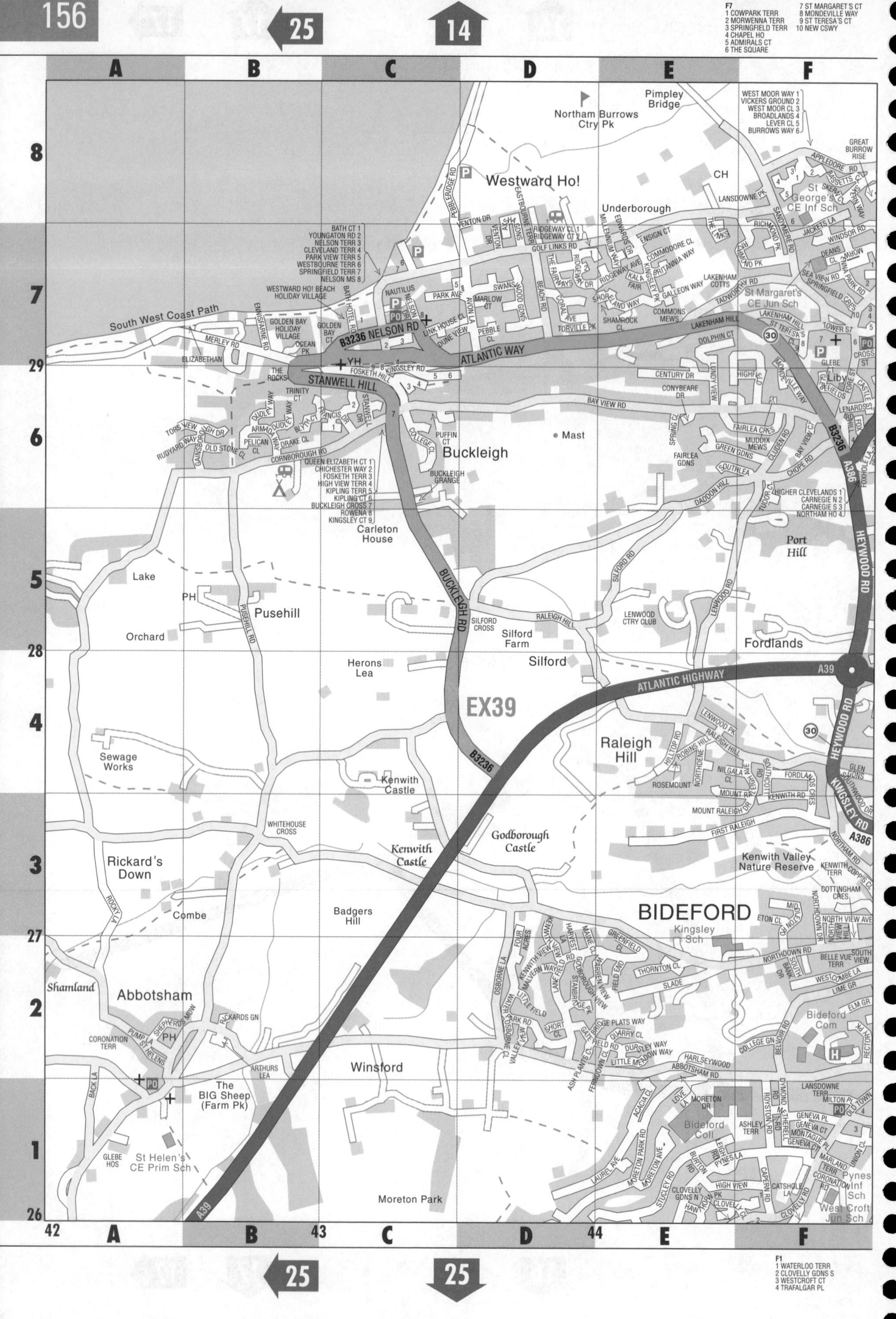

25
14
F7
1 COWPARK TERR
2 MORWENNA TERR
3 SPRINGFIELD TERR
4 CHAPEL HO
5 ADMIRALS CT
6 THE SQUARE
7 ST MARGARET'S CT
8 MONDEVILLE WAY
9 ST TERESA'S CT
10 NEW CSWY
A
B
C
D
E
F
8
7
29
6
5
28
4
3
27
2
1
26
42
43
44
Northam Burrows Ctry Pk
Pimpley Bridge
WEST MOOR WAY 1
VICKERS GROUND 2
WEST MOOR CL 3
BROADLANDS 4
LEVER CL 5
BURROWS WAY 6
GREAT BURROW RISE
APPLEDORE RD
Westward Ho!
Underborough
CH
LANSDOWNE TER
St George's CE Inf Sch
BATH CT 1
YOUNGATON RD 2
NELSON TERR 3
CLEVELAND TERR 4
PARK VIEW TERR 5
WESTBOURNE TERR 6
SPRINGFIELD TERR 7
NELSON MS 8
WESTWARD HO! BEACH HOLIDAY VILLAGE
South West Coast Path
GOLDEN BAY HOLIDAY VILLAGE
GOLDEN BAY CT
OCEAN PK
MERLEY RD
ELIZABETHAN
B3236 NELSON RD
ATLANTIC WAY
STANWELL HILL
THE ROCKS
TRINITY CT
YH
FOSKETH HILL
KINGSLEY RD
LINK HOUSE CL
DUNE VIEW
PEBBLE CL
MARLOW CT
SWANS
WOOD GDNS
BEACH RD
PARK AVE
PEBBLERIDGE RD
VENTON DR
EASTBOURNE TERR
RIDGEWAY CL 1
RIDGEWAY CT 2
GOLF LINKS RD
THE FAIRWAYS
RIDGEWAY DR
RIDGEWAY AVE
KALA FAIR
ENSIGN CT
COMMODORE CL
BRITANNIA WAY
GALLEON WAY
SHORELAND WAY
SHAMROCK CL
COMMONS MEWS
TORVILLE PK
CORAL AVE
LAKENHAM COTTS
TADWORTHY RD
St Margaret's CE Jun Sch
LAKENHAM HILL
DOLPHIN CT
CENTURY DR
CONYBEARE DR
LUNDY VIEW
HIGHFIELD
MONDEVILLE WAY
BAY VIEW RD
SPRING CL
FAIRLEA CRES
MUDDIX MEWS
FAIRLEA GDNS
GREEN GDNS
SOUTHLEA
DADDON HILL
CHOPE RD
TUDOR CL
HIGHER CLEVELANDS 1
CARNEGIE N 2
CARNEGIE S 3
NORTHAM HO 4
B3236
A386
HEYWOOD RD
Port Hill
TORS VIEW
RUDYARD WAY
GAINSBOROUGH DR
OLD STONE CL
PELICAN CL
DRAKE CL
CORNBOROUGH RD
QUEEN ELIZABETH CT 1
CHICHESTER WAY 2
FOSKETH TERR 3
HIGH VIEW TERR 4
KIPLING TERR 5
KIPLING CT 6
BUCKLEIGH CROSS 7
ROWENA 8
KINGSLEY CT 9
Buckleigh
PUFFIN CT
COLLEGE CL
BUCKLEIGH GRANGE
Mast
Carleton House
Lake
PH
Pusehill
PUSEHILL RD
Orchard
BUCKLEIGH RD
SILFORD CROSS
Silford Farm
RALEIGH HILL
Silford
SILFORD RD
LENWOOD RD
LENWOOD CTRY CLUB
Fordlands
Herons Lea
ATLANTIC HIGHWAY
A39
EX39
Raleigh Hill
Sewage Works
Kenwith Castle
WHITEHOUSE CROSS
Godborough Castle
ROSEMOUNT
MOUNT RALEIGH DR
FIRST RALEIGH
KENWITH RD
KINGSLEY RD
Rickard's Down
Kenwith Valley Nature Reserve
BIDEFORD
Kingsley Sch
Badgers Hill
Combe
ROCKY LA
Shamland
Abbotsham
NORTHDOWN RD
THORNTON CL
SLADE
BELLE VUE TERR
WESTCOMBE LA
Bideford Com
CORONATION TERR
RICKARDS GN
PH
ST HELENS
ARTHURS LEA
The BIG Sheep (Farm Pk)
Winsford
COLLEGE GN
HARLSEYWOOD
ABBOTSHAM RD
MORETON DR
Bideford Coll
ASHLEY TERR
LANSDOWNE TERR
MILTON PL
GENEVA PL
GENEVA CT
MONTAGUE PL
BACK LA
GLEBE HOS
St Helen's CE Prim Sch
Moreton Park
LAUREL AVE
MORETON PARK RD
MORETON AVE
STUCLEY RD
BURTON RD
PYNES LA
HIGH VIEW
CLOVELLY GDNS N
CLOVELLY RD
CAPERN RD
CATSHOLE LA
Pynes Inf Sch
West Croft Jun Sch
F1
1 WATERLOO TERR
2 CLOVELLY GDNS S
3 WESTCROFT CT
4 TRAFALGAR PL

25
25

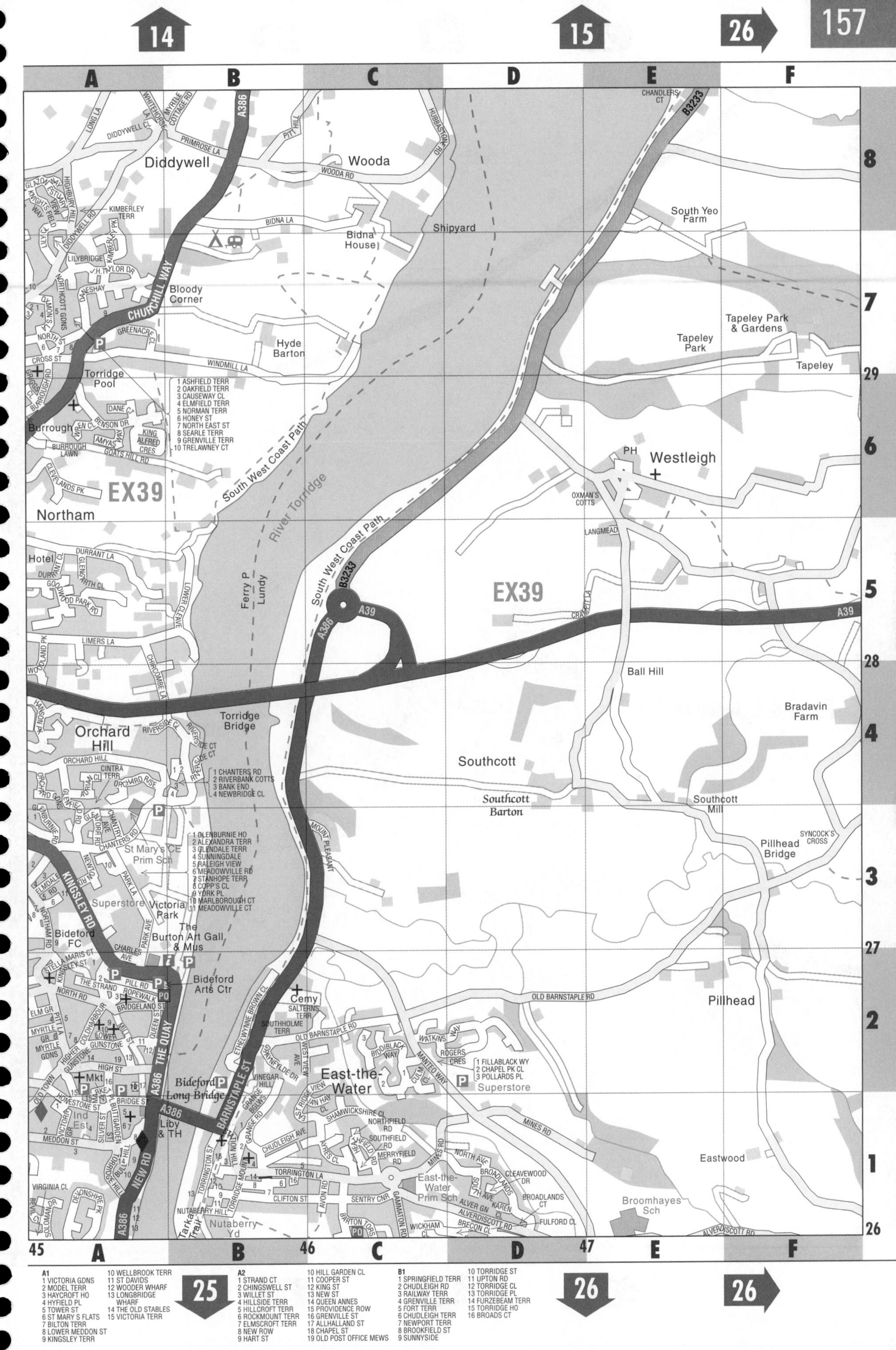

A1
1 VICTORIA GDNS
2 MODEL TERR
3 HAYCROFT HO
4 HYFIELD PL
5 TOWER ST
6 ST MARY S FLATS
7 BILTON TERR
8 LOWER MEDDON ST
9 KINGSLEY TERR
10 WELLBROOK TERR
11 ST DAVIDS
12 WOODER WHARF
13 LONGBRIDGE WHARF
14 THE OLD STABLES
15 VICTORIA TERR

25

A2
1 STRAND CT
2 CHINGSWELL ST
3 WILLET ST
4 HILLSIDE TERR
5 HILLCROFT TERR
6 ROCKMOUNT TERR
7 ELMSCROFT TERR
8 NEW ROW
9 HART ST
10 HILL GARDEN CL
11 COOPER ST
12 KING ST
13 NEW ST
14 QUEEN ANNES
15 PROVIDENCE ROW
16 GRENVILLE ST
17 ALLHALLAND ST
18 CHAPEL ST
19 OLD POST OFFICE MEWS

B1
1 SPRINGFIELD TERR
2 CHUDLEIGH RD
3 RAILWAY TERR
4 GRENVILLE TERR
5 FORT TERR
6 CHUDLEIGH TERR
7 NEWPORT TERR
8 BROOKFIELD ST
9 SUNNYSIDE
10 TORRIDGE ST
11 UPTON RD
12 TORRIDGE CL
13 TORRIDGE PL
14 FURZEBEAM TERR
15 TORRIDGE HO
16 BROADS CT

26
26

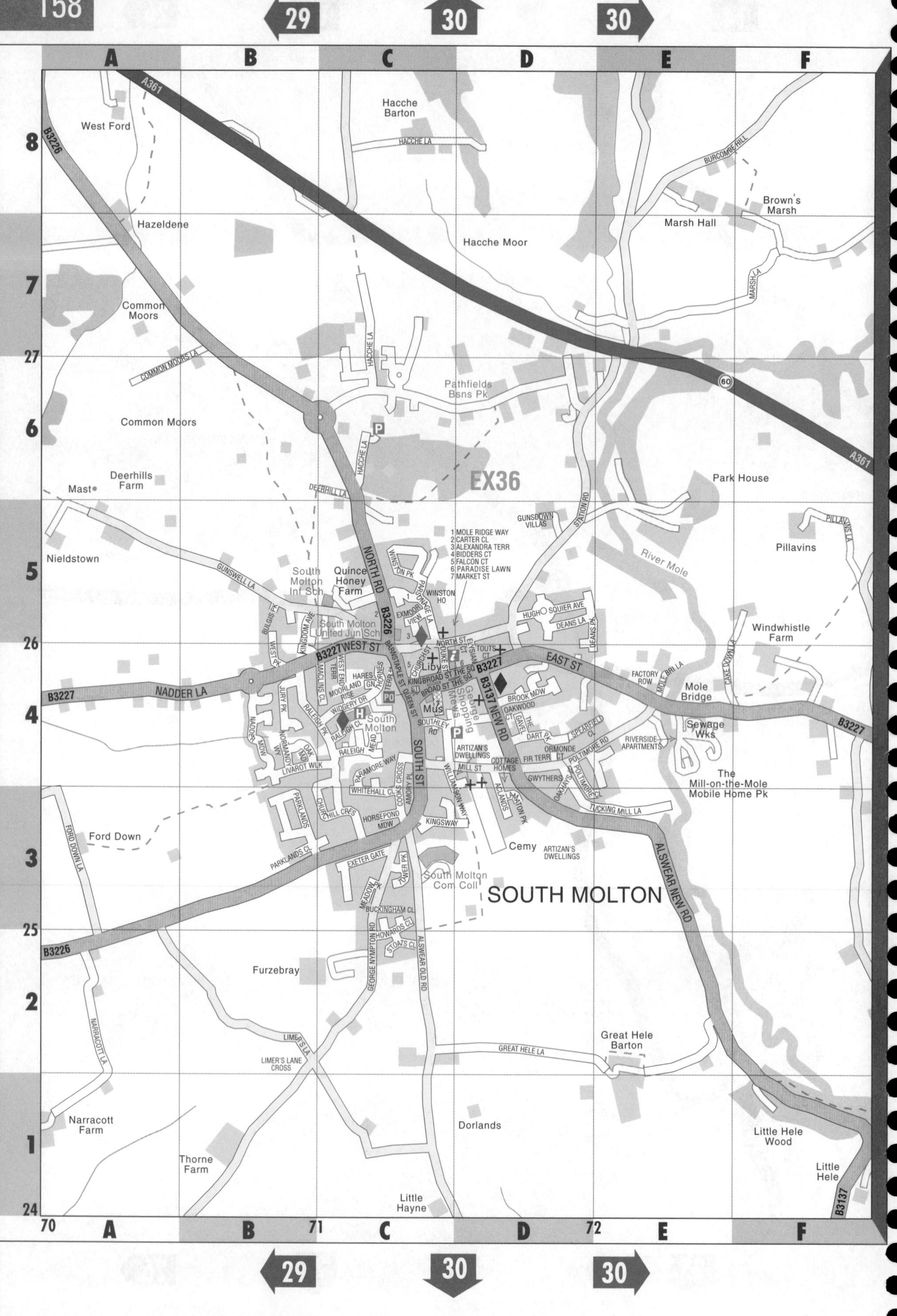

29
30
30
A361
B3226
West Ford
Hacche Barton
HACCHE LA
BURCOMBE HILL
Brown's Marsh
Marsh Hall
Hazeldene
Hacche Moor
MARSH LA
Common Moors
COMMON MOORS LA
HACCHE LA
Pathfields Bsns Pk
Common Moors
EX36
Deerhills Farm
Mast
DEERHILL LA
Park House
GUNSDOWN VILLAS
STATION RD
PILLAVINS LA
Nieldstown
GUNSWELL LA
1 MOLE RIDGE WAY
2 CARTER CL
3 ALEXANDRA TERR
4 BIDDERS CT
5 FALCON CT
6 PARADISE LAWN
7 MARKET ST
River Mole
Pillavins
South Molton Inf Sch
Quince Honey Farm
NORTH RD
WINSTON PK
PARSONAGE LA
WINSTON HO
HUGH SQUIER AVE
DEANS LA
DEANS PK
Windwhistle Farm
South Molton United Jun Sch
EXMOOR VIEW
B3226
NORTH ST
B3227 WEST ST
KINGDOM AVE
BULGIS PK
WEST PK
TOUTS CT
EAST ST
FACTORY ROW
MOLE BRI LA
CAKE DOWN LA
Mole Bridge
B3227
NADDER LA
JURY PK
MACLINS CL
WEST END TERR
HARES GN
MOORLAND RISE
HORNES
CHURCH ST
Liby
DUKE ST
BROAD ST THE SQ
KINGBROAD ST
B3227
B3137 NEW RD
BROOK MDW
OAKWOOD CT
WIDGERY DR
PO
Mus
George Shopping Mews
South Molton
RALEIGH PK
RALEIGH CL
SOUTHLEY RD
GAVEL
DART PK
SPEARFIELD CL
Sewage Wks
NADDER MDW
NORMAND WY
OAK MDW
RALEIGH
MEAD
SOUTH ST
ARTIZAN'S DWELLINGS
COTTAGE HOMES
FIR TERR
ORMONDE CT
POLTIMORE RD
RIVERSIDE APARTMENTS
LIVAROT WLK
PARAMORE WAY
COOKS CROSS
MILL ST
GWYTHERS
POLTIMORE CL
The Mill-on-the-Mole Mobile Home Pk
WHITEHALL CL
AMORY PL
WILLIAMSON WAY
ACLANDS
PATON PK
OAKHAYS
PARKLANDS
CHURCHILL CRES
HORSEPOND MDW
KINGSWAY
TUCKING MILL LA
FORD DOWN LA
Ford Down
Cemy
ARTIZAN'S DWELLINGS
ALSWEAR NEW RD
PARKLANDS CL
EXETER GATE
TOWER PK
South Molton Com Coll
SOUTH MOLTON
MEADOW
BUCKINGHAM CL
HOWARDS CL
STOATS CL
GEORGE NYMPTON RD
ALSWEAR OLD RD
B3226
Furzebray
NARRACOTT LA
LIMERS LA
LIMER'S LANE CROSS
GREAT HELE LA
Great Hele Barton
Narracott Farm
Dorlands
Little Hele Wood
Little Hele
Thorne Farm
Little Hayne
B3137
8
7
27
6
5
26
4
3
25
2
1
24
70
71
72
A
B
C
D
E
F
29
30
30

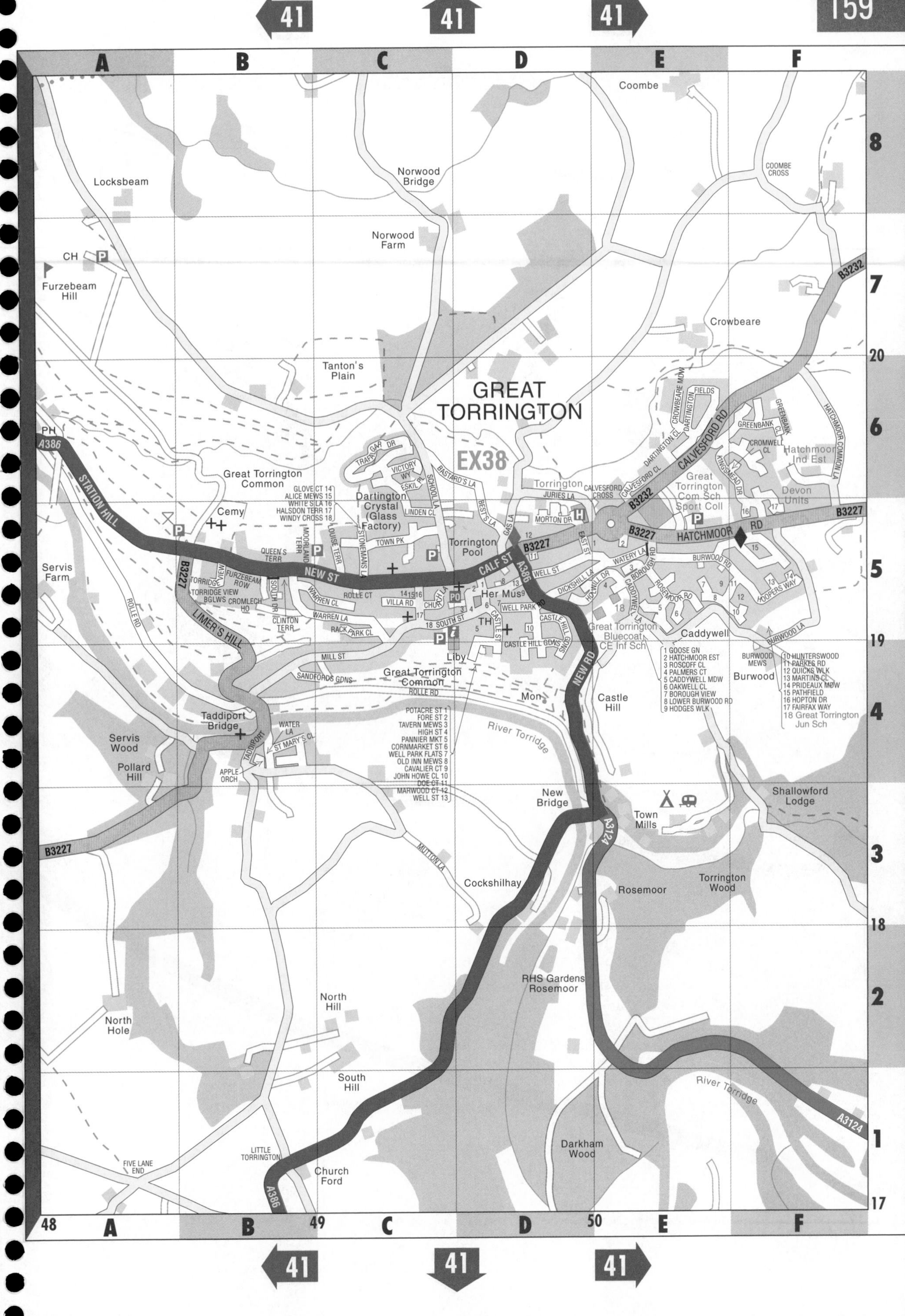
41
41
41
A
B
C
D
E
F
8
7
20
6
5
19
4
3
18
2
1
17
48
49
50
Coombe
Locksbeam
Norwood Bridge
Norwood Farm
COOMBE CROSS
CH
Furzebeam Hill
Crowbeare
B3232
Tanton's Plain
GREAT TORRINGTON
EX38
PH
A386
STATION HILL
Great Torrington Common
Cemy
Dartington Crystal (Glass Factory)
GLOVE CT 14
ALICE MEWS 15
WHITE'S LA 16
HALSDON TERR 17
WINDY CROSS 18
TRAFALGAR DR
VICTORY WY
ESKIL PL
SCHOOL LA
BASTARD'S LA
LINDEN CL
STONEMANS LA
LOUISE TERR
MOORLAND TERR
QUEEN'S TERR
TOWN PK
Torrington Pool
BEST'S LA
GAS LA
NEW ST
CALF ST
B3227
Servis Farm
TORRIDGE VIEW
FURZEBEAM ROW
SOUTH DR
TORRIDGE VIEW BGLWS
CROMLECH HO
ROLLE RD
LIMER'S HILL
CLINTON TERR
WARREN CL
WARREN LA
ROLLE CT
VILLA RD
CHURCH LA
PO
Her Mus
RACK PARK CL
SOUTH ST
TH
CASTLE ST
WELL PARK RD
CASTLE HILL GDNS
Liby
MILL ST
SANDFORDS GDNS
Great Torrington Common
ROLLE RD
Mon
Torrington
JURIES LA
CALVESFORD CROSS
MORTON DR
H
EAST ST
WELL ST
DICKSHILL LA
HOWHILL DR
WATERY LA
BOROUGH RD
CADDYWELL LA
ROSEMOOR RD
Great Torrington Bluecoat CE Inf Sch
CROWBEARE MDW
DARTINGTON FIELDS
DARTINGTON CL
CALVESFORD CL
CALVESFORD RD
Great Torrington Com Sch
Sport Coll
HATCHMOOR RD
GREENBANK CL
GREENBANK
CROWNWELL CL
KINGSMEAD DR
Hatchmoor Ind Est
HATCHMOOR COMMON LA
Devon Units
BURWOOD RD
HOOPERS WAY
Caddywell
BURWOOD LA
1 GOOSE GN
2 HATCHMOOR EST
3 ROSCOFF CL
4 PALMERS CT
5 CADDYWELL MDW
6 OAKWELL CL
7 BOROUGH VIEW
8 LOWER BURWOOD RD
9 HODGES WLK
BURWOOD MEWS
Burwood
10 HUNTERSWOOD
11 PARKES RD
12 QUICKS WLK
13 MARTINS CL
14 PRIDEAUX MDW
15 PATHFIELD
16 HOPTON DR
17 FAIRFAX WAY
18 Great Torrington Jun Sch
NEW RD
Castle Hill
Taddiport Bridge
TADDIPORT
WATER LA
ST MARY'S CL
APPLE ORCH
Servis Wood
Pollard Hill
POTACRE ST 1
FORE ST 2
TAVERN MEWS 3
HIGH ST 4
PANNIER MKT 5
CORNMARKET ST 6
WELL PARK FLATS 7
OLD INN MEWS 8
CAVALIER CT 9
JOHN HOWE CL 10
DOE CT 11
MARWOOD CT 12
WELL ST 13
River Torridge
New Bridge
Town Mills
Shallowford Lodge
A3124
MUTTON LA
Cockshilhay
Rosemoor
Torrington Wood
RHS Gardens Rosemoor
North Hill
North Hole
South Hill
River Torridge
Darkham Wood
FIVE LANE END
LITTLE TORRINGTON
Church Ford
41
41
41

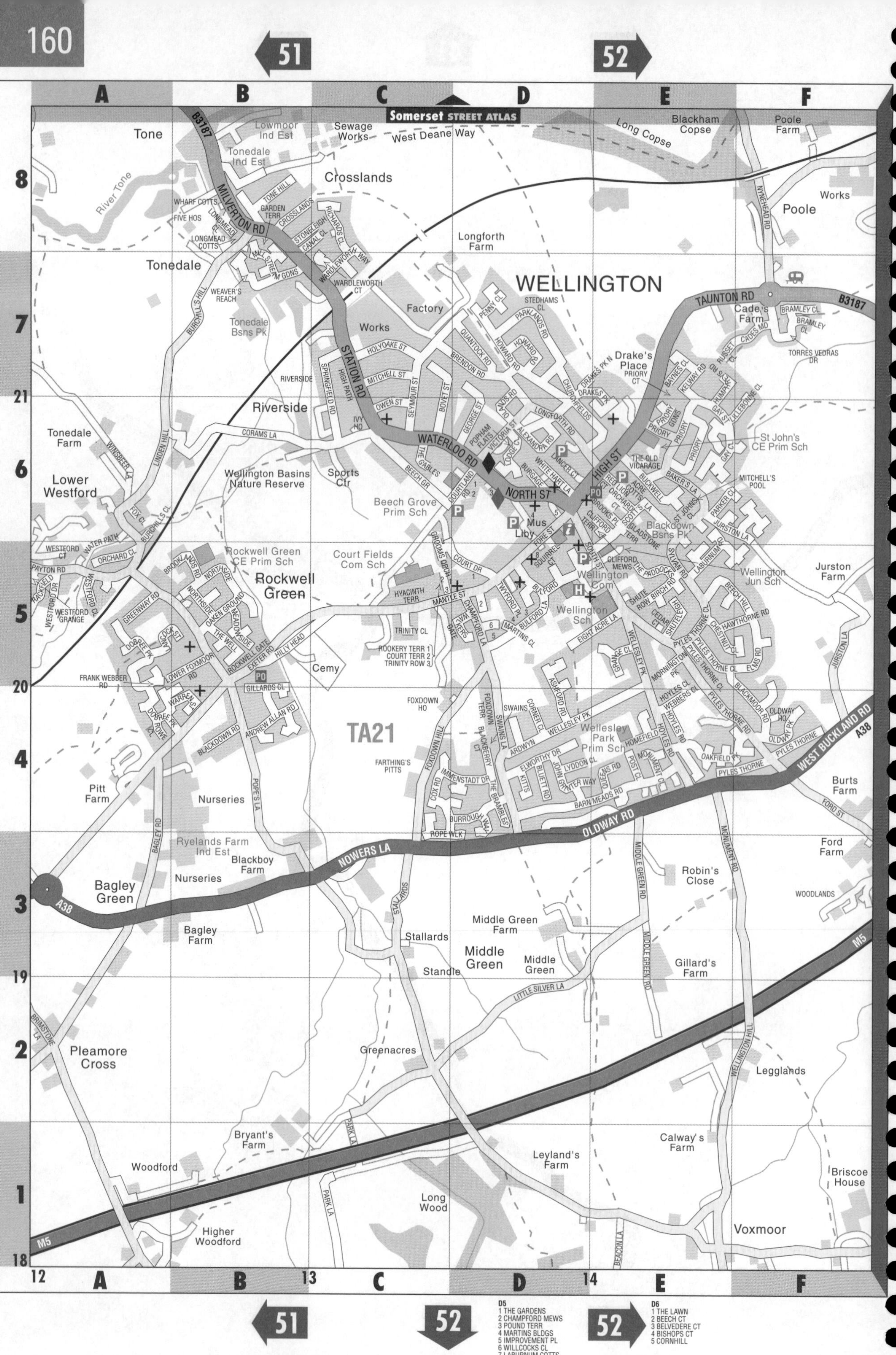
51
52
Somerset STREET ATLAS
A
B
C
D
E
F
8
7
21
6
5
20
4
3
19
2
1
18
12
13
14
Tone
Lowmoor Ind Est
Sewage Works
West Deane Way
Long Copse
Blackham Copse
Poole Farm
Tonedale Ind Est
Crosslands
River Tone
Works
Poole
MILVERTON RD
B3187
Longforth Farm
Tonedale
WELLINGTON
TAUNTON RD
Cade's Farm
Factory
Tonedale Bsns Pk
Works
STATION RD
Drake's Place
Riverside
Tonedale Farm
WATERLOO RD
St John's CE Prim Sch
Lower Westford
Wellington Basins Nature Reserve
Sports Ctr
Beech Grove Prim Sch
HIGH ST
NORTH ST
Mus
Liby
Blackdown Bsns Pk
Rockwell Green CE Prim Sch
Court Fields Com Sch
Rockwell Green
Wellington Com
Wellington Jun Sch
Jurston Farm
Wellington Sch
Cemy
TA21
Wellesley Park Prim Sch
Pitt Farm
Nurseries
Burts Farm
WEST BUCKLAND RD
A38
OLDWAY RD
Ryelands Farm Ind Est
Blackboy Farm
NOWERS LA
Ford Farm
Robin's Close
Bagley Green
Nurseries
Bagley Farm
Middle Green Farm
Stallards
Middle Green
Middle Green
Standle
Gillard's Farm
WOODLANDS
M5
Pleamore Cross
Greenacres
Leggland
Bryant's Farm
Calway's Farm
Woodford
Leyland's Farm
Briscoe House
Long Wood
Higher Woodford
Voxmoor
D5
1 THE GARDENS
2 CHAMPFORD MEWS
3 POUND TERR
4 MARTINS BLDGS
5 IMPROVEMENT PL
6 WILLCOCKS CL
7 LABURNUM COTTS
8 JUBILEE CT
D6
1 THE LAWN
2 BEECH CT
3 BELVEDERE CT
4 BISHOPS CT
5 CORNHILL

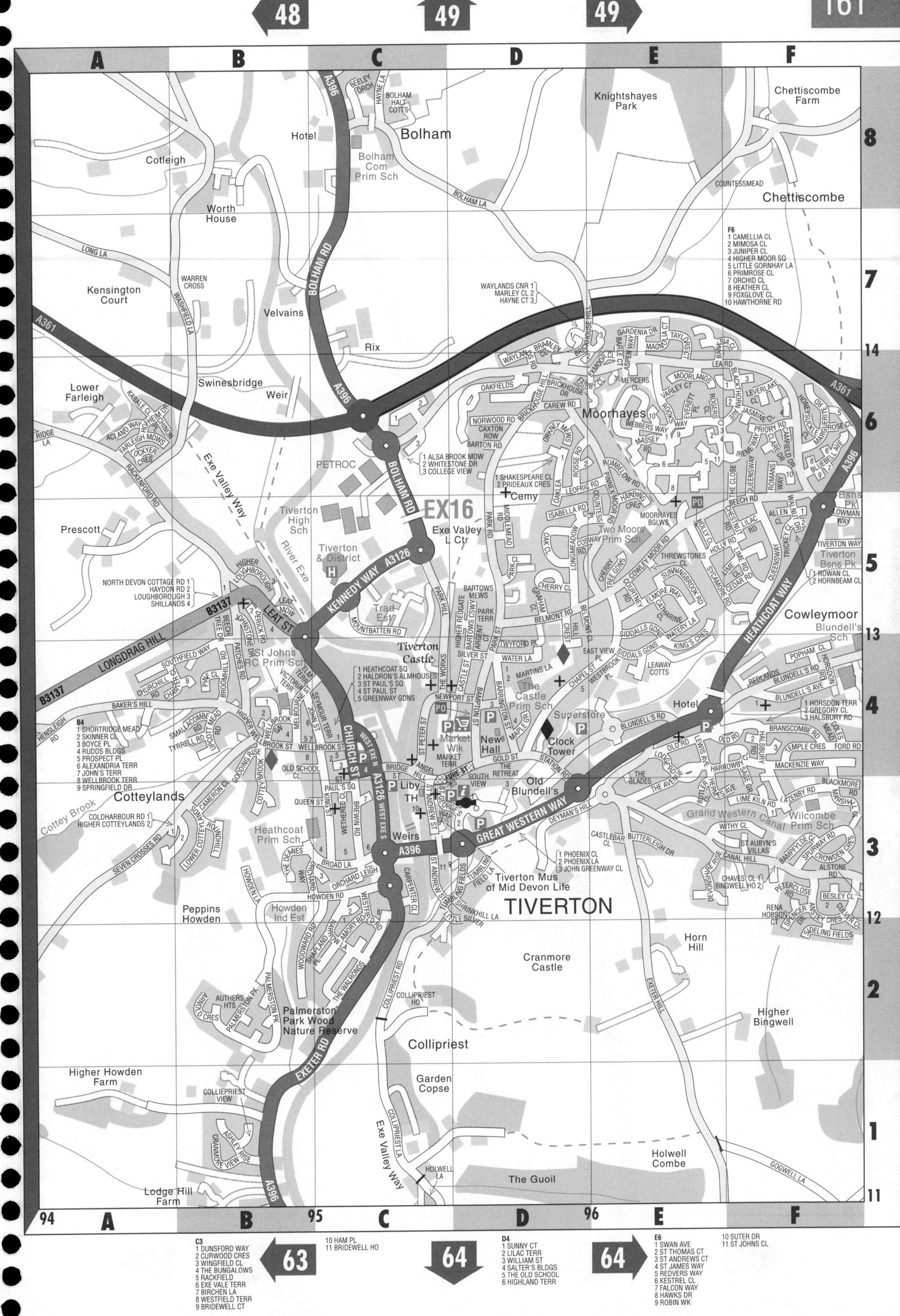
48
49
49
A
B
C
D
E
F
8
7
6
5
4
3
2
1
14
13
12
11
94
95
96
Bolham
Hotel
Bolham Com Prim Sch
BEELEY ORCH
HAYNE LA
BOLHAM HALT COTTS
BOLHAM LA
Knightshayes Park
Chettiscombe Farm
Chettiscombe
COUNTESSMEAD
F6
1 CAMELLIA CL
2 MIMOSA CL
3 JUNIPER CL
4 HIGHER MOOR SQ
5 LITTLE GORNHAY LA
6 PRIMROSE CL
7 ORCHID CL
8 HEATHER CL
9 FOXGLOVE CL
10 HAWTHORNE RD
Cotleigh
Worth House
LONG LA
Kensington Court
WARREN CROSS
WASHFIELD LA
Velvains
BOLHAM RD
A396
A361
Rix
WAYLANDS CNR 1
MARLEY CL 2
HAYNE CT 3
Lower Farleigh
Swinesbridge
Weir
RIDGE LA
KABALE CL
ACLAND WAY
FARLEIGH MDWS
COCKYER CRES
RACKENFORD RD
Exe Valley Way
PETROC
1 ALSA BROOK MDW
2 WHITESTONE DR
3 COLLEGE VIEW
Moorhayes
OAKFIELDS
BRICKHOUSE HILL
BRICKHOUSE DR
CAREW RD
NORWOOD RD
CAXTON ROW
BARTON RD
1 SHAKESPEARE CL
2 PRIDEAUX CRES
Cemy
MOORLANDS
MERCERS CL
WEBBERS WAY
MASSEY RD
LEA RD
BLACKHORN AVE
JASMINE CL
LEVERLAKE
PRIORY RD
BLUEBELL AVE
HONEYSUCKLE
THE CLOSE
QUEENSWAY
ROMANS WAY
PO
BEECH RD
EX16
Prescott
Tiverton High Sch
River Exe
Exe Valley L Ctr
Tiverton & District
H
KENNEDY WAY
A3126
PARK HILL
Trad Est
MOUNTBATTEN RD
BARTOWS MEWS
ISABELLA RD
OAK CL
CHERRY CL
Two Moors Prim Sch
MOORHAYES BGLWS
COWLEY MOOR RD
THREWSTONES CL
SUNNINGBROOK RD
HOLLY CL
LILAC RD
ALLEN CL
TRICKEY CL
TIVERTON WAY
Tiverton Bsns Pk
1 ROWAN CL
2 HORNBEAM CL
Bsns Pk
LOWMAN WAY
HEATHCOAT WAY
Cowleymoor
Blundell's Sch
NORTH DEVON COTTAGE RD 1
HAYDON RD 2
LOUGHBOROUGH 3
SHILLANDS 4
HIGHER LOUGHBOROUGH
B3137
LONGDRAG HILL
LEAT ST
DERICK RD
JOHNSTONE DR
BEECH TREE DR
SOUTHFIELD WAY
CHURCHILL RD
St Johns RC Prim Sch
BELMONT RD
ELMORE WAY
CATHARINE CL
WATERY LA
KING'S CRES
SIDDALLS GDNS
LEAWAY COTTS
EAST VIEW PL
POPHAM CL
BLUNDELL'S RD
BLUNDELL'S AVE
REDLANDS
Tiverton Castle
TWYFORD PL
WATER LA
MARTINS LA
The Castle Prim Sch
1 HEATHCOAT SQ
2 HALDRON'S ALMHOUSES
3 ST PAUL'S SQ
4 ST PAUL ST
5 GREENWAY GDNS
THE WORKS
NEWPORT ST
Superstore
Clock Tower
Hotel
1 HORSDON TERR
2 GREGORY CL
3 HALSBURY RD
HENSLEIGH RD
BAKER'S HILL
B4
1 SHORTRIDGE MEAD
2 SKINNER CL
3 BOYCE PL
4 RUDDS BLDGS
5 PROSPECT PL
6 ALEXANDRIA TERR
7 JOHN'S TERR
8 WELLBROOK TERR
9 SPRINGFIELD DR
SMALLACOMBE RD
TYRRELL RD
WELLBROOK ST
CHURCH ST
Market Wlk
MARKET TERR
New Hall
GOLD ST
THE RETREAT
STATION RD
OLD RD
BRANSCOMBE RD
TEMPLE CRES
FORD RD
MACKENZIE WAY
HARROWBY
BLACKMORE RD
Cotteylands
OLD SCHOOL CL
QUEEN ST
PAUL'S SQ
BRIDGE ST
ANGEL HILL
FORE ST
Liby
TH
SOUTH VIEW
Old Blundell's
GREAT WESTERN WAY
DEYMAN'S HILL
THE GLADES
THE AVENUE
LIME KILN RD
Grand Western Canal
Wilcombe Prim Sch
Cottey Brook
COLDHARBOUR RD 1
HIGHER COTTEYLANDS 2
SEVEN CROSSES RD
Heathcoat Prim Sch
Weirs
A396
BROAD LA
ORCHARD LEIGH
HOWDEN RD
TUMBLING FIELDS
TUMBLING FIELD LA
1 PHOENIX CL
2 PHOENIX LA
3 JOHN GREENWAY CL
CASTLEBAR CL
BUTTERLEIGH DR
WITHY CL
ST AUBYN'S VILLAS
CANAL HILL
CHAVES CL 1
BINGWELL HO 2
ALSTONE RD
BESLEY CL
Tiverton Mus of Mid Devon Life
TIVERTON
Peppins Howden
Howden Ind Est
SHRINKHILL LA
LITTLE SILVER
RENA HOBSON CT
SIDELING FIELDS
Horn Hill
Cranmore Castle
AUTHERS HTS
PALMERSTON PK
Palmerston Park Wood Nature Reserve
THE WALRONDS
WOODWARD RD
COLLIPRIEST RD
COLLIPRIEST HO
Colliprest
EXETER HILL
Higher Bingwell
Higher Howden Farm
EXETER RD
COLLIEPRIEST VIEW
ASHLEY RISE
CRANMORE VIEW RISE
Garden Copse
Exe Valley Way
COLLIPRIEST LA
HOLWELL LA
The Guoil
Holwell Combe
GOGWELL LA
Lodge Hill Farm
C3
1 DUNSFORD WAY
2 CURWOOD CRES
3 WINGFIELD CL
4 THE BUNGALOWS
5 RACKFIELD
6 EXE VALE TERR
7 BIRCHEN LA
8 WESTFIELD TERR
9 BRIDEWELL CT
10 HAM PL
11 BRIDEWELL HO
63
64
D4
1 SUNNY CT
2 LILAC TERR
3 WILLIAM ST
4 SALTER'S BLDGS
5 THE OLD SCHOOL
6 HIGHLAND TERR
64
E6
1 SWAN AVE
2 ST THOMAS CT
3 ST ANDREWS CT
4 ST JAMES WAY
5 REDVERS WAY
6 KESTREL CL
7 FALCON WAY
8 HAWKS DR
9 ROBIN WK
10 SUTER DR
11 ST JOHNS CL

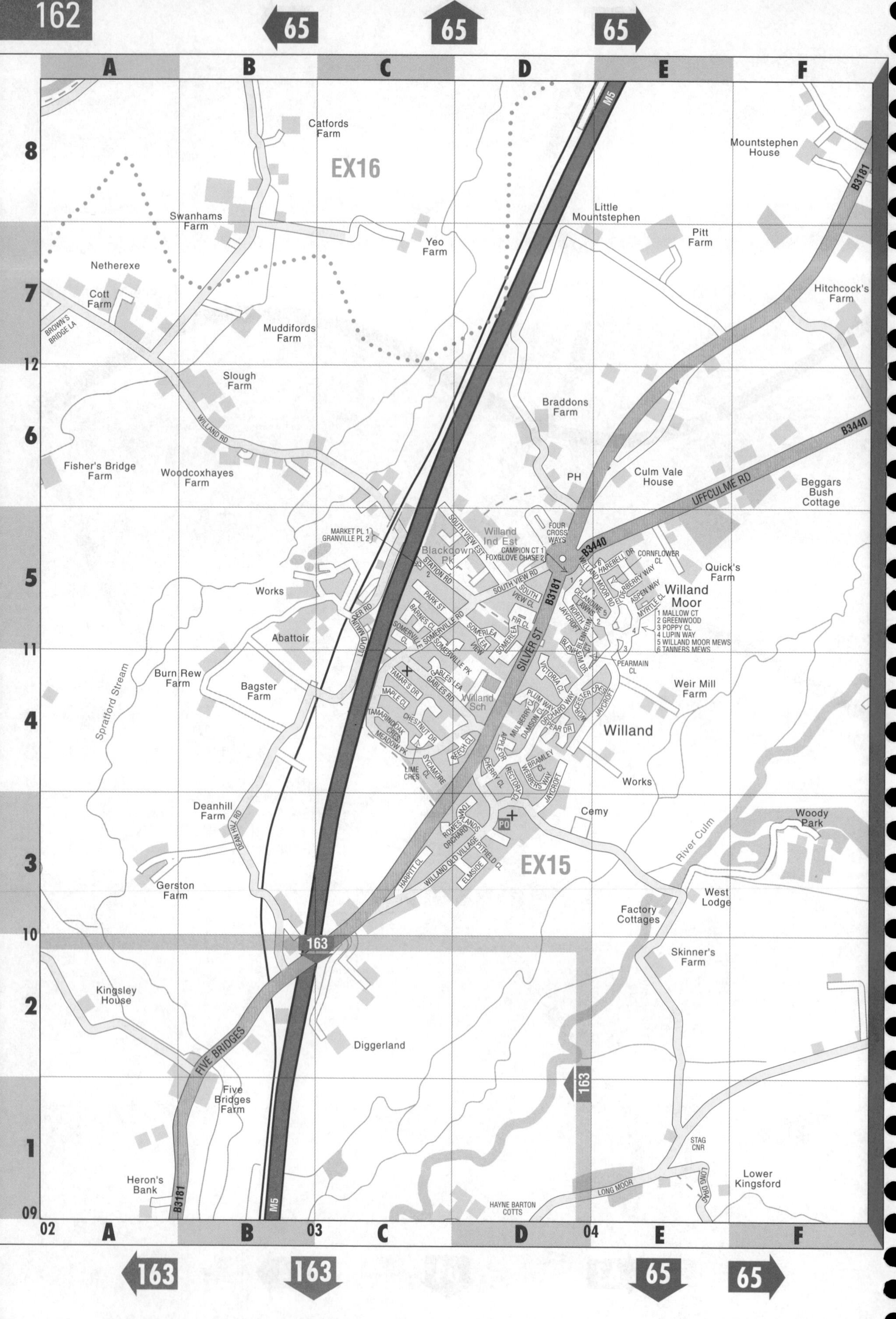

65
65
65
Catfords Farm
EX16
Mountstephen House
B3181
Swanhams Farm
Yeo Farm
Little Mountstephen
Pitt Farm
Netherexe
Cott Farm
Hitchcock's Farm
BROWN'S BRIDGE LA
Muddifords Farm
Slough Farm
Braddons Farm
WILLAND RD
B3440
Fisher's Bridge Farm
Woodcoxhayes Farm
Culm Vale House
PH
UFFCULME RD
Beggars Bush Cottage
Willand Ind Est
FOUR CROSS WAYS
Blackdown Pk
MARKET PL 1
GRANVILLE PL 2
CAMPION CT 1
FOXGLOVE CHASE 2
Quick's Farm
Willand Moor
1 MALLOW CT
2 GREENWOOD
3 POPPY CL
4 LUPIN WAY
5 WILLAND MOOR MEWS
6 TANNERS MEWS
Works
Abattoir
SILVER ST
PEARMAIN CL
Burn Rew Farm
Bagster Farm
Spratford Stream
Willand Sch
Weir Mill Farm
Willand
Works
Deanhill Farm
DEAN HILL RD
Cemy
Woody Park
EX15
River Culm
Gerston Farm
West Lodge
Factory Cottages
163
Skinner's Farm
Kingsley House
FIVE BRIDGES
Diggerland
Five Bridges Farm
163
STAG CNR
Heron's Bank
LONG MOOR
LONG DRAG
Lower Kingsford
HAYNE BARTON COTTS
B3181
M5

163 163 65 65

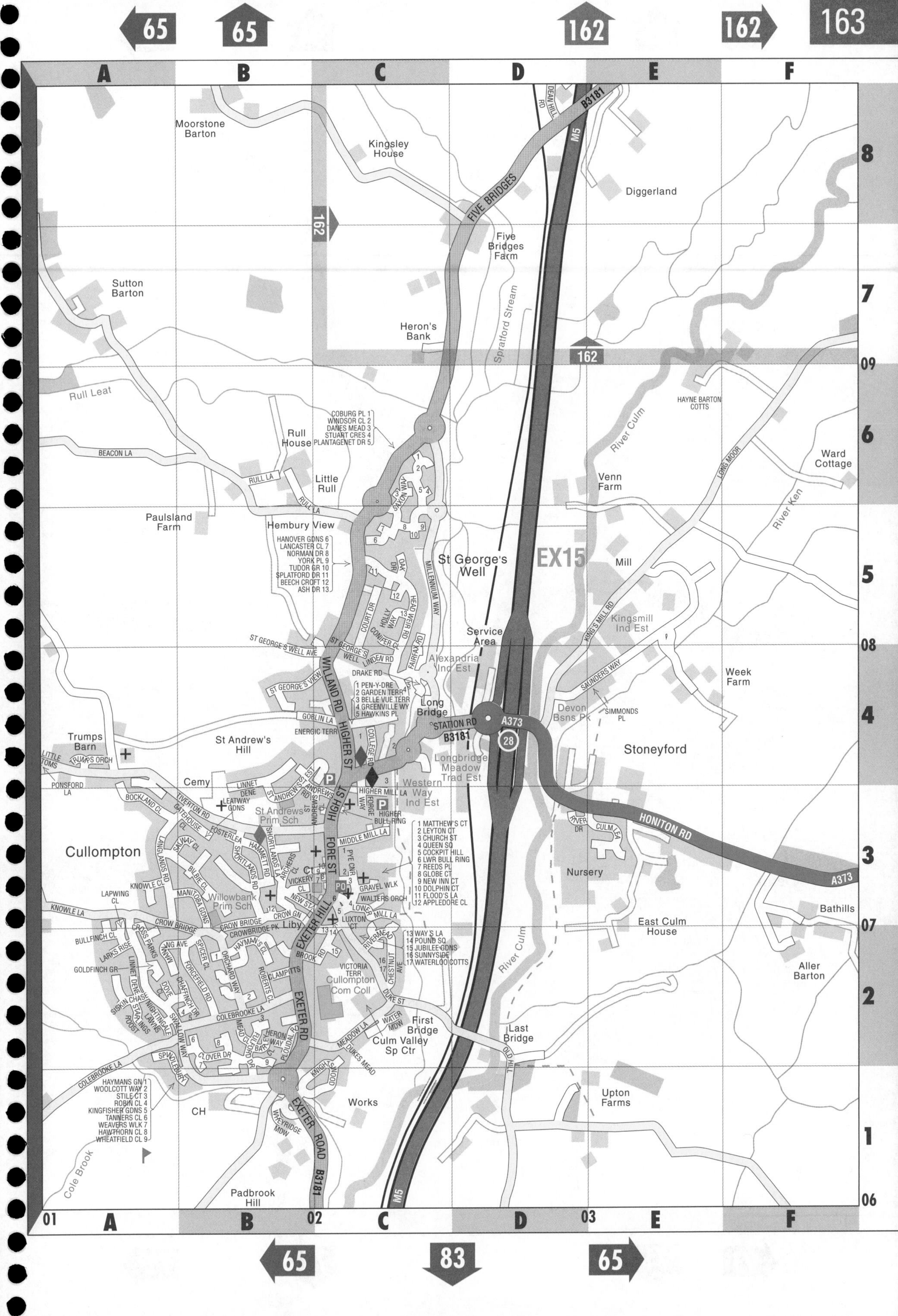
65
65
162
162
A
B
C
D
E
F
8
7
09
6
5
08
4
3
07
2
1
06
01
02
03
Moorstone Barton
Kingsley House
Diggerland
FIVE BRIDGES
B3181
M5
DEAN HILL RD
Five Bridges Farm
Sutton Barton
Heron's Bank
Spratford Stream
Rull Leat
HAYNE BARTON COTTS
River Culm
COBURG PL 1
WINDSOR CL 2
DANES MEAD 3
STUART CRES 4
PLANTAGENET DR 5
Rull House
BEACON LA
Ward Cottage
Little Rull
RULL LA
Venn Farm
LONG MOOR
River Ken
Paulsland Farm
Hembury View
HANOVER GDNS 6
LANCASTER CL 7
NORMAN DR 8
YORK PL 9
TUDOR GR 10
SPLATFORD DR 11
BEECH CROFT 12
ASH DR 13
St George's Well
EX15
Mill
MILLENNIUM WAY
SAXON WAY
OAK DR
COURT DR
HOLLY WAY
HEAD WEIR RD
CONIFER CL
FAIRFAX RD
LINDEN RD
Service Area
Kingsmill Ind Est
KING'S MILL RD
ST GEORGE'S WELL AVE
ST GEORGE'S WELL
Alexandria Ind Est
SAUNDERS WAY
Week Farm
WILLAND RD
DRAKE RD
ST GEORGE'S VIEW
1 PEN-Y-DRE
2 GARDEN TERR
3 BELLE VUE TERR
4 GREENVILLE WY
5 HAWKINS PL
Long Bridge
STATION RD
A373
28
Devon Bsns Pk
SIMMONDS PL
GOBLIN LA
HIGHER ST
ENERGIC TERR
Trumps Barn
St Andrew's Hill
COLLEGE RD
Longbridge Meadow Trad Est
Stoneyford
LITTLE TOMS
TRUMPS ORCH
PONSFORD LA
Cemy
LINNET DENE
ST ANDREWS RD
ST ANDREWS EST
Western Way Ind Est
HIGHER MILL LA
FORGE WAY
BOCKLAND CL
LEATWAY GDNS
TIVERTON RD
GATEHOUSE CL
St Andrews Prim Sch
HIGH ST
HIGHER BULL RING
RIVER DR
CULM LEA
HONITON RD
FOSTERLEA
HAMMETT RD
SHORTLANDS LA
MIDDLE MILL LA
1 MATTHEW'S CT
2 LEYTON CT
3 CHURCH ST
4 QUEEN SQ
5 COCKPIT HILL
6 LWR BULL RING
7 REEDS PL
8 GLOBE CT
9 NEW INN CT
10 DOLPHIN CT
11 FLOOD'S LA
12 APPLEDORE CL
Cullompton
LANGLANDS RD
SALWAY CL
BILBIE CL
SHORTLANDS RD
ARCHERS CL
FORE ST
PYE CNR
Nursery
A373
KNOWLE CL
MANITOBA GDNS
VICKERY CL
Ct
PO
GRAVEL WLK
LAPWING CL
Willowbank Prim Sch
NEW ST
WALTERS ORCH
Bathills
KNOWLE LA
CROW BRIDGE
CROW GN
LOWER MILL LA
LUXTON CT
East Culm House
Liby
CROWBRIDGE PK
EXETER HILL
RIVERMEAD
13 WAY'S LA
14 POUND SQ
15 JUBILEE GDNS
16 SUNNYSIDE
17 WATERLOO COTTS
BULLFINCH CL
LARKS RISE
CROSS PARKS
MAVIN WAY
SPICER CL
HAYMAN'S CL
BROOK RD
River Culm
Aller Barton
GOLDFINCH GR
FORCEFIELD RD
ORCHARD WAY
ROBERTS CL
CLAMPITTS
VICTORIA TERR
CHESTNUT AVE
Cullompton Com Coll
LINNET DENE
DOVE CL
CHAFFINCH DR
EXETER RD
DUKE ST
SISKIN CHASE
NIGHTINGALE LAWNS
SWALLOW WAY
STARLINGS ROOST
COLEBROOKE LA
WATER MDW
First Bridge
Last Bridge
MEAD CL
HERON WAY
PLOUDAL RD
MEADOW LA
Culm Valley Sp Ctr
DUKES MEAD
OLD HILL
CLOVER DR
SPINDLEBURY
COLEBROOKE LA
KNIGHTS MEAD
HAYMANS GN 1
WOOLCOTT WAY 2
STILE CT 3
ROBIN CL 4
KINGFISHER GDNS 5
TANNERS CL 6
WEAVERS WLK 7
HAWTHORN CL 8
WHEATFIELD CL 9
CH
Works
Upton Farms
WHEYRIDGE MDW
EXETER ROAD
Cole Brook
Padbrook Hill
B3181
M5
65
83
65

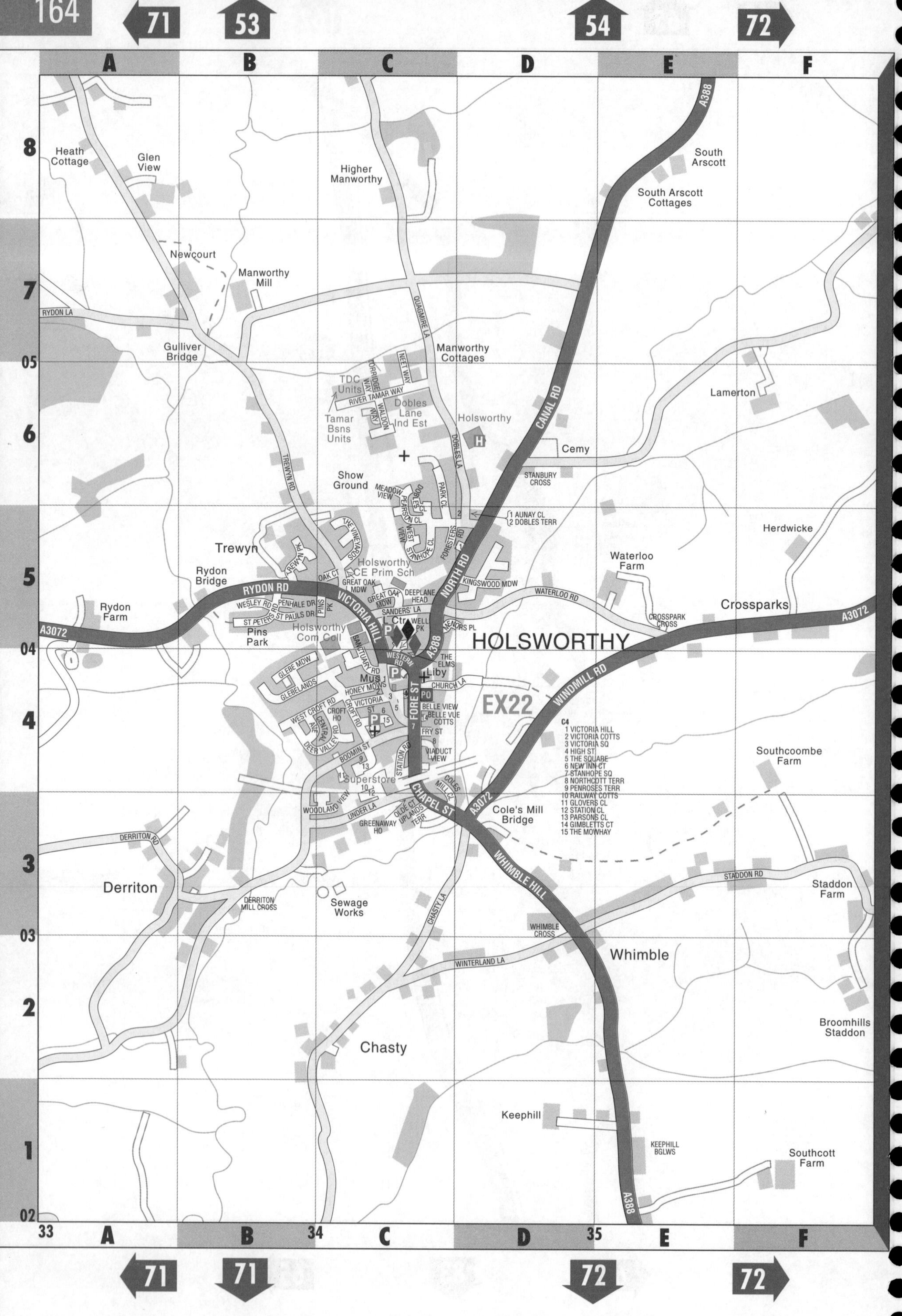
71
53
54
72
A
B
C
D
E
F
8
7
05
6
5
04
4
3
03
2
1
02
33
34
35
Heath Cottage
Glen View
Higher Manworthy
South Arscott
South Arscott Cottages
Newcourt
Manworthy Mill
RYDON LA
Gulliver Bridge
QUAGMIRE LA
Manworthy Cottages
TDC Units
RIVER TAMAR WAY
TORRIDGE WAY
NEET WAY
WALDON WAY
Dobles Lane Ind Est
Tamar Bsns Units
Holsworthy
DOBLES LA
CANAL RD
Lamerton
Cemy
STANBURY CROSS
Show Ground
MEADOW VIEW
PEARSON CL
DOBLES CL
PARK CL
WEST VIEW
STANHOPE CL
FORESTERS RD
1 AUNAY CL
2 DOBLES TERR
TREWYN RD
THE VINEYARDS
Trewyn
NEW PK
Holsworthy CE Prim Sch
Herdwicke
Waterloo Farm
Rydon Bridge
NORTH RD
KINGSWOOD MDW
WATERLOO RD
Crossparks
RYDON RD
OAK CT
GREAT OAK MDW
DEEPLANE HEAD
VICTORIA HILL
CROSSPARK CROSS
A3072
Rydon Farm
WESLEY RD
PENHALE DR
ST PETERS RD
ST PAULS DR
PINS PK
SANDERS' LA
L Ctr
WELL PK
MENORS PL
Pins Park
Holsworthy Com Coll
HOLSWORTHY
A388
SANCTUARY RD
WESTERN RD
THE ELMS
GLEBE MDW
GLEBELANDS
Mus
Liby
CHURCH LA
HONEY MDWS
PO
EX22
WINDMILL RD
WEST CROFT RD
CROFT HO
CROFT RD
VICTORIA ST
FORE ST
BELLE VIEW
BELLE VUE COTTS
FRY ST
CENTRAL AVE
DEER VALLEY RD
BODMIN ST
VIADUCT VIEW
STATION RD
Superstore
C4
1 VICTORIA HILL
2 VICTORIA COTTS
3 VICTORIA SQ
4 HIGH ST
5 THE SQUARE
6 NEW INN CT
7 STANHOPE SQ
8 NORTHCOTT TERR
9 PENROSES TERR
10 RAILWAY COTTS
11 GLOVERS CL
12 STATION CL
13 PARSONS CL
14 GIMBLETTS CT
15 THE MOWHAY
Southcoombe Farm
COLES MILL CL
CHAPEL ST
WOODLAND VIEW
UNDER LA
OLDE CT
UPLANDS TERR
GREENAWAY HO
Cole's Mill Bridge
DERRITON RD
WHIMBLE HILL
STADDON RD
Staddon Farm
Derriton
DERRITON MILL CROSS
Sewage Works
CHASTY LA
WHIMBLE CROSS
Whimble
WINTERLAND LA
Broomhills Staddon
Chasty
Keephill
KEEPHILL BGLWS
Southcott Farm

71
71
72
72

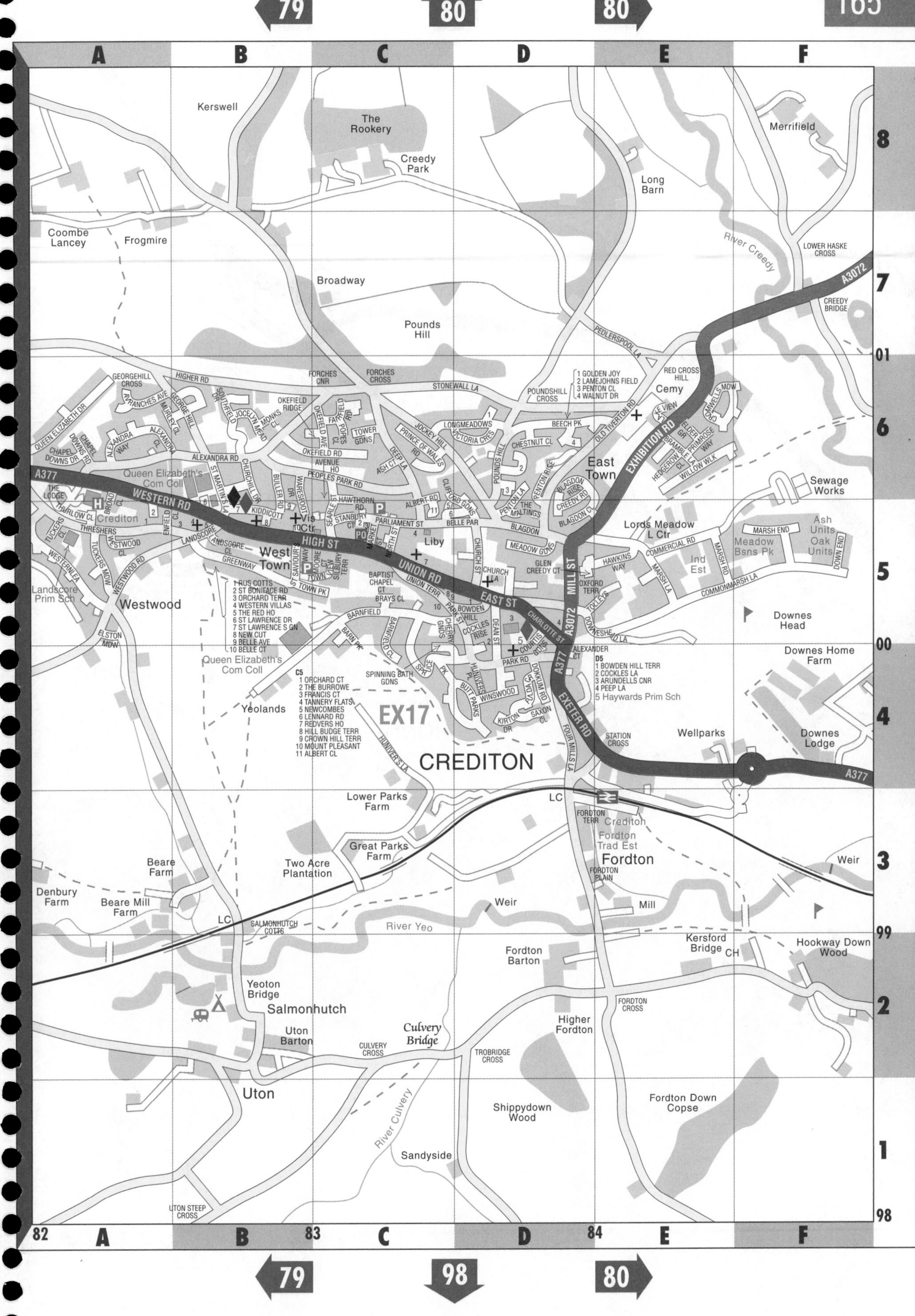
79
80
80
A
B
C
D
E
F
8
7
01
6
5
00
4
3
99
2
1
98
82
83
84
Kerswell
The Rookery
Creedy Park
Merrifield
Long Barn
Coombe Lancey
Frogmire
Broadway
River Creedy
LOWER HASKE CROSS
A3072
CREEDY BRIDGE
Pounds Hill
PEDLERSPOOL LA
GEORGEHILL CROSS
HIGHER RD
FORCHES CNR
FORCHES CROSS
STONEWALL LA
POUNDSHILL CROSS
1 GOLDEN JOY
2 LAMEJOHNS FIELD
3 PENTON CL
4 WALNUT DR
RED CROSS HILL
Cemy
OKEFIELD RIDGE
OKEFIELD RD
TOWER GDNS
JOCKEY HILL
PRINCE OF WALES RD
LONGMEADOWS
VICTORIA CRES
BEECH PK
OLD TIVERTON RD
EXHIBITION RD
CHESTNUT CL
East Town
QUEEN ELIZABETH DR
CHAPEL DOWNS DR
ALEXANDRA WAY
ALEXANDRA RD
Queen Elizabeth's Com Coll
AVENUE HO
PEOPLES PARK RD
HAWTHORN RD
ALBERT RD
PENTON LA
PENTON RISE
THE MALTINGS
BLAGDON RISE
CREEDY RD
BLAGDON CL
Sewage Works
A377
WESTERN RD
THE LODGE
THURLOW CL
Crediton
KIDDICOTT
Vis Ctr
PARLIAMENT ST
BELLE PAR
BLAGDON
Lords Meadow L Ctr
MARSH END
Ash Units
Oak Units
THRESHERS
STANBURY CT
Liby
CHURCH ST
MEADOW GDNS
COMMERCIAL RD
Meadow Bsns Pk
DOWN END
HIGH ST
UNION RD
GLEN CREEDY CT
HAWKINS WAY
Ind Est
MARSH RD
TUCKERS CL
WESTERNLEA
LANDSCORE
West Town
GREENWAY
CHURCH LA
MILL ST
A3072
OXFORD TERR
COMMONMARSH LA
Landscore Prim Sch
Westwood
TUCKERS MDW
WESTWOOD RD
1 RUS COTTS
2 ST BONIFACE RD
3 ORCHARD TERR
4 WESTERN VILLAS
5 THE RED HO
6 ST LAWRENCE DR
7 ST LAWRENCE S GN
8 NEW CUT
9 BELLE AVE
10 BELLE CT
BAPTIST CHAPEL CT
UNION TERR
BRAYS CL
EAST ST
BOWDEN HILL
TOLLEYS
Downes Head
ELSTON MDW
BARNFIELD
BARN PK
COCKLES RISE
DEAN ST
CHARLOTTE ST
DOWNESHEAD LA
ALEXANDER CT
COURTIS GDNS
PARK RD
D5
1 BOWDEN HILL TERR
2 COCKLES LA
3 ARUNDELLS CNR
4 PEEP LA
5 Haywards Prim Sch
Downes Home Farm
Queen Elizabeth's Com Coll
C5
1 ORCHARD CT
2 THE BURROWE
3 FRANCIS CT
4 TANNERY FLATS
5 NEWCOMBES
6 LENNARD RD
7 REDVERS HO
8 HILL BUDGE TERR
9 CROWN HILL TERR
10 MOUNT PLEASANT
11 ALBERT CL
SPINNING BATH GDNS
Yeolands
EX17
WINSWOOD
KIRTON DR
SAXON CL
BUTT PARKS
EXETER RD
FOUR MILLS LA
STATION CROSS
Wellparks
Downes Lodge
HUNTERS LA
CREDITON
Lower Parks Farm
LC
FORDTON TERR
Crediton
Fordton Trad Est
Fordton
FORDTON PLAIN
Great Parks Farm
Two Acre Plantation
Beare Farm
Weir
Denbury Farm
Beare Mill Farm
Weir
Mill
LC
SALMONHUTCH COTTS
River Yeo
Kersford Bridge
CH
Hookway Down Wood
Fordton Barton
Yeoton Bridge
Salmonhutch
FORDTON CROSS
Higher Fordton
Uton Barton
Culvery Bridge
CULVERY CROSS
TROBRIDGE CROSS
Uton
Shippydown Wood
Fordton Down Copse
River Culvery
Sandyside
UTON STEEP CROSS

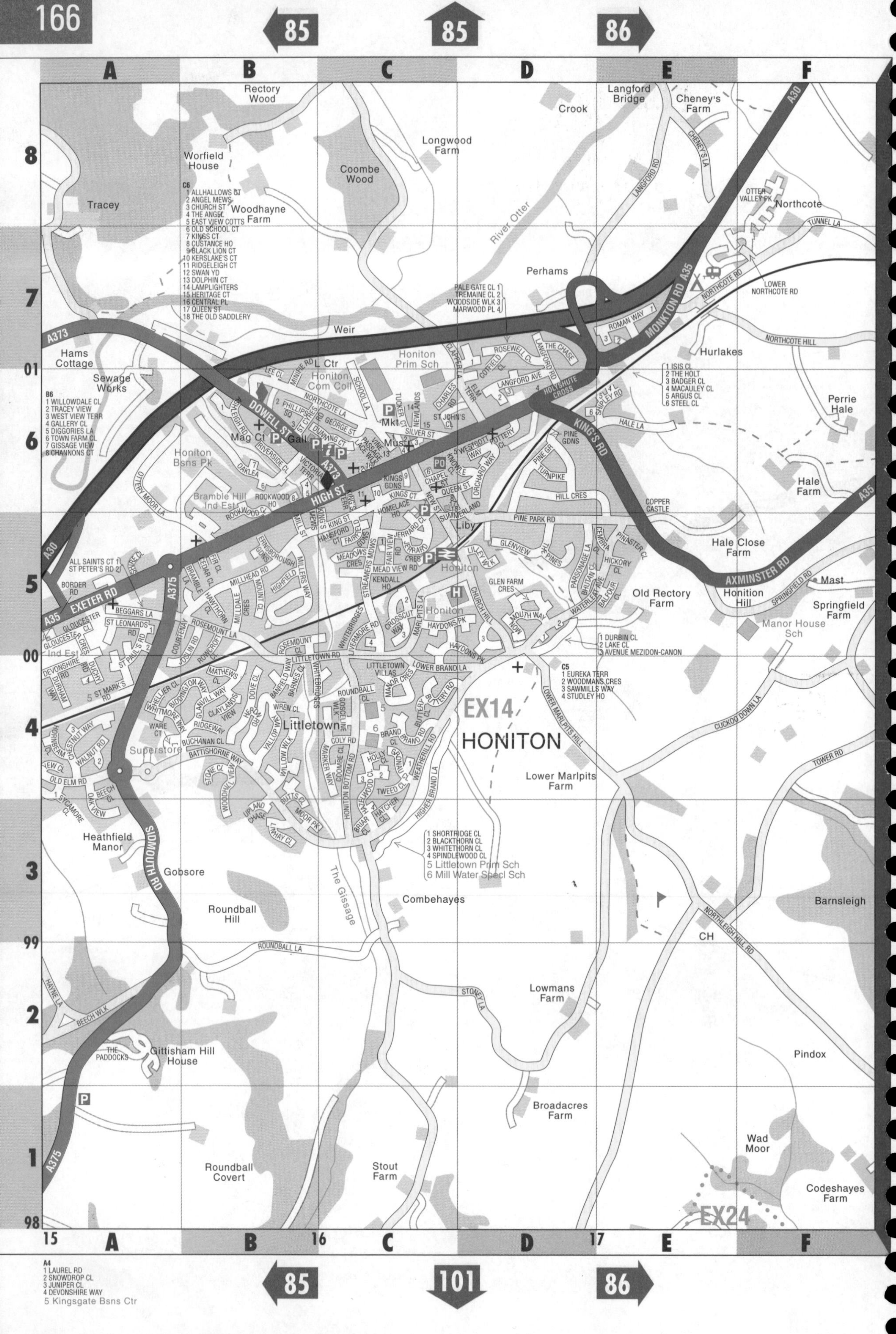

166
85
85
86
A
B
C
D
E
F
8
7
01
6
5
00
4
3
99
2
1
98
15
16
17
Rectory Wood
Crook
Langford Bridge
Cheney's Farm
Worfield House
Coombe Wood
Longwood Farm
Tracey
Woodhayne Farm
C6
1 ALLHALLOWS CT
2 ANGEL MEWS
3 CHURCH ST
4 THE ANGEL
5 EAST VIEW COTTS
6 OLD SCHOOL CT
7 KINGS CT
8 CUSTANCE HO
9 BLACK LION CT
10 KERSLAKE'S CT
11 RIDGELEIGH CT
12 SWAN YD
13 DOLPHIN CT
14 LAMPLIGHTERS
15 HERITAGE CT
16 CENTRAL PL
17 QUEEN ST
18 THE OLD SADDLERY
River Otter
Perhams
Northcote
OTTER VALLEY PK
TUNNEL LA
NORTHCOTE RD
LOWER NORTHCOTE RD
PALE GATE CL 1
TREMAINE CL 2
WOODSIDE WLK 3
MARWOOD PL 4
ROMAN WAY
MONKTON RD
A35
A30
A373
Weir
Hams Cottage
Sewage Works
L Ctr
Honiton Com Coll
Honiton Prim Sch
NORTHCOTE HILL
Hurlakes
1 ISIS CL
2 THE HOLT
3 BADGER CL
4 MACAULEY CL
5 ARGUS CL
6 STEEL CL
B6
1 WILLOWDALE CL
2 TRACEY VIEW
3 WEST VIEW TERR
4 GALLERY CL
5 DIGGORIES LA
6 TOWN FARM CL
7 GISSAGE VIEW
8 CHANNONS CT
DOWELL ST
Mag Ct
Gall
Mkt
Mus
HIGH ST
Honiton Bsns Pk
Bramble Hill Ind Est
KING'S RD
HOLYSHUTE CROSS
HALE LA
Perrie Hale
PINE GDNS
HILL CRES
PINE PARK RD
COPPER CASTLE
Hale Farm
Hale Close Farm
AXMINSTER RD
Liby
Honiton
ALL SAINTS CT 1
ST PETER'S RD 2
BORDER RD
EXETER RD
BEGGARS LA
A375
Ind Est
GLEN FARM CRES
Old Rectory Farm
Honition Hill
Mast
Springfield Farm
SPRINGFIELD RD
Manor House Sch
1 DURBIN CL
2 LAKE CL
3 AVENUE MEZIDON-CANON
C5
1 EUREKA TERR
2 WOODMANS CRES
3 SAWMILLS WAY
4 STUDLEY HO
EX14
HONITON
Littletown
Superstore
CUCKOO DOWN LA
TOWER RD
Lower Marlpits Farm
LOWER MARLPITS HILL
Heathfield Manor
SIDMOUTH RD
Gobsore
1 SHORTRIDGE CL
2 BLACKTHORN CL
3 WHITETHORN CL
4 SPINDLEWOOD CL
5 Littletown Prim Sch
6 Mill Water Specl Sch
The Gissage
Combehayes
Roundball Hill
Barnsleigh
NORTHLEIGH HILL RD
CH
ROUNDBALL LA
HAYNE LA
BEECH WLK
Lowmans Farm
STONEY LA
THE PADDOCKS
Gittisham Hill House
Pindox
Broadacres Farm
Wad Moor
Roundball Covert
Stout Farm
Codeshayes Farm
EX24
A4
1 LAUREL RD
2 SNOWDROP CL
3 JUNIPER CL
4 DEVONSHIRE WAY
5 Kingsgate Bsns Ctr
101

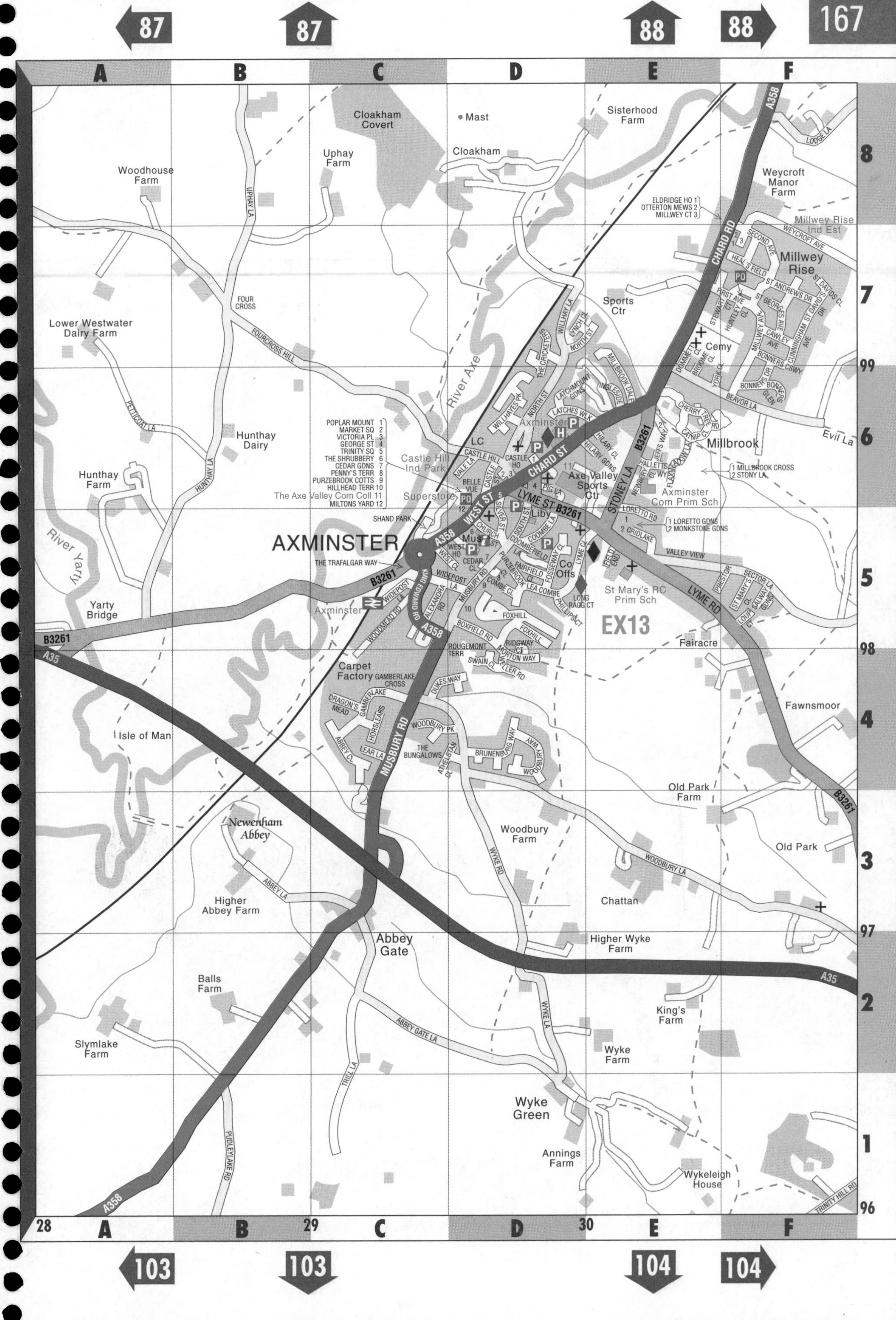

87
87
88
88
AXMINSTER
EX13
Cloakham Covert
Mast
Cloakham
Sisterhood Farm
Uphay Farm
Woodhouse Farm
Weycroft Manor Farm
ELDRIDGE HO 1
OTTERTON MEWS 2
MILLWEY CT 3
Millwey Rise Ind Est
Millwey Rise
Lower Westwater Dairy Farm
FOUR CROSS
Sports Ctr
Cemy
River Axe
Hunthay Dairy
Hunthay Farm
River Yarty
POPLAR MOUNT 1
MARKET SQ 2
VICTORIA PL 3
GEORGE ST 4
TRINITY SQ 5
THE SHRUBBERY 6
CEDAR GDNS 7
PENNY'S TERR 8
PURZEBROOK COTTS 9
HILLHEAD TERR 10
The Axe Valley Com Coll 11
MILTONS YARD 12
Castle Hill Ind Park
Superstore
Axe Valley Sports Ctr
Millbrook
Evil La
1 MILLBROOK CROSS
2 STONY LA
Axminster Com Prim Sch
1 LORETTO GDNS
2 MONKSTONE GDNS
VALLEY VIEW
SHAND PARK
THE TRAFALGAR WAY
Yarty Bridge
Axminster
St Mary's RC Prim Sch
Fairacre
Carpet Factory
GAMBERLAKE CROSS
Fawnsmoor
Isle of Man
THE BUNGALOWS
Old Park Farm
Newenham Abbey
Woodbury Farm
Old Park
Higher Abbey Farm
Chattan
Abbey Gate
Higher Wyke Farm
Balls Farm
King's Farm
Slymlake Farm
Wyke Farm
Wyke Green
Annings Farm
Wykeleigh House
A358
A35
B3261
CHARD RD
LYME RD
MUSBURY RD
WOODBURY LA
ABBEY LA
ABBEY GATE LA
WYKE RD
WYKE LA
TRILL LA
PUDLEYLAKE RD
FOURCROSS HILL
UPHAY LA
HUNTHAY LA
PETTICOAT LA
BEAVOR LA
STONEY LA
WEST ST
CHARD ST
LYME ST
TRINITY HILL RD
LODGE LA
28
29
30
A
B
C
D
E
F
8
7
99
6
5
98
4
3
97
2
1
96

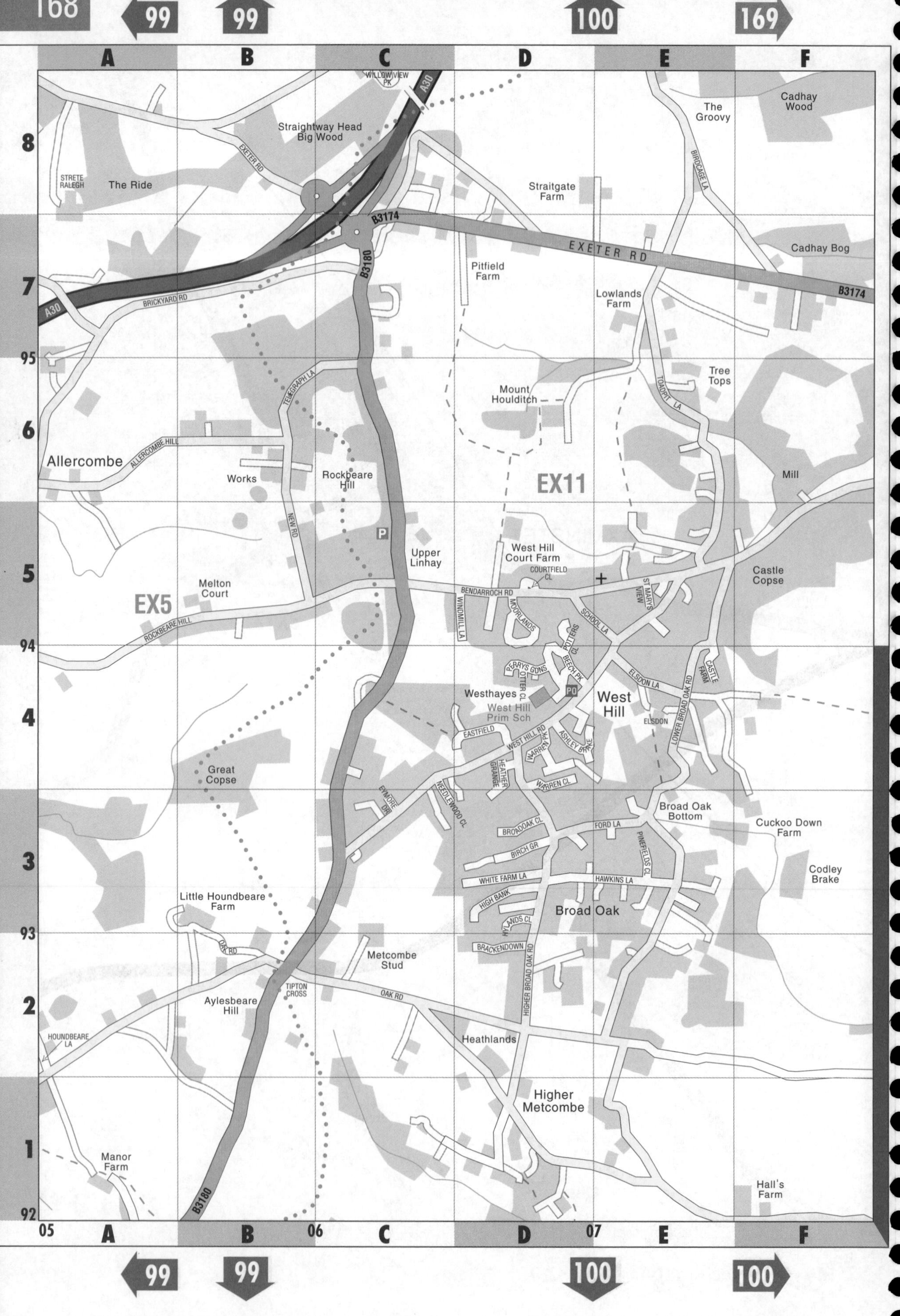
99
99
100
169
Straightway Head
Big Wood
The Ride
Straitgate
Farm
The
Groovy
Cadhay
Wood
Cadhay Bog
EXETER RD
B3174
Pitfield
Farm
Lowlands
Farm
A30
B3180
BRICKYARD RD
Tree
Tops
Mount
Houlditch
Allercombe
Works
Rockbeare
Hill
EX11
Mill
Upper
Linhay
West Hill
Court Farm
Castle
Copse
Melton
Court
EX5
ROCKBEARE HILL
BENDARROCH RD
SCHOOL LA
Westhayes
West Hill
Prim Sch
West
Hill
ELSDON LA
LOWER BROAD OAK RD
Great
Copse
WEST HILL RD
Broad Oak
Bottom
Cuckoo Down
Farm
Codley
Brake
FORD LA
BIRCH GR
WHITE FARM LA
HAWKINS LA
Little Houndbeare
Farm
Broad Oak
Metcombe
Stud
OAK RD
Aylesbeare
Hill
TIPTON
CROSS
Heathlands
Higher
Metcombe
Manor
Farm
Hall's
Farm
05
06
07
92
93
94
95
A
B
C
D
E
F
1
2
3
4
5
6
7
8
99
99
100
100

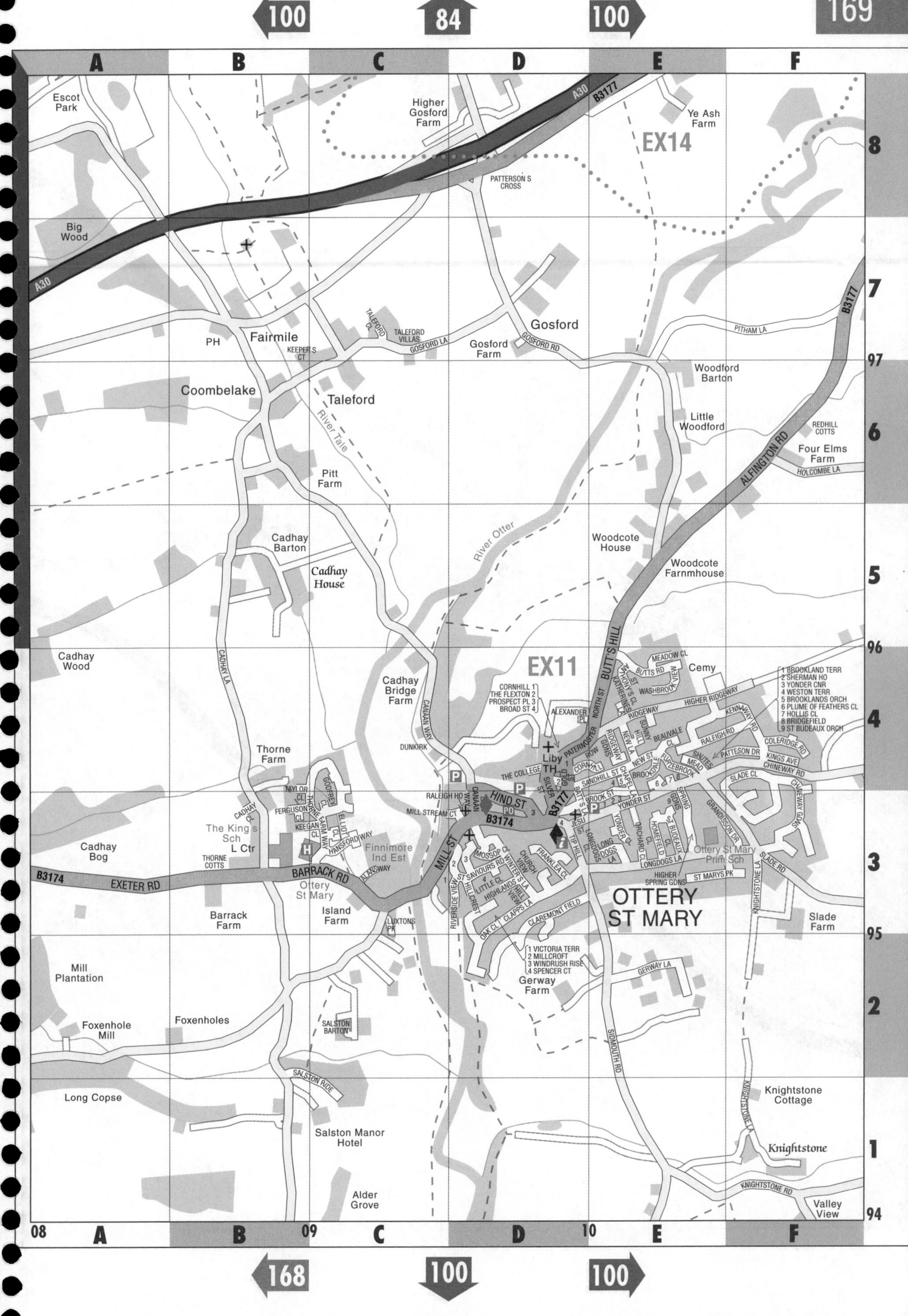

100
84
100
A
B
C
D
E
F
Escot Park
Higher Gosford Farm
Ye Ash Farm
EX14
A30
B3177
PATTERSON S CROSS
Big Wood
Gosford
Gosford Farm
GOSFORD RD
GOSFORD LA
TALEFORD VILLAS
TALEFORD CL
KEEPER S CT
PITHAM LA
PH
Fairmile
Coombelake
Taleford
River Tale
Woodford Barton
Little Woodford
REDHILL COTTS
Four Elms Farm
HOLCOMBE LA
ALFINGTON RD
Pitt Farm
Cadhay Barton
Cadhay House
River Otter
Woodcote House
Woodcote Farnmhouse
Cadhay Wood
CADHAY LA
EX11
BUTT'S HILL
Cemy
MEADOW CL
BUTTS RD
WASHBROOK VIEW
Cadhay Bridge Farm
CANAAN WAY
CORNHILL 1
THE FLEXTON 2
PROSPECT PL 3
BROAD ST 4
ALEXANDER PL
NORTH ST
HIGHER RIDGEWAY
RIDGEWAY
1 BROOKLAND TERR
2 SHERMAN HO
3 YONDER CNR
4 WESTON TERR
5 BROOKLANDS ORCH
6 PLUME OF FEATHERS CL
7 HOLLIS CL
8 BRIDGEFIELD
9 ST BUDEAUX ORCH
Thorne Farm
DUNKIRK
Liby
TH
PATERNOSTER ROW
RALEIGH RD
PATTESON DR
COLERIDGE RD
KINGS AVE
CHINEWAY RD
THE COLLEGE
SANDHILL ST
SLADE CL
TAYLOR CL
GODFREY CL
FERGUSON CL
KEEGAN CL
ELLIOT CL
HANSFORD WAY
RALEIGH HO
MILL STREAM CT
HIND ST
B3174
PO
BROOK ST
YONDER ST
GRANDISSON DR
CHINEWAY GDNS
The King's Sch
L Ctr
Cadhay Bog
THORNE COTTS
Finnimore Ind Est
MILL ST
MOSSOP CL
SAVIOURS RD
LITTLE CL
HIGHLANDS
CHURCH VIEW
FRANKLEA CL
JESU ST
TIP HILL
LONGDOGS LA
ORCHARD CL
HOMEFIELD CL
ST BUDEAUX CL
Ottery St Mary Prim Sch
HIGHER SPRING GDNS
ST MARYS PK
KNIGHTSTONE LA
SLADE RD
B3174
EXETER RD
BARRACK RD
Ottery St Mary
RIVERSIDE VIEW
HILLCREST
CLAPPS LA
OAK CL
CLAREMONT FIELD
OTTERY ST MARY
Slade Farm
Barrack Farm
Island Farm
LUXTONS PK
1 VICTORIA TERR
2 MILLCROFT
3 WINDRUSH RISE
4 SPENCER CT
Gerway Farm
GERWAY LA
Mill Plantation
Foxenhole Mill
Foxenholes
SALSTON BARTON
SIDMOUTH RD
SALSTON RIDE
Long Copse
Knightstone Cottage
KNIGHTSTONE LA
Salston Manor Hotel
Knightstone
KNIGHTSTONE RD
Alder Grove
Valley View
8
7
97
6
5
96
4
3
95
2
1
94
08
09
10
168
100
100

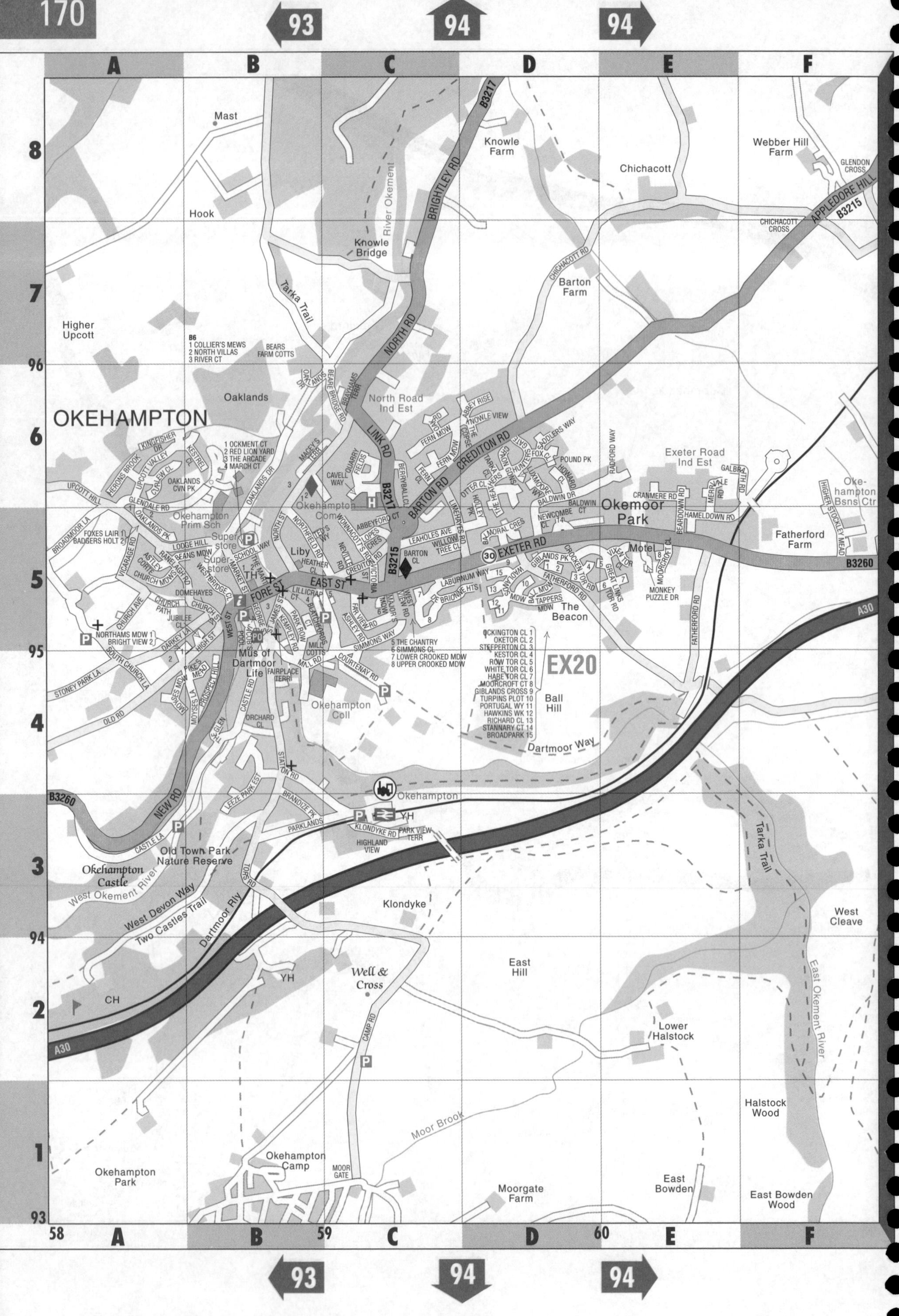
93
94
94
OKEHAMPTON
Okehampton Park
Okehampton Camp
Okehampton Castle
Old Town Park Nature Reserve
Okehampton Coll
Mus of Dartmoor Life
Okemoor Park
The Beacon
Ball Hill
Klondyke
East Hill
Well & Cross
Moorgate Farm
Lower Halstock
East Bowden
Halstock Wood
East Bowden Wood
West Cleave
Fatherford Farm
Exeter Road Ind Est
Chichacott
Barton Farm
Knowle Farm
Knowle Bridge
Webber Hill Farm
Hook
Mast
Higher Upcott
Oaklands
North Road Ind Est
EX20
B6
1 COLLIER'S MEWS
2 NORTH VILLAS
3 RIVER CT
1 OCKMENT CT
2 RED LION YARD
3 THE ARCADE
4 MARCH CT
5 THE CHANTRY
6 SIMMONS CL
7 LOWER CROOKED MDW
8 UPPER CROOKED MDW
OCKINGTON CL 1
OKETOR CL 2
STEEPERTON CL 3
KESTOR CL 4
ROW TOR CL 5
WHITE TOR CL 6
HARE TOR CL 7
MOORCROFT CT 8
GIBLANDS CROSS 9
TURPINS PLOT 10
PORTUGAL WY 11
HAWKINS WK 12
RICHARD CL 13
STANNARY CT 14
BROADPARK 15
FOXES LAIR 1
BADGERS HOLT 2
NORTHAMS MDW 1
BRIGHT VIEW 2
Dartmoor Way
Dartmoor Rly
Tarka Trail
West Devon Way
Two Castles Trail
West Okement River
East Okement River
River Okement
Moor Brook
B3260
B3215
B3217
A30
FORE ST
EAST ST
EXETER RD
CREDITON RD
BARTON RD
LINK RD
NORTH RD
BRIGHTLEY RD
APPLEDORE HILL
58
59
60
93
94
95
96
A
B
C
D
E
F

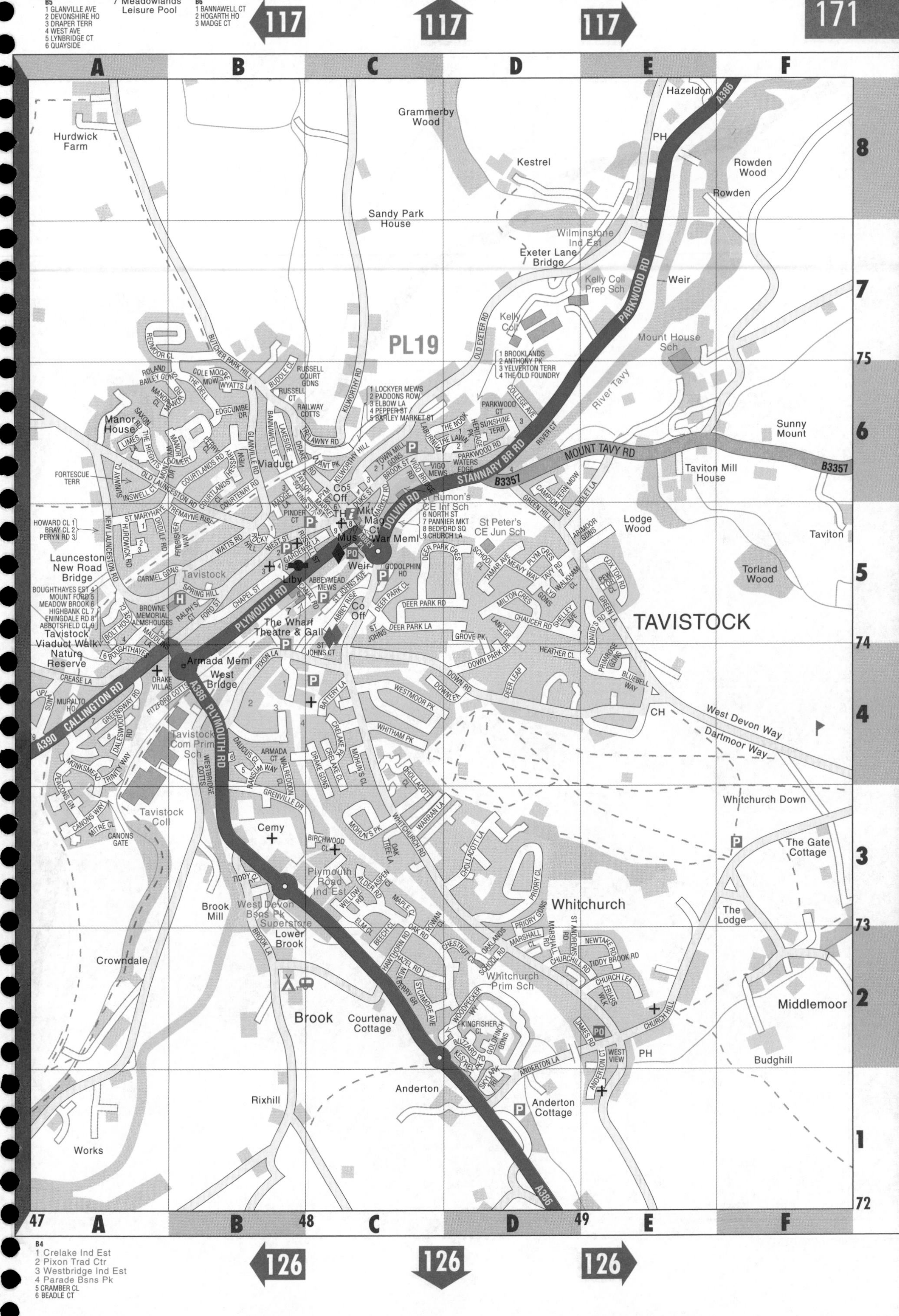
B5
1 GLANVILLE AVE
2 DEVONSHIRE HO
3 DRAPER TERR
4 WEST AVE
5 LYNBRIDGE CT
6 QUAYSIDE
7 Meadowlands Leisure Pool
B6
1 BANNAWELL CT
2 HOGARTH HO
3 MADGE CT
117
117
117
A
B
C
D
E
F
Hazeldon
A386
Grammerby Wood
Hurdwick Farm
PH
Kestrel
Rowden Wood
Rowden
Sandy Park House
Wilminstone Ind Est
Exeter Lane Bridge
PARKWOOD RD
Weir
Kelly Coll Prep Sch
Kelly Coll
PL19
OLD EXETER RD
Mount House Sch
River Tavy
1 BROOKLANDS
2 ANTHONY PK
3 YELVERTON TERR
4 THE OLD FOUNDRY
REDMOOR CL
BUTCHER PARK HILL
RUSSELL COURT GDNS
BUDDLE CL
KILWORTHY RD
ROLAND BAILEY GDNS
COLE MOORE MDW
WYATTS LA
THE DELL
MANOR CL
RUSSELL CT
RAILWAY COTTS
1 LOCKYER MEWS
2 PADDONS ROW
3 ELBOW LA
4 PEPPER ST
5 BARLEY MARKET ST
PARKWOOD CT
COLLEGE AVE
Manor House
SAXON RD
LIMES
THE HEIGHTS
EDGCUMBE DR
GLANVILLE RD
BANNAWELL ST
LAKESIDE
DRAKE RD
TRELAWNY RD
KILWORTHY HILL
TOWN MILL GDNS
LABURNUM
THE NOOK
THE LAWN
HERITAGE PK
SUNSHINE TERR
PARKWOOD RD
RIVER CT
MOUNT TAVY RD
Sunny Mount
Viaduct
BROOK ST
VIGO BRIDGE RD
VIGO MEWS
WATERS EDGE
STANNARY BR RD
B3357
Taviton Mill House
B3357
FORTESCUE TERR
OLD LAUNCESTON RD
COURTLANDS RD
COURTENAY RD
Co Off
DOLVIN RD
St Rumon's CE Inf Sch
GREEN HILL
CAMPION RISE
FERN MDW
VIOLET LA
Lodge Wood
HOWARD CL 1
BRAY CL 2
PERYN RD 3
ST MARYHAYE
TREMAYNE RISE
PINDER CT
TH
Mkt
Mag Ct
6 NORTH ST
7 PANNIER MKT
8 BEDFORD SQ
9 CHURCH LA
St Peter's CE Jun Sch
ARMADOR GDNS
Taviton
Launceston New Road Bridge
NEW LAUNCESTON RD
HURDWICK RD
WATTS RD
ROCKY HILL
WEST ST
Mus
War Meml
DEER PARK CRES
SCHOOL CL
TAMAR AVE
MEAVY WAY
PLYM CRES
TAVY RD
COX TOR RD
Torland Wood
BOUGHTHAYES EST 4
MOUNT FORD 5
MEADOW BROOK 6
HIGHBANK CL 7
ENINGDALE RD 8
ABBOTSFIELD CL 9
CARMEL GDNS
Tavistock
SPRING HILL
CHAPEL ST
PLYMOUTH RD
Liby
Weir
GODOLPHIN HO
ABBEYMEAD MEWS
ST JOHNS AVE
DEER PARK CL
DEER PARK RD
WALKHAM CL
LYD GDNS
MILTON CRES
SHELLEY AVE
GREEN LA
TAVISTOCK
BROWNE MEMORIAL ALMSHOUSES
RALPH'S CT
FORD ST
ABBEY RISE
Co Off
DEER PARK LA
CHAUCER RD
ST DAVIDS RD
Tavistock Viaduct Walk Nature Reserve
BOLT HO
The Wharf Theatre & Gall
ST JOHNS
GROVE PK
LANG GR
PRIMROSE GDNS
6 BOUGHTHAYES
Armada Meml
ST JOHNS CT
PIXON LA
HEATHER CL
DOWN PARK DR
BLUEBELL WAY
CREASE LA
West Bridge
DRAKE VILLAS
DOWN RD
DEER LEAP
UPLANDS
MURALTO HO
CALLINGTON RD
FITZFORD COTTS
A386 PLYMOUTH RD
BATTERY LA
WESTMOOR PK
CH
West Devon Way
Dartmoor Way
GREENSWAY RD
DALESWOOD RD
A390
Tavistock Com Prim Sch
CRELAKE PK
WHITHAM PK
DAUCUS CL
ARMADA CT
WALREDDON CL
DRAKE GDNS
CRELAKE CL
MOHUN'S CL
CHOLLACOTT CL
MONKSMEAD
TRINITY WAY
WESTBRIDGE COTTS
RANSUM WAY
DEACONS GN
CANONS WAY
MITRE CL
CANONS GATE
Tavistock Coll
GRENVILLE DR
WARRAN LA
Whitchurch Down
Cemy
MOHUN'S PK
OAK TREE LA
WHITCHURCH RD
CHOLLACOTT LA
The Gate Cottage
BIRCHWOOD CL
TIDDY CL
Plymouth Road Ind Est
ALDER
ASPEN CL
PRIORY CL
Brook Mill
West Devon Bsns Pk
Superstore
WILLOW RD
MAPLE CL
Whitchurch
The Lodge
ELM CL
BEECH CL
OAK RD
ROWAN CL
PRIORY GDNS
MARSHALL RD
ST ANDREWS RD
Lower Brook
BROOK LA
Crowndale
CHESTNUT CL
OAKLANDS
MARSHALL CL
NEWTAKE RD
HAWTHORN RD
HAZEL RD
SCHOOL RD
CHURCHILL RD
TIDDY BROOK RD
Whitchurch Prim Sch
CHURCH LEA
FRIARS WLK
Middlemoor
MILL GR
BERRY GR
SYCAMORE AVE
WOODPECKER WY
Brook
Courtenay Cottage
KINGFISHER CL
GOLDFINCH GDNS
JAMES RD
CHURCH HILL
PO
BUZZARD RD
KESTREL PK
WEST VIEW
PH
Budghill
ANDERTON LA
SKYLARK RISE
ANDERTON CT
Anderton
Rixhill
Anderton Cottage
Works
A386
8
7
6
5
4
3
2
1
75
74
73
72
47
48
49
B4
1 Crelake Ind Est
2 Pixon Trad Ctr
3 Westbridge Ind Est
4 Parade Bsns Pk
5 CRAMBER CL
6 BEADLE CT
126
126
126

98 81

A B C D E F
8 7 6 5 4 3 2 1
97 96 95 94
88 89 90
A377
COURT BARTON LA
PUMP ST
TYTHEING CL
Newton St Cyres
LILLY LA
Lilly Farm
1 SHUTTERN CL
2 WOODLANDS
SAND DOWN LA
Newton St Cyres Prim Sch
Ford Farm
FORD LA
OLDAWAY LA
Ashfields
MARSH BARTON LA
MARSH MILL CT
CASTLANDS
Half Moon Village
NEW BARN CROSS
Hayne Farm
Bidwell La
BIDWELL CROSS
Langford
Jackmoor Brook
LANGFORD RD
Langford Park
GLEBE CL
Lake's Down
BRAMPFORD CROSS
Pulleton
Hill Copse
Scrawthorn Plantation
Well Down Copse
Horwell Down
Oakford Farm
Newbridge
Oakford Copse
UPTON PYNE HILL
NEWBRIDGE CROSS
NEWBRIDGE HILL
Bodley's Farm
Bodley's Plantation
EX5
Duryardwood Copse
River Creedy
Down Head Plantation
Cawley Plantation
Three Horse Shoes
Gossiford Copse
REDSIDE TERR
TURLAKE MEWS
TURLAKE HO
Halfbrake Copse
PH
DURYARDWOOD LA
Duryardwood Brook
BAILEY LA
Bailey
Nursery
COWLEY HILL
Barn Cottage
UPTON PYNE CROSS
Cold Stub Brake
Barn Copse
STAR BARTON LA
Hill Close Copse
Cowley
Star Barton Brook
Newton Wood
Star Barton
Lower Plantation
COWLEY PL
Exe Valley Way
Cowley Bridge
STOKE RD
A396
Higher Park Plantation
WREFORD'S DR
Moxey's Copse
WREFORD'S CL
COWLEY BRIDGE RD
WEST GARTH CT
WEST GARTH RD
A377
Rowhorne House Farm
Wood End
Exwick Wood
Exwick Barton
East Rowhorne
ST ANDREW'S RD
River Exe
Higher Plantation
ROWHORNE RD
Exwick Leat
EX4
Bolsters Wood
The Knap
Friars Ball Farm
Eastern Plateau
Hamlyns Farm

98 176

81
174

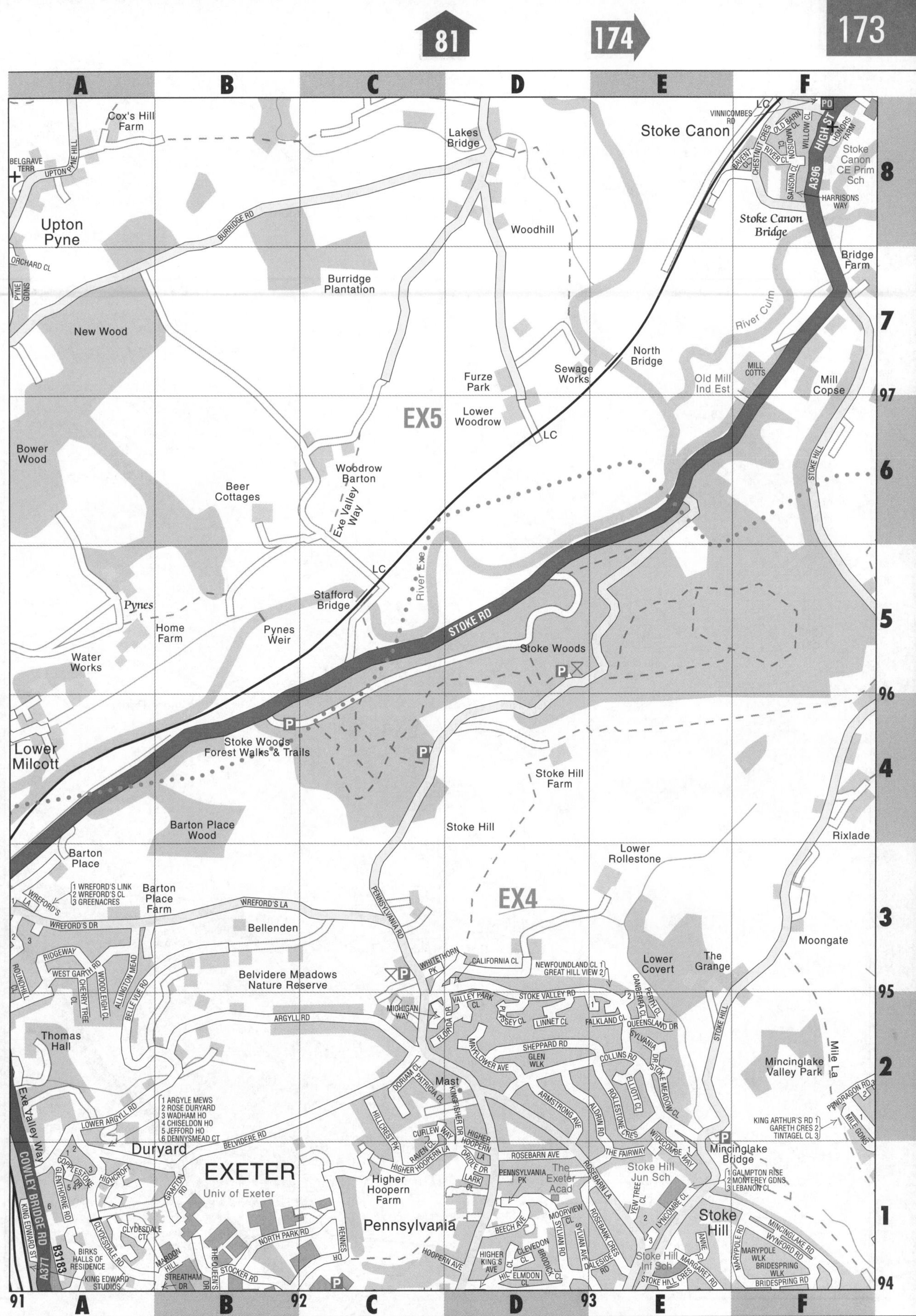

177
174

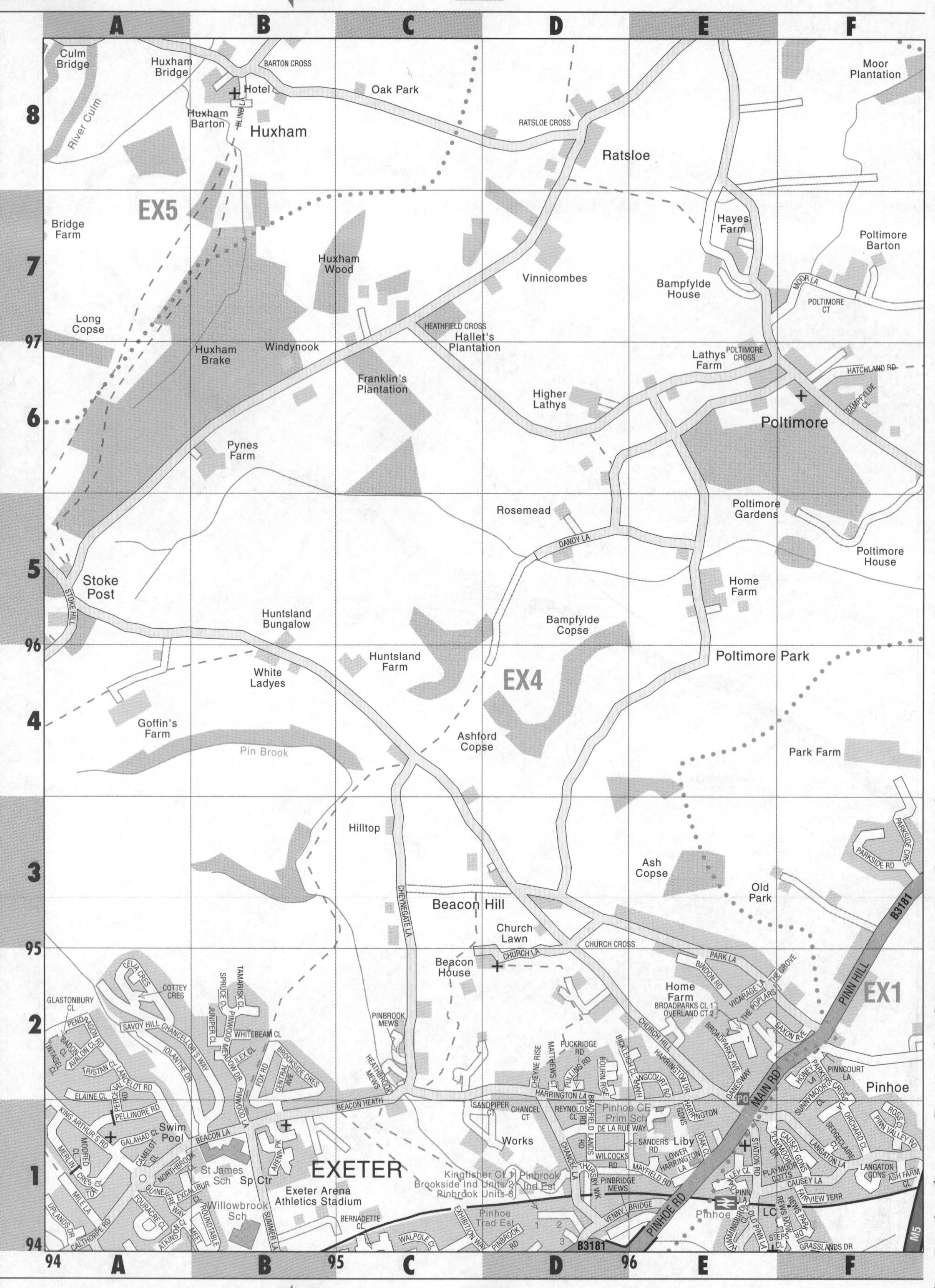
173
82
A B C D E F
8
7
97
6
5
96
4
3
95
2
1
94
Culm Bridge
Huxham Bridge
BARTON CROSS
Hotel
Oak Park
Huxham Barton
Huxham
RATSLOE CROSS
Ratsloe
Moor Plantation
River Culm
EX5
Bridge Farm
Hayes Farm
Poltimore Barton
Huxham Wood
Vinnicombes
Bampfylde House
MOOR LA
POLTIMORE CT
Long Copse
HEATHFIELD CROSS
Hallet's Plantation
Huxham Brake
Windynook
Lathys Farm
POLTIMORE CROSS
HATCHLAND RD
Franklin's Plantation
Higher Lathys
BAMPFYLDE CL
Poltimore
Pynes Farm
Rosemead
Poltimore Gardens
DANDY LA
Poltimore House
Stoke Post
STOKE HILL
Home Farm
Huntsland Bungalow
Bampfylde Copse
Huntsland Farm
Poltimore Park
White Ladyes
EX4
Goffin's Farm
Ashford Copse
Park Farm
Pin Brook
Hilltop
PARKSIDE CRES
PARKSIDE RD
Ash Copse
Old Park
CHEYNEGATE LA
Beacon Hill
B3181
Church Lawn
CHURCH CROSS
CHURCH LA
Beacon House
PARK LA
THE GROVE
BINDON RD
VICARAGE LA
EX1
PINN HILL
Home Farm
BROADPARKS CL 1
OVERLAND CT 2
THE POPLARS
SAXON AVE
GLASTONBURY CL
CELIA CRES
COTTEY CRES
TAMARISK CL
SPRUCE CL
JUNIPER CL
PINWOOD MEADOW DR
SAVOY HILL
CHANCELLOR'S WAY
WHITEBEAM CL
PENDRAGON RD
BADON CL
AVALON CL
TINTAGEL CL
IOLANTHE DR
ILEX CL
PINBROOK MEWS
PUCKRIDGE RD
CHEYNE RISE
MATTHEWS CT
PULLING RD
BOURN RISE
BICKLEIGH CL
KINGCOURT RD
CHURCH HILL
HARRINGTON DR
BROADPARKS AVE
DANESWAY
MAIN RD
PINNCOURT LA
HONEY PARK LA
SUNNYMOOR CROSS
ORCHARD CL
Pinhoe
TRISTAN CL
LANCELOT RD
FOX RD
PINWOOD LA
CENTRAL AVE
BROOKSIDE CRES
HEATHBROOK MEWS
HARRINGTON LA
ELAINE CL
PERCEVAL RD
PELLINORE RD
BEACON HEATH
SANDPIPER CT
CHANCEL CT
REYNOLDS CL
BRADFIELD RD
LANDS RD
Pinhoe CE Prim Sch
HARRINGTON GDNS
PO
KING ARTHUR'S RD
Swim Pool
BEACON LA
GALAHAD CL
CAMELOT CL
DE LA RUE WAY
SANDERS RD
Liby
WILCOCKS RD
LOWER HARRINGTON LA
OAK CL
STATION RD
SEDGECLAIRE CL
ROSS CL
PINN VALLEY RD
CAUSEY GDNS
PENMOOR DR
LANGATON LA
Works
MODRED CL
MERLIN CRES
NORTHBROOK CL
St James Sch
Sp Ctr
ARENA PK
EXETER
CHANCEL LA
THURSBY WK
MAYFIELD RD
Kingfisher Ct 1
Brookside Ind Units 2
Pinbrook Units 3
Pinbrook Ind Est
PLAYMOOR COTTS
LANGATON GDNS
ASH FARM CL
ISOLDE CL
MILE LA
EXCALIBUR CL
GUINEVERE WAY
FOURACRE CL
Willowbrook Sch
Exeter Arena Athletics Stadium
PINBRIDGE MEWS
PINHOE RD
VENNY BRIDGE
Pinhoe
PINN LA
CAUSEY LA
FAIRVIEW TERR
UPLANDS DR
CALTHORPE RD
ATKINSON CL
MEET
ROUNDTABLE
SUMMER LA
BERNADETTE CL
WALPOLE CL
EXHIBITION WAY
Pinhoe Trad Est
PINBROOK RD
LC
HUMMINGBIRD CL
OLD PINN LA
REWS MDW
REWS PARK DR
STEPS CL
GRASSLANDS DR
M5
94 A B 95 C D 96 E F
173
178

82
99

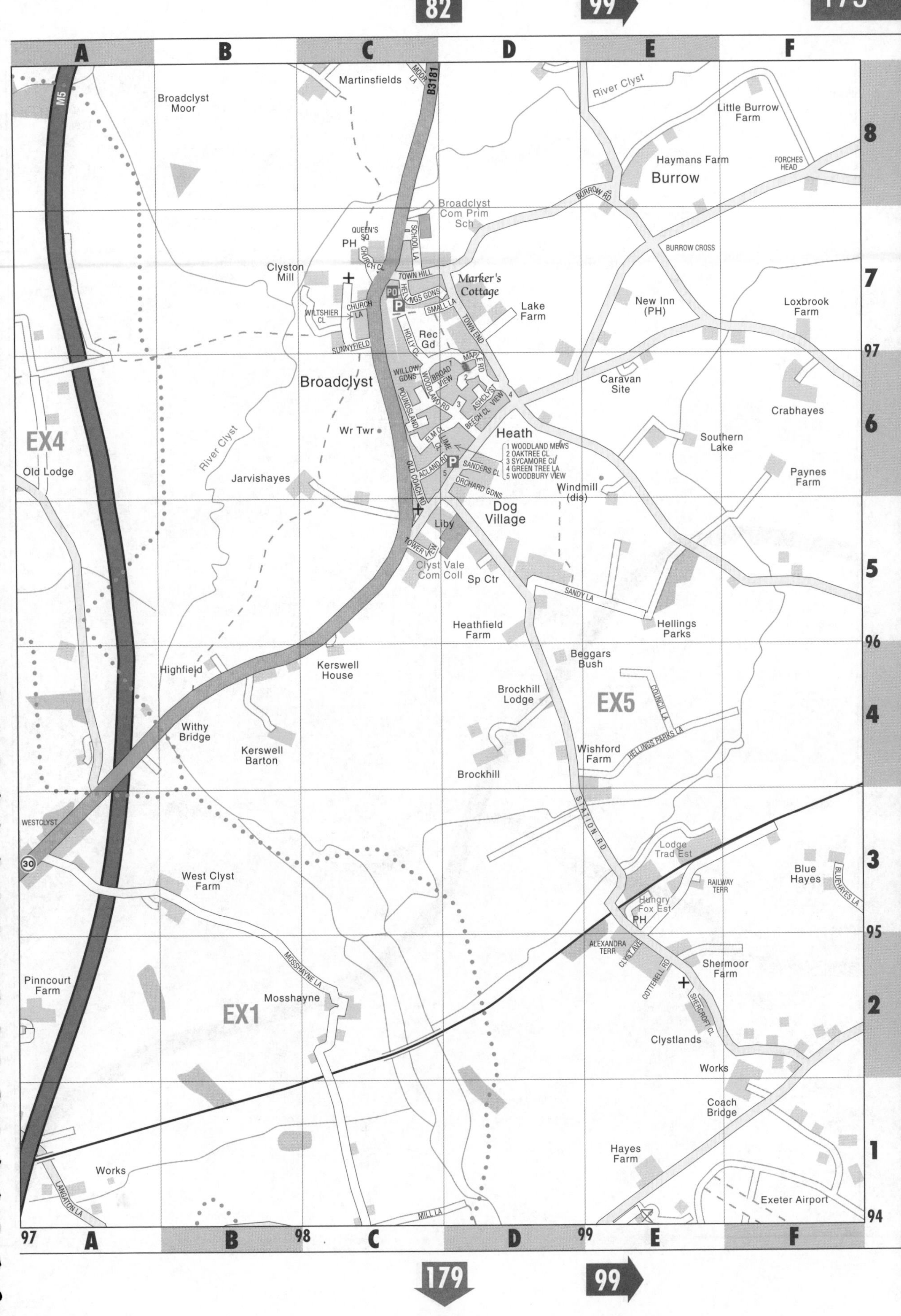
A
B
C
D
E
F
8
7
97
6
5
96
4
3
95
2
1
94
97
98
99
M5
B3181
Broadclyst Moor
Martinsfields
MOOR LA
River Clyst
Little Burrow Farm
Haymans Farm
FORCHES HEAD
Burrow
BURROW RD
Broadclyst Com Prim Sch
QUEEN'S SQ
SCHOOL LA
PH
CHURCH CL
TOWN HILL
BURROW CROSS
Clyston Mill
Marker's Cottage
HELLINGS GDNS
SMALL LA
WILTSHIER CL
CHURCH LA
New Inn (PH)
Loxbrook Farm
Lake Farm
TOWN END
HOLLY CL
Rec Gd
SUNNYFIELD
MAPLE RD
WILLOW GDNS
BROAD VIEW
Broadclyst
WOODLAND RD
POUNDSLAND
ASHCLYST VIEW
BEECH CL
Caravan Site
Crabhayes
EX4
Wr Twr
ELM CL
LIME
Heath
1 WOODLAND MEWS
2 OAKTREE CL
3 SYCAMORE CL
4 GREEN TREE LA
5 WOODBURY VIEW
Southern Lake
River Clyst
Old Lodge
Jarvishayes
ACLAND RD
SANDERS CL
OLD COACH RD
ORCHARD GDNS
Windmill (dis)
Paynes Farm
Dog Village
Liby
TOWER VIEW
Clyst Vale Com Coll
Sp Ctr
SANDY LA
Heathfield Farm
Hellings Parks
Highfield
Kerswell House
Beggars Bush
Brockhill Lodge
COUNCIL LA
EX5
Withy Bridge
Kerswell Barton
Wishford Farm
HELLINGS PARKS LA
Brockhill
STATION RD
WESTCLYST
30
Lodge Trad Est
West Clyst Farm
RAILWAY TERR
Blue Hayes
BLUEHAYES LA
Hungry Fox Est
PH
ALEXANDRA TERR
CLYST AVE
COTTERELL RD
Shermoor Farm
MOSSHAYNE LA
Pinncourt Farm
Mosshayne
EX1
SHERCROFT CL
Clystlands
Works
Coach Bridge
Hayes Farm
Works
LANGATON LA
MILL LA
Exeter Airport

179
99

98
172

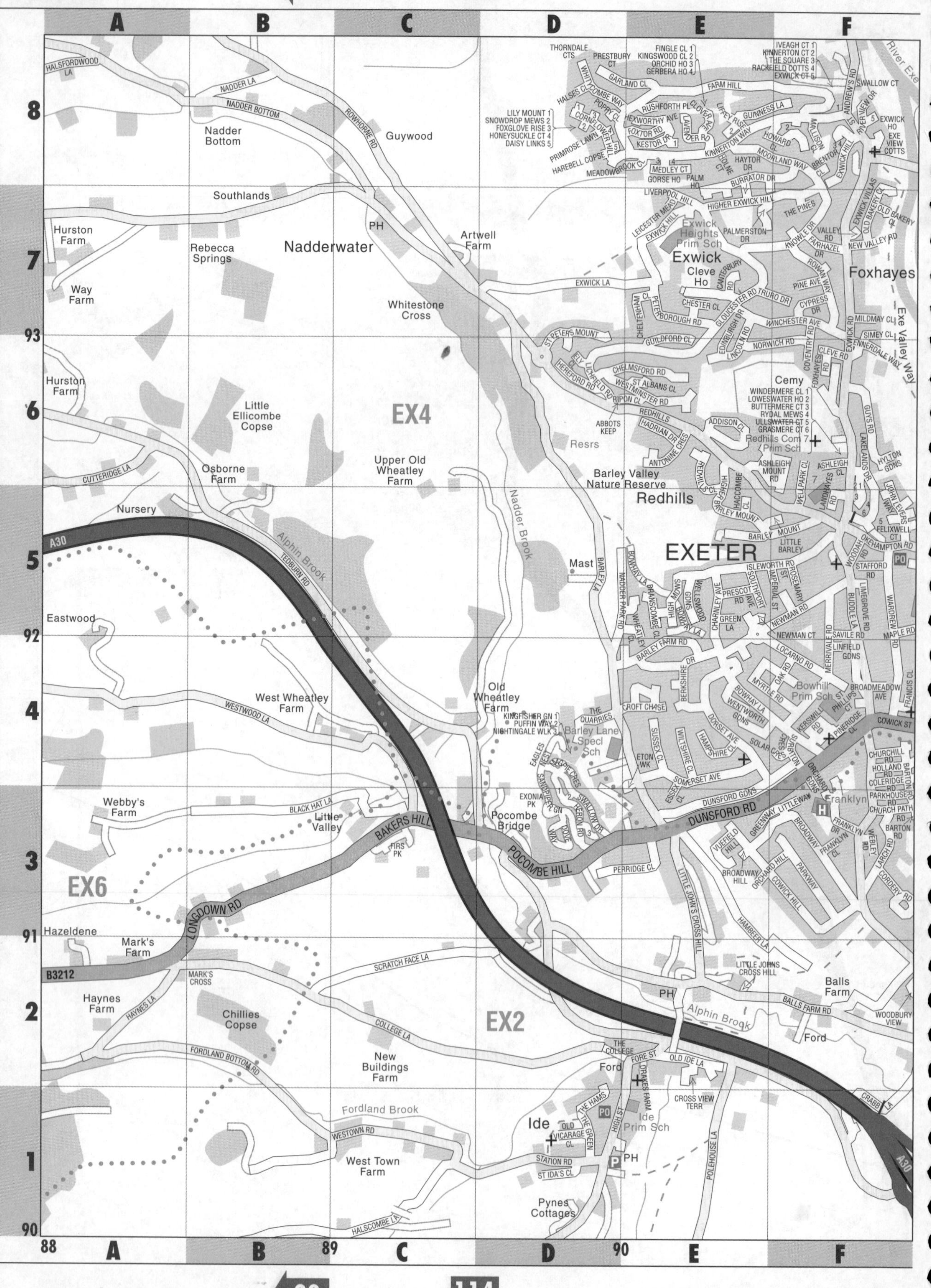
A
B
C
D
E
F
8
7
93
6
5
92
4
3
91
2
1
90
88
89
90
HALSFORDWOOD LA
NADDER LA
NADDER BOTTOM
Nadder Bottom
ROWHORNE RD
Guywood
Southlands
Hurston Farm
Rebecca Springs
PH
Nadderwater
Artwell Farm
Way Farm
Whitestone Cross
EXWICK LA
Hurston Farm
Little Ellicombe Copse
EX4
Upper Old Wheatley Farm
CUTTERIDGE LA
Osborne Farm
Nursery
A30
Alphin Brook
TEDBURN RD
Nadder Brook
Mast
BARLEY LA
Eastwood
West Wheatley Farm
WESTWOOD LA
Old Wheatley Farm
KINGFISHER GN 1
PUFFIN WAY 2
NIGHTINGALE WLK 3
THE QUARRIES
Barley Lane Specl Sch
Webby's Farm
BLACK HAT LA
Little Valley
BAKERS HILL
FIRS PK
Pocombe Bridge
EXONIA PK
POCOMBE HILL
PERRIDGE CL
EX6
LONGDOWN RD
Hazeldene
Mark's Farm
B3212
MARK'S CROSS
SCRATCH FACE LA
Haynes Farm
HAYNES LA
Chillies Copse
COLLEGE LA
EX2
FORDLAND BOTTOM RD
New Buildings Farm
Fordland Brook
WESTOWN RD
West Town Farm
HALSCOMBE LA
THE COLLEGE
Ford
FORE ST
OLD IDE LA
DRAKES FARM
CROSS VIEW TERR
THE HAMS
THE GREEN
PO
HIGH ST
Ide
Ide Prim Sch
OLD VICARAGE CL
STATION RD
ST IDA'S CL
PH
P
POLEHOUSE LA
Pynes Cottages
THORNDALE CTS
PRESTBURY CT
FINGLE CL 1
KINGSWOOD CL 2
ORCHID HO 3
GERBERA HO 4
IVEAGH CT 1
KINNERTON CT 2
THE SQUARE 3
RACKFIELD COTTS 4
EXWICK CT 5
River Exe
GARLAND CL
FARM HILL
SWALLOW CT
HALSES CL
WHITYCOMBE WAY
POPPY CL
RUSHFORTH PL
CLOVER AVE
LIFFEY RISE
GUINNESS LA
ANDREW'S RD
RIVER VIEW DR
LILY MOUNT 1
SNOWDROP MEWS 2
FOXGLOVE RISE 3
HONEYSUCKLE CT 4
DAISY LINKS 5
HEXWORTHY AVE
FOXTOR RD
KESTOR DR
LAVENDER RD
KINNERTON WAY
HOWARD CL
MALLISON CL
EXWICK HO
EXE VIEW COTTS
PRIMROSE LAWN
HAREBELL COPSE
CORNFLOWER HILL
MEADOWBROOK CL
MEDLEY CT
HAYTOR DR
MOORLAND WAY
BRENTOR
EXWICK HILL
GORSE HO
PALM HO
BURRATOR DR
LIVERPOOL HILL
HIGHER EXWICK HILL
THE PINES
EXWICK VILLAS
OLD BAKERY CL
LEICESTER MEAD
EXWICK HILL
Exwick Heights Prim Sch
PALMERSTON DR
KNOWLE DR
VALLEY RD
FAIRHAZEL DR
NEW VALLEY RD
Exwick
Cleve Ho
CANTERBURY RD
ROWAN WAY
Foxhayes
PINE AVE
CHESTER CL
TRURO DR
CYPRESS DR
CHELTENHAM CL
PETERBOROUGH RD
GLOUCESTER RD
MILDMAY CL
Exe Valley Way
ST PETERS MOUNT
WINCHESTER AVE
GUILDFORD CL
EDINBURGH DR
LINCOLN RD
NORWICH RD
SIMEY CL
ENNERDALE WAY
COVENTRY RD
CLEVE RD
EXWICK RD
ELY CL
HEREFORD RD
LICHFIELD RD
CHELMSFORD RD
ST ALBANS CL
WESTMINSTER RD
RIPON CL
Cemy
FOXHAYES RD
WINDERMERE CL 1
LOWESWATER HO 2
BUTTERMERE CT 3
RYDAL MEWS 4
ULLSWATER CT 5
GRASMERE CT 6
REDHILLS
ABBOTS KEEP
HADRIAN DR
ADDISON CL
Resrs
Redhills Com Prim Sch
ANTONINE CRES
GUYS RD
LAKELANDS DR
HYLTON GDNS
Barley Valley Nature Reserve
ASHLEIGH MOUNT RD
ASHLEIGH CL
REDHILLS CL
HIGHER BARLEY MOUNT
HACCOMBE CL
WELLPARK CL
LANDHAYES RD
JOHN LEVERS WAY
Redhills
BARLEY MOUNT
FELIXWELL CT
LITTLE BARLEY
OKEHAMPTON RD
EXETER
ISLEWORTH RD
WOODAH RD
STAFFORD RD
PO
BOWHAY LA
NADDER PARK RD
BRANSCOMBE CL
HIGH MDW
SMYTHEN ST
WELLSWOOD GDNS
CHARNLEY AVE
PRESCOT RD
SOUTHPORT AVE
IMPERIAL ST
ROSEMARY ST
BUDDLE LA
LIMEGROVE RD
WARDREW RD
WHEATLEY CL
BOWHAY LA
GREEN LA
NEWMAN RD
NEWMAN CT
MERRIVALE RD
SAVILE RD
MAPLE RD
LINFIELD GDNS
BARLEY FARM RD
LOCARNO RD
BERKSHIRE DR
OAK RD
MYRTLE RD
Bowhill Prim Sch
BROADMEADOW AVE
FRANCIS CL
CROFT CHASE
WENTWORTH GDNS
ST PHILLIPS CT
COWICK ST
KERSWILL RD
PINERIDGE CL
EAGLES NEST
SANDPIPER GN
DORSET AVE
SUSSEX CL
WILTSHIRE CL
HAMPSHIRE CL
SOLAR CRES
SURBITON CRES
CHURCHILL RD
HOLLAND RD
BARTON RD
COLERIDGE RD
ETON WK
SOMERSET AVE
ORCHARD GDNS
PARKHOUSE RD
ESSEX CL
DUNSFORD GDNS
GREENWAY
LITTLEWAY
Franklyn
CHURCH PATH RD
DUNSFORD RD
BROADWAY
FRANKLYN DR
FRANKLYN CL
BARTON RD
H
VUEFIELD HILL
WEBLEY RD
LARCH RD
ORCHARD HILL
CORDERY RD
BROADWAY HILL
PARKWAY
COWICK HILL
LITTLE JOHN'S CROSS HILL
HAMBEER LA
LITTLE JOHNS CROSS HILL
Balls Farm
PH
BALLS FARM RD
Alphin Brook
WOODBURY VIEW
Ford
CRABB LA
A30

98
114

A5
1 EMMANUEL CL
2 EMMANUEL RD
3 LANDSCORE RD
4 CAMBRIDGE ST
5 CORNWALL ST
6 CLARENCE RD
7 CLEVELAND ST
8 OKEHAMPTON PL
9 PRINCESS ALEXANDRA CT
10 SWAN MAISONETTES
11 Montgomery Comb Sch

173

D8
1 VICTORIA RD
2 WILLOW WLK
3 NEW BLDGS
4 BRIDGE COTTS
5 ROSEWOOD TERR
6 ALMSHOUSES

178

E7
1 WATERMORE CT
2 PROSPECT GDNS
3 SYDENHAM HO
4 NICHOLS WY

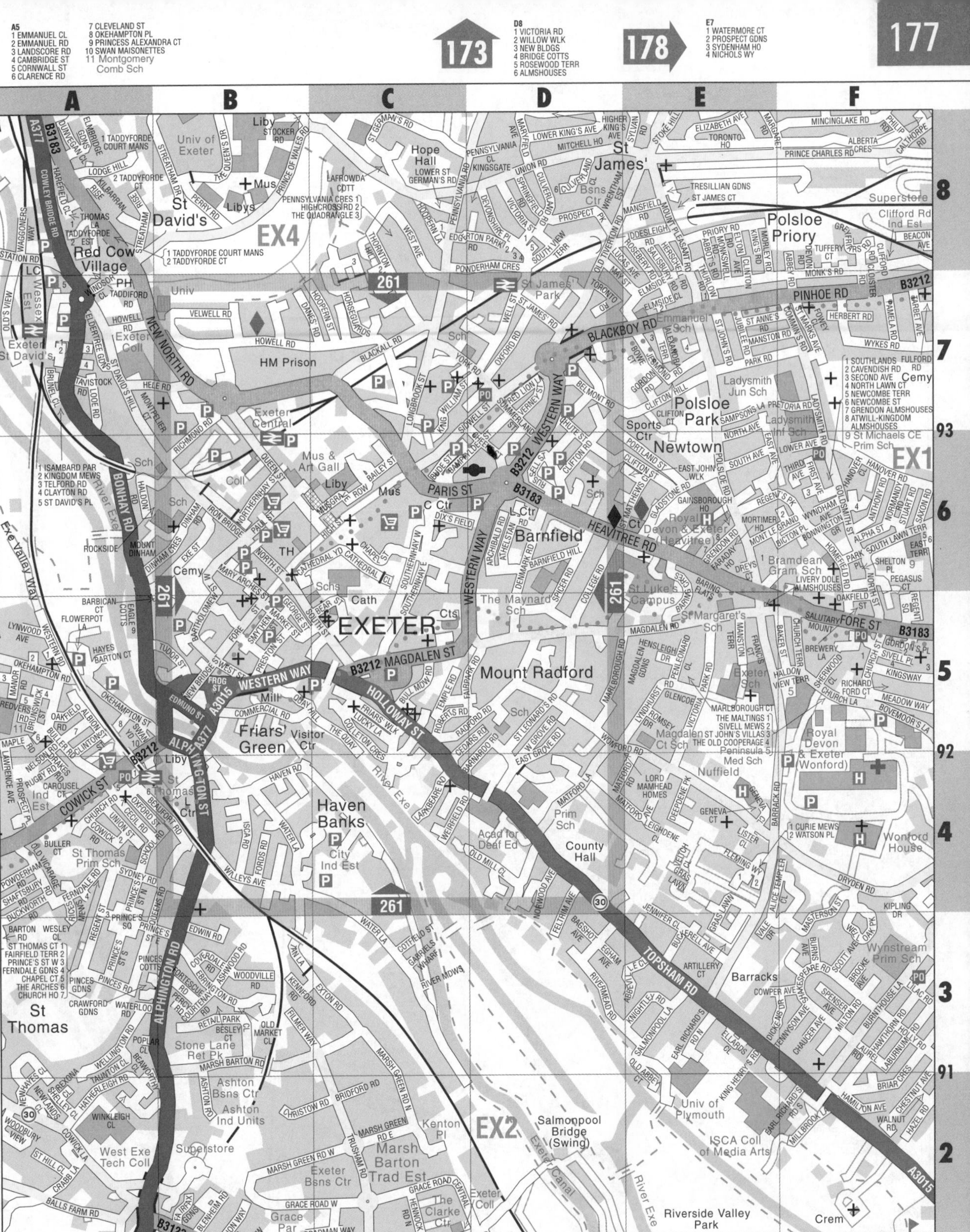

181

178

For full street detail of the highlighted area see page 261.

177
174

C8
1 MARK TWAIN HO
2 FLAYES ALMSHOUSES
3 PEEL ROW
4 ROYSTON CT
5 THE SEASONS
6 WILLOWBROOK AVE
7 MARGARET CT

D5
1 NELSON WAY
2 WELLINGTON CL
3 THE SQUARE
4 ALEXANDER WLK
5 DRAKE AVE
6 MONTGOMERY RD
7 CROMWELL TERR
8 3RD AVE
9 MARLBOROUGH DR
10 BADGER CL
11 RINGSWELL PK

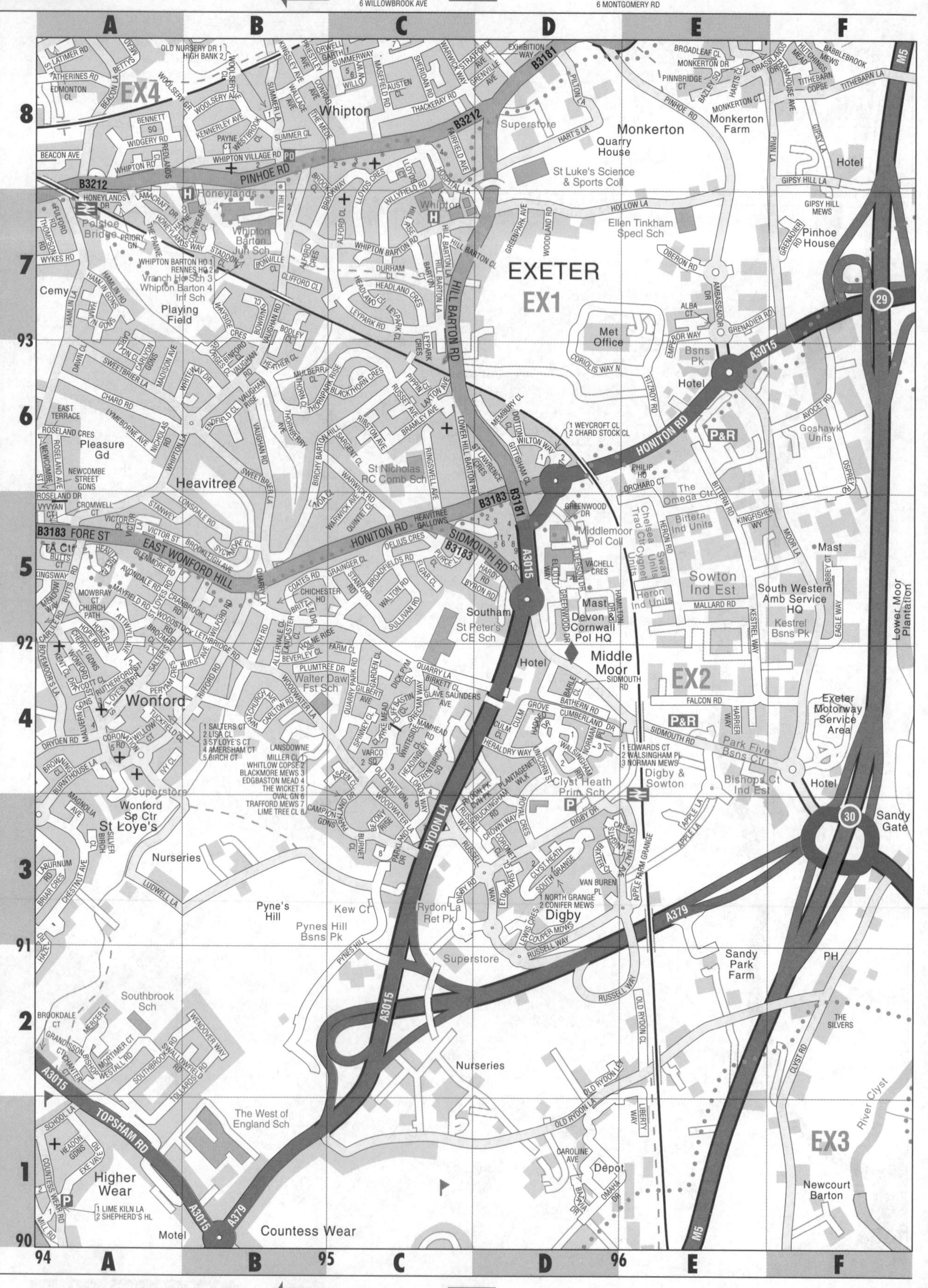

177
182

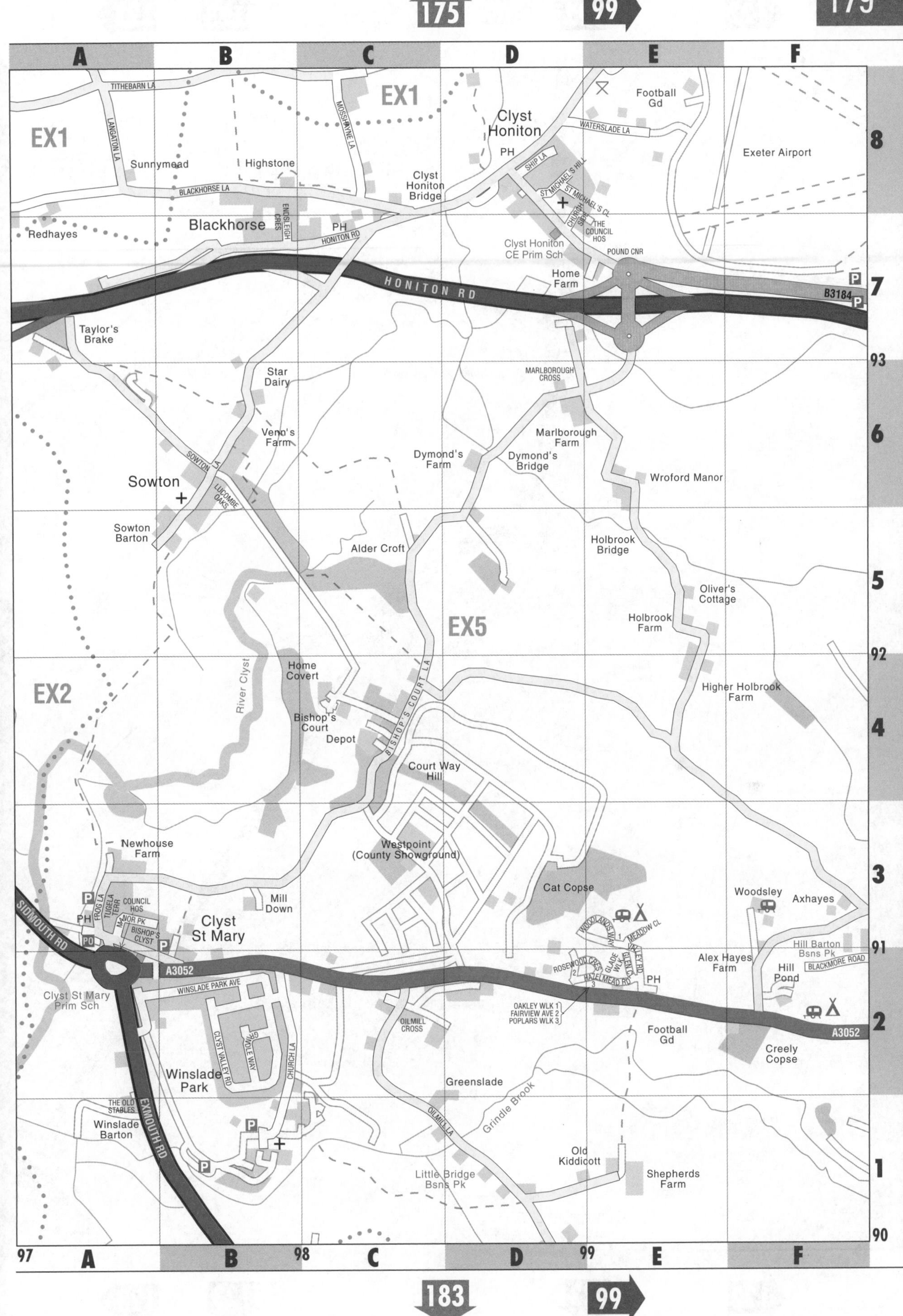
175
99
A
B
C
D
E
F
EX1
Tithebarn La
Langaton La
Sunnymead
Highstone
Mosshayne La
Clyst Honiton
PH
Football Gd
Waterslade La
Exeter Airport
Blackhorse La
Clyst Honiton Bridge
Ship La
St Michael's Hill
St Michael's Cl
Church Side
The Council Hos
Redhayes
Blackhorse
Endsleigh Cres
Honiton Rd
Clyst Honiton CE Prim Sch
Pound Cnr
Home Farm
B3184
Taylor's Brake
Marlborough Cross
Star Dairy
Venn's Farm
Marlborough Farm
Dymond's Farm
Dymond's Bridge
Wroford Manor
Sowton
Sowton La
Lucombe Oaks
Sowton Barton
Alder Croft
Holbrook Bridge
Oliver's Cottage
EX5
Holbrook Farm
River Clyst
Home Covert
EX2
Bishop's Court La
Higher Holbrook Farm
Bishop's Court
Depot
Court Way Hill
Newhouse Farm
Westpoint (County Showground)
Cat Copse
Woodsley
Axhayes
Frog La
Tugela Terr
Council Hos
Manor Pk
Bishop's Clyst
Mill Down
Clyst St Mary
Woodlands Way
Meadow Cl
Hill Barton Bsns Pk
Sidmouth Rd
PH
PO
A3052
Rosewood Cres
Glade Wlk
Glen Cl
Valley Rd
Hazelmead Rd
PH
Alex Hayes Farm
Blackmore Road
Hill Pond
Clyst St Mary Prim Sch
Winslade Park Ave
Oakley Wlk 1
Fairview Ave 2
Poplars Wlk 3
Oilmill Cross
Clyst Valley Rd
Dingle Way
Church La
Football Gd
Creely Copse
Winslade Park
Greenslade
Grindle Brook
The Old Stables
Exmouth Rd
Winslade Barton
Oilmill La
Old Kiddicott
Shepherds Farm
Little Bridge Bsns Pk
8
7
93
6
5
92
4
3
91
2
1
90
97
98
99
183

122 122 123 123

C8
1 SOUTHBROOK LA
2 SOUTHBROOK CL
3 ATWAY CL
4 BULLANDS CL
5 MORETONHAMPSTEAD RD

D8
1 ORCHARD WAY
2 VICTORIA TERR
3 ORCHARD TERR
4 TOWN HALL PL
5 SOUTHDOWN HO
6 TORVIEW FLATS
7 THE ALMSHOUSES

122 122 123 123

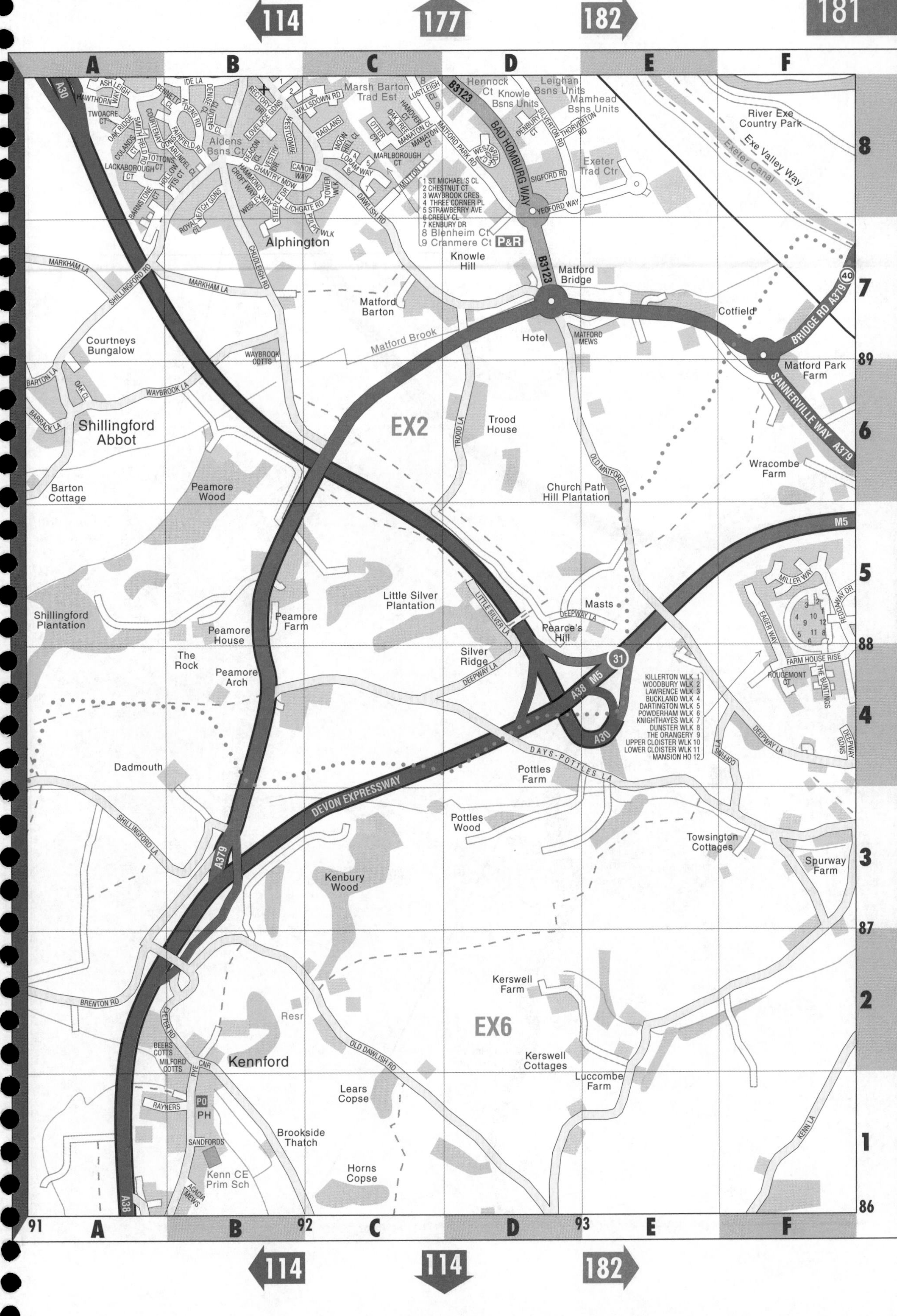
114
177
182
A
B
C
D
E
F
8
7
89
6
5
88
4
3
87
2
1
86
91
92
93
Marsh Barton Trad Est
Hennock Ct
Knowle Bsns Units
Leighan Bsns Units
Mamhead Bsns Units
River Exe Country Park
Exe Valley Way
Exeter Canal
Aldens Bsns Ct
Exeter Trad Ctr
BAD HOMBURG WAY
B3123
1 ST MICHAEL'S CL
2 CHESTNUT CT
3 WAYBROOK CRES
4 THREE CORNER PL
5 STRAWBERRY AVE
6 CREELY CL
7 KENBURY DR
8 Blenheim Ct
9 Cranmere Ct
P&R
Alphington
Knowle Hill
Matford Bridge
Matford Barton
Matford Brook
Courtneys Bungalow
Hotel
Cotfield
BRIDGE RD A379
Matford Park Farm
SANNERVILLE WAY A379
Shillingford Abbot
EX2
Trood House
Wracombe Farm
Barton Cottage
Peamore Wood
Church Path Hill Plantation
M5
Little Silver Plantation
Shillingford Plantation
Peamore Farm
Peamore House
Masts
Pearce's Hill
The Rock
Silver Ridge
Peamore Arch
31
KILLERTON WLK 1
WOODBURY WLK 2
LAWRENCE WLK 3
BUCKLAND WLK 4
DARTINGTON WLK 5
POWDERHAM WLK 6
KNIGHTHAYES WLK 7
DUNSTER WLK 8
THE ORANGERY 9
UPPER CLOISTER WLK 10
LOWER CLOISTER WLK 11
MANSION HO 12
Dadmouth
Pottles Farm
DEVON EXPRESSWAY
Pottles Wood
Towsington Cottages
Spurway Farm
Kenbury Wood
Kerswell Farm
EX6
Resr
Kennford
Kerswell Cottages
Luccombe Farm
Lears Copse
Brookside Thatch
Horns Copse
Kenn CE Prim Sch
PO
PH
A38
A30
A379

181 178

181 194

179
184

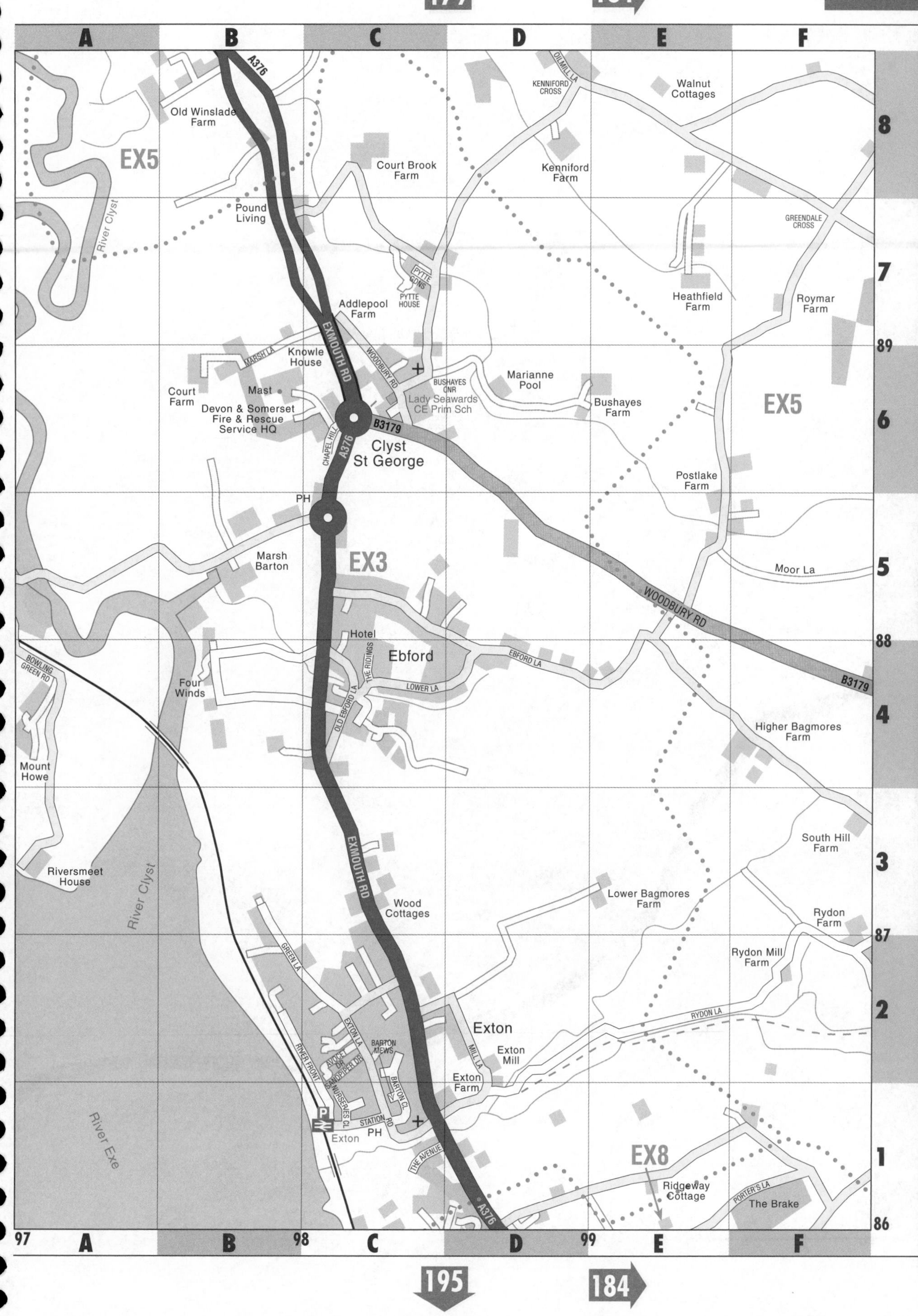

195
184

183
99

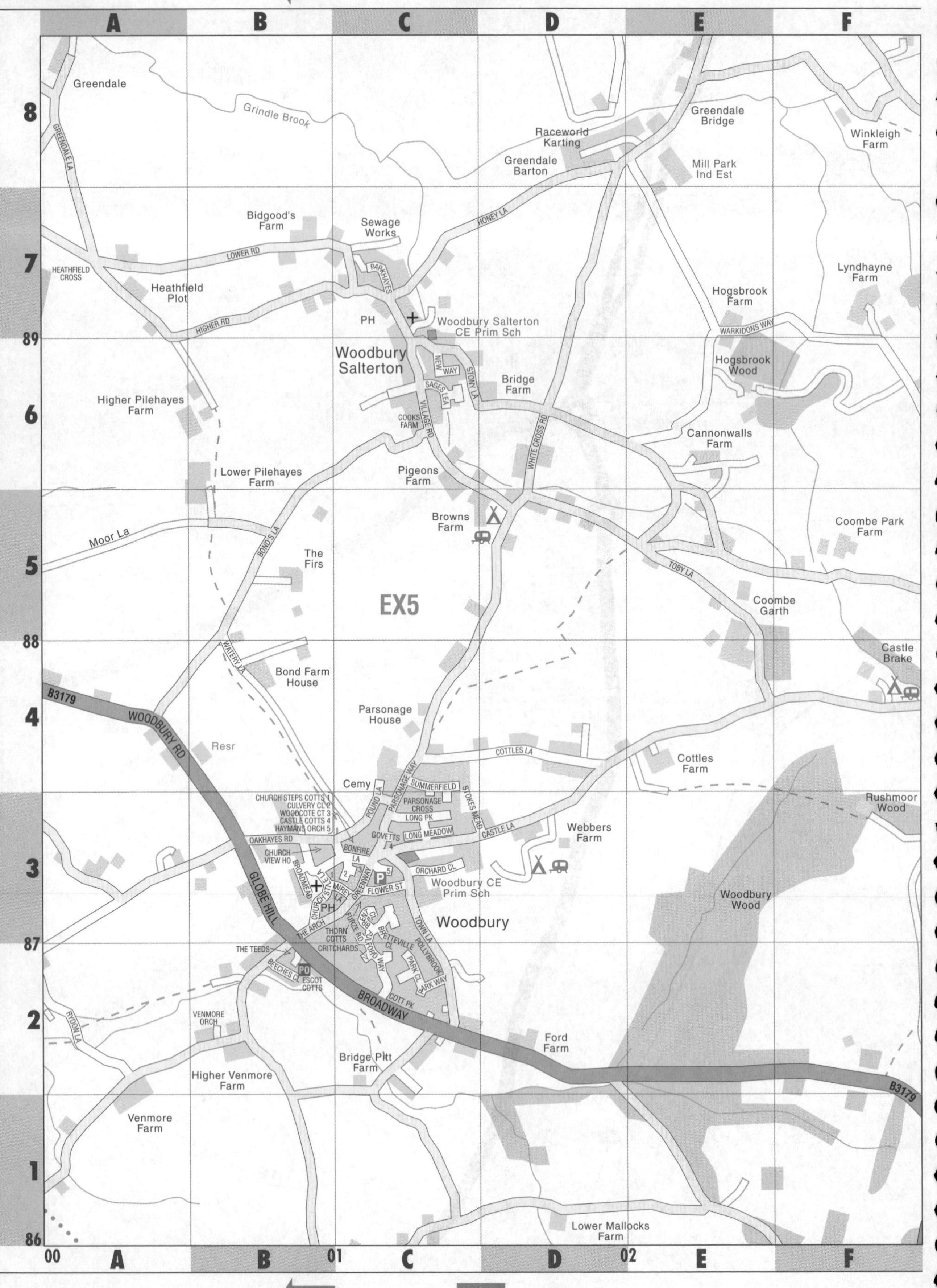

183
196

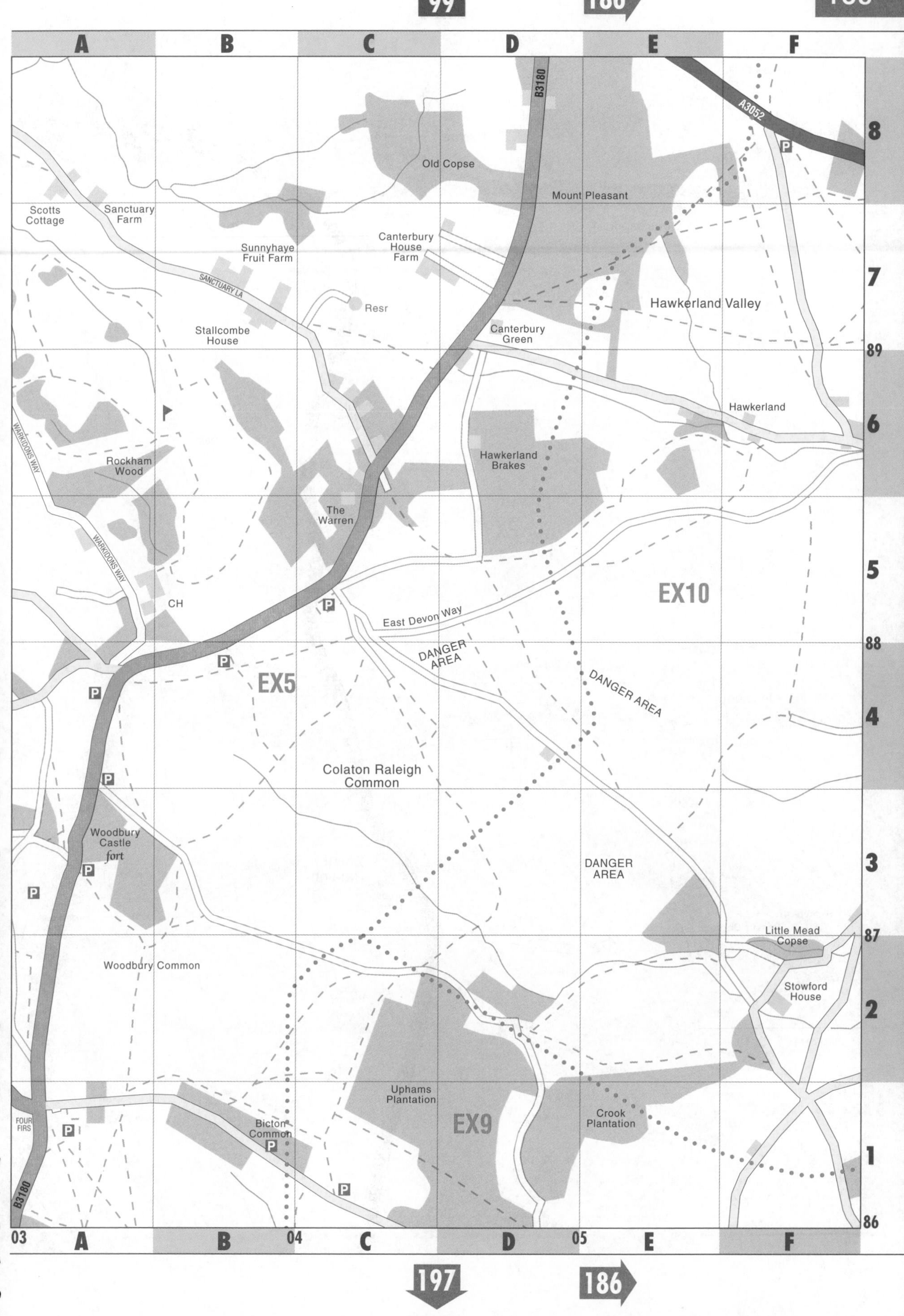

99
186
A
B
C
D
E
F
8
7
89
6
5
88
4
3
87
2
1
86
03
04
05
B3180
A3052
Old Copse
Mount Pleasant
Scotts Cottage
Sanctuary Farm
Sunnyhaye Fruit Farm
Canterbury House Farm
SANCTUARY LA
Resr
Hawkerland Valley
Stallcombe House
Canterbury Green
Hawkerland
Hawkerland Brakes
Rockham Wood
WARKIDONS WAY
The Warren
CH
East Devon Way
EX10
DANGER AREA
EX5
Colaton Raleigh Common
Woodbury Castle fort
Little Mead Copse
Stowford House
Woodbury Common
Uphams Plantation
EX9
Crook Plantation
Bicton Common
FOUR FIRS
197

185
100

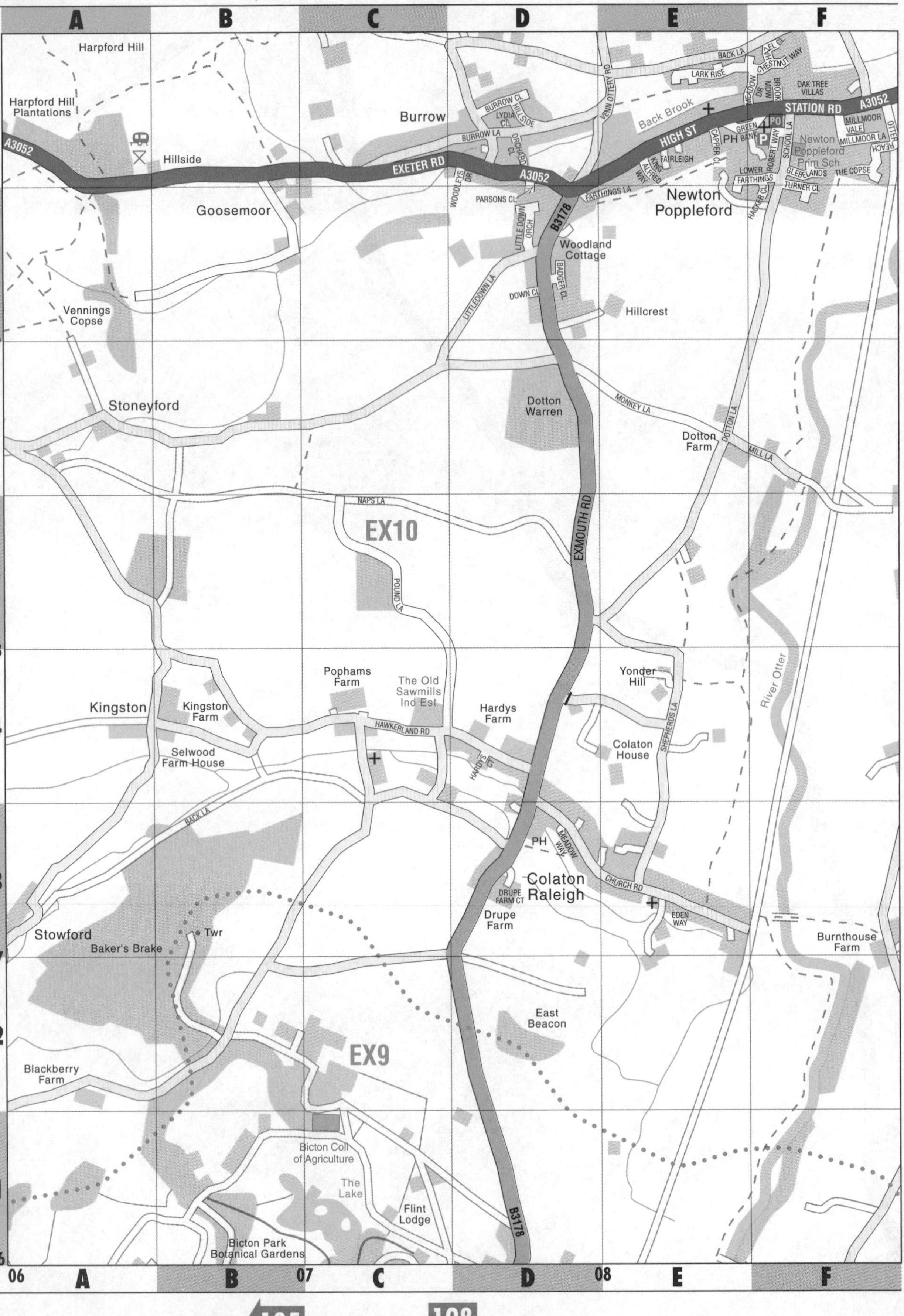
A
B
C
D
E
F
8
7
89
6
5
88
4
3
87
2
1
86
06
07
08
Harpford Hill
Harpford Hill
Plantations
A3052
Hillside
Goosemoor
Vennings
Copse
Stoneyford
Burrow
BURROW CL
LYDIA CL
HILLSIDE
BURROW LA
ORCHARD CL
EXETER RD
A3052
WOODLEYS DR
PARSONS CL
LITTLE DOWN ORCH
LITTLEDOWN LA
DOWN CL
BADGER CL
B3178
Woodland
Cottage
Hillcrest
VENN OTTERY RD
Back Brook
HIGH ST
KING ALFRED WAY
FAIRLEIGH
FARTHINGS LA
Newton
Poppleford
BACK LA
LARK RISE
HAZEL CL
CHESTNUT WAY
MEADOW DR
MDW BROOK
OAK TREE
VILLAS
STATION RD
A3052
MILLMOOR
VALE
MILLMOOR LA
OTTER REACH
PO
P
PH
GREEN BANK
CAPPER CL
ROBERT WAY
SCHOOL LA
Newton
Poppleford
Prim Sch
LOWER
FARTHINGS
GLEBELANDS
THE COPSE
TURNER CL
HACKER CL
Dotton
Warren
MONKEY LA
Dotton
Farm
DOTTON LA
MILL LA
NAPS LA
EX10
POUND LA
EXMOUTH RD
River Otter
Pophams
Farm
The Old
Sawmills
Ind Est
Hardys
Farm
Yonder
Hill
Kingston
Kingston
Farm
Selwood
Farm House
HAWKERLAND RD
HARDYS CT
Colaton
House
SHEPHERDS LA
BACK LA
PH
MEADOW WAY
Colaton
Raleigh
DRUPE
FARM CT
Drupe
Farm
CHURCH RD
EDEN
WAY
Stowford
Twr
Baker's Brake
Burnthouse
Farm
East
Beacon
EX9
Blackberry
Farm
Bicton Coll
of Agriculture
The
Lake
Flint
Lodge
B3178
Bicton Park
Botanical Gardens

100
188

A B C D E F

Bowd
A3052
B3176
Bridge End
FOUR ELMS HILL
LOWER WAY
HIGHER WAY
River Otter
STOWFORD GATE
Wool Brook
Stowford
HAWTHORN DR 1
BLACKTHORN CL 2
LE LOCLE CL 3
SEDEMUDA RD 4
ANDREW CL 5
HIGH ST
A3052
8
GREENWAY LA
FOUR ELMS
NORTHMOSTOWN CT
Northmostown
BACK LA
LADYMEAD
STOWFORD RISE
WHITETHORN CL
FAIRMEAD
MOOR VIEW
BARN HAYES
WOOLBROOK RD
WHITTON CT
WOOLBROOK MEAD
Bulverton Plantation
Northmostown Goyle
HIGHER GREENWAY LA
SPITUP LA
HIGHER WOOLBROOK PK
RIDGEWAY MEAD
BENNETTS HILL
7
Higher Woolbrook
Longmeadow
KITTS CROSS
ICE HOUSE LA
WOOLBROOK PK
KITTS LA
SALTER'S CROSS
Bulverton Hill
89
DARK LA
BULVERTON PK
B3176
Bulverton
6
Calm La
Stoney Hill
Manor Park
Pitson Farm
Bulverton Bottom
PITSON LA
Ashtree Farm
Otterton Hill Plantation
Moor Park La
BICKWELL LA
Wheat Hill
Bickwell Farm
Houghton Farm
Muttersmoor Plantation
MUTTERSMOOR RD
BICKWELL HOUSE LA
BALFOUR MANOR CT
5
St John's Sch
BROADWAY
STINTWAY LA
HOUGHTON LA
EX10
88
KNOWLE GDNS
CONVENT FIELDS
Mutter's Moor
CONVENT RD
KNOWLE DR
BICKWELL VALLEY
Greystone Hill Plantation
4
GORSE WAY
CHEESE LA
Passaford Farm
SEATON BURN
BOUGHMORE RD
Cotmaton
BOUGHMORE LA
WATERPARK CT 1
COLATON TERR 2
GLEN RD 3
PAUNTLEY GDN 4
CUNNINGHAM'S LA 5
THE MARINO
Pinn Beacon Plantation
COTLANDS
SIDMOUTH
ST HELEN'S CT
WITHEBY
P
3
CH
MOOR CT
MOORCOURT CL
COTMATON RD
ORCHARD CL
THE OLD VICARAGE
PEAK HILL RD
Peak Hill
Peak House
87
WILLOUGHBY HO
Peak Hill Llamas
Pinn Barton Farm
Horstone
KINGSLADE LA
FOX'S CNR
2
Weeks Farm
Windgate
South West Coast Path
PINN LA
PINN LANE CNR
Lower Pinn Farm
SOUTHBROOK LA
Otterton Brook
Tortiseshell Rocks
1
Wheel Rock
EX9
BAR'S LA
High Peak
86
09 A B 10 C D 11 E F

199
188

A7
1 St Nicholas
CE Jun Sch

187
101

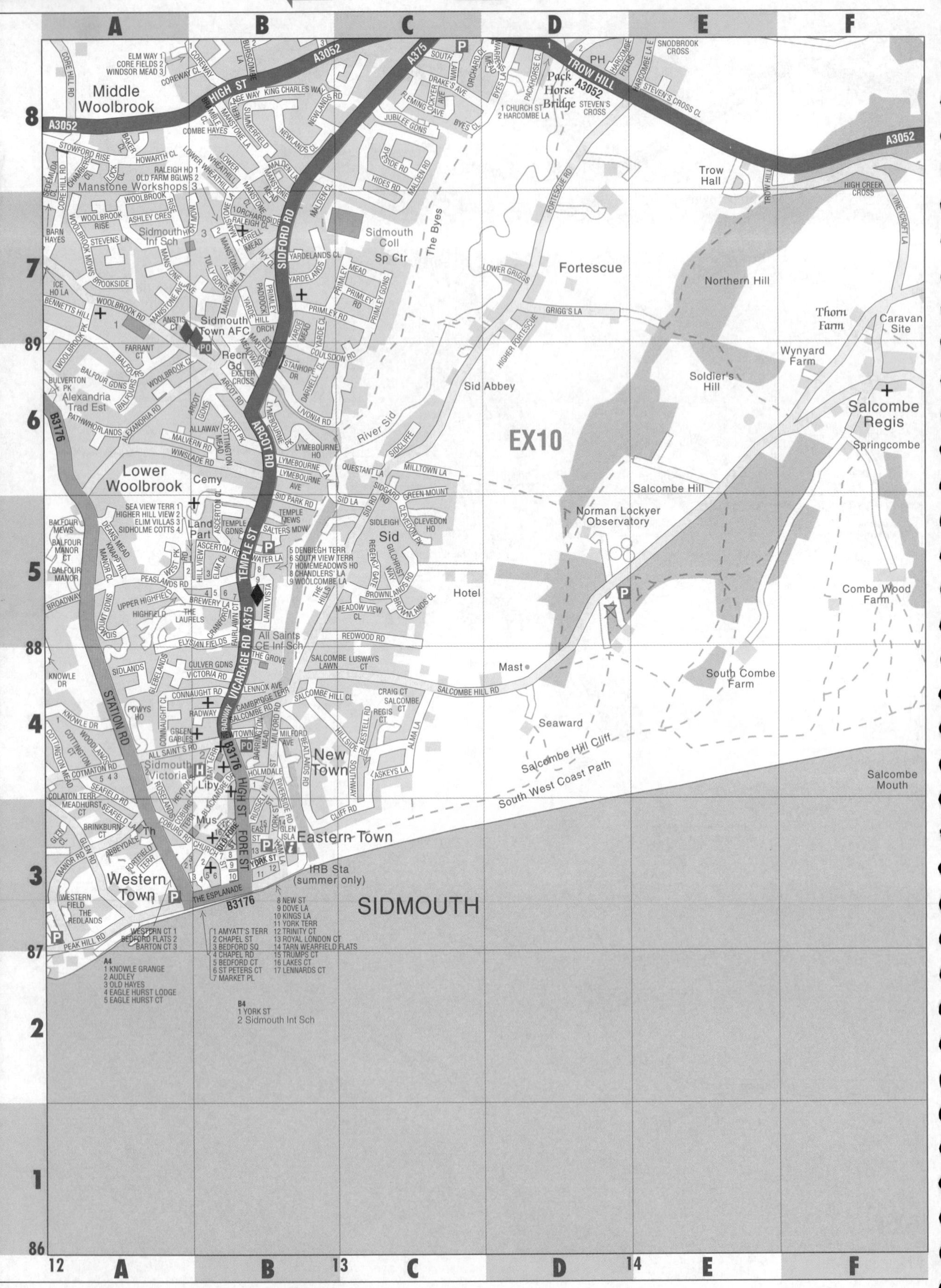

187

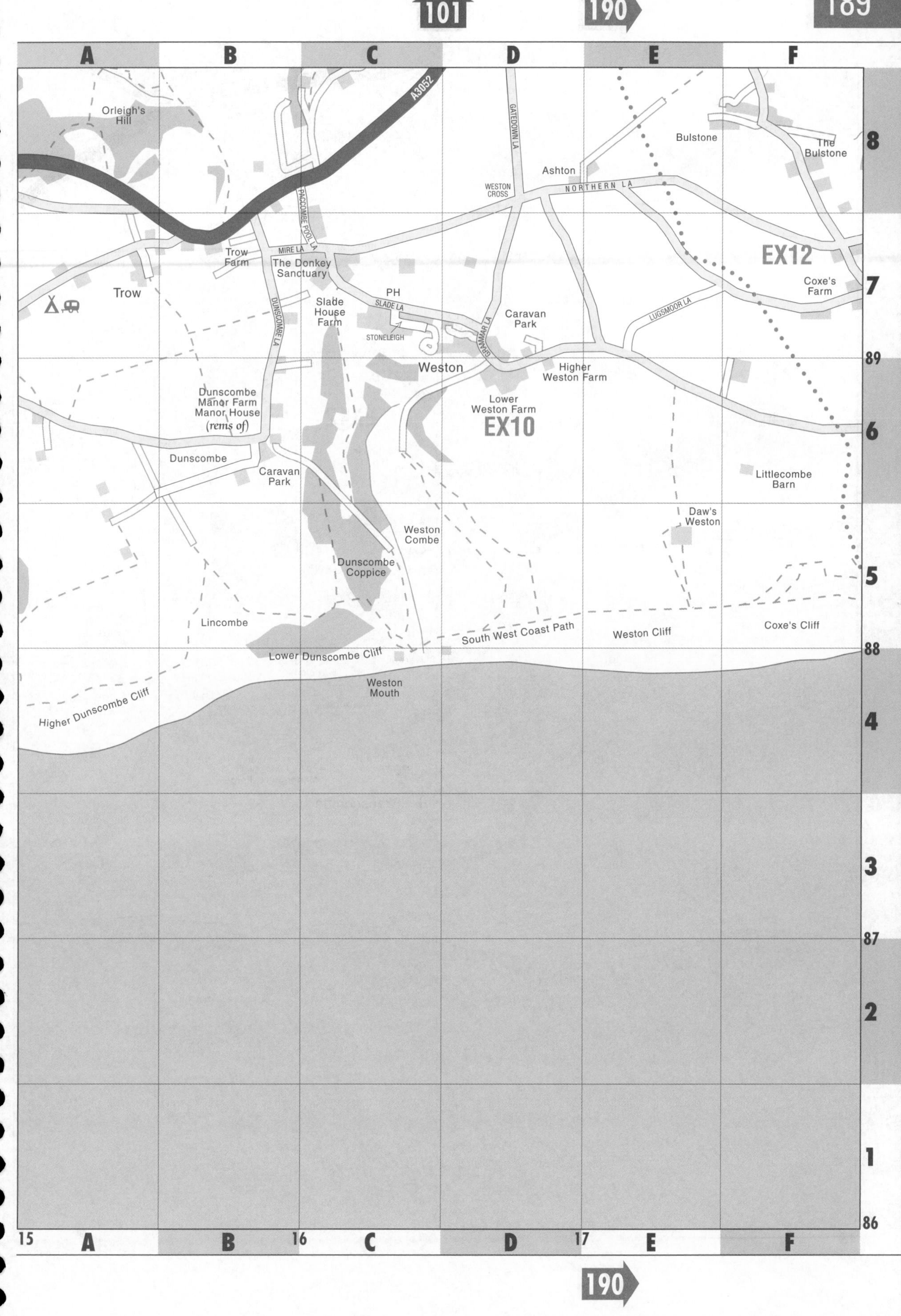

101
190
A
B
C
D
E
F
A3052
Orleigh's Hill
GATEDOWN LA
Bulstone
The Bulstone
Ashton
WESTON CROSS
NORTHERN LA
PACCOMBE POOL LA
MIRE LA
Trow Farm
The Donkey Sanctuary
EX12
Coxe's Farm
Trow
PH
SLADE LA
Slade House Farm
STONELEIGH
GRAMMAR LA
Caravan Park
LUGSMOOR LA
DUNSCOMBE LA
Weston
Higher Weston Farm
Dunscombe Manor Farm
Manor House
(rems of)
Lower Weston Farm
EX10
Dunscombe
Caravan Park
Littlecombe Barn
Daw's Weston
Weston Combe
Dunscombe Coppice
Lincombe
South West Coast Path
Weston Cliff
Coxe's Cliff
Lower Dunscombe Cliff
Weston Mouth
Higher Dunscombe Cliff
8
7
89
6
5
88
4
3
87
2
1
86
15
16
17
190

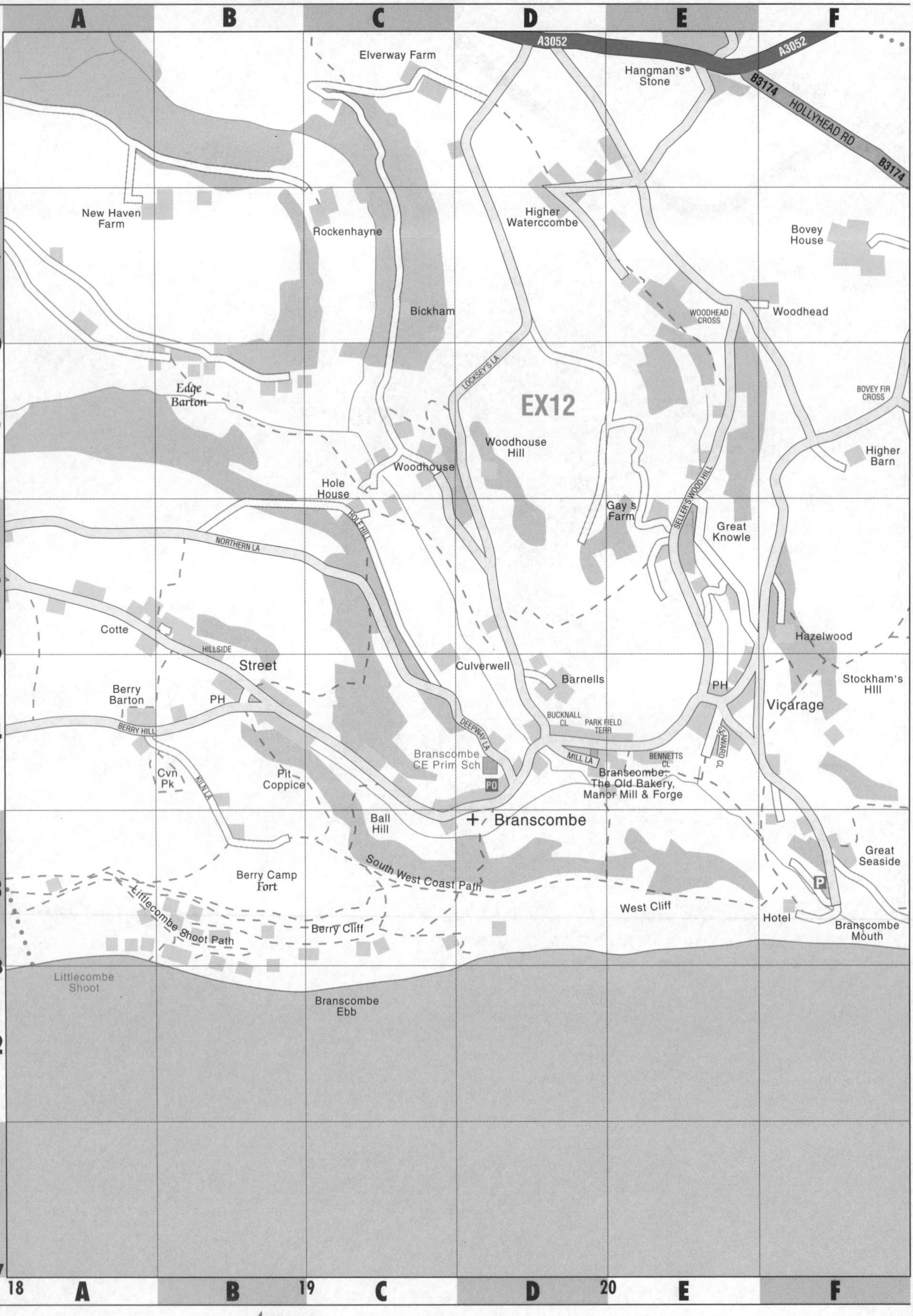

A
B
C
D
E
F
8
7
90
6
5
89
4
3
88
2
1
87
18
19
20
A3052
Elverway Farm
Hangman's Stone
B3174
HOLLYHEAD RD
New Haven Farm
Rockenhayne
Higher Waterccombe
Bovey House
Bickham
WOODHEAD CROSS
Woodhead
Edge Barton
LOCKSEY'S LA
EX12
BOVEY FIR CROSS
Woodhouse Hill
Higher Barn
Hole House
Woodhouse
HOLE HILL
Gay's Farm
SELLER'S WOOD HILL
Great Knowle
NORTHERN LA
Cotte
HILLSIDE
Street
Culverwell
Barnells
Hazelwood
Stockham's Hill
Berry Barton
PH
BERRY HILL
DEEPWAY LA
BUCKNALL CL
PARK FIELD TERR
Vicarage
SEAWARD CL
Branscombe CE Prim Sch
MILL LA
BENNETTS CL
Branscombe: The Old Bakery, Manor Mill & Forge
Cvn Pk
KILN LA
Pit Coppice
PO
Ball Hill
Branscombe
Great Seaside
South West Coast Path
Berry Camp Fort
West Cliff
Littlecombe Shoot Path
Berry Cliff
Hotel
Branscombe Mouth
Littlecombe Shoot
Branscombe Ebb

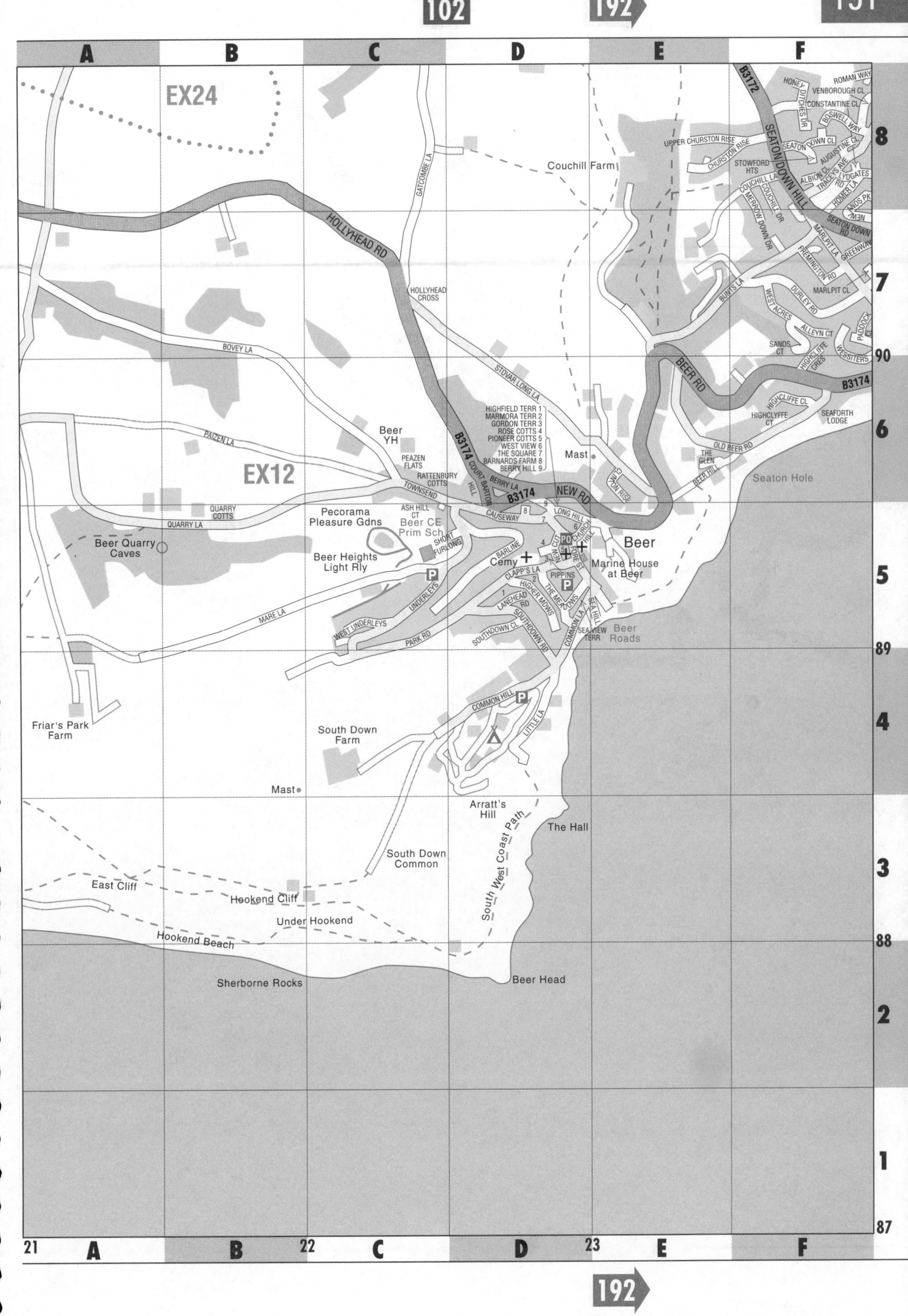
A
B
C
D
E
F
EX24
EX12
HOLLYHEAD RD
GATCOMBE LA
Couchill Farm
HOLLYHEAD CROSS
BOVEY LA
STOVAR LONG LA
PAIZEN LA
Beer YH
PEAZEN FLATS
RATTENBURY COTTS
TOWNSEND
QUARRY COTTS
QUARRY LA
Beer Quarry Caves
Pecorama Pleasure Gdns
ASH HILL CT
Beer CE Prim Sch
SHORT FURLONG
Beer Heights Light Rly
B3174
COURT BARTON HILL
BERRY LA
NEW RD
HIGHFIELD TERR 1
MARMORA TERR 2
GORDON TERR 3
ROSE COTTS 4
PIONEER COTTS 5
WEST VIEW 6
THE SQUARE 7
BARNARDS FARM 8
BERRY HILL 9
Mast
CAUSEWAY
LONG HILL
CHURCH HILL
FORE ST
NEW CUT
BARLINE
Cemy
CLAPP'S LA
PIPPINS
HIGHER MDWS
THE MEADOWS
LANEHEAD RD
SOUTHDOWN RD
SOUTHDOWN CL
COMMON LA
SEA HILL
SEA VIEW TERR
Beer Roads
Beer
Marine House at Beer
CLINTON RISE
MARE LA
UNDERLEYS
WEST UNDERLEYS
PARK RD
COMMON HILL
LITTLE LA
Friar's Park Farm
South Down Farm
Mast
Arratt's Hill
The Hall
South West Coast Path
South Down Common
East Cliff
Hookend Cliff
Under Hookend
Hookend Beach
Sherborne Rocks
Beer Head
B3172
SEATON DOWN HILL
HONEY DITCHES DR
ROMAN WAY
VENBOROUGH CL
CONSTANTINE CL
BOSWELL WAY
UPPER CHURSTON RISE
CHURSTON RISE
SEATON DOWN CL
AUGUSTINE CL
STOWFORD HTS
ALBION CL
TRACEYS AVE
LYDGATES RD
COUCHILL LA
COUCHILL DR
MERROW DOWN DR
HOMER LA
SEATON DOWN RD
MARLPIT LA
GREENWAY
FREMINGTON RD
BUNTS LA
MARLPIT CL
WEST ACRES
DURLEY RD
ALLEYN CT
SANDS CT
HIGHCLIFFE CRES
WESSITERS
PADDOCK
BEER RD
B3174
HIGHCLIFFE CL
HIGHCLYFFE CT
SEAFORTH LODGE
OLD BEER RD
THE GLEN
BEER HILL
Seaton Hole
8
7
90
6
5
89
4
3
88
2
1
87
21
22
23

102
103

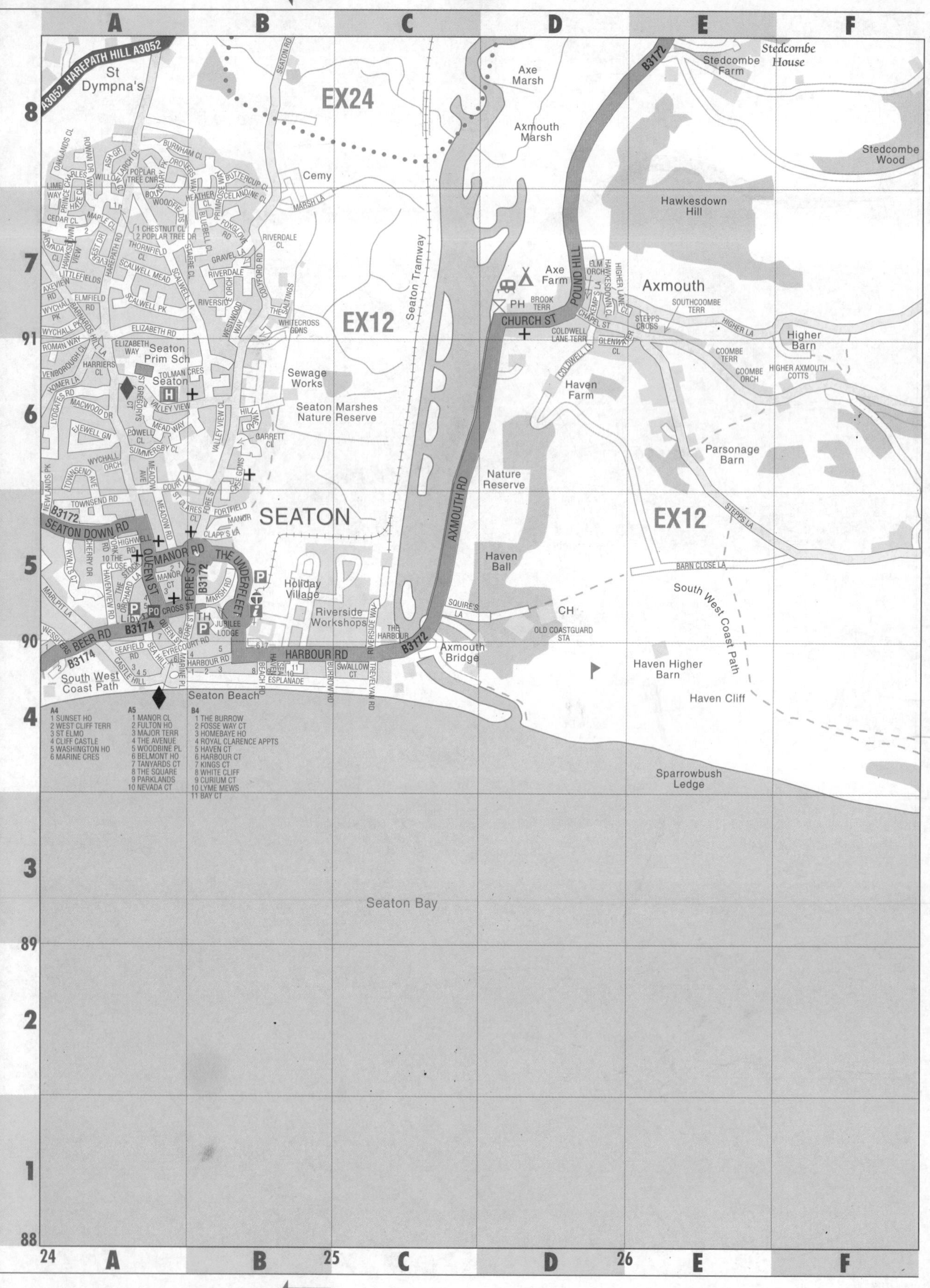
A
B
C
D
E
F
8
7
91
6
5
90
4
3
89
2
1
88
24
25
26
A3052 HAREPATH HILL A3052
St Dympna's
SEATON RD
EX24
Axe Marsh
Axmouth Marsh
Stedcombe Farm
Stedcombe House
Stedcombe Wood
B3172
Hawkesdown Hill
Cemy
MARSH LA
Seaton Tramway
EX12
Axe Farm
POUND HILL
Axmouth
PH
BROOK TERR
CHURCH ST
CHAPEL ST
COLDWELL LANE TERR
SOUTHCOOMBE TERR
HIGHER LA
Higher Barn
COOMBE TERR
COOMBE ORCH
HIGHER AXMOUTH COTTS
STEPPS CROSS
Haven Farm
Seaton Prim Sch
Seaton
Sewage Works
Seaton Marshes Nature Reserve
Nature Reserve
Parsonage Barn
EX12
STEPPS LA
AXMOUTH RD
SEATON
SEATON DOWN RD
B3172
MANOR RD
THE UNDERFLEET
QUEEN ST
FORE ST
Holiday Village
Riverside Workshops
Haven Ball
BARN CLOSE LA
South West Coast Path
CH
OLD COASTGUARD STA
SQUIRE'S LA
Axmouth Bridge
THE HARBOUR
HARBOUR RD
B3172
BEER RD
B3174
Liby
PO
TH
JUBILEE LODGE
South West Coast Path
Seaton Beach
Haven Higher Barn
Haven Cliff
Sparrowbush Ledge
Seaton Bay
A4
1 SUNSET HO
2 WEST CLIFF TERR
3 ST ELMO
4 CLIFF CASTLE
5 WASHINGTON HO
6 MARINE CRES
A5
1 MANOR CL
2 FULTON HO
3 MAJOR TERR
4 THE AVENUE
5 WOODBINE PL
6 BELMONT HO
7 TANYARDS CT
8 THE SQUARE
9 PARKLANDS
10 NEVADA CT
B4
1 THE BURROW
2 FOSSE WAY CT
3 HOMEBAYE HO
4 ROYAL CLARENCE APPTS
5 HAVEN CT
6 HARBOUR CT
7 KINGS CT
8 WHITE CLIFF
9 CURIUM CT
10 LYME MEWS
11 BAY CT

191

103
104

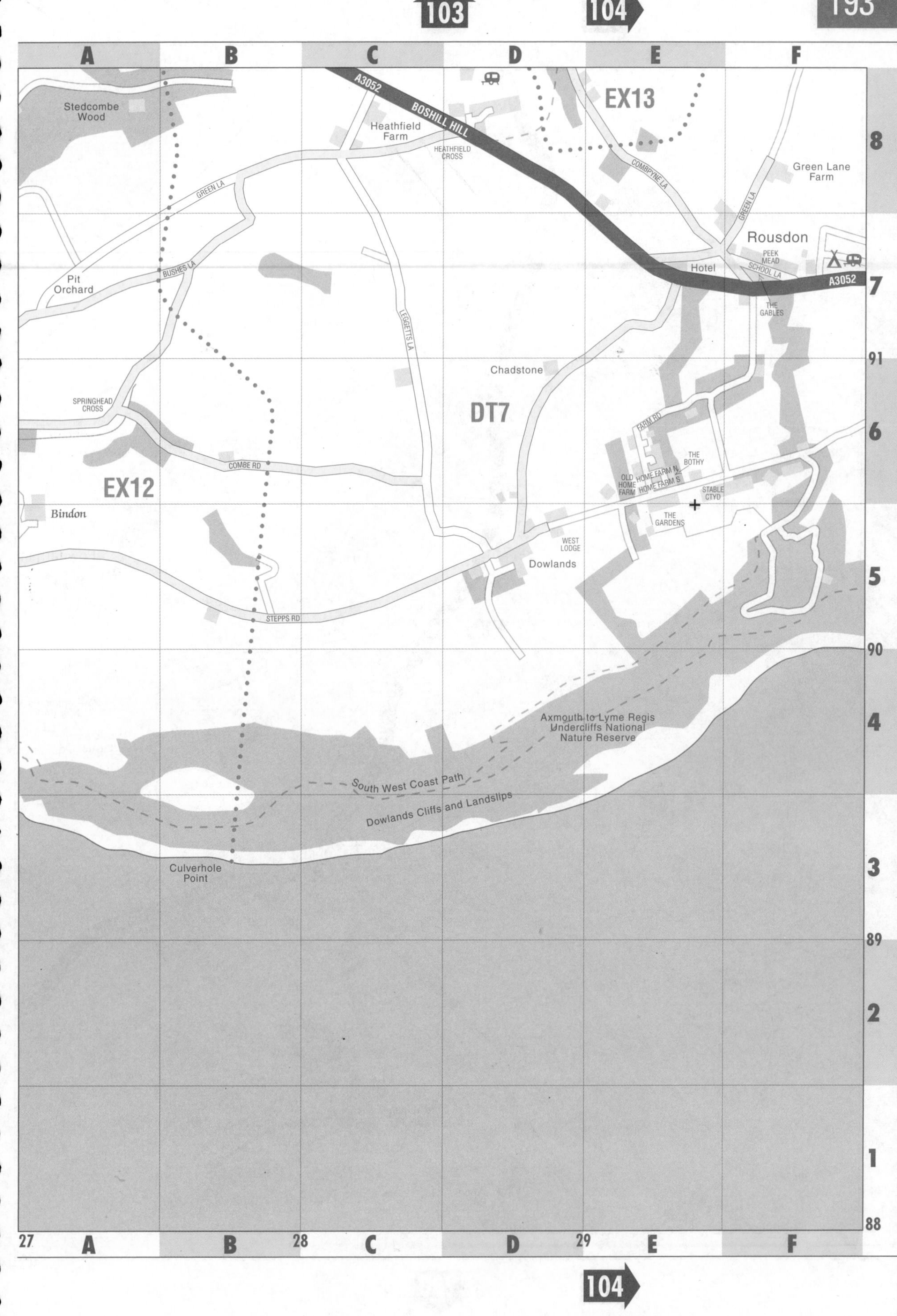
A
B
C
D
E
F
A3052
BOSHILL HILL
EX13
Stedcombe Wood
Heathfield Farm
HEATHFIELD CROSS
COMBPYNE LA
Green Lane Farm
GREEN LA
Rousdon
PEEK MEAD
SCHOOL LA
Hotel
A3052
THE GABLES
GREEN LA
Pit Orchard
BUSHES LA
LEGGETTS LA
Chadstone
SPRINGHEAD CROSS
DT7
FARM RD
THE BOTHY
COMBE RD
OLD HOME FARM
HOME FARM N
HOME FARM S
STABLE CTYD
EX12
Bindon
THE GARDENS
WEST LODGE
Dowlands
STEPPS RD
Axmouth to Lyme Regis Undercliffs National Nature Reserve
South West Coast Path
Dowlands Cliffs and Landslips
Culverhole Point
8
7
91
6
5
90
4
3
89
2
1
88
27
28
29

104

114 182

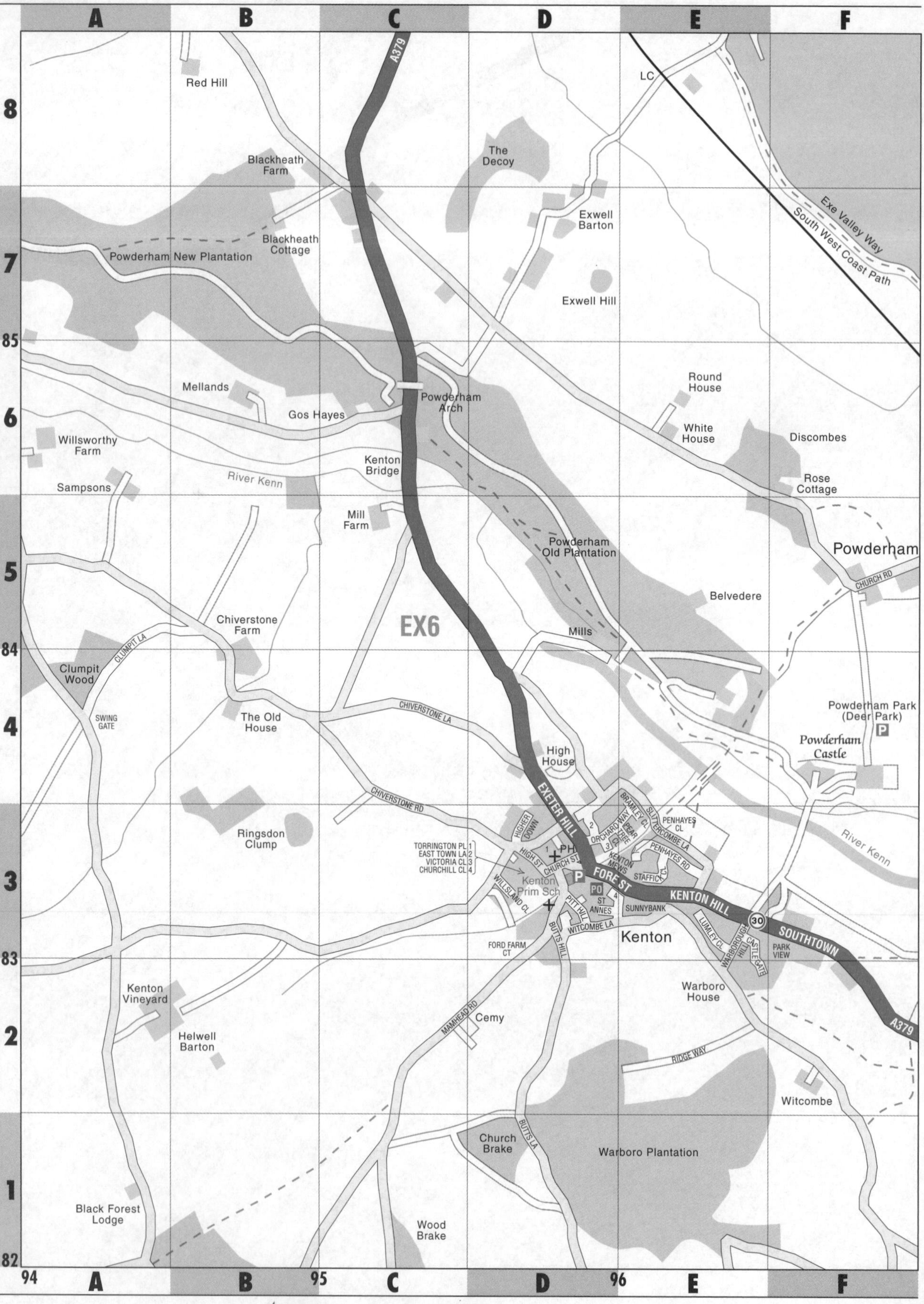

114 200

183
196

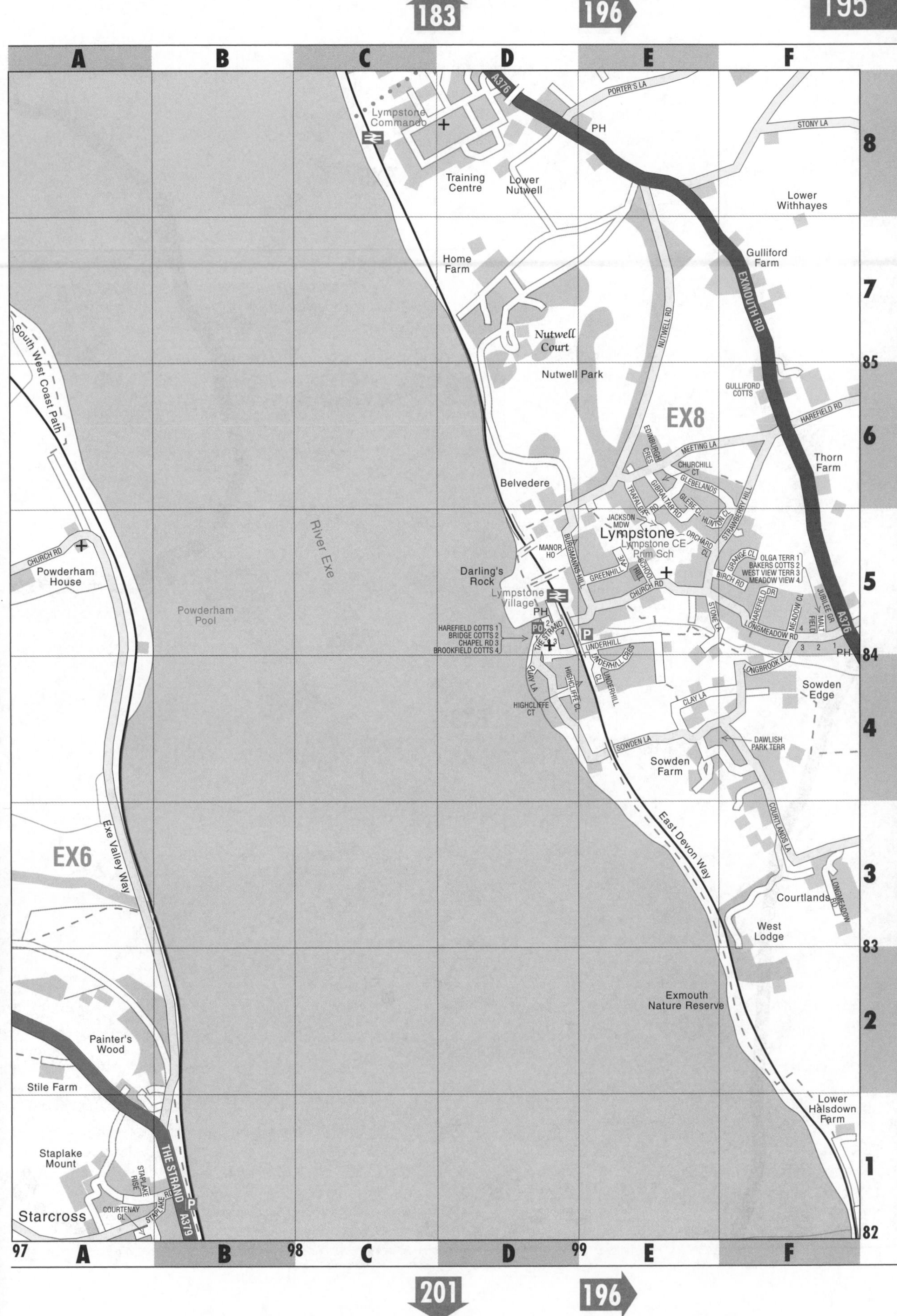

201
196

195
184

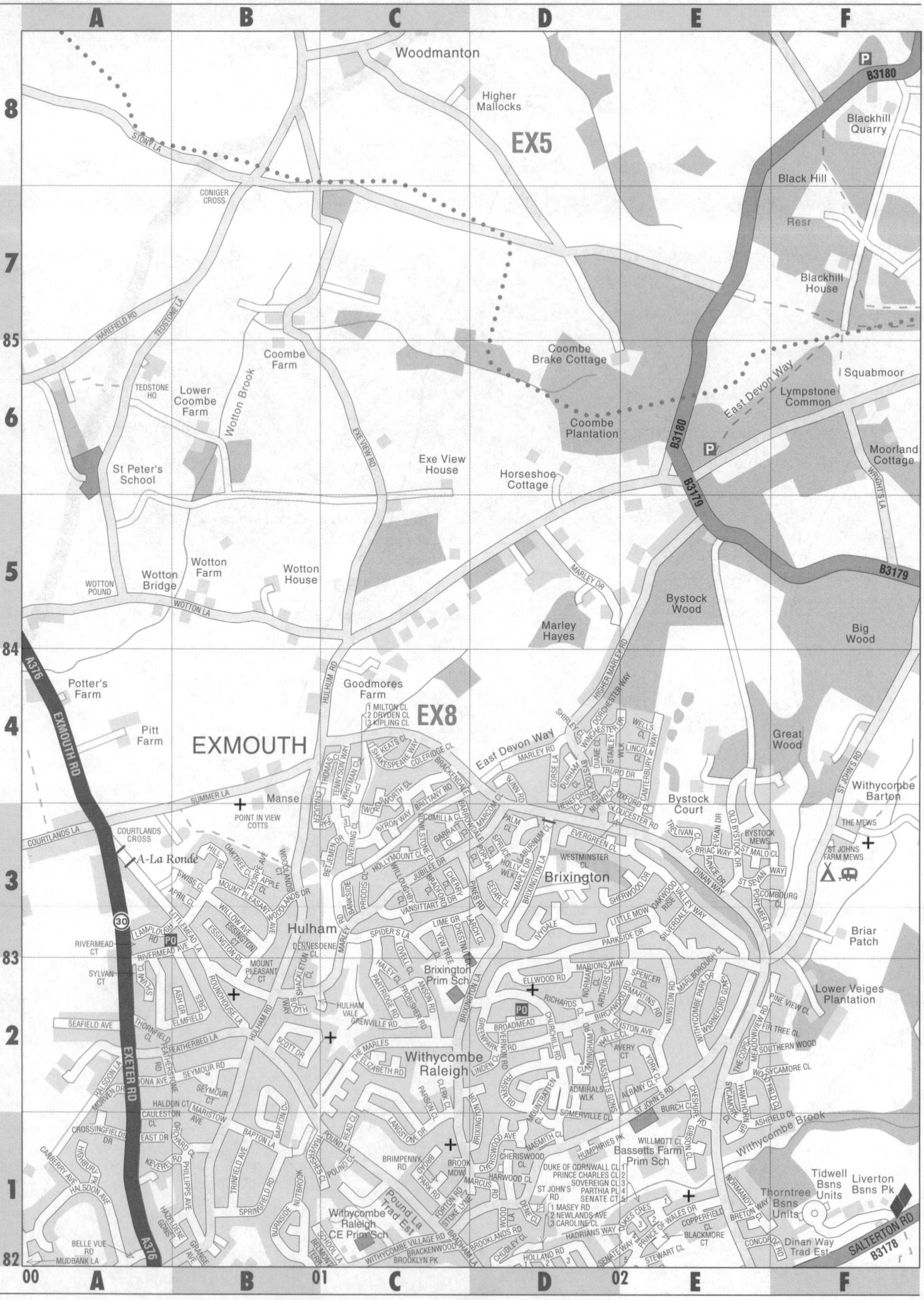
A
B
C
D
E
F
8
7
85
6
5
84
4
3
83
2
1
82
00
01
02
Woodmanton
Higher Mallocks
EX5
B3180
Blackhill Quarry
STONY LA
CONIGER CROSS
Black Hill
Resr
Blackhill House
HAREFIELD RD
TEDSTONE LA
Coombe Farm
Coombe Brake Cottage
Squabmoor
East Devon Way
Lympstone Common
TEDSTONE HO
Lower Coombe Farm
Wotton Brook
Coombe Plantation
B3180
Moorland Cottage
St Peter's School
EXE VIEW RD
Exe View House
Horseshoe Cottage
B3179
WRIGHT'S LA
Wotton Farm
Wotton House
WOTTON POUND
Wotton Bridge
WOTTON LA
MARLEY DR
B3179
Bystock Wood
Marley Hayes
Big Wood
A376
Potter's Farm
HULHUM RD
Goodmores Farm
HIGHER MARLEY RD
EXMOUTH RD
EX8
Pitt Farm
EXMOUTH
Great Wood
East Devon Way
Withycombe Barton
SUMMER LA
Manse
Bystock Court
POINT IN VIEW COTTS
COURTLANDS LA
COURTLANDS CROSS
A-La Ronde
THE MEWS
ST JOHNS FARM MEWS
Brixington
Hulham
Briar Patch
RIVERMEAD CT
SYLVAN CT
Lower Veiges Plantation
Brixington Prim Sch
SEAFIELD AVE
Withycombe Raleigh
EXETER RD
Withycombe Brook
Bassetts Farm Prim Sch
Tidwell Bsns Units
Liverton Bsns Pk
Thorntree Bsns Units
Withycombe Raleigh CE Prim Sch
Pound La Trad Est
Dinan Way Trad Est
SALTERTON RD
B3178
A376
BELLE VUE RD
MUDBANK LA

185
198

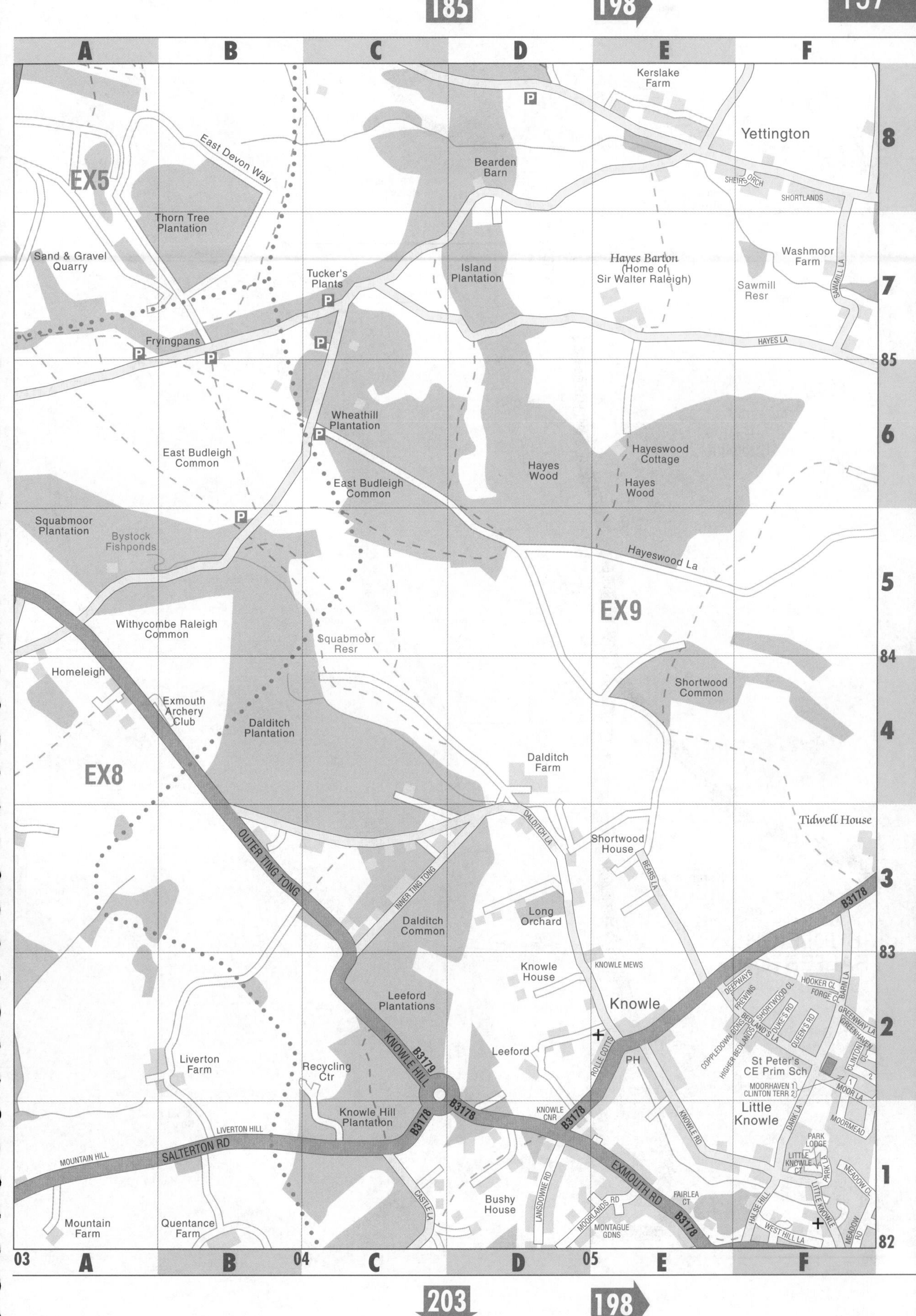

203
198

197
186

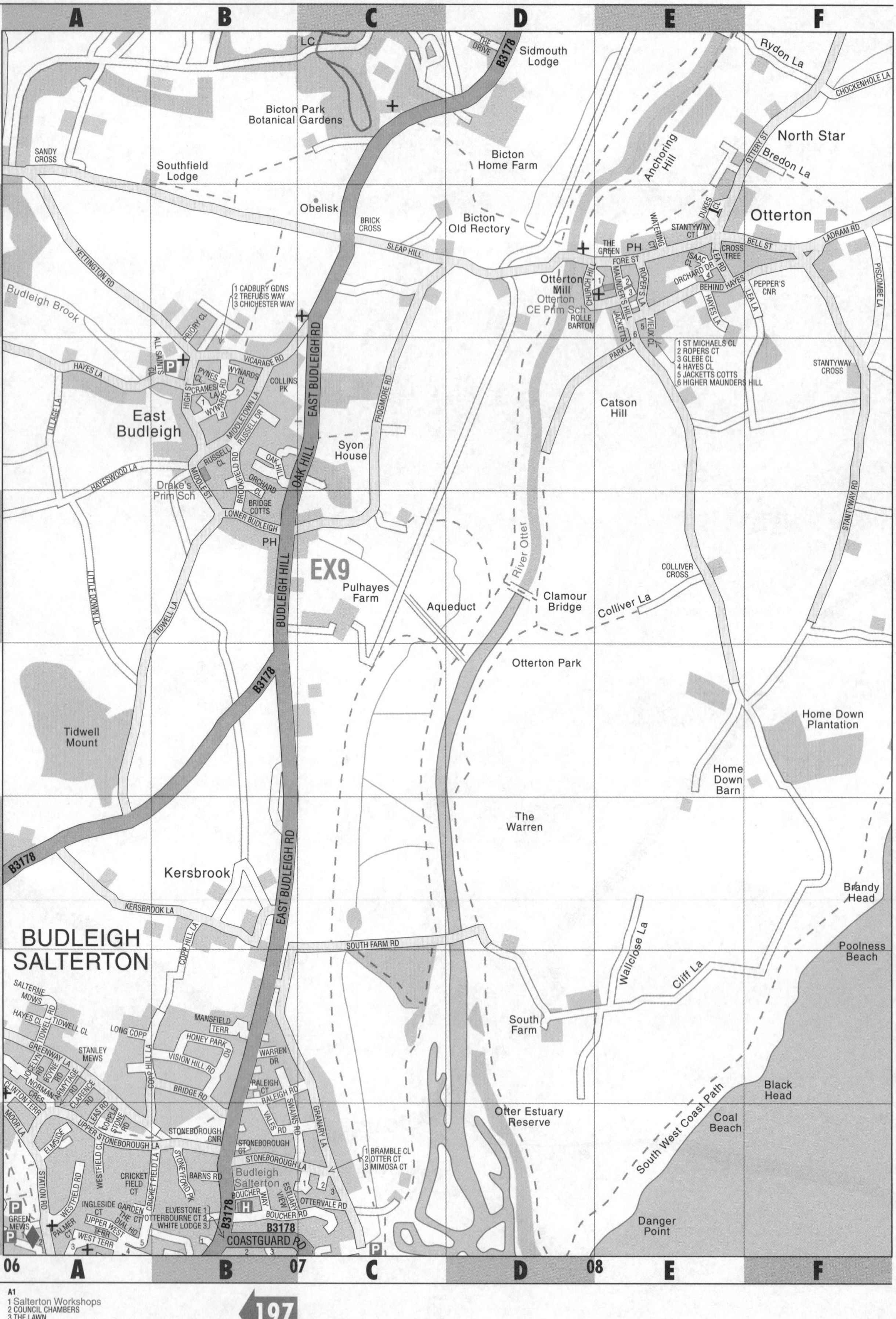

197

A1
1 Salterton Workshops
2 COUNCIL CHAMBERS
3 THE LAWN
4 EAST TERR
5 CHAPEL HILL

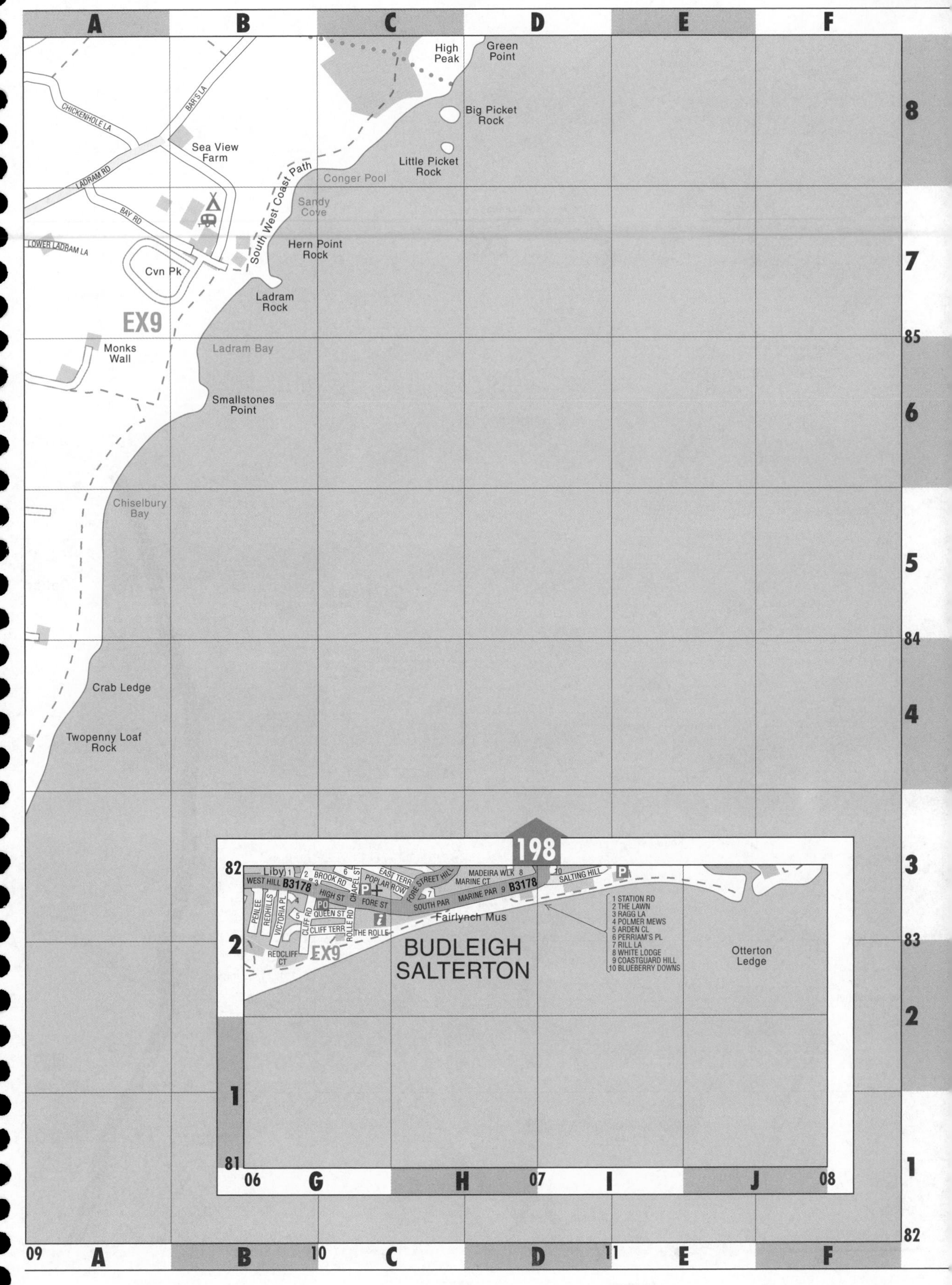
187
A
B
C
D
E
F
High
Peak
Green
Point
CHICKENHOLE LA
BAR'S LA
Big Picket
Rock
8
Sea View
Farm
LADRAM RD
Little Picket
Rock
South West Coast Path
Conger Pool
Sandy
Cove
BAY RD
Hern Point
Rock
LOWER LADRAM LA
7
Cvn Pk
Ladram
Rock
EX9
85
Monks
Wall
Ladram Bay
Smallstones
Point
6
Chiselbury
Bay
5
84
Crab Ledge
4
Twopenny Loaf
Rock
198
3
82
Liby
WEST HILL
B3178
BROOK RD
POPLAR ROW
EAST TERR
FORE STREET HILL
MADEIRA WLK
MARINE CT
B3178
SALTING HILL
HIGH ST
CHAPEL ST
FORE ST
SOUTH PAR
MARINE PAR
PENLEE
REDHILLS
VICTORIA PL
CLIFF RD
QUEEN ST
ROLLE RD
Fairlynch Mus
CLIFF TERR
THE ROLLE
1 STATION RD
2 THE LAWN
3 RAGG LA
4 POLMER MEWS
5 ARDEN CL
6 PERRIAM'S PL
7 RILL LA
8 WHITE LODGE
9 COASTGUARD HILL
10 BLUEBERRY DOWNS
83
2
BUDLEIGH
SALTERTON
REDCLIFF
CT
EX9
Otterton
Ledge
2
1
81
06
G
H
07
I
J
08
1
82
09
A
B
10
C
D
11
E
F

124 194

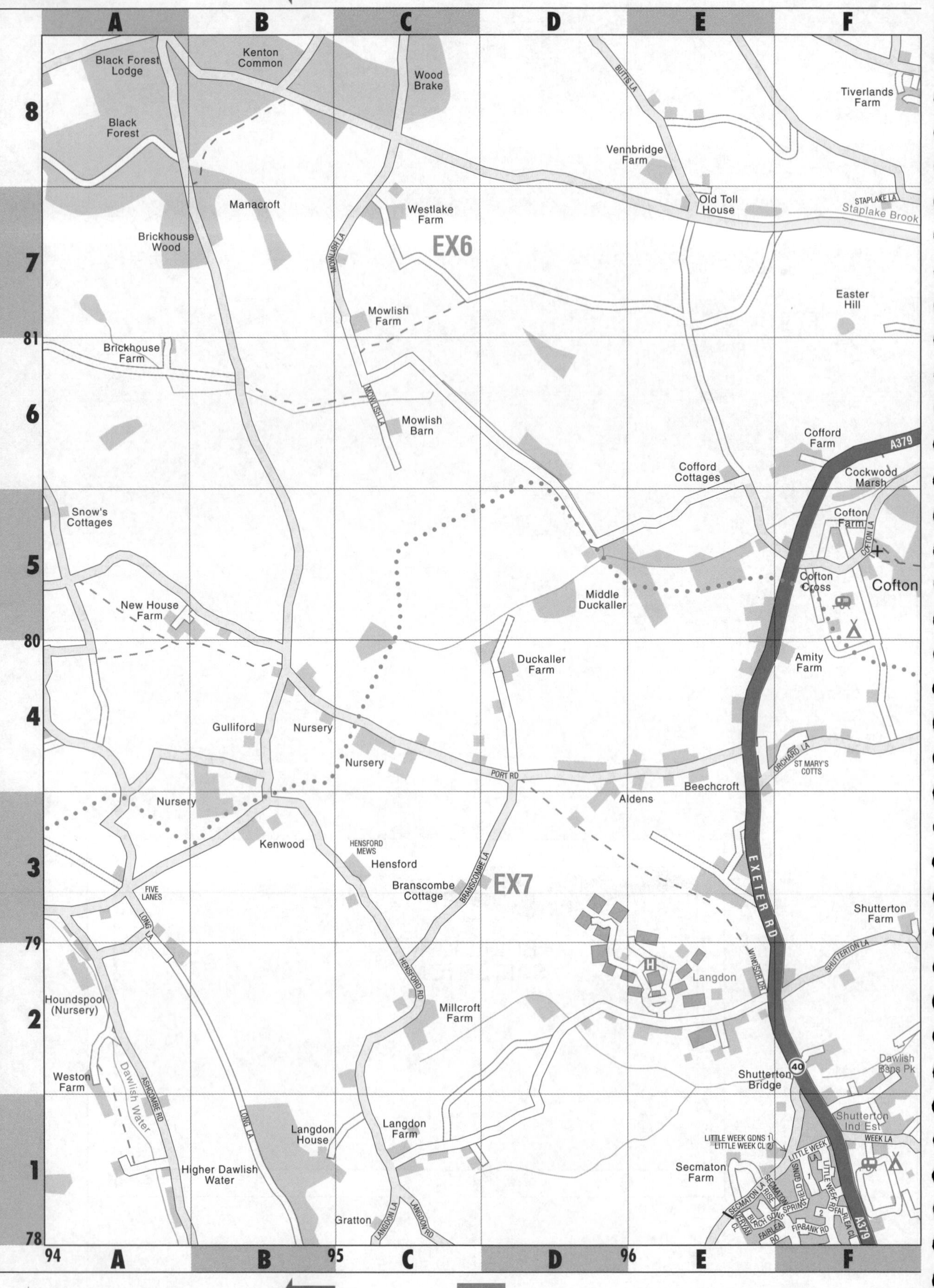

124 204

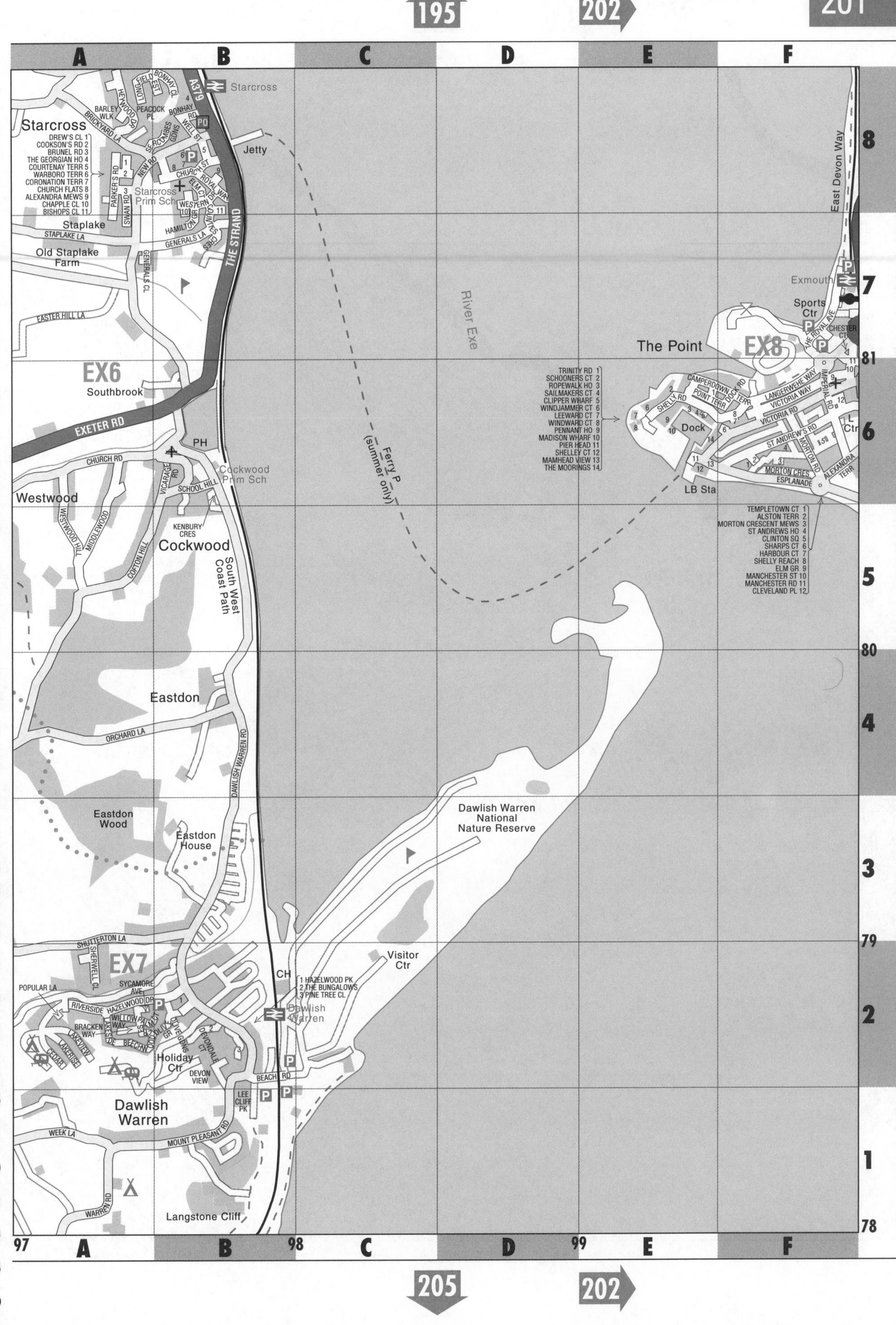
195
202
A
B
C
D
E
F
Starcross
DREW'S CL 1
COOKSON'S RD 2
BRUNEL RD 3
THE GEORGIAN HO 4
COURTENAY TERR 5
WARBORO TERR 6
CORONATION TERR 7
CHURCH FLATS 8
ALEXANDRA MEWS 9
CHAPPLE CL 10
BISHOPS CL 11
BARLEY WLK
BRICKYARD LA
HENWOOD DR
LONGFIELD EST
BONHAY CL
PEACOCK PL
BONHAY RD
WELL ST
SEARLE'S CL
NEW RD
CHURCH ST
PARKER'S RD
SWAN RD
ROYAL WAY
ELM CT
WESTERN DR
HAMILTON GR
COUNTESS CRES
GENERALS LA
GENERALS CL
Starcross Prim Sch
Starcross
A379
Jetty
THE STRAND
Staplake
STAPLAKE LA
Old Staplake Farm
EASTER HILL LA
EX6
Southbrook
EXETER RD
PH
CHURCH RD
VICARAGE RD
SCHOOL HILL
Cockwood Prim Sch
Westwood
WESTWOOD HILL
MIDDLEWOOD
COFTON HILL
KENBURY CRES
Cockwood
South West Coast Path
Eastdon
ORCHARD LA
DAWLISH WARREN RD
Eastdon Wood
Eastdon House
River Exe
Ferry P (summer only)
East Devon Way
Exmouth
Sports Ctr
THE ROYAL AVE
CHESTER CT
The Point
EX8
TRINITY RD 1
SCHOONERS CT 2
ROPEWALK HO 3
SAILMAKERS CT 4
CLIPPER WHARF 5
WINDJAMMER CT 6
LEEWARD CT 7
WINDWARD CT 8
PENNANT HO 9
MADISON WHARF 10
PIER HEAD 11
SHELLEY CT 12
MAMHEAD VIEW 13
THE MOORINGS 14
CAMPERDOWN TERR
POINT TERR
DOCK RD
SHELLY RD
Dock
LANGERWEHE WAY
VICTORIA WAY
IMPERIAL RD
VICTORIA RD
ST ANDREW'S RD
MORTON RD
MORTON CRES
ESPLANADE
ALEXANDRA TERR
L Ctr
LB Sta
TEMPLETOWN CT 1
ALSTON TERR 2
MORTON CRESCENT MEWS 3
ST ANDREWS HO 4
CLINTON SQ 5
SHARPS CT 6
HARBOUR CT 7
SHELLY REACH 8
ELM GR 9
MANCHESTER ST 10
MANCHESTER RD 11
CLEVELAND PL 12
Dawlish Warren National Nature Reserve
Visitor Ctr
SHUTTERTON LA
SHERWELL CL
EX7
SYCAMORE AVE
POPULAR LA
RIVERSIDE
HAZELWOOD DR
WILLOW WAY
BRACKEN WAY
LAKESIDE
LAKEVIEW
LAKERISE
CEDAR
BEECH
OLIVE GR
OLIVE GDNS
DEVONDALE CT
CH
1 HAZELWOOD PK
2 THE BUNGALOWS
3 PINE TREE CL
Dawlish Warren
Holiday Ctr
DEVON VIEW
BEACH RD
LEE CLIFF PK
Dawlish Warren
WEEK LA
MOUNT PLEASANT RD
WARREN RD
Langstone Cliff
8
7
81
6
5
80
4
3
79
2
1
78
97
98
99
205
202

A7
1 GEORGE ST
2 SHUTE MEADOW ST
3 CHARLES ST
4 STAPLES MEWS
5 GLENORCHY CT
6 ALBION CT
7 HENRIETTA PL
8 HENRIETTA RD
9 ALBION TERR
10 PALACE COTTS
11 ALL SAINTS MEWS

201
196

EXMOUTH

EX8

Littleham

A6
1 CHAPEL ST
2 MAGNOLIA WLK
3 LOWER FORE ST
4 MARGARET ST
5 UNION ST
6 VICTORIA PL
7 HELENA PL
8 KING ST
9 UPPER CHURCH ST
10 MAGNOLIA HO
11 QUEEN ST
12 QUEEN'S CT
13 TOWER ST
14 CRITERION PL
15 CHAPEL HILL
16 BEACON HILL
17 ALEXANDRA TERR
18 LITTLE BICTON CT
19 THE OLD WEIGHBRIDGE
20 ST SAVIOURS HO21 DRAY CT
22 ADMIRALS CT
23 PRINCES ST
24 The Beacon CE Prim Sch
25 MYRTLE ROW

B6
1 MONTPELLIER CT
2 ASHLEY HO
3 HIGHFIELD CT
4 HAMILTON CT
5 MAGNOLIA CT
6 The Dolphin Sch

B5
MADEIRA CT 1
MAER BAY CT 2
MARINA CT 3

A5
PENCARWICK HO 1
ADELAIDE CT 2
LION HO 3
EXECLIFF 4

201

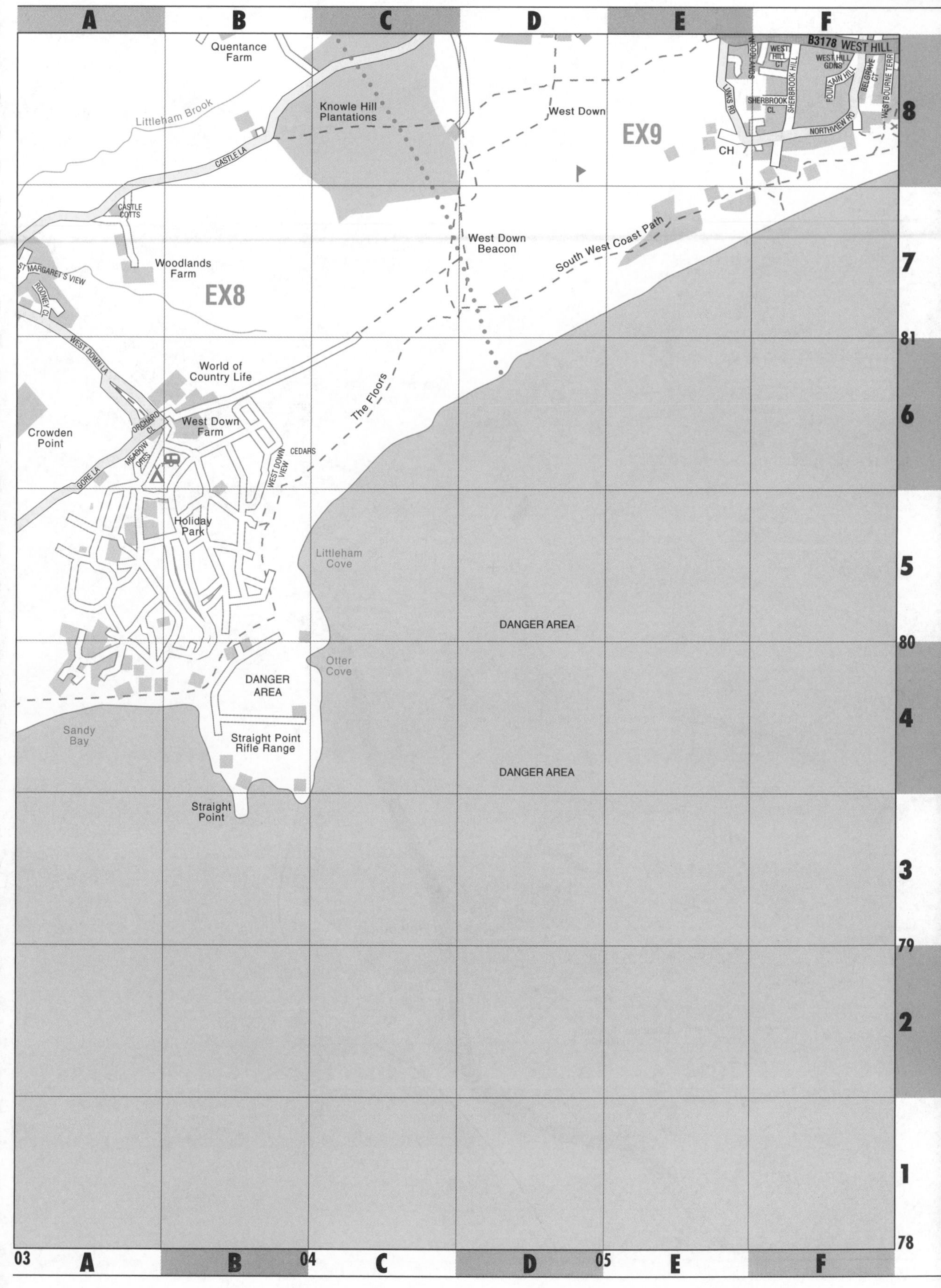
A
B
C
D
E
F
Quentance Farm
Littleham Brook
Knowle Hill Plantations
West Down
EX9
B3178 WEST HILL
WOODLANDS
WEST HILL CT
SHERBROOK HILL
WEST HILL GDNS
FOUNTAIN HILL
BELGRAVE CT
WESTBOURNE TERR
LINKS RD
SHERBROOK CL
NORTHVIEW RD
CH
CASTLE LA
CASTLE COTTS
West Down Beacon
South West Coast Path
Woodlands Farm
ST MARGARET'S VIEW
RODNEY CL
EX8
WEST DOWN LA
World of Country Life
The Floors
Crowden Point
ORCHARD CL
West Down Farm
MEADOW CRES
CEDARS
WEST DOWN VIEW
GORE LA
Holiday Park
Littleham Cove
DANGER AREA
Otter Cove
DANGER AREA
Sandy Bay
Straight Point Rifle Range
DANGER AREA
Straight Point
8
7
81
6
5
80
4
3
79
2
1
78
03
04
05

124

200

D6
1 PENFIELD GDNS
2 RED LION PL
3 SIDNEY CT
4 HOOPERN TERR
5 MANOR CT
6 FREDERICK TERR
7 SCHOOL HILL
8 QUEEN LA
9 STOCKTON LA
10 HATCHER ST
11 BLACKSWAN PL
12 LUSCOMBE TERR
13 PRIORY PARK RD
14 HALDON TERR
15 ORCHARD GDNS
16 PRINCES ST
17 KING ST
18 ALBERT ST
19 TOWN TREE HILL
20 GOLDEN TERR
21 OLD MANOR CT
22 WEDLAKE MEWS
23 ALEXANDER RD
24 BROOKLANDS
25 LAWN TERR
26 Lanherne Fst Sch

A B C D E F

8 7 77 6 5 76 4 3 75 2 1 74

Rixdale Farm
Radfords
Ford
Fairfield House
The Rise
LUSCOMBE HILL
Luscombe Castle
Luscombe Park
Dawlish Water
EX7
Westcote
Gatehouse Farm
Gatehouse Cty Prim Sch
Pathfields Nursery
Oakwood Court Coll
Dawlish Com Coll
L Ctr
DAWLISH
Dawlish
Breakwater
Dawlish Com
Westcliff Prim Sch
Cemy
Ford
Aller Farm
Ford
Oaklands Park Specl Sch
Ratcliffe Specl Sch
Coryton's Cove
Horse Cove
Holcombe Farm
HOLCOMBE DOWN RD
Westbrook
Oakleigh Farm
PH
South West Coast Path
Holcombe
Caravan Pk
East Down
Hole Head
The Parson and Clerk
Higher Holcombe House
Higher Holcombe Farm
Middle Holcombe House
TQ14
TEIGNMOUTH RD
DAWLISH RD
A379
EXETER RD

LEYFIELD WLK 1
WESTERN HO 2
STEWART HO 3
HIGH TREES 4
SWALLOWS ACRE 5
STANMORE RISE 6
HIGH HOUSE CL 7
KINGSDOWN CL 8

STONELANDS TERR 1
STONELANDS MEWS 2
CHURCH VIEW 3
TOWN MILLS 4

1 SUNNYLANDS WAY
2 HOLCOMBE CROSS
3 WINWARD RI

RIVIERA TERR
SEA LAWN TERR
SAN REMO TERR
COASTGUARD COTTS
BURSLEDON CT
CHARLTON HO
LANHERNE
BURNS CT
LEA MOUNT RD

E6
1 PRIORY GDNS
2 PRIORY HILL
3 LAWN HILL
4 MALTING CT
5 BELVEDERE CT
6 CARLTON TERR
7 LEIGHAM CT
8 CLEVELAND PL
9 COMMERCIAL RD
10 IDDESLEIGH TERR
11 WHITE CT
12 BEACH ST
13 MARINERS CT
14 RICHMOND CT
15 RICHMOND PL
16 BRUNEL CT
17 STATION RD
18 BROOKDALE TERR
19 MEWS CT
20 ST MARKS
21 SHAFTESBURY CL
22 SEFTON CT
23 MANOR GDNS

210

210

94 A B 95 C D 96 E F

124

210

A
B
C
D
E
F
EX7
WARREN RD
South West Coast Path
Langstone Rock
PINEWOOD CL
PO
THE ROCKSTONE
8
7
77
6
5
76
4
3
75
2
1
74
97
98
99

131
123

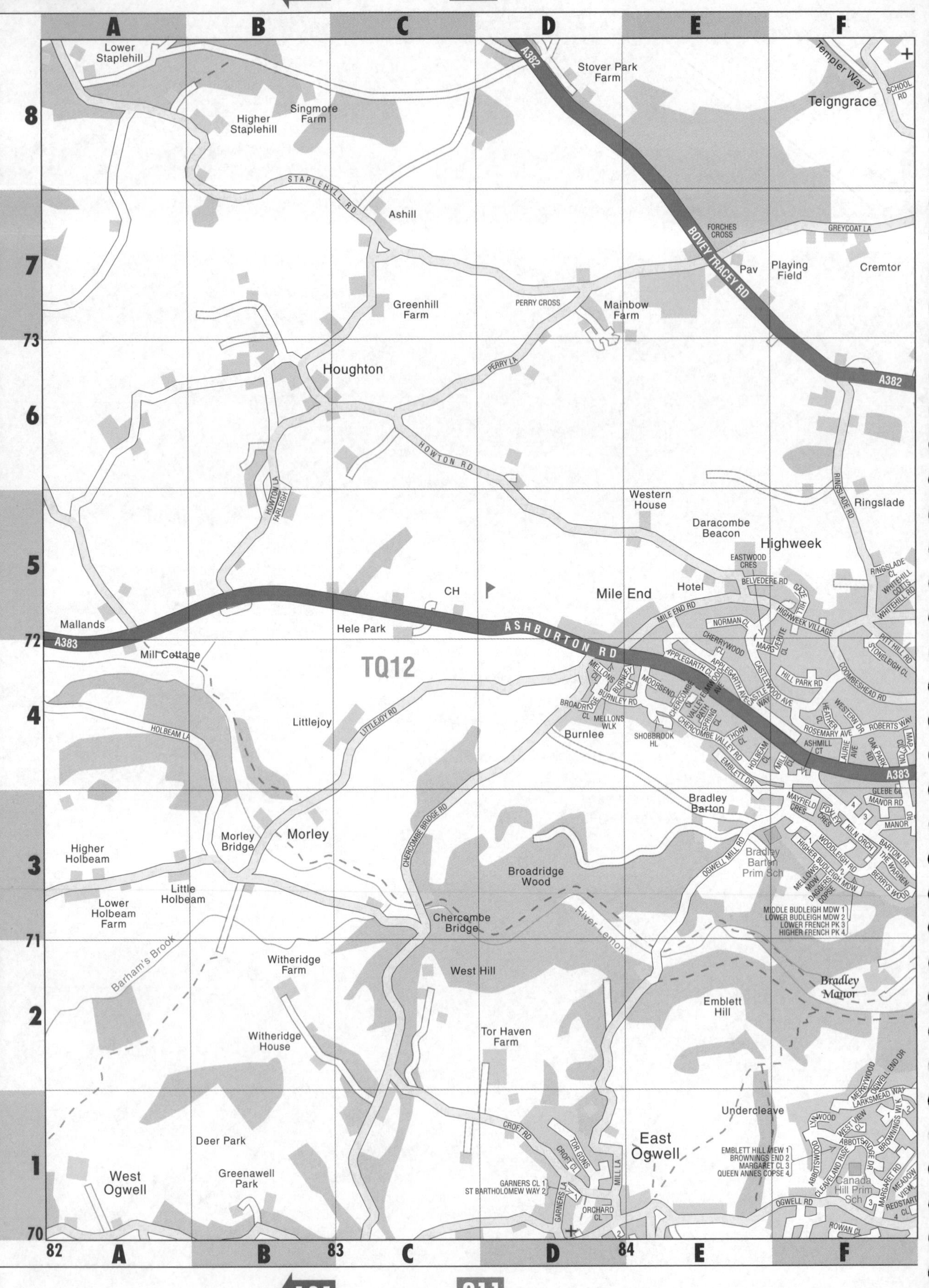

131
211

123
208

B3
1 CORONATION RD
2 POLLYBLANK RD
3 HIGHWEEK RD
4 ST MARY'S CT
5 CHAPEL HILL
6 BRADLEY CT
7 MARKET WLK
8 BEARNE'S LA
9 SUN CT
10 BESIGHEIM PL
11 TUDOR CL
12 GRAFTON RD
13 NEWFOUNDLAND WAY
14 CHURCH CT
15 MANOR COTTS
16 ST LEONARD'S CL
17 HAYTOR TERR
18 ROOKLANDS
19 POUND PL
20 POWDERHAM CT
21 WOODVALE CT
22 ORCHARD CT

B4
1 PAYNSFORD RD
2 BRUNSWICK HO
3 THURLESTONE RD

C2
1 ALEXANDRA RD
2 MILTON CT

C3
1 BRIDGE HO
2 PEARL ASSURANCE HO
3 HOPKINS CT
4 CARLISLE ST
5 SUMMERLAND COTTS
6 SUMMERLAND CT
7 CAULFIELD CT
8 ELM RD
9 CRICKET FIELD RD
10 ALBANY ST
11 GLADSTONE PL
12 IMPERIAL MEWS
13 KINGS COTTS
14 ALBERT TERR
15 ST PAUL'S RD
16 ST PAUL'S CT
17 NORTHERNHAY

212
208

C3
18 Wolborough CE Prim Sch
19 Bearne's Prim Sch
20 South Devon Coll

F2
1 HALDON RISE
2 HALDON CL
3 THE GLEN
4 ELIZABETH SQ
5 WOODLANDS GDNS
6 HACCOMBE PATH

207
124

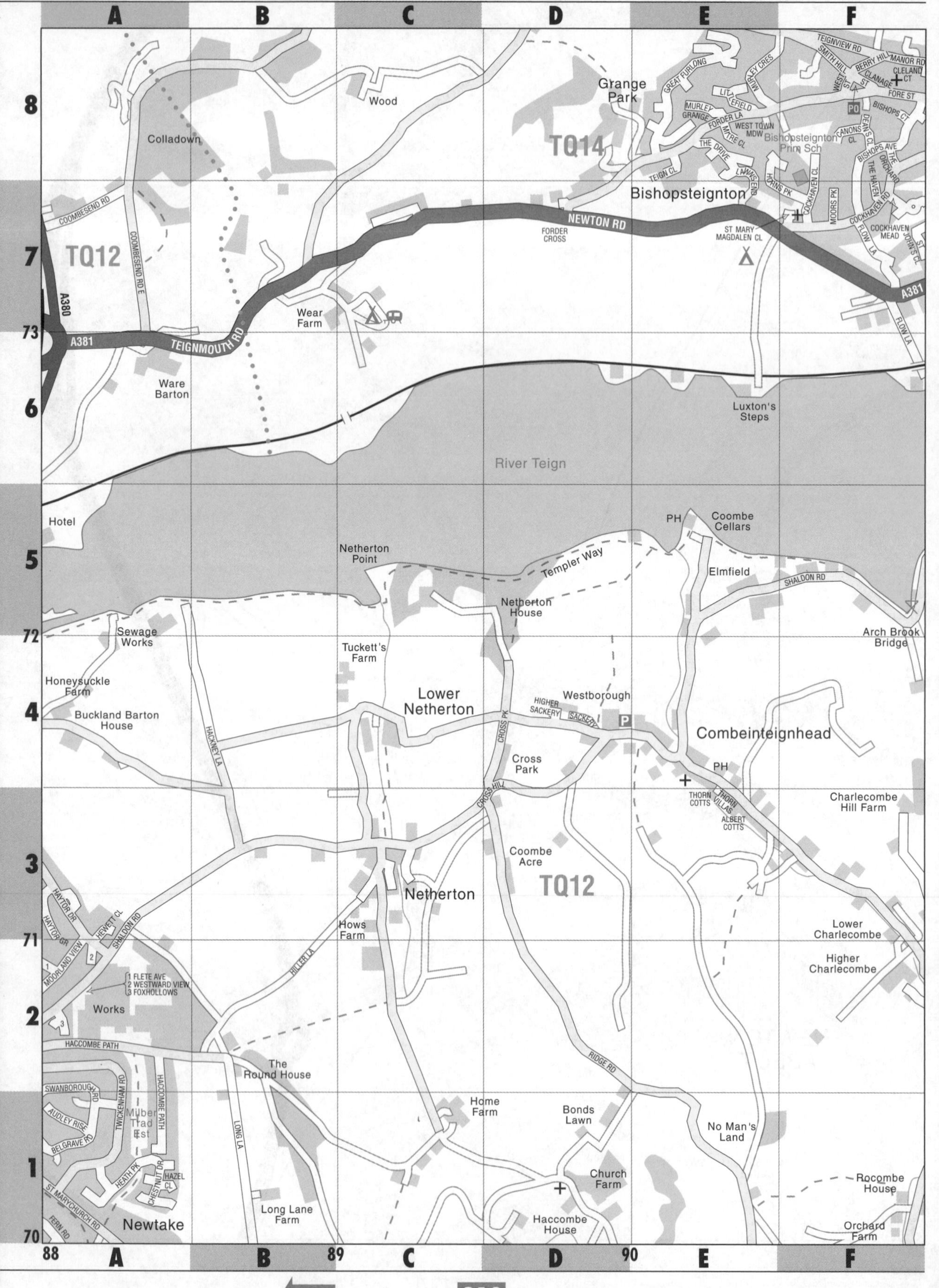

207
213

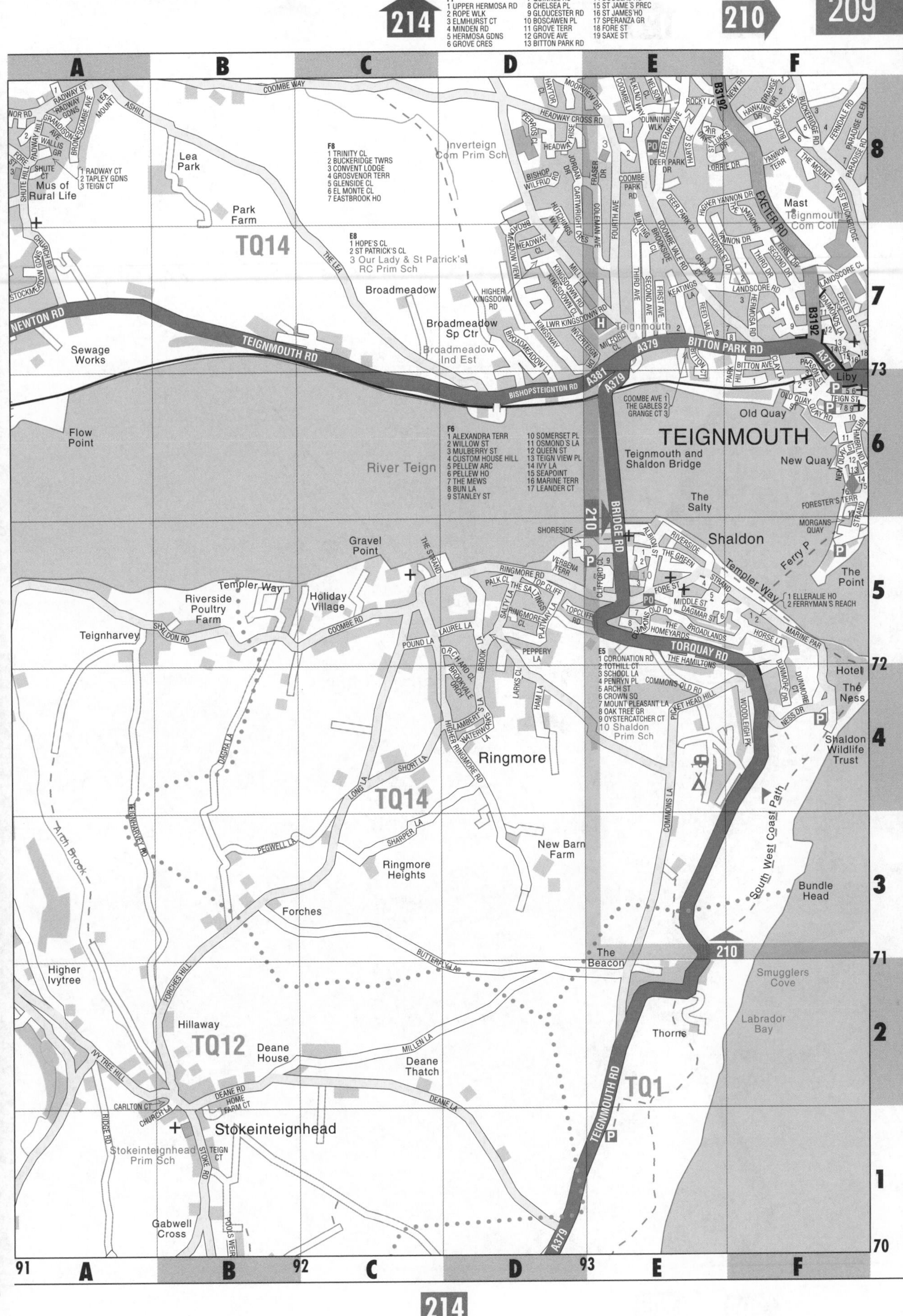
214
F7
1 UPPER HERMOSA RD
2 ROPE WLK
3 ELMHURST CT
4 MINDEN RD
5 HERMOSA GDNS
6 GROVE CRES
7 QUINNEL HO
8 CHELSEA PL
9 GLOUCESTER RD
10 BOSCAWEN PL
11 GROVE TERR
12 GROVE AVE
13 BITTON PARK RD
14 DOUGLAS HO
15 ST JAME'S PREC
16 ST JAMES HO
17 SPERANZA GR
18 FORE ST
19 SAXE ST
210
F8
1 TRINITY CL
2 BUCKERIDGE TWRS
3 CONVENT LODGE
4 GROSVENOR TERR
5 GLENSIDE CL
6 EL MONTE CL
7 EASTBROOK HO
E8
1 HOPE'S CL
2 ST PATRICK'S CL
3 Our Lady & St Patrick's RC Prim Sch
1 RADWAY CT
2 TAPLEY GDNS
3 TEIGN CT
Mus of Rural Life
Lea Park
Park Farm
TQ14
Inverteign Com Prim Sch
Broadmeadow
Broadmeadow Sp Ctr
Broadmeadow Ind Est
Sewage Works
TEIGNMOUTH RD
NEWTON RD
BISHOPSTEIGNTON RD
A381
A379
BITTON PARK RD
B3192
EXETER RD
Mast
Teignmouth Com Coll
Teignmouth
Liby
COOMBE AVE 1
THE GABLES 2
GRANGE CT 3
Old Quay
TEIGNMOUTH
Teignmouth and Shaldon Bridge
New Quay
Flow Point
River Teign
F6
1 ALEXANDRA TERR
2 WILLOW ST
3 MULBERRY ST
4 CUSTOM HOUSE HILL
5 PELLEW ARC
6 PELLEW HO
7 THE MEWS
8 BUN LA
9 STANLEY ST
10 SOMERSET PL
11 OSMOND'S LA
12 QUEEN ST
13 TEIGN VIEW PL
14 IVY LA
15 SEAPOINT
16 MARINE TERR
17 LEANDER CT
The Salty
BRIDGE RD
Shaldon
Ferry P
Templer Way
1 ELLERALIE HO
2 FERRYMAN'S REACH
The Point
Gravel Point
Riverside Poultry Farm
Holiday Village
Teignharvey
TORQUAY RD
E5
1 CORONATION RD
2 TOTHILL CT
3 SCHOOL LA
4 PENRYN PL
5 ARCH ST
6 CROWN SQ
7 MOUNT PLEASANT LA
8 OAK TREE GR
9 OYSTERCATCHER CT
10 Shaldon Prim Sch
Hotel
The Ness
Shaldon Wildlife Trust
Ringmore
TQ14
New Barn Farm
Ringmore Heights
Forches
South West Coast Path
Bundle Head
Arch Brook
The Beacon
Smugglers Cove
Labrador Bay
Higher Ivytree
Hillaway
TQ12
Deane House
Deane Thatch
Thorns
TQ1
TEIGNMOUTH RD
Stokeinteignhead
Stokeinteignhead Prim Sch
Gabwell Cross
A B C D E F
1 2 3 4 5 6 7 8
70 71 72 73
91 92 93
214

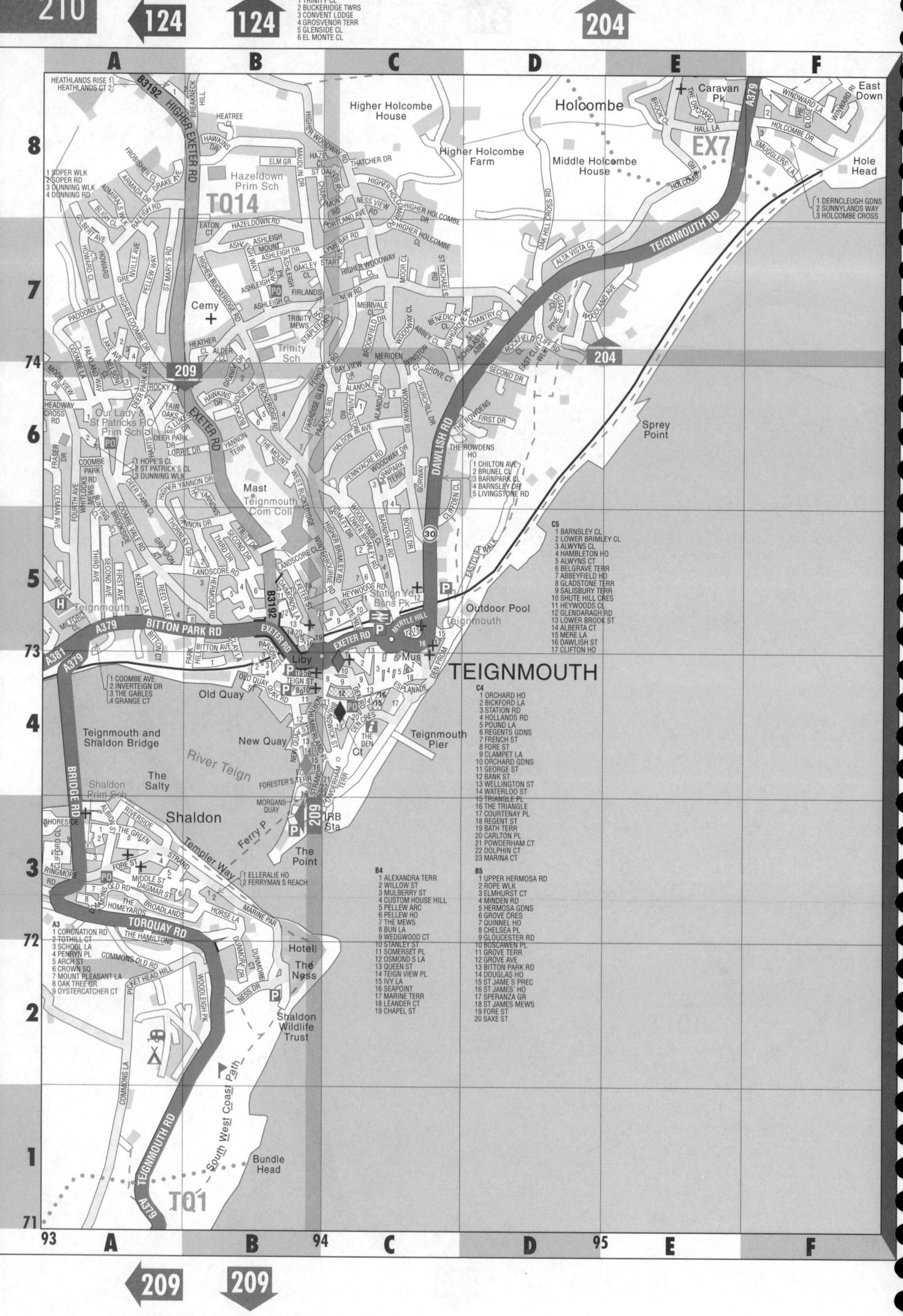

124
124
204
B6
1 TRINITY CL
2 BUCKERIDGE TWRS
3 CONVENT LODGE
4 GROSVENOR TERR
5 GLENSIDE CL
6 EL MONTE CL
7 EASTBROOK HO
A
B
C
D
E
F
Holcombe
Higher Holcombe House
Higher Holcombe Farm
Middle Holcombe House
Caravan Pk
East Down
Hole Head
EX7
TQ14
Hazeldown Prim Sch
Cemy
Trinity Sch
Mast
Teignmouth Com Coll
1 DERNCLEUGH GDNS
2 SUNNYLANDS WAY
3 HOLCOMBE CROSS
1 SOPER WLK
2 SOPER RD
3 DUNNING WLK
4 DUNNING RD
HEATHLANDS RISE 1
HEATHLANDS CT 2
1 HOPE'S CL
2 ST PATRICK'S CL
3 DUNNING WLK
Our Lady & St Patricks RC Prim Sch
1 CHILTON AVE
2 BRUNEL CL
3 BARNPARK CL
4 BARNSLEY DR
5 LIVINGSTONE RD
Sprey Point
C5
1 BARNSLEY CL
2 LOWER BRIMLEY CL
3 ALWYNS CL
4 HAMBLETON HO
5 ALWYNS CT
6 BELGRAVE TERR
7 ABBEYFIELD HO
8 GLADSTONE TERR
9 SALISBURY TERR
10 SHUTE HILL CRES
11 HEYWOODS CL
12 GLENDARAGH RD
13 LOWER BROOK ST
14 ALBERTA CT
15 MERE LA
16 DAWLISH ST
17 CLIFTON HO
Station Yd Bsns Pk
Outdoor Pool
Teignmouth
TEIGNMOUTH
1 COOMBE AVE
2 INVERTEIGN DR
3 THE GABLES
4 GRANGE CT
Old Quay
New Quay
Teignmouth and Shaldon Bridge
River Teign
The Salty
Shaldon Prim Sch
Shaldon
Teignmouth Pier
C4
1 ORCHARD HO
2 BICKFORD LA
3 STATION RD
4 HOLLANDS RD
5 POUND LA
6 REGENTS GDNS
7 FRENCH ST
8 FORE ST
9 CLAMPET LA
10 ORCHARD GDNS
11 GEORGE ST
12 BANK ST
13 WELLINGTON ST
14 WATERLOO ST
15 TRIANGLE PL
16 THE TRIANGLE
17 COURTENAY PL
18 REGENT ST
19 BATH TERR
20 CARLTON PL
21 POWDERHAM CT
22 DOLPHIN CT
23 MARINA CT
IRB Sta
The Point
Ferry P
Templer Way
1 ELLERALIE HO
2 FERRYMAN S REACH
B4
1 ALEXANDRA TERR
2 WILLOW ST
3 MULBERRY ST
4 CUSTOM HOUSE HILL
5 PELLEW ARC
6 PELLEW HO
7 THE MEWS
8 BUN LA
9 WEDGWOOD CT
10 STANLEY ST
11 SOMERSET PL
12 OSMOND S LA
13 QUEEN ST
14 TEIGN VIEW PL
15 IVY LA
16 SEAPOINT
17 MARINE TERR
18 LEANDER CT
19 CHAPEL ST
B5
1 UPPER HERMOSA RD
2 ROPE WLK
3 ELMHURST CT
4 MINDEN RD
5 HERMOSA GDNS
6 GROVE CRES
7 QUINNEL HO
8 CHELSEA PL
9 GLOUCESTER RD
10 BOSCAWEN PL
11 GROVE TERR
12 GROVE AVE
13 BITTON PARK RD
14 DOUGLAS HO
15 ST JAME S PREC
16 ST JAMES' HO
17 SPERANZA GR
18 ST JAMES MEWS
19 FORE ST
20 SAXE ST
A3
1 CORONATION RD
2 TOTHILL CT
3 SCHOOL LA
4 PENRYN PL
5 ARCH ST
6 CROWN SQ
7 MOUNT PLEASANT LA
8 OAK TREE GR
9 OYSTERCATCHER CT
Hotel
The Ness
Shaldon Wildlife Trust
South West Coast Path
Bundle Head
TQ1
TEIGNMOUTH RD
DAWLISH RD
BITTON PARK RD
BRIDGE RD
TORQUAY RD
HIGHER EXETER RD
EXETER RD
93
94
95
71
72
73
74
8
7
6
5
4
3
2
1
209
209

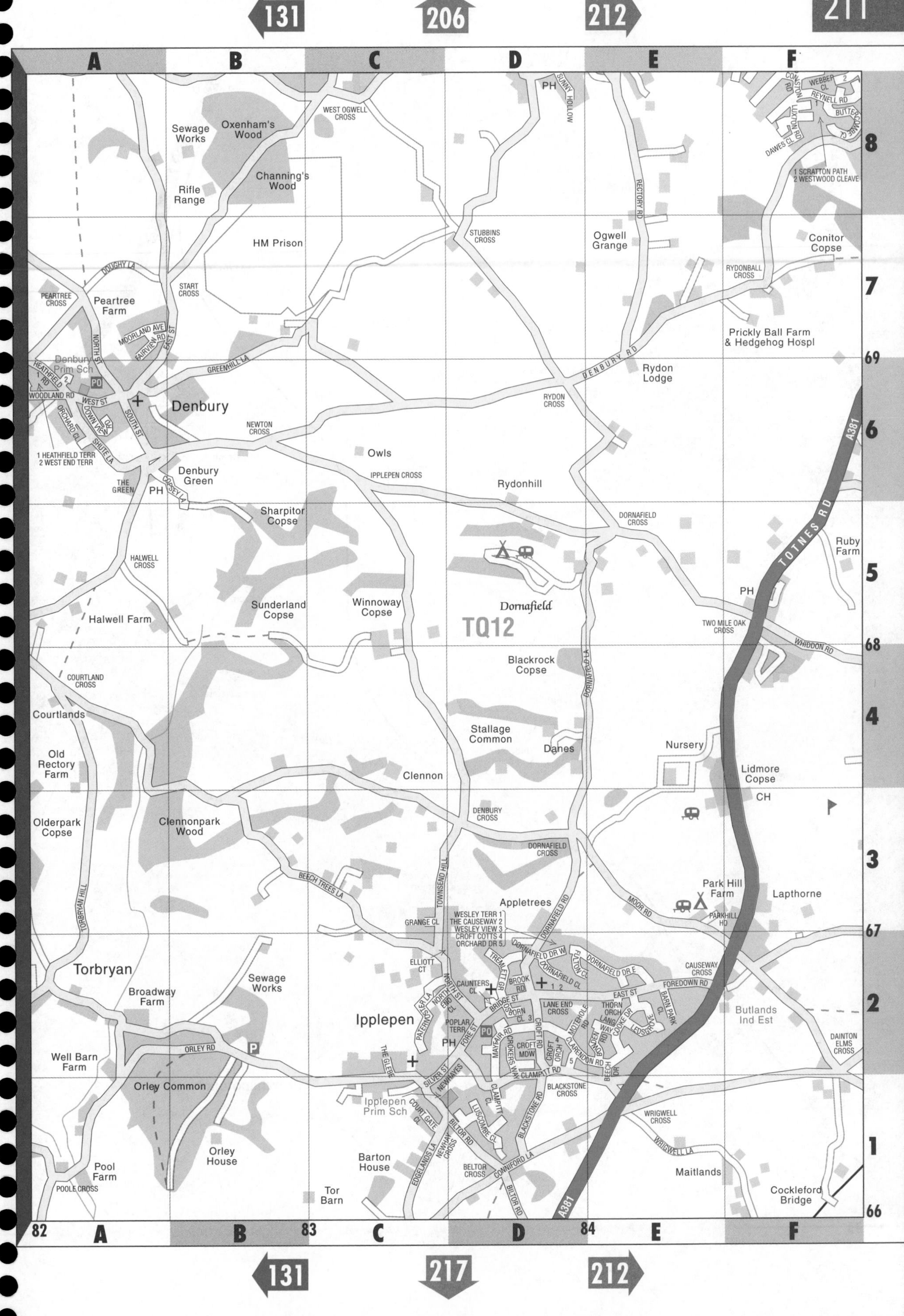
131
206
212
A
B
C
D
E
F
8
7
69
6
5
68
4
3
67
2
1
66
82
83
84
Sewage Works
Oxenham's Wood
Channing's Wood
Rifle Range
HM Prison
WEST OGWELL CROSS
PH
SUNNY HOLLOW
STUBBINS CROSS
Ogwell Grange
RECTORY RD
CONISTON RD
WEBBER CL
REYNELL RD
BUTTERCOMBE CL
LUXTON RD
DAWES CL
1 SCRATTON PATH
2 WESTWOOD CLEAVE
Conitor Copse
RYDONBALL CROSS
Prickly Ball Farm & Hedgehog Hospl
DOUGHY LA
START CROSS
PEARTREE CROSS
Peartree Farm
MOORLAND AVE
FAIRVIEW RD
EAST ST
NORTH ST
Denbury Prim Sch
HEATHFIELD RD
WOODLAND RD
PO
GREENHILL LA
Denbury
WEST ST
DOWN VIEW
ORCHARD CL
SOUTH ST
SHUTE LA
1 HEATHFIELD TERR
2 WEST END TERR
THE GREEN
Denbury Green
COPSEY LA
NEWTON CROSS
DENBURY RD
Rydon Lodge
RYDON CROSS
Owls
IPPLEPEN CROSS
Rydonhill
A381
Sharpitor Copse
DORNAFIELD CROSS
HALWELL CROSS
TOTNES RD
Ruby Farm
Dornafield
TQ12
Sunderland Copse
Winnoway Copse
Halwell Farm
TWO MILE OAK CROSS
WHIDDON RD
Blackrock Copse
COURTLAND CROSS
Courtlands
DORNAFIELD LA
Stallage Common
Danes
Nursery
Old Rectory Farm
Clennon
Lidmore Copse
CH
Olderpark Copse
Clennonpark Wood
DENBURY CROSS
DORNAFIELD CROSS
TOWNSEND HILL
BEECH TREES LA
Park Hill Farm
Lapthorne
Appletrees
MOOR RD
PARKHILL HO
DORNAFIELD RD
GRANGE CL
WESLEY TERR 1
THE CAUSEWAY 2
WESLEY VIEW 3
CROFT COTTS 4
ORCHARD DR 5
TORBRYAN HILL
Torbryan
ELLIOTT CT
DORNAFIELD DR W
FULTON CL
DORNAFIELD DR E
DORNAFIELD CL
TREMLETT GR
CAUSEWAY CROSS
FOREDOWN RD
Sewage Works
Broadway Farm
CAUNTERS CL
BROOK RD
EAST ST
NORTH END CL
BRIDGE ST
OSBORN CL
LANE END CROSS
THORN ORCH
BARN PARK
Butlands Ind Est
Ipplepen
PATERNOSTER LA
POPLAR TERR
FORE ST
MAYFAIR RD
CROFT RD
LANG WAY
COOKE DR
LEDSGROVE
MOTEHOLE RD
BOWDEN RD
CROFT ORCH
CLARENDON RD
CROKERS WAY
CROFT MDW
DAINTON ELMS CROSS
Well Barn Farm
ORLEY RD
P
THE GLEBE
CLAMPITT RD
BEECH DR
Orley Common
SILVER ST
NEWHAYES
BLACKSTONE CROSS
Ipplepen Prim Sch
COURT GATE CL
CLAMPITT CL
LUSCOMBE CL
BLACKSTONE RD
WRIGWELL CROSS
WRIGWELL LA
Pool Farm
Orley House
BILTOR RD
NEWHAYES CROSS
EDGELANDS LA
Barton House
BELTOR CROSS
CONNIFORD LA
Maitlands
Cockleford Bridge
POOLE CROSS
Tor Barn
BILTOR RD
131
217
212

211
207

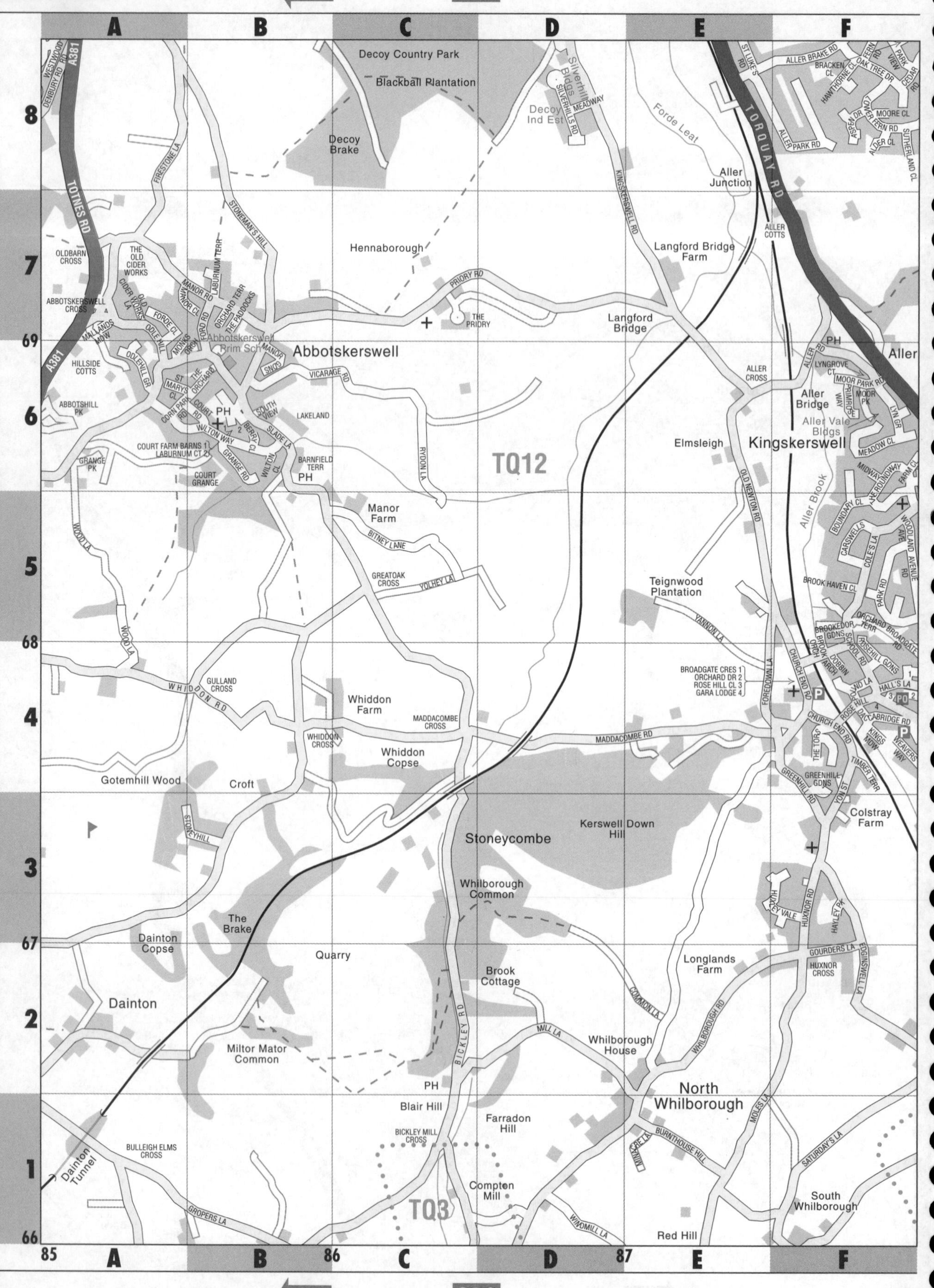
A B C D E F
8 7 6 5 4 3 2 1
69 68 67 66
85 86 87
Decoy Country Park
Blackball Plantation
Decoy Brake
Decoy Ind Est
Silverhill Bldgs
Forde Leat
Aller Junction
TORQUAY RD
TOTNES RD
A381
Hennaborough
Langford Bridge Farm
Langford Bridge
ALLER COTTS
OLDBARN CROSS
ABBOTSKERSWELL CROSS
HILLSIDE COTTS
ABBOTSHILL PK
Abbotskerswell
Abbotskerswell Prim Sch
PRIORY RD
THE PRIORY
VICARAGE RD
LAKELAND
RYDON LA
TQ12
ALLER CROSS
Aller Bridge
Aller Vale Bldgs
Aller
Elmsleigh
Kingskerswell
OLD NEWTON RD
Aller Brook
COURT FARM BARNS 1
LABURNUM CT 2
GRANGE PK
COURT GRANGE
BARNFIELD TERR
PH
Manor Farm
BITNEY LANE
GREATOAK CROSS
YOLHEY LA
Teignwood Plantation
VANNON LA
BROADGATE CRES 1
ORCHARD DR 2
ROSE HILL CL 3
GARA LODGE 4
WOOD LA
GULLAND CROSS
WHIDDON RD
Whiddon Farm
MADDACOMBE CROSS
WHIDDON CROSS
Whiddon Copse
MADDACOMBE RD
Gotemhill Wood
Croft
STONEYHILL
Stoneycombe
Kerswell Down Hill
Colstray Farm
Whilborough Common
The Brake
Dainton Copse
Quarry
Brook Cottage
Longlands Farm
GOURDERS LA
HUXNOR CROSS
Dainton
Miltor Mator Common
BICKLEY RD
MILL LA
COMMON LA
Whilborough House
WHILBOROUGH RD
North Whilborough
PH
Blair Hill
Farradon Hill
BICKLEY MILL CROSS
BURNTHOUSE HILL
MOLES LA
SATURDAY'S LA
Dainton Tunnel
BULLEIGH ELMS CROSS
GROPERS LA
Compton Mill
TQ3
WINDMILL LA
Red Hill
South Whilborough

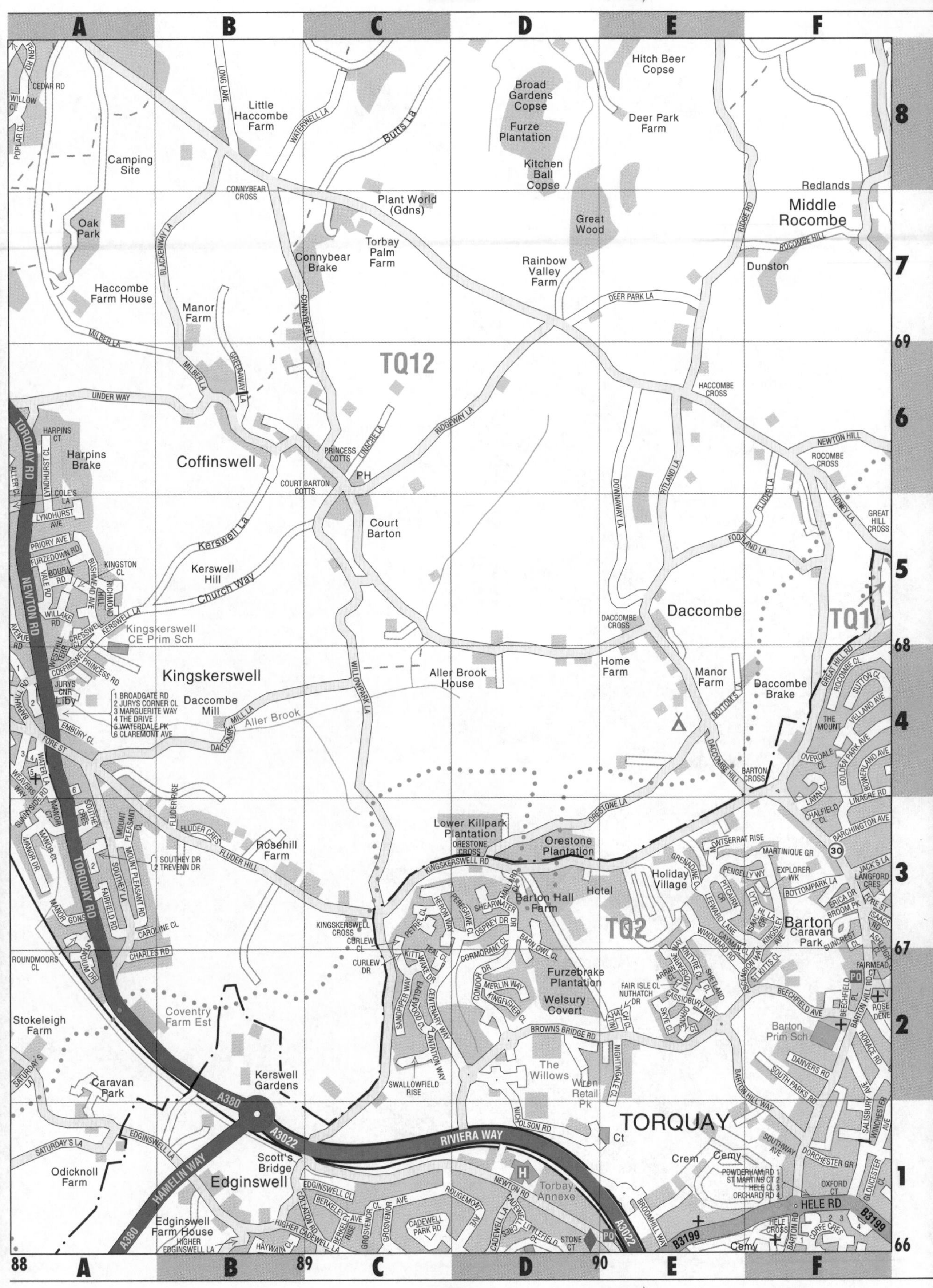
Hitch Beer Copse
Broad Gardens Copse
Furze Plantation
Little Haccombe Farm
Deer Park Farm
Kitchen Ball Copse
Camping Site
Plant World (Gdns)
Oak Park
Redlands
Middle Rocombe
Great Wood
Torbay Palm Farm
Connybear Brake
Rainbow Valley Farm
Dunston
Haccombe Farm House
Manor Farm
TQ12
Harpins Brake
Coffinswell
PH
Court Barton
Kerswell Hill
Daccombe
TQ1
Kingskerswell CE Prim Sch
Kingskerswell
Daccombe Mill
Aller Brook House
Home Farm
Manor Farm
Daccombe Brake
Aller Brook
Lower Killpark Plantation
Orestone Plantation
Rosehill Farm
Holiday Village
Barton Hall Farm
Hotel
TQ2
Barton Caravan Park
Furzebrake Plantation
Welsury Covert
Coventry Farm Est
Stokeleigh Farm
Barton Prim Sch
Kerswell Gardens
Caravan Park
The Willows
Wren Retail Pk
TORQUAY
Odicknoll Farm
Scott's Bridge
Edginswell
Crem
Cemy
Torbay Annexe
Edginswell Farm House
RIVIERA WAY
HAMELIN WAY
TORQUAY RD
NEWTON RD
A380
A3022
B3199
HELE RD
1 BROADGATE RD
2 JURYS CORNER CL
3 MARGUERITE WAY
4 THE DRIVE
5 WATERDALE PK
6 CLAREMONT AVE
1 SOUTHEY DR
2 TREVENN DR
1 POWDERHAM RD
2 ST MARTINS CT
3 HELE CL
4 ORCHARD RD

213
209
Lower Gabwell
TQ12
Higher Gabwell
Hafod Farm
Herring Cove
Mackerel Cove
Higher Rocombe Barton
Ross Hill
Blackaller's Cove
Maidencombe
Maidencombe Beach
TQ1
South West Coast Path
Babbacombe Bay
Great Hill
Rock House
Valley of Rocks
Whitsand Beach
Watcombe Head
Watcombe Beach
TQ2
Watcombe Prim Sch
Mayfield Specl Sch
Combe Pafford Sch
Smugglers' Hole
Watcombe
Playing Field
TORQUAY
Shag Cliff
Roundhouse Point
Petit Tor Beach
Combe Pafford Playing Field
Ind Est
Petit Tor
St Marychurch
St Marychurch CE Prim Sch
Petit Tor Point
St Cuthbert Mayne Sch
TEIGNMOUTH RD
ST MARYCHURCH RD
A379
B3199
1 STABLE LA
2 HILLY GARDENS RD
3 PETIT WELL LA
4 ST MARY'S CT
5 CHARLOTTE CT
6 THE PADDOCK
7 PETITOR MEWS
8 CAMPION CT
9 CHURCH RD
1 STADDON GDNS
2 CORNFIELD GN
91
92
93
66
67
68
69
220

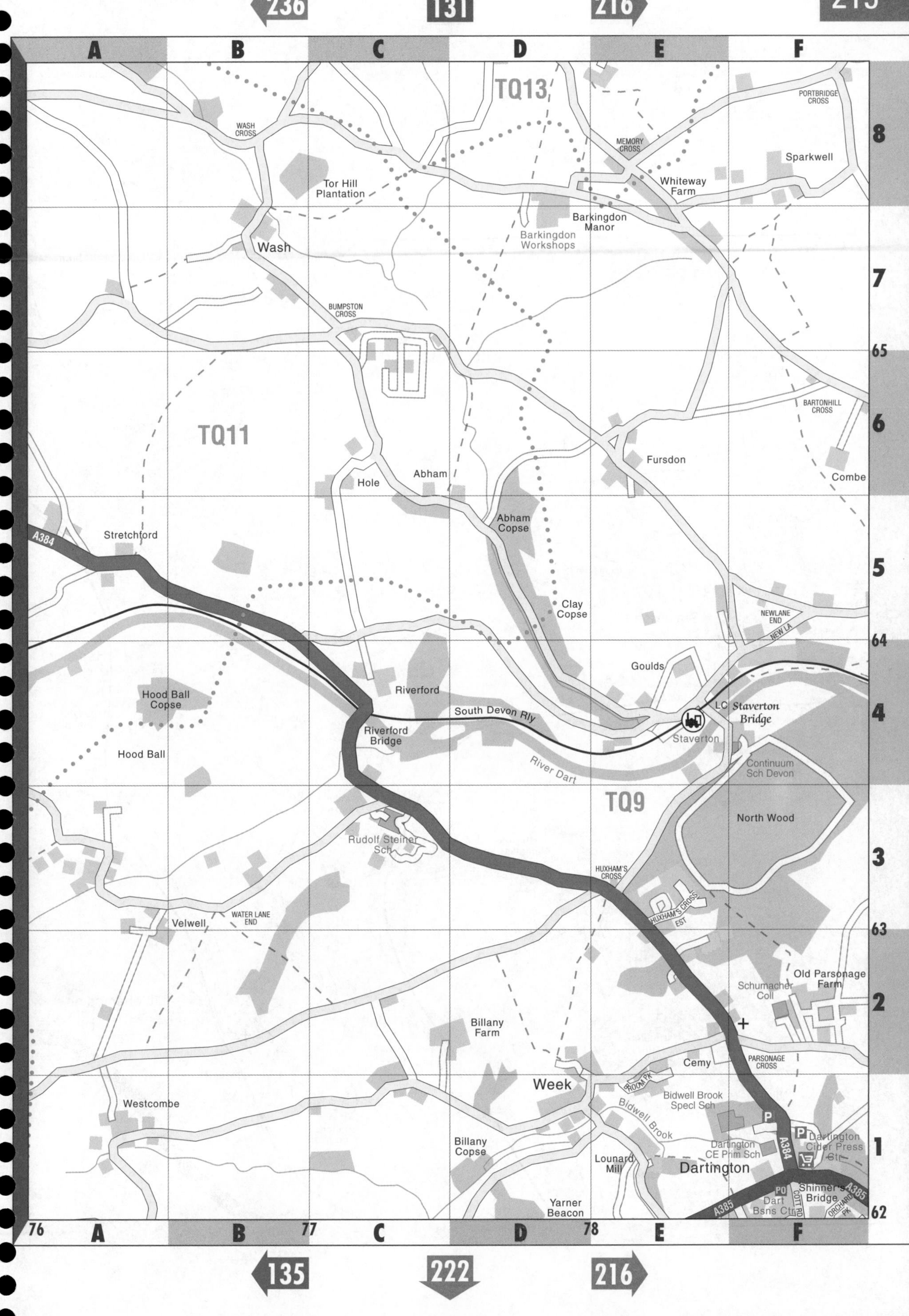
236
131
216
A
B
C
D
E
F
TQ13
WASH CROSS
MEMORY CROSS
PORTBRIDGE CROSS
Sparkwell
8
Tor Hill Plantation
Whiteway Farm
Barkingdon Manor
Barkingdon Workshops
Wash
7
BUMPSTON CROSS
65
BARTONHILL CROSS
TQ11
6
Fursdon
Hole
Abham
Combe
Abham Copse
A384
Stretchford
5
Clay Copse
NEWLANE END
NEW LA
64
Goulds
Riverford
Hood Ball Copse
LC
Staverton Bridge
South Devon Rly
4
Riverford Bridge
Staverton
Hood Ball
Continuum Sch Devon
River Dart
TQ9
North Wood
Rudolf Steiner Sch
3
HUXHAM'S CROSS
HUXHAM'S CROSS EST
Velwell
WATER LANE END
63
Old Parsonage Farm
Schumacher Coll
2
Billany Farm
PARSONAGE CROSS
Cemy
Week
BROOM PK
Bidwell Brook Specl Sch
Westcombe
Bidwell Brook
P
P
Billany Copse
Dartington CE Prim Sch
Dartington Cider Press Ctr
1
Lounard Mill
Dartington
Shinner's Bridge
Dart Bsns Ctr
A385
PO
COTT RD
ORCHARD PK
Yarner Beacon
62
76
77
78
135
222
216

215
131

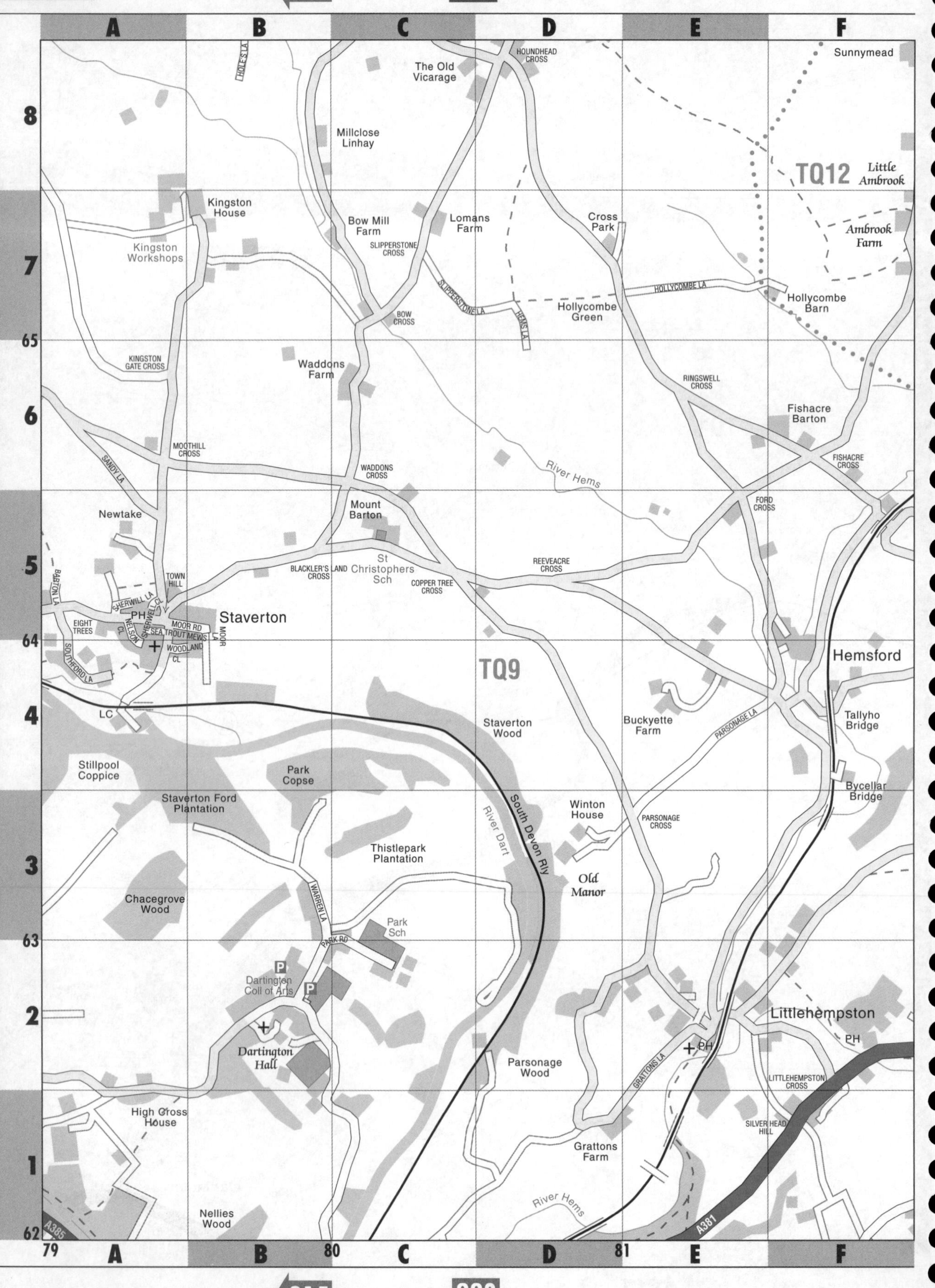

215
223

211
218

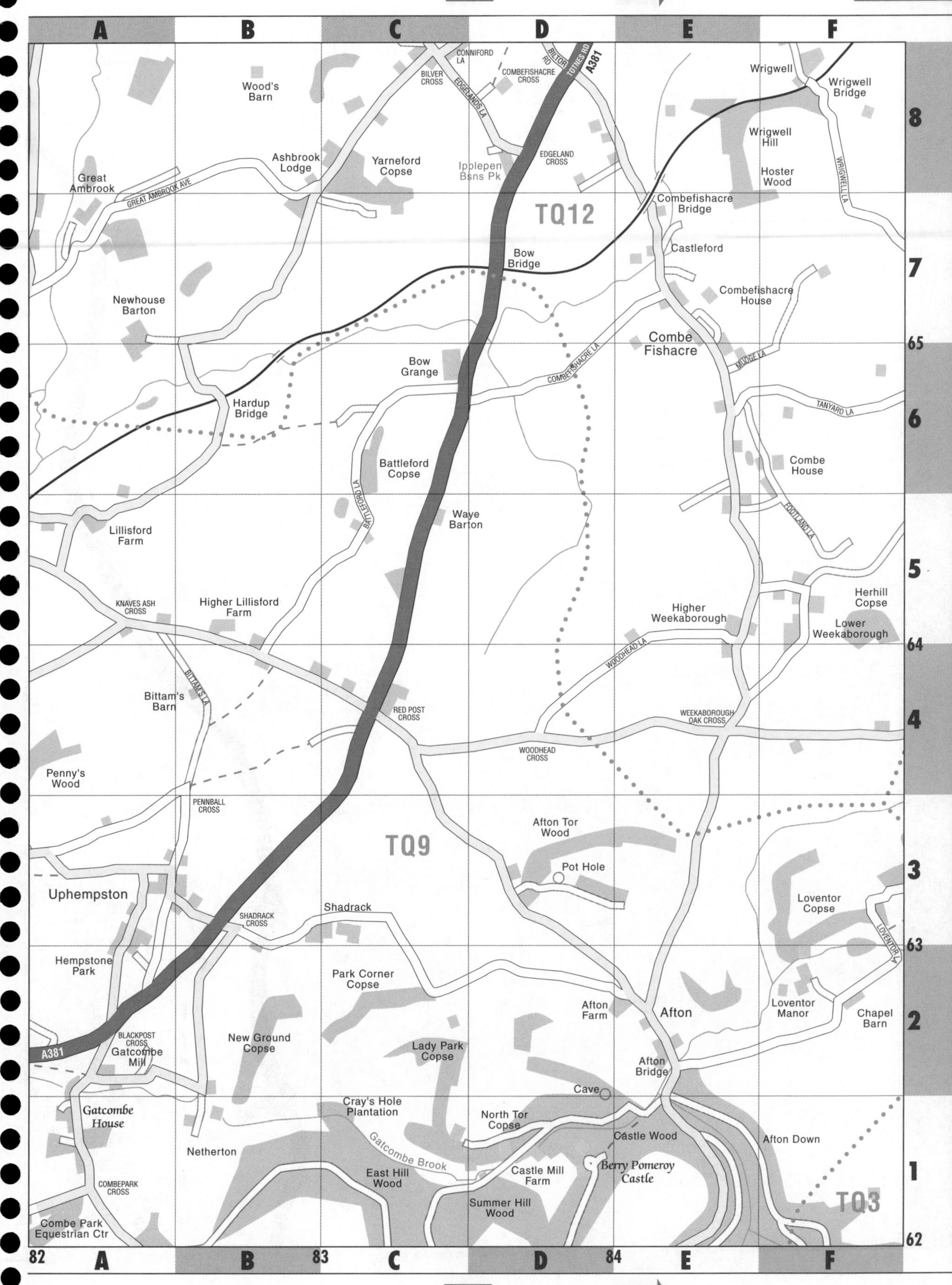

224
218

217 212

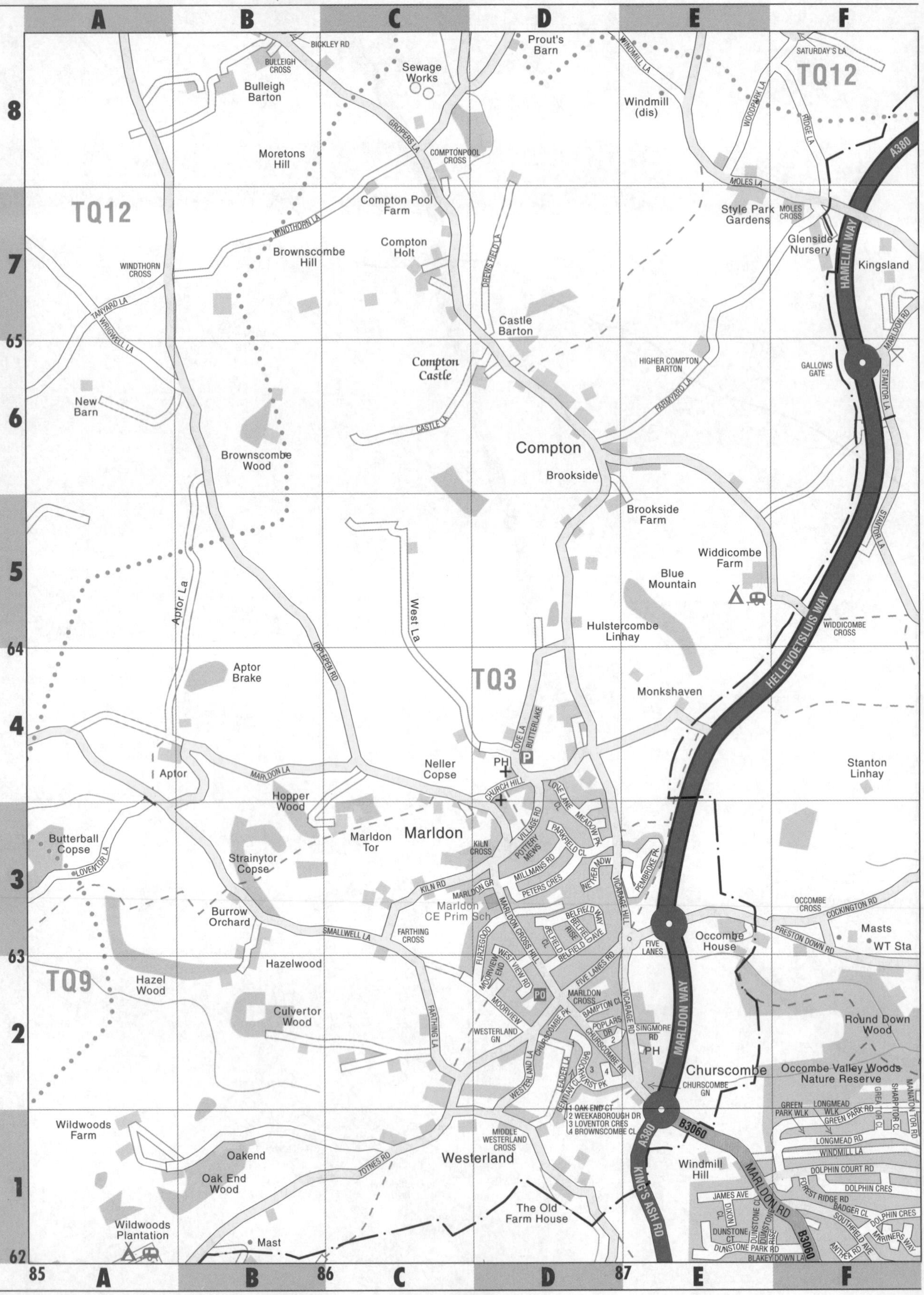

217 225

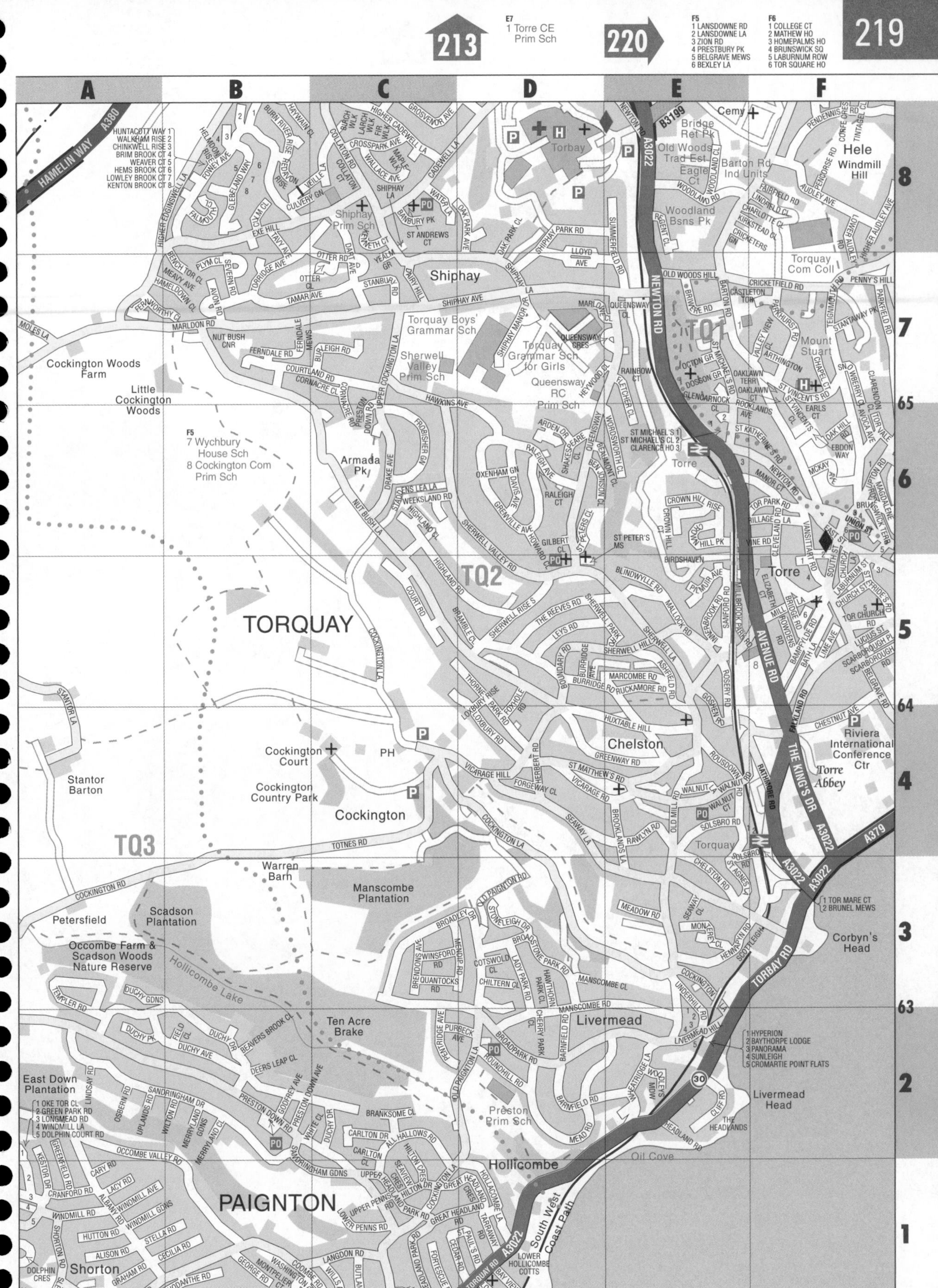
A
B
C
D
E
F
8
7
65
6
5
64
4
3
63
2
1
62
88
89
90
HUNTACOTT WAY 1
WALKHAM RISE 2
CHINKWELL RISE 3
BRIM BROOK CT 4
WEAVER CT 5
HEMS BROOK CT 6
LOWLEY BROOK CT 7
KENTON BROOK CT 8
HAMELIN WAY
A380
Torbay
Shiphay
Shiphay Prim Sch
Bridge Ret Pk
Old Woods Trad Est
Eagle Ct
Barton Rd Ind Units
Woodland Bsns Pk
Cemy
Hele
Windmill Hill
Torquay Com Coll
TQ1
Mount Stuart
Torquay Boys' Grammar Sch
Torquay Grammar Sch for Girls
Sherwell Valley Prim Sch
Queensway RC Prim Sch
Cockington Woods Farm
Little Cockington Woods
F5
7 Wychbury House Sch
8 Cockington Com Prim Sch
Armada Pk
ST MICHAEL'S 1
ST MICHAEL'S CL 2
CLARENCE HO 3
Torre
TQ2
TORQUAY
Chelston
Riviera International Conference Ctr
Torre Abbey
Cockington Court
PH
Cockington Country Park
Cockington
Stanton Barton
TQ3
Torquay
Warren Barn
Manscombe Plantation
Petersfield
Scadson Plantation
Occombe Farm & Scadson Woods Nature Reserve
Hollicombe Lake
1 TOR MARE CT
2 BRUNEL MEWS
Corbyn's Head
Ten Acre Brake
Livermead
1 HYPERION
2 BAYTHORPE LODGE
3 PANORAMA
4 SUNLEIGH
5 CROMARTIE POINT FLATS
Livermead Head
East Down Plantation
1 OKE TOR CL
2 GREEN PARK RD
3 LONGMEAD RD
4 WINDMILL LA
5 DOLPHIN COURT RD
Preston Prim Sch
Oil Cove
Hollicombe
PAIGNTON
Shorton
South West Coast Path
LOWER HOLLICOMBE COTTS
NEWTON RD
AVENUE RD
THE KING'S DR
TORBAY RD
A3022
B3199
A379
SHIPHAY AVE
MARLDON RD
TOTNES RD
COCKINGTON RD
COCKINGTON LA
OLD PAIGNTON RD
PRESTON DOWN RD
OCCOMBE VALLEY RD
SHORTON VALLEY RD

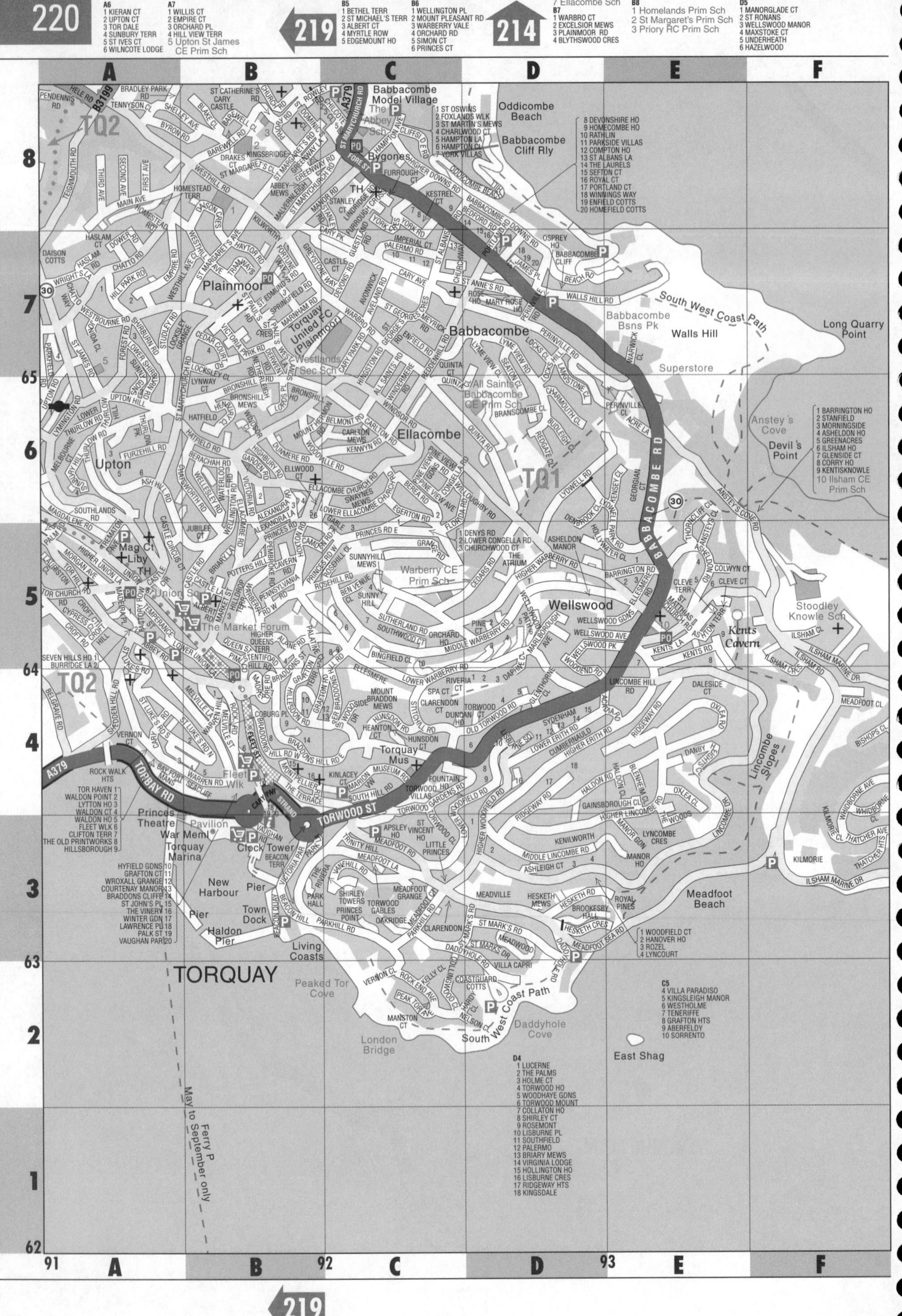

A6
1 KIERAN CT
2 UPTON CT
3 TOR DALE
4 SUNBURY TERR
5 ST IVES CT
6 WILNCOTE LODGE
A7
1 WILLIS CT
2 EMPIRE CT
3 ORCHARD PL
4 HILL VIEW TERR
5 Upton St James CE Prim Sch
219
B5
1 BETHEL TERR
2 ST MICHAEL'S TERR
3 ALBERT CT
4 MYRTLE ROW
5 EDGEMOUNT HO
B6
1 WELLINGTON PL
2 MOUNT PLEASANT RD
3 WARBERRY VALE
4 ORCHARD RD
5 SIMON CT
6 PRINCES CT
214
7 Ellacombe Sch
B7
1 WARBRO CT
2 EXCELSIOR MEWS
3 PLAINMOOR RD
4 BLYTHSWOOD CRES
B8
1 Homelands Prim Sch
2 St Margaret's Prim Sch
3 Priory RC Prim Sch
D5
1 MANORGLADE CT
2 ST RONANS
3 WELLSWOOD MANOR
4 MAXSTOKE CT
5 UNDERHEATH
6 HAZELWOOD
A B C D E F
8 7 65 6 5 64 4 3 63 2 1 62
91 92 93
TQ2
TQ1
Babbacombe Model Village
Oddicombe Beach
Babbacombe Cliff Rly
1 ST OSWINS
2 FOXLANDS WLK
3 ST MARTIN'S MEWS
4 CHARLWOOD CT
5 HAMPTON LA
6 HAMPTON CL
7 YORK VILLAS
8 DEVONSHIRE HO
9 HOMECOMBE HO
10 RATHLIN
11 PARKSIDE VILLAS
12 COMPTON HO
13 ST ALBANS LA
14 THE LAURELS
15 SEFTON CT
16 ROYAL CT
17 PORTLAND CT
18 WINNINGS WAY
19 ENFIELD COTTS
20 HOMEFIELD COTTS
Bygones
Plainmoor
Torquay United FC (Plainmoor)
Westlands Sec Sch
Babbacombe
Babbacombe Bsns Pk
South West Coast Path
Walls Hill
Long Quarry Point
Superstore
All Saints Babbacombe CE Prim Sch
Ellacombe
Upton
Anstey's Cove
Devil's Point
1 BARRINGTON HO
2 STANFIELD
3 MORNINGSIDE
4 ASHELDON HO
5 GREENACRES
6 ILSHAM HO
7 GLENSIDE CT
8 CORRY HO
9 KENTISKNOWLE
10 Ilsham CE Prim Sch
BABBACOMBE RD
1 DENYS RD
2 LOWER CONGELLA RD
3 CHURCHWOOD CT
Warberry CE Prim Sch
Wellswood
Stoodley Knowle Sch
Kents Cavern
Mag Ct
Liby
TH
Union Sq
The Market Forum
Torquay Mus
Lincombe Slopes
TORBAY RD
TORWOOD ST
TOR HAVEN 1
WALDON POINT 2
LYTTON HO 3
WALDON CT 4
WALDON HO 5
FLEET WLK 6
CLIFTON TERR 7
THE OLD PRINTWORKS 8
HILLSBOROUGH 9
Princes Theatre
Pavilion
War Meml
Torquay Marina
Clock Tower
HYFIELD GDNS 10
GRAFTON CT 11
WROXALL GRANGE 12
COURTENAY MANOR 13
BRADDONS CLIFFE 14
ST JOHN'S PL 15
THE VINERY 16
WINTER GDN 17
LAWRENCE PL 18
PALK ST 19
VAUGHAN PAR 20
New Harbour
Pier
Town Dock
Haldon Pier
Living Coasts
Meadfoot Beach
1 WOODFIELD CT
2 HANOVER HO
3 ROZEL
4 LYNCOURT
TORQUAY
Peaked Tor Cove
C5
4 VILLA PARADISO
5 KINGSLEIGH MANOR
6 WESTHOLME
7 TENERIFFE
8 GRAFTON HTS
9 ABERFELDY
10 SORRENTO
South West Coast Path
Daddyhole Cove
London Bridge
East Shag
D4
1 LUCERNE
2 THE PALMS
3 HOLME CT
4 TORWOOD HO
5 WOODHAYE GDNS
6 TORWOOD MOUNT
7 COLLATON HO
8 SHIRLEY CT
9 ROSEMOUNT
10 LISBURNE PL
11 SOUTHFIELD
12 PALERMO
13 BRIARY MEWS
14 VIRGINIA LODGE
15 HOLLINGTON HO
16 LISBURNE CRES
17 RIDGEWAY HTS
18 KINGSDALE
Ferry P
May to September only
219

A
B
C
D
E
F
8
7
65
6
5
64
4
3
63
2
1
62
94
95
96
Bishop's Wlk
Black Head
Brandy Cove
RICHMOND CL
BISHOPS CL
BISHOPS RISE
Hope Cove
TQ1
WHIDBORNE AVE
ILSHAM MARINE DR
Hope's Nose
THATCHER AVE
THATCHER AVE
MARINE MOUNT
Lead Stone or Flat Rock
Thatcher House
COMPASS SOUTH
South West Coast Path
Thatcher Point
Ore Stone
Thatcher Rock

135
215

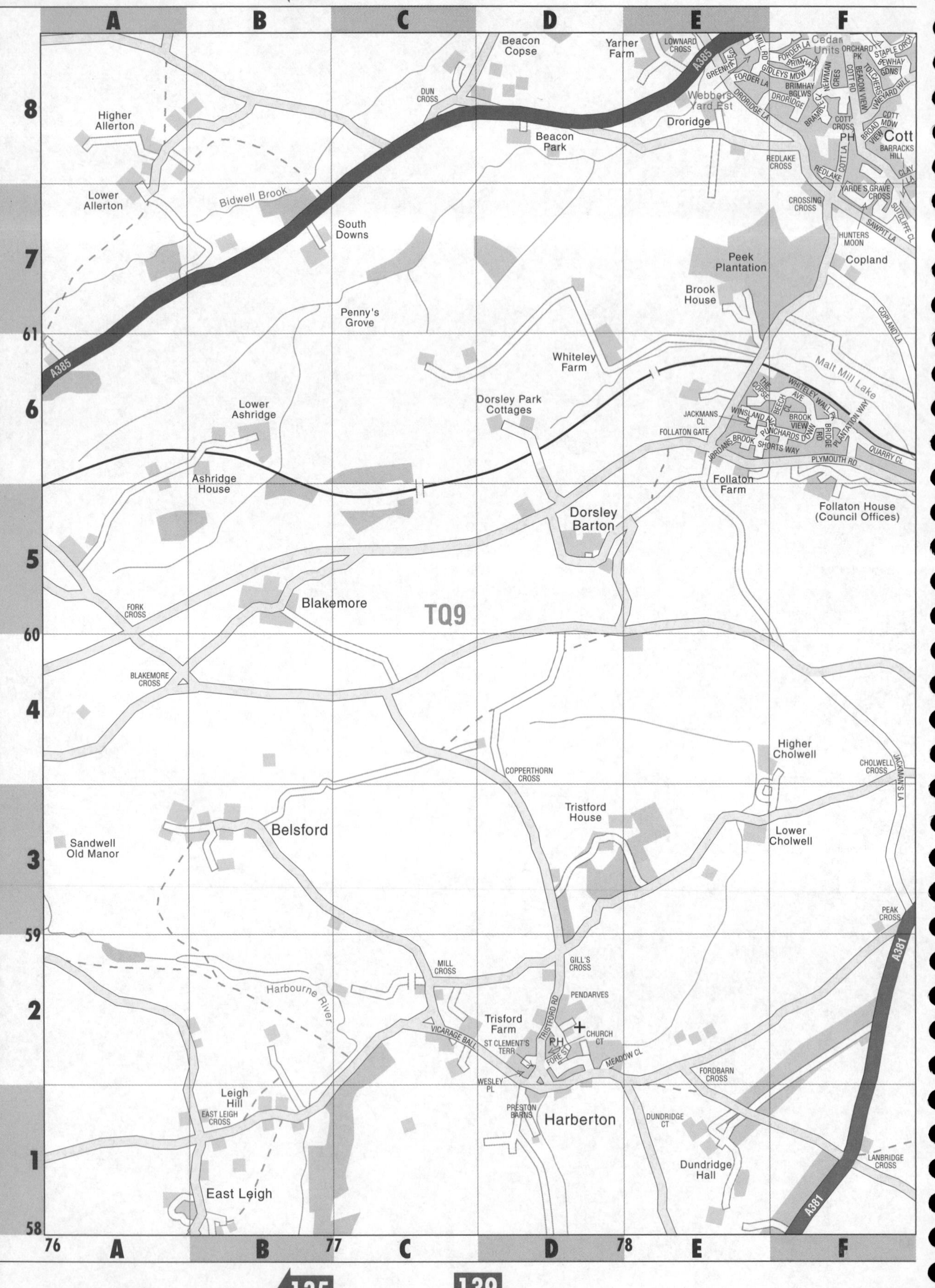

135
139

216
224

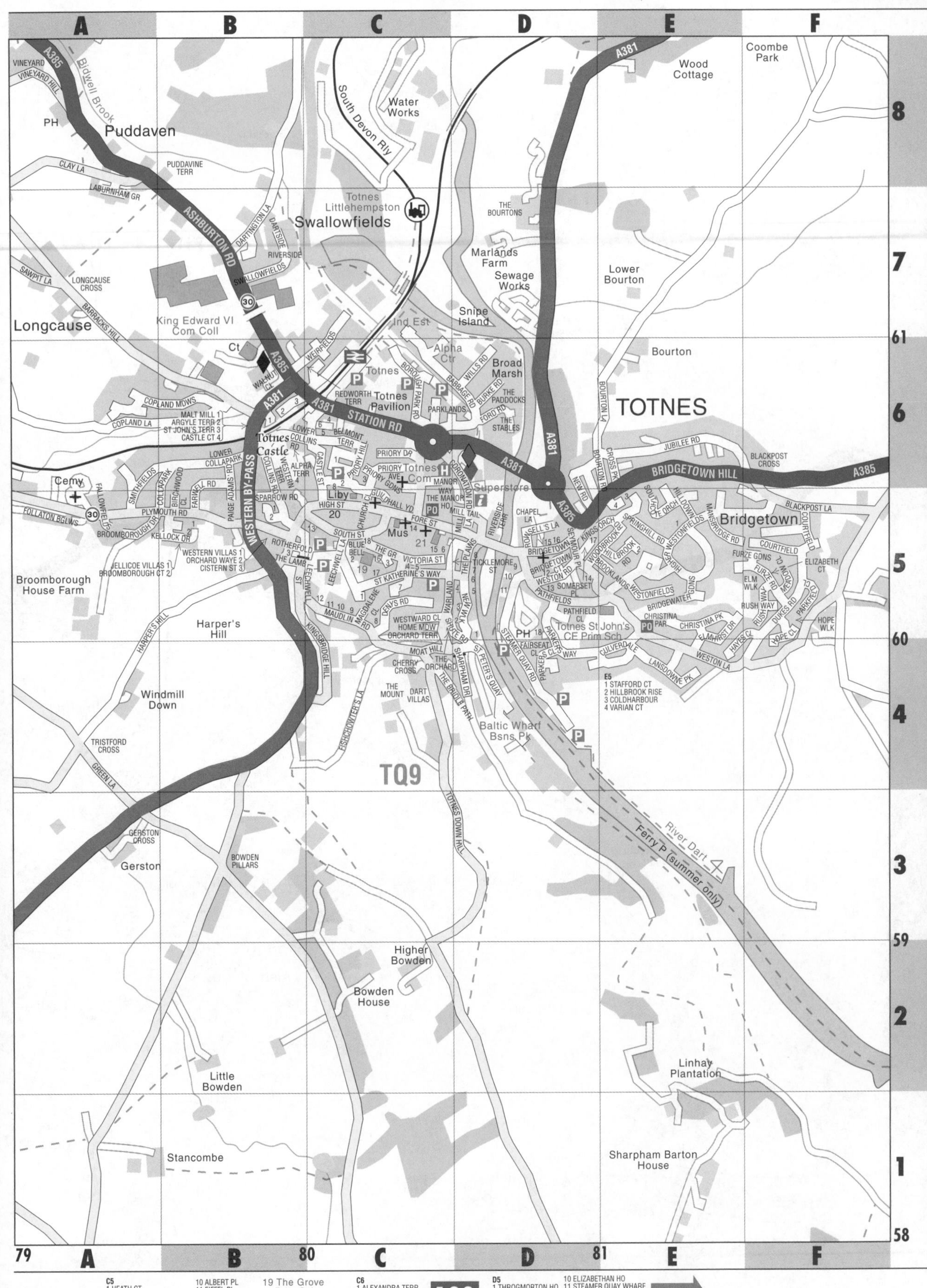

A B 80 C D 81 E F

C5
1 HEATH CT
2 MOUNT VIEW TERR
3 GROVE CL
4 VICTORIA CT
5 ST KATHERINE S MEWS
6 BANK LA
7 THE CARRIONS
8 SUNNYMEAD TERR
9 SHAFTSBURY PL
10 ALBERT PL
11 EIFFEL PL
12 GARFIELD PL
13 GILLS NURSERY
14 ATHERTON LA
15 TIMES MEWS
16 GROVE MEWS
17 MOORASHES
18 BLUEBALL HL
19 The Grove Prim Sch
20 Totnes Costume Mus
21 King Edward VI Com Coll

C6
1 ALEXANDRA TERR
2 NORTH ST
3 PRIORY CT
4 QUEEN'S TERR
5 ANTRIM TERR
6 GLENARM TERR
7 PRIORY TERR
8 NORTH CASTLE MEWS

139

D5
1 THROGMORTON HO
2 TAUNTON CT
3 REEVES CL
4 WINDEATT SQ
5 THE MALTHOUSE
6 APPLE WHARF
7 THE CHAPEL
8 WATERSIDE HO
9 SEYMOUR CT
10 ELIZABETHAN HO
11 STEAMER QUAY WHARF
12 TOLLIT GDN
13 BROAD OAK CRES
14 BARING COTTS
15 DEVON PL
16 DEVON TERR
17 SOMERSET CT
18 MEADOW BROOK

224

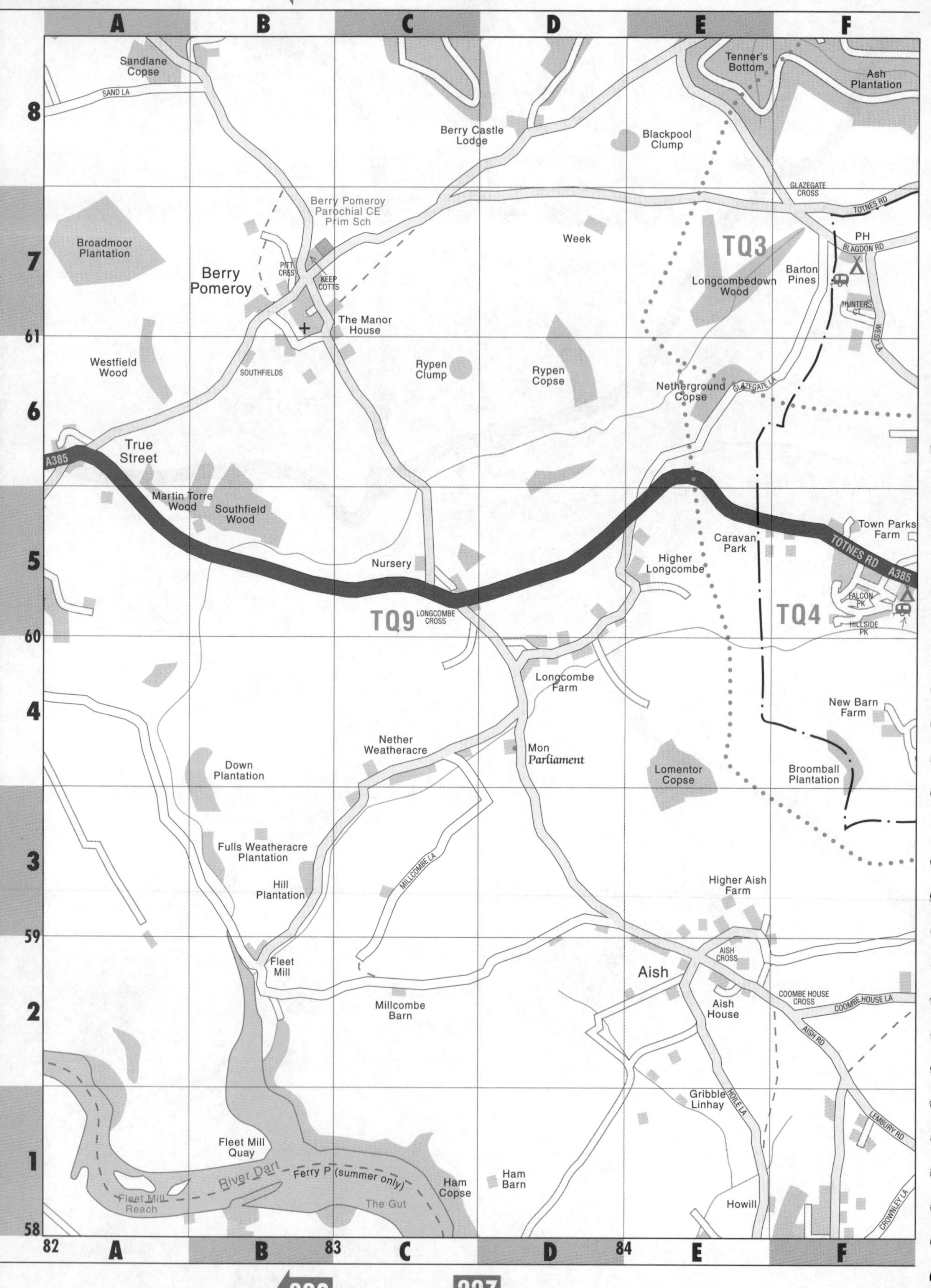
A B C D E F
8 7 61 6 5 60 4 3 59 2 1 58
82 83 84
Sandlane Copse
SAND LA
Tenner's Bottom
Ash Plantation
Berry Castle Lodge
Blackpool Clump
GLAZEGATE CROSS
TOTNES RD
Berry Pomeroy Parochial CE Prim Sch
Broadmoor Plantation
Week
PH
BLAGDON RD
TQ3
Berry Pomeroy
PITT CRES
KEEP COTTS
Longcombedown Wood
Barton Pines
HUNTERS CT
WEST LA
The Manor House
Westfield Wood
SOUTHFIELDS
Rypen Clump
Rypen Copse
Netherground Copse
GLAZEGATE LA
True Street
A385
Martin Torre Wood
Southfield Wood
Caravan Park
Town Parks Farm
Nursery
Higher Longcombe
TOTNES RD
A385
FALCON PK
TQ9
LONGCOMBE CROSS
TQ4
HILLSIDE PK
Longcombe Farm
New Barn Farm
Nether Weatheracre
Mon
Parliament
Down Plantation
Lomentor Copse
Broomball Plantation
Fulls Weatheracre Plantation
Hill Plantation
MILLCOMBE LA
Higher Aish Farm
Fleet Mill
AISH CROSS
Aish
COOMBE HOUSE CROSS
COOMBE HOUSE LA
Millcombe Barn
Aish House
AISH RD
Gribble Linhay
HOILE LA
LEMBURY RD
Fleet Mill Quay
River Dart
Ferry P (summer only)
Ham Copse
Ham Barn
Fleet Mill Reach
The Gut
Howill
CROWNLEY LA

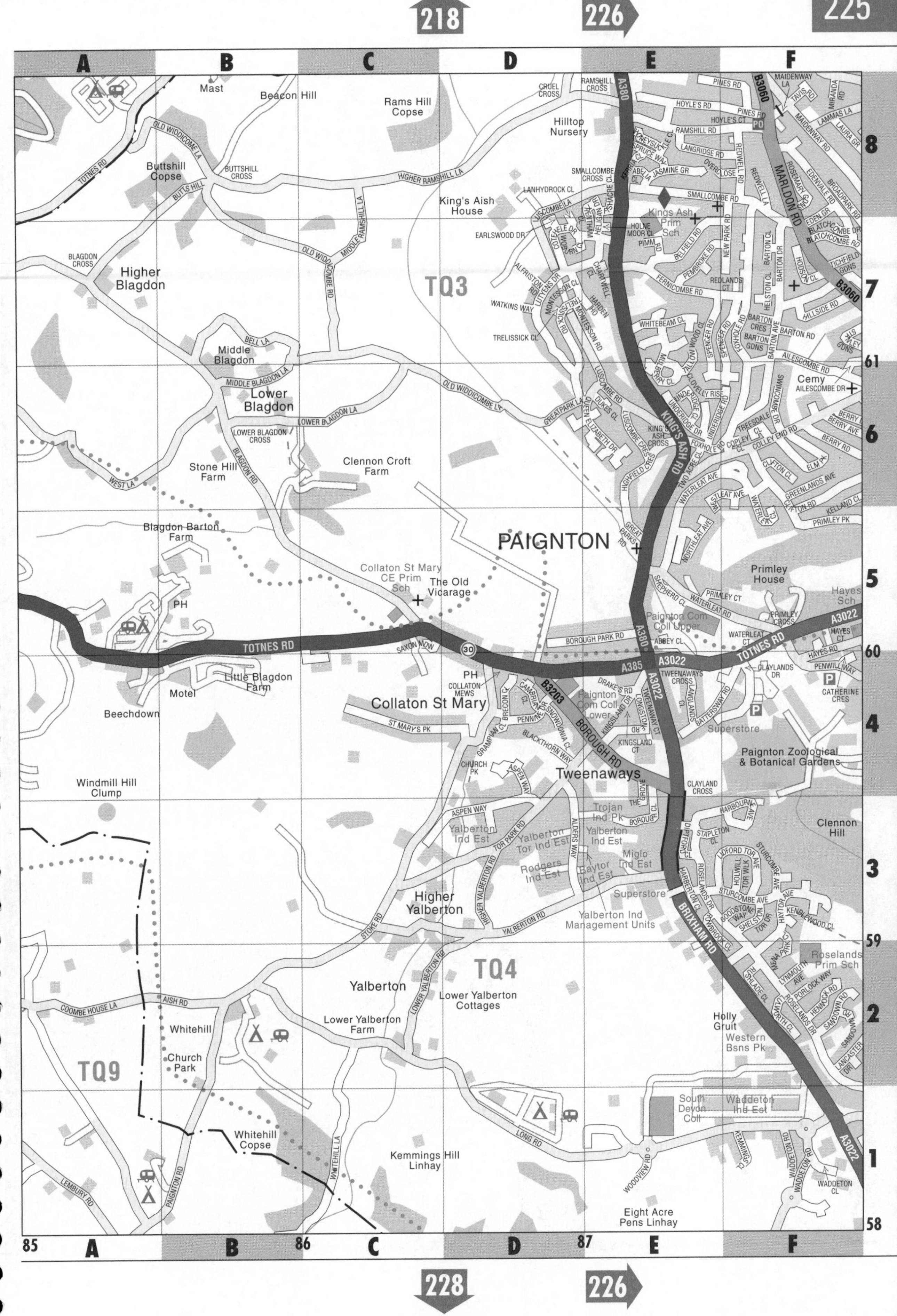
218
226
PAIGNTON
TQ3
TQ4
TQ9
Beacon Hill
Rams Hill Copse
Hilltop Nursery
Buttshill Copse
King's Aish House
Higher Blagdon
Middle Blagdon
Lower Blagdon
Stone Hill Farm
Clennon Croft Farm
Blagdon Barton Farm
Collaton St Mary CE Prim Sch
The Old Vicarage
Collaton St Mary
Little Blagdon Farm
Motel
Beechdown
Windmill Hill Clump
Tweenaways
Primley House
Paignton Com Coll Upper
Paignton Com Coll Lower
Paignton Zoological & Botanical Gardens
Superstore
Clennon Hill
Yalberton Ind Est
Yalberton Tor Ind Est
Rodgers Ind Est
Baytor Ind Est
Miglo Ind Est
Trojan Ind Pk
Yalberton Ind Management Units
Higher Yalberton
Yalberton
Lower Yalberton Cottages
Lower Yalberton Farm
Whitehill
Church Park
Whitehill Copse
Kemmings Hill Linhay
Holly Gruit
Western Bsns Pk
South Devon Coll
Waddeton Ind Est
Eight Acre Pens Linhay
Roselands Prim Sch
Kings Ash Prim Sch
Hayes Sch
Cemy
TOTNES RD
KING'S ASH RD
BRIXHAM RD
MARLDON RD
BOROUGH RD
OLD WIDDICOMBE LA
HIGHER RAMSHILL LA
LOWER BLAGDON LA
BLAGDON RD
COOMBE HOUSE LA
LONG RD
YALBERTON RD
STOKE RD
A380
A385
A3022
B3203
B3060
58
59
60
61
1
2
3
4
5
6
7
8
85
86
87
A
B
C
D
E
F
228
226

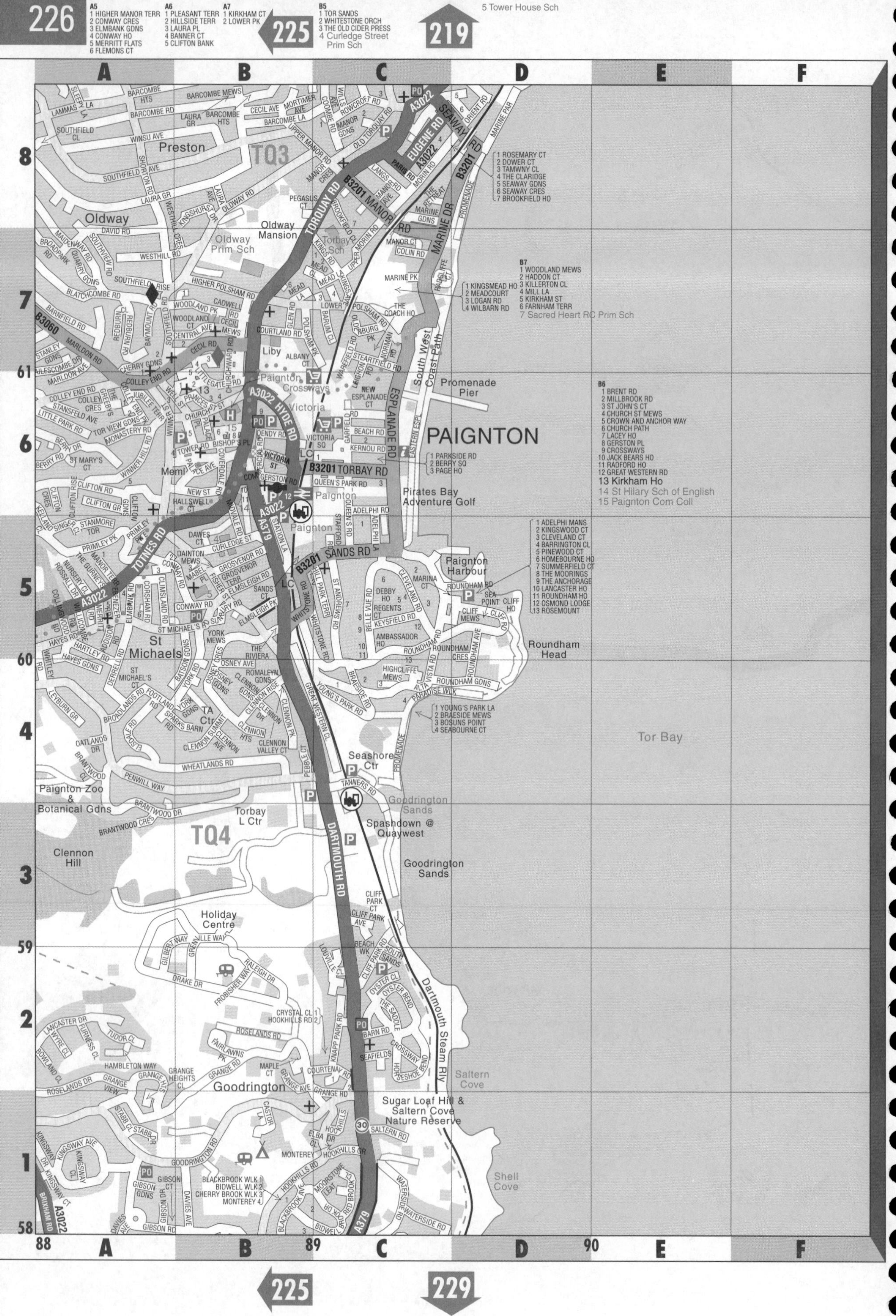
A5
1 HIGHER MANOR TERR
2 CONWAY CRES
3 ELMBANK GDNS
4 CONWAY HO
5 MERRITT FLATS
6 FLEMONS CT
A6
1 PLEASANT TERR
2 HILLSIDE TERR
3 LAURA PL
4 BANNER CT
5 CLIFTON BANK
A7
1 KIRKHAM CT
2 LOWER PK
225
B5
1 TOR SANDS
2 WHITESTONE ORCH
3 THE OLD CIDER PRESS
4 Curledge Street Prim Sch
219
5 Tower House Sch
A B C D E F
Preston
TQ3
Oldway
Oldway Mansion
Oldway Prim Sch
Torbay Sch
1 ROSEMARY CT
2 DOWER CT
3 TAMWNY CL
4 THE CLARIDGE
5 SEAWAY GDNS
6 SEAWAY CRES
7 BROOKFIELD HO
B7
1 WOODLAND MEWS
2 HADDON CT
3 KILLERTON CL
4 MILL LA
5 KIRKHAM ST
6 FARNHAM TERR
7 Sacred Heart RC Prim Sch
1 KINGSMEAD HO
2 MEADCOURT
3 LOGAN RD
4 WILBARN RD
Liby
Paignton Crossways
Victoria
Promenade Pier
South West Coast Path
PAIGNTON
B6
1 BRENT RD
2 MILLBROOK RD
3 ST JOHN'S CT
4 CHURCH ST MEWS
5 CROWN AND ANCHOR WAY
6 CHURCH PATH
7 LACEY HO
8 GERSTON PL
9 CROSSWAYS
10 JACK BEARS HO
11 RADFORD HO
12 GREAT WESTERN RD
13 Kirkham Ho
14 St Hilary Sch of English
15 Paignton Com Coll
1 PARKSIDE RD
2 BERRY SQ
3 PAGE HO
Pirates Bay Adventure Golf
Paignton
1 ADELPHI MANS
2 KINGSWOOD CT
3 CLEVELAND CT
4 BARRINGTON CL
5 PINEWOOD CT
6 HOMEBOURNE HO
7 SUMMERFIELD CT
8 THE MOORINGS
9 THE ANCHORAGE
10 LANCASTER HO
11 ROUNDHAM HO
12 OSMOND LODGE
13 ROSEMOUNT
Paignton Harbour
Roundham Head
St Michaels
1 YOUNG'S PARK LA
2 BRAESIDE MEWS
3 BOSUNS POINT
4 SEABOURNE CT
Tor Bay
Seashore Ctr
Paignton Zoo & Botanical Gdns
Torbay L Ctr
TQ4
Goodrington Sands
Spashdown @ Quaywest
Clennon Hill
Holiday Centre
Dartmouth Steam Rly
Saltern Cove
Goodrington
Sugar Loaf Hill & Saltern Cove Nature Reserve
Shell Cove
88 89 90
225
229

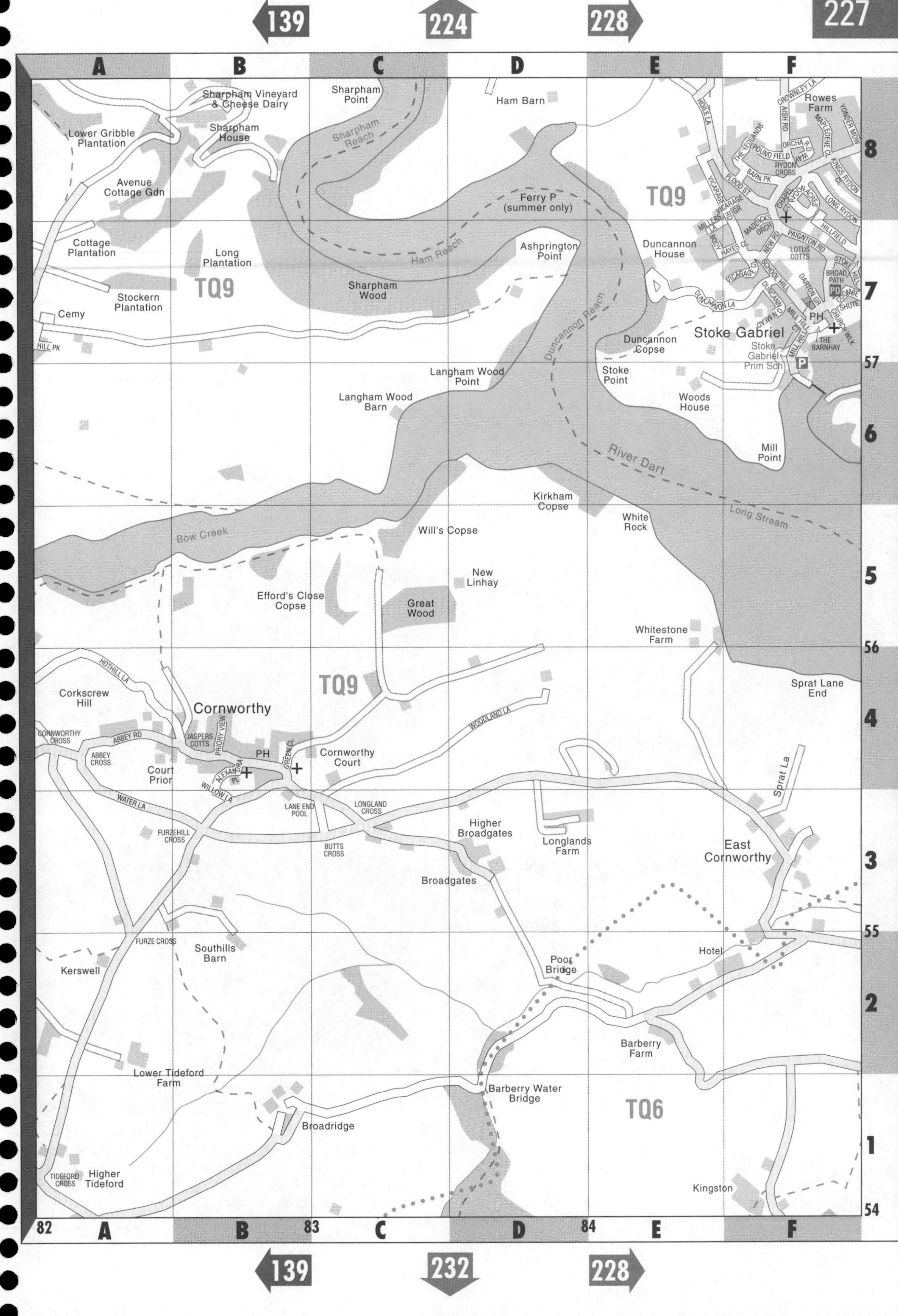
139
224
228
A
B
C
D
E
F
Sharpham Vineyard & Cheese Dairy
Sharpham Point
Sharpham Reach
Ham Barn
Lower Gribble Plantation
Sharpham House
Rowes Farm
Avenue Cottage Gdn
Ferry P (summer only)
TQ9
Cottage Plantation
Long Plantation
Ham Reach
Ashprington Point
Duncannon House
Stockern Plantation
Sharpham Wood
Cemy
HILL PK
Duncannon Reach
Duncannon Copse
Stoke Gabriel
Stoke Gabriel Prim Sch
Langham Wood Point
Stoke Point
Langham Wood Barn
Woods House
River Dart
Mill Point
Kirkham Copse
White Rock
Long Stream
Will's Copse
Bow Creek
New Linhay
Efford's Close Copse
Great Wood
Whitestone Farm
Sprat Lane End
Corkscrew Hill
Cornworthy
Cornworthy Court
Court Prior
PH
Higher Broadgates
Longlands Farm
East Cornworthy
Broadgates
Sprat La
Southills Barn
Kerswell
Poor Bridge
Hotel
Barberry Farm
Lower Tideford Farm
Barberry Water Bridge
TQ6
Broadridge
Higher Tideford
Kingston
8
7
57
6
5
56
4
3
55
2
1
54
82
83
84
232

227 225

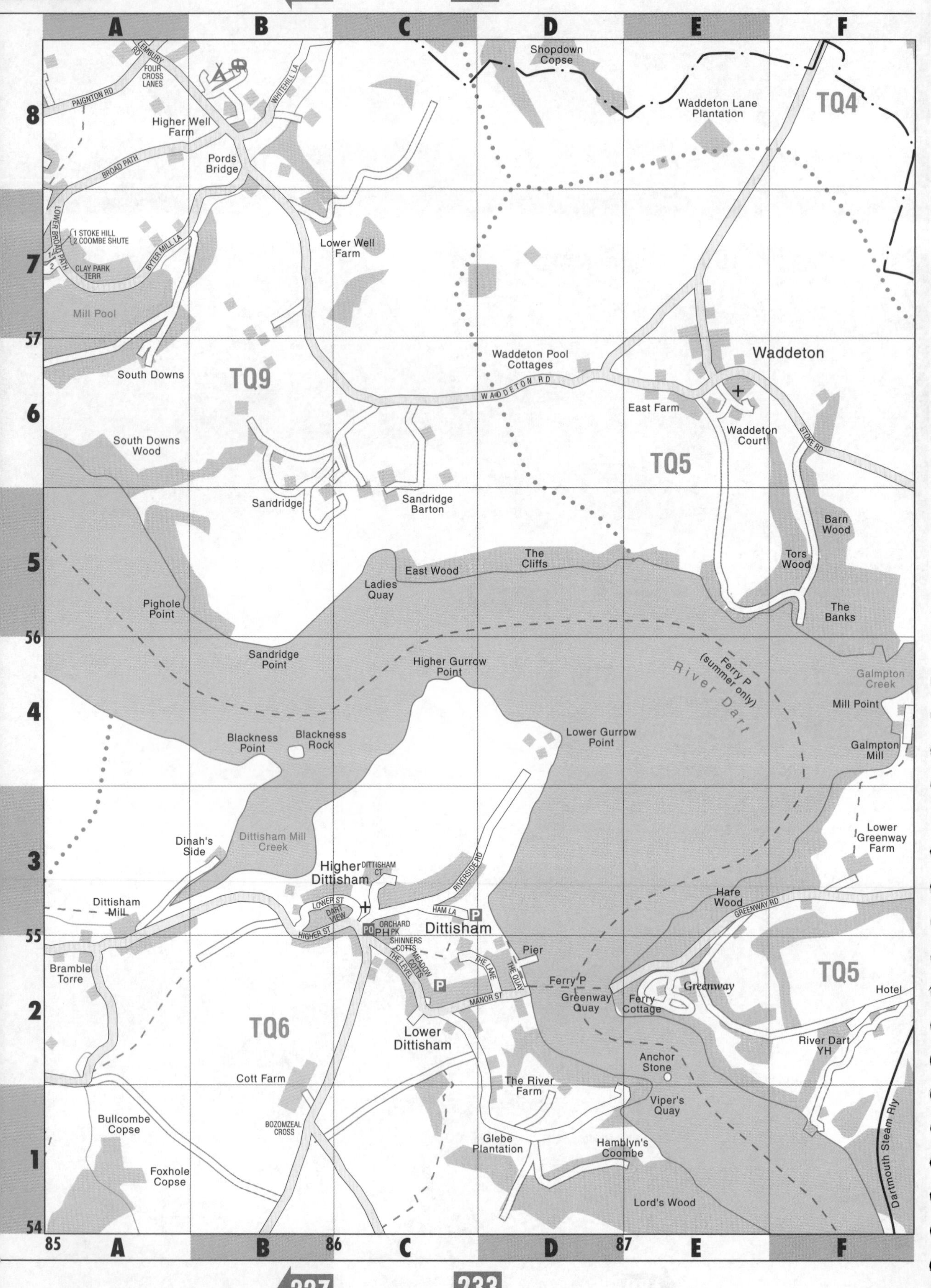

227 233

226
230

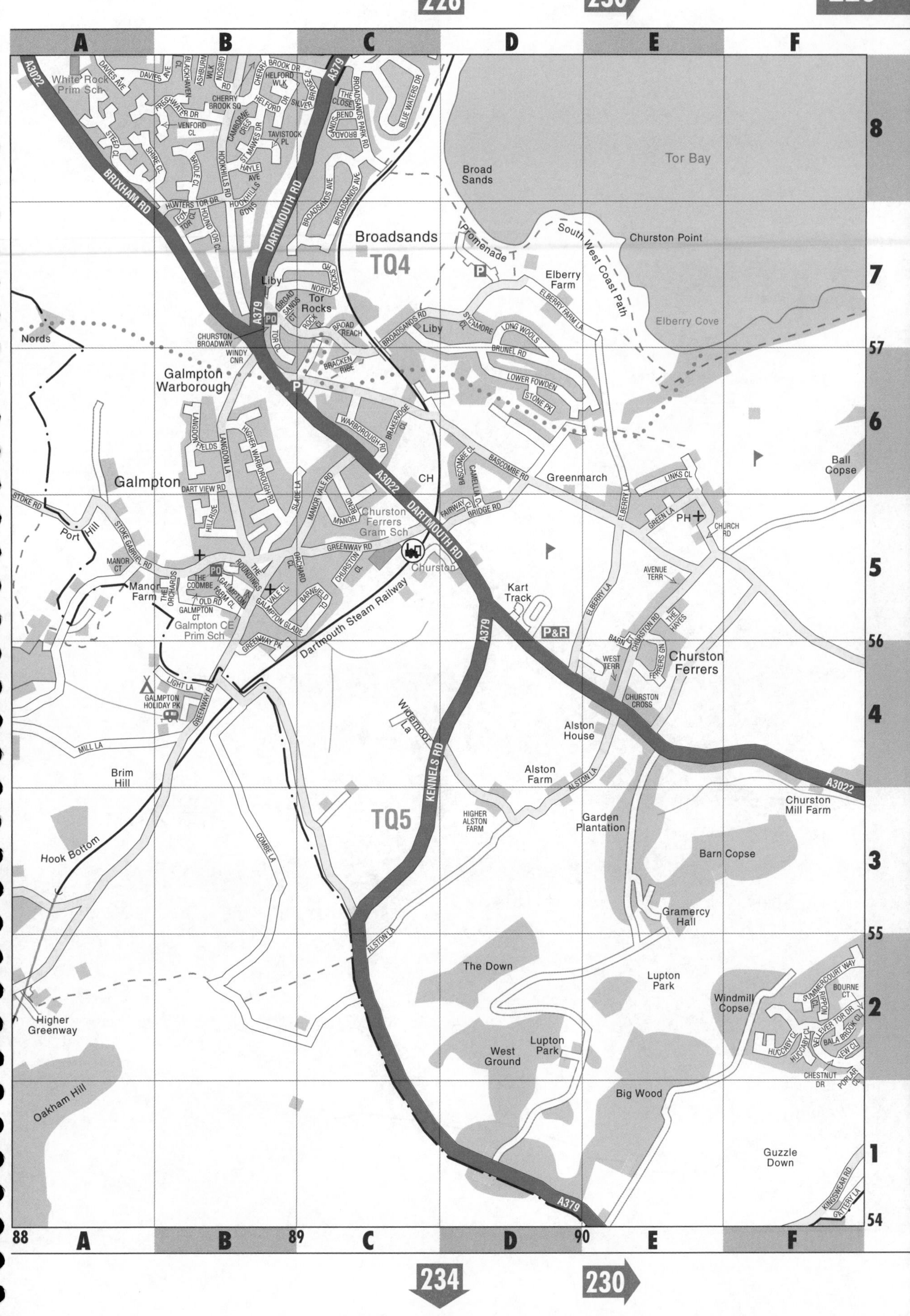

234
230

229

C3
1 GARROW CL
2 EVELEIGH CL
3 DOCTORS RD
4 GREENSWOOD RD
5 CLENNON CT
6 MAYFLOWER DR
7 HANOVER CL
8 ORCHARD CL
9 GREENSWOOD CL

C4
1 PRINCE WILLIAM CT
2 SAXON HTS
3 CAVERN RD
4 TINKERS WOOD CT
5 WATERMILL CT
6 PARKHAM TWRS
7 CHURCHILL CT
8 BOLTON CT
9 WINDMILL CT
10 WREN CT
11 GREAT GATE FLATS
12 PARKHAM TERR

C5
1 HARBOUR VIEW CL
2 LINDEN CT
3 PROSPECT RD
4 CHURCH ST
5 CHURCH HILL W
6 CHURCH HILL E
7 APTERS HILL
8 MARKET ST
9 UNION LA
10 SOMERSET CT
11 BANK LA
12 BREWERY LA
13 PRINGS CT

D5
1 PARADISE PL
2 FURZE LA
3 THE STRAND
4 PUMP ST
5 ST PETER'S HILL
6 TEMPERANCE PL
7 MARINERS CT
8 HEADLAND CT
9 RANSCOMBE CT

A B C D E F

8

Tor Bay

Ferry P

7

Fishcombe Point

Churston Cove

South West Coast Path

Jetty

Outer Harbour

57

The Breakwater

The Grove

Shoalstone Point

6

1 THE MOUNT
2 VICTORIA PL
3 FAIRLEA
4 TRAFALGAR TERR
5 BELLA VISTA RD
6 DALVERTON CT
7 SEA VIEW TERR
8 DOLPHIN CT

Oxen Cove

LB Sta

1 DEVONCOURT
2 HEATH CT

BREAKWATER CT

Marina

Berry Head Farm

Beacon

VIX CT 1
PILLAR FLATS 2
PILLAR CT 3
FURZEHAM CT 4

PRINCE WILLIAM QUAY

The Golden Hind

MOORINGS REACH

Furzeham Prim Sch

Mkt

5

Northfields Ind Est

1 RIDGEMARK CL
2 ANCHORAGE CL
3 TORBAY CT
4 HEATH RISE

Liby

Her Mus

TH & Theatre

56

1 Torbay Trad Est

Rea Hill

Brixham Coll

Holiday Village

Brixham CE Prim Sch

4

Brixham Enterprise Est

Brixham RFC

Brixham

A3022

NEW RD

BRIMLANDS CT 1
SEAWAY CT 2
BROOKDALE CT 3

Higher Brixham

BRIXHAM

Metherell Ave Ind Est

3

Eden Park Prim Sch

1 ST MARY'S DR
2 THE CRESCENT
3 SHARKHAM CT
4 MARCENT ROW
5 ST MARY'S HILL
6 PENN VIEW
7 BRISEHAM CL

St Mary's Bay

St Margaret Clitherow RC Prim Sch

TQ5

Sharkham Village

Mussel Rock

55

EVENTIDE HOMES

UPTON MANOR CT

2

Sharkham Point National Nature Reserve

Chestnut Prim Sch

Holiday Park

South West Coast Path

Sharkham Point

Redwells

1

SOUTHDOWN CROSS

CHALLEYCROFT RD

GATTERY LA

MILL LA

SOUTHDOWN RD

54

91 A B 92 C D 93 E F

229

235

A
B
C
D
E
F
8
7
57
6
Quay
Berry Head
Berry Head National Nature Reserve
TQ5
Berry Head Fort
Berry Head Common
Berry Head Country Park
P
5
56
Mew Stone
Cod Rock
4
Durl Head
Durl Rock
3
55
2
1
54
94
95
96

139
227

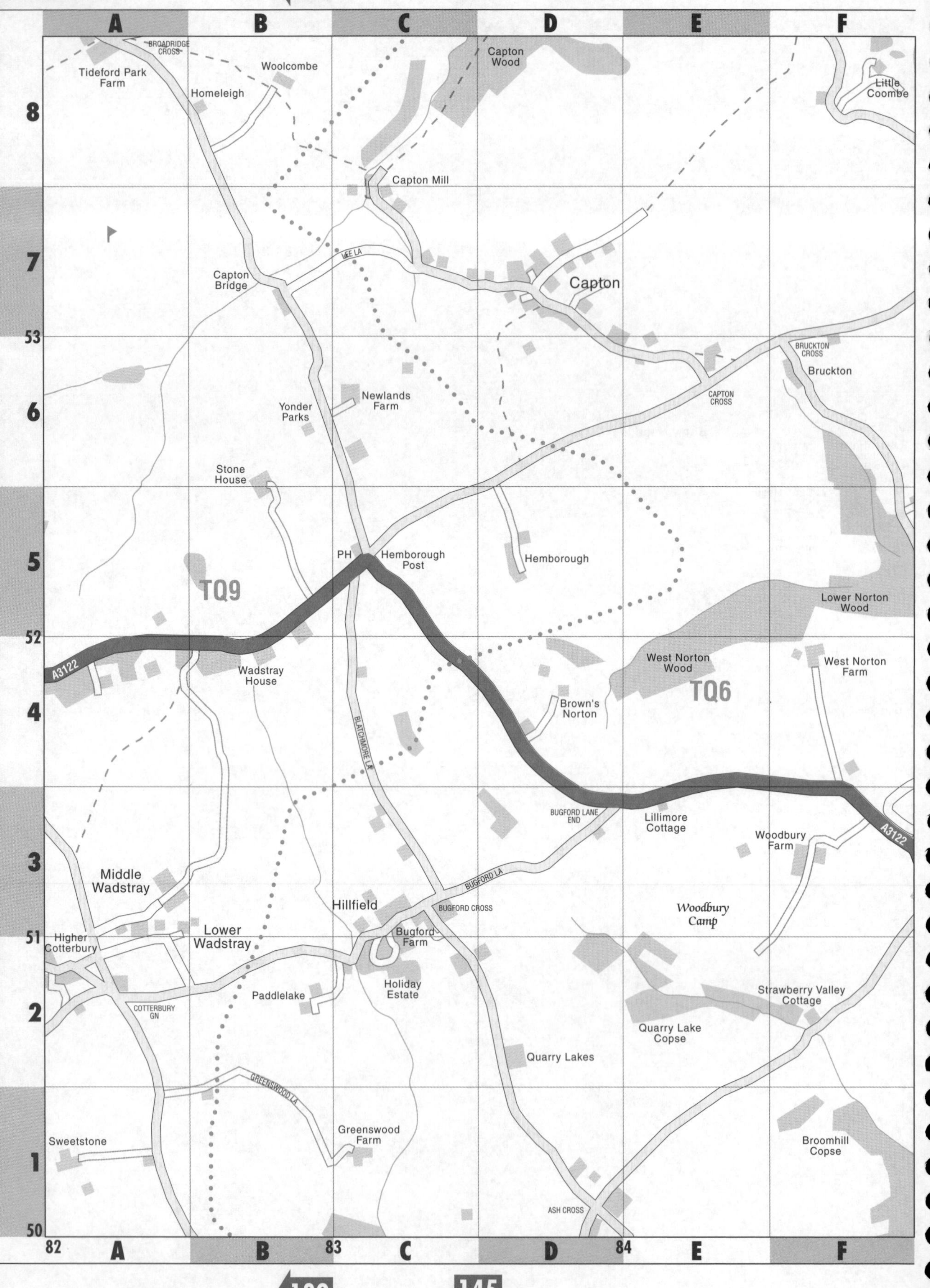

139
145

228
234

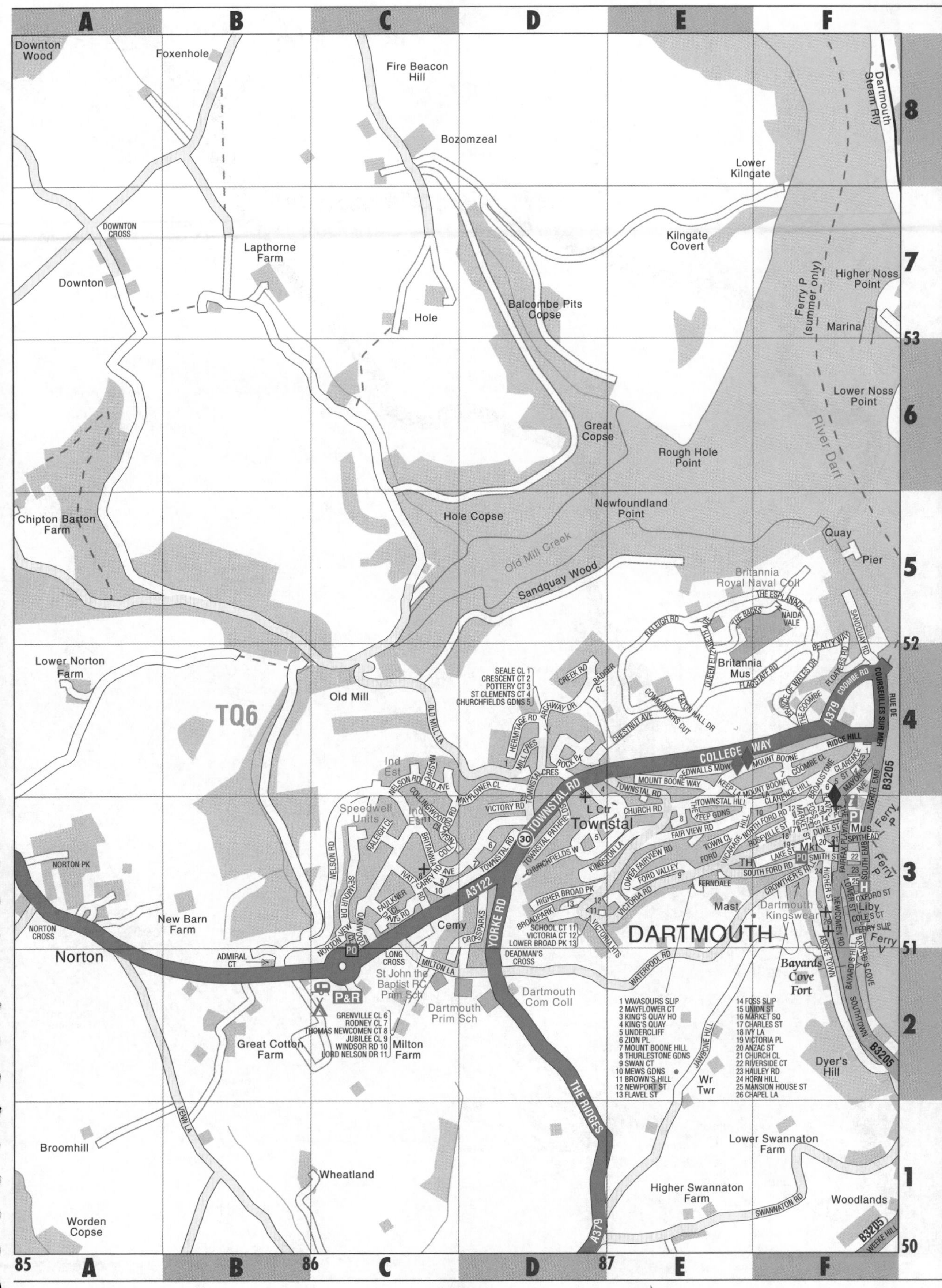

146
234

233
229

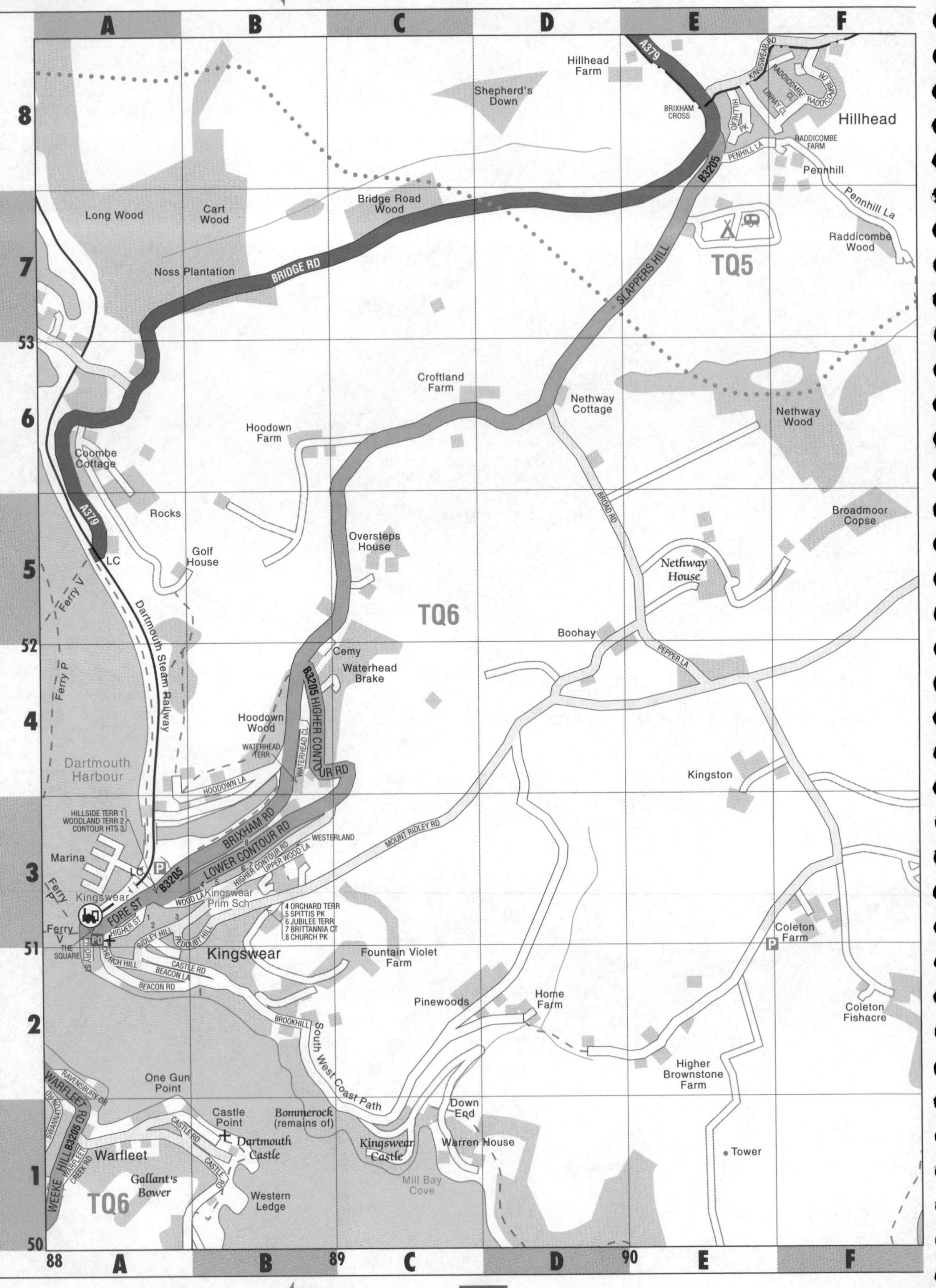

233
146

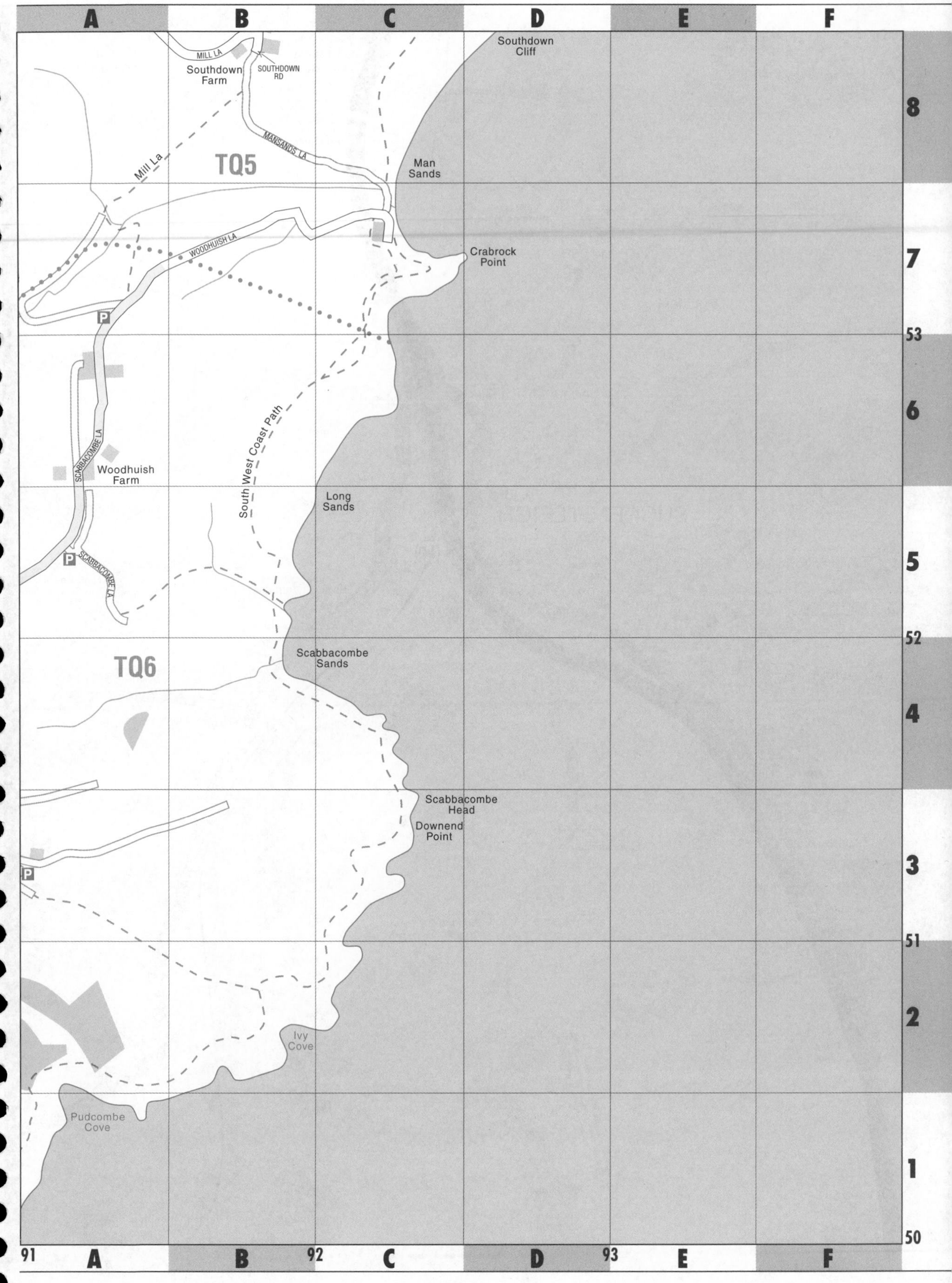
A
B
C
D
E
F
Southdown Cliff
MILL LA
Southdown Farm
SOUTHDOWN RD
MANSANDS LA
Mill La
TQ5
Man Sands
8
WOODHUISH LA
Crabrock Point
7
53
6
SCABBACOMBE LA
Woodhuish Farm
South West Coast Path
Long Sands
SCABBACOMBE LA
5
52
TQ6
Scabbacombe Sands
4
Scabbacombe Head
Downend Point
3
51
2
Ivy Cove
Pudcombe Cove
1
50
91
92
93

130 130 131

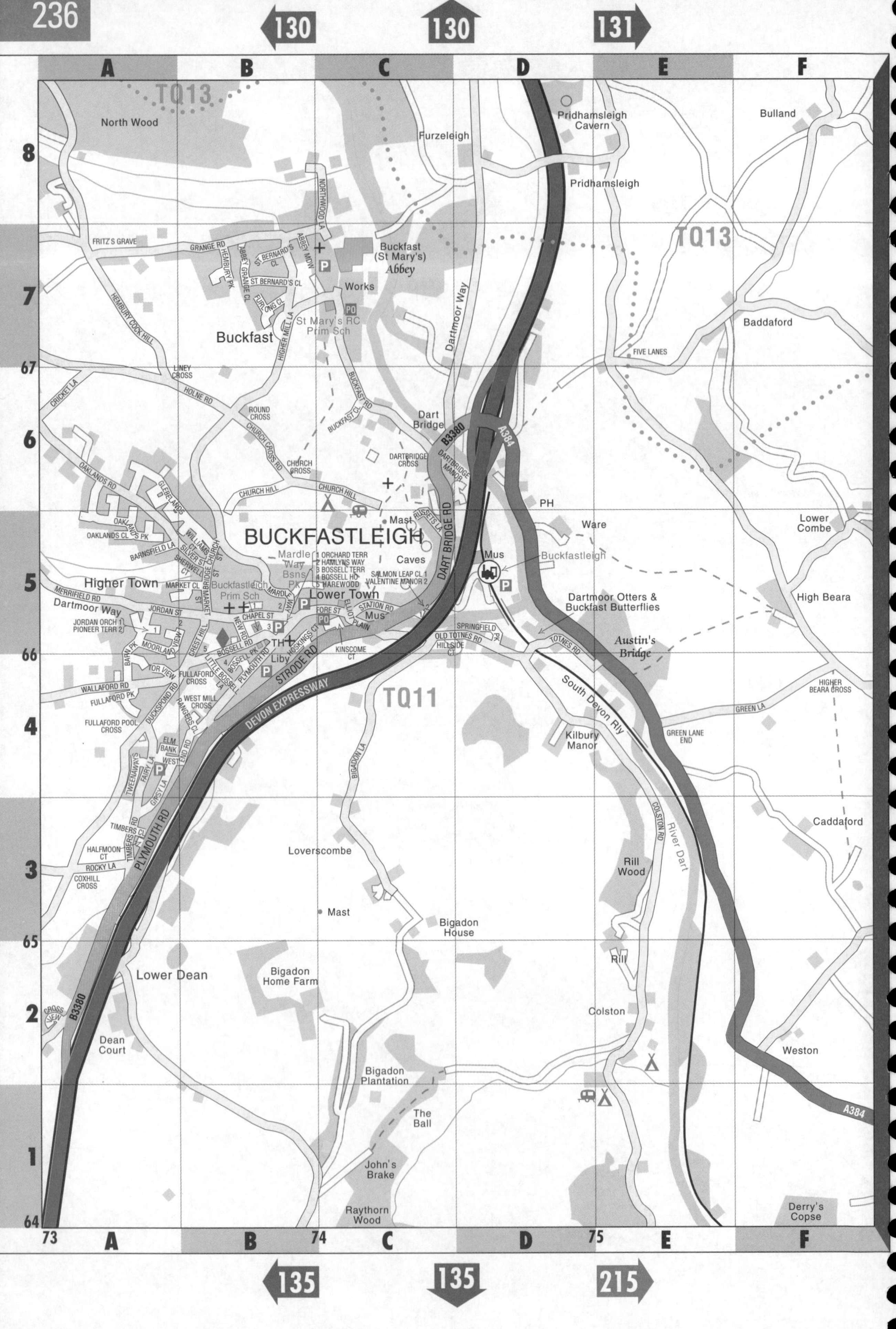

135 135 215

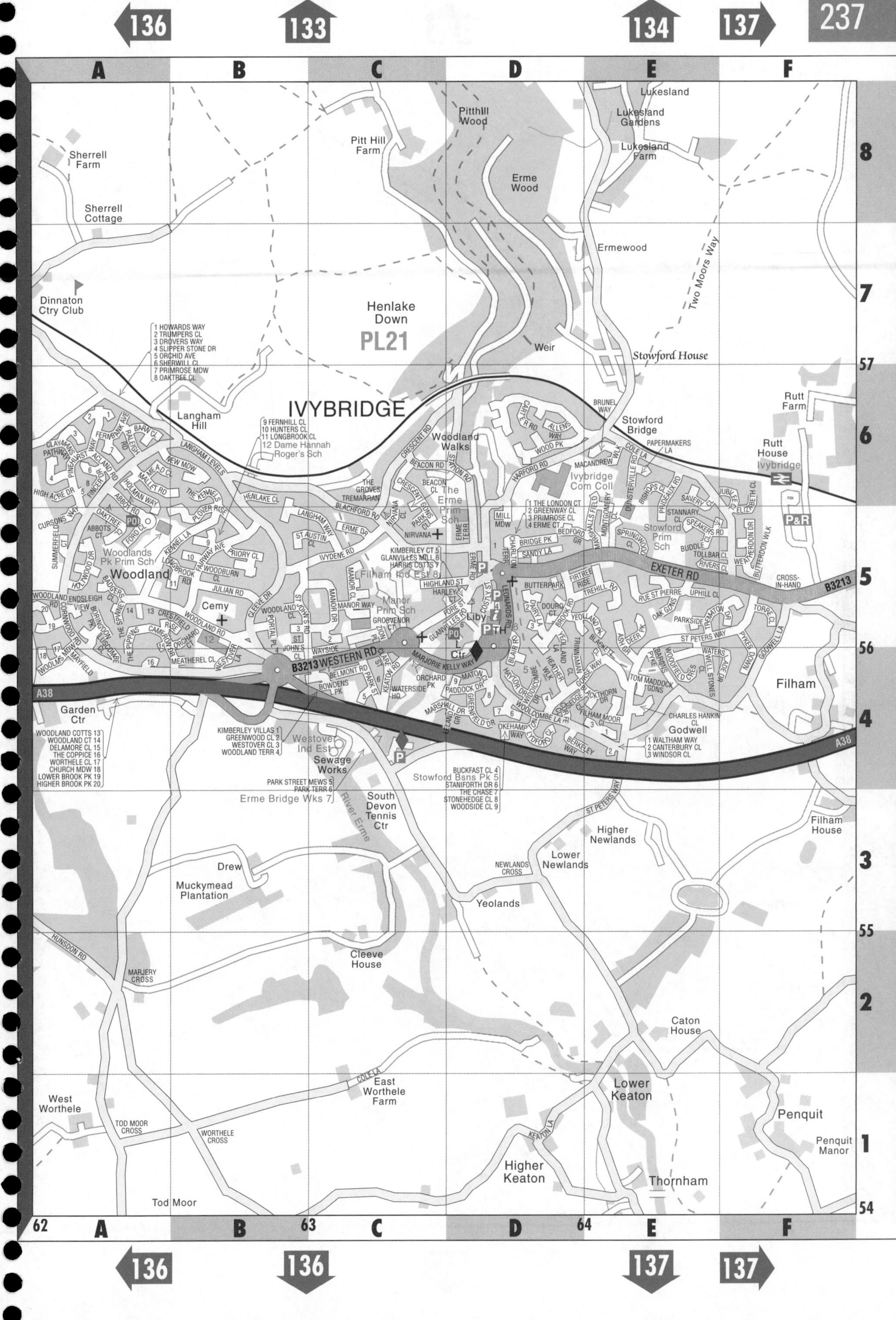

237
136
133
134
137
A
B
C
D
E
F
Lukesland
Lukesland Gardens
Lukesland Farm
Pitthill Wood
Pitt Hill Farm
Erme Wood
Sherrell Farm
Sherrell Cottage
Ermewood
Two Moors Way
Dinnaton Ctry Club
Henlake Down
PL21
Weir
Stowford House
1 HOWARDS WAY
2 TRUMPERS CL
3 DROVERS WAY
4 SLIPPER STONE DR
5 ORCHID AVE
6 SHERWILL CL
7 PRIMROSE MDW
8 OAKTREE CL
IVYBRIDGE
Langham Hill
9 FERNHILL CL
10 HUNTERS CL
11 LONGBROOK CL
12 Dame Hannah Roger's Sch
Woodland Walks
Stowford Bridge
Rutt Farm
Rutt House
Ivybridge
Ivybridge Com Coll
1 THE LONDON CT
2 GREENWAY CL
3 PRIMROSE CL
4 ERME CT
The Erme Prim Sch
Stowford Prim Sch
P&R
Woodlands Pk Prim Sch
Woodland
Cemy
Filham Ind Est 8
Manor Prim Sch
KIMBERLEY CT 5
GLANVILLES MILL 6
HARRIS COTTS 7
EXETER RD
B3213
CROSS-IN-HAND
Liby
Ctr
TH
B3213 WESTERN RD
A38
Filham
Godwell
Garden Ctr
WOODLAND COTTS 13
WOODLAND CT 14
DELAMORE CL 15
THE COPPICE 16
WORTHELE CL 17
CHURCH MDW 18
LOWER BROOK PK 19
HIGHER BROOK PK 20
KIMBERLEY VILLAS 1
GREENWOOD CL 2
WESTOVER CL 3
WOODLAND TERR 4
Westover Ind Est
Sewage Works
PARK STREET MEWS 5
PARK TERR 6
Erme Bridge Wks 7
BUCKFAST CL 4
STANIFORTH DR 5
THE CHASE 7
STONEHEDGE CL 8
WOODSIDE CL 9
Stowford Bsns Pk 5
1 WALTHAM WAY
2 CANTERBURY CL
3 WINDSOR CL
South Devon Tennis Ctr
River Erme
Higher Newlands
Lower Newlands
NEWLANDS CROSS
Filham House
Drew
Muckymead Plantation
Yeolands
Cleeve House
HUNSDON RD
MARJERY CROSS
Caton House
East Worthele Farm
West Worthele
TOD MOOR CROSS
WORTHELE CROSS
Lower Keaton
Higher Keaton
Thornham
Penquit
Penquit Manor
Tod Moor
8
7
57
6
5
56
4
3
55
2
1
54
62
63
64

125

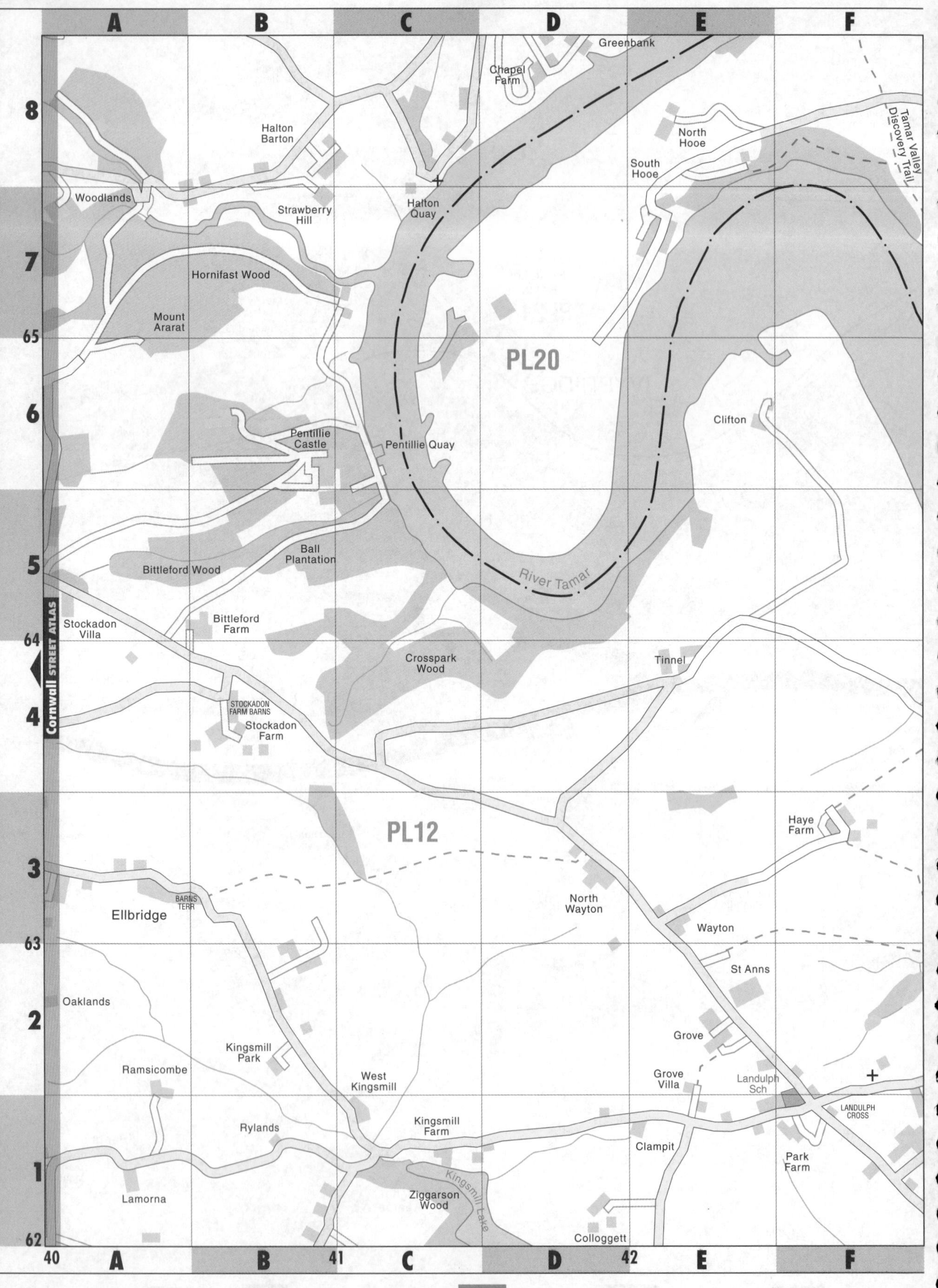

A
B
C
D
E
F
8
7
65
6
5
64
4
3
63
2
1
62
40
41
42
Greenbank
Chapel Farm
Halton Barton
North Hooe
South Hooe
Tamar Valley Discovery Trail
Woodlands
Strawberry Hill
Halton Quay
Hornifast Wood
Mount Ararat
PL20
Clifton
Pentillie Castle
Pentillie Quay
Ball Plantation
Bittleford Wood
River Tamar
Stockadon Villa
Bittleford Farm
Crosspark Wood
Tinnel
Cornwall STREET ATLAS
STOCKADON FARM BARNS
Stockadon Farm
PL12
Haye Farm
BARNS TERR
Ellbridge
North Wayton
Wayton
St Anns
Oaklands
Grove
Kingsmill Park
Ramsicombe
West Kingsmill
Grove Villa
Landulph Sch
LANDULPH CROSS
Rylands
Kingsmill Farm
Clampit
Park Farm
Kingsmill Lake
Lamorna
Ziggarson Wood
Colloggett

242

125
240

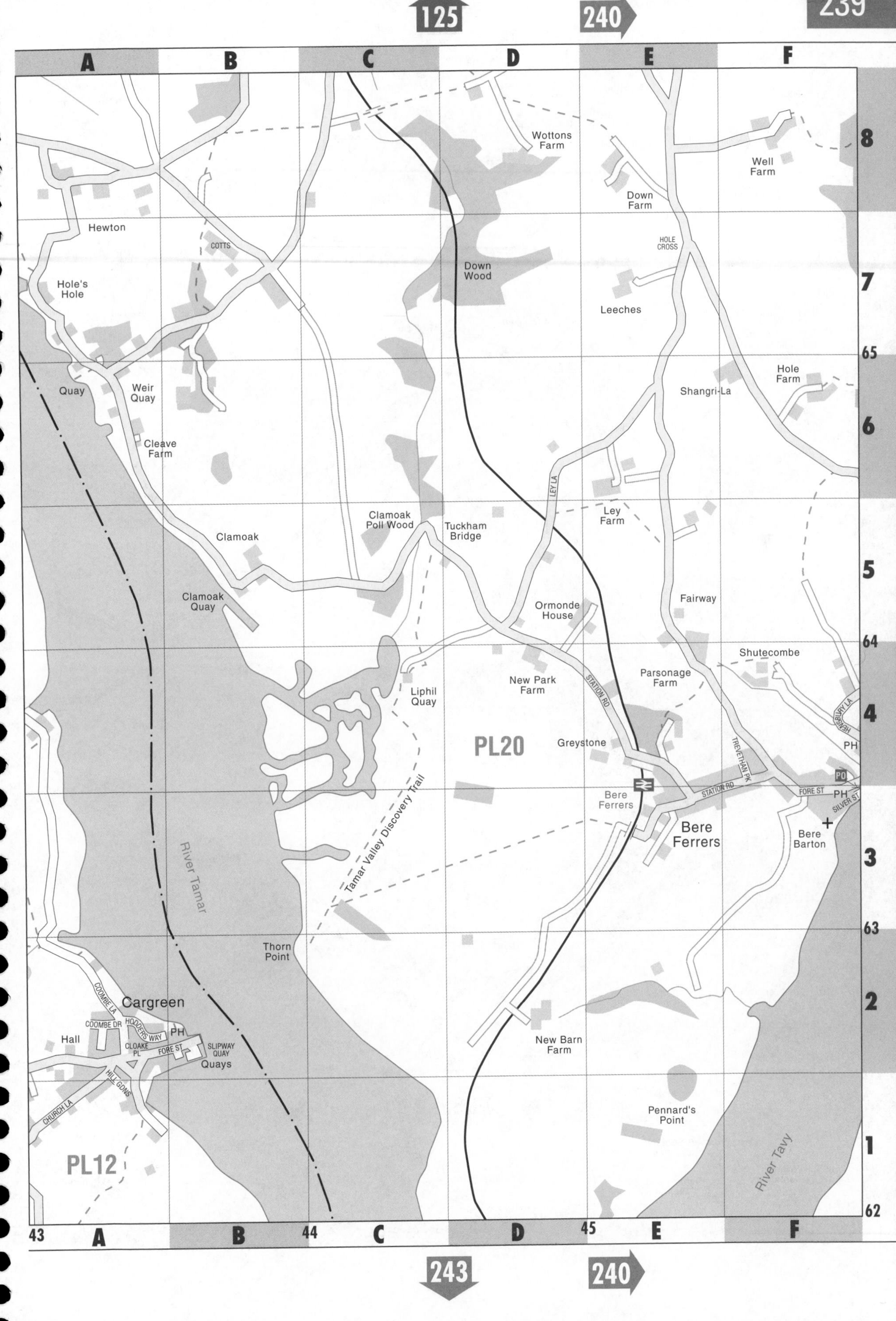

243
240

239
126

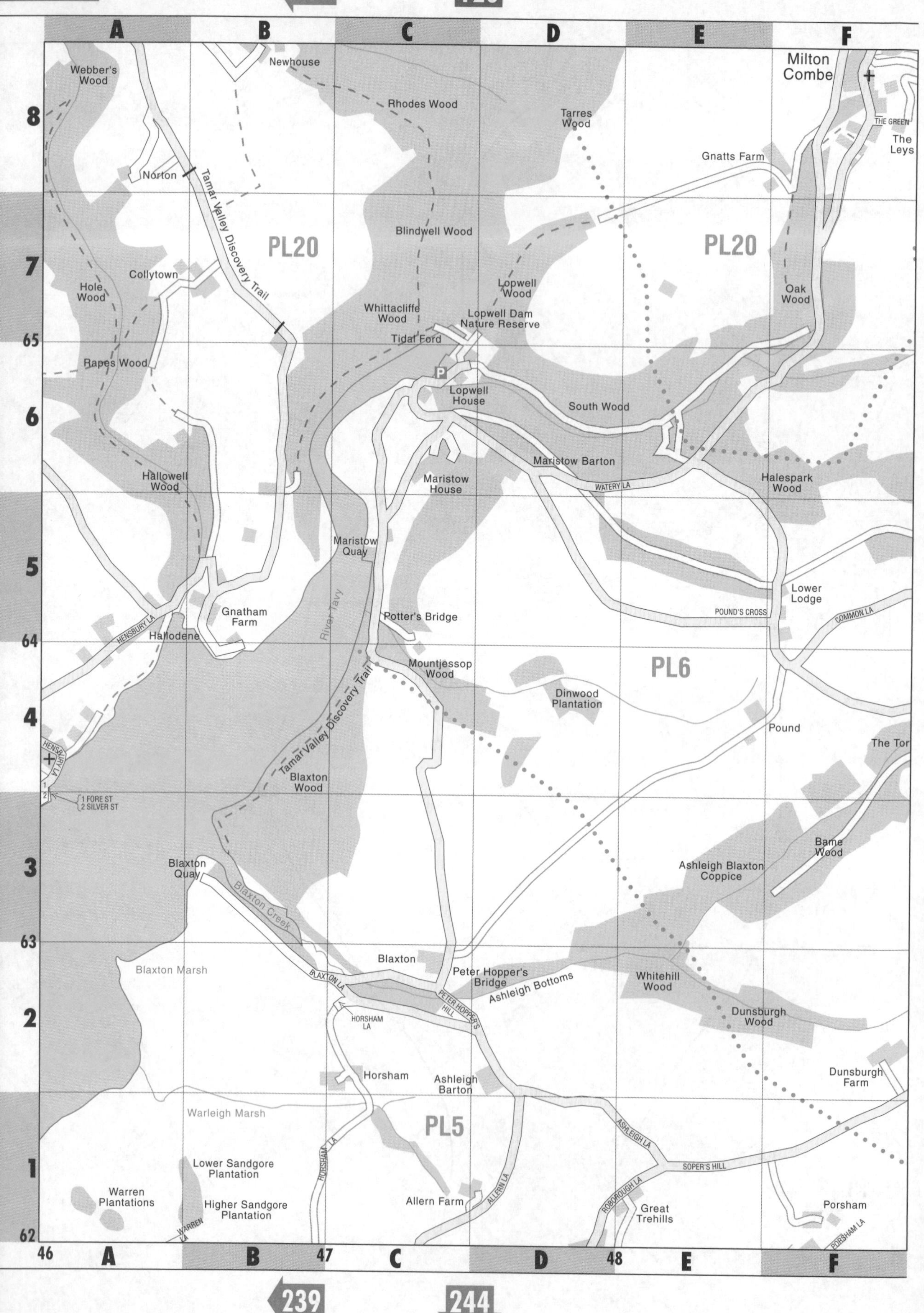

239
244

126
132

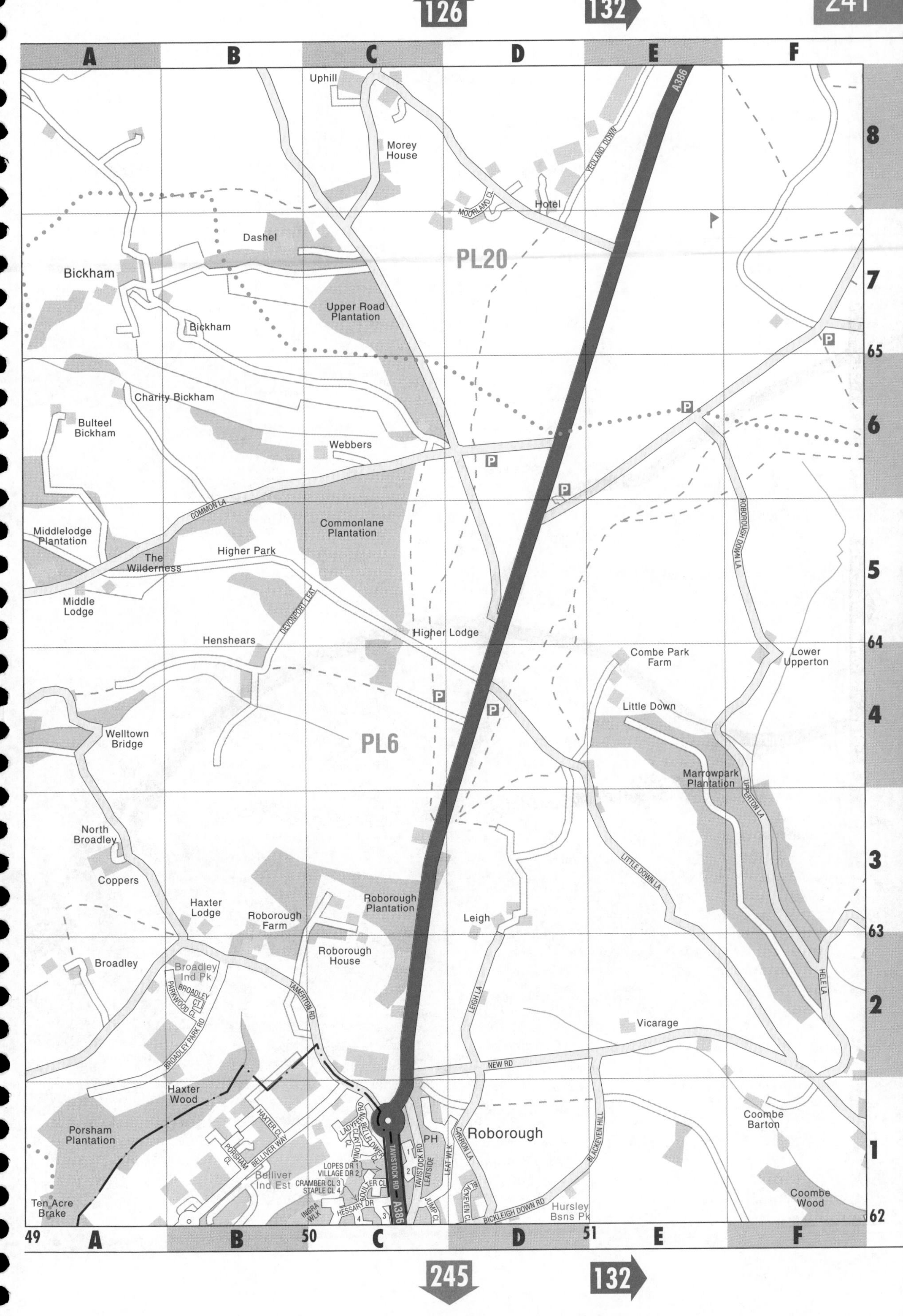

245
132

238

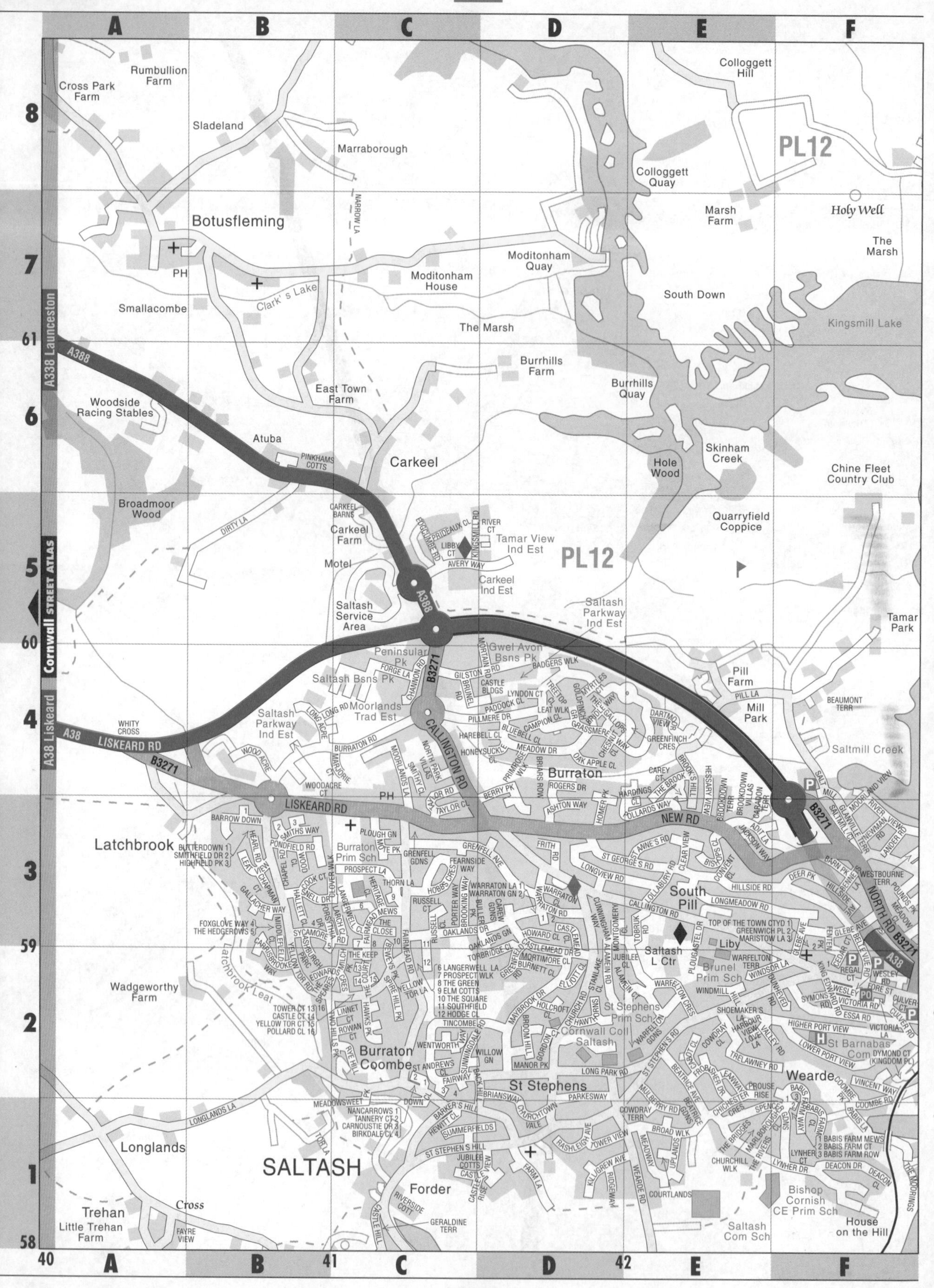

Cross Park Farm
Rumbullion Farm
Sladeland
Marraborough
Botusfleming
Colloggett Hill
PL12
Colloggett Quay
Marsh Farm
Holy Well
The Marsh
Moditonham Quay
Moditonham House
South Down
Kingsmill Lake
Smallacombe
Clark's Lake
The Marsh
Burrhills Farm
Burrhills Quay
East Town Farm
Woodside Racing Stables
Atuba
Carkeel
Hole Wood
Skinham Creek
Chine Fleet Country Club
Broadmoor Wood
Carkeel Farm
Tamar View Ind Est
Quarryfield Coppice
PL12
Motel
Carkeel Ind Est
Saltash Service Area
Saltash Parkway Ind Est
Tamar Park
Peninsular Pk
Gwel Avon Bsns Pk
Saltash Bsns Pk
Pill Farm
Mill Park
Moorlands Trad Est
Saltash Parkway Ind Est
Saltmill Creek
Burraton
Latchbrook
Burraton Prim Sch
South Pill
Saltash L Ctr
Liby
Brunel Prim Sch
Wadgeworthy Farm
Latchbrook Leat
St Stephens Prim Sch
Cornwall Coll Saltash
Burraton Coombe
St Barnabas Com
Wearde
St Stephens
Longlands
SALTASH
Forder
Trehan
Cross
Little Trehan Farm
Bishop Cornish CE Prim Sch
Saltash Com Sch
House on the Hill
A388
A38
B3271
LISKEARD RD
CALLINGTON RD
NEW RD
NORTH RD
A38 Launceston
A38 Liskeard
Cornwall STREET ATLAS

239
244

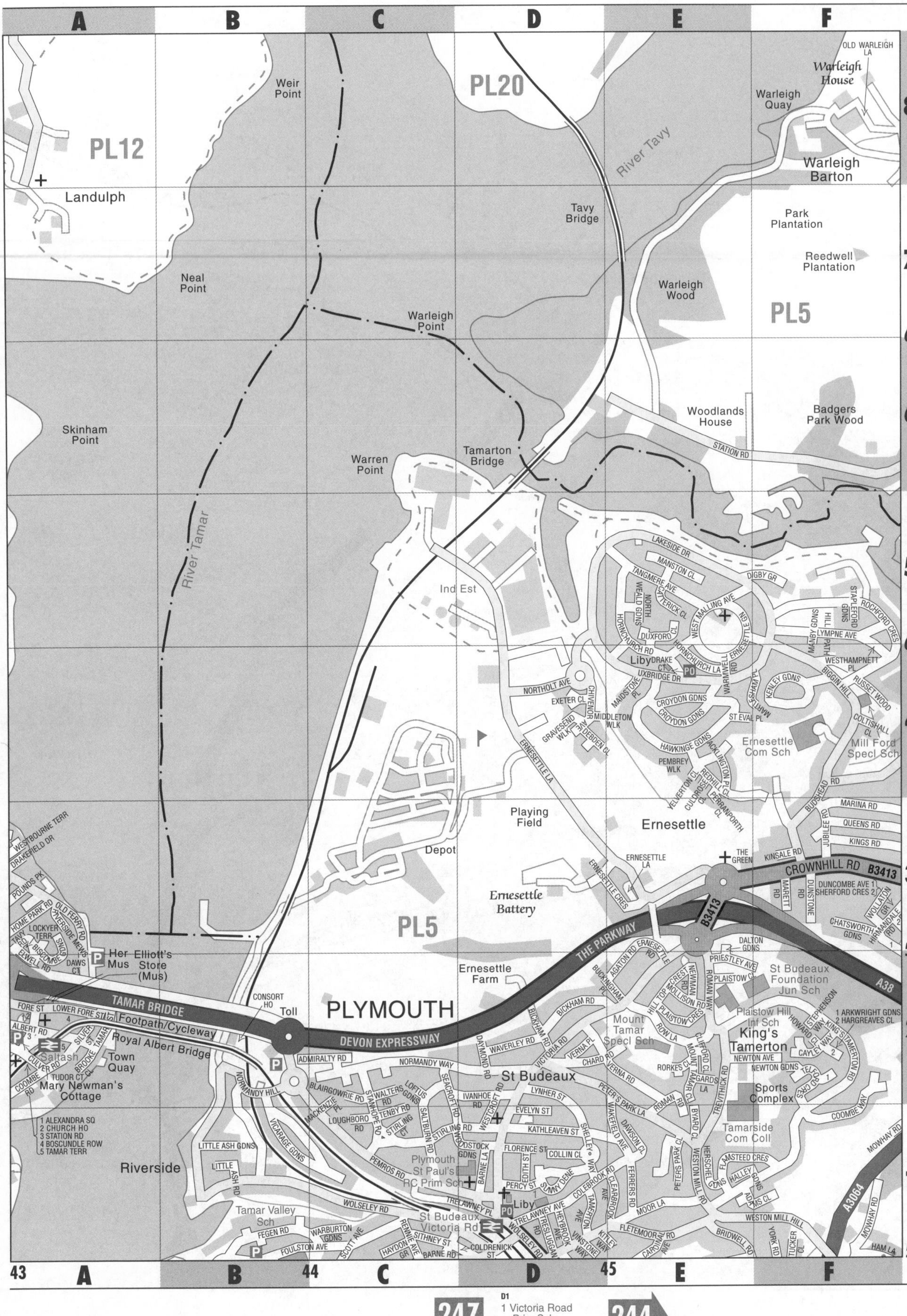

A B C D E F

8 7 61 6 5 60 4 3 59 2 1 58

43 A B 44 C D 45 E F

D1
1 Victoria Road Prim Sch

247
244

243 240

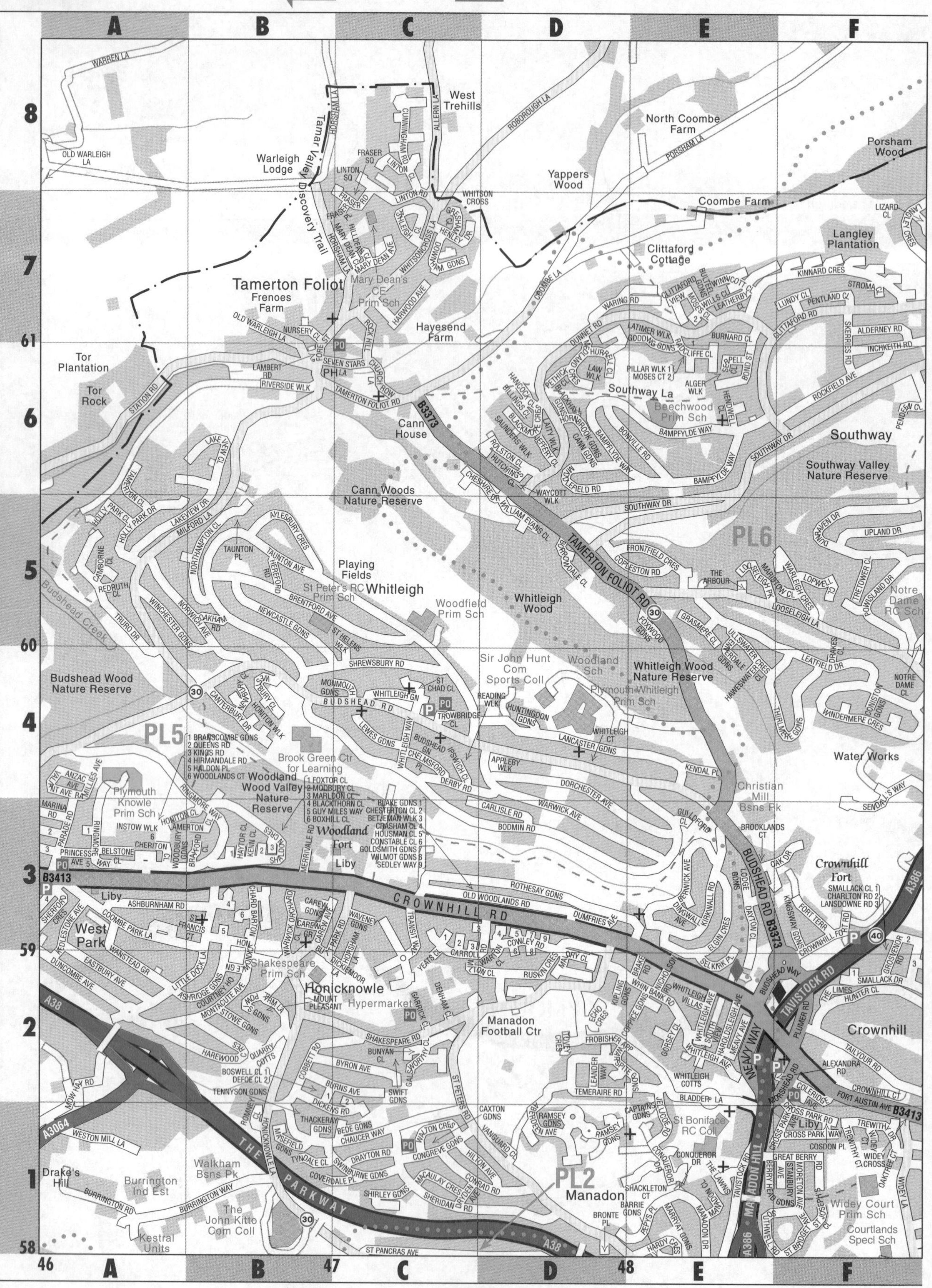

243 248

241 132

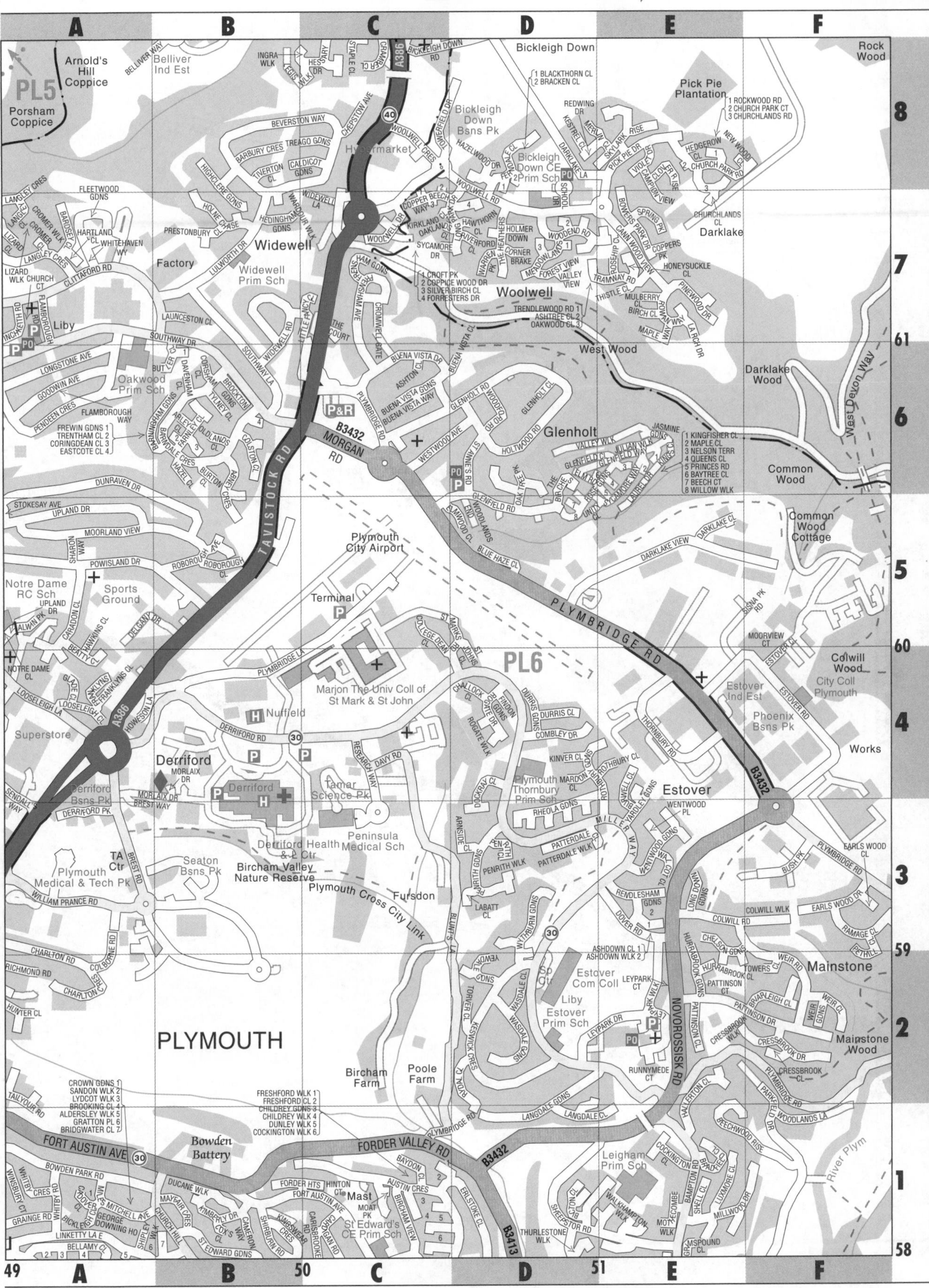

249 132

242

A
B
C
D
E
F
Trehan
Castle Farm
CASTLE HILL
Trematon Castle
PL12
WEARDE RD
Merryfield View
Henn Point
Forder Lake
PL12
Marsh Coombe
Piers
Wearde Quay
Shillingham Manor
Antony Passage
Quay
Beggar's Island
St Germans or Lynher River
Jupiter Point
Jetty
Higher Wearlands Plantation
Shillingham Point
Wivelscombe Lake
Jupiter Plantation
Antony Woodland Garden
Tomboy Hill
Great Kithill Plantation
North Wilcove
Wilcove
Ince Castle
Ince Point
Bath House
Wilderness
Antony House
FERRY LA
Antony Park
WILCOVE LA
PENGELLY PK
PENGELLY CL
Maryfield
Coombe Pk
A374
Cornwall STREET ATLAS
Borough Farm House
Sports Gd
1 FISTRAL CL
2 GWITHIAN CL
Bulland Quay
Horson House
Horson Plantation
Mast
BOROUGH CT
THE MEADOWS
PRIMROSE CL
KYNANCE CL
MULLION CL
TREVITHICK AVE
SENNEN CL
BOROUGH PK
PENLEE PK
LAMORNA PK
TREMATON CL
INCE CL
CARADON CL
PENDENNIS CL
Clift Quay
PL11
GROVE PK
LANGDON DOWN WAY
CLEGG AVE
WESTLAKE CL
PENTIRE RD
WOODLAND WAY
Bulland
KERNOW CT 3
TRELAWNEY WAY 4
GOAD AVE
WAVISH PK
ADAMS CRES
West Clift
Trevol Bsns Pk
WAY
FISGARD
FROBISHER WAY
HMS Fisgard
Longlands Plantation
Cemy
TRELAWNEY RISE
MURDOCK RD
GOAD CL
TRENGROUSE AVE
DAVY CL
GURNEY CL
SYCAMORE DR
Trevol Ho
TREVOL RD
TREVOL PL
HAWTHORN AVE
CHESTNUT CL
Hay
CEDAR DR
PENCAIR AVE
TREGONING RD
Trinaway Plantation
TREVORDER RD
TREVORDER CL
PENDILLY AVE
A374
A374 Looe (A387)
HMS Raleigh
ABBOTSCOURT LA
Sports Gd
West Antony
Rifle Range
ST JOHNS LA
Eastdowns Lake
Sewage Wks
Deadman's Point
River Tamar Hamoaze
Efford's Bridge
DANGER AREA
Wolsdon House
St John's Lake
8
7
57
6
5
56
4
3
55
2
1
54
40
41
42

243

248

F5
1 NEPEAN ST
2 ADELAIDE ST
3 BRUNEL TERR
4 EPWORTH TERR
5 SUSSEX TERR
6 RAILWAY COTTS
7 YORK TERR
8 ST MAWES TERR

253

F3
1 CLARENDON HO
2 GARFIELD TERR
3 TRAFALGAR PL
4 THE MEWS
5 NELSON GDNS
6 BEYROUT PL
7 ST MICHAEL'S CT

248

8 ST MICHAEL'S TERR
9 PORTLAND CT
10 MOLYNEAUX PL
11 CLARENDON LA

F4
1 ST GEORGES CT
2 HORNBY ST
3 PHILLIMORE ST
4 FREMANTLE GDNS
5 FAIRFAX TERR
6 HARGOOD TERR
7 HARRISON ST
8 KEPPEL TERR
9 HEALY CT
10 BRUNSWICK PL

A5
1 MELVILLE PL
2 Wolseley Bsns Pk
3 AUCKLAND RD
4 HALEY BARTON
5 GREATLANDS PL
6 WADHAM TERR
7 CRANTOCK TERR
E5
1 Hyde Park Jun & Inf Schs
247
E6
1 BRENT KNOLL RD
2 LUDLOW RD
3 SWAINDALE RD
4 TYTHING WLK
5 GLENHURST RD
6 VENN CL
244
E8
1 Manadon Vale Prim Sch
F4
1 GROSVENOR COTTS
2 HILLSBOROUGH
3 PEARSON AVE
4 PENLEE PL
5 PENROSE VILLAS
6 CROZIER RD
7 MARINA TERR
8 KENSINGTON PL
9 SIDMOUTH CTS
F6
1 RESERVOIR LA
2 PEARN COTTS
3 BRANDRETH RD
4 GLENEAGLE AVE
5 GLENEAGLE VILLAS
6 HENDERS CNR
7 ROSEVEAN HO
8 ROSEVEAN CT
9 MANNAMEAD CT
10 FOSBROOKE CT
A B C D E F
8 7 57 6 5 56 4 3 55 2 1 54
46 47 48
Pennycross
Manadon Wood
Ham
Hartley
North Prospect
Peverell
Home Park (Plymouth Argyle FC)
Mannamead
Ford
PLYMOUTH
Ford Park
Central Park
Mutley
Stoke
Royal Eye Infirmary
Pennycomequick
Plymouth
Victoria Park
Cath
Univ of Plymouth
Stonehouse
Pavilions
Guildhall
Barbican
Millbay
Millbay Docks
Barracks
Sutton Harbour
Aquarium
PL1 PL2 PL3 PL4 PL5 PL6
A38 A386 A3064 A374 B3250 B3396 B3214 B3238 B3240
UNION ST
EXETER ST
NOTTE ST
VAUXHALL ST
262 263
A3
1 UNDERHILL VILLAS
2 OSBORNE VILLAS
3 EDGCUMBE CT
4 NELSON GDNS
5 COLLINGWOOD VILLAS
6 PAVILAND GRANGE
7 FITZROY TERR
A4
1 WESLEY PL
2 MASTERMAN RD
3 DUCKWORTH ST
4 DUNDAS ST
5 BROMLEY PL
6 BROMLEY HO
7 LEESIDE CT
8 BELMONT CT
9 Stoke Damerel Bsns Ctr
247
A4
10 SOMERSET COTTS
11 SOMERSET PLACE LA
12 PARK PLACE LA
254
E4
1 HERMITAGE CT
2 WARLEIGH RD
3 ROCHESTER RD
4 CHESTER PL
5 ALEXANDRA PL
6 CONNAUGHT LA
For full street detail of the highlighted area see pages 262 and 263.

245
250

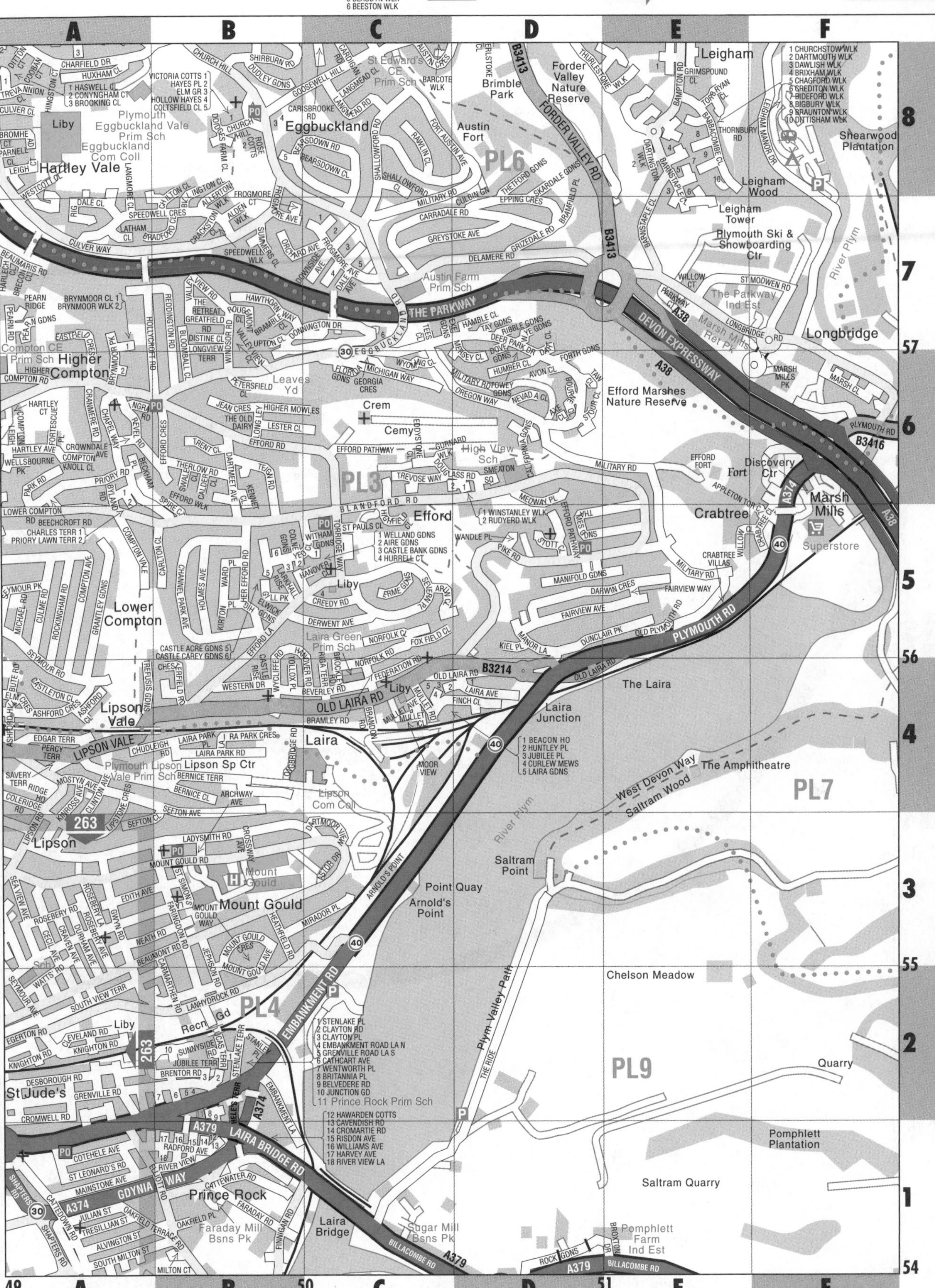

255
250
For full street detail of the highlighted area see page 263.

249
132

E7
1 PERSEVERANCE COTTS
2 BLANCHARD PL

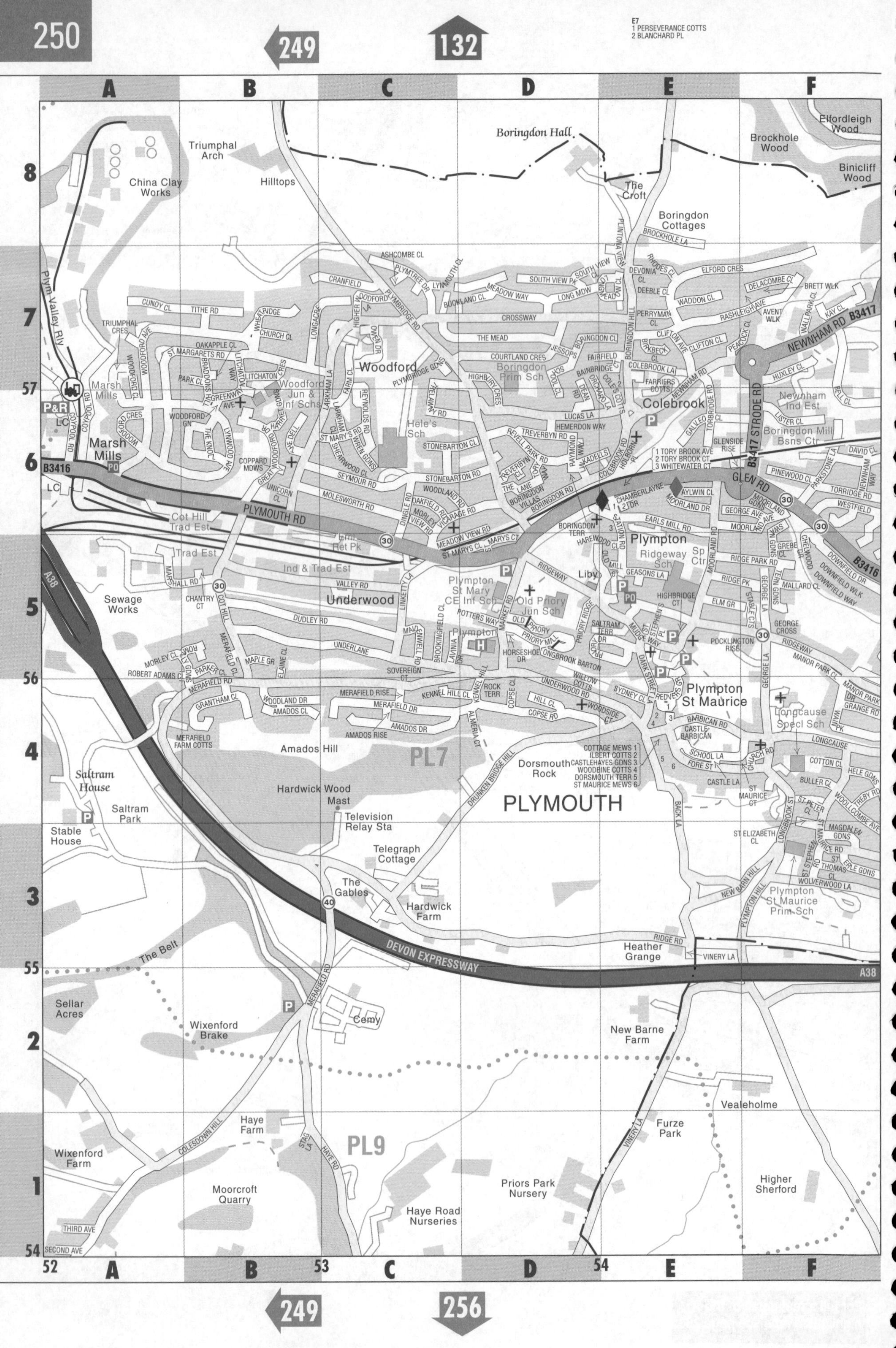

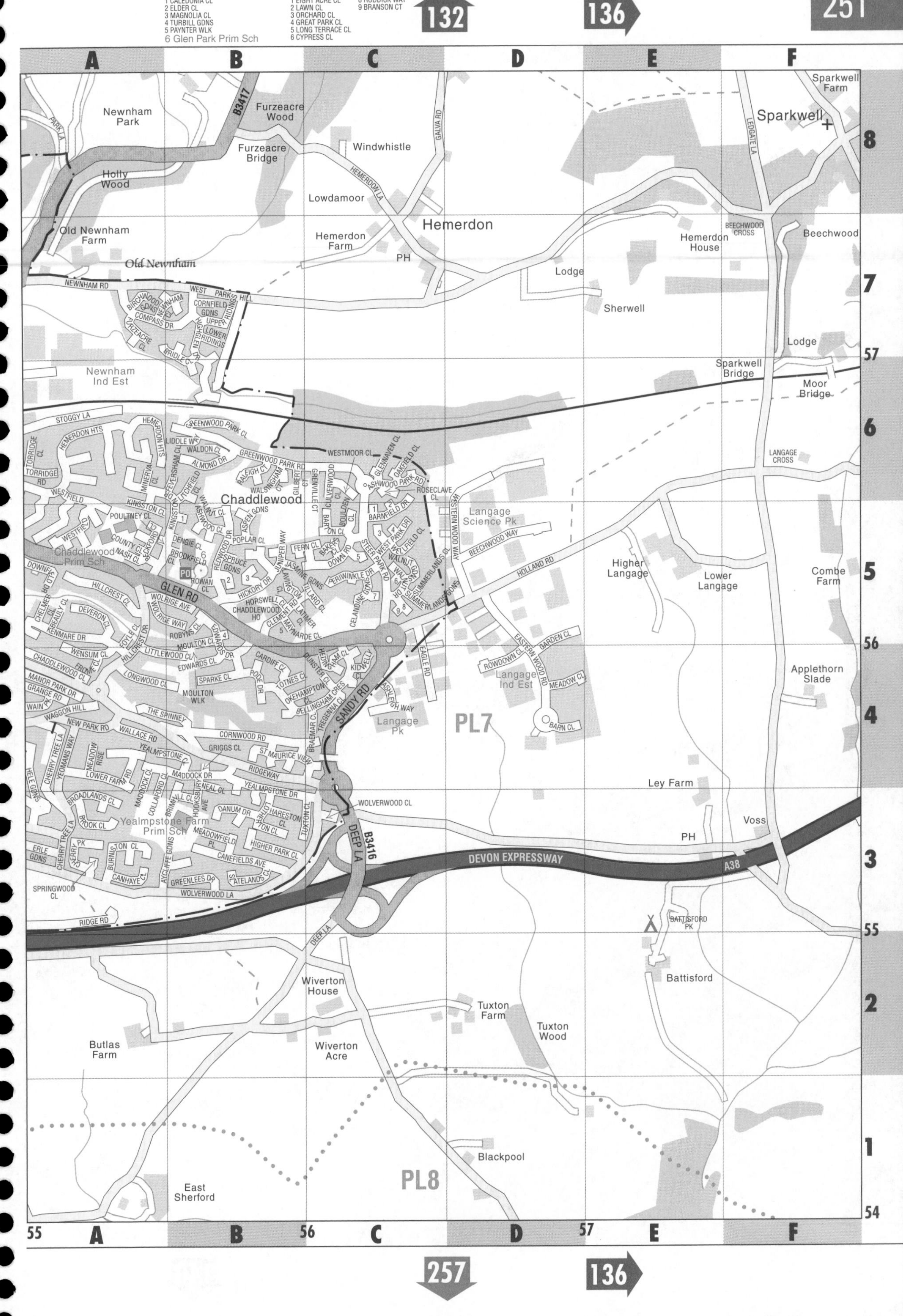
B5
1 CALEDONIA CL
2 ELDER CL
3 MAGNOLIA CL
4 TURBILL GDNS
5 PAYNTER WLK
6 Glen Park Prim Sch
C5
1 EIGHT ACRE CL
2 LAWN CL
3 ORCHARD CL
4 GREAT PARK CL
5 LONG TERRACE CL
6 CYPRESS CL
7 CAMPION CL
8 RODDICK WAY
9 BRANSON CT
132
136
A
B
C
D
E
F
8
7
57
6
5
56
4
3
55
2
1
54
55
56
57
Newnham Park
Furzeacre Wood
Furzeacre Bridge
Windwhistle
Holly Wood
Lowdamoor
Old Newnham Farm
Hemerdon Farm
Hemerdon
PH
Old Newnham
Sparkwell Farm
Sparkwell
Hemerdon House
Beechwood
Lodge
Sherwell
Newnham Ind Est
Sparkwell Bridge
Moor Bridge
Chaddlewood
Langage Science Pk
Chaddlewood Prim Sch
Higher Langage
Lower Langage
Combe Farm
Langage Ind Est
Langage Pk
PL7
Applethorn Slade
Ley Farm
Voss
PH
Yealmpstone Farm Prim Sch
DEVON EXPRESSWAY
A38
B3416
B3417
Battisford
Wiverton House
Tuxton Farm
Tuxton Wood
Butlas Farm
Wiverton Acre
Blackpool
PL8
East Sherford
GLEN RD
SANDY RD
DEEP LA
HOLLAND RD
NEWNHAM RD
GALVA RD
HEMERDON LA
LEDGATE LA
257
136

246

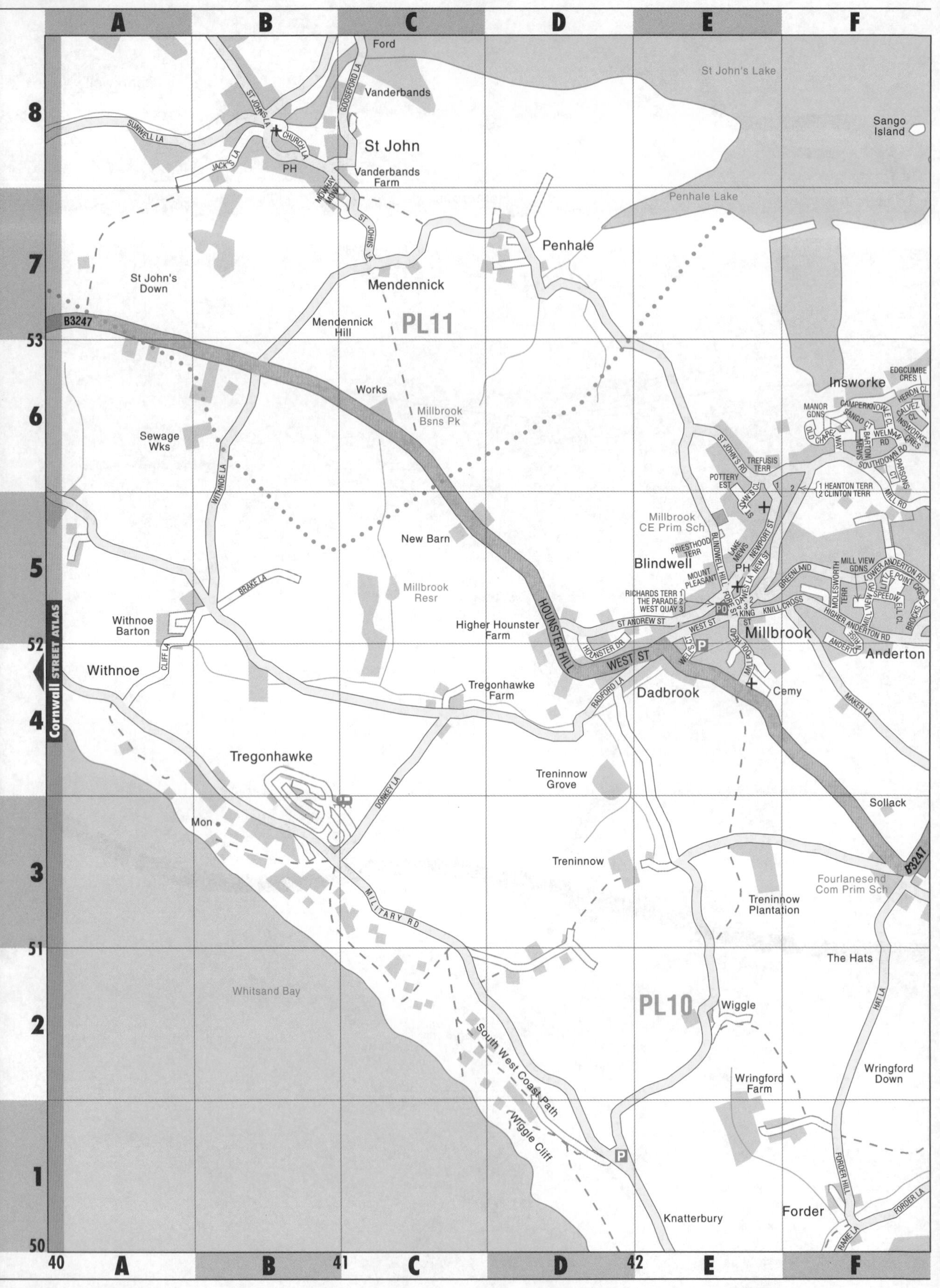

Ford
St John's Lake
Vanderbands
Sango Island
St John
Vanderbands Farm
PH
SUNWELL LA
JACK'S LA
CHURCH LA
ST JOHN'S LA
GOOSEFORD LA
Penhale Lake
Penhale
St John's Down
Mendennick
Mendennick Hill
PL11
B3247
Works
Millbrook Bsns Pk
Sewage Wks
Insworke
New Barn
Millbrook CE Prim Sch
Blindwell
Millbrook Resr
Withnoe Barton
Withnoe
Higher Hounster Farm
HOUNSTER HILL
WEST ST
Millbrook
Anderton
Dadbrook
Cemy
Tregonhawke Farm
Tregonhawke
Treninnow Grove
Sollack
Mon
Treninnow
Fourlanesend Com Prim Sch
Treninnow Plantation
MILITARY RD
Whitsand Bay
The Hats
PL10
Wiggle
South West Coast Path
Wringford Farm
Wringford Down
Wiggle Cliff
Knatterbury
Forder
DONKEY LA
WITHNOE LA
BRAKE LA
CLIFF LA
RADFORD LA
MAKER LA
HAT LA
FORDER HILL
FORDER LA
RAME LA
Cornwall STREET ATLAS

140

247
254

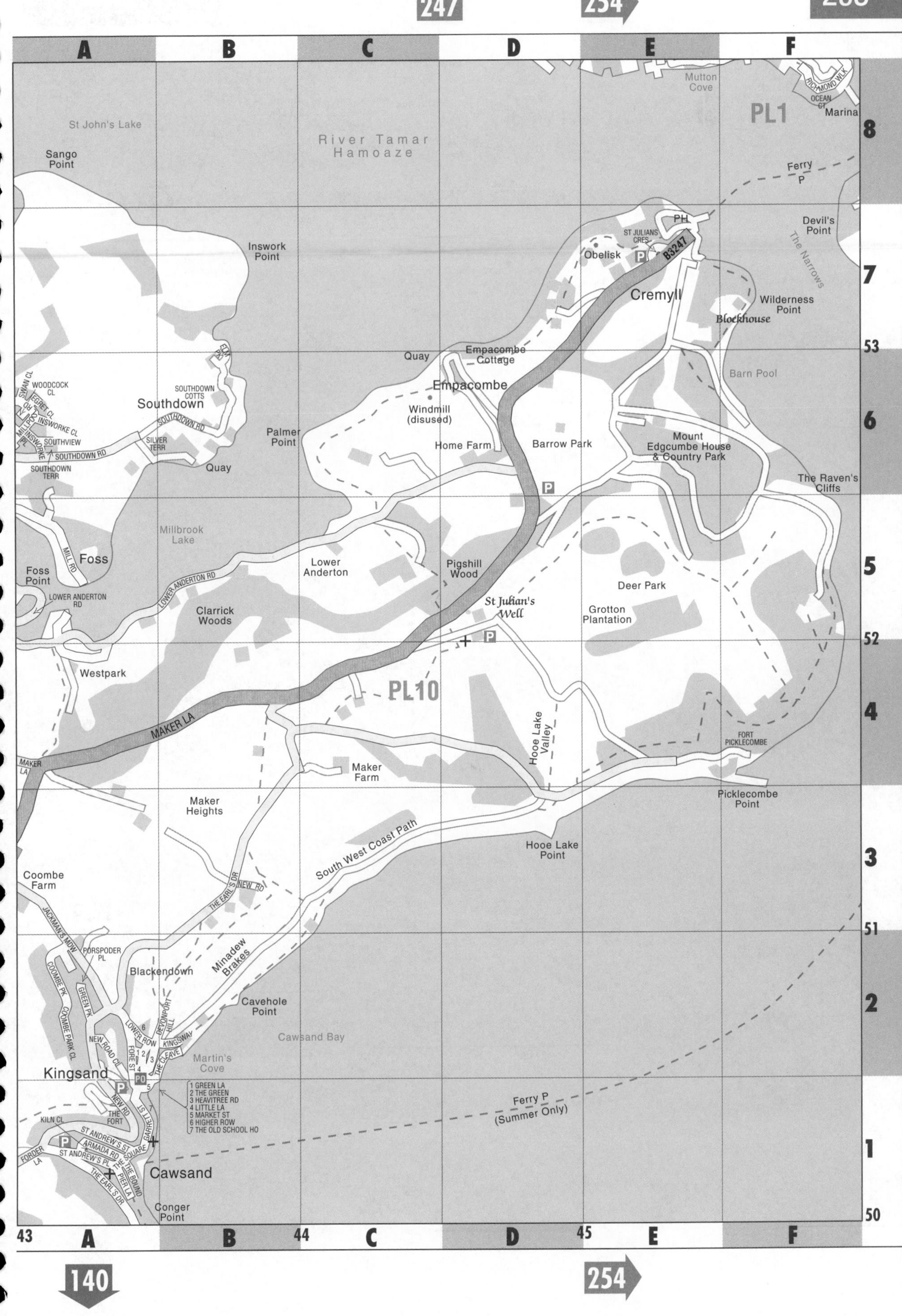

140
254

253
248
For full street detail of the highlighted area see pages 262 and 263.

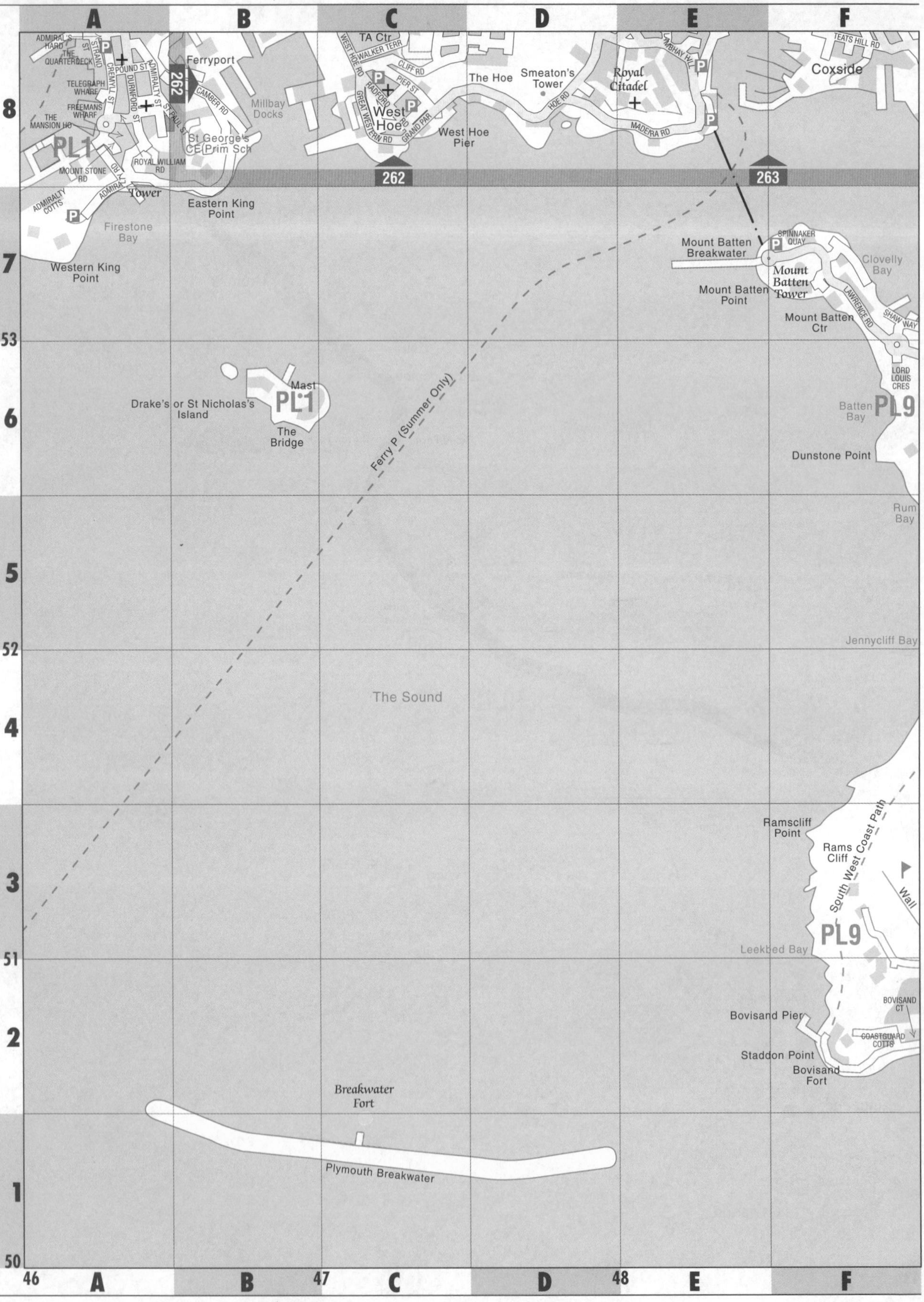

253

For full street detail of the highlighted area see page 263.

249

256

F5
1 CHALLGOOD CL
2 ORCHARDTON TERR

F7
1 THE DUKES RYDE
2 MAPLE CT
3 MAGNOLIA CT
4 HORN LANE FLATS
5 SELKIRK HO

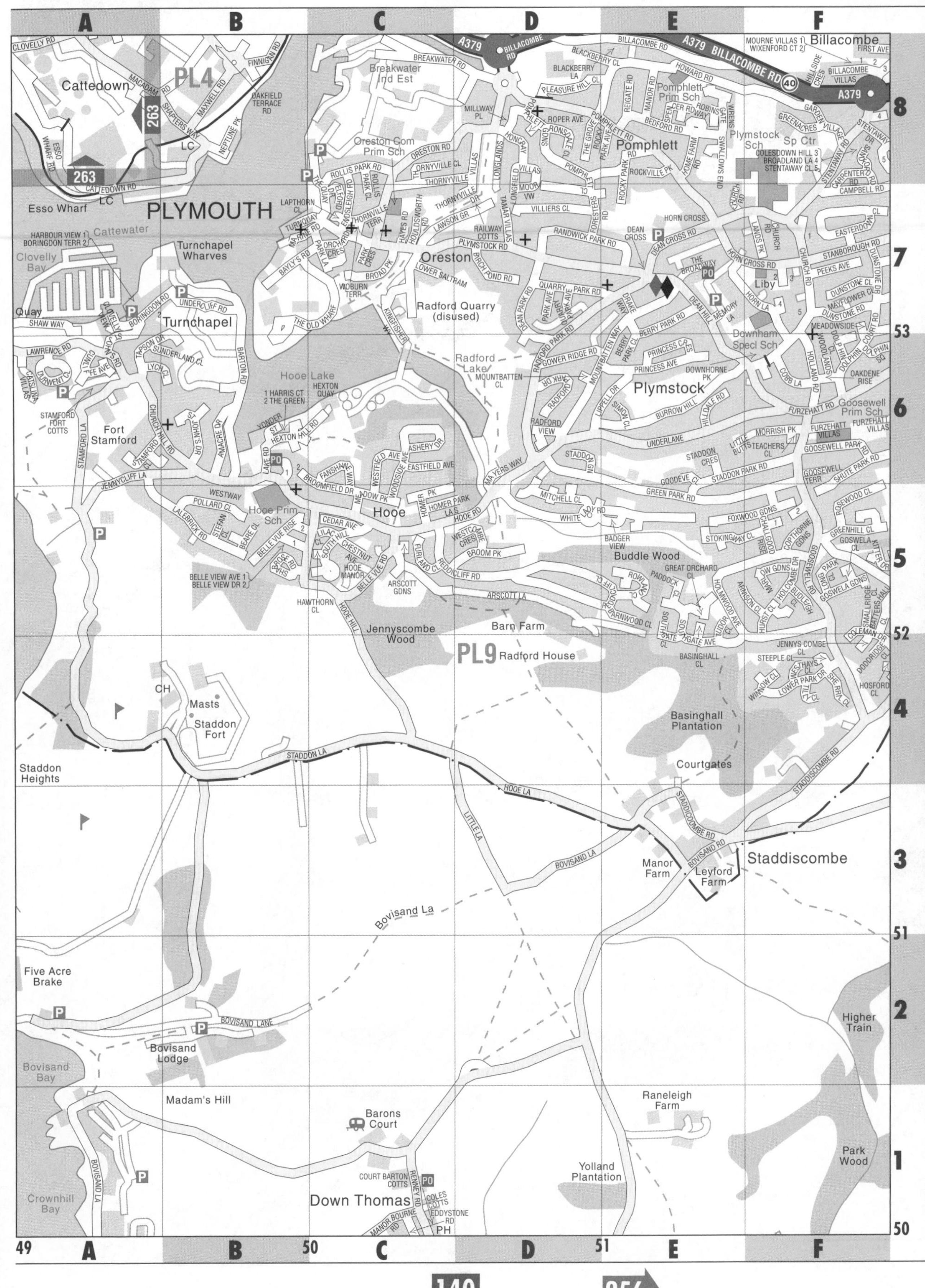

140

256

255
250

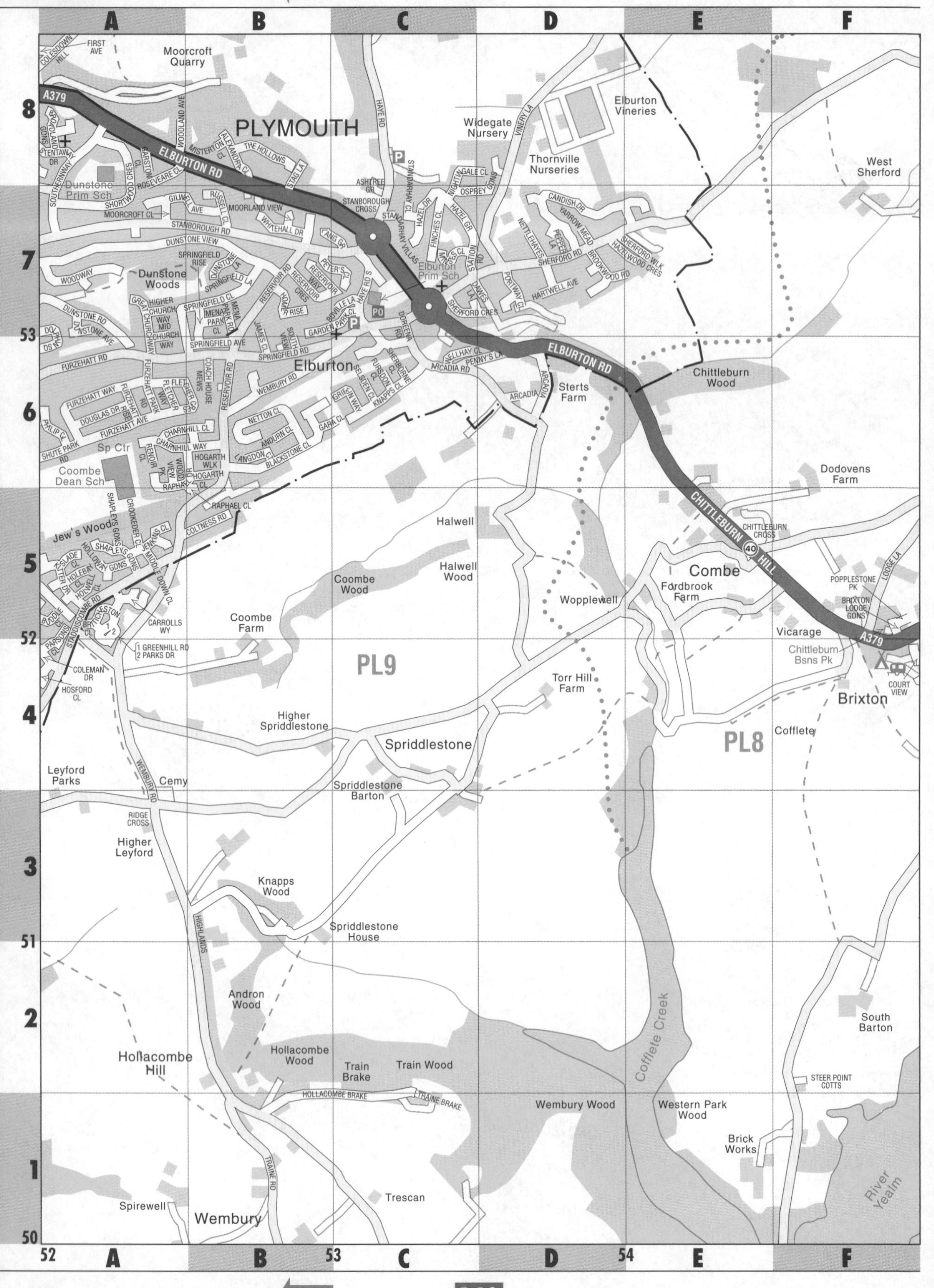

255
140

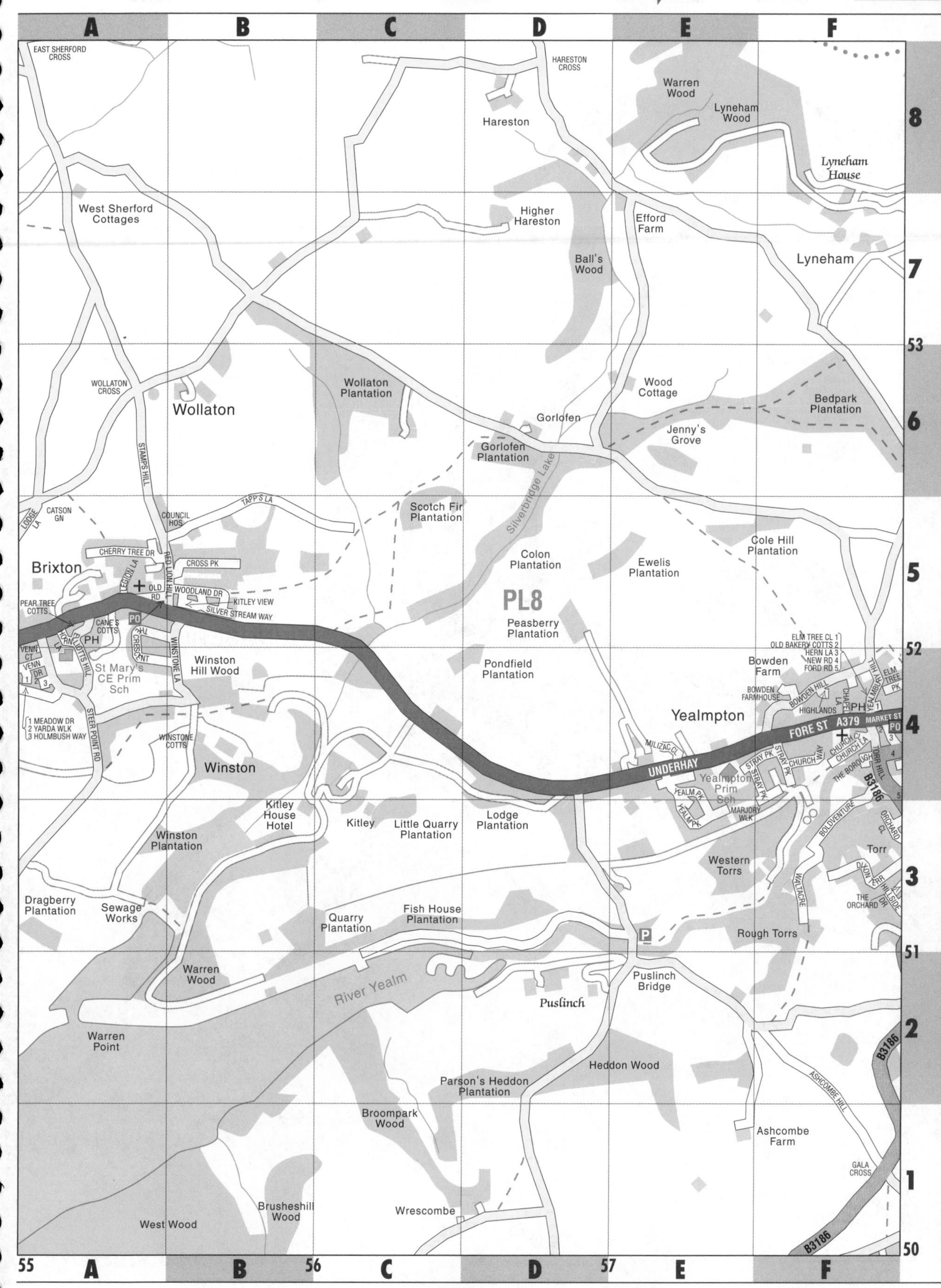
A
B
C
D
E
F
8
7
53
6
5
52
4
3
51
2
1
50
55
56
57
EAST SHERFORD CROSS
HARESTON CROSS
Warren Wood
Lyneham Wood
Hareston
Lyneham House
West Sherford Cottages
Higher Hareston
Efford Farm
Ball's Wood
Lyneham
WOLLATON CROSS
Wollaton
Wollaton Plantation
Wood Cottage
Gorlofen
Bedpark Plantation
Jenny's Grove
Gorlofen Plantation
Silverbridge Lake
STAMPS HILL
CATSON GN
LODGE LA
COUNCIL HOS
TAPP'S LA
Scotch Fir Plantation
Cole Hill Plantation
CHERRY TREE DR
Brixton
CROSS PK
Colon Plantation
Ewelis Plantation
OLD RD
WOODLAND DR
PL8
PEAR TREE COTTS
KITLEY VIEW
SILVER STREAM WAY
Peasberry Plantation
CANE'S COTTS
PH
St Mary's CE Prim Sch
Winston Hill Wood
WINSTONE LA
Pondfield Plantation
Bowden Farm
ELM TREE CL
OLD BAKERY COTTS
HERN LA
NEW RD
FORD RD
BOWDEN FARMHOUSE
BOWDEN HILL
HIGHLANDS
ELM TREE PK
1 MEADOW DR
2 YARDA WLK
3 HOLMBUSH WAY
STEER POINT RD
WINSTONE COTTS
Winston
Yealmpton
FORE ST
A379
MARKET ST
MILIZAC CL
UNDERHAY
CHURCH CL
CHURCH LA
THE BOROUGH
TORR HILL
B3186
Yealmpton Prim Sch
STRAY PK
YEALM PK
MARJORY WLK
Kitley House Hotel
Kitley
Little Quarry Plantation
Lodge Plantation
Winston Plantation
BOLDVENTURE
ORCHARD CL
Torr
Western Torrs
Dragberry Plantation
Sewage Works
Quarry Plantation
Fish House Plantation
WALTACRE
THE ORCHARD
HILLSIDE DR
Rough Torrs
Warren Wood
River Yealm
Puslinch Bridge
Puslinch
Warren Point
Heddon Wood
Parson's Heddon Plantation
ASHCOMBE HILL
Broompark Wood
Ashcombe Farm
GALA CROSS
Brusheshill Wood
Wrescombe
West Wood

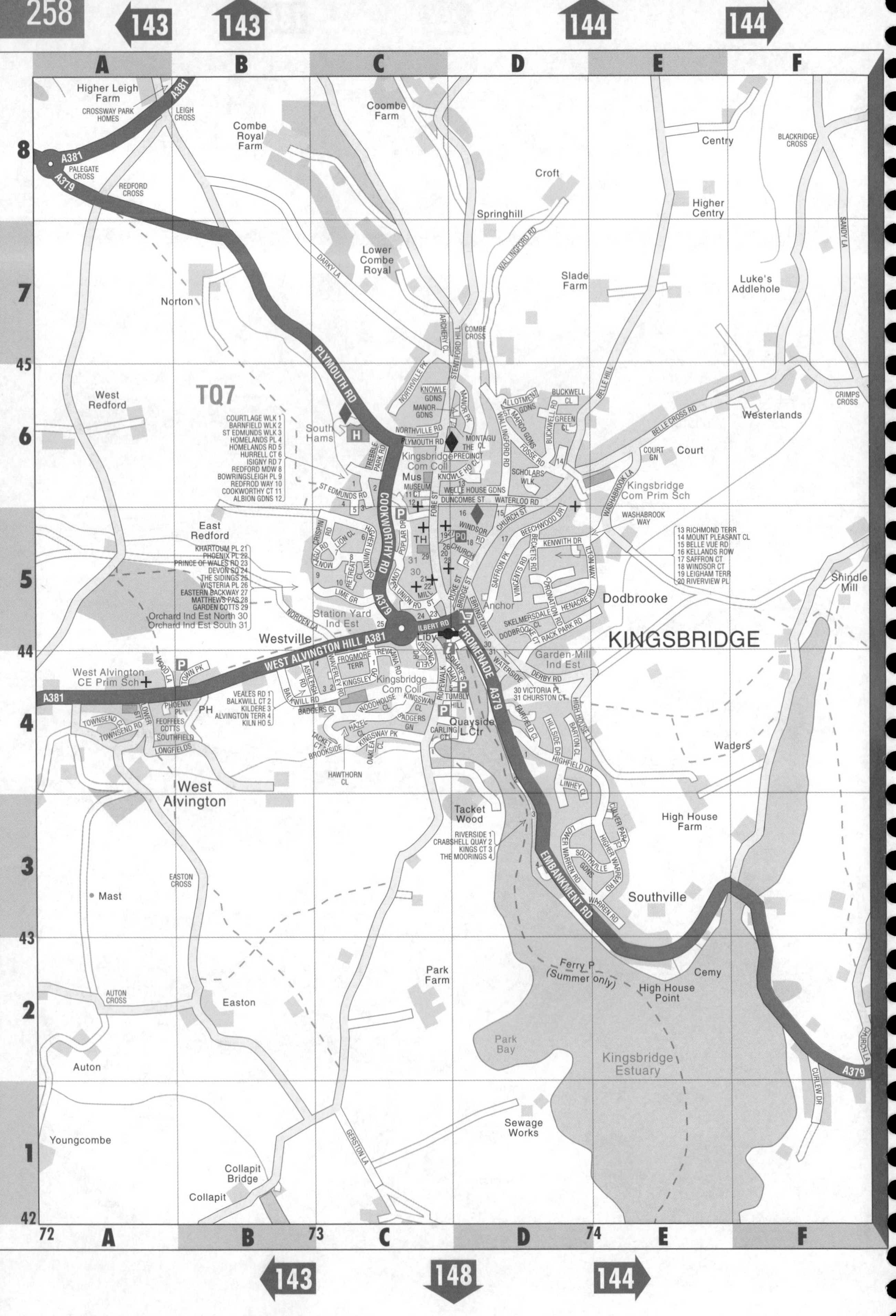
143
143
144
144
A
B
C
D
E
F
8
7
45
6
5
44
4
3
43
2
1
42
72
73
74
Higher Leigh Farm
CROSSWAY PARK HOMES
LEIGH CROSS
A381
PALEGATE CROSS
A379
REDFORD CROSS
Combe Royal Farm
Coombe Farm
Croft
Springhill
Centry
BLACKRIDGE CROSS
Higher Centry
Lower Combe Royal
DARKY LA
WALLINGFORD RD
Slade Farm
Luke's Addlehole
Norton
PLYMOUTH RD
ARCHERY CL
STENTIFORD HILL
COMBE CROSS
SANDY LA
TQ7
West Redford
BELLE HILL
BELLE CROSS RD
CRIMPS CROSS
Westerlands
South Hams
Kingsbridge Com Coll
Mus
Court
COURT GN
Kingsbridge Com Prim Sch
WASHABROOK LA
WASHABROOK WAY
COURTLAGE WLK 1
BARNFIELD WLK 2
ST EDMUNDS WLK 3
HOMELANDS PL 4
HOMELANDS RD 5
HURRELL CT 6
ISIGNY RD 7
REDFORD MDW 8
BOWRINGSLEIGH PL 9
REDFROD WAY 10
COOKWORTHY CT 11
ALBION GDNS 12
13 RICHMOND TERR
14 MOUNT PLEASANT CL
15 BELLE VUE RD
16 KELLANDS ROW
17 SAFFRON CT
18 WINDSOR CT
19 LEIGHAM TERR
20 RIVERVIEW PL
East Redford
KHARTOUM PL 21
PHOENIX PL 22
PRINCE OF WALES RD 23
DEVON SQ 24
THE SIDINGS 25
WISTERIA PL 26
EASTERN BACKWAY 27
MATTHEWS PAS 28
GARDEN COTTS 29
Orchard Ind Est North 30
Orchard Ind Est South 31
COOKWORTHY RD
Shindle Mill
Dodbrooke
Station Yard Ind Est
Anchor
Westville
KINGSBRIDGE
WEST ALVINGTON HILL A381
PROMENADE
Garden Mill Ind Est
West Alvington CE Prim Sch
Kingsbridge Com Coll
VEALES RD 1
BALKWILL CT 2
KILDERE 3
ALVINGTON TERR 4
KILN HO 5
30 VICTORIA PL
31 CHURSTON CT
Quayside L Ctr
Waders
West Alvington
HAWTHORN CL
Tacket Wood
RIVERSIDE 1
CRABSHELL QUAY 2
KINGS CT 3
THE MOORINGS 4
High House Farm
EMBANKMENT RD
Southville
EASTON CROSS
Mast
Ferry P (Summer only)
Cemy
Park Farm
High House Point
AUTON CROSS
Easton
Park Bay
Kingsbridge Estuary
Auton
A379
Sewage Works
GERSTON LA
Youngcombe
Collapit Bridge
Collapit
CURLEW DR
CHURCH LA

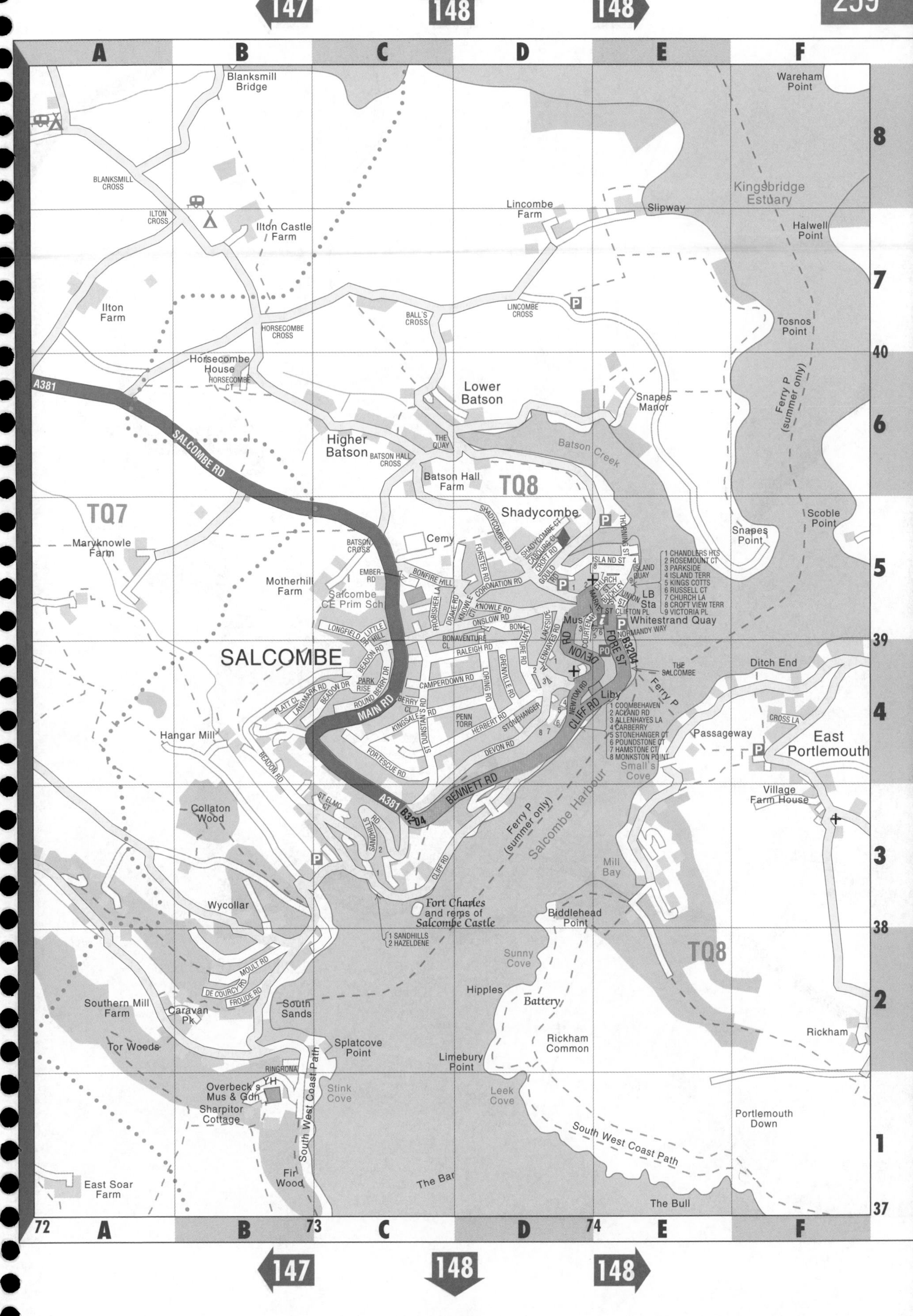
147
148
148
A B C D E F
Blanksmill Bridge
BLANKSMILL CROSS
ILTON CROSS
Ilton Castle Farm
Ilton Farm
HORSECOMBE CROSS
Horsecombe House
HORSECOMBE CT
A381
SALCOMBE RD
Lincombe Farm
Slipway
Kingsbridge Estuary
Wareham Point
Halwell Point
Tosnos Point
BALL'S CROSS
LINCOMBE CROSS
Lower Batson
Snapes Manor
Ferry P (summer only)
Higher Batson
BATSON HALL CROSS
THE QUAY
Batson Creek
Batson Hall Farm
TQ8
Shadycombe
TQ7
Maryknowle Farm
Cemy
BATSON CROSS
Motherhill Farm
Salcombe CE Prim Sch
Scoble Point
Snapes Point
1 CHANDLERS HTS
2 ROSEMOUNT CT
3 PARKSIDE
4 ISLAND TERR
5 KINGS COTTS
6 RUSSELL CT
7 CHURCH LA
8 CROFT VIEW TERR
9 VICTORIA PL
ISLAND QUAY
LB Sta
Whitestrand Quay
Mus
NORMANDY WAY
SALCOMBE
FORE ST
B3204
DEVON RD
THE SALCOMBE
Ferry P
Ditch End
Liby
1 COOMBEHAVEN
2 ACLAND RD
3 ALLENHAYES LA
4 CARBERRY
5 STONEHANGER CT
6 POUNDSTONE CT
7 HAMSTONE CT
8 MONKSTON POINT
MAIN RD
CLIFF RD
Hangar Mill
Passageway
East Portlemouth
CROSS LA
Small's Cove
Village Farm House
BENNETT RD
A381 B3204
Salcombe Harbour
Collaton Wood
Mill Bay
Fort Charles and rems of Salcombe Castle
1 SANDHILLS
2 HAZELDENE
Wycollar
Biddlehead Point
TQ8
Sunny Cove
Southern Mill Farm
Caravan Pk
South Sands
Hipples
Battery
Rickham
Tor Woods
Splatcove Point
Limebury Point
Rickham Common
Overbeck's Mus & Gdn
YH
Sharpitor Cottage
Stink Cove
Leek Cove
South West Coast Path
Portlemouth Down
East Soar Farm
Fir Wood
The Bar
The Bull
8 7 40 6 5 39 4 3 38 2 1 37
72 73 74
147
148
148

104 104 104

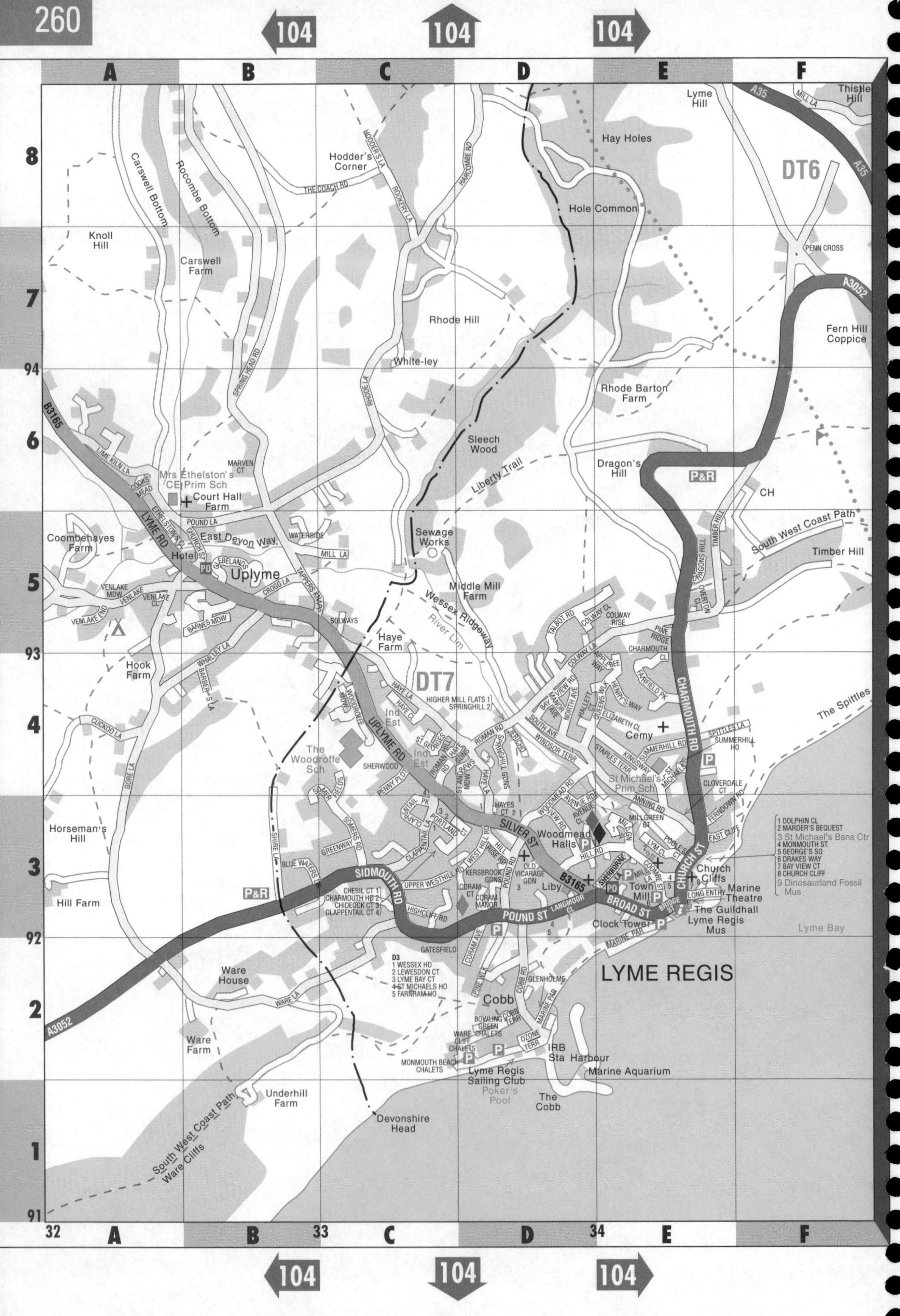

104 104 104

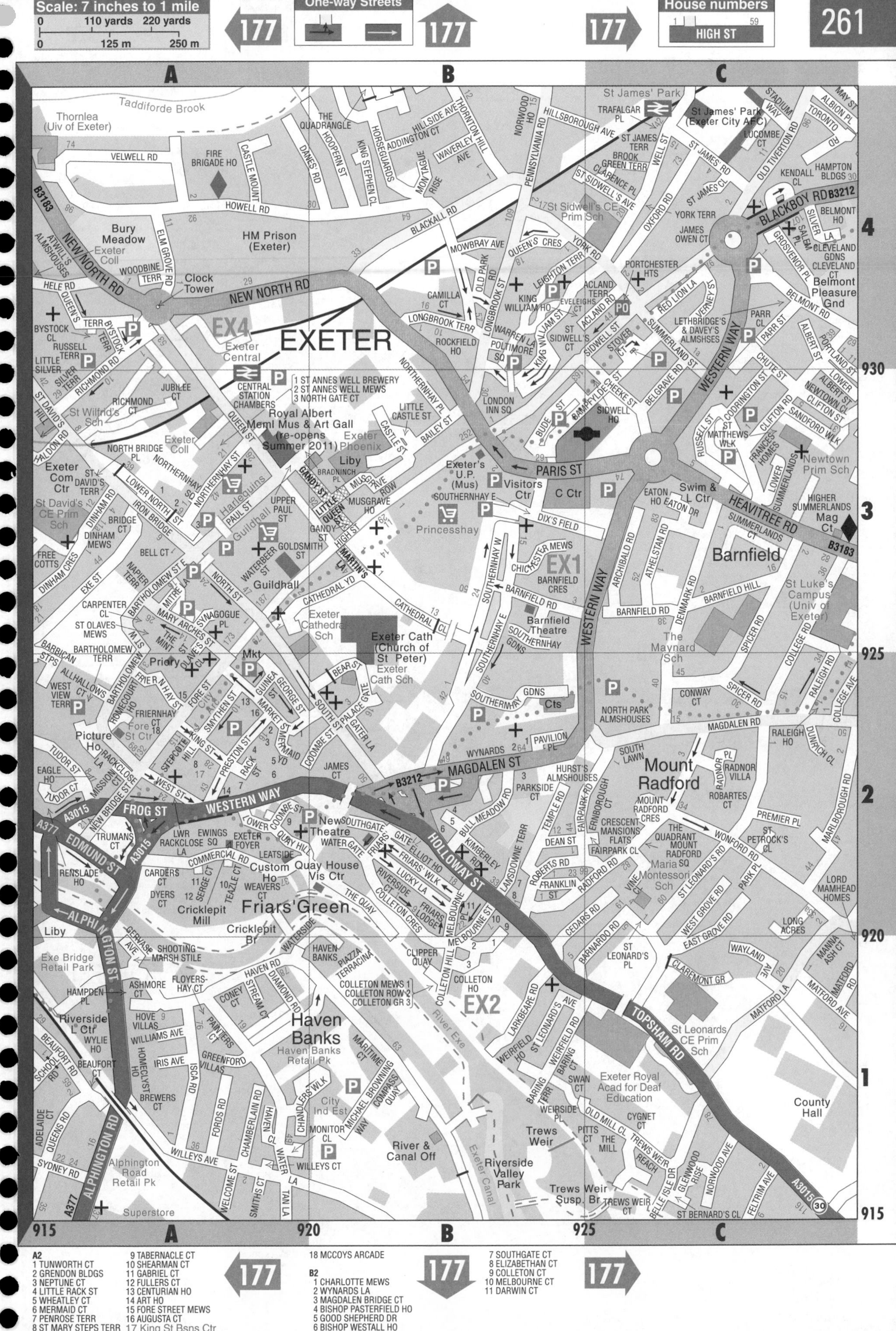

Scale: 7 inches to 1 mile
0
110 yards
220 yards
0
125 m
250 m
177
One-way Streets
177
177
House numbers
1
59
HIGH ST
261
A
B
C
EXETER
EX4
EX1
EX2
Taddiforde Brook
Thornlea
(Uiv of Exeter)
VELWELL RD
FIRE BRIGADE HO
HOWELL RD
Bury Meadow
HM Prison (Exeter)
Exeter Coll
Clock Tower
NEW NORTH RD
HELE RD
BYSTOCK CL
RUSSELL TERR
LITTLE SILVER
RICHMOND RD
Exeter Central
CENTRAL STATION CHAMBERS
JUBILEE CT
1 ST ANNES WELL BREWERY
2 ST ANNES WELL MEWS
3 NORTH GATE CT
Royal Albert Meml Mus & Art Gall (re-opens Summer 2011)
Exeter Phoenix
Liby
St Wilfrid's Sch
NORTH BRIDGE PL
Exeter Com Ctr
St David's CE Prim Sch
DINHAM MEWS
FREE COTTS
DINHAM CRES
BELL CT
Harlequins
Guildhall
UPPER PAUL ST
GOLDSMITH ST
WATERBEER ST
CATHEDRAL YD
Exeter Cathedral Sch
Exeter Cath (Church of St Peter)
Exeter Cath Sch
Exeter's U.P. (Mus)
SOUTHERNHAY E
Princesshay
Visitors Ctr
PARIS ST
C Ctr
DIX'S FIELD
CHICHESTER MEWS
BARNFIELD CRES
BARNFIELD RD
Barnfield Theatre
SOUTHERNHAY GDNS
Cts
WESTERN WAY
Barnfield
HEAVITREE RD
Swim & L Ctr
St Luke's Campus (Univ of Exeter)
The Maynard Sch
SPICER RD
MAGDALEN RD
Mount Radford
NORTH PARK ALMSHOUSES
HURST'S ALMSHOUSES
MAGDALEN ST
HOLLOWAY ST
TOPSHAM RD
St James' Park
St James' Park (Exeter City AFC)
BLACKBOY RD B3212
Belmont Pleasure Gnd
Newtown Prim Sch
Higher Summerlands Mag Ct
St Sidwell's CE Prim Sch
SIDWELL HO
Priory
Mkt
FORE ST
Fore St Ctr
Picture Ho
FROG ST
EDMUND ST
ALPHINGTON ST
New Theatre
Custom Ho
Quay House Vis Ctr
Friars' Green
Cricklepit Mill
Cricklepit Br
Liby
Exe Bridge Retail Park
Riverside L Ctr
Haven Banks
Haven Banks Retail Pk
City Ind Est
River & Canal Off
Riverside Valley Park
Trews Weir
Trews Weir Susp. Br
Exeter Canal
River Exe
Alphington Road Retail Pk
Superstore
ALPHINGTON RD
WILLEYS AVE
Exeter Royal Acad for Deaf Education
St Leonards CE Prim Sch
Maria Montessori Sch
County Hall
915
920
925
930
1
2
3
4
A2
1 TUNWORTH CT
2 GRENDON BLDGS
3 NEPTUNE CT
4 LITTLE RACK ST
5 WHEATLEY CT
6 MERMAID CT
7 PENROSE TERR
8 ST MARY STEPS TERR
9 TABERNACLE CT
10 SHEARMAN CT
11 GABRIEL CT
12 FULLERS CT
13 CENTURIAN HO
14 ART HO
15 FORE STREET MEWS
16 AUGUSTA CT
17 King St Bsns Ctr
18 MCCOYS ARCADE
B2
1 CHARLOTTE MEWS
2 WYNARDS LA
3 MAGDALEN BRIDGE CT
4 BISHOP PASTERFIELD HO
5 GOOD SHEPHERD DR
6 BISHOP WESTALL HO
7 SOUTHGATE CT
8 ELIZABETHAN CT
9 COLLETON CT
10 MELBOURNE CT
11 DARWIN CT

248 ← 248 ↑

One-way Streets

House numbers 1 59 HIGH ST

A B C

4 3 2 1

550 545 540 535

465 470 475

PL3 PL4 PL1

Pennycomequick

PLYMOUTH

Millbay

West Hoe

The Hoe

A3
1 WYNDHAM MEWS
2 HOLLYWOOD TERR
3 NORBURY CT
4 THE NORTH COURTS
5 THE EAST COURTS
6 GORDON CT
7 FELLOWES CT
8 THE SOUTH COURTS
9 LYSTER CT
10 HOWESON CT
11 Millfields Trust Bus Units
12 MCDONALD CT
13 STONLEY CT

← 254

B3
1 ANSON HO
2 MELBOURNE GN
3 ETON TERR
4 OXFORD TERR
5 CAMBRIDGE LA W
6 FREDERICK ST W
7 ALICE LA
8 HARWELL CT
9 FRANKFORT GATE
10 COLIN CAMPBELL CT

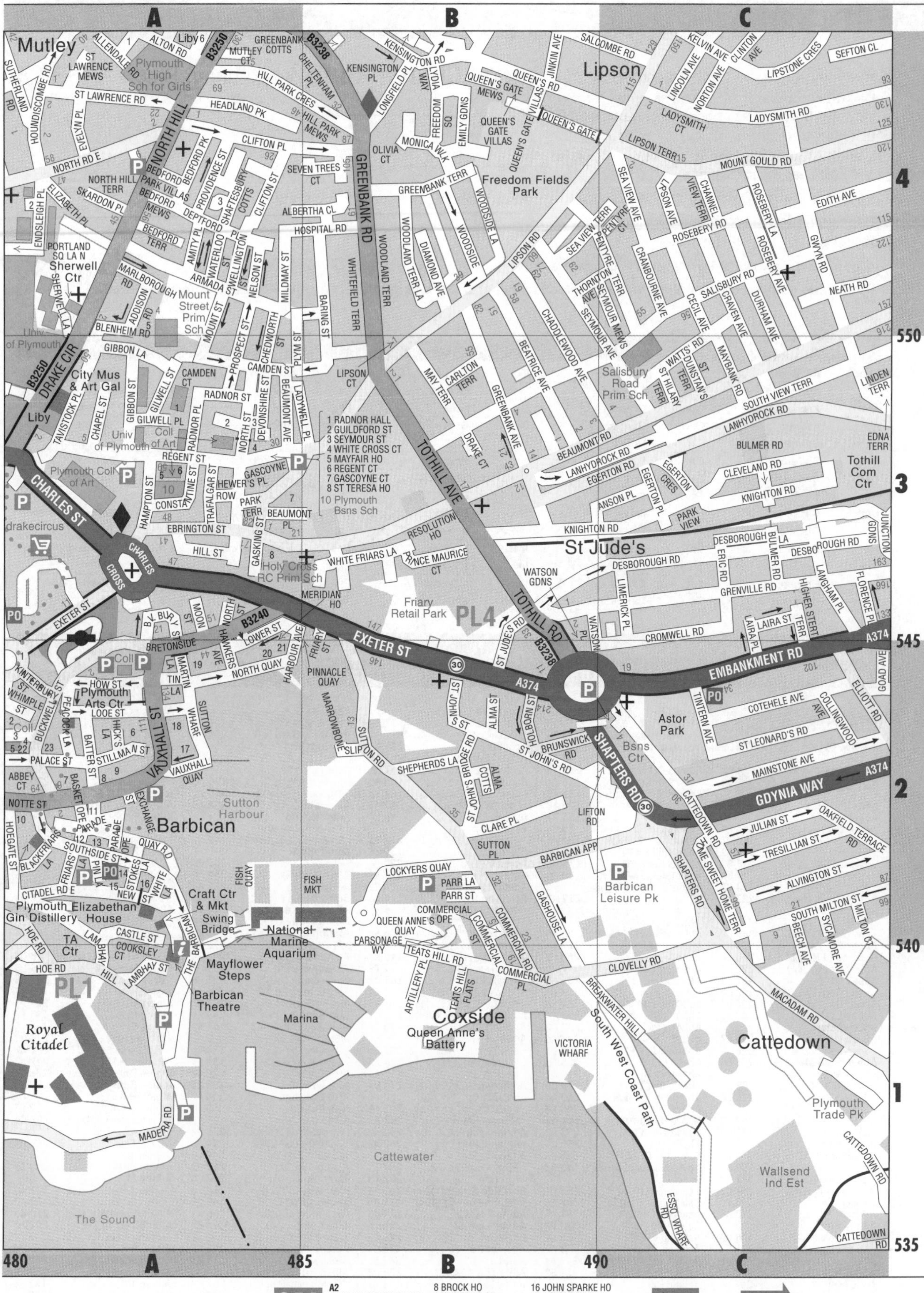

Scale: 7 inches to 1 mile
0 110 yards 220 yards
0 125 m 250 m

248 249 249

A4
1 ABINGDON RD
2 ENDSLEIGH GDNS
3 SHAFTESBURY CT
4 The Old Tannery Bsns Pk
5 WINIFRED BAKER CT
6 ROCHESTER RD

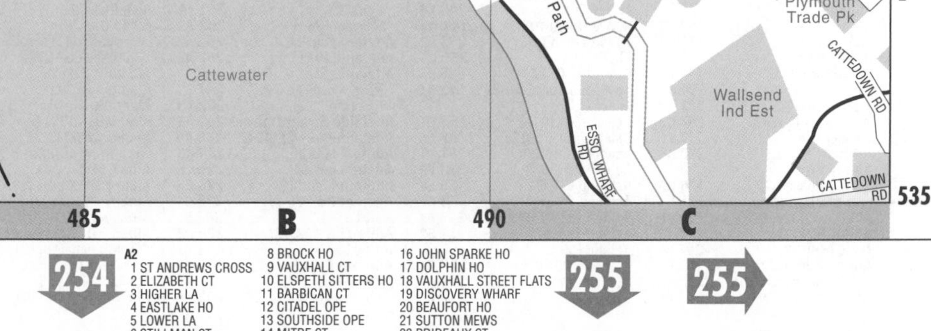

A2
1 ST ANDREWS CROSS
2 ELIZABETH CT
3 HIGHER LA
4 EASTLAKE HO
5 LOWER LA
6 STILLMAN CT
7 WOOLSTER CT
8 BROCK HO
9 VAUXHALL CT
10 ELSPETH SITTERS HO
11 BARBICAN CT
12 CITADEL OPE
13 SOUTHSIDE OPE
14 MITRE CT
15 HANOVER CT
16 JOHN SPARKE HO
17 DOLPHIN HO
18 VAUXHALL STREET FLATS
19 DISCOVERY WHARF
20 BEAUFORT HO
21 SUTTON MEWS
22 PRIDEAUX CT
23 PALACE CT

254 255 255

Index

Place name May be abbreviated on the map
Location number Present when a number indicates the place's position in a crowded area of mapping
Locality, town or village Shown when more than one place has the same name
Postcode district District for the indexed place
Page and grid square Page number and grid reference for the standard mapping

Church Rd 6 Beckenham BR2..........**53** C6

Cities, towns and villages are listed in CAPITAL LETTERS
Public and commercial buildings are highlighted in magenta **Places of interest** are highlighted in blue with a star★

Abbreviations used in the index

Acad	Academy	Comm	Common	Gd	Ground	L	Leisure	Prom	Promenade
App	Approach	Cott	Cottage	Gdn	Garden	La	Lane	Rd	Road
Arc	Arcade	Cres	Crescent	Gn	Green	Liby	Library	Recn	Recreation
Ave	Avenue	Cswy	Causeway	Gr	Grove	Mdw	Meadow	Ret	Retail
Bglw	Bungalow	Ct	Court	H	Hall	Meml	Memorial	Sh	Shopping
Bldg	Building	Ctr	Centre	Ho	House	Mkt	Market	Sq	Square
Bsns, Bus	Business	Ctry	Country	Hospl	Hospital	Mus	Museum	St	Street
Bvd	Boulevard	Cty	County	HQ	Headquarters	Orch	Orchard	Sta	Station
Cath	Cathedral	Dr	Drive	Hts	Heights	Pal	Palace	Terr	Terrace
Cir	Circus	Dro	Drove	Ind	Industrial	Par	Parade	TH	Town Hall
Cl	Close	Ed	Education	Inst	Institute	Pas	Passage	Univ	University
Cnr	Corner	Emb	Embankment	Int	International	Pk	Park	Wk, Wlk	Walk
Coll	College	Est	Estate	Intc	Interchange	Pl	Place	Wr	Water
Com	Community	Ex	Exhibition	Junc	Junction	Prec	Precinct	Yd	Yard

Index of towns, villages, streets, hospitals, industrial estates, railway stations, schools, shopping centres, universities and places of interest

3rd–Ald

A

C

D

E

F

H

M

N

O

P

S

T